BARRON'S

TOEFL

PRACTICE EXERCISES

TEST OF ENGLISH AS A FOREIGN LANGUAGE

NINTH EDITION

Pamela J. Sharpe, Ph.D.

BARRON'S

To my students,
with best wishes for success on the
TOEFL and after the TOEFL

Published by Kaplan, Inc., d/b/a Barron's Educational Series
750 Third Avenue
New York, NY 10017
www.barronseduc.com

ISBN: 978-1-4380-1259-9

10 9 8 7 6 5 4 3 2 1

Kaplan, Inc., d/b/a Barron's Educational Series print books are available at special quantity discounts to use for sales
promotions, employee premiums, or educational purposes. For more information or to purchase books, please call the
Simon & Schuster special sales department at 866-506-1949.

Contents

Acknowledgments

I am fortunate to have been associated with so many talented collaborators. Heartfelt thanks to

Lillie Sharpe, my mother
for the lifelong example of positive thinking that inspired Chapter One of this book;

Robert Sharpe, my dad
for wise counsel and a good laugh at just the right times;

Kristen Girardi, Editor at Kaplan
for managing the production of many previous editions at Barron's Educational Series Inc., with intelligence, kindness, and extraordinary expertise, as well as for collaborating in the development of this revision;

Christine Ricketts, Production Editor at Kaplan
for bringing a new perspective to the ninth edition, for selecting an exceptional team, and for coordinating the production with enthusiasm, patience, and outstanding professionalism;

Kathy Russell Telford, Proofreader's Plus
for reading the manuscript prior to submission, for her positive approach to errors, and her friendship over the years;

Nancy de Guerre, Copyeditor
for making many improvements, large and small, in the new material, especially in the revised reading passages;

Michael Popper, Proofreader
for reading the previous edition with a meticulous eye and making suggestions for useful changes in the ninth;

Aptara, Typesetter
for skillfully formatting the pages and making the corrections that support our readers;

Brendan Feeney and Gavin Skal at Audiomedia Production
for casting the talented studio voices and bringing the characters to life;

John T. Osterman, my husband
for making countless cups of tea, supplying a copy machine, and living without complaint among the paper storms that I created while completing the manuscript. Life with John continues to be the best chapter in my life story.

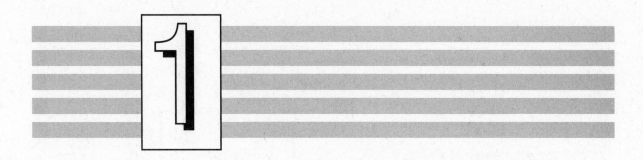

PLAN FOR SUCCESS

Introduction

The TOEFL examination is currently administered at test sites around the world in two different formats: the Institutional TOEFL® (ITP) and the Internet-Based TOEFL (iBT®). Similar language proficiency skills are tested on both formats, but they are tested in different ways.

Ask yourself three questions as you prepare for the TOEFL.

1 Which TOEFL test do you plan to take?

Institutional TOEFL® Program (ITP)

The Institutional TOEFL® Program (ITP) is a paper-based TOEFL test. Colleges or other schools use the ITP to test students in their institutions. Schools use the ITP for placement in their English programs and for progress evaluations to promote students to the next level of their programs. Institutional TOEFL scores are not valid outside of the school where they are administered, but a college or school may accept your ITP score for admission to the school where you take the test. The ITP cannot be used for admission to other schools. Some government agencies also use ITP scores to select scholarship recipients. The Institutional TOEFL has three parts: Listening Comprehension, Structure and Written Expression, and Reading Comprehension. In addition, schools and agencies often require an essay score.

Internet-Based TOEFL (iBT®)

In contrast, the Internet-Based TOEFL (iBT®) is a computer-based TOEFL test that is used for admission to schools throughout the world as well as for licensing and other official purposes. The iBT has four parts: Reading, Listening, Speaking, and Writing. On the four-part iBT, most of the questions are independent, but some of the questions are integrated. For example, you may be asked to listen to a lecture or read a passage, and then speak or write a response.

It is important that you take the test that furthers your goals, and that you know which test you will take, because the ITP and the iBT have different parts and require somewhat different preparation.

Are you confused about the two TOEFL formats? Then take a few minutes to look at the chart on page 4. This chart gives you a quick comparison of the two TOEFL formats. Still not sure? Then look at the model tests in Chapter 8. Don't try to read or answer the questions. Just get a general idea of the formats for the two tests.

	INSTITUTIONAL TOEFL® ITP			INTERNET-BASED TOEFL iBT®		
Listening	30 Short Conversations 2 Longer Conversations 3 Short Talks	50 Questions	35 Minutes	2–3 Conversations 3–4 Lectures	23–39 Questions	41–57 Minutes
Speaking		NO Questions		1 Independent Task 3 Integrated Tasks	4 Questions	17 Minutes
Structure	15 Fill-in 25 Error Recognition	40 Questions	25 Minutes		NO Questions	
Reading	5 Passages	50 Questions	55 Minutes	3–4 Passages	30–40 Questions	54–72 Minutes
Writing	1 Optional Essay	1 Question	30 Minutes	1 Integrated Essay 1 Independent Essay	2 Questions	50 Minutes
			TIME 2 Hours			**TIME 3 Hours**

The TOEFL iBT® has been shortened. Before August 1, 2019, the test was almost four hours long but is now about three hours long. The kinds of questions that you will see are similar to those from the longer test, but there are fewer questions in the Reading, Listening, and Speaking Sections. Refer to the chart above for details.

2 How can you use this book to prepare for your TOEFL test?

This book offers practice for both formats of the TOEFL, and all the exercises will help you improve the skills that you need to succeed on both TOEFL tests. However, if you have limited time, and you know which sections of the test are more difficult for you, you can spend more time on the chapters that provide practice for those sections. Or, if you know which test you plan to take—either the ITP or iBT—then you can focus on those exercises that will give you practice for the specific format that you will see on test day. Choose the study plan that is most convenient for you.

Three Study Plans

To *schedule* means to plan your time. If you plan your time and follow a schedule, you will be able to review and study everything in this book before you take the TOEFL. For help in preparing your schedule, choose one of the study plans outlined below. Then, stay on schedule.

"Diligence is the Mother of Good Luck."—Benjamin Franklin

Intensive Study Plan

If you have time to do all of the exercises in this book, that is the best study plan. All of the skills you practice will help you prepare for the Institutional TOEFL Program (ITP) and the Internet-Based TOEFL (iBT®).

Skills Study Plan

If you have already taken the TOEFL, you will know which section or sections are the most difficult for you. Even if you have not taken the TOEFL, you probably know your strong and weak points. You can select only those exercises that correspond to the TOEFL section in which you need to improve. Choose the chapters that correspond to Listening, Speaking, Structure, Reading, or Writing. This will give you specific experience with the types of items that are the most challenging for you.

Format Study Plan

If you have limited time, you can select only those exercises that correspond to the TOEFL format that you intend to take. This will give you specific experience with the type of items that are found on the test you plan to take.

Icons

Four icons are included in the book to help you.

 When you see headphones, you should turn on the audio track. The track number is referenced in parentheses beside the icon. On the audio, you will hear the scripts for the Listening Exercises, the Speaking Exercises, and some of the Writing Exercises. In addition, you will hear the scripts for the ITP and iBT model tests.

 When you see a pencil, you know that the format of the exercise is the Institutional ITP because it is a pencil-and-paper test. The skills you learn will prepare you for both the ITP and iBT, but the format will give you practice for the Institutional ITP format.

 When you see a computer mouse, you know that the format of the exercise is the Internet iBT because it is a computer test. The skills you learn will prepare you for both the iBT and ITP, but the format will give you practice for the Internet iBT format.

 When you see a computer mouse with a pencil, you know that the format of the exercise is generally the same for both the Institutional ITP and the Internet iBT. The skills you learn will prepare you for both the ITP and iBT, and the format will give you practice for both TOEFL tests.

3 How can you succeed on the TOEFL?

Develop a Positive Attitude

To succeed on the TOEFL, begin with a positive attitude, learn what to expect on the test, use your time well to prepare, and gain experience by reviewing English and practicing test items. Here is some specific advice.

<u>Visualize</u>

"Imagination is the beginning of creation. You imagine what you desire. You will what you imagine. And, at last, you create what you will."—George Bernard Shaw

To *visualize* means to see a picture of something in your mind. Spend one minute visualizing your success before each study session. Close your eyes and see what you want to happen. See yourself sitting at the TOEFL administration, visualize that you are relaxed, moving through the test confidently, completing it within the time limits. Now you are viewing the computer screen with your range of scores. See the score that you want on the computer screen. See yourself smiling. Now picture yourself achieving the goal that motivated you to take the TOEFL. If you are a student, see yourself on a university campus, going to class. If you are in the medical profession, see yourself working in a hospital. See your success. Enjoy your visualizations.

<u>Affirm</u>

"People become really quite remarkable when they start thinking that they can do things. When they believe in themselves, they have the first secret of success."—Norman Vincent Peale

To *affirm* means to have a positive conversation with yourself. Say in words what you have visualized. Spend 30 seconds repeating affirmations. For example, you might say, "I am confident."

This affirmation is from *Barron's TOEFL iBT® Seventeenth Edition*:

"I know more today than I did yesterday.
I am preparing.
I will succeed."

Formulate a Plan
"As a general rule, the most successful man in life is the one who has the best information."
—Benjamin Disraeli

You need to know what to expect on the TOEFL. If you are informed, you will not be surprised and confused on the day of the exam. Visit the official TOEFL web site at *www.toefl.org*. Download the *TOEFL Bulletin of Information* from the site, or order it by mail. Be sure to download the format that you intend to take—the Institutional TOEFL (ITP) or the Internet-Based TOEFL (iBT®) TOEFL. If you have also purchased the current edition of *Barron's TOEFL iBT®*, read Chapter One, "Questions and Answers About the TOEFL." Study the chart on page 4 of this book for a summary and comparison of the two TOEFL exams.

Review
"To climb steep hills requires a slow pace at first."—*William Shakespeare*

To *review* is to study something that you have studied before. To succeed on the TOEFL, you must have studied English already. It is not possible to achieve an excellent score if you are just beginning to study English. However, it is possible to make a higher score by reviewing what you have already studied, especially when you concentrate on the type of English that appears most often on the TOEFL. For an extensive review of every section of the TOEFL, along with eight online model tests, you can use the current edition of *Barron's TOEFL iBT®*.

Practice
"Practice makes perfect."—*Anonymous*

Practice is very important in order to succeed on the TOEFL. By practicing exercises that simulate the items on the TOEFL exam, you gain valuable experience. Because you understand the directions for each section, you know what to do on the official TOEFL without trying to figure it out under the stress of an actual test. You can learn test strategies as well—how to manage your time on each section, how to eliminate possible answer choices, and when to guess.

Work through the practice exercises in this book systematically, using the study plan that you have selected. Spend time practicing every day for at least an hour instead of sitting down to review once a week for seven hours. Even though you are studying for the same amount of time, research shows that shorter sessions every day produce better results on the test. Refer to the explanatory and example answers in Chapter 7 for each exercise. By studying the explanations, you will begin to understand the way that good test takers think. Why is the answer correct? Is it like other questions you have seen before? Can you explain the answer to someone else? This will help you to answer the test items correctly when you take the official TOEFL.

Evaluate

"Nothing great was ever achieved without enthusiasm."—Ralph Waldo Emerson

Estimating your score before you take the TOEFL is important because the test is costly. You will want to take it at the point when you have the best opportunity to succeed. Use the answer keys on pages 445 for the Institutional TOEFL and 493 for the Internet-Based TOEFL, respectively, for your final model test. Then estimate your score using the charts and rubrics in Chapter 9. By scoring your model test, you will know whether you should register to take the official TOEFL or continue to prepare. Whatever you do, go forward with enthusiasm.

Best wishes.
Dr. Pamela J. Sharpe
www.teflprep.com

2

PRACTICE EXERCISES
FOR LISTENING

Listening Section

Overview of the TOEFL iBT® Listening Section

The Listening Section tests your ability to understand spoken English that is typical of interactions and academic speech on college campuses. During the test, you will listen to conversations and lectures, and you will answer questions about them. In some of the lectures, the professor is speaking, and the students are listening. In other lectures, the professor is speaking, and the students are participating.

Most of the time, the speaker will have a North American dialect, but sometimes the speaker will have a British or Australian dialect.

There are two formats for the Listening Section. On the short format, you will listen to two conversations and three lectures. On the long format, you will listen to three conversations and four lectures. After each listening passage, you will answer five to six questions about it. Only two conversations and three lectures will be graded. The other passages are part of an experimental section for future tests. Because you will not know which conversations and lectures will be graded, you must try to do your best on all of them.

You will hear each passage one time. You may take notes while you listen, but notes are not graded. You may use your notes to answer the questions.

Choose the best answer for multiple-choice questions. Follow the directions on the page or on the screen for computer-assisted questions. Click on **Next** and then on **OK** to go to the next question. You cannot return to previous questions.

The Listening Section is divided into parts. Each part includes one conversation and one or two lectures. You will have 41 minutes to listen to the conversations and lectures and answer all of the questions on the short format, and 57 minutes to listen to the conversations and lectures and answer all of the questions on the long format. A clock on the screen will show you how much time you have to complete your answers for the section. To complete all of the questions within the time limit, you should try to answer two questions in about one minute. As you practice, use the model tests in this book, and you will learn how to pace yourself so that you can finish the Listening Section on time.

Overview of the TOEFL® ITP Listening Comprehension Section

The Listening Section tests your ability to understand spoken English that is representative of classroom and interpersonal interactions both on college campuses and in other settings off campus. The topics are both academic and general.

The Listening Section is divided into three parts. In Part A, you will hear 30 short conversations between two people. After each conversation, you will hear one question. In Part B, you will hear two longer conversations between two people. After each conversation, you will hear three to five questions. In Part C, you will hear three short talks by one person. After each talk, you will hear three to five questions.

You will hear each conversation, talk, and question only one time. You may take notes while you listen, but notes are not graded. You may use your notes to answer the questions.

The questions are all multiple-choice with four possible answer choices. After every question, choose the best answer choice. You should not mark your answers in the test book. Fill in the oval that corresponds to the letter of your answer on a separate answer sheet, using a soft lead pencil. If you change your answer, be sure to erase your first answer completely.

You will have about 35 minutes to listen to the conversations and talks and answer all of the questions.

Exercise 1: Short Conversations—Topics

 (Track 1)

In some dialogues in the Listening Comprehension Section on the Institutional TOEFL, you will be asked to identify the main topic from among several secondary subjects in the conversations. Choose the best answer.

1. What are the man and woman talking about?
   - Ⓐ A health club
   - Ⓑ A class
   - Ⓒ A game
   - Ⓓ A dentist

2. What are these two people most probably discussing?
   - Ⓐ Food and grocery items
   - Ⓑ Gasoline prices
   - Ⓒ Weights and measures
   - Ⓓ Money

3. What are the two people talking about?
   - Ⓐ A vacation
   - Ⓑ The mail
   - Ⓒ The newspaper
   - Ⓓ The office

4. What are the two people discussing?
   - Ⓐ A new doctor
   - Ⓑ A party they attended
   - Ⓒ Their friend Mary
   - Ⓓ A graduate program

5. What are the man and the woman discussing?
   - Ⓐ An exchange program
   - Ⓑ The man's trip to England
   - Ⓒ The man's illness
   - Ⓓ Their friend Nancy

6. What are the man and woman talking about?
   - Ⓐ The professor's lecture
   - Ⓑ The woman's children
   - Ⓒ The chairs they are sitting in
   - Ⓓ The size of the lecture room

7. What are the two people discussing?
   - Ⓐ The woman's computer
   - Ⓑ The woman's paper
   - Ⓒ The man's hometown
   - Ⓓ The man's job

8. What are the two people talking about?
   - Ⓐ The campus
   - Ⓑ Registration week
   - Ⓒ The parking situation
   - Ⓓ The woman's class

9. What are the man and the woman discussing?
   - Ⓐ The professor, Dr. Smith
   - Ⓑ The lab reports
   - Ⓒ The attendance policy
   - Ⓓ The teaching assistant

10. What are the man and the woman talking about?
    - Ⓐ The chemistry department
    - Ⓑ The woman's house
    - Ⓒ The man's employer
    - Ⓓ Having lunch on campus

Refer to pages 239–240 for the Explanatory Answers.

EXERCISE 2: Short Conversations—Details

 **(Track 2)**

In some dialogues in the Listening Comprehension Section on the Institutional TOEFL, you will be asked to remember details that are directly stated. Choose the best answer.

1. What is the man's problem?
   - (A) He is tired.
   - (B) He is drunk.
   - (C) He is thirsty.
   - (D) He is busy.

2. How does the woman want to pay?
   - (A) She wants to pay by check.
   - (B) She prefers to use a credit card.
   - (C) She has cash.
   - (D) She will need a loan.

3. Why did Sharon stop seeing the man?
   - (A) He was too short for her.
   - (B) She didn't know him very well.
   - (C) The gift made her uncomfortable.
   - (D) The man never gave her gifts.

4. Why did the man look through the woman's purse?
   - (A) He thought she was a thief.
   - (B) He wanted to secure it for her.
   - (C) His job was to check belongings.
   - (D) He was looking for a standard size.

5. What does the woman want the man to do?
   - (A) Study with her
   - (B) Help her on the test
   - (C) Take a break
   - (D) Lend her his notebook

6. Who is driving Steve's car?
   - (A) Steve's girlfriend
   - (B) Steve's sister
   - (C) Steve
   - (D) Mary Anne

7. Why won't the door open?
   - (A) The door is locked.
   - (B) The woman doesn't have the right key.
   - (C) The door is stuck.
   - (D) The doorknob is broken.

8. What does the man want to do?
   - (A) Check the calculators.
   - (B) Use a calculator to do his test.
   - (C) Purchase a calculator.
   - (D) Borrow a calculator.

9. What is the woman's advice?
   - (A) She thinks the man should pay the bills.
   - (B) She thinks the man should ask his family for help.
   - (C) She thinks the man should contact his roommate's family.
   - (D) She thinks the man should leave.

10. How will the woman help the man?
    - (A) By filling out forms
    - (B) By filing his taxes
    - (C) By advising him about student loans
    - (D) By completing his application

Refer to pages 241–242 for the Explanatory Answers.

EXERCISE 3: Short Conversations—Selections

 (Track 3)

In some dialogues in the Listening Comprehension Section on the Institutional TOEFL, you will be asked to select the correct detail from among several similar alternatives, all of which have been mentioned in different contexts in the conversation. Choose the best answer.

1. What is the relationship between Jack and the man?
   - Ⓐ They are brothers.
   - Ⓑ They are good friends.
   - Ⓒ They are cousins.
   - Ⓓ They are classmates.

2. What does the woman suggest?
   - Ⓐ That the man room with Frank and Geoff
   - Ⓑ That the man ask Geoff to be his roommate
   - Ⓒ That the man and Steve be roommates
   - Ⓓ That the man share a room with Frank

3. What grade did the woman receive?
   - Ⓐ She earned an *A*.
   - Ⓑ She received a *B*.
   - Ⓒ Her grade was *C*.
   - Ⓓ She got a *D* or *F*.

4. What advice does the woman give the man?
   - Ⓐ Buy the computer at a discount store
   - Ⓑ Put an ad in the newspaper for a computer
   - Ⓒ Go to a computer store to buy the computer
   - Ⓓ Buy the computer at the university as part of a special offer

5. Why didn't the woman receive a grade for the course?
   - Ⓐ She didn't pay her fees.
   - Ⓑ She didn't register for the class.
   - Ⓒ She didn't attend the class.
   - Ⓓ She didn't have her name on the roster.

6. What size will the man probably bring?
   - Ⓐ He will probably bring her a size 5½.
   - Ⓑ He will probably bring her a size 6.
   - Ⓒ He will probably bring her a size 7.
   - Ⓓ He will probably bring her a size 7½.

7. What does the man suspect?
   - Ⓐ The woman needs new glasses.
   - Ⓑ The woman has high blood pressure.
   - Ⓒ The woman has serious headaches.
   - Ⓓ The woman is suffering from stress.

8. For which class must the woman begin to prepare?
   - Ⓐ She must begin writing a paper for her history class.
   - Ⓑ She must start her laboratory assignments for her chemistry class.
   - Ⓒ She must begin studying for her English examination.
   - Ⓓ She must begin studying for her French examination.

9. Where does the man live?
   - Ⓐ In New York
   - Ⓑ In Boston
   - Ⓒ In Michigan
   - Ⓓ In Washington

10. Which gear needs to be fixed?
    - Ⓐ First gear
    - Ⓑ Second gear
    - Ⓒ Reverse
    - Ⓓ Drive

Refer to pages 243–244 for the Explanatory Answers.

EXERCISE 4: Short Conversations—Reversals

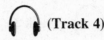 **(Track 4)**

In some dialogues in the Listening Comprehension Section on the Institutional TOEFL, you will be asked to identify the speaker's final choice or decision after a change of opinion. Choose the best answer.

1. How will the woman get to the airport?
   - Ⓐ She will get a ride with the man.
   - Ⓑ She will ride the airport shuttle.
   - Ⓒ She will drive her car.
   - Ⓓ She will rent a car.

2. What does the woman want to eat?
   - Ⓐ She would like eggs and potatoes.
   - Ⓑ She wants eggs and pancakes.
   - Ⓒ She wants to eat potato pancakes.
   - Ⓓ Pancakes is what she would like to eat.

3. How many boxes of cookies did the man order?
   - Ⓐ The man bought one box of cookies.
   - Ⓑ The man ordered four boxes of cookies.
   - Ⓒ He purchased five boxes of cookies.
   - Ⓓ He did not order any cookies this year.

4. What is the correct area code for the woman?
   - Ⓐ The number is 6-9-1.
   - Ⓑ The area code is 1-9-6.
   - Ⓒ 9-1-6 is the area code.
   - Ⓓ 6-1-9 is the correct number.

5. How much per copy will the woman pay?
   - Ⓐ She will pay eight cents per page.
   - Ⓑ The price is ten cents a copy.
   - Ⓒ She owes fifteen cents per copy.
   - Ⓓ Twenty cents per page is the price.

6. How much will the woman pay?
   - Ⓐ One dollar a minute
   - Ⓑ One dollar a page
   - Ⓒ Two dollars and fifty cents a minute
   - Ⓓ Two dollars and fifty cents a page

7. What does the woman want to do?
   - Ⓐ See a documentary
   - Ⓑ Change the channel
   - Ⓒ Watch television
   - Ⓓ Go to a movie

8. What does the man want the woman to do?
   - Ⓐ He wants all twenty-dollar bills.
   - Ⓑ He wants all fifty-dollar bills.
   - Ⓒ He wants all large bills.
   - Ⓓ He wants some twenty- and some fifty-dollar bills.

9. Where will the man and woman eat lunch?
   - Ⓐ The Country Kitchen
   - Ⓑ The Country Home
   - Ⓒ The Old House
   - Ⓓ The Old Kitchen

10. When will the man be home?
    - Ⓐ He will be home at six o'clock.
    - Ⓑ He will not be home late.
    - Ⓒ He will be home a little after seven.
    - Ⓓ He will be home earlier than usual.

Refer to pages 245–246 for the Explanatory Answers.

EXERCISE 5: Short Conversations—Idioms

 **(Track 5)**

In some dialogues in the Listening Comprehension Section on the Institutional TOEFL, you will be asked to paraphrase idiomatic expressions. Choose the best answer.

1. What does the woman mean?
   - Ⓐ She does not think that the man is serious.
   - Ⓑ She thinks that the man is going to take her to Florida.
   - Ⓒ She thinks that the man has a good idea.
   - Ⓓ She thinks that the man does not have any money.

2. What does the woman mean?
   - Ⓐ She needs one more semester.
   - Ⓑ She needs a hundred dollars.
   - Ⓒ The increase will be difficult for her.
   - Ⓓ The paper is not dependable.

3. What did the man do?
   - Ⓐ He has left the lecture.
   - Ⓑ He has used his last piece of paper.
   - Ⓒ He has said good-bye to the woman.
   - Ⓓ He has finished giving the lecture.

4. How does the man feel about the test?
   - Ⓐ He feels that the test was fair.
   - Ⓑ He agrees with the woman about the test.
   - Ⓒ He does not want the woman to tease him about the test.
   - Ⓓ He is not worried about the test.

5. What does the woman mean?
   - Ⓐ The man does not pay attention.
   - Ⓑ The man is very honest.
   - Ⓒ The man has gone away.
   - Ⓓ The man needs to repeat.

6. What does the man mean?
   - Ⓐ He does not remember what is in his notes.
   - Ⓑ He is very sure about the title of the book.
   - Ⓒ He is making a good guess at information.
   - Ⓓ He is in a hurry to get back to his room.

7. What does the woman mean?
   - Ⓐ She does not want the man to come for her.
   - Ⓑ She thinks that the man is a bother.
   - Ⓒ She does not want to go to class.
   - Ⓓ She accepts the man's offer.

8. What does the man mean?
   - Ⓐ The man likes ice cream.
   - Ⓑ The man will tell the woman later whether he wants ice cream.
   - Ⓒ The man does not want to say whether he likes ice cream.
   - Ⓓ The man will get some ice cream for the woman.

9. What does the woman mean?
   - Ⓐ She is glad Joan is moving.
   - Ⓑ She does not believe that Joan will move.
   - Ⓒ She saw Joan move.
   - Ⓓ She believes Joan is moving because she saw her.

10. What does the man mean?
   - Ⓐ He is angry with the woman.
   - Ⓑ He wants to talk with the woman.
   - Ⓒ It was a bad day for the man.
   - Ⓓ He does not know what day it is.

Refer to pages 246–248 for the Explanatory Answers.

EXERCISE 6: Short Conversations—Emotions

 **(Track 6)**

In some dialogues in the Listening Comprehension Section on the Institutional TOEFL, you will be asked to draw conclusions about the feelings or emotions expressed by the speakers. Words and phrases as well as the tone of voice of speakers in the conversation will provide information for your conclusions. Choose the best answer.

1. How does the man feel?
   Ⓐ He is worried.
   Ⓑ He is happy.
   Ⓒ He feels confident.
   Ⓓ He feels tired.

2. How did the man feel about the movie?
   Ⓐ He thought it was a very unrealistic movie.
   Ⓑ He was impressed with the movie.
   Ⓒ He agreed with the woman about the movie.
   Ⓓ He liked the movie because it was a fairy tale.

3. How does the woman feel about the TOEFL?
   Ⓐ She does not know whether she did well.
   Ⓑ She thinks that she improved her score.
   Ⓒ She believes that she scored about 90.
   Ⓓ She is concerned about the reading comprehension.

4. How does the woman feel about the man?
   Ⓐ She believes that he is having a bad day.
   Ⓑ She does not like the man.
   Ⓒ She thinks that he never pays attention.
   Ⓓ She likes to help the man every day.

5. How does the man feel about Rick?
   Ⓐ He forgot who he was.
   Ⓑ He thinks that Rick and Lucy will forget to come.
   Ⓒ He likes Rick, but not Lucy.
   Ⓓ He does not want to invite them.

6. What is the man's reaction to the news?
   Ⓐ He is surprised.
   Ⓑ He is confused.
   Ⓒ He does not agree.
   Ⓓ He does not want to know.

7. How does the man feel about the assignments?
   Ⓐ He does not care.
   Ⓑ He does not like the lab assistant.
   Ⓒ He does not like the grading system.
   Ⓓ He does not agree with the woman.

8. What best describes the man's opinion of Terry?
   Ⓐ He feels protective of Terry.
   Ⓑ The man is supportive.
   Ⓒ He has his doubts about Terry.
   Ⓓ He feels hostile toward Terry.

9. How does the man feel about the review session?
   Ⓐ He wants to go, but he won't.
   Ⓑ He does not want to go, but he will.
   Ⓒ He wants to go, and he will.
   Ⓓ He does not want to go, and he won't.

10. How does the man feel about Janine?
    Ⓐ He thinks Janine would be difficult to live with.
    Ⓑ He thinks Janine and the woman will like living together.
    Ⓒ He thinks it would be better to live with Janine than with Carol.
    Ⓓ He thinks that Janine and Carol should live together.

Refer to pages 248–250 for the Explanatory Answers.

EXERCISE 7: Short Conversations—Suggestions

 **(Track 7)**

In some dialogues in the Listening Comprehension Section on the Institutional TOEFL, you will be asked to recognize a suggestion. Words and phrases such as "you should" or "why don't you" or "why not" introduce a suggestion. Choose the best answer.

1. What does the man suggest that the woman do?
   Ⓐ Buy dinner
   Ⓑ Pay for part of the dinner
   Ⓒ Tip the waiter after dinner
   Ⓓ Prepare the dinner

2. What does the man suggest that the woman do?
   Ⓐ Return later
   Ⓑ Call the security guard
   Ⓒ Stay at the dorm
   Ⓓ Look for the key

3. What does the woman suggest that the man do?
   Ⓐ Find another bathroom
   Ⓑ Use the bathroom in the main lobby
   Ⓒ Ask the custodian to unlock the bathroom
   Ⓓ Go to another building to locate a bathroom

4. What does the man suggest that the woman do?
   Ⓐ Get in line behind him
   Ⓑ Take a number
   Ⓒ Come back later
   Ⓓ Go to the end of the line

5. What does the woman suggest that the man do?
   Ⓐ Go to another bank
   Ⓑ Open an account with the bank
   Ⓒ Cash his check
   Ⓓ Make out the check for twenty dollars

6. What does the woman suggest that the man do?
   Ⓐ Pick her up at 11:35 A.M.
   Ⓑ Wait for her at the airport
   Ⓒ Wait for her to call him
   Ⓓ Call the airport for the schedule

7. What does the man suggest that the woman do?
   Ⓐ Refer to the syllabus
   Ⓑ Go to Dr. Watson's office
   Ⓒ See Dr. Watson at 2:00 P.M.
   Ⓓ Ask someone else

8. What does the man suggest that they do?
   Ⓐ Stay home
   Ⓑ Go out after dinner
   Ⓒ Find a babysitter
   Ⓓ Take the children out to dinner

9. What does the woman suggest that the man do?
   Ⓐ Ask for an extension
   Ⓑ Use the interlibrary loan
   Ⓒ Look for references in the library
   Ⓓ Try the internet

10. What does the woman suggest that the man do?
    Ⓐ Buy a larger wallet
    Ⓑ Keep the cards in his book bag
    Ⓒ Carry fewer cards
    Ⓓ Organize the cards

Refer to pages 250–252 for the Explanatory Answers.

EXERCISE 8: Short Conversations—Assumptions

 **(Track 8)**

In some dialogues in the Listening Comprehension Section on the Institutional TOEFL, you must be able to recognize remarks that register surprise and draw conclusions about the assumptions that the speaker may have made. Choose the best answer.

1. What had the man assumed about the test?
   Ⓐ The test would not be timed.
   Ⓑ The test could be taken home to complete.
   Ⓒ He would be able to use his book during the test.
   Ⓓ He would have to study very hard for the test.

2. What had the man assumed?
   Ⓐ The woman would not receive her deposit.
   Ⓑ The old apartment was not safe.
   Ⓒ The new apartment would require a deposit.
   Ⓓ The woman would not move.

3. What had the man assumed about the woman?
   Ⓐ She would not have lunch.
   Ⓑ She would not start dating Phil again.
   Ⓒ She would have lunch with him.
   Ⓓ She would have to go before lunch.

4. What had the man assumed about the woman's daughter?
   Ⓐ She was younger.
   Ⓑ She was having a birthday party.
   Ⓒ She was joking with him.
   Ⓓ She would invite him to her house.

5. What had the woman assumed about the presentation?
   Ⓐ There would not be any handouts.
   Ⓑ Anne would finish the handouts.
   Ⓒ Anne would not make the presentation.
   Ⓓ The presentation had already been made.

6. What had the woman assumed about the health center?
   Ⓐ The health center was in the student services building.
   Ⓑ The health center was in the union.
   Ⓒ The health center was on North Campus.
   Ⓓ The health center was not on campus.

7. What had the man assumed about Bill?
   Ⓐ Bill did not do much traveling.
   Ⓑ Bill did not take the class.
   Ⓒ Bill did not read novels.
   Ⓓ Bill did not like to read.

8. What had the woman assumed about John?
   Ⓐ He was serious about becoming a doctor.
   Ⓑ He was not serious about changing majors.
   Ⓒ He was serious about going into the family business.
   Ⓓ He was not serious about applying for the business program.

9. What had the woman assumed about Mr. Brown?
   Ⓐ He would be late getting to the lab.
   Ⓑ He would be in the lab working.
   Ⓒ He would not set up the equipment.
   Ⓓ He would not have time to set up the equipment.

10. What had the woman assumed about Dr. Peterson?
   Ⓐ She would not meet with their study group.
   Ⓑ She would not give them an outline of the book.
   Ⓒ She would not give them a break.
   Ⓓ She would not let them use the book.

Refer to pages 252–254 for the Explanatory Answers.

EXERCISE 9: Short Conversations—Predictions

 (Track 9)

In some dialogues in the Listening Comprehension Section on the Institutional TOEFL, you will be asked to make predictions about the future activities of the speakers. Your prediction should be based on evidence in the conversation from which you can draw a logical conclusion. Choose the best answer.

1. What will the man probably do?
   Ⓐ Leave the restaurant
   Ⓑ Order the size orange juice they have
   Ⓒ Not have any orange juice
   Ⓓ Have orange juice instead of hot tea

2. What will the woman probably do?
   Ⓐ Go to the kitchen to study
   Ⓑ Go to her chemistry class
   Ⓒ Go to the library to look for her book
   Ⓓ Go to the table to eat

3. What will the woman probably do?
   Ⓐ Call London about the charges
   Ⓑ Accept the charges for the call
   Ⓒ Refuse the call from London
   Ⓓ Charge the call to someone in London

4. What will the man probably do?
   Ⓐ Ask the woman to make a copy for him
   Ⓑ Go across the street to make a copy
   Ⓒ Ask the woman for directions to the building
   Ⓓ Take his copies to the other building

5. What will the woman probably do?
   Ⓐ Join the club
   Ⓑ Pay five dollars for a DVD
   Ⓒ Rent ten DVDs
   Ⓓ Go to the DVD exchange

6. What does the man probably want to do?
   Ⓐ Get directions
   Ⓑ Make a call
   Ⓒ Make a reservation
   Ⓓ Talk to the woman

7. What will the woman probably do?
   Ⓐ Walk to the mall
   Ⓑ Get on the bus
   Ⓒ Cross the street to wait for the bus
   Ⓓ Take a taxi to the mall

8. What will the woman probably do?
   Ⓐ Leave at once
   Ⓑ Call the highway patrol
   Ⓒ Go home with the man
   Ⓓ Drive carefully

9. What will the man do?
   Ⓐ Take the delivery to the university
   Ⓑ Refuse to make the delivery to the woman
   Ⓒ Make the delivery to the woman if she is close to the university
   Ⓓ Deliver to a main location three miles from the university where the woman can pick it up

10. What will the man probably do?
   Ⓐ Wait twenty minutes to be seated
   Ⓑ Wait five minutes to be seated
   Ⓒ Go right in to be seated
   Ⓓ Go outside while he waits to be seated

Refer to pages 254–256 for the Explanatory Answers.

EXERCISE 10: Short Conversations—Implications

(Track 10)

In some dialogues in the Listening Comprehension Section on the Institutional TOEFL, you will be asked to draw general conclusions about the speakers or the situation. Words and phrases and the tone of voice of speakers in the conversation will provide information for your conclusions. Choose the best answer.

1. What does the man imply?
    - (A) He will not use the book.
    - (B) He will use the book in the library for two hours.
    - (C) He will check the book out before closing.
    - (D) He will reserve the book.

2. What does the man imply?
    - (A) The woman cannot get a soda.
    - (B) He will go downstairs to get the woman a soda.
    - (C) The woman should go downstairs to get a soda.
    - (D) He does not know where to get a soda.

3. What do we know about the woman?
    - (A) She thought she had applied to the right school.
    - (B) She attends an American university now.
    - (C) She does not have to take the TOEFL.
    - (D) She graduated from an American high school.

4. What did the man mean?
    - (A) The woman was in line for a long time.
    - (B) The man was in line longer than the woman.
    - (C) The man registered quickly.
    - (D) The woman did not register.

5. What does the man prefer to do?
    - (A) He prefers staying at home because he doesn't like to travel.
    - (B) He prefers taking a plane because the bus is too slow.
    - (C) He prefers taking a bus because the plane makes him nervous.
    - (D) He prefers traveling with the woman.

6. Where does this conversation most likely take place?
    - (A) On a reservation
    - (B) At a party
    - (C) At a restaurant
    - (D) In a bakery

7. What conclusion does the man want us to draw from his statement?
    - (A) Sally is serious about Bob.
    - (B) Bob is serious about Sally.
    - (C) Sally is not serious about Bob.
    - (D) Bob is not serious about Sally.

8. What are these people most probably discussing?
    - (A) Weights and measurements
    - (B) Political systems
    - (C) Employment
    - (D) Money

9. What does the man think about Jane?
    - (A) She will go away.
    - (B) She will be sorry.
    - (C) She will not quit her job.
    - (D) She will not buy him a present.

10. What do we learn about Betty from this conversation?
    - (A) She does not like plays.
    - (B) She went to see the play with the man and woman.
    - (C) She had not planned to attend the play.
    - (D) She was not at the play.

Refer to pages 256–258 for the Explanatory Answers.

EXERCISE 11: Short Conversations—Problems

 (Track 11)

In some dialogues in the Listening Comprehension Section on the Institutional TOEFL, you will be asked to identify the problem that the speakers are discussing. This may be more difficult because different aspects of the problem may be included in the conversation. Choose the best answer.

1. What is the man's problem?
   - Ⓐ He does not have a checking account.
   - Ⓑ He does not have any checks.
   - Ⓒ He does not have the money to pay his rent.
   - Ⓓ There is a line at the cashier's window.

2. What is the woman's problem?
   - Ⓐ She does not like to live alone.
   - Ⓑ Her roommate will be moving out.
   - Ⓒ She wants to get married.
   - Ⓓ She does not have any messages.

3. What is the man's problem?
   - Ⓐ He needs his advisor to sign the registration form.
   - Ⓑ He does not have an academic advisor.
   - Ⓒ He does not know how to register for next semester.
   - Ⓓ He can't find his registration.

4. What is the woman's problem?
   - Ⓐ She does not have a car.
   - Ⓑ She needs a ride.
   - Ⓒ She is late to class.
   - Ⓓ She has to go shopping.

5. What is the problem that the man and woman are talking about?
   - Ⓐ They don't have a good book for their class.
   - Ⓑ They don't like Professor Jones.
   - Ⓒ The professor changed the book this semester.
   - Ⓓ Books are very expensive.

6. What is the woman's problem?
   - Ⓐ She has to wait for the telephone to be installed.
   - Ⓑ She does not have a telephone.
   - Ⓒ She has already seen the movie.
   - Ⓓ She cannot go to the movie because she has company.

7. What is the man's problem?
   - Ⓐ He has gained weight.
   - Ⓑ The sweatshirt is too big.
   - Ⓒ He does not have the receipt.
   - Ⓓ The clerk cannot authorize exchanges.

8. What is the woman's problem?
   - Ⓐ She needs child care that is closer to the university.
   - Ⓑ She needs someone to take care of her children while she is in class.
   - Ⓒ She needs the man to help her more with the children.
   - Ⓓ She needs to spend more time with the children.

9. What is the man's problem?
   - Ⓐ He does not like his job.
   - Ⓑ He wants to work more hours.
   - Ⓒ He cannot change jobs.
   - Ⓓ He needs to spend more time studying.

10. What is the woman's problem?
   - Ⓐ She needs to get more sleep.
   - Ⓑ She is starting to feel sick.
   - Ⓒ She did not finish her papers and projects.
   - Ⓓ She is tired of schoolwork.

Refer to pages 258–260 for the Explanatory Answers.

EXERCISE 12: Conversations—Friends on Campus

 (Track 12)

In some conversations in the Listening Comprehension Section on the Institutional TOEFL, you will be asked to recall information exchanged in conversations among friends in a variety of settings on campus. Choose the best answer.

Conversation One

1. What do the speakers mainly discuss?
   - Ⓐ The use of photographs in painting
   - Ⓑ A TV program about Norman Rockwell
   - Ⓒ *The Saturday Evening Post* magazine
   - Ⓓ Exhibits of art at the library

2. How did Rockwell paint such interesting faces?
   - Ⓐ He imagined them.
   - Ⓑ He used magazine covers.
   - Ⓒ He hired models.
   - Ⓓ He read stories.

3. What do we know about Rockwell?
   - Ⓐ He was a prolific painter.
   - Ⓑ He was an eccentric person.
   - Ⓒ He was an avid reader.
   - Ⓓ He was a good teacher.

4. What do the students plan to do for extra credit?
   - Ⓐ Watch a video on reserve at the college library.
   - Ⓑ Write a proposal to bring an art exhibit to the library.
   - Ⓒ Take photographs of models like Norman Rockwell did.
   - Ⓓ Submit photos of the Rockwell exhibit.

5. What will the couple probably do?
   - Ⓐ They will probably go to the exhibit.
   - Ⓑ They will probably see the special on television.
   - Ⓒ They will probably turn off the TV.
   - Ⓓ They will probably go to Miami.

Conversation Two

1. What are the students mainly discussing?
   - Ⓐ Taking notes
   - Ⓑ Studying for a test
   - Ⓒ The woman's grades
   - Ⓓ The reading assignments

2. Why does Bill mention colonial art?
   - Ⓐ It was an example of a question from the handouts.
   - Ⓑ It was an example of a question he had missed on the midterm.
   - Ⓒ It was an example of a topic that he had in his notes.
   - Ⓓ It was an example of a topic in the textbook assignments.

3. How does Linda usually study for a test?
   - Ⓐ She takes notes from the book.
   - Ⓑ She rewrites her class notes.
   - Ⓒ She makes handouts.
   - Ⓓ She rereads the highlights.

4. What kind of student is Linda?
   - Ⓐ She tries to get Bs.
   - Ⓑ She is an average student.
   - Ⓒ She is often absent.
   - Ⓓ She can make an A.

5. What will Bill probably do?
   - Ⓐ He will borrow Linda's class notes.
   - Ⓑ He will rewrite all his class notes.
   - Ⓒ He will take notes from the textbook.
   - Ⓓ He will organize his lecture notes.

Refer to pages 260–262 for the Explanatory Answers.

EXERCISE 13: Conversations—Campus Personnel/Students

 **(Track 13)**

In some conversations in the Listening Comprehension Section on the Institutional TOEFL, you will be asked to recall information from conversations between personnel and students in a variety of settings on campus. Choose the best answer.

Conversation One

1. What do the speakers mainly discuss?
    - Ⓐ A sick friend
    - Ⓑ A math class
    - Ⓒ School policy
    - Ⓓ The man's test

2. Why can't the woman give Terry Young's test to the man?
    - Ⓐ It is against the law.
    - Ⓑ The man is not a member of Terry's family.
    - Ⓒ The woman cannot find the test.
    - Ⓓ Terry was too sick to take the test.

3. What is the man's last name?
    - Ⓐ Young
    - Ⓑ Purcell
    - Ⓒ Raleigh
    - Ⓓ Kelly

4. How does the woman feel about the policy?
    - Ⓐ She agrees with it.
    - Ⓑ She thinks it is odd.
    - Ⓒ She does not enforce it.
    - Ⓓ She is angry about it.

5. What will the man most probably do?
    - Ⓐ Call his friend
    - Ⓑ Go to the office to get his test
    - Ⓒ Send the woman a letter
    - Ⓓ Take the test later

Conversation Two

1. What is the purpose of this conversation?
    - Ⓐ To register the student for classes
    - Ⓑ To register the student for placement tests
    - Ⓒ To help the student change his major field of study
    - Ⓓ To advise the student about the orientation to engineering program

2. How many classes does the woman advise the man to take?
    - Ⓐ Two
    - Ⓑ Five
    - Ⓒ Three
    - Ⓓ Seventeen

3. What does the man need to be admitted to the examination?
    - Ⓐ A driver's license
    - Ⓑ A permission slip
    - Ⓒ A registration card
    - Ⓓ Nothing

4. What does the woman suggest?
    - Ⓐ The man should return Friday afternoon.
    - Ⓑ The man should complete his registration now.
    - Ⓒ The man should take five classes.
    - Ⓓ The man should schedule the Math 130 class.

5. What do we know about the student?
    - Ⓐ He is majoring in mathematics.
    - Ⓑ He has never taken a chemistry course.
    - Ⓒ He is a freshman.
    - Ⓓ He does not like his advisor.

Refer to pages 262–265 for the Explanatory Answers.

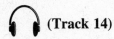

EXERCISE 14: Conversations—Campus Personnel/Students

(Track 14)

In some conversations in the Listening Section on the Internet-Based TOEFL, you will be asked to recall information from conversations between personnel and students in a variety of settings on campus. The conversations will include natural pauses and will be at a normal rate for a conversation between native speakers. Choose the best answer.

Conversation One

1. What is the purpose of this conversation?
   Ⓐ The woman is asking the man's opinion of Professor Hendrix.
   Ⓑ The woman is buying books for a college course.
   Ⓒ The man is training the woman to work in the bookstore.
   Ⓓ The man is helping the woman with her packages.

2. Why didn't the woman use her roommate's book?
   Ⓐ She was taking the course with a different professor.
   Ⓑ The professor was using a different book.
   Ⓒ The book had a lot of marks in it.
   Ⓓ Her roommate had already sold the book.

3. According to the man, what is the problem with using an older edition?
   Ⓐ The instructor refers to different page numbers.
   Ⓑ It is usually very marked up from use.
   Ⓒ The professor doesn't order them.
   Ⓓ They aren't much cheaper than the new edition.

4. Why does the woman buy the style manual?
   Ⓐ The manual is required.
   Ⓑ The price is not expensive.
   Ⓒ The instructor will refer to it.
   Ⓓ The man found one.

5. Why does the woman say this: "Wouldn't you know?"
   Ⓐ She is asking the man if he knows what her roommate did.
   Ⓑ She is confirming that the man knows her roommate.
   Ⓒ She is commenting about her bad luck.
   Ⓓ She is trying to get the man to laugh.

6. What can we infer about the woman?
   Ⓐ She is happy with her purchase.
   Ⓑ She is friends with the man.
   Ⓒ She is an A student.
   Ⓓ She is angry with her roommate.

Refer to pages 265–267 for the Explanatory Answers.

Conversation Two

1. What is the main topic of this conversation?
   - Ⓐ The internet
   - Ⓑ Research methods online
   - Ⓒ The school home page
   - Ⓓ Library computer terminals

2. What is *Oasis*?
   - Ⓐ The online library catalog
   - Ⓑ The name of the school
   - Ⓒ A website for books
   - Ⓓ The password for Netlibrary

3. How does the man set up an account for Netlibrary?
   - Ⓐ He tells his password to the librarian.
   - Ⓑ He logs in on his home computer.
   - Ⓒ He uses the computer in the library.
   - Ⓓ He does it by telephoning the library.

4. How does the man pay for Netlibrary?
   - Ⓐ There is a one-time fee.
   - Ⓑ He will be charged every month.
   - Ⓒ The service is free for students.
   - Ⓓ He pays a fee per book.

5. Why does the man say this: "Let me see if I've got this."
   - Ⓐ To check whether he has understood the woman
   - Ⓑ To look for something he has lost at school
   - Ⓒ To ask the woman to show him some books
   - Ⓓ To find out if he has a job at the library

6. What will the man probably do now?
   - Ⓐ Go back to his apartment
   - Ⓑ Open an account
   - Ⓒ Use Netlibrary
   - Ⓓ Ask the librarian for help

Refer to pages 267–269 for the Explanatory Answers.

EXERCISE 15: Conversations—Professors/Students

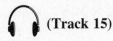 **(Track 15)**

In some conversations in the Listening Comprehension Section on the Institutional TOEFL, you will be asked to recall information exchanged in conversations between professors and students in a variety of settings on campus. Choose the best answer.

Conversation One

1. What is the main subject of the conversation?
   - Ⓐ The man's last appointment
   - Ⓑ Professor Irwin's office hours
   - Ⓒ Student advisement during registration
   - Ⓓ The man's health problems

2. When is the man's new appointment scheduled?
   - Ⓐ Tuesday at two o'clock
   - Ⓑ Thursday at two o'clock
   - Ⓒ This afternoon at three o'clock
   - Ⓓ Now

3. What should the man have done about his first appointment?
   - Ⓐ He should have made an appointment.
   - Ⓑ He should have called to cancel his appointment.
   - Ⓒ He should have come for his appointment.
   - Ⓓ He should have stayed at home until he was well.

4. What is the man's excuse?
   - Ⓐ He wasn't well.
   - Ⓑ He was out of town.
   - Ⓒ He didn't know what to do.
   - Ⓓ He forgot the time.

5. What word best describes Professor Irwin's attitude toward the student?
   - Ⓐ Uninterested
   - Ⓑ Apologetic
   - Ⓒ Sick
   - Ⓓ Annoyed

Conversation Two

1. What is the woman's main purpose in this conversation?
   - Ⓐ To take her final exam
   - Ⓑ To apologize to the professor
   - Ⓒ To change the date of her exam
   - Ⓓ To schedule her flight

2. Why does the woman have a problem?
   - Ⓐ She is taking too many classes.
   - Ⓑ She lives too far from her family.
   - Ⓒ She made an error when she scheduled her trip.
   - Ⓓ She did not do well on her final exam.

3. On what day is the exam scheduled?
   - Ⓐ Monday
   - Ⓑ Tuesday
   - Ⓒ Wednesday
   - Ⓓ Thursday

4. What does the professor decide to do?
   - Ⓐ Allow the woman to repeat the exam.
   - Ⓑ Reschedule the woman's exam for another day.
   - Ⓒ Let the woman skip the final exam.
   - Ⓓ Give the woman a grade of incomplete.

5. When does this conversation most probably take place?
   - Ⓐ In March
   - Ⓑ In May
   - Ⓒ In November
   - Ⓓ In December

Refer to pages 269–272 for the Explanatory Answers.

EXERCISE 16: Conversations—Professors/Students

 (Track 16)

In some conversations in the Listening Section on the Internet-Based TOEFL, you will be asked to recall information exchanged between professors and students in a variety of settings on campus. The conversations will include natural pauses and will be at a normal rate for a conversation between native speakers. Choose the best answer.

Conversation One

1. What is the main topic of this conversation?
   Ⓐ The man's health
   Ⓑ The makeup test
   Ⓒ The man's classes
   Ⓓ The course syllabus

2. Why did the man need to take the test?
   Ⓐ He was absent when the test was given in class.
   Ⓑ He will have to miss class on the day of the test.
   Ⓒ He is taking an independent-study course.
   Ⓓ He has to complete a placement test to take the class.

3. What kind of test will the man take?
   Ⓐ True-false
   Ⓑ Multiple-choice
   Ⓒ Essay
   Ⓓ Oral recitation

4. How long does he have to complete the test?
   Ⓐ 10 minutes
   Ⓑ 45 minutes
   Ⓒ 50 minutes
   Ⓓ 1 hour

5. Why does the professor say this: "But, knowing you, I think you'll probably finish long before that."
   Ⓐ To tell the student to finish the test as quickly as possible
   Ⓑ To give the student self-confidence for the test
   Ⓒ To let the student have more time to complete the test
   Ⓓ To find out how long the student needs to finish the test

6. What can we assume about the man?
   Ⓐ He is not a serious student.
   Ⓑ He is still sick.
   Ⓒ He has a syllabus.
   Ⓓ He is prepared for the test.

Refer to pages 272–274 for the Explanatory Answers.

Conversation Two

1. What is the purpose of this conversation?
   - Ⓐ The woman's grade in biology
   - Ⓑ The woman's major field of study
   - Ⓒ The woman's workload
   - Ⓓ The woman's lab reports

2. What does Marge mean when she says she is "over her head"?
   - Ⓐ She does not understand the biology class.
   - Ⓑ She does not have time to complete the assignments.
   - Ⓒ She does not like the class because of the lab.
   - Ⓓ She is not majoring in biology for premed.

3. Why does Marge want to drop the biology class?
   - Ⓐ It is not her favorite class.
   - Ⓑ Her grades in the class are low.
   - Ⓒ She would not mind taking it again.
   - Ⓓ She does not like the professor.

4. Why does Marge need the professor's signature?
   - Ⓐ She wants to take an exam instead of attending the class.
   - Ⓑ She would like to withdraw from the professor's biology class.
   - Ⓒ She needs an excused absence from the laboratory sessions.
   - Ⓓ She has to notify her advisor that she is failing the class.

5. Why does the professor say this: "Well, have you considered taking an incomplete?"
   - Ⓐ He is finding out about the student's academic record.
   - Ⓑ He is asking whether the student can finish the class.
   - Ⓒ He is making a suggestion for the student to think about.
   - Ⓓ He is trying to understand the student's problem.

6. Why does Dr. Jones want Marge to write a memo to her advisor?
   - Ⓐ So that she will not register for so many hours again
   - Ⓑ So that her advisor will know that she failed the class
   - Ⓒ So that Marge will complete the course in January
   - Ⓓ So that the advisor will fill out the paperwork

Refer to pages 274–276 for the Explanatory Answers.

EXERCISE 17: Conversations—Professors/Students

 (Track 17)

In some conversations in the Listening Section on the Internet-Based TOEFL, you will be asked to recall information exchanged between professors and students in a variety of settings on campus. The conversations will include natural pauses and will be at a normal rate for a conversation between native speakers. Choose the best answer.

Conversation One

1. What is the purpose of this conversation?
   - Ⓐ The student needs help finding a job.
   - Ⓑ The student wants to apply for law school.
   - Ⓒ The student needs another student loan.
   - Ⓓ The student is looking for advice about his major.

2. Why did the man decide to major in history?
   - Ⓐ He wanted to teach history.
   - Ⓑ He liked reading history books.
   - Ⓒ He planned to be a librarian.
   - Ⓓ He had taken a lot of history courses.

3. Why does the professor say this:
   "Okay. Scratch the teaching jobs."
   - Ⓐ She is eliminating teaching as an option for Paul.
   - Ⓑ She is agreeing that Paul would not be a good teacher.
   - Ⓒ She is upset that Paul does not want to teach.
   - Ⓓ She is surprised at Paul's attitude about teaching.

4. According to the student, what is the problem with law school?
   - Ⓐ He would have to take on more student loans.
   - Ⓑ He isn't very interested in studying law.
   - Ⓒ He would have to change his major to history.
   - Ⓓ He doesn't think he would be a good lawyer.

5. What is Professor Watson's final recommendation for the student?
   - Ⓐ He should go to graduate school.
   - Ⓑ He should major in economics.
   - Ⓒ He should work to pay for his tuition.
   - Ⓓ He should go to law school.

6. What will Paul probably do?
   - Ⓐ Return in a few days to see Professor Watson
   - Ⓑ Continue with the program that he is studying
   - Ⓒ Withdraw from school and work as a researcher
   - Ⓓ Change his program to a major in history

Refer to pages 276–278 for the Explanatory Answers.

Conversation Two

1. What is the main purpose of this conversation?
   - Ⓐ To explore options for scholarships
   - Ⓑ To get information about the engineering program
   - Ⓒ To ask the man for a letter of reference
   - Ⓓ To discuss the woman's transcripts

2. How has the woman been paying for her tuition?
   - Ⓐ Her family has been funding her education.
   - Ⓑ She has been receiving a general scholarship.
   - Ⓒ An international agency gave her an award.
   - Ⓓ Her brother has been sending her money.

3. Why does the man say this: 🎧 "…but I'll be honest with you, they are very competitive."
   - Ⓐ He is trying to gain the student's trust.
   - Ⓑ He wants the student to be realistic.
   - Ⓒ He is encouraging the student to compete.
   - Ⓓ He is sorry about the woman's problem.

4. What can we assume about the university?
   - Ⓐ It is most probably a very small school.
   - Ⓑ It does not have many international students.
   - Ⓒ It is most likely in the state of Wisconsin.
   - Ⓓ It must be difficult to be admitted.

5. What does the man tell the student about the Danburry scholarship?
   - Ⓐ It is based on financial need, not on merit.
   - Ⓑ It is for women in the engineering program.
   - Ⓒ It covers the entire cost of student tuition.
   - Ⓓ It requires a meeting with the Danburry family.

6. What will the woman probably do to apply for the Danburry scholarship?
   - Ⓐ Take her transcripts to the man
   - Ⓑ Fill out an application form online
   - Ⓒ Write an essay about herself
   - Ⓓ Wait until next semester

Refer to pages 278–279 for the Explanatory Answers.

EXERCISE 18: Conversations—Professors/Students

 (Track 18)

In some conversations in the Listening Comprehension Section on the Institutional TOEFL, you will be asked to recall information from consultations between professors and students about classroom content or policies. Choose the best answer.

Conversation One

1. What is the purpose of this conversation?
   Ⓐ To discuss the results of the lab experiment
   Ⓑ To answer the students' questions about the lab experiment
   Ⓒ To explain the method of collection by water displacement
   Ⓓ To prepare the students to do the lab experiment

2. What was deposited on the bottom of the gas bottle?
   Ⓐ Magnesium
   Ⓑ Limestone
   Ⓒ Carbon
   Ⓓ Water

3. What caused the deposits?
   Ⓐ The hydrochloric acid broke the carbon bonds in the carbon dioxide.
   Ⓑ The magnesium oxide broke the carbon-oxygen bonds in the carbon dioxide.
   Ⓒ The burning magnesium broke the carbon-oxygen bonds in the carbon dioxide.
   Ⓓ The gas collection method broke the carbon-oxygen bonds in the carbon dioxide.

4. Where does this conversation take place?
   Ⓐ In the lab
   Ⓑ In the classroom
   Ⓒ In the hallway
   Ⓓ In Professor Smith's office

5. What can we infer from this conversation?
   Ⓐ Bob does not get along with his lab partner.
   Ⓑ The students performed the experiment correctly.
   Ⓒ The students had problems, and could not complete the lab experiment.
   Ⓓ There was a fire in the lab during the experiment.

Conversation Two

1. What prompted the conversation?
   Ⓐ The students did not understand the course requirements.
   Ⓑ The students wanted to do a research paper instead of a final exam.
   Ⓒ The professor changed the requirements for the course.
   Ⓓ The professor offered to listen to the students' suggestions for the course.

2. What kind of research paper has Dr. Anderson assigned?
   Ⓐ A report
   Ⓑ A book review
   Ⓒ An original study
   Ⓓ A five-page composition

3. What kind of examination has Dr. Anderson prepared?
   Ⓐ An essay examination
   Ⓑ An objective examination
   Ⓒ An open-book examination
   Ⓓ A take-home examination

4. Which option do the students choose?
   Ⓐ A lecture series
   Ⓑ A paper
   Ⓒ A reading list
   Ⓓ An examination

5. Based on the conversation, which course does Dr. Anderson most probably teach?
   Ⓐ English 355
   Ⓑ Psychology 201
   Ⓒ Political Science 400
   Ⓓ Chemistry 370

Refer to pages 279–282 for the Explanatory Answers.

EXERCISE 19: Conversations—Professors/Students

 (Track 19)

In some conversations in the Listening Section on the Internet-Based TOEFL, you will be asked to recall information from consultations between professors and students about classroom content or policies. The interactions will include natural pauses and will be at a normal rate for a conversation between native speakers. Choose the best answer for multiple-choice questions. For computer-assisted questions, follow the directions on screen.

Conversation One

1. What is the purpose of the conversation?
   Ⓐ Larry has some questions before the quiz.
   Ⓑ Larry wants to know more about Hawaii.
   Ⓒ Larry is concerned about his grade on the last quiz.
   Ⓓ Larry is asking for help because he missed the lecture.

2. What is the main topic of this conversation?
   Ⓐ Topography
   Ⓑ Volcanoes
   Ⓒ Hawaii
   Ⓓ Hot spots

3. What is the altitude of Hawaii?
   Ⓐ 400–500 meters
   Ⓑ 4,500 meters
   Ⓒ 5,500 meters
   Ⓓ 10,000 meters

4. What does the professor say about the newest Hawaiian island?
   Ⓐ It has not yet been given an official scientific name.
   Ⓑ It will appear in 10–40 years according to estimates.
   Ⓒ It is already a few feet above sea level when the ocean is calm.
   Ⓓ It will already be very high when it appears above the water.

5. Why does the professor say this:
   ". . . and you and I won't see it at all . . ."
   Ⓐ He is sad that he won't see it.
   Ⓑ He is giving a concrete example.
   Ⓒ He is making a little joke.
   Ⓓ He is disagreeing with the student.

6. Put the following events in order to explain how island chains are formed.
   Ⓐ Lithospheric plates move over the hot spot, carrying the island with them.
   Ⓑ Active volcanoes in a hot spot erupt to build the first island.
   Ⓒ Island building occurs in a second place close to the first island.
   Ⓓ The plates move again while the hot spot remains in place.

1.	
2.	
3.	
4.	

Refer to pages 282–284 for the Explanatory Answers.

Conversation Two

1. What is Ronda's problem?
   - Ⓐ She does not have a topic for her term paper.
   - Ⓑ The topic that she has selected is too broad.
   - Ⓒ The professor does not like the topic for her paper.
   - Ⓓ She cannot find information about the topic she has chosen.

2. How long should the paper be?
   - Ⓐ Five pages
   - Ⓑ Ten to twelve pages
   - Ⓒ Fifteen to twenty pages
   - Ⓓ Twenty-five pages

3. What does Dr. Gilbert suggest?
   - Ⓐ Ronda should choose a different topic for her paper.
   - Ⓑ Ronda should use the resources that he has given her.
   - Ⓒ Ronda should talk with him again after she has a title.
   - Ⓓ Ronda should show him her first draft in class tomorrow.

4. Where did Ronda's family live five years ago?
   - Ⓐ Italy
   - Ⓑ Spain
   - Ⓒ France
   - Ⓓ England

5. Why does the student ask this:
   "Are you busy?"
   - Ⓐ She wonders what Dr. Gilbert is doing.
   - Ⓑ She is chatting with Dr. Gilbert.
   - Ⓒ She is interrupting Dr. Gilbert politely.
   - Ⓓ She would like to help Dr. Gilbert.

6. What will Ronda most probably do?
   - Ⓐ Write her paper about the Hall of Mirrors.
   - Ⓑ Try to find more sources for her term paper.
   - Ⓒ Change her topic to some other period of art.
   - Ⓓ Revise her second draft to make it longer.

Refer to pages 284–287 for the Explanatory Answers.

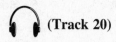 # EXERCISE 20: Conversations—Professors/Students

(Track 20)

In some conversations in the Listening Section on the Internet-Based TOEFL, you will be asked to recall information exchanged between professors and students about classroom content or policies. The interactions will include natural pauses and will be at a normal rate for a conversation between native speakers. Choose the best answer for multiple-choice questions. For computer-assisted questions, follow the directions on the screen.

Conversation One

1. What is the student mainly discussing with his professor?
   Ⓐ Transfer to another college
   Ⓑ Prerequisites for a class
   Ⓒ The summaries in the e-book
   Ⓓ Answering questions on a test

2. When will the test be given?
   Ⓐ Monday
   Ⓑ Wednesday
   Ⓒ Friday
   Ⓓ Today

3. Why is the man worried about the test?
   Choose 2 answers.
   Ⓐ It is his first test in this professor's class.
   Ⓑ He is used to multiple-choice tests.
   Ⓒ This test is much longer than previous ones.
   Ⓓ He is not confident about his writing.

4. What does the professor suggest?
   Ⓐ Study the summaries after each chapter.
   Ⓑ Spend time going over the notes from class.
   Ⓒ Review the terms at the end of the book.
   Ⓓ Write an essay instead of taking the test.

5. What does Jim mean when he says this: "Oh, I think I get it now."
   Ⓐ He will take the test right away.
   Ⓑ He understands the explanation.
   Ⓒ He may need another example.
   Ⓓ He is ready to leave the office.

6. What can we assume about the man?
   Ⓐ He is going to change roommates.
   Ⓑ He is adjusting to the larger school.
   Ⓒ He did not take the prerequisite.
   Ⓓ He didn't take notes in class.

Refer to pages 287–288 for the Explanatory Answers.

Conversation Two

1. Why did the professor want to see the student?
   - (A) To lend her a book for her paper
   - (B) To talk with her about the library
   - (C) To help her find a research topic
   - (D) To discuss her use of citations

2. Why did the student lose points on her last paper?
   - (A) It was not well written.
   - (B) She had too few citations.
   - (C) The sources were not good.
   - (D) The paper wasn't long enough.

3. How does the student do her research now?
   - (A) She does a general Google search.
   - (B) She purchases articles online.
   - (C) She uses Google Scholar.
   - (D) She goes to the library.

4. Why does the professor say this: "But?"
   - (A) He is encouraging the student to continue.
   - (B) He expresses surprise that she doesn't want help.
   - (C) He is changing the subject they are discussing.
   - (D) He indicates that he has stopped offering help.

5. How will the professor help the student?
   - (A) He will read her paper and correct any errors.
   - (B) He plans to give her a list of sources to use.
   - (C) He is going to make suggestions for citations.
   - (D) He does not need to help her with her paper.

6. When will they meet again?
   - (A) Next Monday
   - (B) Friday after class
   - (C) During office hours
   - (D) Tuesday morning

Refer to pages 289–290 for the Explanatory Answers.

EXERCISE 21: Talks—Professor

(Track 21)

In some talks in the Listening Comprehension Section on the Institutional TOEFL, you will be asked to recall information in announcements and explanations that might be heard at the beginning or end of a college class. Choose the best answer.

Lecture One

1. What is the purpose of the announcement?
   - Ⓐ To give an overview of the course
   - Ⓑ To explain how to prepare for the test
   - Ⓒ To cover the material from the textbooks
   - Ⓓ To assist students with their lab assignments

2. On the test, how much will the multiple-choice questions count?
   - Ⓐ Ten percent
   - Ⓑ Twenty-five percent
   - Ⓒ Forty percent
   - Ⓓ Fifty percent

3. For what percentage of the total grade will the test count?
   - Ⓐ Ten percent
   - Ⓑ Twenty-five percent
   - Ⓒ Forty percent
   - Ⓓ Fifty percent

4. What does the speaker say about math problems?
   - Ⓐ The students should not review their notes.
   - Ⓑ There won't be any math problems on the test.
   - Ⓒ There will be fifty math problems on the test.
   - Ⓓ The math formulas will not be necessary for the test.

5. In which class would this announcement occur?
   - Ⓐ An English class
   - Ⓑ A history class
   - Ⓒ A chemistry class
   - Ⓓ A foreign language class

Lecture Two

1. What is the main topic of this talk?
   - Ⓐ The difference between plagiarism and legitimate writing strategies
   - Ⓑ The penalties for plagiarism
   - Ⓒ The use of quotations in term papers
   - Ⓓ The requirement for a term paper on plagiarism

2. What is *plagiarizing*?
   - Ⓐ Using your own ideas
   - Ⓑ Quoting someone's exact words and citing the source
   - Ⓒ Enclosing someone's exact words in quotation marks
   - Ⓓ Copying ideas without citing the source

3. What are two legitimate writing strategies?
   - Ⓐ Paraphrasing and plagiarizing
   - Ⓑ Quoting and plagiarizing
   - Ⓒ Paraphrasing and quoting
   - Ⓓ Copying and paraphrasing

4. What will happen to a student who plagiarizes on the term paper?
   - Ⓐ He will receive a lower grade.
   - Ⓑ He will be asked to repeat the course.
   - Ⓒ He will be asked to rewrite the paper.
   - Ⓓ He will fail the course.

5. Who is the speaker?
   - Ⓐ A writer
   - Ⓑ A student
   - Ⓒ A librarian
   - Ⓓ A teacher

Refer to pages 290–292 for the Explanatory Answers.

 # EXERCISE 22: Lectures—Professor

(Track 22)

In some lectures in the Listening Section on the Internet-Based TOEFL, you will be asked to recall information in announcements and explanations that might be heard at the beginning or end of a college class. The lectures will include natural pauses, and will be at a normal rate for a lecture between native speakers. Choose the best answer.

Lecture One

1. What is the main purpose of this lecture?
   - Ⓐ To discuss incomplete grades
   - Ⓑ To arrange for makeup exams
   - Ⓒ To explain course policies and procedures
   - Ⓓ To give an overview of the course content

2. What is the professor's policy for late assignments?
   - Ⓐ He will allow the students one day after the due date before marking them down.
   - Ⓑ He will not accept late assignments.
   - Ⓒ He will subtract one letter from the grade for each day that the paper is late.
   - Ⓓ He will excuse students who are ill.

3. What is the professor's attendance policy?
   - Ⓐ He calls the roll before every session.
   - Ⓑ He does not take attendance in class.
   - Ⓒ He has each student check in after class.
   - Ⓓ He uses a seating chart to take attendance.

4. What is the procedure for a student to receive a grade of incomplete?
   - Ⓐ The student must submit a request form explaining why the incomplete is necessary.
   - Ⓑ The student must call the professor to explain.
   - Ⓒ The student must arrange for the incomplete within one week of the final exam.
   - Ⓓ The student must register to take the course again.

5. Why does the professor say this: "Remember that attendance is 10 percent . . . sorry . . . 15 percent of the grade . . ."
   - Ⓐ He is acknowledging that his policy is unpopular.
   - Ⓑ He is announcing a change in policy.
   - Ⓒ He is correcting an error that he made.
   - Ⓓ He is reminding students to attend.

6. What can we infer about the professor?
   - Ⓐ He is not very organized.
   - Ⓑ He does not like his students.
   - Ⓒ He does not mind if his students call him at home.
   - Ⓓ He does not give many exams.

Refer to pages 292–294 for the Explanatory Answers.

Lecture Two

1. What is the purpose of this lecture?
   - Ⓐ The professor is announcing the grades for the group project.
   - Ⓑ The students are asking questions about the group project.
   - Ⓒ The professor is explaining how he will grade the group project.
   - Ⓓ The students are protesting their grades on the group project.

2. How will the written report be graded?
   - Ⓐ Each individual will receive a separate grade.
   - Ⓑ The same grade will be given to every member of the group.
   - Ⓒ The professor will give three grades for the report.
   - Ⓓ Three grades will be averaged for the evaluation of the report.

3. How will the final grade be calculated for each student?
   - Ⓐ The professor will average the grades of each member of the group.
   - Ⓑ Two group grades and one individual grade will be averaged.
   - Ⓒ The self-evaluation for each member of the group will be averaged.
   - Ⓓ The grades of all three groups will be averaged.

4. How will the professor know what each individual has contributed?
   - Ⓐ He will supervise each student closely.
   - Ⓑ He will rely on each individual to report.
   - Ⓒ The group will verify a report by each member.
   - Ⓓ The group leader will report each member's work.

5. Why does the professor ask this: 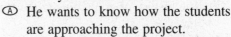 "How do you divide the work?"
   - Ⓐ He wants to know how the students are approaching the project.
   - Ⓑ He does not understand what the students are doing.
   - Ⓒ He asks a question in order to provide an answer for the students.
   - Ⓓ He disapproves of the way that the students organized the work.

6. Why does the professor most probably use such a complicated grading system?
   - Ⓐ He is trying to be fair.
   - Ⓑ He has used it before.
   - Ⓒ He does not like to evaluate.
   - Ⓓ He can explain it easily.

Refer to pages 294–296 for the Explanatory Answers.

EXERCISE 23: Talks—Professor

 **(Track 23)**

In some talks in the Listening Comprehension Section on the Institutional TOEFL, you will be asked to understand content from short lectures that might be heard in a college classroom. Choose the best answer.

Lecture One

1. What is the main topic of this lecture?
   - Ⓐ The American eagle as a symbol on coins
   - Ⓑ The history of gold coins in the United States
   - Ⓒ The United States Mint
   - Ⓓ The value to collectors of gold coins

2. What was the value of the original gold eagle?
   - Ⓐ $20.00
   - Ⓑ $10.00
   - Ⓒ $5.00
   - Ⓓ $2.50

3. What was the value of silver to gold in 1792?
   - Ⓐ Fifteen to one
   - Ⓑ Fifteen and a quarter to one
   - Ⓒ Fifteen and three quarters to one
   - Ⓓ Fifteen to three

4. What happened after the law of 1834?
   - Ⓐ The Great Depression occurred.
   - Ⓑ The size of gold coins was reduced.
   - Ⓒ All gold coins were turned in to the government.
   - Ⓓ The collecting of gold was severely reduced.

5. What are the restrictions on collecting gold coins today?
   - Ⓐ Gold coins may be imported without restrictions.
   - Ⓑ Gold coins may be collected but not exported.
   - Ⓒ There are few restrictions on the collection of gold coins.
   - Ⓓ Only certain kinds of gold coins may be purchased and sold.

Lecture Two

1. What kind of music is associated with Stephen Foster?
   - Ⓐ Sentimental tunes
   - Ⓑ Plantation songs
   - Ⓒ Hymns for churches
   - Ⓓ Serious society music

2. Which piece was the most successful song written by an American?
   - Ⓐ "Open Thy Lattice, Love"
   - Ⓑ "Oh, Susanna"
   - Ⓒ "Old Folks at Home"
   - Ⓓ "Beautiful Dreamer"

3. Why did Stephen Foster withhold his name from the cover to some of his sheet music?
   - Ⓐ He was too young to publish music at that time.
   - Ⓑ His name was not yet very well known.
   - Ⓒ He knew that some songs would not be approved by high society.
   - Ⓓ He reserved his name for his most popular music.

4. What best describes Stephen Foster's most popular songs?
   - Ⓐ Easy to remember
   - Ⓑ Written for the piano
   - Ⓒ Appropriate for society events
   - Ⓓ Very serious

5. What do we know about Stephen Foster?
   - Ⓐ He wrote many songs during his career.
   - Ⓑ Only a few of his songs were popular.
   - Ⓒ He was not successful in his lifetime.
   - Ⓓ He wrote most of his music for children.

Refer to pages 296–298 for the Explanatory Answers.

Exercise 24: Talks—Professor

 **(Track 24)**

In some talks in the Listening Comprehension Section on the Institutional TOEFL, you will be asked to understand content from short lectures that might be heard in a college classroom. Choose the best answer.

Lecture One

1. What is the main subject of this lecture?
   - Ⓐ Heredity
   - Ⓑ Environment
   - Ⓒ Birth order
   - Ⓓ Motivation

2. What should the students know before they hear this lecture?
   - Ⓐ Birth order may influence personality.
   - Ⓑ Heredity and environment play a role in the development of the personality.
   - Ⓒ There is research on birth order at the University of Texas at Arlington.
   - Ⓓ Firstborn children and only children have similar personalities.

3. Which one of the people would probably be the most comfortable interacting with a member of the opposite sex?
   - Ⓐ A man with younger sisters
   - Ⓑ A man with older sisters
   - Ⓒ A woman with younger sisters
   - Ⓓ A woman with older sisters

4. What personality trait will firstborn children probably exhibit?
   - Ⓐ Likable
   - Ⓑ Ambitious
   - Ⓒ Sociable
   - Ⓓ Talkative

5. According to the research, what might be the dominant personality trait of the youngest child?
   - Ⓐ Charming
   - Ⓑ Shy
   - Ⓒ Motivated
   - Ⓓ Happy

Lecture Two

1. What is the main focus of this lecture?
   - Ⓐ The Knickerbocker School
   - Ⓑ The character of Natty Bumppo
   - Ⓒ The *Leatherstocking Tales*
   - Ⓓ Writers for the *New York Evening Post*

2. What are the *Leatherstocking Tales*?
   - Ⓐ Stories by Washington Irving
   - Ⓑ Five novels about frontier life
   - Ⓒ Serials in the *New York Evening Post*
   - Ⓓ Poems by the Knickerbocker group

3. What kind of character is Natty Bumppo?
   - Ⓐ A frontier hero
   - Ⓑ An inept settler on the frontier
   - Ⓒ The son of an Indian chief
   - Ⓓ The last member of his tribe

4. Who was one of the most important members of the Knickerbocker School?
   - Ⓐ Rip Van Winkle
   - Ⓑ Washington Irving
   - Ⓒ Forrest Mohican
   - Ⓓ Diedrich Knickerbocker

5. Which of the following best describes James Fenimore Cooper?
   - Ⓐ Author, the *Leatherstocking Tales*
   - Ⓑ Author, "The Legend of Sleepy Hollow"
   - Ⓒ Editor, the *New York Evening Post*
   - Ⓓ Professor, the Knickerbocker School

Refer to pages 299–301 for the Explanatory Answers.

EXERCISE 25: Lectures—Professor

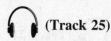 **(Track 25)**

In some lectures in the Listening Section on the Internet-Based TOEFL, you will be asked to understand academic content similar to that of short lectures that might be heard in a college classroom. The lectures will include natural pauses, and will be at a normal rate for a talk by a native speaker. Choose the best answer for multiple-choice questions. For computer-assisted questions, follow the directions.

Lecture One

1. What is the main topic of this lecture?
   - Ⓐ Popcorn
   - Ⓑ Radiometric dating
   - Ⓒ Carbon-14
   - Ⓓ Geological formations

2. What is the definition of a *half-life*?
   - Ⓐ The average time it takes for half of a group to decay
   - Ⓑ Half the time it takes for a group to decay
   - Ⓒ Half an hour for an individual nucleus to decay
   - Ⓓ Half of the carbon present in a living organism

3. Why does the professor mention popcorn?
   - Ⓐ Because it was an example in the textbook
   - Ⓑ Because he is using popcorn in a laboratory demonstration
   - Ⓒ Because popcorn is a good analogy for half-lives
   - Ⓓ Because popcorn is a carbon-based life form

4. What do we know about carbon-14?
   - Ⓐ It is the only accurate isotope for radiometric dating.
   - Ⓑ It represents most of the carbon in living things.
   - Ⓒ It has a half-life of almost 50 billion years.
   - Ⓓ It is used to estimate the age of carbon-based life forms.

5. Why does the professor ask this question: "So what about rocks that are millions or even billions of years old?"
   - Ⓐ He is preparing to suggest an answer to the question that he has just asked.
   - Ⓑ He is trying to encourage the students to answer a difficult question.
   - Ⓒ He is expressing doubt about the concept that he has been discussing.
   - Ⓓ He is probing to see whether the students have understood the lecture so far.

6. Which of the following would NOT be dated using carbon-14?
   - Ⓐ A fossilized shellfish
   - Ⓑ An animal skull
   - Ⓒ A dead tree
   - Ⓓ A giant crystal

Refer to pages 301–303 for the Explanatory Answers.

Lecture Two

1. What is this lecture mainly about?
   Ⓐ Ancient cities
   Ⓑ Three types of cities
   Ⓒ City planning
   Ⓓ Urban sprawl

2. What feature of ancient cities appears throughout most of the world?
   Ⓐ Walls and fortifications
   Ⓑ A central marketplace
   Ⓒ Plazas and parks
   Ⓓ A pattern of square blocks

3. When were symmetrical streets with circular patterns introduced?
   Ⓐ During Roman colonization
   Ⓑ During the Renaissance
   Ⓒ During the Industrial Revolution
   Ⓓ During the Modern Era

4. What was the problem for city planners during the Industrial Revolution?
   Choose 2 answers.
   Ⓐ Housing for immigrants from the countryside
   Ⓑ Inadequate sanitation services for the population
   Ⓒ Reconstruction of cities devastated by war
   Ⓓ The growth of sprawling suburban areas

5. Why did the professor say this: "I advise you to refer to the three types of cities in your book"?
   Ⓐ She wants the students to spend more time reading their books.
   Ⓑ She did not have time to talk about the concept in depth.
   Ⓒ She is going to read some important information to the students.
   Ⓓ She wants the students to prepare for the next class.

6. Classify each of these cities by matching them with their type.
   Ⓐ Singapore
   Ⓑ Mexico City
   Ⓒ Los Angeles

Decentralized	Centralized	Densely populated

Refer to pages 303–305 for the Explanatory Answers.

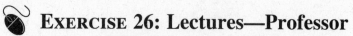

EXERCISE 26: Lectures—Professor

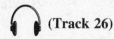 (Track 26)

In some lectures in the Listening Section on the Internet-Based TOEFL, you will be asked to understand academic content similar to that of short lectures that might be heard in a college classroom. The lectures will include natural pauses and will be at a normal rate for a talk by a native speaker. Choose the best answer for multiple-choice questions. For computer-assisted questions, follow the directions.

Lecture One

1. What is this lecture mainly about?
   Ⓐ An overview of fuel cell technology
   Ⓑ A process for producing fuel cells
   Ⓒ A comparison of fuel cell models
   Ⓓ Some problems in fuel cell distribution

2. What do we know about hydrogen?
   Ⓐ It produces energy through combustion.
   Ⓑ It must be used with other energy sources.
   Ⓒ It is not as efficient as a combustion engine.
   Ⓓ It is possible to produce it from water.

3. Why does the professor mention the STEP program in Australia?
   Ⓐ He has personal experience in this project.
   Ⓑ He is referring to information from a previous discussion.
   Ⓒ He is comparing it to a successful program in Japan.
   Ⓓ He thinks it is a very good example of a project.

4. Why does the professor say this: "... if memory serves, it was 2003..."
   Ⓐ To indicate that the date is not important
   Ⓑ To provide a specific date for the contract
   Ⓒ To correct a previous statement about the date
   Ⓓ To show that he is uncertain about the date

5. What are some of the problems associated with fuel cell technology?
   Choose 2 answers.
   Ⓐ Noise pollution
   Ⓑ Public acceptance
   Ⓒ Supplies of hydrogen
   Ⓓ Investment in infrastructures

6. What is the professor's attitude toward fuel cells?
   Ⓐ He thinks that the technology is not very efficient.
   Ⓑ He is hopeful about their development in the future.
   Ⓒ He is doubtful that fuel cells will replace fossil fuels.
   Ⓓ He is discouraged because of the delays in production.

Refer to pages 305–308 for the Explanatory Answers.

Lecture Two

1. What does this lecturer mainly discuss?
   - Ⓐ Transcendentalism
   - Ⓑ Puritanism
   - Ⓒ Ralph Waldo Emerson
   - Ⓓ Nature

2. Why does the professor say this: "Which, come to think of it, isn't an unusual attitude for students when they talk about their professors."
   - Ⓐ She is joking with the students.
   - Ⓑ She is drawing a conclusion.
   - Ⓒ She is correcting the students' behavior.
   - Ⓓ She is reasoning aloud.

3. According to the professor, what was true about the Puritans?
   - Ⓐ They stressed the essential importance of the individual.
   - Ⓑ They supported the ideals of the Transcendental Club.
   - Ⓒ They believed that society should be respected above persons.
   - Ⓓ They thought that people should live in communes like Brook Farm.

4. Why did the church oppose the transcendental movement?
   - Ⓐ The authority of the church would be challenged by a code of personal ethics.
   - Ⓑ The leaders of the transcendentalists were not as well educated as the clergy.
   - Ⓒ Church members were competing with transcendentalists for teaching positions.
   - Ⓓ Professors at Harvard College convinced the church to support their position.

5. Why did the professor mention *Walden*?
   - Ⓐ It is probably well-known to many of the students in the class.
   - Ⓑ It is considered an excellent example of transcendental literature.
   - Ⓒ It is required reading for the course that she is teaching.
   - Ⓓ It is her personal favorite of nineteenth-century essays.

6. According to the professor, what was the most lasting contribution of transcendentalism?
   - Ⓐ Educational reorganization
   - Ⓑ Religious reformation
   - Ⓒ Experimental communities
   - Ⓓ Political changes

Refer to pages 308–310 for the Explanatory Answers.

EXERCISE 27: Talks—Professors/Students

 (Track 27)

In some talks in the Listening Comprehension Section on the Institutional TOEFL, you will be asked to understand content from short discussions that might be heard in a college classroom. Both the professor and the students will be contributing to the class. Choose the best answer.

Lecture One

1. What do the speakers mainly discuss?
   - Ⓐ Admissions standards at the University of Michigan
   - Ⓑ The use of standardized tests for college admissions
   - Ⓒ The TOEFL (Test of English as a Foreign Language)
   - Ⓓ Evaluation without standardized tests

2. What is Paul's opinion about the TOEFL and the Michigan Test?
   - Ⓐ He believes that the tests are good.
   - Ⓑ He believes that the required test scores are too low.
   - Ⓒ He believes that they are more important than academic preparation.
   - Ⓓ He believes that the tests should not be used.

3. What does Sally say about the admissions officers?
   - Ⓐ They don't always use the TOEFL and the Michigan Test scores correctly.
   - Ⓑ They look at transcripts instead of scores.
   - Ⓒ They should insist on a rigid cut-off score.
   - Ⓓ They are looking for an appropriate alternative.

4. How does the professor handle the disagreement?
   - Ⓐ He agrees with Sally.
   - Ⓑ He restates both opinions.
   - Ⓒ He asks the class to vote.
   - Ⓓ He disagrees with both students.

5. Where did this discussion most probably take place?
   - Ⓐ In a college classroom
   - Ⓑ At the Office of International Services
   - Ⓒ In the cafeteria
   - Ⓓ At a party

Lecture Two

1. What do the speakers mainly discuss?
   - Ⓐ Making friends in a foreign country
   - Ⓑ Spanish and French
   - Ⓒ Foreign TV, radio, and other media
   - Ⓓ Learning a foreign language

2. Why does Professor Baker begin the discussion by calling on Betty?
   - Ⓐ Because she is not a shy person
   - Ⓑ Because she studied languages in high school
   - Ⓒ Because she knows several languages
   - Ⓓ Because she agrees with him

3. What helped Betty most in learning Spanish?
   - Ⓐ The language laboratory
   - Ⓑ Travel in other countries
   - Ⓒ Studying in high school
   - Ⓓ Going to movies and watching TV

4. What is Professor Baker's opinion?
   - Ⓐ He believes that it is a good idea to do all of the things that Betty and Bill suggested.
   - Ⓑ He agrees with Betty's idea for learning languages.
   - Ⓒ He believes that going to class is the best way to learn.
   - Ⓓ He believes that it is ideal to live in a country where the language is spoken.

5. How can we best describe Professor Baker?
   - Ⓐ He is not very knowledgeable.
   - Ⓑ He is respectful of his students.
   - Ⓒ He has a very formal manner in class.
   - Ⓓ He has traveled extensively.

Refer to pages 310–312 for the Explanatory Answers.

EXERCISE 28: Lectures—Professor/Students

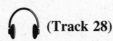 (Track 28)

In some lectures in the Listening Section on the Internet-Based TOEFL, you will be asked to understand academic content similar to that of short lectures that might be heard in a college classroom. The lectures will include natural pauses, and will be at a normal rate for a conversation between native speakers. Both the professor and the students will be contributing to the class. Choose the best answer for multiple-choice questions. For computer-assisted questions, follow the directions.

Lecture One

1. What is this lecture mainly about?
   - Ⓐ Pop artists of the 1960s
   - Ⓑ Andy Warhol's art
   - Ⓒ Portraits of famous people
   - Ⓓ The use of color in pop art

2. According to the lecturer, why did Warhol paint objects in the environment?
   - Ⓐ He was once a commercial artist.
   - Ⓑ He was a very logical person.
   - Ⓒ He used the objects in his daily routine.
   - Ⓓ He was tired of painting landscapes.

3. Whose faces did Warhol paint?
   Choose 2 answers.
   - Ⓐ Marilyn Monroe
   - Ⓑ Elvis Presley
   - Ⓒ John Kennedy
   - Ⓓ Andy Warhol

4. What problem does Tom mention?
   - Ⓐ The colors that pop artists used were grotesque.
   - Ⓑ The paintings were used as commercial advertisements.
   - Ⓒ The paintings were too large for private collectors.
   - Ⓓ The subjects might not be of interest in the future.

5. Why did the professor say this: "So, Tom, you're saying that since pop art . . . since it depends on the popular culture, which by its very nature is uh, transient, you're asking . . . will the subject matter of the pop art movement doom its artists to temporary recognition?"
   - Ⓐ He asks the student to repeat his idea because it is interesting.
   - Ⓑ He disagrees with the student's statement about pop art.
   - Ⓒ He asks the student another question to continue the discussion.
   - Ⓓ He restates the student's comment to refine and clarify it.

6. Choose the drawing that is done in the Andy Warhol style.

   A.   B.   C.

Refer to pages 313–315 for the Explanatory Answers.

Lecture Two

1. What is the main topic of today's lecture?
   Ⓐ The climax association
   Ⓑ Pioneer plants
   Ⓒ A forest fire
   Ⓓ A disturbance in the balance of nature

2. How does the scientific community view the theory of a stable climax community?
   Ⓐ They no longer support it.
   Ⓑ They were never interested in it.
   Ⓒ They named it *dynamic equilibrium.*
   Ⓓ They proposed it to replace *polyclimax.*

3. According to the lecturer, why is pioneer life important?
   Ⓐ It prepares the environment for the forms that will replace it.
   Ⓑ It is a stable environment that remains undisturbed in spite of conditions.
   Ⓒ It assures that plants, animals, and minerals are replaced by exactly the same flora and fauna.
   Ⓓ It is the only life that will ever be able to grow in areas where the balance of nature has been disturbed.

4. What is Dr. Green's opinion of a *controlled burn*?
   Ⓐ He agrees with using a *cool fire* to control wildfires.
   Ⓑ He disagrees with the author of the textbook they are using.
   Ⓒ He thinks that using a *controlled burn* is the only reasonable opinion.
   Ⓓ He does not think that fire-prevention strategies influence forest fires.

5. Why did the student ask this question: "Excuse me, Dr. Green, would that be what the book refers to as *ecological succession*?"
   Ⓐ Because the book is difficult to understand
   Ⓑ Because he is trying to relate the lecture to the book
   Ⓒ Because Dr. Green's lecture was not very clear
   Ⓓ Because he wants to interrupt Dr. Green

6. The professor describes the process of ecological succession that occurs after the balance of nature has been disturbed. Summarize the process by putting the events in order.
   Ⓐ Pioneer flora and fauna appear.
   Ⓑ The climax association occurs.
   Ⓒ More stable plant and animal life is established.
   Ⓓ Other forms of temporary plants and animals replace the early ones.

1.	
2.	
3.	
4.	

Refer to pages 315–317 for the Explanatory Answers.

EXERCISE 29: Talks—Professor/Visuals

 (Track 29)

In some talks in the Listening Comprehension Section on the Institutional TOEFL, you will be asked to understand academic content similar to that of short lectures that might be heard in a college classroom. Drawings, charts, or other visuals will support the talk. Choose the best answer.

Lecture One

1. What is the main purpose of this lecture?
   - Ⓐ The life of Louis Tiffany
   - Ⓑ The work of Louis Tiffany
   - Ⓒ The art nouveau movement
   - Ⓓ *Favrile* glass art objects

2. What characterized Tiffany's jewelry?
   - Ⓐ Iridescent glass
   - Ⓑ Precious stones
   - Ⓒ Traditional styles
   - Ⓓ Floral designs

3. How did Tiffany help aspiring artists?
   - Ⓐ He was a teacher.
   - Ⓑ He founded a school.
   - Ⓒ He provided scholarships.
   - Ⓓ He sold their work in his shop.

4. For which interior design was Tiffany NOT commissioned?
   - Ⓐ A glass curtain at the National Theater in Mexico
   - Ⓑ The altar in the Cathedral of Saint John the Divine
   - Ⓒ The reception rooms in the White House
   - Ⓓ Exclusive stores on Fifth Avenue in Manhattan

5. Select the example of a Tiffany *favrile* design. Choose the letter of the drawing that was described in the talk.

Refer to pages 317–319 for the Explanatory Answers.

Lecture Two

1. What is the lecture mainly about?
   - Ⓐ The structure of the cactus
   - Ⓑ Extreme climates
   - Ⓒ Water storage in cactus plants
   - Ⓓ The nutritive functions of leaves

2. What is assumed about cactus plants millions of years ago?
   - Ⓐ They were probably much larger.
   - Ⓑ They probably had leaves like other plants.
   - Ⓒ They probably grew underground.
   - Ⓓ They probably had fruit as well as flowers.

3. According to the lecturer, why have cacti developed spines and needles?
   - Ⓐ They grew closer to the surface.
   - Ⓑ They could absorb water more quickly.
   - Ⓒ They protected the plant from animals.
   - Ⓓ They supported beautiful blossoms.

4. Where is the nutritive function of the cactus carried out?
   - Ⓐ Leaves
   - Ⓑ Blossoms
   - Ⓒ Stems
   - Ⓓ Roots

5. Select the Saguaro cactus from among the choices pictured. Choose the letter of the drawing that was described in the talk.
   - Ⓐ
   - Ⓑ
   - Ⓒ

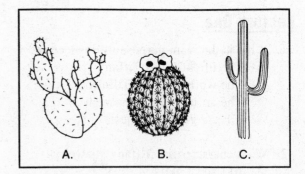

A.   B.   C.

Refer to pages 319–320 for the Explanatory Answers.

EXERCISE 30: Lectures—Professor/Visuals

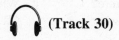 **(Track 30)**

In some lectures in the Listening Section on the Internet-Based TOEFL, you will be asked to understand academic content similar to that of short lectures that might be heard in a college classroom. The lectures will include natural pauses, and will be at a normal rate for a talk by a native speaker. Drawings, charts, or other visuals will support the lecture. Choose the best answer for multiple-choice questions. For computer-assisted questions, follow the directions on screen.

Lecture One

1. What is the main purpose of this lecture?
   - Ⓐ To make arrangements for the field trip
   - Ⓑ To introduce the students to some common petroglyphs
   - Ⓒ To discuss legends from the Hohokam culture
   - Ⓓ To classify the different clans in Hohokam culture

2. What are *petroglyphs*?
   - Ⓐ An early alphabet
   - Ⓑ Art on rocks
   - Ⓒ Anthropologists
   - Ⓓ Religious ceremonies

3. How are anthropologists able to interpret the symbols?
   Choose 2 answers.
   - Ⓐ Early inhabitants left a history.
   - Ⓑ The descendants of early people know the stories.
   - Ⓒ Some of the symbols are common to many cultures.
   - Ⓓ The symbols are pictures that represent objects.

4. What might be represented by a *zoomorph*?
   Choose 2 answers.
   - Ⓐ A religious ceremony
   - Ⓑ The history of a successful hunt
   - Ⓒ The name of a family clan
   - Ⓓ The symbol of a group of spirits

5. Why did the professor say this: "But, um . . . why were they carved in the first place?"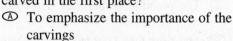
   - Ⓐ To emphasize the importance of the carvings
   - Ⓑ To ask a question that she will answer
   - Ⓒ To check on students' comprehension
   - Ⓓ To begin a discussion among the students

6. Choose the petroglyph that is a spiritual symbol of life.

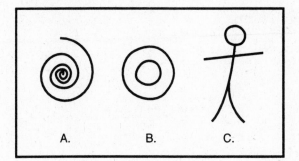

A.   B.   C.

Refer to pages 320–323 for the Explanatory Answers.

Lecture Two

1. What is the main purpose of this lecture?
   - Ⓐ To contrast short-period and long-period comets
   - Ⓑ To discuss the structure and nature of comets
   - Ⓒ To explain the orbit of planets
   - Ⓓ To predict the probability of collisions between planets and comets

2. What causes the tail of a comet to point away from the Sun?
   - Ⓐ The orbit of the comet
   - Ⓑ The solar wind
   - Ⓒ The coma of the comet
   - Ⓓ The cloud that lies beyond Pluto

3. What is the difference between a short-period comet and a long-period comet?
   - Ⓐ The shape of their orbits
   - Ⓑ The size of their tails
   - Ⓒ The probability that they will collide with planets
   - Ⓓ The time they take to orbit the Sun

4. What is *capture*?
   - Ⓐ The gravitational pull of a planet permanently attracts a comet.
   - Ⓑ A long-period comet is converted into a short-period comet.
   - Ⓒ The orbits of planets and comets intersect at one point.
   - Ⓓ The impact of comets on planets and moons causes craters.

5. Why does the professor say this: "Let me say that again."
   - Ⓐ He wants the students to write down the definition.
   - Ⓑ He did not say it correctly the first time.
   - Ⓒ He does not think that students are paying attention.
   - Ⓓ He believes in class participation.

6. Choose the orbit of a comet.

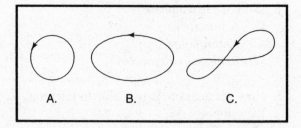

Refer to pages 323–326 for the Explanatory Answers.

PRACTICE EXERCISES
FOR SPEAKING

Speaking Section

The Speaking Section of the TOEFL tests your ability to speak in English about a variety of general and academic topics. The Speaking Section is not included in the Institutional TOEFL. It is included only in the Internet-Based TOEFL.

Overview of the TOEFL iBT® Speaking Section

The Speaking Section tests your ability to communicate in English in an academic setting. During the test, you will be presented with four speaking questions. The questions ask for a response to a single question, a talk, or a lecture. The prompts and questions are presented only one time.

You may take notes as you listen, but notes are not graded. You may use your notes to answer the questions. Some of the questions ask for a response to a reading passage and a talk or a lecture. The reading passages and the questions are written, but the directions will be spoken.

Your speaking will be evaluated on both the fluency of the language and the accuracy of the content. You will have 15–30 seconds to prepare and 45–60 seconds to respond to each question. Typically, a good response will require all of the response time, and the answer will be complete by the end of the response time.

You will have about 17 minutes to complete the Speaking Section. A clock on the screen will show you how much time you have to prepare each of your answers and how much time you have to record each response.

EXERCISE 31: Independent Task 1—Agree or Disagree

 (Track 31)

In Task 1 of the Speaking Section on the Internet-Based TOEFL, you may be asked to agree or disagree with a statement. Most of the time, the speaker will have a North American dialect, but sometimes, as in Topic Two, the speaker will have an Australian dialect. You have 15 seconds to prepare after you have heard the question. Then, you have 45 seconds to record your answer.

Topic One

Question:
State whether you agree or disagree with the following position.

A college education should be free for all qualified students.

Be sure to use specific reasons and examples to support your opinion.

Preparation Time: 15 seconds
Recording Time: 45 seconds

Notes

Refer to pages 328–329 for the Example Answer.

<u>Topic Two</u>

Question:
State whether you agree or disagree with the following position.

Young people spend too much time on their phones.

Be sure to use specific reasons and examples to support your opinion.

Preparation Time: 15 seconds
Recording Time: 45 seconds

Notes

Refer to page 329 for the Example Answer.

EXERCISE 32: Independent Task 1—Two Options

 (Track 32)

In Task 1 of the Speaking Section on the Internet-Based TOEFL, you may be asked to make a choice between two options, and defend your opinion. Most of the time, the speaker will have a North American dialect, but sometimes, as in Topic Two, the speaker will have a British dialect. You have 15 seconds to prepare after you have heard the question. Then, you have 45 seconds to record your answer.

Topic One

Question:

Some teachers encourage competition among their students. Others help students learn how to collaborate and study in groups. Which approach do you think is better for learning and why do you think so? Be sure to use specific reasons and examples to support your opinion.

Preparation Time: 15 seconds
Recording Time: 45 seconds

Notes

Refer to page 330 for the Example Answer.

Topic Two

Question:

Some people cope with stress by exercising. Others talk with family or friends. How do you handle stressful situations? Be sure to use specific reasons and examples to support your opinion.

Preparation Time: 15 seconds
Recording Time: 45 seconds

Notes

Refer to page 331 for the Example Answer.

EXERCISE 33: Independent Task 1—Three Options

 (Track 33)

In Task 1 of the Speaking Section on the Internet-Based TOEFL, you may be asked to make a choice among three options, and defend your opinion. You have 15 seconds to prepare after you have heard the question. Then, you have 45 seconds to record your answer.

Topic One

Question:

You are applying for a work-study job on campus, and you have three opportunities: a job in the library, in the cafeteria, or in a professor's office. For which job would you apply? Be sure to give specific reasons and examples for your choice.

Preparation Time: 15 seconds
Recording Time: 45 seconds

Notes

Refer to page 332 for the Example Answer.

Topic Two

Question:
The International Student Association is planning a fund-raiser. Three possibilities are being considered: a talent show with music and dancing from around the world, a dinner with food from various countries, and a fair with booths featuring international items for sale. Which option would you support, and why? Be sure to give specific reasons and examples for your choice.

Preparation Time: 15 seconds
Recording Time: 45 seconds

Notes

Refer to page 333 for the Example Answer.

EXERCISE 34: Integrated Task 2—Campus Reports

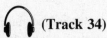 **(Track 34)**

In Task 2 of the Speaking Section on the Internet-Based TOEFL, you will be asked to make a connection between a short reading passage and a talk. You have 30 seconds to prepare after you have read the passage and heard the talk. Then, you have 60 seconds to record your answer.

Topic One

Reading Time: 50 seconds

Accelerated Bachelor's Program

City College currently requires all bachelor's degree students to complete their degrees by fulfilling the course requirements in a four-year program plan. A three-year bachelor's degree program is being proposed to allow selected students to accelerate their programs, completing their degrees in three-fourths the time. If there is sufficient interest, the program will be offered to students in forty major fields of study. Classes will be limited to twenty students as compared with more than one hundred in the large lecture classes for students enrolled in the four-year program. To find out whether you qualify for this opportunity, contact an advisor in the Millennium Program Office in the Old Main Building.

Now listen to a student who is speaking to an advisor. She is expressing her opinion about the new program.

Question:
The student expresses her opinion about the college's plans for an accelerated three-year degree program. Summarize her opinion and the reasons she gives for having that opinion.

Preparation Time: 30 seconds
Recording Time: 60 seconds

Notes

Refer to pages 335–336 for the Example Answer.

<u>Topic Two</u>

Reading Time: 50 seconds

<u>Notice concerning dorm closing</u>

State University is considering a proposal to close all but one of the dormitories over spring break. The Office of University Research reports that only 10 percent of the dorm students maintain their residence on campus over the break, whereas the other 90 percent go home or leave for vacations. The cost of keeping all of the dorms open is difficult to justify; however, Norman Hall would offer a temporary living situation for those students who chose to remain on campus. This proposal will be discussed at a public meeting in the Little Theater at 7 P.M. on January 10.

Now listen to a student who is speaking at the meeting. He is expressing his opinion about the new policy.

Question:
The student expresses his opinion about the proposal for closing the dorms over spring break. Summarize his opinion and the reasons he gives for having that opinion.

Preparation Time: 30 seconds
Recording Time: 60 seconds

Notes

Refer to pages 336–337 for the Example Answer.

EXERCISE 35: Integrated Task 2—Campus Reports

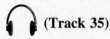 **(Track 35)**

In Task 2 of the Speaking Section on the Internet-Based TOEFL, you will be asked to make a connection between a short reading passage and a conversation. You have 30 seconds to prepare after you have read the passage and heard the conversation. Then, you have 60 seconds to record your answer.

Topic One

Reading Time: 50 seconds

Registration hours shortened

The hours for on-site registration at City College have traditionally been from 7 A.M. to 7 P.M. Monday through Friday the week before classes. However, since many students have been taking advantage of on-line registration, next term registration week will be shortened to three days, starting at 7 A.M. the Wednesday before classes begin and ending at 7 P.M. on Friday. Late registration during the first two days of classes will not be affected. Both on-site and on-line registration will be open for late scheduling and drop-add scheduling as usual on the first Monday and Tuesday of the semester.

Now listen to a conversation between two students. The man is expressing his opinion about the change.

Question:
The man expresses his opinion about the changes in the registration procedure. Report his opinion and explain the reasons that he gives for having that opinion.

Preparation Time: 30 seconds
Recording Time: 60 seconds

Notes

Refer to pages 337–338 for the Example Answer.

Topic Two

Reading Time: 50 seconds

Notice concerning the fall career fair

More than 100 representatives from business and industry will be participating in the annual career fair on Saturday, October 7, including high-level officers from a number of international companies. Booths and exhibits will be set up in the college auditorium between 9 A.M. and 3 P.M. To take full advantage of this opportunity, bring copies of your resume and transcripts with you to the fair. Representatives will be collecting applications so that they can contact students to arrange interviews. Most of the representatives will return to campus next month to complete the screening process, although some companies have announced that they will interview immediately after the exhibits are closed on Saturday.

Now listen to a conversation between two students. The woman is expressing her opinion about the career fair.

Question:
The woman expresses her opinion about the career fair. Report her opinion and explain the reasons that she gives for having that opinion.

Preparation Time: 30 seconds
Recording Time: 60 seconds

Notes

Refer to pages 338–340 for the Example Answer.

EXERCISE 36: Integrated Task 3—Academic Concepts

 (Track 36)

In Task 3 of the Speaking Section on the Internet-Based TOEFL, you will be asked to make a connection between a short reading passage and a lecture. In most of these items, you will be required to relate an example to a general concept. You have 30 seconds to prepare after you have read the passage and heard the lecture. Then, you have 60 seconds to record your answer.

Topic One

Reading Time: 50 seconds

A Village

A traditional village is self-contained, which means that within the village, facilities for daily life such as sleeping, eating, health care, and social activities are constructed. Furthermore, nearly all the essential supplies of goods and services are stored within the confines of the village, although one village may trade with another to secure certain items. In addition, the residents of the village interact closely with each other and have common goals and interests that are reflected in their activities. Finally, it is said the outward appearance of a village expresses the essence of who the inhabitants believe themselves to be.

Now listen to part of a lecture on the same topic.

Question:
Refer to Thomas Jefferson's definition of a college campus presented in the lecture, and explain how the information in the anthropology text supported Jefferson's view.

Preparation Time: 30 seconds
Recording Time: 60 seconds

Notes

Refer to pages 340–341 for the Example Answer.

Topic Two

Reading Time: 50 seconds

Entrepreneurs

Numerous studies of small-business owners in the United States reveal that about 50 percent of them come from poor or lower middle-class families. Most begin their working life early and are already employed full time by the age of 18. Most have already established their businesses by the age of 30. In general, they tend to display three characteristics, including a strong desire for independence, a high level of initiative, and the ability to react quickly to take advantage of an opportunity. Another interesting characteristic is the fact that so many successful small-business owners establish their businesses as a result of a coincidence rather than by following a business plan.

Now listen to part of a lecture on the same topic. The professor is talking about Levi Strauss.

Question:
Referring to both the lecture and the reading passage, explain why the experience of Levi Strauss is typical of small-business owners.

Preparation Time: 30 seconds
Recording Time: 60 seconds

Notes

Refer to pages 341–342 for the Example Answer.

EXERCISE 37: Integrated Task 3—Academic Concepts

 (Track 37)

In Task 3 of the Speaking Section on the Internet-Based TOEFL, you will be asked to make a connection between a short reading passage and a lecture. In most of these items, you will be required to relate an example to a general concept. You have 30 seconds to prepare after you have read the passage and heard the lecture. Then, you have 60 seconds to record your answer.

Topic One

Reading Time: 50 seconds

Expressionism

Expressionistic architecture was part of the early modernist movement which emerged in Europe around 1910 and continued through 1930, but today it has been redefined to encompass architecture created much later. Novel materials, formal innovation, and unusual masses and colors inspired by natural biomorphic forms were front and center in the buildings that the architects created. Another important aspect of expressionistic architecture was that engineering based on new technologies and materials offered novel possibilities for unique forms. All of these features of expressionism combined to provide architects with the opportunity to create individual structures designed to evoke an emotional response.

Now listen to part of a lecture. The professor is talking about architecture.

Question:
Referring to both the lecture and the reading passage, explain why the Sydney Opera House is an example of expressionism.

Preparation Time: 30 seconds
Recording Time: 60 seconds

Notes

Refer to pages 342–344 for the Example Answer.

Topic Two

Reading Time: 50 seconds

The Pygmalion Effect

The Pygmalion effect is a psychological phenomenon that occurs when high expectations lead to improved performance. Whether the expectation comes from ourselves or from others, the result seems to be the same. Even when the expectations are the result of bias or are irrational, we are influenced by them. Certainly, the effect is contingent upon being physically or mentally capable of achieving what is expected, and overly high expectations can be stressful and may cause us to give up. Nevertheless, if we are challenged but capable of what is expected, then high expectations can support higher achievement.

Now listen to part of a lecture on the same topic.

Question:
Referring to both the lecture and the reading passage, explain how the Pygmalion effect was demonstrated in the Rosenthal and Jacobson experiment.

Preparation Time: 30 seconds
Recording Time: 60 seconds

Notes

Refer to pages 344–345 for the Example Answer.

EXERCISE 38: Integrated Task 4—Academic Summaries

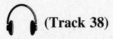 **(Track 38)**

In Task 4 of the Speaking Section on the Internet-Based TOEFL, you will be asked to summarize the main points in a short lecture. In most of these summaries, you will be required to explain a term or a concept. You have 20 seconds to prepare after you have heard the lecture. Then, you have 60 seconds to record your answer.

Topic One

Question:
Referring to the main points and examples from the lecture, describe the two general groups of flowering plants. Then explain the problem for classification that the professor presents.

Preparation Time: 20 seconds
Recording Time: 60 seconds

Notes

Refer to pages 345–347 for the Example Answer.

Topic Two

Question:

Referring to the main points and examples from the lecture, describe the two types of bridge construction presented by the professor. Then explain the specific advantages and disadvantages of each type.

Preparation Time: 20 seconds
Recording Time: 60 seconds

Notes

Refer to pages 347–348 for the Example Answer.

EXERCISE 39: Integrated Task 4—Academic Summaries

 **(Track 39)**

In Task 4 of the Speaking Section on the Internet-Based TOEFL, you will be asked to summarize the main points in a short lecture. In most of these summaries, you will be required to explain a term or a concept. You have 20 seconds to prepare after you have heard the lecture. Then, you have 60 seconds to record your answer.

Topic One

Question:
Referring to the main points and examples from the lecture, describe the three basic functions of the liver presented by the professor.

Preparation Time: 20 seconds
Recording Time: 60 seconds

Notes

Refer to pages 348–350 for the Example Answer.

Topic Two

Question:
Referring to the main points and examples from the lecture, describe two types of research correlations that the professor presents. Then explain causality.

Preparation Time: 20 seconds
Recording Time: 60 seconds

Notes

Refer to pages 350–351 for the Example Answer.

EXERCISE 40: Integrated Task 4—Academic Summaries

 (Track 40)

In Task 4 of the Speaking Section on the Internet-Based TOEFL, you will be asked to summarize the main points in a short lecture. In most of the summaries, you will be required to explain a term or a concept. You have 20 seconds to prepare after you have heard the lecture. Then, you have 60 seconds to record your answer.

Topic One

Question:
Referring to the main points and examples from the lecture, describe the two classifications of crimes presented by the lecturer, and the reasons why it is difficult to distinguish between them.

Preparation Time: 20 seconds
Recording Time: 60 seconds

Notes

Refer to pages 351–352 for the Example Answer.

Topic Two

Question:
Referring to the main points and examples from the lecture, explain the issues surrounding the continuing use of fossil fuels.

Preparation Time: 20 seconds
Recording Time: 60 seconds

Notes

Refer to pages 353–354 for the Example Answer.

PRACTICE EXERCISES
FOR STRUCTURE

Structure and Written Expression Section

The Structure and Written Expression Section of the TOEFL tests your ability to recognize standard written English as it is used in North America. The Structure Section is included in the Institutional TOEFL, but it is not included as a separate section in the Internet-Based TOEFL. This chapter is not intended to teach you all the grammar that you will need to succeed on the TOEFL. These exercises will give you practice answering the most frequently tested items. For a more comprehensive review of structure and written expression, you should take a class or study an English grammar book.

Overview of the TOEFL® ITP Structure and Written Expression Section

The Structure and Written Expression Section in the TOEFL® ITP tests your ability to recognize standard written English.

There are two parts in the section. In Part 1 Structure, you will see 15 incomplete sentences with four possible answer choices below each of them. You are to choose the answer that best completes the sentence. In Part 2 Written Expression, you will see 25 incorrect sentences with four underlined words or phrases marked (A), (B), (C), and (D). Choose the one word or phrase that must be changed to correct the sentence.

You will have 25 minutes to read and answer all of the questions in this section.

EXERCISE 41: Sentences—Verbs

In some sentences in the Structure and Written Expression Section on the Institutional TOEFL, you will be asked to identify the correct verb. In fact, most of the sentences in the Structure Section are verb problems. A verb is a word or phrase that expresses action or condition. A verb can be classified as transitive or intransitive according to whether it requires a complement; it can be classified further according to the kind of complement it requires, including not only nouns, pronouns, adjectives, and adverbs but also *-ing* forms or infinitives. Choose the correct answer in the incomplete sentences. Choose the incorrect word or phrase in the underlined choices.

1. Almost everyone fails _____ the driver's test on the first try.
   Ⓐ passing
   Ⓑ to have passed
   Ⓒ to pass
   Ⓓ in passing

2. When <u>the silkworm</u> gets through <u>to lay</u> <u>its</u>
         Ⓐ   Ⓑ Ⓒ

   eggs, <u>it dies</u>.
      Ⓓ

3. If endangered species _____ saved, rain forests must be protected.
   Ⓐ are to be
   Ⓑ be
   Ⓒ can be
   Ⓓ will be

4. The average spoken sentence in conversational English takes 2.5 seconds _____.
   Ⓐ for to complete
   Ⓑ completing
   Ⓒ to complete
   Ⓓ by completing

5. At one time, most doctors agreed _____ truthful with their terminally ill patients, a trend that has reversed itself in modern medical practice.
   Ⓐ don't to be
   Ⓑ not to be
   Ⓒ we shouldn't been
   Ⓓ not to been

6. William Torrey Harris was one of the first educators interested _____ a logical progression of topics in the school curriculum.
   Ⓐ in establishing
   Ⓑ for establishing
   Ⓒ establishing
   Ⓓ to establish

7. North American Indian tribes used sign language _____ with tribes that spoke a different language or dialect.
   Ⓐ to communicating
   Ⓑ for communicate
   Ⓒ to communicate
   Ⓓ for communicated

8. Art tends to be _____ more after the death of the artist, but most literary works tend to decrease in value when the writer dies.
   Ⓐ price
   Ⓑ worthy
   Ⓒ worth
   Ⓓ value

9. Adult eagles let their offspring _____ nests near their original nesting area.
   Ⓐ build
   Ⓑ builds
   Ⓒ building
   Ⓓ to build

10. <u>A barometer</u> is a device with a <u>sealed metal</u>
        Ⓐ   Ⓑ

    chamber designed <u>to reading</u> the changes
                  Ⓒ

    in the pressure of <u>air</u> in the atmosphere.
               Ⓓ

11. If a person does not have an attorney, the court _____ one.
    Ⓐ will appoint
    Ⓑ appointed
    Ⓒ would appoint
    Ⓓ appointing

12. Since lightning was probably significant in the formation of life, understanding it
    Ⓐ
    might help us to understanding life itself.
    Ⓑ   Ⓒ   Ⓓ

13. Iowa _____ of flat-topped hills erected by the ancient Mound Builder people as temples and burial sites.
    Ⓐ with a larger number
    Ⓑ has a large number
    Ⓒ having a large number
    Ⓓ a large number

14. If the oxygen supply in the atmosphere was
    Ⓐ   Ⓑ
    not replenished by plants, it would soon be
    Ⓒ
    exhausted.
    Ⓓ

15. _____ the eight Ivy League schools are among the most prestigious colleges in the United States.
    Ⓐ It is generally accepted that
    Ⓑ That it is accepted
    Ⓒ Accepting that it is
    Ⓓ That is accepted

16. The Girl Scouts, which was found by
    Ⓐ
    Juliette Gordon Low in 1912, has grown to
    Ⓑ   Ⓒ
    a current membership of more than three
    Ⓓ
    million girls.

17. To relieve pain caused by severe burns, prevent infection, and treat for shock, _____ immediate steps.
    Ⓐ taking
    Ⓑ to take
    Ⓒ taken
    Ⓓ take

18. If gasoline vapor _____ with air, combustion will occur.
    Ⓐ mixed
    Ⓑ had mixed
    Ⓒ mixes
    Ⓓ mixture

19. Vermont, commonly known as the Green Mountain State, refused _____ until 1791.
    Ⓐ to join the Union
    Ⓑ joining the Union
    Ⓒ the joining of the Union
    Ⓓ join the Union

20. Air constricted between the vocal chords makes them _____, producing sounds.
    Ⓐ to vibrate
    Ⓑ vibrating
    Ⓒ vibrate
    Ⓓ the vibration

Refer to pages 355–356 for the Explanatory Answers.

EXERCISE 42: Sentences—Auxiliary Verbs

In some sentences in the Structure and Written Expression Section on the Institutional TOEFL, you will be asked to select the correct auxiliary verb. An auxiliary verb is a verb that accompanies the main verb and makes distinctions in the meaning of the main verb. Some examples of auxiliary verbs are BE, HAVE, or a modal. Choose the correct answer in the incomplete sentences. Choose the incorrect word or phrase in the underlined choices.

1. On the average, a healthy heart _____ to pump five tablespoons of blood with every beat.
   Ⓐ must
   Ⓑ ought
   Ⓒ can
   Ⓓ should

2. It is generally believed that Thomas
           Ⓐ

   Jefferson was the one who had researched

   and wrote the *Declaration of Independence*
      Ⓑ

   during the months prior to its signing
                 Ⓒ

   in July 1776.
     Ⓓ

3. In general, by the second year of production, the price of a new piece of technology _____ significantly.
   Ⓐ will decreased
   Ⓑ has decreased
   Ⓒ will have decreased
   Ⓓ will has decreased

4. Although higher structures
           Ⓐ

   have been build in New York City, none
         Ⓑ

   characterizes the skyline better than the
       Ⓒ   Ⓓ

   Empire State Building.

5. Research in genetics and DNA having had a
                       Ⓐ

   profound influence on the direction of
      Ⓑ   Ⓒ

   treatment for a large number of diseases.
             Ⓓ

6. Bones composed chiefly of calcium,
       Ⓐ   Ⓑ   Ⓒ

   phosphorous, and a fibrous substance

   known as collagen.
       Ⓓ

7. A cure for juvenile diabetes _____ until more funds are allocated to basic research.
   Ⓐ won't develop
   Ⓑ aren't developing
   Ⓒ don't develop
   Ⓓ won't be developed

8. During the past decade, college graduates
       Ⓐ

   spended more than twice as much for
     Ⓑ   Ⓒ   Ⓓ

   student loans as in the previous decade.

9. Civil engineers had better _____ steel supports in concrete structures built on unstable geophysical sites.
   Ⓐ include
   Ⓑ including
   Ⓒ inclusion
   Ⓓ included

10. There is no limit to the diversity to be
          Ⓐ

    finding in the cultures of people
      Ⓑ   Ⓒ   Ⓓ

    throughout the world.

11. The cones of pine trees _____ two or three years to reach maturity.
    Ⓐ to take
    Ⓑ taking
    Ⓒ may take
    Ⓓ takes

12. The government requires that a census <u>taken</u>
⒜

   every <u>ten years</u> so that accurate <u>statistics</u>
⒝   ⒞

   <u>may be compiled</u>.
⒟

13. It is important that cancer <u>is</u> <u>diagnosed</u> and
⒜   ⒝

   treated <u>as early as possible</u> in order
⒞

   <u>to assure</u> a successful cure.
⒟

14. Although the scientific community had
   hoped that the field of transplantation
   _____, the shortage of organ donors has
   curtailed research.
   ⒜ progress
   ⒝ had progressed
   ⒞ would progress
   ⒟ progressing

15. Before <u>railroad lines</u> were <u>extended</u> from
⒜   ⒝

   Missouri to New Mexico, millions of

   dollars in trade <u>was used to be carried</u> over
⒞

   the Santa Fe Trail <u>by wheeled wagons</u>.
⒟

16. Based on a decline in vehicular deaths

   during the past decade, <u>driver assist</u>
⒜

   and other safety features in <u>newer</u>
⒝

   automobiles must be <u>save</u> <u>lives</u>.
⒞   ⒟

17. <u>The gold</u> used in jewelry is not
⒜

   <u>strong enough</u> unless <u>it</u> <u>be</u> alloyed.
⒝   ⒞ ⒟

18. Even without strong wings, the ostrich has
   survived because it _____ at high speeds
   to escape predators.
   ⒜ to run
   ⒝ can run
   ⒞ running
   ⒟ run

19. General damage that <u>been caused</u>
⒜

   <u>by aphids</u> or pollution <u>is sometimes</u>
⒝   ⒞

   <u>known as</u> blight.
⒟

20. Shakespeare <u>is said</u> to <u>had been</u>
⒜   ⒝

   the most <u>popular playwright</u> of the
⒞

   Renaissance era, as well as a <u>talented</u>
⒟

   poet and actor.

Refer to page 356 for the Explanatory Answers.

EXERCISE 43: Sentences—Nouns

In some sentences in the Structure and Written Expression Section on the Institutional TOEFL, you will be asked to identify the correct noun. A noun is a word that names persons, objects, and ideas. There are two basic classifications of nouns in English: count nouns and noncount nouns. Count nouns are those that can be made plural by -s, -es, or an irregular form. They are used in agreement with either singular or plural verbs. Noncount nouns are those that cannot be made plural in these ways. They are used in agreement with singular verbs. It is necessary to know whether a noun is count or noncount to maintain verb agreement and to choose correct adjective modifiers. Choose the correct answer in the incomplete sentences. Choose the incorrect word or phrase in the underlined choices.

1. The understanding electricity depends on a
      (A)   (B)   (C)

   knowledge of atoms and the subatomic

   particles of which they are composed.
                    (D)

2. The cost of delivering mails is estimated
      (A)   (B)

   at 600 percent more for mass mailing
                     (C)

   campaigns using the U.S. Post Office as

   compared with e-mail advertising.
                 (D)

3. The two main _____ are permanent magnets and electromagnets.
   - (A) kinds of magnets
   - (B) kind of magnets
   - (C) kind magnets
   - (D) kinds magnets

4. When water is frozen, it becomes _____.
   - (A) ice
   - (B) ices
   - (C) the ice
   - (D) an ice

5. _____ can live to be more than fifteen years old.
   - (A) That it is dogs
   - (B) That dogs
   - (C) Dogs that
   - (D) Dogs

6. One of the most distinctive plant found in
           (A)   (B) (C)

   the desert is the Saguaro cactus.
              (D)

7. In the fall, deciduous trees lose _____, which have, by then, turned from green to gold and orange.
   - (A) their leaf
   - (B) their leaves
   - (C) the leaf
   - (D) the leafs

8. Doctors have concluded that in addition to regular exercise, a diet rich in _____ is good for the heart.
   - (A) fruits and vegetable
   - (B) a fruit and vegetable
   - (C) the fruits and vegetables
   - (D) fruit and vegetables

9. A thunder usually follows lightning by five
     (A)   (B)

   seconds for every mile between the flash
            (C)   (D)

   and the observer.

10. Canada stretches from the Atlantic Ocean to the Pacific Ocean and covers _____ of almost four million square miles.
    - (A) a area
    - (B) an area
    - (C) the area
    - (D) area

11. During the early nineteenth century, _____ were hunted for their pelts.
    - (A) a beaver
    - (B) beavers
    - (C) the beaver
    - (D) that beavers

12. The stories of Dr. Seuss have been enjoyed
    Ⓐ   Ⓑ

    by millions of childrens.
    Ⓒ   Ⓓ

13. Collections of simple and functional
    Ⓐ

    Shaker furniture can be seen in museum
          Ⓑ   Ⓒ   Ⓓ

    throughout the United States.

14. The decathlon is a two-day
                         Ⓐ

    athletic competition that consists of
        Ⓑ   Ⓒ

    ten types track and field events.
    Ⓓ

15. _____ designs on a wall, also called
    graffiti, has become associated with gang
    activity in many neighborhoods.
    Ⓐ Spraying of
    Ⓑ The spraying of
    Ⓒ Spray the
    Ⓓ Sprays

16. _____ by the author John Grisham are
    frequently on the best-seller list.
    Ⓐ The novel
    Ⓑ Novels
    Ⓒ A novel
    Ⓓ Some novel

17. _____ have made communication faster
    and easier through the use of e-mail and
    the internet is widely recognized.
    Ⓐ It is that computers
    Ⓑ That it is computers
    Ⓒ Computers that
    Ⓓ That computers

18. Provide pensions for retired persons is
    Ⓐ   Ⓑ   Ⓒ

    the primary function of the Social Security
            Ⓓ

    system.

19. New equipments for medical diagnosis
        Ⓐ

    have made many formerly unpleasant
    Ⓑ   Ⓒ

    procedures quite painless.
    Ⓓ

20. Termites can do _____ to the wood in
    homes before they are detected.
    Ⓐ an extensive damage
    Ⓑ extensive damages
    Ⓒ the extensive damage
    Ⓓ extensive damage

Refer to pages 356–357 for the Explanatory Answers.

EXERCISE 44: Sentences—Pronouns

In some sentences in the Structure and Written Expression Section on the Institutional TOEFL, you will be asked to identify the correct pronoun. A pronoun is a word that can be used instead of a noun, usually to avoid repeating the noun. A pronoun may be singular or plural; masculine, feminine, or neuter; and first, second, or third person to agree with the noun to which it refers. A pronoun may be used as the subject of a sentence or a clause or as the object of a sentence, a clause, or a preposition. In English, pronouns are also used to express possessives and reflexives. Choose the correct answer in the incomplete sentences. Choose the incorrect word or phrase in the underlined choices.

1. The crime rate has begun to decline in New York City due to efforts on the part of both government and private citizens to curb _____.
   Ⓐ them
   Ⓑ him
   Ⓒ its
   Ⓓ it

2. Sloths spend most of its time hanging upside
                    Ⓐ   Ⓑ
   down from trees and feeding on leaves and
                          Ⓒ
   fruit.
   Ⓓ

3. When the European settlers came

   in the seventeenth century, the newcomers
   _____
                      Ⓐ
   began a systematic effort to push the Native
                              Ⓑ
   Americans into the wilderness and to take

   their land from their.
   Ⓒ   Ⓓ

4. Seals can _____ because they have a thick layer of blubber under their fur.
   Ⓐ keep them warm
   Ⓑ keep themselves warm
   Ⓒ they keep warm
   Ⓓ keep their warm

5. After Dr. Werner Arber discovered
                              Ⓐ
   restriction enzymes, Drs. Daniel Nathan,

   Hamilton Smith, and him were awarded the
                        Ⓑ   Ⓒ
   Nobel Prize for their research in that field.
                      Ⓓ

6. There are not many people which adapt
         Ⓐ   Ⓑ   Ⓒ
   to a new culture without feeling some
                            Ⓓ
   disorientation at first.

7. In order for people who speak different languages to engage in trade _____, they often develop a simplified language called *pidgin*.
   Ⓐ with each the other
   Ⓑ with each to the other
   Ⓒ with each another
   Ⓓ with each other

8. Those of us who have a family history of
             Ⓐ
   heart disease should make yearly
                 Ⓑ   Ⓒ
   appointments with their doctors.
                        Ⓓ

9. Domestic cats often show loyalty to their owners by leaving freshly killed prey such as birds for _____ to find.
   Ⓐ they
   Ⓑ he
   Ⓒ them
   Ⓓ their

10. The United States and Canada have many trade agreements that benefit _____.
    Ⓐ one the other
    Ⓑ other
    Ⓒ other one
    Ⓓ each other

11. George Herman Ruth, <u>which</u> was <u>better</u>
      Ⓐ   Ⓑ

    <u>known as</u> Babe Ruth, <u>began</u> his baseball
    Ⓒ   Ⓓ

    career in 1914 with the Baltimore Orioles.

12. The constellation Orion is easily
    recognized by _____ three vertical stars.
    Ⓐ your
    Ⓑ its
    Ⓒ their
    Ⓓ her

13. <u>The first</u> full-length animated movie, *Snow*
      Ⓐ

    White, <u>was produced</u> by Walt Disney <u>whom</u>
           Ⓑ   Ⓒ

    creative genius also inspired <u>such</u> animated
                                  Ⓓ

    classics as *Bambi* and *Cinderella*.

14. Wolves, which are known to travel in
    packs, both provide for and defend _____
    through group cooperation.
    Ⓐ himself
    Ⓑ themselves
    Ⓒ itself
    Ⓓ theirselves

15. Although orchids give the appearance of
    being very fragile, they are actually very
    hardy plants _____ indoors during the
    winter months.
    Ⓐ which may be grown
    Ⓑ what may grow
    Ⓒ who may be grow
    Ⓓ where may be growing

16. Hyperactivity in children may result from
    _____ some food additives.
    Ⓐ their eating
    Ⓑ they eat
    Ⓒ to eat
    Ⓓ them eating

17. In <u>advanced</u> stages of anorexia, <u>the patient</u> is
       Ⓐ   Ⓑ

    <u>unable to feed</u> <u>themself</u>.
    Ⓒ   Ⓓ

18. <u>It is documented</u> that Custer <u>led</u> his troops
       Ⓐ   Ⓑ

    into a ravine near the Little Big Horn, where

    a huge army of Sioux Indians <u>was waiting</u>
                                 Ⓒ

    for <u>they</u>.
        Ⓓ

19. The sea horse is unique <u>among fish</u> <u>because</u>
                          Ⓐ   Ⓑ

    the female deposits <u>their eggs</u> in a pouch
                        Ⓒ

    that the male carries until the small sea

    horses <u>are hatched</u>.
           Ⓓ

20. Hawkeye was a character _____ James
    Fenimore Cooper created for *The Last of
    the Mohicans*.
    Ⓐ who
    Ⓑ whom
    Ⓒ which
    Ⓓ whose

Refer to pages 357–358 for the Explanatory Answers.

EXERCISE 45: Sentences—Modifiers

In some sentences in the Structure and Written Expression Section on the Institutional TOEFL, you will be asked to identify the correct modifier. A modifier can be an adjective or an adjectival phrase that describes a noun or an *-ing* form. A modifier can also be an adverb or an adverbial phrase that adds information about the verb, adjective, or another verb. Adjectives do not change form to agree with the nouns or *-ing* forms that they describe, but some adjectives are used only with count nouns and others are used only with noncount nouns. Choose the correct answer in the incomplete sentences. Choose the incorrect word or phrase in the underlined choices.

1. The data on the winter migration patterns of the monarch butterfly is very _____.
   A interested
   B interest
   C interesting
   D of interest

2. There are more potatoes cultivated than any
   —A—   —B—
   the other vegetable crop worldwide.
   —C—   —D—

3. Marian Anderson, recognized both in the

   U.S. and in Europe as a real great
       —A—   —B—
   vocalist, was the first black singer to appear
           —C— —D—
   with the Metropolitan Opera Company.

4. The New England states have had _____ serious earthquakes since the Ice Age.
   A none
   B not any
   C not
   D no

5. _____ orangutans live alone.
   A Near all
   B Almost all
   C The all
   D The most all

6. Some hybrid flowers retain the fragrant scent of the nonhybrid, and _____ are bred without fragrance.
   A anothers
   B the other
   C some other
   D others

7. At the core of a star, temperatures and
      —A—
   pressures are so great as particles collide and
              —B—
   connect in a process called fusion.
            —C—   —D—

8. The Cartwheel Galaxy is 500 million
                            —A—
   light year away from Earth.
   —B—   —C—   —D—

9. According to a recent survey, _____ doctors do not have a personal physician.
   A a large amount of
   B large amount of
   C a large number of
   D large number of

10. Because none of food is as nutritious for a
                 —A—   —B—
    baby as its mother's milk, many women are
           —C—   —D—
    returning to the practice of breast feeding.

11. John F. Kennedy was the youngest president elected to that office and _____ to be assassinated.
    A the fourth
    B fourth
    C four
    D the four

12. Euthanasia, the practice of assisting the

    death of a person suffering from an
                        —A—
    incurable disease, is such a controversial

    issue as it is illegal in most countries.
         —B— —C—   —D—

13. _____ in the world export diamonds.
    - Ⓐ Only little nations
    - Ⓑ Only few nations
    - Ⓒ Only a little nations
    - Ⓓ Only a few nations

14. Uranus is just _____ to be seen on a clear night with the naked eye.
    - Ⓐ bright enough
    - Ⓑ enough brightly
    - Ⓒ as enough bright
    - Ⓓ bright as enough

15. The conversations on the TOEFL

    will be spoken just one time; therefore, you
    ‾‾‾‾‾‾‾‾‾‾‾‾
        Ⓐ

    must listen very careful in order
    ‾‾‾‾‾‾‾‾‾‾‾‾‾‾
            Ⓑ

    to understand what the speakers have said.
    ‾‾‾‾‾‾‾‾‾‾ ‾‾‾‾
        Ⓒ   Ⓓ

16. Gold, silver, and copper coins are often

    alloyed with harder metals to make
    ‾‾‾‾‾‾   ‾‾‾‾
            Ⓐ   Ⓑ

    them hard as enough to withstand wear.
    ‾‾‾ ‾‾‾‾‾‾‾‾‾‾‾
     Ⓒ   Ⓓ

17. _____ like McDonald's and Kentucky Fried Chicken have used franchising to extend their sales internationally.
    - Ⓐ Chain's restaurants
    - Ⓑ Chains restaurants
    - Ⓒ Chain restaurant
    - Ⓓ Chain restaurants

18. Thirty-six years after his first flight, at the age of 77, John Glenn proved that he was not _____ to return to his role as an astronaut.
    - Ⓐ so old
    - Ⓑ too old
    - Ⓒ oldest
    - Ⓓ very older

19. _____ that is known as art deco culminated in the exhibits and expositions at the World's Fair in 1939.
    - Ⓐ The art
    - Ⓑ Arts
    - Ⓒ An art
    - Ⓓ Artist

20. The brightest body in the constellation Hydra, Alphard is only _____.
    - Ⓐ a second-magnitude star
    - Ⓑ a magnitude second star
    - Ⓒ a star of the magnitude second
    - Ⓓ a second magnitudes star

Refer to pages 358–359 for the Explanatory Answers.

EXERCISE 46: Sentences—Comparatives

In some sentences in the Structure and Written Expression Section on the Institutional TOEFL, you will be asked to identify the correct comparative. A comparative can be a word or phrase that expresses similarity or difference. A comparative can also be a word ending like -er or -est that expresses a degree of comparison with adjectives and adverbs. Choose the correct answer in the incomplete sentences. Choose the incorrect word or phrase in the underlined choices.

1. Tuition at an American university runs
   _____ fifty thousand dollars a year.
   Ⓐ so high as
   Ⓑ as high to
   Ⓒ as high as
   Ⓓ as high than

2. Alligators are <u>about the same color than</u>
                    Ⓐ   Ⓑ
   crocodiles, although the adults <u>may be</u>
                                       Ⓒ
   slightly darker with broader heads and

   <u>blunter</u> noses.
      Ⓓ

3. It has been <u>argued</u> that the PNG format is
                 Ⓐ
   <u>a good choice</u> for line art, text, and images
       Ⓑ
   with <u>few</u> colors, but JPEG is considered a
          Ⓒ
   <u>best</u> format for photographs.
      Ⓓ

4. The cost of a thirty-second commercial on
   a network television station is _____ for
   most businesses.
   Ⓐ so much
   Ⓑ much
   Ⓒ very much
   Ⓓ much too much

5. The New York City <u>subway system</u> is
                          Ⓐ
   <u>the most longest</u> <u>underground railroad</u>
        Ⓑ   Ⓒ
   <u>operating</u> in the United States.
      Ⓓ

6. School children in <u>the same grade</u> in
                          Ⓐ
   American schools <u>are</u> <u>usually</u> <u>the same old</u>
                       Ⓑ   Ⓒ   Ⓓ
   as their classmates.

7. The seed heads of teasel plants raise the
   nap on coarse tweed cloth _____ than do
   the machine tools invented to replace them.
   Ⓐ more efficiently
   Ⓑ efficiently
   Ⓒ more efficient
   Ⓓ most efficient

8. Benjamin Franklin <u>was</u> the editor of
                        Ⓐ
   <u>the larger</u> newspaper in the colonies, a
       Ⓑ
   diplomatic representative to France and later

   to England, and <u>the inventor</u> of <u>many</u> useful
                       Ⓒ   Ⓓ
   devices.

9. The standard for cleanliness in the area

   where <u>a microchip</u> <u>is</u> <u>manufactured</u> is
       Ⓐ   Ⓑ   Ⓒ
   <u>same</u> that of an operating room in a hospital.
      Ⓓ

10. The North American robin is only _____
    the European and African robins.
    Ⓐ half big
    Ⓑ as big half
    Ⓒ half as big as
    Ⓓ big by half

11. Mountain bikes <u>differ</u> ordinary bicycles in
    Ⓐ

    that <u>they</u> have ten or more gears, a
          Ⓑ

    <u>more rugged</u> frame, and <u>wider</u> treads on
         Ⓒ   Ⓓ
    the tires.

12. <u>As a rule</u>, <u>the more</u> rapid the <u>heart rate</u>,
        Ⓐ   Ⓑ   Ⓒ

    <u>quicker</u> the pulse.
       Ⓓ

13. In U.S. law, a misdemeanor is a crime that
    is _____ a felony and usually carries a
    term of imprisonment of less than one year
    for most offenses.
    Ⓐ lesser than
    Ⓑ less severe than
    Ⓒ less than severe
    Ⓓ severely lesser

14. Although both are mammals, the early
    stages of development on the part of
    placentals differ from _____.
    Ⓐ marsupials
    Ⓑ that of marsupials
    Ⓒ those of marsupials
    Ⓓ those marsupials

15. Eli Whitney's cotton gin enabled the cotton
    producers of the early nineteenth century to
    increase their production by _____ times
    the amount produced prior to the invention.
    Ⓐ more fifty
    Ⓑ more as fifty
    Ⓒ more than fifty
    Ⓓ most than fifty

16. _____ 250,000 species of fossils have
    been discovered in both organized,
    scientific searches and by sheer accident.
    Ⓐ As much as
    Ⓑ As many as
    Ⓒ As many
    Ⓓ Many as

17. The North's abundance of industry and
    commercial wealth proved to be a greater
    advantage _____ in determining the
    outcome of the Civil War.
    Ⓐ than originally thought
    Ⓑ that originally thought
    Ⓒ as originally thought
    Ⓓ originally thought

18. Every year the Coachella Music Festival
    sells out _____ in the Southwestern
    states.
    Ⓐ fastest than any other musical event
    Ⓑ fast as any other musical event
    Ⓒ than any other events
    Ⓓ faster than any other event

19. <u>Alike</u> her friend and fellow impressionist
       Ⓐ

    artist, Edgar Degas, Mary Cassatt <u>used</u>
         Ⓑ   Ⓒ

    brush strokes and colors in new and

    <u>different ways</u>.
         Ⓓ

20. A dancer, while always graceful and
    precise in her movements, trains _____
    any other athlete.
    Ⓐ as strenuously
    Ⓑ more strenuously as
    Ⓒ as strenuously as
    Ⓓ as strenuously that

Refer to pages 359–360 for the Explanatory Answers.

EXERCISE 47: Sentences—Connectors

In some sentences in the Structure and Written Expression Section of the Institutional TOEFL, you will be asked to identify the correct connector. A connector is a word or phrase that joins words, phrases, or clauses. A connector expresses relationships between the words, phrases, and clauses that it joins. Some common relationships are cause and result, contradiction, substitution, addition, exception, example, and purpose. Choose the correct answer in the incomplete sentences. Choose the incorrect word or phrase in the underlined choices.

1. It is not clear how much students learn _____ television classes without supervision and monitoring.
   - Ⓐ for watching
   - Ⓑ from watching
   - Ⓒ by watch
   - Ⓓ to watch

2. In spite of the fact that 85 percent of all societies allow the men to take more than one wife, most prefer monogamy _____ polygamy.
   - Ⓐ than
   - Ⓑ to
   - Ⓒ for
   - Ⓓ that

3. Some metals <u>such</u> gold, silver, copper, and
   <u>Ⓐ</u>   <u>Ⓑ</u>
   tin occur <u>naturally</u> and are easy <u>to work</u>.
   <u>Ⓒ</u>   <u>Ⓓ</u>

4. Stained glass becomes even more beautiful when it _____ because the corrosion diffuses light.
   - Ⓐ will age
   - Ⓑ ages
   - Ⓒ are aging
   - Ⓓ aged

5. All of the senses _____ smell must pass through intermediate gateways to be processed before they are registered in the brain.
   - Ⓐ until
   - Ⓑ but
   - Ⓒ to
   - Ⓓ for

6. <u>Because</u> the expense of traditional fuels
   <u>Ⓐ</u>
   and the concern that <u>they</u> <u>might run out,</u>
   <u>Ⓑ</u>   <u>Ⓒ</u>
   many countries <u>have been investigating</u>
   <u>Ⓓ</u>
   alternative sources of power.

7. The lights and appliances in most homes use alternating current _____.
   - Ⓐ instead direct current
   - Ⓑ instead of direct current
   - Ⓒ that instead direct current
   - Ⓓ for direct current instead

8. Only seventeen <u>on</u> one hundred
   <u>Ⓐ</u>
   business calls <u>get through</u> to the correct
   <u>Ⓑ</u>   <u>Ⓒ</u>
   person on <u>the first</u> attempt.
   <u>Ⓓ</u>

9. More murders are reported _____ December in the United States than during any other month.
   - Ⓐ on
   - Ⓑ in
   - Ⓒ at
   - Ⓓ for

10. The tendency to develop cancer, even in high-risk individuals, can be decreased _____ the amount of fruit and vegetables in the diet.
   - Ⓐ to increase
   - Ⓑ for increase
   - Ⓒ for increasing
   - Ⓓ by increasing

11. The concept of lift in aerodynamics refers to
    <u>A</u>

    the relationship <u>among</u> the <u>increased</u> speed
    <u>B</u>   <u>C</u>

    of air over the top of a wing and the higher

    pressure of <u>the slower air</u> underneath.
    <u>D</u>

12. If one of the participants in a conversation
    wonders _____, no real communication
    has taken place.
    Ⓐ what said the other person
    Ⓑ what the other person said
    Ⓒ what did the other person say
    Ⓓ what was the other person saying

13. A prism is used to <u>refract</u> light <u>so as</u> <u>it</u>
    <u>A</u>   <u>B</u> <u>C</u>

    spreads out in a continuous spectrum

    <u>of colors</u>.
    <u>D</u>

14. Nuclear power plants are <u>still</u> supported
    <u>A</u>

    <u>by</u> the society of Professional Engineers
    <u>B</u>

    <u>in spite</u> unfortunate accidents like the
    <u>C</u>

    <u>one at</u> Fukushima, Japan.
    <u>D</u>

15. Neptune is an extremely cold planet, and
    _____.
    Ⓐ so does Uranus
    Ⓑ so has Uranus
    Ⓒ so is Uranus
    Ⓓ so Uranus

16. Deserts are often formed _____ they are
    cut off from rain-bearing winds by the
    surrounding mountain ranges.
    Ⓐ because
    Ⓑ in spite of
    Ⓒ so
    Ⓓ due to

17. There are many beautifully preserved
    historic buildings _____.
    Ⓐ in Beacon Street in Boston
    Ⓑ in Beacon Street at Boston
    Ⓒ on Beacon Street in Boston
    Ⓓ at Beacon Street at Boston

18. _____ the original document, the U.S.
    Constitution contains ten amendments
    called the Bill of Rights.
    Ⓐ Beside
    Ⓑ Besides
    Ⓒ In addition
    Ⓓ Also

19. National parks <u>include</u> not only
    <u>A</u>

    <u>the most scenic</u> places in the nation <u>but</u>
    <u>B</u>   <u>C</u>

    places <u>distinguished</u> for their historic or
    <u>D</u>

    scientific interest.

20. Cooking oil made from corn does not
    become saturated when heated, and _____.
    Ⓐ neither oil made from soy
    Ⓑ oil made from soy does either
    Ⓒ neither does oil made from soy
    Ⓓ oil made from soy either

Refer to pages 360–361 for the Explanatory Answers.

EXERCISE 48: Sentences—Sentences and Clauses

In some sentences in the Structure and Written Expression Section of the Institutional TOEFL, you will be asked to distinguish between a sentence, also called a main or independent clause, and a subordinate or dependent clause that is attached to a sentence. Choose the correct answer in the incomplete sentences. Choose the incorrect word or phrase in the underlined choices.

1. Some ancient units, such as the day, the foot, and the pound, _____ today.
   Ⓐ are still in use
   Ⓑ that are still in use
   Ⓒ which are in use still
   Ⓓ still in use

2. Paper money _____ by the Continental Congress in order to finance the American Revolution.
   Ⓐ which was issued
   Ⓑ was issuing
   Ⓒ issued
   Ⓓ was issued

3. The plastic arts, mainly sculpture and
   Ⓐ   Ⓑ
   ceramics, that are produced
             Ⓒ
   by modeling or molding the materials into
             Ⓓ
   interesting shapes.

4. The Scholastic Aptitude Test (SAT) _____ by high school students as a requirement for admission to many colleges.
   Ⓐ which is taken
   Ⓑ is taken
   Ⓒ taken
   Ⓓ is taking

5. Ocean currents that help transfer heat from
                   Ⓐ   Ⓑ
   the equator to the poles, thereby creating
                                        Ⓒ
   a more balanced global environment.
     Ⓓ

6. Camp David _____ the official country home of the U.S. presidents.
   Ⓐ that is
   Ⓑ that it is
   Ⓒ it is
   Ⓓ is

7. Gas and dust that stream away from a comet
     Ⓐ   Ⓑ
   forming one or more tails that may extend
     Ⓒ   Ⓓ
   for millions of miles.

8. The Northwest Ordinances which regulated
                            Ⓐ
   the sale and settlement of land between the
                                    Ⓑ
   Great Lakes and the Mississippi River,

   territories still occupied
                     Ⓒ
   by Native American nations.
            Ⓓ

9. _____ considered strong and reliable, and is favored by investors who are interested in security.
   Ⓐ That blue chip stock
   Ⓑ Blue chip stock is
   Ⓒ It is blue chip stock
   Ⓓ Which is blue chip stock

10. Most botanists have observed _____ a period of dormancy, even when conditions may be favorable for growth.
   Ⓐ that seeds exhibiting
   Ⓑ that seeds exhibit
   Ⓒ seeds that exhibiting
   Ⓓ seeds that they exhibit

11. La Guardia Airport in New York City _____ for Fiorello La Guardia, one of New York's most popular mayors.
   Ⓐ which is named
   Ⓑ named
   Ⓒ which named
   Ⓓ is named

12. In a meritocracy, intelligence and ability
    _____ more than social position or wealth.
    Ⓐ which value
    Ⓑ that are valued
    Ⓒ valuing
    Ⓓ are valued

13. The larva of the boll weevil, which it feeds
        Ⓐ   Ⓑ
    on the immature pods of the cotton plant,
                                Ⓒ
    often destroying an entire crop.
          Ⓓ

14. Of all the lawsuits in the world, _____ in
    U.S. courts.
    Ⓐ filed 95 percent of them
    Ⓑ 95 percent of them are filed
    Ⓒ that filed are 95 percent of them
    Ⓓ which of them 95 percent are filed

15. "Chicago" is a poem _____ in praise of
    one of the busiest industrial centers in the
    U.S.
    Ⓐ which by Carl Sandburg
    Ⓑ which was written by Carl Sandburg
    Ⓒ was written by Carl Sandburg
    Ⓓ Carl Sandburg who wrote it

16. _____ are kept as pets in almost every
    country in the world.
    Ⓐ Cats and dogs which
    Ⓑ Which cats and dogs
    Ⓒ Cats and dogs
    Ⓓ That cats and dogs

17. By studying the fossils of pollen, which
       Ⓐ   Ⓑ
    extremely resistant to decay, researchers
    can gain useful information about the
      Ⓒ   Ⓓ
    vegetation of the past.

18. The PTA _____ parents and teachers who
    support the school by fund-raising and
    other activities.
    Ⓐ it is a group of
    Ⓑ that is a group of
    Ⓒ which group of
    Ⓓ is a group of

19. The attribution of human characteristics to
        Ⓐ
    animals or inanimate objects appears in the
                             Ⓑ
    mythologies of many cultures is a literary
                 Ⓒ
    device called anthropomorphism.
         Ⓓ

20. The jet stream _____ usually occurs at
    about thirty-five to sixty degrees latitude.
    Ⓐ a narrow band of wind that
    Ⓑ is a narrow band of wind that
    Ⓒ a narrow band of wind
    Ⓓ it is a narrow band of wind that

Refer to pages 361–362 for the Explanatory Answers.

EXERCISE 49: Sentences—Point of View

In some sentences in the Structure and Written Expression Section of the Institutional TOEFL, you will be asked to identify errors in point of view. Point of view is the relationship between the verb in the main clause of a sentence and other verbs, or between the verbs in a sentence and the adverbs that express time. Choose the correct answer in the incomplete sentences. Choose the incorrect word or phrase in the underlined choices.

1. Although there <u>are</u> <u>approximately</u> 120
          Ⓐ   Ⓑ
   intensive language institutes <u>in</u> the United
                        Ⓒ
   States in 1970, there are more than

   <u>five times as many</u> now.
          Ⓓ

2. Cartographers cannot make an accurate map

   because the political situation in many

   areas changes <u>so</u> rapidly that they <u>were</u> not
                 Ⓐ   Ⓑ
   able <u>to draw</u> the boundaries <u>correctly</u>.
        Ⓒ   Ⓓ

3. Although Emily Dickinson <u>publishes</u> <u>only</u>
                      Ⓐ   Ⓑ
   three of her verses before she died, today

   there <u>are</u> <u>more than</u> one thousand of her
       Ⓒ   Ⓓ
   poems printed in many important

   collections.

4. Dew <u>usually</u> <u>disappeared</u> <u>by</u> seven o'clock
        Ⓐ   Ⓑ   Ⓒ
   <u>in the morning</u> when the sun comes up.
        Ⓓ

5. Before the 1800s, when William Young
   made different shoes for right and left feet,
   shoes _____ on either foot.
   Ⓐ can wear
   Ⓑ are wearing
   Ⓒ could be worn
   Ⓓ worn

6. Seven months before the <u>stock</u> market
                     Ⓐ
   crashed <u>in</u> 1929, President Hoover said that
          Ⓑ
   the economy of the nation <u>is</u> <u>secure</u>.
                      Ⓒ Ⓓ

7. In the Middle Ages, the word
   "masterpiece" referred to a work that
   _____ by a journeyman in order to qualify
   as a master artisan.
   Ⓐ completed
   Ⓑ is completed
   Ⓒ was completed
   Ⓓ complete

8. <u>Most</u> archaeologists agree that humans
    Ⓐ
   <u>are living</u> in the area around Philadelphia
      Ⓑ
   <u>for</u> <u>about</u> twelve thousand years.
    Ⓒ   Ⓓ

9. Although we once thought that Saturn <u>has</u>
                                Ⓐ
   only seven rings, we now know that <u>it</u>
                             Ⓑ
   has hundreds of rings <u>extending</u> for
                      Ⓒ
   thousands of <u>miles</u>.
             Ⓓ

10. Before his death in 1943, in an effort
    to encourage less dependence on one
    crop by the South, George Washington
    Carver _____ for developing hundreds
    of industrial uses for peanuts and sweet
    potatoes.
    Ⓐ has responsibility
    Ⓑ were responsibility
    Ⓒ is responsible
    Ⓓ was responsible

11. The Greek historian Herodotus reported that one hundred thousand men _____ for twenty years to build the Great Pyramid at Gizeh.
    - Ⓐ employ
    - Ⓑ employed
    - Ⓒ are employed
    - Ⓓ were employed

12. In 1900, <u>according</u> to the National Center
    Ⓐ
    for Health Statistics, the average life
    expectancy for people <u>born</u> <u>during</u> that
    Ⓑ   Ⓒ
    year <u>is</u> less than 50 years.
    Ⓓ

13. Champlain <u>founded</u> a base at Port Royal
    Ⓐ
    <u>in 1605</u>, and <u>builds</u> a fort at <u>Quebec</u> three
    Ⓑ   Ⓒ   Ⓓ
    years later.

14. <u>According</u> to the Congressional Record,
    Ⓐ
    almost one-third of <u>all new laws</u> in 2000
    Ⓑ
    <u>are passed</u> <u>to celebrate</u> some day, week, or
    Ⓒ   Ⓓ
    month for a special interest group's
    purposes, such as Music Week.

15. <u>The first</u> significant engagement of the
    Ⓐ
    American Revolution <u>occurs</u>
    Ⓑ
    on June 17, 1775, and <u>has been referred to</u>
    Ⓒ   Ⓓ
    as the Battle of Bunker Hill.

16. Evolutionary changes in the speech organs probably _____ the development of language in humanoids.
    - Ⓐ to contribute
    - Ⓑ contribute to
    - Ⓒ contribution to
    - Ⓓ contributed to

17. <u>Originally</u>, the purpose of a sampler <u>is</u>
    Ⓐ   Ⓑ
    <u>to record</u> complex stitches so that <u>they</u>
    Ⓒ   Ⓓ
    could be duplicated later.

18. Before he died, Armand Hammer _____ an extraordinarily diverse business empire, including interests in oil, livestock, cattle, grain, and art.
    - Ⓐ established
    - Ⓑ establishing
    - Ⓒ establishes
    - Ⓓ establish

19. <u>Many</u> ancient cultures <u>begin</u> <u>their</u> spiritual
    Ⓐ   Ⓑ   Ⓒ
    life <u>by worshipping</u> the Sun.
    Ⓓ

20. Many people cannot remember when _____ without a computer terminal.
    - Ⓐ they have to work
    - Ⓑ they had to work
    - Ⓒ their working
    - Ⓓ working

Refer to pages 362–363 for the Explanatory Answers.

EXERCISE 50: Sentences—Agreement

In some sentences in the Structure and Written Expression Section of the Institutional TOEFL, you will be asked to identify errors in agreement. Agreement is the relationship between a subject and verb or between a pronoun and noun, or between a pronoun and another pronoun. To agree, a subject and verb must both be singular or both be plural. To agree, a pronoun and the noun or pronoun to which it refers must both be singular or plural and both be masculine or feminine or neuter. Choose the correct answer in the incomplete sentences. Choose the incorrect word or phrase in the underlined choices.

1. Both a term paper <u>and</u> a final exam <u>is</u> often
   (A)   (B)
   <u>required</u> <u>for</u> a college class.
   (C)   (D)

2. The popularity of soccer in the United States

   <u>were increased</u> <u>significantly</u> by <u>the playing</u>
   (A)   (B)   (C)
   of the World Cup in cities throughout the

   country <u>in 1994.</u>
   (D)

3. How many musical notes of the 11,000
   tones that the human ear can distinguish
   _____ in the musical scale?
   (A) it is
   (B) is it
   (C) there are
   (D) are there

4. Not one <u>in a hundred</u> seeds <u>develop</u> <u>into</u> a
   (A)   (B)   (C)
   healthy plant, <u>even</u> under laboratory
   (D)
   conditions.

5. Nine of every ten people in the world
   _____ in the country in which they were
   born.
   (A) living
   (B) they are living
   (C) lives
   (D) live

6. Benjamin Franklin <u>strongly</u> objected <u>to the</u>
   (A)   (B)
   eagle's being chosen as the national bird

   <u>because of</u> <u>their</u> predatory nature.
   (C)   (D)

7. In order to grow <u>well</u>, the Blue Spruce,
   (A)
   <u>like</u> <u>other</u> pine trees, <u>require</u> a temperate
   (B) (C)   (D)
   climate.

8. Few airports in the United States <u>is</u> as
   (A)
   modern as <u>that</u> <u>of</u> Denver.
   (B) (C) (D)

9. In the ocean, _____ more salt in the
   deeper water.
   (A) is there
   (B) it may be
   (C) there is
   (D) it is

10. Work <u>on improving</u> the depletion of the
    (A)
    ozone layer <u>were</u> begun in the late 1980s,
    (B)
    shortly after the Montreal Protocol

    <u>was ratified</u> <u>by 196 nations.</u>
    (C)   (D)

11. The average temperature of rocks on the
    surface of the earth _____ 55 degrees F.
    (A) be
    (B) are
    (C) is
    (D) been

12. The officials of the Board of Elections asked

    that each voter <u>present</u> <u>their</u> registration
    (A)   (B)
    card and a valid <u>driver's</u> license before
    (C)
    <u>receiving</u> a ballot.
    (D)

13. If one <u>has</u> a special medical condition such
    Ⓐ

    as diabetes, epilepsy, or allergy, it is

    advisable that <u>they</u> <u>carry</u> some kind of
    Ⓑ Ⓒ

    identification in order to avoid <u>being</u> given
    Ⓓ

    improper medication in an emergency.

14. A large percentage of federal employees

    <u>are participating</u> in an experimental
    Ⓐ

    <u>four-day</u> <u>work week</u> aimed at curbing
    Ⓑ   Ⓒ

    gasoline consumption and pollution, two of

    <u>the most urgent problems</u> facing cities today.
    Ⓓ

15. A mature grove of Aspen trees often
    _____ that supports numerous trunks.
    Ⓐ have a single system of roots
    Ⓑ has a single root system
    Ⓒ make a single system from roots
    Ⓓ making a single roots system

16. <u>One-cent</u> coins <u>issued</u> in the United States
    Ⓐ   Ⓑ

    <u>since 1982</u> <u>is</u> 96 percent zinc.
    Ⓒ   Ⓓ

17. <u>According to</u> <u>a team of scientists,</u> <u>there are</u>
    Ⓐ   Ⓑ   Ⓒ

    evidence that Mount Everest is still <u>rising</u>.
    Ⓓ

18. <u>The urinary system,</u> <u>including</u> both the
    Ⓐ   Ⓑ

    bladder <u>and</u> the kidneys, <u>are contained in</u>
    Ⓒ   Ⓓ

    the cavities of the trunk.

19. The smallest flying dinosaurs _____ of a
    robin.
    Ⓐ about the size
    Ⓑ was about the size
    Ⓒ were about the size
    Ⓓ have been about the size

20. In the 1920s, art deco, <u>known</u> for plastic
    Ⓐ   Ⓑ

    and <u>chrome-plated</u> objects, <u>were</u> very
    Ⓒ   Ⓓ

    popular.

Refer to pages 363–364 for the Explanatory Answers.

EXERCISE 51: Sentences—Introductory Verbal Modifiers

In some sentences in the Structure and Written Expression Section of the Institutional TOEFL, you will be asked to identify errors in introductory verbal modifiers and the subjects that they modify. Introductory verbal modifiers are *-ing* forms, participles, and infinitives. A phrase with an introductory verbal modifier occurs at the beginning of a sentence and is followed by a comma. The subject modified by an introductory verbal modifier must follow the comma. If the correct subject does not follow the comma, then the meaning of the sentence is changed. Often the changed meaning is not logical. Choose the correct answer in the incomplete sentences. Choose the incorrect word or phrase in the underlined choices.

1. After finishing *Roots*, the one-hundred-year
   Ⓐ   Ⓑ
   history of an African-American family,

   the Nobel Prize committee awarded author
                              Ⓒ
   Alex Haley a special citation for literary
                                    Ⓓ
   excellence.

2. A competitive sport, gymnasts perform
   Ⓐ
   before officials who must use their judgment
                     Ⓑ
   along with their knowledge of the rules
   Ⓒ
   to determine the relative skill of each
   Ⓓ
   participant.

3. To remove stains from permanent press
                     Ⓐ
   clothing, carefully soaking in cold water
             Ⓑ
   before washing with a regular detergent.
   Ⓒ   Ⓓ

4. An abstract painter and pioneer of
   Surrealism, _____ and symbolic images.
   Ⓐ Miro's works are characterized by
      bright colors
   Ⓑ the works of Miro are characterized by
      bright colors
   Ⓒ Miro is famous for works characterized
      by bright colors
   Ⓓ bright colors characterize the works of
      Miro

5. Found in Tanzania by Mary Leakey, some
                        Ⓐ
   archeologists estimated that the

   three-million-year-old fossils were the oldest
            Ⓑ   Ⓒ
   human remains to be discovered.
                  Ⓓ

6. Originally having been buried in Spain,
   Ⓐ   Ⓑ   Ⓒ
   and later moved to Santo Domingo

   in the Dominican Republic,

   Columbus's final resting place is in
                    Ⓓ
   Andalucia, Spain.

7. Arguably the largest hotel on Earth, _____.
   Ⓐ the First World Hotel in Pahang, Malaysia, has 7,350 rooms between two towers
   Ⓑ there are 7,350 rooms between two towers in the First World Hotel in Pahang, Malaysia
   Ⓒ 7,350 rooms are between two towers in the First World Hotel in Pahang, Malaysia
   Ⓓ it is the First World Hotel in Pahang, Malaysia, that has 7,350 rooms between two towers

8. With music <u>written</u> by Andrew Lloyd
       Ⓐ

    Webber, <u>audiences are still thrilled by</u>
                        Ⓑ

    Phantom of the Opera, <u>the longest-running</u>

    <u>musical on the Broadway stage,</u>
                    Ⓒ

    <u>a hit that premiered</u> in 1986.
             Ⓓ

9. To prevent cavities,

    <u>dental floss should be used</u> <u>daily</u> after
            Ⓐ   Ⓑ

    <u>brushing</u> <u>one's</u> teeth.
         Ⓒ   Ⓓ

10. While researching the problem of violent

    crime, <u>the Senate committee's discovery</u>
                        Ⓐ

    that handguns <u>were used</u> <u>to commit</u> 67
                    Ⓑ   Ⓒ

    percent of <u>all murders</u> in the United States.
                    Ⓓ

11. One of the world's greatest rivers, _____.
    Ⓐ one-third of North America is linked
        by the water of the Mississippi
    Ⓑ the Mississippi links one third of North
        America by water
    Ⓒ North America is linked by the Missis-
        sippi in one third of the water
    Ⓓ the water is linked in North America
        by one third of the Mississippi

12. <u>After reviewing the curriculum,</u> <u>several</u>
            Ⓐ   Ⓑ

    significant changes <u>were</u> made by the
                         Ⓒ

    faculty <u>in</u> traditional business programs at
            Ⓓ

    Harvard University.

13. Having <u>hit</u> more home runs in his career
           Ⓐ

    <u>than</u> <u>any other player</u> in the history of
     Ⓑ   Ⓒ

    baseball, <u>Barry Bond's record</u> is famous.
                        Ⓓ

14. <u>Banned in the U.S.,</u> the effect of
            Ⓐ

    fluorocarbons <u>continues</u> at a level that could
                     Ⓑ

    <u>eventually</u> damage the ozone layer, and
        Ⓒ

    bring about <u>such</u> serious results as high risk
                  Ⓓ

    of skin cancer and global climate changes.

15. While trying to build a tunnel through the
    Blue Ridge Mountains, _____.
    Ⓐ coal was discovered by workmen at
        the construction site
    Ⓑ workmen discovered coal at the con-
        struction site
    Ⓒ the construction site was where coal
        was discovered by workmen
    Ⓓ it was the construction site where
        workmen discovered coal

16. <u>To avoid jet lag,</u> many doctors recommend
         Ⓐ

    that their patients <u>begin</u> adjusting one week
                         Ⓑ

    before departure time <u>by shifting</u> one hour
                              Ⓒ

    each day toward the new <u>time schedule.</u>
                                Ⓓ

17. <u>Traditionally</u> <u>named for women,</u>
        Ⓐ   Ⓑ

    Bob <u>was chosen</u> as <u>the first</u> male name for a
            Ⓒ   Ⓓ

    hurricane.

18. Published by Pocket Books almost eighty
    years ago, _____ offered to the public.
    Ⓐ Pearl Buck wrote *The Good Earth* in
        1938 as the first paperback book
    Ⓑ *The Good Earth* it was the first paper-
        back book by Pearl Buck
    Ⓒ Pearl Buck's *The Good Earth* was the
        first paperback book
    Ⓓ it was *The Good Earth* by Pearl Buck
        that was the first paperback book

19. Born in 1892, _____ while he wrote the poems and plays that made him famous.

    (A) the Library of Congress is where Archibald MacLeish worked as a librarian

    (B) Archibald MacLeish worked as a librarian at the Library of Congress

    (C) a librarian at the Library of Congress, Archibald MacLeish worked

    (D) at the Library of Congress, Archibald MacLeish worked as a librarian

20. Founded in 1919, students and teachers who
       <u>A</u>   <u>B</u>
    are interested in spending several months

    abroad <u>may benefit</u> from educational
              C
    programs <u>administered by</u> the Institute
                    D
    for International Education.

Refer to pages 364–365 for the Explanatory Answers.

EXERCISE 52: Sentences—Parallel Structure

In some sentences in the Structure and Written Expression Section of the Institutional TOEFL, you will be asked to identify errors in parallel structure. Parallel structure is the use of the same grammatical structures for related ideas of equal importance. Related ideas of equal importance often occur in the form of a list. Sometimes related ideas of equal importance are connected by conjunctions, such as *and*, *but*, and *or*. Choose the correct answer in the incomplete sentences. Choose the incorrect word or phrase in the underlined choices.

1. Country music is not only popular in the
   Ⓐ   Ⓑ   Ⓒ Ⓓ
   United States but also abroad.

2. To control quality and making decisions
                           Ⓐ
   about production are among the many
   Ⓑ   Ⓒ   Ⓓ
   responsibilities of an industrial engineer.

3. Most of the Cajun French who live in
   Louisiana can neither read _____ the
   French variety that they speak fluently.
   Ⓐ nor they write
   Ⓑ nor write
   Ⓒ or writing
   Ⓓ neither write

4. The six main parts of a business letter are
       Ⓐ   Ⓑ   Ⓒ
   the address, the inside address, the

   salutation, the body, the closing, and

   signing your name.
       Ⓓ

5. Microwaves are used for cooking,
   telecommunications, and _____.
   Ⓐ to diagnose medically
   Ⓑ medical diagnosing
   Ⓒ diagnosed medically
   Ⓓ medical diagnosis

6. To read literature and being introduced to a
                       Ⓐ   Ⓑ
   different culture are two excellent
                   Ⓒ
   reasons for studying a foreign language.
           Ⓓ

7. Ice skating and to go skiing are popular
       Ⓐ   Ⓑ
   winter sports in the northern United States.
           Ⓒ   Ⓓ

8. To treat minor diarrhea, drink plenty of
   Ⓐ
   liquids, especially tea, water, and carbonated

   beverages, eat soup, yogurt, salty crackers,
              Ⓑ

   and bananas, and avoiding milk, butter,
                   Ⓒ

   eggs, and meat for twenty-four hours.
                   Ⓓ

9. A vacuum will neither conduct heat nor

   _____.
   Ⓐ transmit sound waves
   Ⓑ transmitting sound waves
   Ⓒ sound waves are transmitted
   Ⓓ the transmission of sound waves

10. The Smithsonian Institute is famous because

    it contains such interesting exhibits as the

    flag that was raised over Fort McHenry
            Ⓐ

    in 1812, the airplane that the Wright
    Ⓑ

    brothers built for their first flight at Kitty
            Ⓒ

    Hawk, and there are the gowns worn by
              Ⓓ

    every first lady since Martha Washington.

11. In order to become a law, a bill
    Ⓐ
    must be passed not only by the Senate but
         Ⓑ   Ⓒ

    also the House of Representatives.
           Ⓓ

12. The color of a star depends on the heat and
    _____.
    - Ⓐ how much energy produced
    - Ⓑ the energy it produces
    - Ⓒ production of the energy
    - Ⓓ producing energy

13. The cloverleaf is a common engineering
    design for expressways that <u>permits</u> traffic
                                         Ⓐ
    <u>between</u> two intersecting highways <u>to move</u>
      Ⓑ   Ⓒ
    more safely, efficiently, and <u>with ease.</u>
                                     Ⓓ

14. A new product <u>should be judged</u> not by the
                          Ⓐ
    promises made in commercials <u>and</u>
                                 Ⓑ
    advertisements, <u>but also</u> by the results
                    Ⓒ
    <u>demonstrated</u> in actual use.
      Ⓓ

15. The artisans of the southwestern United
    States are famous for their beautiful art
    work, especially handmade jewelry cast
    from silver, carved from stones, or _____
    with beads and feathers.
    - Ⓐ decorations
    - Ⓑ decorating
    - Ⓒ decorated
    - Ⓓ decorate

16. <u>Snakes</u> stick out <u>their</u> tongues, move them
      Ⓐ   Ⓑ
    around, and <u>also they</u> retract them
                Ⓒ
    quickly <u>to pick up</u> odor molecules that aid in
           Ⓓ
    detecting direction.

17. <u>Thought</u> by some to be the first <u>labor</u> party,
     Ⓐ   Ⓑ
    the Workingman's Party struggled not
    only for better working conditions <u>also</u> for
                                      Ⓒ
    public schools for <u>all children.</u>
                     Ⓓ

18. The cerebellum's <u>main functions</u> <u>are</u>
                    Ⓐ   Ⓑ
    <u>the maintenance</u> of posture and <u>move</u> the
        Ⓒ   Ⓓ
    body.

19. The Cabinet consists of secretaries of
    departments who report to the president,
    give him advice, and _____ decisions.
    - Ⓐ helping him making
    - Ⓑ helping him make
    - Ⓒ help him making
    - Ⓓ help him make

20. Increasing involvement in agriculture
    <u>by large corporations</u> <u>has resulted in</u>
        Ⓐ   Ⓑ
    what is <u>known as</u> agribusiness—that is,
           Ⓒ
    agriculture with business techniques,
    including heavy capitalization,
    specialization of production, and <u>to control</u>
                                       Ⓓ
    all stages of the operation.

Refer to pages 365–366 for the Explanatory Answers.

EXERCISE 53: Sentences—Redundancy

In some sentences in the Structure and Written Expression Section of the Institutional TOEFL, you will be asked to identify errors in redundancy. Redundancy is the unnecessary repetition of words and phrases. Choose the correct answer in the incomplete sentences. Choose the incorrect word or phrase in the underlined choices.

1. Some international students use their
   Ⓐ
   phones to make recordings of their classes
   Ⓑ
   so that they can repeat the lectures again.
   Ⓒ   Ⓓ

2. Blood plasma it is the transportation system
   Ⓐ
   for all of the widely separated organs in
   Ⓑ   Ⓒ
   the human body.
   Ⓓ

3. Whereas a gas expands _____ in all
   directions, a vapor remains somewhat more
   concentrated.
   Ⓐ in a uniform manner
   Ⓑ uniformly
   Ⓒ uniformly in manner
   Ⓓ uniform

4. Appointed by the General Assembly for a
   Ⓐ   Ⓑ
   five-year term, the Secretary-General of the
   United Nations must act in an impartial manner
   Ⓒ   Ⓓ
   toward all members.

5. Humans who lived thousands of years ago,
   Ⓐ   Ⓑ
   long before alphabets were devised, they
   Ⓒ
   used pictures to record events and
   to communicate ideas.
   Ⓓ

6. If one does not pick up the dry cleaning
   Ⓐ
   within thirty days, the management is
   Ⓑ
   usually not obligated to return it back.
   Ⓒ   Ⓓ

7. That witches cause disasters and
   misfortunes _____ among the colonists in
   Salem, Massachusetts.
   Ⓐ it was widely believed
   Ⓑ was widely believed
   Ⓒ was believed in a wide way
   Ⓓ they widely believed

8. The southern part of the United States has
   ideal conditions for raising cotton because
   Ⓐ
   the climate is sufficiently warm enough
   Ⓑ
   to allow a six-month growing period.
   Ⓒ   Ⓓ

9. People who are competitive in nature are
   Ⓐ   Ⓑ
   more likely to suffer from the effects of
   Ⓒ
   stress on their health.
   Ⓓ

10. International law is made up of the rules and
    Ⓐ
    customs that they deal with the relationships
    Ⓑ Ⓒ
    between different nations and the citizens of
    Ⓓ
    different nations.

11. Found in and near the Mohave Desert,
    _____ has a limited habitat.
    Ⓐ is the Joshua tree that it
    Ⓑ it is the Joshua tree
    Ⓒ the Joshua tree
    Ⓓ the Joshua tree it

12. Traditionally, the South has been mostly Democrat _____, while the North has been divided between Democrats and Republicans.
    Ⓐ in the politics
    Ⓑ politically
    Ⓒ politics-wise
    Ⓓ in a political way

13. It was Isadora Duncan who was responsible
    Ⓐ   Ⓑ

    for many of the new innovations that have
                   Ⓒ

    made modern dance different from classical
                       Ⓓ

    ballet.

14. *Little House on the Prairie*, a successful

    television program, was adapted from a

    series of books by a young pioneer woman
    Ⓐ

    whose life was similar to that of the
    Ⓑ   Ⓒ

    character called by name Laura.
                    Ⓓ

15. In recent years great advances forward have
    Ⓐ   Ⓑ   Ⓒ

    been made in the field of genetic research.
                              Ⓓ

16. Today the United States is one of the few
                           Ⓐ

    countries in the Western Hemisphere that

    it has laws providing for the death penalty.
    ⒷⒸ   Ⓓ

17. Because of special cells with colored
                Ⓐ

    pigment in them layered under their skin,
                    Ⓑ

    chameleons can change color with rapidity,
                                  Ⓒ

    sometimes in as little as twenty seconds.
               Ⓓ

18. Digital clocks, however precise, _____ because the earth's rotation changes slightly over the year.
    Ⓐ they cannot be perfectly accurate
    Ⓑ cannot be perfectly accurate
    Ⓒ not perfectly accurate
    Ⓓ not be perfectly accurate

19. Natural gas often occurs _____ petroleum in the minute pores of rocks such as sandstone and limestone.
    Ⓐ both together with
    Ⓑ both together
    Ⓒ with
    Ⓓ both with

20. World hunger it is one of the most urgent
                 ⒶⒷ   Ⓒ

    problems that we face today.
                  Ⓓ

Refer to page 367 for the Explanatory Answers.

EXERCISE 54: Sentences—Word Choice

In some sentences in the Structure and Written Expression Section of the Institutional TOEFL, you will be asked to identify errors in word choice. Word choice is the selection of words that express the exact meaning of an idea. Sometimes it is necessary to make a choice between words that are very similar in appearance but very different in meaning. Choose the correct answer in the incomplete sentences. Choose the incorrect word or phrase in the underlined choices.

1. According to the Pythagorean theorem, the
   A
   sum of the squares of the two sides

   of a triangle is equal as the square of the
   B   C   D
   hypotenuse.

2. The flag over the White House is risen
                A   B
   at dawn every day by a color guard from the
   C   D
   United States armed forces.

3. Commercials on the educational television

   network are generally shorter comparing
           A   B   C
   those on other networks.
         D

4. The Pilgrims _____ seven thousand dollars
   at 43 percent interest to make their journey
   in 1620.
   A lent
   B borrowing
   C to lend
   D borrowed

5. The Food and Drug Administration does not

   declare a drug a carcinogen until it has
                                    A
   been proven conclusively that the effects in
               B   C
   rats can be generalized for human beings.
          D

6. In some states, the law allows drivers to turn
                                          A
   right at a red light, but in other states,
                             B
   the law does not leave them do it.
                    C   D

7. The effective of a project on the general
         A
   population is difficult to measure unless a
                          B
   statistician is employed to tabulate the
                 C   D
   variables.

8. When a person is arrested, the cops must
                              A
   let him make one telephone call.
   B C   D

9. Although blood _____ in urine and stool
   samples, it cannot always be detected
   without the aid of a microscope.
   A lets residue
   B leaves residue
   C residues
   D making residue

10. The audible range of frequencies for
    human beings _____ between 20 and
    20,000 Hz.
    A lies
    B lays
    C lying
    D laying

11. If the owner of a bar suspicions that
                         A
    someone's identification is not valid, he can
                            B
    refuse to serve the order.
          C   D

12. The condition of menkind has been
                     A   B
    improved by recent technological advances.
            C   D

13. _____ mammals, once weaned, do not routinely drink milk.
    - Ⓐ As a whole,
    - Ⓑ As whole,
    - Ⓒ Wholly,
    - Ⓓ On a whole,

14. The classify of plants begins with those
       Ⓐ   Ⓑ

    having the simplest structure and progresses

    to include the most highly organized forms
                    Ⓒ

    in four divisions called phylums.
                        Ⓓ

15. With the develop of a cheap process
                 Ⓐ

    for desalination, 97 percent of
        Ⓑ

    the Earth's water could become available
         Ⓒ   Ⓓ

    for freshwater purposes.

16. People with exceptionally high intelligence quotients may not be the best employees since they _____ unless the job is constantly changing.
    - Ⓐ become bored of work
    - Ⓑ are becoming boring in work
    - Ⓒ become bored with their work
    - Ⓓ work becoming bored

17. An understand of calculus is essential
        Ⓐ   Ⓑ

    to the study of engineering.
        Ⓒ   Ⓓ

18. Henry Wadsworth Longfellow not only

    wrote poems and stories but also presided
                                Ⓐ   Ⓑ

    the modern language department at Harvard

    University for more than eighteen years.
              Ⓒ   Ⓓ

19. In cold weather, growers place wind machines _____ the groves to keep the air circulating and to warm up the citrus crops.
    - Ⓐ near to
    - Ⓑ near of
    - Ⓒ next to
    - Ⓓ nearly

20. Almost all life depends to chemical
        Ⓐ   Ⓑ

    reactions with oxygen to produce energy.
                        Ⓒ   Ⓓ

Refer to pages 367–368 for the Explanatory Answers.

EXERCISE 55: Sentences—Comprehensive Structures

In the Structure and Written Expression Section of the Institutional TOEFL, the items will be organized into two parts—completion sentences and correction sentences. The test will include a comprehensive selection of structures. This exercise is an example of the Institutional TOEFL format. Choose the correct answer in the incomplete sentences. Choose the incorrect word or phrase in the underlined choices.

Part 1

1. In simple animals, _____ reflex movement or involuntary response to stimuli.
   - Ⓐ behavior mostly
   - Ⓑ most is behavior
   - Ⓒ most behavior is
   - Ⓓ the most behavior

2. Although the weather in Martha's Vineyard isn't _____ to have a year-round tourist season, it has become a favorite summer resort.
   - Ⓐ goodly enough
   - Ⓑ good enough
   - Ⓒ good as enough
   - Ⓓ enough good

3. According to the wave theory, _____ population of the Americas may have been the result of a number of separate migrations.
   - Ⓐ the
   - Ⓑ their
   - Ⓒ that
   - Ⓓ whose

4. It is presumed that rules governing the sharing of food influenced _____ that the earliest cultures evolved.
   - Ⓐ that the way
   - Ⓑ is the way
   - Ⓒ the way
   - Ⓓ which way

5. Calculus, _____ elegant and economical symbolic system, can reduce complex problems to simple terms.
   - Ⓐ it is an
   - Ⓑ that an
   - Ⓒ an
   - Ⓓ is an

6. Before 2009, Canada did not require that U.S. citizens obtain passports to enter the country, and _____.
   - Ⓐ Mexico did neither
   - Ⓑ Mexico didn't either
   - Ⓒ neither Mexico did
   - Ⓓ either did Mexico

7. The poet _____ just beginning to be recognized as an important influence at the time of his death.
   - Ⓐ being Walt Whitman
   - Ⓑ who was Walt Whitman
   - Ⓒ Walt Whitman
   - Ⓓ Walt Whitman was

8. _____ the formation of the Sun, the planets, and other stars began with the condensation of an interstellar cloud.
   - Ⓐ It accepted that
   - Ⓑ Accepted that
   - Ⓒ It is accepted that
   - Ⓓ That is accepted

9. As a general rule, the standard of living _____ by the average output of each person in society.
   - Ⓐ is fixed
   - Ⓑ fixed
   - Ⓒ has fixed
   - Ⓓ fixes

10. The *Consumer Price Index* lists _____.
    - Ⓐ how much costs every car
    - Ⓑ how much does every car cost
    - Ⓒ how much every car costs
    - Ⓓ how much are every car cost

11. The Ford Theater where Lincoln was shot _____ because it looks like it did in 1863.
    - Ⓐ must restore
    - Ⓑ must be restoring
    - Ⓒ must have been restored
    - Ⓓ must restored

12. Fast-food restaurants have become popular because many working people want _____.
    - Ⓐ to eat quickly and cheaply
    - Ⓑ eating quickly and cheaply
    - Ⓒ eat quickly and cheaply
    - Ⓓ the eat quickly and cheaply

13. After seeing the Harry Potter movies, _____.
    - Ⓐ the books were read by many people
    - Ⓑ the books made many people want to read them
    - Ⓒ many people wanted to read the books
    - Ⓓ the reading of the books interested many people

14. _____, Carl Sandburg is also well-known for his multivolume biography of Lincoln.
    - Ⓐ An eminent American poet
    - Ⓑ He is an eminent American poet
    - Ⓒ An eminent American poet who is
    - Ⓓ Despite an eminent American poet

15. The examiner will make you _____ your identification in order to be admitted to the test center.
    - Ⓐ showing
    - Ⓑ show
    - Ⓒ showed
    - Ⓓ to show

Part 2

16. A swarm of locusts <u>is responsible</u> the
    Ⓐ
    consumption of <u>enough plant material</u>
    Ⓑ
    to feed a million <u>and a half</u> people.
    Ⓒ   Ⓓ

17. Oyster <u>farming</u> has been <u>practice</u> in <u>most</u>
    Ⓐ   Ⓑ   Ⓒ
    parts of the world <u>for</u> many years.
    Ⓓ

18. <u>Those</u> of us <u>who</u> smoke should have
    Ⓐ   Ⓑ
    <u>their</u> lungs x-rayed <u>regularly</u>.
    Ⓒ   Ⓓ

19. After the team of geologists had drawn

    diagrams in <u>their</u> notebooks and <u>wrote</u>
    Ⓐ   Ⓑ
    explanations of the formations <u>which</u> they
    Ⓒ
    had observed, they returned to their

    campsite <u>to compare</u> notes.
    Ⓓ

20. If Robert Kennedy <u>would have lived</u>
    Ⓐ
    <u>a little longer</u>, he <u>probably</u> would have
    Ⓑ   Ⓒ
    <u>won</u> the election.
    Ⓓ

21. <u>It</u> was Shirley Temple Black <u>which</u>
    Ⓐ   Ⓑ
    <u>represented</u> her country in the United
    Ⓒ
    Nations and <u>later</u> became an ambassador.
    Ⓓ

22. The prices <u>at</u> online stores <u>are</u> as
    Ⓐ   Ⓑ
    reasonable, <u>if not more</u> reasonable, <u>as</u> those
    Ⓒ   Ⓓ
    at discount stores.

23. <u>It</u> is <u>extremely</u> important <u>for</u> an engineer
    Ⓐ   Ⓑ   Ⓒ
    <u>to know</u> to use up-to-date computer
    Ⓓ
    programs.

24. Historically there has been only two major
    (A)   (B)   (C)   (D)

    factions in the Republican Party—the

    liberals and the conservatives.

25. Whitman wrote *Leaves of Grass* as a

    tribute to the Civil War soldiers who

    had laid on the battlefields and whom he
    (A)   (B)

    had seen while serving as an army nurse.
    (C)   (D)

26. One of the first and ultimately the most
                        (A)

    important purposeful of a reservoir is
              (B)

    to control flooding.
    (C)   (D)

27. The Chinese were the first and large ethnic
    (A)   (B)

    group to work on the construction of the
          (C)   (D)

    transcontinental railroad system.

28. The range of plant life on a mountainside

    is a results of differences in temperature
    (A) (B)   (C)

    and precipitation at varying altitudes.
                        (D)

29. Even a professional psychologist may have
    (A)

    difficulty talking calm and logically about
                       (B)   (C)

    his own problems.
    (D)

30. The more the relative humidity reading

    rises, the worst the heat affects us.
    (A)   (B)   (C) (D)

31. Because correlations are not causes,
                              (A)

    statistical data which are extremely easy
                    (B)   (C)

    to misuse.
    (D)

32. Lectures for the week of March 22–26
               (A)

    will include the following: The Causes of
    (B)   (C)

    the Civil War, The Economy of the South,

    Battle Strategies, and The Assassinate
                            (D)

    Lincoln.

33. Despite of many attempts to introduce a
    (A)   (B)   (C)

    universal language, notably Esperanto and

    Idiom Neutral, the effort has met with very

    little success.
    (D)

34. As every other nation, the United States
    (A)   (B)

    used to define its unit of currency, the
        (C)   (D)

    dollar, in terms of the gold standard.

35. In most states, it is necessary that one met
                                          (A)

    with a judge before signing the final papers
                  (B)   (C)

    for a divorce.
    (D)

36. Until recently, the Inuit people are
                                 (A)

    primarily nomadic, sheltering in temporary
    (B)   (C)

    domes made from blocks of ice.
          (D)

37. According to the graduate catalog, student
    (A)

    housing is more cheaper than housing off
    (B)   (C)   (D)

    campus.

38. John Dewey thought that children

    will learn better through participating in
    (A)   (B)

    experiences rather than through listening to
               (C)   (D)

    lectures.

39. <u>In England</u> <u>as early</u> as the <u>twelfth century</u>,
    Ⓐ   Ⓑ   Ⓒ

young boys enjoyed <u>to play</u> football.
                Ⓓ

40. <u>Some methods</u> <u>to prevent</u> soil erosion <u>are</u>
    Ⓐ   Ⓑ   Ⓒ

plowing parallel with the slopes of hills,

<u>to plant</u> trees on unproductive land, and
  Ⓓ

rotating crops.

Refer to pages 368–370 for the Explanatory Answers.

PRACTICE EXERCISES
FOR READING

Reading Section

The Reading Section of the TOEFL tests your ability to understand written English as it is presented in textbooks and other academic materials in North America. This section is included in the Institutional TOEFL and the Internet-Based TOEFL. The section is different for each of the TOEFL formats.

Overview of the TOEFL iBT® Reading Section

The Reading Section tests your ability to understand reading passages like those in college textbooks. The reading passages are presented in one complete section, which allows you to move to the next passage or return to a previous passage to change questions or answers that you may have left blank throughout the entire section. The passages are about 700 words in length.

There are two formats for the Reading Section. On the short format, you will read three passages. On the long format, you will read four passages. After each passage, you will answer 10 questions about it. Only three passages will be graded. The other passage is part of an experimental section for future tests. Because you will not know which passages will be graded, you must try to do your best on all of them. You may take notes while you read, but notes are not graded. You may use your notes to answer the questions. Some passages may include a word or phrase that is underlined in blue. Click on the word or phrase to see a glossary definition or explanation.

Choose the best answer for multiple-choice questions. Follow the directions on the page or on the screen for computer-assisted questions. Most questions are worth 1 point, but the last question in each passage is worth more than 1 point.

Click on **Next** to go to the next question. Click on **Back** to return to previous questions. You may return to previous questions for all of the passages.

You can click on **Review** to see a chart of the questions you have answered and the questions you have not answered. From this screen, you can return to the question you want to answer.

Although you can spend more time on one passage and less time on another passage, you should try to pace yourself so that you take about 18 minutes to read each passage and answer the questions for that passage. You will have 54 minutes to complete all of the passages and answer all of the questions on the short format and 72 minutes to read all of the passages and answer all of the questions on the long format. A clock on the screen will show you how much time you have left to complete the Reading Section.

Overview of the TOEFL® ITP Reading Comprehension Section

The Reading Comprehension Section tests your ability to understand short reading passages based on both general interest and academic topics. The passages are about 300–350 words in length.

There are five passages in the Reading Comprehension Section. After each passage, you will answer nine to eleven questions about it. You may take notes while you read, but notes are not graded. You may use your notes to answer the questions.

All 50 questions are multiple-choice with four possible answer choices. After each question, choose the best answer. You should not mark your answers in the test book. Fill in the oval that corresponds to the letter of your answer on a separate answer sheet, using a soft lead pencil. Be sure to erase your first answer completely if you change your answer.

You will have 55 minutes to read all of the passages and answer the questions about them.

EXERCISE 56: Narration/Sequence—Popular Culture

In some questions in the Reading Comprehension Section on the Institutional TOEFL, you will be asked to recall and relate information and content from narration or sequence passages about popular culture. Choose the best answer.

Basketball

Although he created the game of basketball at the YMCA in Springfield, Massachusetts, Dr. James A. Naismith was a Canadian. Working as a physical education instructor at the International
Line YMCA, now Springfield College, Dr. Naismith noticed a lack of
5   interest in exercise among students during the wintertime. The New England winters were fierce, and the students balked at participating in outdoor activities. Naismith determined that a fast-moving game that could be played indoors would fill a void after the baseball and football seasons had ended.
10   First he attempted to adapt outdoor games such as soccer and rugby to indoor play, but he soon found them unsuitable for confined areas. Finally, he determined that he would have to invent a game.

In December of 1891, Dr. Naismith hung two old peach baskets at either end of the gymnasium at the school, and, using a soccer
15   ball and nine players on each side, organized the first basketball game. The early rules allowed three points for each basket and made running with the ball a violation. Every time a goal was made, someone had to climb a ladder to retrieve the ball.

Nevertheless, the game became popular. In less than a year,
20   basketball was being played in both the United States and Canada. Five years later, a championship tournament was staged in New York City, which was won by the Brooklyn Central YMCA.

The teams had already been reduced to seven players, and five became standard in the 1897 season. When basketball was introduced
25   as a demonstration sport in the 1904 Olympic Games in St. Louis, it quickly spread throughout the world. In 1906, a metal hoop was used for the first time to replace the basket, but the name basketball has remained.

1. What does this passage mainly discuss?
   Ⓐ The Olympic Games in St. Louis in 1904
   Ⓑ The development of basketball
   Ⓒ The YMCA athletic program
   Ⓓ Dr. James Naismith

2. When was the first demonstration game of basketball held during the Olympics?
   Ⓐ 1891
   Ⓑ 1892
   Ⓒ 1897
   Ⓓ 1904

3. The phrase "balked at" in line 6 could best be replaced by
   Ⓐ resisted
   Ⓑ enjoyed
   Ⓒ excelled at
   Ⓓ were exhausted by

4. The word "fierce" in line 6 is closest in meaning to
   Ⓐ long
   Ⓑ boring
   Ⓒ extreme
   Ⓓ dark

5. The word "them" in line 11 refers to
   Ⓐ indoors
   Ⓑ seasons
   Ⓒ games
   Ⓓ areas

6. Where in the passage does the author discuss the first basketball championship tournament?
   Ⓐ Lines 10–12
   Ⓑ Lines 13–15
   Ⓒ Lines 21–22
   Ⓓ Lines 24–26

7. What does the author mean by the statement in lines 24–26: "When basketball was introduced as a demonstration sport in the 1904 Olympic Games in St. Louis, it quickly spread throughout the world"?
   Ⓐ Basketball was not considered an Olympic sport at the St. Louis games.
   Ⓑ Basketball became popular worldwide after its introduction at the Olympic Games in St. Louis.
   Ⓒ Basketball players from many countries competed in the Olympic Games in St. Louis.
   Ⓓ Basketball was one of the most popular sports at the Olympic Games in St. Louis.

8. Why did Naismith decide to invent basketball?
   Ⓐ He did not like soccer or rugby.
   Ⓑ He was tired of baseball and football.
   Ⓒ He wanted his students to exercise during the winter.
   Ⓓ He could not convince his students to play indoors.

9. The author mentions all of the following as typical of the early game of basketball EXCEPT
   Ⓐ three points were scored for every basket
   Ⓑ running with the ball was not a foul
   Ⓒ nine players were on a team
   Ⓓ the ball had to be retrieved from the basket after each score

10. It can be inferred from the passage that the original baskets
    Ⓐ were not placed very high
    Ⓑ had a metal rim
    Ⓒ did not have a hole in the bottom
    Ⓓ were hung on the same side

Refer to page 371 for the Explanatory Answers.

EXERCISE 57: Definition/Illustration—Popular Culture

In some questions in the Reading Comprehension Section on the Institutional TOEFL, you will be asked to recall and relate information and content from definition or illustration passages about popular culture. Choose the best answer.

Mickey Mouse

Mickey Mouse was not Walt Disney's first successful cartoon creation, but he is certainly his most famous one. It was on a cross-country train trip from New York to California in 1927 that Disney
Line first drew the mouse with the big ears. Supposedly, he took his
5   inspiration from the tame field mice that used to scamper into his old studio in Kansas City. No one is quite sure why he dressed the mouse in the now-familiar shorts with two buttons and gave him the yellow shoes. But we do know that Disney had intended to call him Mortimer until his wife Lillian intervened and christened him Mickey
10 Mouse.

Capitalizing on the interest in Charles Lindbergh, Disney planned Mickey's debut in the short cartoon Plane Crazy, with Minnie as a co-star. In the third short cartoon, *Steamboat Willie*, Mickey was whistling and singing through the miracle of the modern soundtrack.
15 By the 1930s Mickey's image had circled the globe. He was a superstar at the height of his career.

Although he has received a few minor changes throughout his lifetime, most notably the addition of white gloves and the alterations to achieve the rounder forms of a more childish body, he
20 has remained true to his nature since those first cartoons. Mickey is appealing because he is nice. He may get into trouble, but he takes it on the chin with a grin. He is both good-natured and resourceful. Perhaps that was Disney's own image of himself. Why else would he have insisted on doing Mickey's voice in all the cartoons for twenty
25 years? When interviewed, he would say. "There is a lot of the mouse in me." And that mouse has remained one of the most pervasive images in American popular culture.

1. Which of the following is the main topic of the passage?
   - Ⓐ The image of Mickey Mouse
   - Ⓑ The life of Walt Disney
   - Ⓒ The history of cartoons
   - Ⓓ The definition of American culture

2. What distinguished *Steamboat Willie* from earlier cartoons?
   - Ⓐ Better color
   - Ⓑ A sound track
   - Ⓒ Minnie Mouse as co-star
   - Ⓓ The longer format

3. The word "pervasive" in line 26 could best be replaced by
   - Ⓐ well loved
   - Ⓑ widespread
   - Ⓒ often copied
   - Ⓓ expensive to buy

4. The word "appealing" in line 21 is closest in meaning to
   - Ⓐ attractive
   - Ⓑ famous
   - Ⓒ exceptional
   - Ⓓ distinguishable

5. The word "those" in line 20 refers to
   - Ⓐ cartoons
   - Ⓑ forms
   - Ⓒ gloves
   - Ⓓ changes

6. Where in the passage does the author relate how Mickey got his name?
   - Ⓐ Lines 8–10
   - Ⓑ Lines 11–13
   - Ⓒ Lines 15–16
   - Ⓓ Lines 17–20

7. What does the author mean by the statement in lines 17–20: "Although he has received a few minor changes throughout his lifetime, most notably the addition of white gloves and the alterations to achieve the rounder forms of a more childish body, he has remained true to his nature since those first cartoons"?
   - Ⓐ The current version of Mickey Mouse is different in every way from the early cartoons.
   - Ⓑ The original Mickey Mouse was one of the first cartoon characters.
   - Ⓒ In the first cartoons, Mickey Mouse looked more like a child.
   - Ⓓ The personality of Mickey Mouse has not changed over the years.

8. What did Disney mean when he said, "There is a lot of the mouse in me?"
   - Ⓐ He was proud of the mouse that he created.
   - Ⓑ He knew that the mouse would be a famous creation.
   - Ⓒ He created the mouse with many of his own qualities.
   - Ⓓ He had worked very hard to create the mouse.

9. The first image of Mickey Mouse is described as all of the following EXCEPT
   - Ⓐ he was dressed in shorts with two buttons
   - Ⓑ he had big ears
   - Ⓒ he wore yellow shoes
   - Ⓓ he was wearing white gloves

10. The paragraph following the passage most probably discusses
    - Ⓐ the history of cartoons
    - Ⓑ other images in popular culture
    - Ⓒ Walt Disney's childhood
    - Ⓓ the voices of cartoon characters

Refer to pages 371–372 for the Explanatory Answers.

EXERCISE 58: Narration/Sequence—Social Sciences

In some questions in the Reading Comprehension Section on the Institutional TOEFL, you will be asked to recall and relate information and content from narration or sequence passages in various fields of study. Choose the best answer.

Federal Policies for Native Peoples

Federal policy toward the Native Americans has a long history of inconsistency, reversal, and failure. In the late 1700s, the United States government owned and operated factories, exchanging
Line manufactured goods for furs and horses with the hope that mutual
5 satisfaction with trade would result in peace between Native Americans and the rush of settlers who were moving west. At the same time, the government supported missionary groups in their efforts to build churches, schools, and model farms for those tribes that permitted them to live in their midst.
10 By the 1800s, federal negotiators were trying to convince many tribes to sell their land and move out of the line of frontier expansion, a policy that culminated in the forced expulsion of the major Southeastern tribes to the west. Over protests by Congress and the Supreme Court, President Andrew Jackson ordered the Native
15 Americans to be removed to what is now Oklahoma. On the forced march, which the Cherokee Nation refers to as the "Trail of Tears," many Native Americans died of disease, exposure, and hunger.
By the end of the 1800s, the government had discovered that some of the land allocated as permanent reservations for the Native
20 Americans contained valuable resources. Congress passed the Dawes Severalty Act, and for the next forty years Indian agents and missionaries attempted to destroy the tribal system by separating the members. It was during this time that the government boarding schools were established to educate Native-American youth outside
25 of the home environment.
Under the Indian Reorganization Act of 1934, scattered tribes were encouraged to reorganize their tribal governments. Anti-Indian sentiment resurfaced only ten years later, and by the 1950s relocation centers to move Native Americans from the reservations to urban
30 areas were established.
Today, government policies are unclear. Many officials want to remove the federal government completely from Native-American governance. Others believe that the government should support Native-American efforts to maintain their culture. Not surprisingly,
35 the Native Americans themselves are ambivalent about the role of the federal government in their affairs.

1. What is the author's main point?
   - Ⓐ Government policies for Native Americans have not changed many times during the past three hundred years.
   - Ⓑ Today government officials are in agreement about their role in Native-American affairs.
   - Ⓒ The federal government has been inconsistent and unclear in its policies for Native Americans.
   - Ⓓ The Indian Reorganization Act was a failure.

2. What was involved in the "Trail of Tears"?
   - Ⓐ Native-American children were separated from their families and sent to boarding schools.
   - Ⓑ Native-American families living in the Southeast were forced to move to Oklahoma.
   - Ⓒ Native-American families were resettled on reservations.
   - Ⓓ Native Americans were moved from reservations to cities.

3. The word "ambivalent" in line 35 refers to
   - Ⓐ exhibiting suspicion
   - Ⓑ experiencing contradictory feelings
   - Ⓒ expressing concern
   - Ⓓ demonstrating opposition

4. The word "culminated" in line 12 is closest in meaning to
   - Ⓐ ended
   - Ⓑ failed
   - Ⓒ belonged
   - Ⓓ caused

5. The word "them" in line 9 refers to
   - Ⓐ missionary groups
   - Ⓑ efforts
   - Ⓒ model farms
   - Ⓓ tribes

6. Where in the passage does the author refer to the congressional act that allowed Native-American students to be sent to boarding schools?
   - Ⓐ Lines 6–9
   - Ⓑ Lines 13–15
   - Ⓒ Lines 20–25
   - Ⓓ Lines 26–30

7. What does the author mean by the statement in lines 13–15: "Over protests by Congress and the Supreme Court, President Andrew Jackson ordered the Native Americans to be removed to what is now Oklahoma?"
   - Ⓐ Oklahoma objected to the president's order to move Native Americans to their state.
   - Ⓑ The Native Americans had to move to Oklahoma because Congress and the Supreme Court objected to the president's order.
   - Ⓒ The president ordered the Native Americans in Oklahoma to move despite opposition by Congress and the Supreme Court.
   - Ⓓ Despite objections by Congress and the Supreme Court, Native Americans were forced to move to Oklahoma by the president.

8. Why did Congress pass the Dawes Severalty Act?
   - Ⓐ Because the government agencies wanted to exploit the resources on reservations
   - Ⓑ Because missionaries wanted to convert the Native Americans to Christianity
   - Ⓒ Because teachers wanted to set up schools for Native Americans in urban areas
   - Ⓓ Because officials on the reservations wanted to preserve Native-American culture

9. Native-American policies are described as all of the following EXCEPT
   - Ⓐ inconsistent
   - Ⓑ destructive
   - Ⓒ permanent
   - Ⓓ unclear

10. The paragraph following the passage most probably discusses
   - Ⓐ the Native-American point of view regarding government policies today
   - Ⓑ the efforts by Native Americans to maintain their culture
   - Ⓒ the results of the reservation system
   - Ⓓ the intertribal councils that Native Americans have established

Refer to page 372 for the Explanatory Answers.

EXERCISE 59: Narration/Sequence—Arts/Architecture

In some questions in the Reading Comprehension Section on the Institutional TOEFL, you will be asked to recall and relate information and content from narration or sequence passages in various fields of study. Choose the best answer.

Eugene O'Neill

Universally acclaimed as America's greatest playwright, Eugene O'Neill was born in 1888 in the heart of the theater district in New York City. As the son of an actor, he had early exposure to the world
Line of the theater. He attended Princeton University briefly in 1906, but
5 returned to New York to work in a variety of jobs before joining the crew of a freighter as a seaman. Upon returning from voyages to South Africa and South America, he was hospitalized for six months to recuperate from tuberculosis. While he was recovering, he determined to write a play about his adventures on the sea.
10 He went to Harvard, where he wrote the one-act *Bound East for Cardiff*. It was produced in 1916 on Cape Cod by the Provincetown Players, an experimental theater group that was later to settle in the famous Greenwich Village theater district in New York City. The Players produced several more of his one-acts in the years between
15 1916–1920. With the full-length play *Beyond the Horizon*, produced on Broadway in 1920, O'Neill's success was assured. The play won the Pulitzer Prize for the best play of the year. O'Neill was to be awarded the prize again in 1922, 1928, and 1957 for *Anna Christie*, *Strange Interlude*, and *Long Day's Journey Into Night*. Although he
20 did not receive the Pulitzer Prize for it, *Mourning Becomes Electra*, produced in 1931, is arguably his most lasting contribution to the American theater. In 1936, he was awarded the Nobel Prize for literature.
O'Neill's plays, forty-five in all, cover a wide range of dramatic
25 subjects, but several themes emerge, including the ambivalence of family relationships, the struggle between the sexes, the conflict between spiritual and material desires, and the vision of modern man as a victim of uncontrollable circumstances. Most of O'Neill's characters are seeking meaning in their lives. According to his
30 biographers, most of the characters were portraits of himself and his family. In a sense, his work chronicled his life.

1. This passage is a summary of O'Neill's
   - Ⓐ work
   - Ⓑ life
   - Ⓒ work and life
   - Ⓓ family

2. How many times was O'Neill awarded the Pulitzer Prize?
   - Ⓐ One
   - Ⓑ Three
   - Ⓒ Four
   - Ⓓ Five

3. The word "briefly" in line 4 is closest in meaning to
   - Ⓐ seriously
   - Ⓑ for a short time
   - Ⓒ on scholarship
   - Ⓓ without enthusiasm

4. The word "struggle" in line 26 is closest in meaning to
   - Ⓐ influence
   - Ⓑ conflict
   - Ⓒ appreciation
   - Ⓓ denial

5. The word "it" in line 20 refers to
   - Ⓐ Harvard
   - Ⓑ one-act play
   - Ⓒ theater group
   - Ⓓ theater district

6. Where in the passage does the author indicate the reason for O'Neill's hospitalization?
   - Ⓐ Lines 3–4
   - Ⓑ Lines 6–8
   - Ⓒ Lines 10–13
   - Ⓓ Lines 16–19

7. What does the author mean by the statement in lines 29–31: "According to his biographers, most of the characters were portraits of himself and his family"?
   - Ⓐ He used his family and his own experiences in his plays.
   - Ⓑ His biography contained stories about him and his family.
   - Ⓒ He had paintings of himself and members of his family.
   - Ⓓ His biographers took pictures of him with his family.

8. According to the passage, which of O'Neill's plays was most important to the American theater?
   - Ⓐ *Anna Christie*
   - Ⓑ *Beyond the Horizon*
   - Ⓒ *Long Day's Journey Into Night*
   - Ⓓ *Mourning Becomes Electra*

9. The author mentions all of the following as themes for O'Neill's plays EXCEPT
   - Ⓐ life in college
   - Ⓑ adventures at sea
   - Ⓒ family life
   - Ⓓ relationships between men and women

10. We can infer from information in the passage that O'Neill's plays were not
    - Ⓐ controversial
    - Ⓑ autobiographical
    - Ⓒ optimistic
    - Ⓓ popular

Refer to page 373 for the Explanatory Answers.

EXERCISE 60: Narration/Sequence—Humanities/Business

In some questions in the Reading Section on the Internet-Based TOEFL, you will be asked to recall and relate information and content from narration or sequence passages found in college textbooks. Choose the best answer for multiple-choice questions. For computer-assisted questions, follow the directions on the screen.

The History of Printing

Paragraph 1   The history of printing began as early as 3500 B.C.E. with cylinder seals, used by the Persian and Mesopotamians civilizations to certify documents written in clay. For the most part, however, writing was performed by scribes or clerks who were schooled in this laborious art. Sacred documents, governmental laws and notices, and commercial records and transactions were all copied by hand. In the Far East, however, especially in present-day China, Korea, and Japan, examples of wooden block printing on paper have been identified and dated as early as 704 and 751 C.E. Several forms of moveable type were invented in China in the eleventh century, using clay and glue to create individual characters, which when fired became durable porcelain squares. Later, iron plates were used to hold them, making it possible to print an entire page. However, the Chinese preferred block printing even into the modern period, perhaps because the nature of Chinese writing lent itself to the production of an entire page of characters on one block instead of the arrangement of many small pieces of type on lines. In contrast, German and other European languages with a relatively small number of characters, were much easier to set in moveable type.

2   It has been speculated that Marco Polo may have seen examples of block printing and even moveable type during his voyages to the Far East in the thirteenth century, a time period that fits with the introduction of block printing in fourteenth-century Europe to create religious images and prayers. Egyptians had also used block printing for seals on their documents, some of which may have been transported to Europe, and several early cultures had begun using block printing for paper money. However, there is no direct evidence that typesetting in any form was transferred from either China or Egypt to Europe. It seems more likely that European inventors independently experimented with block printing as a way to replace manuscript copying, and discovered that it, too, was expensive and slow.

3   It was not until the middle of the fifteenth century that Johannes Gutenberg invented the printing press, using durable, reusable lead alloy pieces that provided for uniform lettering. The printing process that he developed required the solution of complicated problems at each stage. Gutenberg used his knowledge of metallurgy, learned from an apprenticeship as a goldsmith with his father, and

developed a set of metal letters, but the crucial innovation was a mold for each letter into which molten metal was poured, thereby producing a single letter of type. Using this ingenious method, Gutenberg could make hundreds of pieces of type daily. [A] Gutenberg also adapted the technology of his time, repurposing the screw press that was already successful in the production of linen, paper, and wine. [B] By combining soot and linseed oil with his ink, he was able to thicken it so that it would adhere smoothly to the metal type.

4   Although no date actually appears in the Gutenberg Bible, it was probably completed in the mid 1450s. The first dated version from the press in 1457 appears in two colors—black for the print and red for initial letters. Sadly, after the successful publication of his first books, Gutenberg had to give the equipment and remaining Bibles in his possession to his business partner, Johann Fust, a businessman who had advanced him money to carry out the lengthy experiments that would finally result in a functioning printing press. [C]

5   The revolutionary process, which produced more than a thousand copies in one printing, cost only a fraction of the price of texts copied by hand. By 1500, there were printers in sixty German towns, and printing was well established throughout Europe. [D]

6   Gutenberg had changed European culture in a number of important ways. Never before had it been possible for information and ideas to be shared simultaneously across such long distances. Furthermore, books became available in many parts of Europe outside of the large cities where previously it had been almost impossible to find manuscript copies.

7   Moreover, owning books was no longer the exclusive privilege of scholars. Although the classics were still available in the ancient languages, William Caxton began printing books in English as early as the 1470s. Martin Luther's translation of the Bible into German fifty years later solidified the popularity of vernacular languages and encouraged more consistent spelling. In short, the printing press had promoted literacy throughout Europe.

8   Oral history, stories, and songs were standardized in print and shared by a wide readership. News pages and newspapers became popular. Not only the language, but also the breadth of the readership and the character of the content had been changed. It has even been argued that without the printing press, the political changes that took place in Europe and the American continent may not have been possible.

1. According to the passage, what was NOT true of block printing?
   - Ⓐ It was an expensive method.
   - Ⓑ The process was very slow.
   - Ⓒ It replaced many scribes.
   - Ⓓ Marco Polo brought it to Europe.

2. The word them in the passage refers to
   - Ⓐ individual characters
   - Ⓑ iron plates
   - Ⓒ clay and glue
   - Ⓓ porcelain squares

3. According to paragraph 2, how did the author believe that block printing was introduced in Europe?

    Ⓐ They saw examples that were brought from China by explorers and soldiers.

    Ⓑ A German goldsmith invented it at the beginning of the fifteenth century.

    Ⓒ It was first devised in Europe in order to print paper money.

    Ⓓ The Egyptians used the blocks for documents that the Europeans received.

4. The word crucial in the passage is closest in meaning to

    Ⓐ totally new

    Ⓑ very significant

    Ⓒ greatly debated

    Ⓓ highly complex

5. It can be inferred that Gutenberg

    Ⓐ had probably traveled to China and western Asia

    Ⓑ did not live to see his invention succeed

    Ⓒ was a painter before he became an inventor

    Ⓓ worked for a long time to perfect his printing process

6. Four squares (☐) indicate where the following sentence can be added to the passage.

    Although he did not receive the financial remuneration that he deserved, history has recorded his name among the most influential inventors of all time.

    Where would the sentence best fit into the passage?

    Ａ

    Ｂ

    Ｃ

    Ｄ

7. Which of the sentences below best expresses the information in the highlighted statement in the passage? The other choices change the meaning or leave out important information.

    Ⓐ Scholars owned more books than other people.

    Ⓑ Scholars were not the only people who could own books.

    Ⓒ Scholars preserved books for use by other people.

    Ⓓ Scholars owned some exclusive books.

8. The author mentions all of the following advantages of the print revolution EXCEPT

    Ⓐ the standardization of written languages throughout Europe

    Ⓑ the advancement of literacy among Europeans

    Ⓒ the dissemination of information to European towns

    Ⓓ the restoration of many ancient European manuscripts

9. How was popular culture affected by printing?

    Ⓐ The oral tradition required editing of printed documents.

    Ⓑ Stories and songs changed less often.

    Ⓒ More folk histories were preserved.

    Ⓓ Traditional performers became more popular.

10. Complete a summary of the passage by selecting THREE answer choices that express the most important ideas. The other three sentences do not belong in the summary because they express ideas that are not in the passage or they do not refer to the major ideas. *This question is worth 2 points.*

    Printing not only changed the way information was transmitted but also changed the character of the information itself.

    Ⓐ Gutenberg devised reusable type for European languages to replace the block printing that was more appropriate for Asian languages.

    Ⓑ Information and ideas were made available throughout Europe to a large number of people at virtually the same time.

    Ⓒ A new format for books made them more portable and easier for people to handle.

    Ⓓ Block printing continued to be used to print paper money in most of the European countries.

    Ⓔ Many changes in literacy and vernacular languages occurred as a result of the printing press.

    Ⓕ Gutenberg did not realize much from his invention because he had accumulated debts in order to pay for his experiments.

Refer to pages 373–374 for the Explanatory Answers.

EXERCISE 61: Narration/Sequence—Natural Sciences

In some questions in the Reading Section on the Internet-Based TOEFL, you will be asked to recall and relate information and content from narration or sequence passages found in college textbooks. Choose the best answer for multiple-choice questions. For computer-assisted questions, follow the directions on the screen.

Glacial Movement

Paragraph 1   Glacial ice is actually a rock made of one mineral, the crystalline structure of water. It forms when tens of thousands of individual snowflakes fail to melt and begin to accumulate, forming crystals and eventually flowing downhill. It is this ability to move that makes glaciers unique. Whereas the top layer of a glacier looks like normal ice or even snow, just below this crust is a transitional layer, which, because it is less dense, moves more like a river. Finally, at the bottom of a glacier, the ice gets compressed by the layers on top of it and flows in response to the weight and pressure from the ice above it and the steepness of the land mass.

2   In general, glaciers move slowly, covering a distance ranging from imperceptible to a mile or two annually. The base usually moves slower than the internal, more plastic flow of the glacier, which results in something called *basal slip*, or the movement of the upper part of the glacier ahead of the bottom. It is often caused when the bottom of the glacier becomes heated by friction with the bedrock, which in turn causes a small amount of melting, lubricating the area where the rock and ice meet, and causing the glacier to move faster.

3   Basal ice may melt and refreeze in a process called ice *regelation*, which is one way that the glacier secures rock and debris in the basal layer, thus facilitating its movement downhill. The difference in the speed of the flow stretches the surface ice, which is one of the reasons that glaciers may develop crevasses, deep vertical cracks just below the surface. Navigating across a glacier is perilous because snow or a thin layer of ice can hide a crevasse.

4   Although the movement of glaciers is relatively predictable, a glacier will occasionally surge forward without warning. The term *surge* is actually misleading, since the ice doesn't move more than thirty feet in twenty-four hours; however, in glacial time, this movement is considered abrupt because it is more than 100 times faster than usual. Surges are thought to be caused by meltwater at the base of a glacier, which would result in water pressure sufficient to temporarily detach the top of the glacier from the rock in a soft bed of saturated sediment under the glacier. The top then floats forward. However, the precise cause of surges is still under investigation.

5   One spectacular feature of glacial ice is that it can appear blue due to its dense structure, created by years of compression that forces out the air pockets between the crystals. As this occurs, the ice absorbs red light, leaving the blue reflection that is visible to the eye. When glacial ice is white, it usually indicates that the air bubbles are still in the ice.

6   Currently, glaciers account for about 10 percent of the total land
area of the Earth, mostly in the polar regions of Antarctica,
Greenland and the Canadian Arctic. In these and a few other regions,
we find large areas of interconnected glaciers called *ice fields*.
[A] Some of the most famous include the Columbia Ice Field in
Canada, the Harding Ice Field in Alaska, the Northern and Southern
Patagonian Ice Fields in Chile and Argentina, the Dovre and
Jotunheimen Fields in Norway, and the Olivine Ice Plateau in New
Zealand. [B]

7   Even larger than ice fields are the gigantic glacial ice sheets that
cover continental land masses in Antarctica and Greenland. [C] To
understand how enormous the expanse of ice is, consider that the ice
sheet on Antarctica is more than three miles thick in some areas.
[D] It covers almost all of the land features, with the exception of the
Transantarctic Mountains, extending 5.4 million square miles or
approximately the combined area of the United States and Mexico.
Like smaller glaciers and ice fields, ice sheets are constantly in
motion, slowly flowing downhill. When they are near the coast,
the glaciers flow into the sea and form icebergs that float along
like icy mountains; an ice sheet, however, remains stable as long
as the accumulation of snow is about the same as the loss of ice into
the sea.

1. According to paragraph 2, what causes
    basal slip?
    Ⓐ The upper part of the glacier melts
        from exposure to the Sun.
    Ⓑ The lower part of the glacier heats up
        from rubbing against the bedrock.
    Ⓒ The rock breaks through the ice at the
        top of the glacier.
    Ⓓ The glacier moves faster than it
        usually does.

2. What can be inferred about *ice regulation*?
    Ⓐ It prevents dangerous crevasses from
        forming in glaciers.
    Ⓑ It is an important process that
        promotes glacial movement.
    Ⓒ It keeps rock and debris from freezing
        in the glacier.
    Ⓓ It allows scientists to predict the
        direction a glacier will move.

3. According to paragraph 4, why do glacial
    surges usually occur?
    Ⓐ Heavy snow pushes the glacier
        forward.
    Ⓑ Water pressure under the glacier
        causes the ice to float.
    Ⓒ Dry rock and dirt that is packed under
        the glacier moves.
    Ⓓ Earthquakes under the ice sheet pick
        up the glacier.

4. The word abrupt in the passage is closest
    in meaning to
    Ⓐ unexpected
    Ⓑ lengthy
    Ⓒ destructive
    Ⓓ simple

5. The word precise in the passage is closest in meaning to
   Ⓐ exact
   Ⓑ important
   Ⓒ possible
   Ⓓ usual

6. According to paragraph 5, what makes glaciers look blue?
   Ⓐ Air bubbles absorb red light, leaving the blue.
   Ⓑ Blue light is reflected from the ice and red light is absorbed.
   Ⓒ White light is divided into colors but blue light is not reflected.
   Ⓓ The dense ice crystals have blue air pockets between them.

7. Four squares (☐) indicate where the following sentence can be added to the passage.

   These fields are usually found in cold, mountainous regions where there is a lot of snowfall.

   Where would the sentence best be added to the passage?
   A
   B
   C
   D

8. Why does the author mention *the U.S. and Mexico* in paragraph 7?
   Ⓐ To identify the location of the most famous ice fields
   Ⓑ To explain the formation of large icebergs
   Ⓒ To demonstrate the size of the ice sheet in Antarctica
   Ⓓ To provide examples of ice fields near a coast

9. The author mentions all of the following characteristics of glaciers EXCEPT
   Ⓐ glaciers are a major source of fresh water
   Ⓑ glacial ice has all the properties of a mineral
   Ⓒ ice flows below the surface of a glacier
   Ⓓ glaciers cover about 10 percent of the Earth

10. Complete a summary of the passage by selecting THREE answer choices that express the most important ideas. The other three sentences do not belong in the summary because they express ideas that are not in the passage or they do not refer to the major ideas. *This question is worth 2 points.*

How do glaciers move?

Ⓐ A glacial surge can occur unpredictably, moving the ice sheet more abruptly than usual.

Ⓑ A thin layer of snow can sometimes hide the presence of a potentially dangerous crevasse.

Ⓒ Below the surface of a glacier, the ice flows, thereby moving the glacier forward.

Ⓓ Hubbard Glacier in Alaska experienced a sudden and very rapid surge in 1986.

Ⓔ Snow accumulation, temperature, water, or sediment beneath the ice can affect the rate of the movement.

Ⓕ The movement of a glacier is usually so slow that it must be studied over a long period of time.

Refer to pages 374–375 for the Explanatory Answers.

EXERCISE 62: Definition/Illustration—Humanities/Business

In some questions in the Reading Comprehension Section on the Institutional TOEFL, you will be asked to recall and relate information and content from definition or illustration passages about various fields of study. Choose the best answer.

The Canadian Government

Canada is a democracy organized as a constitutional monarchy with a parliamentary system of government modeled after that of Great Britain. The official head of state in Canada is Queen Elizabeth II of Britain, who is also Queen of Canada. The governor-general is the queen's personal representative in Canada and the official head of the Canadian parliament, although with very limited powers.

The federal parliament in Canada consists of the House of Commons and the Senate. The actual head of government is the prime minister, who is responsible for choosing a cabinet. The cabinet consists of a group of ministers of varied expertise who serve with the support of the House of Commons. They are responsible for most legislation and have the sole power to prepare and introduce bills that provide for the expenditure of public funds or taxation. The system is referred to as responsible government, which means that cabinet members sit in the parliament and are directly responsible to it, holding power only as long as a majority of the House of Commons shows confidence by voting with them. If a cabinet is defeated in the House of Commons on a motion of censure or a vote of no confidence, the cabinet must either resign, in which case the governor-general will ask the leader of the opposition to form a new cabinet, or a new election may be called.

The Canadian Senate has 104 members, appointed by the governor-general on the advice of the prime minister. Their actual function is advisory, although they may make minor changes in bills, and no bill may become a law without being passed by the Senate. Senators hold office until age seventy-five unless they are absent from two consecutive sessions of parliament. The real power, however, resides in the House of Commons, the members of which are elected directly by the voters. The seats are allocated on the basis of population, and there are about 300 constituencies. By custom, almost all members of the cabinet must be members of the House of Commons or, if not already members, must win seats within a reasonable time.

General elections must be held at the end of every five years, but they may be conducted whenever issues require it, and most parliaments are dissolved before the end of the five-year term. When a government loses its majority support in a general election, a change of government occurs.

Although major and minor political parties were not created by law, they are recognized by law in Canada. The party that wins the largest number of seats in a general election forms the government, and its leader becomes the prime minister. The second-largest party becomes the official opposition, and its leader is recognized as the leader of the opposition. In this way, the people are assured of an effective alternative government should they become displeased with the one in power.

1. What does this passage mainly discuss?
   - Ⓐ Political parties in Canada
   - Ⓑ The Canadian election process
   - Ⓒ The Canadian system of government
   - Ⓓ The powers of parliament in Canada

2. When does a change of government occur in Canada?
   - Ⓐ When the governor-general decides to appoint a new government
   - Ⓑ When the voters do not return majority support for the government in a general election
   - Ⓒ When the prime minister advises the governor-general to appoint a new government
   - Ⓓ When the House of Commons votes for a new government

3. The word "dissolved" in line 35 could best be replaced by
   - Ⓐ approved
   - Ⓑ evaluated
   - Ⓒ reorganized
   - Ⓓ dismissed

4. The word "varied" in line 10 is closest in meaning to
   - Ⓐ little
   - Ⓑ different
   - Ⓒ good
   - Ⓓ steady

5. The word "it" in line 16 refers to
   - Ⓐ majority
   - Ⓑ parliament
   - Ⓒ cabinet
   - Ⓓ system

6. Where in the passage does the author indicate whose responsibility it is to choose the cabinet in Canada?
   - Ⓐ Lines 4–6
   - Ⓑ Lines 8–9
   - Ⓒ Lines 11–13
   - Ⓓ Lines 27–29

7. What does the author mean by the statement in lines 1–3: "Canada is a constitutional monarchy with a . . . parliamentary system of government modeled after that of Great Britain"?
   - Ⓐ Whereas Canada has a constitutional form of government, Great Britain has a parliamentary system.
   - Ⓑ Canada and Great Britain both have model systems of government.
   - Ⓒ Great Britain and Canada have very similar systems of government.
   - Ⓓ Canada's parliament has adopted Great Britain's constitution.

8. What is the role of political parties in Canada?
   - Ⓐ Until they become powerful, they are not legally recognized.
   - Ⓑ Although they serve unofficial functions, they are not very important.
   - Ⓒ If they win a majority of seats, their leader becomes prime minister.
   - Ⓓ Because they are not elected, they offer the government opposing views.

9. The governor-general is described as all of the following EXCEPT
   - Ⓐ the official head of parliament
   - Ⓑ the head of government
   - Ⓒ the queen's representative in Canada
   - Ⓓ the official who appoints the Senate

10. It can be inferred from the passage that the voters in Canada
    - Ⓐ choose the prime minister and the cabinet
    - Ⓑ do not usually vote in general elections
    - Ⓒ allow their representatives to vote on their behalf
    - Ⓓ determine when a change of government should occur

Refer to page 375 for the Explanatory Answers.

EXERCISE 63: Definition/Illustration—Natural Sciences

In some questions in the Reading Comprehension Section on the Institutional TOEFL, you will be asked to recall and relate information and content from definition or illustration passages about various fields of study. Choose the best answer.

Hydrogen

Hydrogen is the most common element in the universe and was perhaps the first to form. It is among the ten most common elements on Earth as well and one of the most useful for industrial
Line purposes. Under normal conditions of temperature, hydrogen is a gas.
5 Designated as H, hydrogen is the first element in the periodic table because it contains only one proton. Hydrogen can combine with a large number of other elements, forming more compounds than any of the others. Pure hydrogen seldom occurs naturally, but it exists in most organic compounds, that is, compounds that contain carbon,
10 which account for a very large number of compounds. Moreover, hydrogen is found in inorganic compounds. For example, when hydrogen burns in the presence of oxygen, it forms water.

The lightest and simplest of the elements, hydrogen has several properties that make it valuable for many industries. It releases more
15 heat per unit of weight than any other fuel. In rocket engines, tons of hydrogen and oxygen are burned, and hydrogen is used with oxygen for welding torches that produce temperatures as high as 4,000 degrees F and can be used in cutting steel. Fuel cells to generate electricity operate on hydrogen and oxygen.
20 Hydrogen also serves to prevent metals from tarnishing during heat treatments by removing the oxygen from them. Although it would be difficult to remove the oxygen by itself, hydrogen readily combines with oxygen to form water, which can be heated to steam and easily removed. Furthermore, hydrogen is one of the coolest
25 refrigerants. It does not become a liquid until it reaches temperatures of −425 degrees F. Pure hydrogen gas is used in large electric generators to cool the coils.

Future uses of hydrogen include fuel for cars, boats, planes, and other forms of transportation that currently require petroleum
30 products. These fuels would be lighter, a distinct advantage in the aerospace industry, and they would also be cleaner, thereby reducing pollution in the atmosphere.

Hydrogen is also useful in the food industry for a process known as hydrogenation. Products such as margarine and cooking oils are
35 changed from liquids to semisolids by combining hydrogen with their molecules. Soap manufacturers also use hydrogen for this purpose.

In addition, in the chemical industry, hydrogen is used to produce ammonia, gasoline, methyl alcohol, and many other important products.

1. What is the author's main purpose in the passage?
    Ⓐ To explain the industrial uses of hydrogen
    Ⓑ To describe the origin of hydrogen in the universe
    Ⓒ To discuss the process of hydrogenation
    Ⓓ To give examples of how hydrogen and oxygen combine

2. How can hydrogen be used to cut steel?
    Ⓐ By cooling the steel to a very low temperature
    Ⓑ By cooling the hydrogen with oxygen to a very low temperature
    Ⓒ By heating the steel to a very high temperature
    Ⓓ By heating the hydrogen with oxygen to a very high temperature

3. The word "readily" in line 22 could best be replaced by
    Ⓐ completely
    Ⓑ slowly
    Ⓒ usually
    Ⓓ easily

4. The word "combining" in line 35 is closest in meaning to
    Ⓐ trying
    Ⓑ changing
    Ⓒ finding
    Ⓓ adding

5. The word "them" in line 21 refers to
    Ⓐ fuel cells
    Ⓑ metals
    Ⓒ treatments
    Ⓓ products

6. Where in the passage does the author explain why hydrogen is used as a refrigerant?
    Ⓐ Lines 8–10
    Ⓑ Lines 15–18
    Ⓒ Lines 20–21
    Ⓓ Lines 24–26

7. What does the author mean by the statement in lines 21–24: "Although it would be difficult to remove the oxygen by itself, hydrogen readily combines with oxygen to form water, which can be heated to steam and easily removed"?
    Ⓐ It is easy to form steam by heating water.
    Ⓑ Water can be made by combining hydrogen and oxygen.
    Ⓒ Hydrogen cannot be separated from oxygen because it is too difficult.
    Ⓓ Oxygen is removed by combining it with hydrogen and heating it.

8. How does hydrogen generally occur?
    Ⓐ It is freely available in nature.
    Ⓑ It is contained in many compounds.
    Ⓒ It is often found in pure form.
    Ⓓ It is released during hydrogenation.

9. The author mentions all of the following as uses for hydrogen EXCEPT
    Ⓐ to remove tarnish from metals
    Ⓑ to produce fuels such as gasoline and methyl alcohol
    Ⓒ to operate fuel cells that generate electricity
    Ⓓ to change solid foods to liquids

10. It can be inferred from the passage that hydrogen
    Ⓐ is too dangerous to be used for industrial purposes
    Ⓑ has many purposes in a variety of industries
    Ⓒ has limited industrial uses because of its dangerous properties
    Ⓓ is used in many industries for basically the same purpose

Refer to pages 375–376 for the Explanatory Answers.

EXERCISE 64: Definition/Illustration—Social Sciences

In some questions in the Reading Section on the Internet-Based TOEFL, you will be asked to recall and relate information and content from definition or illustration passages found in college textbooks. Choose the best answer for multiple-choice questions. For computer-assisted questions, follow the directions on the screen.

Internet Sales and Retail Stores

Paragraph 1   The impact of the internet on retail sales is more complex than may have been reported initially. At first, it was suggested that physical brick-and-mortar stores would disappear entirely because online options would not have the overhead of a physical location and would be able to offer lower prices as a result. For some large retail chain stores that has been true, and empty buildings testify to the closing of a large percentage of stores, especially in smaller communities. Many retailers, however, began merging online and in-store experiences for their customers with great success.

2   Shoppers can now choose from several options for purchase and delivery, for example, shopping online with either home delivery for a fee or store pickup with no fee, or shopping in a store and either taking home the purchase or having it delivered. Some customers like to check online to see whether a store has a certain item in stock before making the trip to purchase, or to compare prices at several stores before making the trip to the one with the best price.

3   One disadvantage for retail stores is that customers often use them to preview products and then shop online for better prices after they have had the opportunity to see them and even try them out in the store. The internet accommodates shopping when retail stores are traditionally closed, making the concept of store hours obsolete and offering another reason to choose online shopping instead of going to a store. Furthermore, return policies affect the willingness of customers to purchase in stores, since online returns tend to be easier.

4   A large number of small retailers are able to develop products and brands online without the large startup costs of a physical store. Cottage industries are beginning to pop up all over the internet, offering items that are handmade or unusual and that cannot be found in retail chain stores. Small online businesses offer many options for customers looking for something unique. Moreover, the small businessperson doesn't have to rely on local customers, since because the internet offers a global market for their merchandise, and social media provides a cheap and pervasive marketing platform.

5   Online reviews are also influencing the purchases that customers are making when they have a choice among products that are almost alike, whether they buy them online or in a retail setting. By learning whether others have been satisfied with a purchase or what their experience has been with the product, customers may decide to buy or continue looking for a similar item with better reviews.

6   In order to survive in this new and competitive marketplace, many retail stores realized that they could not continue to be warehouses for products that might or might not sell. With a limited amount of space for inventory, retailers had to plan around limited space and figure out what to do when items on the shelf weren't selling. Now retailers that offer both brick-and-mortar as well as online shopping options can ship unwanted items from their retail stores to online warehouses, freeing up space for items that are more popular. Like online stores, brick-and-mortar retailers are also offering home delivery.

7   Many retail stores are trying to create other similarities for customers in their online shopping experiences and the shopping experiences that they have in stores. For example, software allows virtual experiences such as viewing items in different colors or trying on clothes to simulate the experience of going into a dressing room in a store. If customers are shopping for furniture, they may now be able to move the furniture into a space that simulates a room in their homes so they can experience the look before they buy. Using the customer's browsing history, online advertising can predict buying preferences and send special ads and coupons for items that customers are likely to want, and virtual shopping assistants can offer advice through chat or even lifelike interactions.

8   To push back, shopping centers are incorporating options that make going to retail locations more fun. For example, some new malls have safe play areas for children or sports and fitness centers. [A] Convenience is also a way to attract customers. [B] Superstores include banking, dry cleaning, post office, pharmacy, and grocery shopping under one roof. [C] Medical and dental facilities have also enhanced the convenience of shopping malls. [D] Restaurants and entertainment bring in shoppers who may decide to pick something up at a store before or after dinner or a movie.

1. According to paragraph 1, why did some retail stores have to close?
   Ⓐ The towns did not have enough shoppers.
   Ⓑ The prices that they charged were too low.
   Ⓒ They could not compete with the online stores.
   Ⓓ There were not enough buildings available.

2. The word merging in the passage is closest in meaning to
   Ⓐ combining
   Ⓑ identifying
   Ⓒ changing
   Ⓓ improving

3. According to paragraph 3, why do some shoppers go to stores before they purchase online?
   Ⓐ They want to support their local businesses.
   Ⓑ They like to see the item before deciding to buy it.
   Ⓒ They need to get advice from a clerk in the store.
   Ⓓ They shop in several places for a good price.

4. The word obsolete in the passage is closest in meaning to
   Ⓐ temporary
   Ⓑ unusual
   Ⓒ discontinued
   Ⓓ confusing

5. According to paragraph 4, how have small businesses taken advantage of online retail?
   - Ⓐ They have been able to sell real estate to a wider market.
   - Ⓑ They have not had to invest as much initially to sell online.
   - Ⓒ They have been able to use social media to find investors.
   - Ⓓ They have identified and contacted local shoppers.

6. Which of the sentences below best expresses the information in the highlighted statement in the passage? The other choices change the meaning or leave out important information.
   - Ⓐ Products that are the same receive reviews online from customers who have bought them.
   - Ⓑ Shoppers in retail and online stores use reviews to select from among different products.
   - Ⓒ Customers rely on reviews to choose from similar products they will buy in a retail or online store.
   - Ⓓ Reviews online are not helpful unless products are almost the same as those in retail stores.

7. According to paragraph 6, what can be inferred about home delivery options?
   - Ⓐ Online stores offer this service because they have large warehouses.
   - Ⓑ Local retail stores had to offer home delivery to compete with online stores.
   - Ⓒ Stores with limited shelf space decided to offer home delivery to local shoppers.
   - Ⓓ Distribution of unwanted items caused home delivery to become popular.

8. According to paragraph 7, all of the following are ways that online stores are trying to make shopping more like their local retail stores EXCEPT
   - Ⓐ Coupons for specific customers
   - Ⓑ Personal shoppers on chat lines
   - Ⓒ Virtual dressing rooms
   - Ⓓ Spaces with sale items

9. Four squares (□) indicate where the following sentence can be added to the passage.

   Golfers who are not interested in shopping are attracted to putting greens in malls and often drop into a store after they finish practicing.

   Where would the sentence best fit into the passage?
   A
   B
   C
   D

10. Complete the following table below by matching each of the answer choices with the advantages mentioned for each shopping option.
    - Ⓐ Easy to return purchases
    - Ⓑ More convenient hours
    - Ⓒ Immediate pickup
    - Ⓓ Cottage industries
    - Ⓔ Convenient to restaurants

Advantages of Shopping

Local retail stores	Online stores

Refer to pages 376–377 for the Explanatory Answers.

EXERCISE 65: Definition/Illustration—Arts/Architecture

In some questions in the Reading Section on the Internet-Based TOEFL, you will be asked to recall and relate information and content from definition or illustration passages found in college textbooks. Choose the best answer for multiple-choice questions. For computer-assisted questions, follow the directions on the screen.

The Octave

Paragraph 1   The word *octave* is derived from the Latin root *oct* meaning "eight." Most cultures in the world use the octave in their musical compositions; however, the particular division of the octave varies from one culture to another. The octave is the interval between one musical tone and another with double its frequency. So we see that the frequencies are two, not eight times. That means that whether the scale has five, six, seven, eight, thirteen, or even twenty-two or twenty-four notes, the span from the lowest to the highest note, with a frequency ratio of 2:1 is still referred to as an octave. Such subdivisions of the octave are called *scales*.

2   Notes that are separated by an octave or several octaves in Western music have the same letter name. [A] G notes that are an octave apart are both called G and have a similar sound. [B] The C an octave above or to the right of middle C on the keyboard has double the frequency of middle C and is pitched higher, whereas the C an octave below middle C has half the frequency of middle C and is pitched lower. [C] On stringed instruments, if a C string is strummed, it will sound an octave higher if it is divided in half. [D] Furthermore, the frequencies in Hz will be doubled. For example, the frequencies 440 Hz and 880 Hz both correspond to the musical note A, one octave apart.

3   In Western music, the octave is divided into eight tones, represented by seven letters; however, on the piano, you will find thirteen keys in an octave. The reason for this is the traditional half step that divides Western music. These half steps occur between two adjacent keys, either from a white key to a black key, or where there is no black key between them, from a white key to a white key. There are twelve half steps in an octave in this system.

4   In contrast, Persian music recognizes twenty-four quarter steps in the traditional octave. Some classical Persian musicians reject the notion of an octave altogether, insisting that it is an artificial construct, imposed on Persian music to make it more understandable to the Western musical world. Music in the Indian tradition divides the octave into twenty-two tones, but Arabic music divides the octave into twenty-four quarter steps, and Turkish musical tradition recognizes intervals of fifty-three in an octave.

5   In Chinese traditional music, the octave is subdivided into a five-tone scale known as the *pentatonic scale*. The pentatonic scale, which has often been identified as the earliest stage of musical development, is thought to have been developed independently by

many ancient cultures. Ancient musical instruments such as the bone flute had five finger holes and produced pentatonic tones. One of the oldest examples carved from a vulture bone is more than 40,000 years old.

6   The five-tone scale is still widely used in Asian and many African cultures and is still found in different forms in much of the world's music. Native American in North and South America prefer a scale of five tones in their octave. The pentatonic scale is prevalent in modern jazz and rock music as well as folk music that originated in Europe and the British Isles and transplanted to Appalachia. It was even adopted by some western classical composers, including Debussy, Chopin, and Dvorak.

7   According to many music theorists, what makes the pentatonic scale pleasing to so many different cultures is the absence of half steps. In other words, the tones are all whole steps apart, with no possibility of discord. They can be played in any major or minor key. To hear one example on a piano keyboard, play the black keys only.

8   Generally, Western musicians do not regard the scales as meaningful, other than by the occasional observation that the major scales, which are limited to white piano keys, sound happy and that the minor scales, limited to black keys, sound sad. In some cultures, there is a philosophical meaning for individual notes in the scale, and the selection of each note provides not only sound but also deep symbolism.

1. The word particular in the passage is closest in meaning to
   Ⓐ previous
   Ⓑ specific
   Ⓒ changed
   Ⓓ neutral

2. Four squares (□) indicate where the following sentence can be added to the passage.

   Middle C is the note in the middle of a piano keyboard.

   Where would the sentence best fit into the passage?
   Ⓐ
   Ⓑ
   Ⓒ
   Ⓓ

3. How many pitches are in an octave in Western music?
   Ⓐ Seven
   Ⓑ Eight
   Ⓒ Twelve
   Ⓓ Thirteen

4. The word adjacent in the passage is closest in meaning to
   Ⓐ beside each other
   Ⓑ like each other
   Ⓒ without each other
   Ⓓ despite each other

5. Which of the sentences below best expresses the information in the highlighted statement in the passage? The other choices change the meaning or leave out important information.
   - Ⓐ The idea of an octave is not accepted by some Persian musicians because they believe that it is used to interpret their music to Western musicologists.
   - Ⓑ Western musicians insist on using the octave to interpret Persian music because it is so different from music from the Western world.
   - Ⓒ The octave in Persian music is very different from the octave in Western music, which makes it difficult to understand.
   - Ⓓ Understanding Persian music is very difficult because the concept of the octave has not been accepted by some of their musicians.

6. Why is the *bone flute* mentioned in paragraph 5?
   - Ⓐ To provide evidence that the pentatonic scale is an early form of music
   - Ⓑ To introduce the topic of Chinese traditional musical instruments
   - Ⓒ To compare Asian and African musical traditions with those in the Americas
   - Ⓓ To demonstrate the relationship between archaeology and music

7. According to the passage, what is NOT true of the pentatonic scale?
   - Ⓐ It is found in many cultures.
   - Ⓑ There is no discord in the scale.
   - Ⓒ Some classical composers used it.
   - Ⓓ Each note is highly symbolic.

8. According to the passage, what is common to the musical octave in all cultures?
   - Ⓐ The number of tones is an even number in every octave.
   - Ⓑ The highest note is twice the frequency of the lowest note.
   - Ⓒ The scales in the octave are the same for all music.
   - Ⓓ The typical octave has eight notes worldwide.

9. The author mentions all of the following characteristics of the European octave EXCEPT
   - Ⓐ seven letters
   - Ⓑ twelve half steps
   - Ⓒ thirteen keys
   - Ⓓ twenty-four quarter steps

10. Complete a summary of the passage by selecting THREE answer choices that express the most important ideas. The other three sentences do not belong in the summary because they express ideas that are not in the passage or they do not refer to the major ideas. *This question is worth 2 points.*

The audible frequency spectrum offers a large selection of pitches.
   - Ⓐ The pentatonic scale is an early and popular musical form of the octave.
   - Ⓑ In European music, there are eight pitches and thirteen keys to represent the octave.
   - Ⓒ The first seven letters in the alphabet are used to label pitches in Western music.
   - Ⓓ Almost every culture relies on the concept of the octave, although it may be called by a different name.
   - Ⓔ The octave can be divided into more or fewer pitches depending on the distance between them.
   - Ⓕ The progression of a melody is more important in non-Western music than harmony.

Refer to pages 377–378 for the Explanatory Answers.

EXERCISE 66: Classification—Humanities/Business

In some questions in the Reading Comprehension Section on the Institutional TOEFL, you will be asked to recall and relate information and content from classification passages about various fields of study. Choose the best answer.

Competition

Rivalry among businesses and service industries is called competition. This feature of a market economy encourages businesses to improve their goods and services, keep their prices
Line affordable, and offer new products to attract more buyers.
5   There are four basic types of competition in business that form a continuum from *pure competition* through *monopolistic competition* and *oligopoly* to *monopoly*. (See diagram chart.) At one end of the continuum, pure competition results when every company has a similar product. Companies that deal in commodities such
10 as wheat or corn are often involved in pure competition. In *pure competition*, it is often the ease and efficiency of distribution that influences purchase.

    In contrast, in *monopolistic competition*, several companies may compete for the sale of items that may be substituted. The classic
15 example of monopolistic competition is coffee and tea. If the price of one is perceived as too high, consumers may begin to purchase the other. Coupons and other discounts are often used as part of a marketing strategy to influence sales.

    Oligopoly occurs when a few companies dominate the sales of
20 a product or service. For example, only five airline carriers control more than 70 percent of all ticket sales in the United States. In oligopoly, serious competition is not considered desirable because it would result in reduced revenue for every company in the group. Although price wars do occur, in which all companies offer
25 substantial savings to customers, a somewhat similar tendency to raise prices simultaneously is also usual.

    Finally, *monopoly* occurs when only one firm sells the product. Some monopolies have been tolerated for producers of goods and services that have been considered basic or essential, including
30 electricity and water. In these cases, it is government control, rather than competition, that protects and influences sales. The following chart represents the competition continuum.

Most————————————Competition————————————Least
Pure competition————Monopolistic competition—Oligopoly—Monopoly

1. Which of the following would be a better title for the passage?
   Ⓐ Monopolies
   Ⓑ The Commodity Market
   Ⓒ The Competition Continuum
   Ⓓ The Best Type of Competition

2. An example of a product in monopolistic competition is
   Ⓐ corn
   Ⓑ electricity
   Ⓒ airline tickets
   Ⓓ coffee

3. The word "tolerated" in line 28 could best be replaced by
   Ⓐ permitted
   Ⓑ reserved
   Ⓒ criticized
   Ⓓ devised

4. The word "dominate" in line 19 is closest in meaning to
   Ⓐ evaluate
   Ⓑ control
   Ⓒ modify
   Ⓓ oppose

5. The word "it" in line 22 refers to
   Ⓐ competition
   Ⓑ group
   Ⓒ company
   Ⓓ revenue

6. Where in the passage does the author explain pure competition?
   Ⓐ Lines 7–12
   Ⓑ Lines 13–15
   Ⓒ Lines 19–21
   Ⓓ Lines 27–30

7. What does the author mean by the statement in lines 24–26: "Although price wars do occur, in which all companies offer substantial savings to customers, a somewhat similar tendency to raise prices simultaneously is also usual"?
   Ⓐ It is not unusual for all companies to increase prices at the same time.
   Ⓑ It is common for companies to compete for customers by lowering prices.
   Ⓒ Customers may lose money when companies have price wars.
   Ⓓ Prices are lower during price wars, but they are usually higher afterward.

8. Which type of competition is subject to the greatest government control?
   Ⓐ Monopolies
   Ⓑ Oligopolies
   Ⓒ Monopolistic competition
   Ⓓ Pure competition

9. The author mentions all of the following as characteristic of monopoly EXCEPT
   Ⓐ the use of coupons or other discounts
   Ⓑ government control
   Ⓒ basic or essential services
   Ⓓ only one firm

10. It can be inferred that this passage was first printed in
    Ⓐ a business textbook
    Ⓑ a government document
    Ⓒ an airline brochure
    Ⓓ a newspaper

Refer to page 378 for the Explanatory Answers.

EXERCISE 67: Classification—Social Sciences

In some questions in the Reading Comprehension Section on the Institutional TOEFL, you will be asked to recall and relate information and content from classification passages about various fields of study. Choose the best answer.

Sleep Cycles

Whether one is awake or asleep, the brain emits electrical waves. These waves occur in predictable sleep cycles that can be measured with an electroencephalograph, known more commonly as an EEG.
Line During wakefulness, the waves are recorded at about ten small waves
5 per second, but with the onset of sleep, the waves become larger and slower. The largest, slowest waves occur during the first three hours of sleep when mental activity slows down but does not stop. In fact, if awakened from slow-wave sleep, a person can often remember vague thoughts that occurred during that period of sleep, but the
10 sleeper does not generally dream. Referred to as NREM or non-REM sleep, it is characterized by large, slow waves.

During sleep, intervals of small, fast waves also occur in patterns similar to those experienced while awake. The eyes move rapidly, and it appears to the observer that the sleeper is watching some
15 event. Sleepers who are awakened during this rapid-eye-movement sleep will often recall the details of dreams they have been having. Sleep of this kind is called dreaming sleep or rapid-eye-movement sleep, also known as REM sleep. REM sleep is emotionally charged. The heart beats irregularly, and blood pressure may be elevated.
20 In contrast, the body is so still that the dreamer may appear to be paralyzed.

In a period of eight hours, most sleepers experience from three to five instances of REM sleep. Each instance lasts from five to thirty minutes with an interval of at least ninety minutes between each one.
25 Later instances of REM sleep are usually of longer duration than are instances earlier in the eight-hour period.

Since people who suffer sleep deprivation experience fatigue, irritability, and loss of concentration, we must conclude that sleep is essential because in some way it regenerates the brain and the
30 nervous system. NREM sleep increases after physical exertion, whereas REM sleep tends to increase after a stressful day. Studies suggest that non-REM sleep may be especially helpful in restoring muscle control, whereas REM sleep may be more important in revitalizing mental activity. It appears that both kinds of sleep
35 are necessary, and the recuperation of sleep of one kind will not compensate for a lack of the other kind of sleep.

1. What is the author's main purpose in the passage?
   - Ⓐ To describe REM sleep
   - Ⓑ To explain sleep deprivation
   - Ⓒ To discuss the two types of sleep
   - Ⓓ To recommend an increase in the number of hours of sleep

2. How many times per night do most sleepers experience REM sleep?
   - Ⓐ Eight
   - Ⓑ Three to five
   - Ⓒ Five to thirty
   - Ⓓ Ninety

3. The word "vague" in line 9 could best be replaced by
   - Ⓐ familiar
   - Ⓑ indefinite
   - Ⓒ unpleasant
   - Ⓓ detailed

4. The word "essential" in line 29 is closest in meaning to
   - Ⓐ planned
   - Ⓑ natural
   - Ⓒ interesting
   - Ⓓ necessary

5. The word "it" in line 29 refers to
   - Ⓐ deprivation
   - Ⓑ the brain
   - Ⓒ sleep
   - Ⓓ concentration

6. Where in the passage does the author explain why sleep is essential?
   - Ⓐ Lines 4–6
   - Ⓑ Lines 7–10
   - Ⓒ Lines 18–21
   - Ⓓ Lines 27–30

7. What does the author mean by the statement in lines 31–34: "Studies suggest that non-REM sleep may be especially helpful in restoring muscle control, whereas REM sleep may be more important in revitalizing mental activity"?
   - Ⓐ REM sleep is more important than slow-wave sleep for all types of activities.
   - Ⓑ Mental and physical activities require both kinds of sleep.
   - Ⓒ Slow-wave sleep, also called REM sleep, restores mental activity.
   - Ⓓ Physical activity is supported by slow-wave sleep, but mental activity is supported by REM sleep.

8. Which response is NOT typical of REM sleep?
   - Ⓐ Irregular heartbeat
   - Ⓑ Dreams and visions
   - Ⓒ Movements in arms and legs
   - Ⓓ Higher blood pressure

9. The author mentions all the following as characteristics of REM sleep EXCEPT
   - Ⓐ vague thoughts
   - Ⓑ smaller brain waves
   - Ⓒ eye movements
   - Ⓓ dreams

10. It can be inferred from the passage that students who are writing term papers
    - Ⓐ require slow-wave sleep to increase mental activity
    - Ⓑ can stay up all night working and recover the sleep they need by sleeping for a few hours the next afternoon
    - Ⓒ need REM sleep to restore mental functioning
    - Ⓓ do not need as much sleep because of the heightened brain waves involved in creative activity

Refer to pages 378–379 for the Explanatory Answers.

EXERCISE 68: Classification—Arts/Architecture

In some questions in the Reading Section on the Internet-Based TOEFL, you will be asked to recall and relate information and content from classification passages found in college textbooks. Choose the best answer for multiple-choice questions. For computer-assisted questions, follow the directions on the screen.

Classical Architecture

Paragraph 1   *Orders* in classical architecture refer to the form and decoration of Greek and Roman buildings. The three major styles are Doric, Ionic, and Corinthian, which take their names from the location where they originated and are readily identifiable by the proportions of the columns and profiles as well as by the details of the decoration.

Greek Orders
DORIC

2   The Doric order is the earliest of the three styles, appearing on the Greek mainland during the late seventh century B.C.E. It is also the heaviest of the styles and the only one that is constructed with no base on the column, which means that the foot is placed directly on the platform. The simplest of the three styles, the Doric column is either smooth or grooved and the <u>capital</u> on top is often an unornamented circle or square, although the <u>frieze</u> above the columns can be quite complex. The Parthenon is an example of architecture with simple Doric columns but a beautifully carved frieze.

IONIC

3   The Ionic order is taller and thinner, usually standing on a base that separates it from the platform. [A] It became popular in Anatolia in present-day Turkey and was imported to mainland Greece by the fifth century B.C.E. [B] The columns are usually grooved and banded, but sometimes they are replaced by female figures. [C] The graceful Ionic style is beautifully realized in the Athenian Acropolis. [D]

CORINTHIAN

4   The Corinthian order is the latest of the styles and is quite similar to the Ionic; however, the capital is more decorative. It is considered the most ornate and feminine of the orders, with slender columns and elaborate capitals that are often carved with symmetrical scrolls or rows of acanthus leaves. Originally found in the city-state of Corinth around 425 B.C.E., it is complex and ornamental. West of Corinth, Greece, is the Temple of Apollo, which Epicurus thought to be the oldest surviving example of the classical Corinthian column.

Roman Orders

5   The Romans borrowed the Doric, Ionian, and Corinthian orders from the Greeks. In general, when the Romans adapted the Greek orders, they made the columns lighter but more ornate. The Corinthian style decorated with acanthus leaves was probably the most popular in ancient Rome. In addition, the Romans developed

two styles of their own—the Tuscan and the Composite. The Tuscan is, in effect, a simplified variation of the Doric order with a plain column, whereas the Composite is a more elaborate variation of the Corinthian order with some elements of the Ionic order as well. The Romans also created rules for a superimposed order, in which successive stories included multiple orders, one on top of the other. The heaviest orders were constructed on the ground floor, with the lightest on top. Consequently, the Doric order was on the ground floor, the Ionic on the middle floor, and the Corinthian at the top. The Colosseum is a well-known example of the superimposed order.

MATHEMATICS AND ORDERS

6   The relationship between the height of a column and the size of the diameter of the base was governed by strict mathematical calculations. Architects designed the height of their Doric columns to be between four and six times the diameter of the base. In contrast, the Ionic column was nine times and a Corinthian ten times the diameter. It is interesting that the term for *symmetry* in classical architecture meant "mathematical harmony." With such exacting measurements, even an architect of mediocre talent could design and execute a pleasing building.

7   The influence of classical architecture has been far-reaching. The ancient Greeks and Romans transported their architectural styles to the lands that they conquered and colonized. When Greece became a Roman province in the second century, the Romans recognized and admired the architecture, commissioning many of their important buildings to Greek architects. Nevertheless, the Romans did contribute several innovations to their designs. By perfecting the engineering to add strength to the arch and the dome, they were able to bring a dimension to their buildings that the Greeks had not anticipated. Furthermore, the Roman invention of concrete allowed them to build without relying solely on stone or wood.

Doric   Ionic   Corinthian

Glossary
capital: from the word "head" referring to the top of the column
frieze: a band of sculptured or painted decoration

1. Four squares (☐) indicate where the following sentence can be added to the passage.

   In fact, the Ionic column has been compared to a female form, whereas the Doric, with its thicker body and undecorated capital, has been identified as a male figure.

   Where would the sentence best be added to the passage?

   Ⓐ

   Ⓑ

   Ⓒ

   Ⓓ

2. The author mentioned all of the following characteristics of the Corinthian order EXCEPT
   Ⓐ It was the Greek style that the Romans preferred.
   Ⓑ It was always decorated with vertical grooves.
   Ⓒ It was a design that first appeared in Corinth.
   Ⓓ It was often used as the top story above the Doric and Ionic.

3. According to paragraph, which new orders did the Romans add to the architectural styles of the Greeks?

   Choose 2 answers.
   Ⓐ Doric
   Ⓑ Composite
   Ⓒ Tuscan
   Ⓓ Corinthian

4. The phrase the other in the passage refers to
   Ⓐ buildings
   Ⓑ orders
   Ⓒ rules
   Ⓓ stories

5. Which of the following buildings is representative of the superimposed order?
   Ⓐ The Acropolis
   Ⓑ The Parthenon
   Ⓒ The Colosseum
   Ⓓ The Temple of Apollo

6. What is the rule for the height of a Corinthian column?
   Ⓐ Six times the diameter of the base
   Ⓑ Nine times the diameter of the base
   Ⓒ Ten times the diameter of the base
   Ⓓ Twelve times the diameter of the base

7. It can be inferred from the mathematical rules that
   Ⓐ the Ionic column is the heaviest
   Ⓑ the Corinthian column is the slimmest
   Ⓒ the Doric column is the tallest
   Ⓓ the Tuscan column is the most ornate

8. The phrase far-reaching in the passage is closest in meaning to
   Ⓐ very good
   Ⓑ very large
   Ⓒ very beautiful
   Ⓓ very strong

9. According to paragraph 7, what do we know about Roman engineering?
   Ⓐ They borrowed their materials from the Greeks.
   Ⓑ They preferred to build with wood and stone.
   Ⓒ They adapted architectural styles from the colonies.
   Ⓓ They used concrete to strengthen their structures.

10. Complete the table below by classifying each of the answer choices under the order to which it refers. One of the answer choices will not be used.
   - Ⓐ Various leaves and scrolls decorate the column.
   - Ⓑ The column is often painted in bright colors.
   - Ⓒ A column without a base, it sits on the platform.
   - Ⓓ The largest, widest style of the Greek columns.
   - Ⓔ The column is nine times as high as the diameter of the base.
   - Ⓕ Female figures are sometimes substituted for the shaft.
   - Ⓖ Four symmetrical scrolls grace the column.

Doric	Ionic	Corinthian
•	•	•
•	•	•

EXERCISE 69: Classification—Natural Sciences

In some questions in the Reading Section on the Internet-Based TOEFL, you will be asked to recall and relate information and content from classification passages found in college textbooks. Choose the best answer for multiple-choice questions. For computer-assisted questions, follow the directions on the screen.

Galaxies

Paragraph 1   Traditionally, astronomers have classified galaxies into three major types according to their shape.

Spiral Galaxies

2   Our galaxy, the Milky Way, is shaped like a spiral and is classified as a spiral galaxy. All spiral galaxies have a *bulge*, a thin *disk*, and a *halo*. The bulge is the spherical structure in the center of the galaxy, containing mostly older stars, connecting with the halo and extending to a radius of more than 100,000 light years. Although no definitive boundary separates the bulge from the halo, astronomers generally include stars within 10,000 light years from the center in the bulge and those farther away to be part of the halo. Combined, the bulge and the halo form the spheroidal component, which derives its name from the round shape.

3   The disk forms the arms of the structure, cutting through the bulge and the halo and extending thousands of light years from the center. For example, the Milky Way has a disk that stretches out 50,000 light years from the center. All spiral galaxies have disks that contain interstellar gas and dust, differing in the amount and combination from galaxy to galaxy. In general, spiral galaxies with large bulges tend to have less interstellar gas and dust than those with small bulges.

4   Spiral galaxies are further classified into two groups: ordinary and barred. In the ordinary or standard spiral galaxies, the arms emerge directly from the bulge, whereas in the barred spiral galaxies, like the Milky Way, a straight bar runs through the nucleus, and the arms emerge from there.

5   Other differences are evident in spiral galaxies, among the most obvious, the spiral galaxies that have disks but no apparent arms. These are known as lenticular galaxies because when they are viewed from the edges, they look like a lens. Because these galaxies have less cool gas than standard spirals but more than standard ellipticals, and tend to form in clusters of galaxies, some astronomers have classified lenticular galaxies as a different class entirely, forming an intermediary between the spirals and the next class of galaxy, the elliptical.

6   When considering the large galaxies in the universe, most of them are spiral or lenticular, forming about 75 percent of the total. Also characteristic of spiral galaxies is their location in communities of galaxies called groups, extending over several million light years. The Milky Way and the Andromeda Galaxy, for instance, are two large spiral galaxies in our local group. Even more galaxies—hundreds or even thousands—exist in clusters stretching out over ten million or more light years and containing, for the most part, spiral and lenticular galaxies.

Elliptical Galaxies

7   Elliptical galaxies, sometimes known as spheroidal galaxies, are shaped like a sphere. They differ from spiral galaxies in large measure because they

do not have a substantial disk. In fact, it appears rather like a bulge and halo in a spiral galaxy. Some of them have a small, relatively cold, central disk, but it is suspected that they might be remnants of past collision with a spiral galaxy. Moreover, elliptical galaxies have no specific axis of rotation, and they commonly contain very little dust or cool gas, although they are not devoid of them.

8   Elliptical galaxies are often found in clusters of galaxies. [A] Elliptical galaxies comprise about 50 percent of the large galaxies in the center of clusters, but only about 15 percent of the large galaxies outside of clusters. [B] However, ellipticals are more common among small galaxies. [C] Particularly small elliptical galaxies with less than a billion stars, called dwarf elliptical galaxies, are often found near larger spiral galaxies. [D] At least ten dwarf elliptical galaxies belong to our local group.

Irregular Galaxies

9   A small percentage of the large galaxies are neither spiral nor elliptical and appear to have no regular or symmetrical structure. This irregular group of galaxies falls into a miscellaneous classification. This classification of galaxies does have a similar characteristic in that large amounts of dust block much of the light from the stars, making it almost impossible to distinguish individual stars. In addition, it appears that galaxies at a greater distance tend to be irregular as compared with the spirals and ellipticals nearer our own galaxy. Perhaps because the light of distant galaxies represents a more distant past, we may speculate that irregular galaxies were more common in an early universe.

Figure 1

Figure 2

Figure 3

Glossary
bulge: central part of a spiral galaxy in the shape of a football
disk: part of a spiral galaxy in the shape of a disk
halo: region around the disk of a spiral galaxy

1. It may be assumed that stars 15,000 light years away from the center of the Milky Way are
   Ⓐ very bright and easy to see
   Ⓑ part of the halo
   Ⓒ separated from the disk
   Ⓓ without gas and dust

2. Which of the sentences below best expresses the information in the highlighted statement in the passage? The other choices change the meaning or leave out important information.
   Ⓐ Spiral galaxies with small bulges have more gas and dust.
   Ⓑ Spiral galaxies have more gas and dust in their bulges.
   Ⓒ There is less gas and dust in a spiral galaxy with a small bulge.
   Ⓓ Gas and dust collect in the bulges of the large spiral galaxies.

3. What do we know about our Milky Way galaxy?
   Ⓐ It is a common type of galaxy.
   Ⓑ It no longer has a halo in the spiral.
   Ⓒ The interstellar gas has been depleted.
   Ⓓ The arms extend from the bulge.

4. According to paragraph 5, what is NOT true of lenticular galaxies?
   Ⓐ They are spiral galaxies without arms.
   Ⓑ They are found in groups of galaxies.
   Ⓒ They have an irregular shape.
   Ⓓ They could be a separate type of galaxy.

5. The word remnants in the passage is closest in meaning to
   Ⓐ remains
   Ⓑ origin
   Ⓒ damage
   Ⓓ evidence

6. The word devoid in the passage is closest in meaning to
   Ⓐ hidden
   Ⓑ empty
   Ⓒ dense
   Ⓓ bright

7. What distinguishes a spiral galaxy from an elliptical galaxy?
   Ⓐ Elliptical galaxies have a much larger halo.
   Ⓑ Elliptical galaxies have more dust and cool gas.
   Ⓒ Spiral galaxies are more irregularly shaped.
   Ⓓ Spiral galaxies have a more prominent disk.

8. Four squares (☐) indicate where the following sentence can be added to the passage.

   A good example of a dwarf elliptical galaxy is Leo I in our local group.

   Where would the sentence best fit into the passage?
   Ⓐ
   Ⓑ
   Ⓒ
   Ⓓ

9. According to paragraph 9, all of the following characteristics are true of irregular galaxies EXCEPT
   Ⓐ They could have been more common in the past.
   Ⓑ They tend to be located farther away from our galaxy.
   Ⓒ They are not shaped symmetrically like other galaxies.
   Ⓓ They include stars that are very bright and easy to see.

10. Complete the table below by classifying each of the answer choices as a *spiral*, *elliptical*, or *irregular* galaxy. Two of the answer choices will NOT be used.

Ⓐ Less gas or dust is found.
Ⓑ A disk component is prominent.
Ⓒ More radiation is noted.
Ⓓ The stars are older.
Ⓔ Their atmosphere is slightly blue.
Ⓕ The Milky Way is an example.
Ⓖ They are often found in large clusters.
Ⓗ A miscellaneous class of galaxies.

Spiral	Elliptical	Irregular
•	•	•
•	•	•

Refer to pages 379–380 for the Explanatory Answers.

EXERCISE 70: Comparison/Contrast—Humanities/Business

In some questions in the Reading Comprehension Section on the Institutional TOEFL, you will be asked to recall and relate information and content from comparison or contrast passages about various fields of study. Choose the best answer.

Levels of Vocabulary

Most languages have several levels of vocabulary that may be used by the same speakers. In English, at least three have been identified and described.

Line   Standard usage includes those words and expressions understood,
5   used, and accepted by a majority of the speakers of a language in any situation regardless of the level of formality. As such, these words and expressions are well defined and listed in standard dictionaries. Colloquialisms, on the other hand, are familiar words and idioms that are understood by almost all speakers of a language
10   and used in informal speech or writing, but not considered acceptable for more formal situations. Almost all idiomatic expressions are colloquial language. Slang, however, refers to words and expressions understood by a large number of speakers but not accepted as appropriate formal usage by the majority. Colloquial expressions
15   and even slang may be found in standard dictionaries but will be so identified. Both colloquial usage and slang are more common in speech than in writing.

Colloquial speech often passes into standard speech. Some slang also passes into standard speech, but other slang expressions enjoy
20   momentary popularity followed by obscurity. In some cases, the majority never accepts certain slang phrases but nevertheless retains them in their collective memories. Every generation seems to require its own set of words to describe familiar objects and events.

It has been pointed out by a number of linguists that three
25   cultural conditions are necessary for the creation of a large body of slang expressions. First, the introduction and acceptance of new objects and situations in the society; second, a diverse population with a large number of subgroups; third, association among the subgroups and the majority population.

30   Finally, it is worth noting that the terms "standard," "colloquial," and "slang" exist only as abstract labels for scholars who study language. Only a tiny number of the speakers of any language will be aware that they are using colloquial or slang expressions. Most speakers of English will, during appropriate situations, select and use
35   all three types of expressions.

1. Which of the following is the main topic of the passage?
   - Ⓐ Standard speech
   - Ⓑ Idiomatic phrases
   - Ⓒ Different types of vocabulary
   - Ⓓ Dictionary usage

2. How is slang defined by the author?
   - Ⓐ Words and phrases accepted by the majority for formal usage
   - Ⓑ Words and phrases understood by the majority but not found in standard dictionaries
   - Ⓒ Words and phrases that are understood by a restricted group of speakers
   - Ⓓ Words and phrases understood by a large number of speakers but not accepted as formal usage

3. The word "obscurity" in line 20 could best be replaced by
   - Ⓐ disappearance
   - Ⓑ influence
   - Ⓒ qualification
   - Ⓓ tolerance

4. The word "appropriate" in line 14 is closest in meaning to
   - Ⓐ old
   - Ⓑ large
   - Ⓒ correct
   - Ⓓ important

5. The word "them" in line 22 refers to
   - Ⓐ words
   - Ⓑ slang phrases
   - Ⓒ memories
   - Ⓓ the majority

6. Where in the passage does the author explain where colloquial language and slang are most commonly used?
   - Ⓐ Lines 4–6
   - Ⓑ Lines 16–17
   - Ⓒ Lines 24–26
   - Ⓓ Lines 33–35

7. What does the author mean by the statement in lines 8–11: "Colloquialisms, on the other hand, are familiar words and idioms that are understood by almost all speakers of a language and used in informal speech or writing, but not considered acceptable for more formal situations"?
   - Ⓐ Familiar words and phrases are found in both speech and writing in formal settings.
   - Ⓑ Familiar situations that are experienced by most people are called colloquialisms.
   - Ⓒ Informal language contains colloquialisms, which are not found in more formal language.
   - Ⓓ Most of the speakers of a language can use both formal and informal speech in appropriate situations.

8. Which of the following is true of standard usage?
   - Ⓐ It can be used in formal or informal settings.
   - Ⓑ It is limited to written language.
   - Ⓒ It is only understood by the upper classes.
   - Ⓓ It is constantly changing.

9. The author mentions all of the following as requirements for slang expressions to be created EXCEPT
   - Ⓐ new situations
   - Ⓑ a new generation
   - Ⓒ interaction among diverse groups
   - Ⓓ a number of linguists

10. It can be inferred from the passage that the author
    - Ⓐ does not approve of either slang or colloquial speech in any situation
    - Ⓑ approves of colloquial speech in some situations, but not slang
    - Ⓒ approves of slang and colloquial speech in appropriate situations
    - Ⓓ does not approve of colloquial usage in writing

Refer to pages 380–381 for the Explanatory Answers.

EXERCISE 71: Comparison/Contrast—Arts/Architecture

In some questions in the Reading Comprehension Section on the Institutional TOEFL, you will be asked to recall and relate information and content from comparison or contrast passages about various fields of study. Choose the best answer.

The New Photography

In order to establish photography as art, members of the Aesthetic movement modeled their work on classical paintings, even copying the subjects and poses popularized by artists of the Classical

Line Period. As the movement gained in popularity, photographers made

5 a clear distinction between the elegant, artistic photography that conformed to the aesthetic standard used for paintings and the work of more realistic photographers that was beginning to appear. Since they were cloudy because of the gum bichromate plate that allowed for manual intervention, the aesthetic prints were easily

10 distinguished from the more modern prints, which came to be called *straightforward photographs*. In contrast, the straightforward photographers produced images that were sharp and clear. Whereas the proponents of the Aesthetic movement continued to hand-color their photographs, adding details and textures to conform to the art

15 of printmakers, the philosophy that surrounded the new photography rejected manipulation of either the subject matter or the print. The subjects included nature in its undisturbed state and people in everyday situations.

A number of major exhibitions and the formation of photographic

20 clubs during the late nineteenth century provided the impetus for the Photo-Secession movement. Founded by Alfred Steiglitz in New York City in 1902, Photo-Secession had as its proposition the promotion of straightforward photography through exhibits and publications. One of the publications, *Camera Work*, has been

25 recognized among the most beautiful journals ever produced. By the 1920s, the mechanical precision that had once been criticized as a defect by members of the Aesthetic movement had become a hallmark of modern photography. Chiefly through the efforts of Steiglitz, modern photography had seceded from painting and

30 emerged as a legitimate art form. In summary, the Aesthetic movement rejected reality for beauty, but the Photo-Secessionists embraced realism as even more beautiful.

1. Which of the following would be an alternative title for the passage?
   - Ⓐ The Photo-Secession Movement
   - Ⓑ The Aesthetic Movement
   - Ⓒ Alfred Steiglitz
   - Ⓓ Photography as Art

2. How can earlier photographs be distinguished from more modern photographs?
   - Ⓐ They were not the same color.
   - Ⓑ They were not as clear.
   - Ⓒ They did not look like paintings.
   - Ⓓ They were not retouched.

3. The word "defect" in line 27 is closest in meaning to
   - Ⓐ disturbance
   - Ⓑ ideal
   - Ⓒ requirement
   - Ⓓ imperfection

4. The word "chiefly" in line 28 is closest in meaning to
   - Ⓐ only
   - Ⓑ mostly
   - Ⓒ rarely
   - Ⓓ likely

5. The word "they" in line 8 refers to
   - Ⓐ paintings
   - Ⓑ aesthetic prints
   - Ⓒ modern prints
   - Ⓓ straightforward photographs

6. Where in the passage does the author identify the subjects that modern photographers used?
   - Ⓐ Lines 4–7
   - Ⓑ Lines 16–18
   - Ⓒ Lines 25–28
   - Ⓓ Lines 30–32

7. What does the author mean by the statement in lines 25–28: "By the 1920s, the mechanical precision that had once been criticized as a defect by members of the Aesthetic movement had become a hallmark of modern photography"?
   - Ⓐ The defect of the Aesthetic movement was eliminated by the mechanical precision of later photographers.
   - Ⓑ Later photographers used mechanical precision in spite of criticism by earlier photographers in the Aesthetic movement.
   - Ⓒ The modern photographers used hallmarks, unlike the photographers of the earlier Aesthetic movement.
   - Ⓓ Mechanical precision was a defect that later photographers eliminated from their work.

8. What is NOT true of *Camera Work*?
   - Ⓐ It is considered among the most attractive magazines.
   - Ⓑ It encouraged members of the Aesthetic movement.
   - Ⓒ It was promoted by Alfred Steiglitz.
   - Ⓓ It was a vehicle for realistic beauty.

9. The Photo-Secession movement is described as including all of the following EXCEPT
   - Ⓐ straightforward photographs
   - Ⓑ mechanical precision
   - Ⓒ sharp, clear images
   - Ⓓ manipulation of prints

10. It can be inferred from the passage that the author
    - Ⓐ knew Alfred Steiglitz personally
    - Ⓑ was not interested in Alfred Steiglitz
    - Ⓒ disagreed with Alfred Steiglitz
    - Ⓓ admired Alfred Steiglitz

Refer to page 381 for the Explanatory Answers.

EXERCISE 72: Comparison/Contrast—Social Sciences

In some questions in the Reading Section on the Internet-Based TOEFL, you will be asked to recall and relate information and content from comparison or contrast passages found in college textbooks. Choose the best answer for multiple-choice questions. For computer-assisted questions, follow the directions on the screen.

History of Psychology

Paragraph 1   Although psychology can be traced back to the early Greeks, it did not emerge as a distinct discipline until the late 1800s when Wilhelm Wundt began to use scientific research methods to study human thought and behavior. One of his students, Edward Titchener, founded the first major psychological approach, which he identified as *structuralism*, a school that became very popular throughout Europe. According to the structuralists, human consciousness could be dissected into parts, using introspection, or the examination of one's own thoughts and feelings. [A] To state that another way, subjects were encouraged to engage in self-examination, analyzing their personalities and motivations as well as their actions. Of course, as a research tool, the process was very controlled, or structured. [B] Observers were highly trained, and observations were repeated numerous times. [C] In spite of this rigorous methodology, even experienced observers did not work consistently, and complex experiences were difficult to analyze. [D]

2   Across the ocean, in the United States, William James was pioneering a different school of psychology called *functionalism*. Convinced that it was not possible to understand the human mind by breaking it down into small parts, James perceived consciousness to be a process that was continually changing, like a stream. Although introspection was still a popular methodology, James also relied heavily on direct observation. Influenced by Darwin, he argued that it was necessary to understand the purpose of mental operations as well as the way that people adapt their mental operations in order to solve problems. To functionalists, all types of behavior were appropriate for study.

3   Although structuralism and functionalism used different approaches, they both focused on understanding immediate experiences, and to that end, introspection played a fundamental role. It was not until Sigmund Freud proposed his theory of personality at the turn of the twentieth century that unconscious thoughts and feelings were taken into consideration in the study of the mind. Although subjects use defense mechanisms to protect themselves from painful information in their unconscious minds, strategies such as dream analysis and free association helped them to recognize thoughts and recall memories that were previously in their unconscious minds. *Psychoanalysis* went beyond introspection to bring the unconscious into conscious awareness, a process that claimed to provide relief from psychological distress.

4   At about the same time that Freud was studying the unconscious mind in Europe, John Watson began to question the functionalism that was still popular in the United States. According to his theory, the internal conscious or unconscious experiences were unable to

be properly observed, and therefore not subject to scientific study. In contrast, observable behavior was measurable. Highly controlled laboratory experiments with animals and humans demonstrated how behavior could be changed by using reinforcement such as a reward to encourage a certain action, and the study of behavior modification dominated the field of psychology for decades. *Behaviorism*, as it came to be known, is still used today.

5   By the 1950s, in large measure because of a reaction against behaviorism and its dependence on animal research, a new *humanistic psychology* became popular. This approach insisted that the whole person should be studied. Underpinning the study was the assumption that people are basically good and are motivated to improve themselves. Both Carl Rogers and Abraham Maslow argued that objective reality, which was a primary focus of study in early schools of psychology, was less important than each person's subjective perception and understanding of the world. Humanistic psychologists used qualitative research as their primary tool. They talked with their human subjects to determine their needs and support their growth.

6   In the 1950s, in part because of a widespread interest in computers, a new school of psychology emerged. Known as *cognitive psychology*, it focused on the study of mental processes such as memory, problem solving, and language. Cognitive psychologists asserted that information processing in humans was similar to that in computers and was based on storing and retrieving information from memory as well as transforming information as output. One of the most widely known cognitive psychologists of his time was Jean Piaget, who made a systematic study of the stages of cognitive development.

7   Although one school of thought may have dominated the discipline at a particular time in the history of psychology, psychologists today do not generally identify themselves according to any one school of psychology, and most would agree that each has made a significant contribution to the field.

1. Four squares (□) indicate where the following sentence can be added to the passage.

   In many cases, questions elicited responses that were limited to "yes" or "no."

   Where would the sentence best fit into the passage?
   Ⓐ
   Ⓑ
   Ⓒ
   Ⓓ

2. The word consistently in the passage is closest in meaning to
   Ⓐ carefully
   Ⓑ skillfully
   Ⓒ uniformly
   Ⓓ frequently

3. In paragraph 1, what does the author say about self-observation?
   Ⓐ It should be the primary method for psychology.
   Ⓑ It may not provide accurate data.
   Ⓒ It is useful for the study of abnormal psychology.
   Ⓓ It is best to document the experience.

4. The word fundamental in the passage is closest in meaning to
   Ⓐ new
   Ⓑ limited
   Ⓒ surprising
   Ⓓ necessary

5. According to paragraph 4, how did behaviorists modify behaviors?
   Ⓐ By providing a reward for positive responses
   Ⓑ By observing the behavior and encouraging improvement
   Ⓒ By breaking down behavior into smaller parts
   Ⓓ By controlling the behavior in experiments

6. Which of the psychologists studied the purpose of experience?
   Ⓐ Evolutionists
   Ⓑ Behaviorists
   Ⓒ Structuralists
   Ⓓ Functionalists

7. According to paragraph 6, which of the following statements does NOT refer to cognitive psychologists?
   Ⓐ They were interested in computer processing.
   Ⓑ They proposed stages of cognitive development.
   Ⓒ They studied memory and other mental processes.
   Ⓓ They performed experiments with animals.

8. The word each in the passage refers to
   Ⓐ history
   Ⓑ school
   Ⓒ contribution
   Ⓓ fields

9. The author mentions all of the following methods of analysis EXCEPT
   Ⓐ psychoanalysis
   Ⓑ behavior modification
   Ⓒ group therapy
   Ⓓ introspection

10. Complete a summary of the passage by selecting THREE answer choices that express the most important ideas. The other three sentences do not belong in the summary because they express ideas that are not in the passage or they do not refer to the major ideas. *This question is worth 2 points.*

Several theories were influential in the history of psychology.

Ⓐ Unlike those who practiced psychoanalysis, behaviorists advocated the study of observable behaviors.

Ⓑ Structuralism in Europe and functionalism in the U.S. were among the first schools of psychology.

Ⓒ Freud was developing psychoanalysis at about the same time that Watson was experimenting with behaviorism.

Ⓓ Darwin's theory of evolution supported the proponents of functional psychology who observed adaptation.

Ⓔ Animal research was useful to several schools of psychology in the historical development of the discipline.

Ⓕ Humanistic psychology, a reaction against behaviorism, and cognitive psychology emerged in the 1950s.

Refer to pages 381–382 for the Explanatory Answers.

EXERCISE 73: Comparison/Contrast—Natural Sciences

In some questions in the Reading Section on the Internet-Based TOEFL, you will be asked to recall and relate information and content from comparison or contrast passages found in college textbooks. Choose the best answer for multiple-choice questions. For computer-assisted questions, follow the directions on the screen.

Science, Engineering, and Technology

Paragraph 1   Students who excel in mathematics and science have a number of career options, including but not limited to basic scientific research, engineering, and engineering technology. Unfortunately, there is a great deal of confusion when they are choosing a career path, because the three fields are closely related and tend to overlap. In order to make good choices, students need to understand the differences in the roles among these related but distinct careers.

2   Whereas scientists, engineers, and engineering technologists all have to be keen observers, a scientist creates technological questions and searches for the answers to understand why a phenomenon occurs in nature. [A] An engineer also searches for the answers to scientific questions but always with a view to using them for a practical application. [B] Scientists work on the acquisition of new knowledge, and engineers work on the design and development of a new product or service. [C] In contrast, engineering technologists would need to understand how to use tools and materials to make the product, using both the research that the scientist has provided and the design that the engineer has provided. [D] The engineering technologist has the hands-on responsibility.

3   These three careers are quite different, but scientists, engineers, and engineering technologists complement each other and often collaborate on a team. The work of scientists directs the engineers and engineering technologists by giving them new ideas that inspire their designs and products. On the other hand, the engineers report practical observations to the scientists and suggest areas of further research, and the engineering technologists discover problems in the designs that must be resolved by the engineers. Moreover, the engineering technologists are often responsible for making the tools that engineers need to complete their projects and that scientists use to perform their research.

4   As an example of how scientists, engineers, and engineering technologists might collaborate on a project, consider the problem of building a structure that will withstand a specific type of earthquake in a region where earthquakes occur on a regular basis. Scientists would engage in laboratory and field research to understand earthquakes. They would ask questions and devise experiments to learn more about the types of earthquakes in the area. They might also try to determine how these earthquakes could be predicted and what happens to the soil during one of the earthquakes. Engineers would use the basic research results to design safer buildings that could withstand the specific type of earthquakes in the area. They might also include plans for an early warning system in the buildings that would alert the occupants that an earthquake was imminent. Engineering technologists would use computer technology to draw and test the designs as well as machines and tools to actually build the structures and the warning system. They might also assist the engineers in the oversight of the construction.

5   As for the courses and training that students should pursue for these three career choices, those interested in employment as a scientist should be directed to take higher mathematics and advanced science courses; those interested in engineering would need math and science, but would also require specialized courses, depending on which types of engineering programs they were interested in—mechanical, electrical, civil, or chemical, to name only a few. The skills and training required for students choosing a career in engineering technology would include experience operating and troubleshooting tools and equipment or managing computer systems.

6   After graduation, scientists are usually employed either in basic scientific research facilities, such as the National Institutes for Health, or in colleges and universities where they divide their time between professorial duties and research that is often funded by grants.

7   There are some opportunities for employment that would attract both engineers and engineering technologists, such as those in manufacturing where either an engineer or an engineering technologist might supervise assembly-line workers in a factory; however, for the most part, their career paths would lead to different jobs. Engineers often work in partnership with other engineers in firms that offer design services to private, public, and governmental agencies. Engineering technologists are highly sought after for operations management, computer design, or manufacturing.

1. The word roles in the passage is closest in meaning to
   Ⓐ training
   Ⓑ ideas
   Ⓒ problems
   Ⓓ positions

2. The word phenomenon in the passage is closest in meaning to
   Ⓐ hazard
   Ⓑ system
   Ⓒ occurrence
   Ⓓ triumph

3. Four squares (☐) indicate where the following sentence can be added to the passage.

   To say that another way, basic science is concerned with hypotheses and theories, but engineering involves the practical application of science to solve everyday problems.

   Where would the sentence best fit into the passage?
   Ⓐ
   Ⓑ
   Ⓒ
   Ⓓ

4. According to the passage, engineering technologists
   - (A) identify design issues
   - (B) develop new products
   - (C) engage in basic research
   - (D) design specialized tools

5. Which of the sentences below best expresses the information in the highlighted statement in the passage? The other choices change the meaning or leave out important information.
   - (A) It is important for engineering technologists to make tools for engineering projects.
   - (B) Engineers, scientists, and engineering technologists need tools for their work.
   - (C) Responsibilities for projects and research are assumed by engineering technologists.
   - (D) Tools for engineering projects and scientific research are made by engineering technologists.

6. Why does the author talk about *earthquakes* in paragraph 4?
   - (A) To demonstrate how scientists, engineers, and engineering technologists work on projects
   - (B) To provide an example of a successful plan for a complex construction project
   - (C) To offer a suggestion for research that would solve a practical problem
   - (D) To clarify the education that scientists, engineers, and engineering technologists require

7. According to paragraphs 5 and 6, what would probably be true of engineering students?
   - (A) The majority of their courses would include on-site training.
   - (B) They would spend most of their time learning how to use equipment.
   - (C) They could select courses in a number of specialized engineering programs.
   - (D) They would receive funding from grants to pursue their research projects.

8. According to paragraph 7, which of the following jobs would NOT be appropriate for an engineering technologist?
   - (A) Supervisor in a factory
   - (B) Computer designer
   - (C) Assembly-line worker
   - (D) Operations manager

9. It can be inferred that this passage would be published in
   - (A) a mathematics textbook at the college level
   - (B) an orientation book for engineering students
   - (C) a workbook in an advanced science course
   - (D) an engineering technology textbook

10. Complete a summary of the passage by selecting THREE answer choices that express the most important ideas. The other three sentences do not belong in the summary because they express ideas that are not in the passage or they do not refer to the major ideas. *This question is worth 2 points*.

What are the roles of various technology professionals?

Ⓐ An engineer seeks the answers to technological questions to create new technology.

Ⓑ Engineers and technicians provide customer support for technical equipment.

Ⓒ A scientist is involved in basic research to advance scientific knowledge.

Ⓓ Many students who excel in math and science are attracted to engineering fields.

Ⓔ Technicians use skills to accomplish work with existing equipment.

Ⓕ The engineer often works with managers in an office instead of in a laboratory setting.

Refer to pages 382–383 for the Explanatory Answers.

EXERCISE 74: Cause/Effect—Natural Sciences

In some questions in the Reading Comprehension Section on the Institutional TOEFL, you will be asked to recall and relate information and content from cause-and-effect passages about various fields of study. Choose the best answer.

Bioluminescence

Light from a living plant or animal is called bioluminescence, or cold light, to distinguish it from incandescence or heat-generating light. Life forms could not produce incandescent light without being
Line burned. Their light is produced by chemicals combining in such a
5   way that little or no measurable heat is produced, and the life forms generating it are unharmed. Although bioluminescence is a relatively complicated process, it can be reduced to simple terms. Living light occurs when luciferin and oxygen combine in the presence of luciferase. In a few cases, fireflies the most common, an additional
10   compound called ATP is required.

     The earliest recorded experiments with bioluminescence in the late 1800s are attributed to Raphael Dubois, who extracted a luminous fluid from a clam, observing that it continued to glow in the test tube for several minutes. He named the substance *luciferin*,
15   which means "the bearer of light." In further research, Dubois discovered that several chemicals were required for bioluminescence to occur. In his notes, it was recorded that a second important substance, which he called *luciferase*, was always present. In later studies of small, luminous sea creatures, Newton Harvey concluded
20   that *luciferin* was composed of carbon, hydrogen, and oxygen, which are the building blocks of all living cells. He also proved that there are a variety of luciferins and luciferases, specific to the plants and animals that produce them.

     Much remains unknown, but many scientists who are studying
25   bioluminescence now believe that the origin of the phenomenon may be traced to a time when there was no oxygen in the Earth's atmosphere. When oxygen was gradually introduced into the atmosphere, it was actually poisonous to life forms. Plants and animals produced light to use up the oxygen in a gradual but
30   necessary adaptation. It is speculated that millions of years ago, all life may have produced light to survive. As the millennia passed, life forms on Earth became tolerant of, and finally dependent on, oxygen, and the adaptation that produced bioluminescence was no longer necessary, but some primitive plants and animals continued to
35   use the light for new functions such as mating or attracting prey.

1. Which of the following is the main topic of the passage?
    - Ⓐ Cold light
    - Ⓑ Luciferase
    - Ⓒ Primitive plants and animals
    - Ⓓ Earth's atmosphere

2. According to the author, why has bioluminescence continued in modern plants and animals?
    - Ⓐ For survival
    - Ⓑ For mating or attracting prey
    - Ⓒ For producing heat
    - Ⓓ For burning excess oxygen

3. The word "primitive" in line 34 is closest in meaning to
    - Ⓐ very old
    - Ⓑ very large
    - Ⓒ very important
    - Ⓓ very common

4. The word "relatively" in line 6 is opposite in meaning to
    - Ⓐ comparatively
    - Ⓑ moderately
    - Ⓒ exclusively
    - Ⓓ partially

5. The word "it" in line 2 refers to
    - Ⓐ a plant
    - Ⓑ an animal
    - Ⓒ bioluminescence
    - Ⓓ incandescence

6. Where in the passage does the author explain how living light occurs?
    - Ⓐ Lines 1–3
    - Ⓑ Lines 7–9
    - Ⓒ Lines 11–14
    - Ⓓ Lines 18–21

7. What does the author mean by the statement in lines 4–6: "Their light is produced by chemicals combining in such a way that little or no measurable heat is produced, and the life forms generating it are unharmed"?
    - Ⓐ Chemicals combine to produce light without heat.
    - Ⓑ The combination of chemicals produces more heat than light.
    - Ⓒ The chemicals that produce heat and light cannot be measured.
    - Ⓓ Heat and light are measured by chemicals.

8. What is true about luciferin?
    - Ⓐ It was recently discovered.
    - Ⓑ It was found to be poisonous.
    - Ⓒ It occurs in the absence of luciferase.
    - Ⓓ It produces light in animals.

9. Bioluminescence is described as all of the following EXCEPT
    - Ⓐ a complex chemical process
    - Ⓑ an adaptation of early plants and animals to the environment
    - Ⓒ a form of cold light
    - Ⓓ a poisonous substance

10. The paragraph following the passage most probably discusses
    - Ⓐ incandescence in prehistoric plants and animals
    - Ⓑ incandescence in modern plants and animals
    - Ⓒ bioluminescence in prehistoric plants and animals
    - Ⓓ bioluminescence in modern plants and animals

Refer to page 383 for the Explanatory Answers.

EXERCISE 75: Cause/Effect—Social Sciences

In some questions in the Reading Comprehension Section on the Institutional TOEFL, you will be asked to recall and relate information and content from cause-and-effect passages about various fields of study. Choose the best answer.

Why Are Americans Getting Older?

In 2000, persons sixty-five years and over already represented 13 percent of the total population in America, and by 2025, there will be 59 million elderly Americans, representing 21 percent of the population
Line of the United States. Furthermore, the percentage of the population over
5 age eighty-five will increase from about 1 percent currently to 5 percent in 2050. This population trend has been referred to as the graying of America.

To explain this demographic change, we must look to three factors. Fertility, mortality, and immigration in large part influence all
10 demographic trends and the graying of America is no exception. The large number of children born after World War II will increase the pool of elderly between 2010 and 2030. The "baby boom" will have become the "senior boom" sixty-five years later as this large segment of the population ages.
15 Although the increase in the birth rate is the most dramatic factor, the decline in the death rate is also significant. Medical advances have influenced life expectancy. Antibiotics and drug therapies as well as new surgical techniques have made a significant contribution. In addition, technological devices for diagnosis and treatment have saved and
20 extended lives. For example, whereas only 40 percent of those Americans born in 1900 had a life expectancy of sixty-five, in the year 2000, 80 percent reached the classic retirement age. The average male life span in 2000 was 71.4 years and increased to 73.3 by 2005. Among females, the life span increased from 78.3 years in 2000 to 81.3 years by 2005
25 (see chart).

In addition, immigration has contributed to the increasing number of elderly. After World War I, a massive immigration of young adults of child-bearing age occurred. Because the customs and traditions of the immigrants encouraged large families, and birth rates among this
30 specialized population were very high, their children, now among the elderly, are currently a significant segment of the older population.

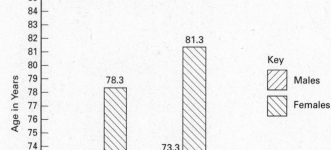

Life Expectancy in the United States in Years

1. Which of the following would be an alternative title for the passage?
   Ⓐ The Graying of America
   Ⓑ Immigration Patterns in America
   Ⓒ Trends in Life Expectancy
   Ⓓ Baby Boomers

2. The average life expectancy for an American woman in 2000 was
   Ⓐ 71.4 years
   Ⓑ 73.3 years
   Ⓒ 78.3 years
   Ⓓ 81.3 years

3. The word "pool" in line 11 refers to
   Ⓐ a group of people
   Ⓑ a general direction
   Ⓒ a negative attitude
   Ⓓ an increase in influence

4. The word "trends" in line 10 is closest in meaning to
   Ⓐ many questions
   Ⓑ small mistakes
   Ⓒ final conclusions
   Ⓓ general directions

5. The word "their" in line 30 refers to
   Ⓐ families
   Ⓑ elderly
   Ⓒ immigrants
   Ⓓ birth rates

6. Where in the passage does the author explain what has influenced life expectancy?
   Ⓐ Lines 12–14
   Ⓑ Lines 16–20
   Ⓒ Lines 22–25
   Ⓓ Lines 26–28

7. What does the author mean by the statement in lines 15–16: "Although the birth rate is the most dramatic factor, the decline in the death rate is also significant"?
   Ⓐ Both the increase in births and the decrease in deaths are significant.
   Ⓑ The higher number of births is less significant than the decrease in deaths.
   Ⓒ Lower birth rates and higher death rates have had dramatic results.
   Ⓓ A significant change in the number of births has balanced the change in the death rates.

8. When will the number of elderly people exceed 20 percent of the population?
   Ⓐ 2010
   Ⓑ 2020
   Ⓒ 2025
   Ⓓ 2030

9. The author mentions all of the following as factors that have influenced population trends EXCEPT
   Ⓐ the "baby boom" after World War II
   Ⓑ the immigration after World War I
   Ⓒ the improvements in health care
   Ⓓ the decline in the birth rate among young Americans

10. It can be inferred from the passage that the word "gray" is a reference to
    Ⓐ the hair color typical of older people
    Ⓑ the last name of the person who has studied the population trends
    Ⓒ the diversity of colors in the population that mix to make gray
    Ⓓ the dismal outlook for the future because of population trends

Refer to pages 383–384 for the Explanatory Answers.

EXERCISE 76: Cause/Effect—Arts/Architecture

In some questions in the Reading Section on the Internet-Based TOEFL, you will be asked to recall and relate information and content from cause-and-effect passages found in college textbooks. Choose the best answer for multiple-choice questions. For computer-assisted questions, follow the directions on the screen.

The Dutch Golden Age

Paragraph 1   The seventeenth century has been called the Golden Age of the Dutch Republic, a time when the Dutch dominated commercial trade and their economy prospered. It was also a time when art was flourishing and major changes were taking place both in the social structure and in the art world.

2   Because commissioning works of art by well-known artists was costly, collecting art had usually been reserved for the aristocracy and very wealthy patrons; however, during the seventeenth century, socioeconomic factors in the Dutch Republic revolutionized art.

3   In the first place, Amsterdam developed into the most important economic center in Europe, and the people enjoyed the highest per capita income in Europe. Trade routes were established with North and South America as well as with Asia, with a concomitant rise of a wealthy middle class made up of tradesmen and owners of large manufacturing enterprises, as well as shipping magnates and other business proprietors. As a result of their affluence and in the absence of a monarch, political power was assumed by the urban upper middle class consisting of the merchants and manufacturers. In addition, their desire to demonstrate their fine taste encouraged them to purchase fine furnishings and art. Consequently, by the end of the baroque period, Dutch artists began to view the middle class as a serious market for their work and started to produce the kind of art that would appeal to them as well as to the aristocracy that had always been major patrons.

4   Furthermore, as the Dutch economy continued to flourish, even the lower middle class began to take an interest in art. Bureaucrats, craftspeople, and military officers began to acquire the pieces that they could afford. These new patrons influenced the development of art during the Dutch baroque period. The rise of puritan Calvinism in the Dutch Republic discouraged the decoration of churches, which resulted in a corresponding reduction in the production of religious art.

5   It was interesting that, in spite of the severe morality that was at the core of Calvinism, the new middle class did not require such stark decoration in their homes, using furniture, tapestries, paintings, and porcelain to display their success in the secular world. Probably in keeping with their ethical and religious standards, art collectors tended to choose smaller works such as landscapes, still lives, and portraits as opposed to the ceiling frescoes and lavish decorations typical at the height of the Italian baroque period, when churches and palaces were being decorated. The themes emphasized ordinary,

contemporary life and realistic treatments. As a result, some scholars refer to Dutch Golden Age painting as Dutch Realism.

6   Perhaps because of their business acumen, the middle class patrons also established new practices for the purchase of art. Unlike the system of commissions, which was the traditional way for artists to sell their works in Europe, the Dutch artists realized that they could expand their market by producing works that would appeal to the new collectors, and they began selling directly to clients through art dealers, exhibitions, and auctions. Artists also began inviting potential buyers to visit them in their studios to view finished pieces as well as works in progress.

7   Without the contract that was a mainstay of the commission system, artists became aware of market preferences and began to develop their own lists of clients. In the case of painters, they started specializing in a particular genre, such as landscapes or portraits, depending on the preference of the collectors who frequented their studios or purchased through their dealers. Thus, the institutions that currently market art, such as dealers, galleries, estate sales, studio sales, and auctions, were all established during the seventeenth century in the Dutch Republic.

8   [A] It would be difficult to determine the precise prices for paintings sold at that time because receipts were not common. [B] The few documents that exist show that historical paintings and landscapes were the most expensive, followed by still lives and, finally, portraits. [C] Prices are also difficult to research because there were many transactions that were conducted without the exchange of money. [D] Many artists settled their debts by decorating businesses with their art. This practice was especially popular among innkeepers and tavern owners, who often became art dealers, even hosting exhibitions in their premises.

1. The word major in the passage is closest in meaning to
   Ⓐ probable
   Ⓑ usual
   Ⓒ important
   Ⓓ recent

2. Which of the sentences below best expresses the information in the highlighted statement in the passage? The other choices change the meaning or leave out important information.
   Ⓐ People engaged in business and trade became politically influential because they were wealthy and no monarch was in power.
   Ⓑ The ruling class lost power when the royal family was forced to leave the city because of politics.
   Ⓒ Many merchants and manufacturers ran for political office after the monarchy fell in the country.
   Ⓓ Since the royal family owed a great deal of money to the patrician class, they could not maintain power.

3. The word acquire in the passage is closest in meaning to
   - Ⓐ achieve
   - Ⓑ publish
   - Ⓒ accept
   - Ⓓ increase

4. According to paragraph 5, why did the Dutch prefer more modest works of art?
   - Ⓐ They appreciated the Italian baroque style.
   - Ⓑ The investment in commissions was smaller.
   - Ⓒ Their religion encouraged restraint.
   - Ⓓ The open market did not offer large works.

5. It can be inferred that the following work would have been purchased in the Dutch Republic.
   - Ⓐ A painting of a family member
   - Ⓑ A large, colorful tapestry
   - Ⓒ An ornate ceiling fresco
   - Ⓓ A biblical story

6. According to paragraph 7, what was NOT true of the way that artists began selling their works in the Dutch Golden Age?
   - Ⓐ They signed a contract with a patron.
   - Ⓑ They contacted clients from a list.
   - Ⓒ They sold their works in art galleries.
   - Ⓓ They sent their art to auction houses.

7. According to paragraph 8, why did tavern owners often become art dealers?
   - Ⓐ Many artists had their studios in local taverns and held exhibits there.
   - Ⓑ Many artists owned taverns and painted when they were not working.
   - Ⓒ Innkeepers had been successful as art dealers.
   - Ⓓ They were trying to sell art that artists had used to cancel debts at their taverns.

8. Four squares (☐) indicate where the following sentence can be added to the passage.

   However, considering the wide diversity of patrons, the prices no doubt ranged from very cheap to extravagantly expensive.

   Where would the sentence best fit into the passage?
   - Ⓐ
   - Ⓑ
   - Ⓒ
   - Ⓓ

9. The author mentions all of the following as reasons for the emergence of the modern art world EXCEPT
   - Ⓐ Subjects for art included decorative as well as religious themes.
   - Ⓑ Wealthy merchants and businesspeople began to collect art.
   - Ⓒ The Dutch Republic sold art to the colonies they had established.
   - Ⓓ Artists started to create works without securing commissions.

10. Complete a summary of the passage by selecting THREE answer choices that express the most important ideas. The other three sentences do not belong in the summary because they express ideas that are not in the passage or they do not refer to the major ideas. *This question is worth 2 points.*

The Golden Age of Dutch art was a time of great productivity and change.

Ⓐ The Dutch Republic extended its influence through global trade routes in the Americas and Asia.

Ⓑ Artists responded to middle-class tastes and produced smaller, more decorative pieces for display in homes.

Ⓒ Direct sales to patrons replaced the commission system, formerly used to market works of art.

Ⓓ The Italian baroque style favored religious themes, which artists executed on a grand scale.

Ⓔ Perhaps the most well-known artists of the Dutch Golden Age were painters, although sculptors and architects also produced works.

Ⓕ Calvinist values encouraged a preference for secular subjects and more modest works of art during the Golden Age.

Refer to pages 384–385 for the Explanatory Answers.

EXERCISE 77: Cause/Effect—Social Sciences

In some questions in the Reading Section on the Internet-Based TOEFL, you will be asked to recall and relate information and content from cause-and-effect passages found in college textbooks. Choose the best answer for multiple-choice questions. For computer-assisted questions, follow the directions on the screen.

The Dust Bowl

Paragraph 1   The *Dust Bowl* was the way that people commonly referred to the ecological and economic disaster of unprecedented proportions that struck the southern Great Plains in the mid 1930s. The region had experienced several years of drought earlier, and the farming families who lived in the area were accustomed to cycles of dry periods that occurred regularly in cycles every twenty years. However, this Dust Bowl event was different. Violent dust storms with high winds swept across Texas and Oklahoma to Nebraska, killing livestock and settlers and devastating their crops.

2   The dust storms were caused by the convergence of several circumstances, including federal land policies and farming practices, technological advances, and unusual weather. In an effort to encourage westward expansion in the late 1800s, the federal government passed the Homestead Act, which provided settlers with 160 acres of public land. Enticed by this opportunity, a stream of inexperienced farmers claimed homesteads. During World War I, when wheat reached record-high prices, the new farmers stripped millions of acres of native grasslands on the plains to plant crops. As prices fell during the depression in the 1920s, farmers plowed up more land in an effort to increase production. As crops began to fail because of the drought, bare land was exposed, and, with no native buffalo grass to protect the soil, the massive dust storms began their destructive path.

3   Ironically, advances in farm equipment also contributed to the problem. The flat land on the plains adapted to the new mechanized farming practices very well. Gasoline-powered tractors, disc plows, and combines increased productivity. Whereas it had formerly taken about sixty hours of manual labor to produce an acre of wheat, with machinery it could be done in less than three hours, with the result that more land could be farmed by the homesteaders.

4   Once the native prairie grass was stripped, there was nothing to prevent soil erosion. Dust storms blew away millions of acres of rich topsoil, and thousands of farm families fled the region. Those who stayed suffered serious economic and psychological losses from the disaster. The most serious destruction occurred in Kansas, Colorado, Oklahoma, the Texas Panhandle, and New Mexico. When a Denver journalist coined the phrase "Dust Bowl," it quickly caught on.

5   Severe dust storms called "black blizzards" rose more than a mile and a half high, blowing across the land, darkening the sky, and settling over hundreds of miles. In many cases, the dust drifted like snow. It made it difficult for farmers and their livestock to breathe and destroyed crops and vegetation, turning day into night. "Dust pneumonia" and other respiratory infections afflicted thousands of people.

6   President Franklin D. Roosevelt worked with several federal agencies to alleviate the suffering and address the environmental issues that had caused the disaster. Many thousands of farm families were given direct emergency relief by the Resettlement Administration. Other federal aid included loans for seeds and temporary jobs with the Works Progress Administration (WPA). It is estimated that as many as one-third of the families in the region applied for assistance.

7   The Agricultural Adjustment Administration paid farmers millions of dollars not to grow wheat and encouraged them to substitute soil-enriching crops such as sorghum for the soil-depleting crops like wheat. To discourage cattle grazing on the depleted prairies, the Drought Relief Service of the Department of Agriculture purchased more than eight million head of cattle in the years between 1934 and 1936, and for a short time, the federal government became the largest cattle owner in the world. The department also provided loans for feed and allowed livestock to graze on public lands. But in spite of these efforts to alter the situation, more than 2.5 million people migrated from the states where the Dust Bowl had hit, moving west to seek work. More than a quarter of a million migrants moved from Oklahoma to California.

8   To change the ways that land was used, to reduce soil erosion, and to nurture new grasslands, the Department of Agriculture encouraged different farming practices. The Soil Conservation Service (SCS) organized research projects and demonstration farms and provided technical assistance, supplies, and equipment to farmers who implemented conservation practices.

9   At the height of the disaster, 100 million acres had been eroded, but by 1940, the acreage vulnerable to erosion in the southern plains had been reduced to less than four million acres. New farm policies had mostly controlled the agricultural market. However, with several consecutive years of good rainfall and the increased demand and higher prices for grain during World War II, many homesteaders abandoned the practices that the SCS had encouraged them to institute on their farms. Wheat farming increased, and farmers pursued commercial agricultural opportunities without consideration for the potential hazard to the prairie land.

1. According to paragraphs 2 and 3, what was NOT a factor that caused the Dust Bowl?
   - Ⓐ The Homestead Act
   - Ⓑ A long dry period
   - Ⓒ Better farm equipment
   - Ⓓ Prairie grasslands

2. Why did the author mention *snow* in paragraph 5?
   - Ⓐ To describe the color of the dust
   - Ⓑ To explain how the dust piled up
   - Ⓒ To refer to the cold temperatures
   - Ⓓ To contrast the black blizzards with it

3. According to paragraph 7, why did the federal government purchase cattle?
   - Ⓐ To become the largest cattle owner in the world
   - Ⓑ To prevent ranchers from grazing their cattle on the prairie
   - Ⓒ To encourage people to stay in Oklahoma
   - Ⓓ To make money for their government programs

4. Which of the sentences below best expresses the information in the highlighted statement in the passage? The other choices change the meaning or leave out important information.

Ⓐ Planting sorghum with wheat saved the government millions of dollars in subsidies.

Ⓑ The government subsidized crops that contributed to the regeneration of the soil.

Ⓒ Farmers sold their wheat crops to the government for a large subsidy.

Ⓓ The soil was depleted because the government had subsidized wheat crops.

5. The word alter in the passage is closest in meaning to

Ⓐ expand
Ⓑ predict
Ⓒ notice
Ⓓ modify

6. The word them in the passage refers to

Ⓐ prices
Ⓑ homesteaders
Ⓒ practices
Ⓓ farms

7. How many acres were affected by the erosion at the height of the storms?

Ⓐ 100 million
Ⓑ 50 million
Ⓒ 8 million
Ⓓ 4 million

8. The word potential in the passage is closest in meaning to

Ⓐ probable
Ⓑ serious
Ⓒ new
Ⓓ temporary

9. It can be inferred from the passage that

Ⓐ ranchers caused the Dust Bowl by grazing too many buffalo on the grasslands

Ⓑ the Dust Bowl was brought to an end by World War II

Ⓒ the Great Plains is a wheat-producing region in the United States

Ⓓ all the homesteaders had to abandon their farms during the Dust Bowl

10. Complete a summary of the passage by selecting THREE answer choices that express the most important ideas. The other three sentences do not belong in the summary because they express ideas that are not in the passage or they do not refer to the major ideas. *This question is worth 2 points.*

In the 1930s, an ecological and economic disaster struck the Great Plains.

Ⓐ The federal government became the largest cattle owner in the world.

Ⓑ Federal agencies intervened to assist farmers and ranchers in the Great Plains.

Ⓒ Many farmers and homesteaders left the Great Plains during the worst drought.

Ⓓ The Works Progress Administration built bridges, roads, and public structures.

Ⓔ Farmers plowed under the natural vegetation in order to grow wheat.

Ⓕ Soil erosion and dust storms combined to create the Dust Bowl.

Refer to page 385 for the Explanatory Answers.

EXERCISE 78: Persuasion/Justification—Natural Sciences

In some questions in the Reading Comprehension Section on the Institutional TOEFL, you will be asked to recall and relate information and content from persuasion or justification passages about various fields of study. Choose the best answer.

Endangered Species

There are three valid arguments to support the preservation of endangered species. An aesthetic justification contends that biodiversity contributes to the quality of life because many of the

Line
5 endangered plants and animals are particularly appreciated for their unique physical beauty. The aesthetic role of nature in all its diverse forms is reflected in the art and literature of every culture, attaining symbolic status in the spiritual life of many groups. According to the proponents of the aesthetic argument, people need nature in all its diverse and beautiful forms as part of the experience of the world.

10 Another argument that has been put forward, especially by groups in the medical and pharmacological fields, is that of ecological self-interest. By preserving all species, we retain a balance of nature that is ultimately beneficial to humankind. Recent research on global ecosystems has been cited as evidence that every

15 species contributes important or even essential functions that may be necessary to the survival of our own species. Some advocates of the ecological argument contend that important chemical compounds derived from rare plants may contain the key to a cure for one of the diseases currently threatening human beings. If we do not protect

20 other species, then they cannot protect us.

Apart from human advantage in both the aesthetic and ecological arguments, the proponents of a moral justification contend that all species have the right to exist, a viewpoint stated in the United Nations World Charter for Nature, created in 1982. Furthermore, if

25 humankind views itself as the stewards of all the creatures on Earth, then it is incumbent upon human beings to protect them and to ensure the continued existence of all species. Moral justification has been extended by a movement called "deep ecology," the members of which rank the biosphere higher than people because the

30 continuation of life depends on this larger perspective. To carry their argument to its logical conclusion, all choices must be made for the biosphere, not for people.

1. Which of the following is the main topic of the passage?
   Ⓐ The beauty of the world
   Ⓑ The quality of life
   Ⓒ The preservation of species
   Ⓓ The balance of nature

2. Which of the arguments supports animal rights?
   Ⓐ Aesthetic justification
   Ⓑ Ecological argument
   Ⓒ Self-interest argument
   Ⓓ Moral justification

3. The word "perspective" in line 30 could best be replaced by
   Ⓐ ideal
   Ⓑ event
   Ⓒ truth
   Ⓓ view

4. The word "unique" in line 5 is closest in meaning to
   Ⓐ strong
   Ⓑ new
   Ⓒ special
   Ⓓ active

5. The word "them" in line 26 refers to
   Ⓐ humankind
   Ⓑ stewards
   Ⓒ creatures
   Ⓓ human beings

6. Where in the passage does the author explain how rare species contribute to the health of the human species?
   Ⓐ Lines 2–5
   Ⓑ Lines 7–9
   Ⓒ Lines 16–19
   Ⓓ Lines 24–27

7. What does the author mean by the statement in lines 7–9: "According to the proponents of the aesthetic argument, people need nature in all its diverse and beautiful forms as part of the experience of the world"?
   Ⓐ The world is experienced by nature in various forms that are equally beautiful.
   Ⓑ People are naturally attracted to beautiful forms rather than to different ones.
   Ⓒ Nature is beautiful because it provides varied experiences for people.
   Ⓓ An appreciation of the Earth requires that people have an opportunity to enjoy the diversity and beauty of nature.

8. According to the passage, what do we know from research on global ecosystems?
   Ⓐ Nature is very diverse.
   Ⓑ A balance of nature is important.
   Ⓒ Humans have a responsibility to nature.
   Ⓓ Nature represents spiritual values.

9. The author mentions all of the following as justifications for the protection of endangered species EXCEPT
   Ⓐ the natural compounds needed for medicines
   Ⓑ the intrinsic value of the beauty of nature
   Ⓒ the control of pollution in the biosphere
   Ⓓ the right to life implied by their existence

10. It can be inferred from the passage that the author
    Ⓐ is a member of the "deep ecology" movement
    Ⓑ does not agree with ecological self-interest
    Ⓒ supports all of the arguments to protect species
    Ⓓ participated in drafting the Charter for Nature

Refer to pages 385–386 for the Explanatory Answers.

Exercise 79: Persuasion/Justification—Social Sciences

In some questions in the Reading Comprehension Section on the Institutional TOEFL, you will be asked to recall and relate information and content from persuasion or justification passages about various fields of study. Choose the best answer.

Prison Reform

In the United States today, there are more than half a million criminals serving time in jails or prisons. Most prisoners are male high school dropouts between the ages of 18 and 29. Even more *Line* shocking is the fact that the number and rate of imprisonment has
5 more than doubled over the past twenty years, and the recidivism— that is, the rate for rearrest—is more than 60 percent.

Although the stated objective of the criminal justice system, on both federal and state levels, is to rehabilitate the inmates and reintegrate them into society, the system itself does not support
10 such a goal. Although most jails are located within the community, prisons are usually geographically or psychologically isolated and terribly overcrowded. Even in the more enlightened prisons, only one-third of the inmates have vocational training opportunities or work release options. Even fewer have access to qualified counselors,
15 psychologists, or social workers.

If prisons are indeed to achieve the goal of rehabilitating offenders, then the prisons themselves will have to change. First, they will have to be smaller, housing no more than five hundred prisoners. It has been shown that crowding in large facilities is
20 not conducive to behavior modification. Second, they will have to be built in or near population centers with community resources available for gradual reintegration into society. This must include social and psychological services. Finally, prison programs must be restructured to provide work release and vocational and
25 academic training for all inmates to prepare them with skills that carry over into their lives after release. In addition to parole terms and community supervised work release, successful models for such collaborative efforts between the criminal justice system and the community already exist in several hundred halfway houses
30 throughout the country where inmates complete their sentences while beginning to reestablish their lives as productive members of society. Studies suggest that imprisonment as it is currently administered must be viewed as punishment rather than reform. Until we approach the problem in terms of changing behaviors rather
35 than segregating offenders, prisoners who are released will probably return to a life of crime.

1. What is the author's main point?
   - Ⓐ Prisons must be restructured if they are to accomplish the goal of rehabilitation.
   - Ⓑ Goals for community collaboration have been successful.
   - Ⓒ Most of the criminals serving time in prison do not have goals.
   - Ⓓ The criminal justice system must establish a better goal.

2. According to the author, how many prisoners are offered training or work release?
   - Ⓐ None
   - Ⓑ 33⅓ percent
   - Ⓒ 50 percent
   - Ⓓ 60 percent

3. The word "recidivism" in line 5 refers to
   - Ⓐ all people who are imprisoned
   - Ⓑ people who return to prison after release
   - Ⓒ people who drop out of high school
   - Ⓓ people who have been in prison for a long time

4. The word "options" in line 14 is closest in meaning to
   - Ⓐ exceptions
   - Ⓑ challenges
   - Ⓒ alternatives
   - Ⓓ benefits

5. The word "them" in line 9 refers to
   - Ⓐ prison systems
   - Ⓑ inmates
   - Ⓒ goals
   - Ⓓ levels

6. Where in the passage does the author explain the rate of imprisonment over the past twenty years?
   - Ⓐ Lines 1–2
   - Ⓑ Lines 3–6
   - Ⓒ Lines 7–10
   - Ⓓ Lines 12–14

7. What does the author mean by the statement in lines 7–10: "Although the stated objective of the criminal justice system, on both federal and state levels, is to rehabilitate the inmates and reintegrate them into society, the systems themselves do not support such a goal"?
   - Ⓐ Inmates in prisons do not participate in rehabilitation programs before they are reintegrated into society.
   - Ⓑ The goal of rehabilitation and reintegration into society is encouraged by the prison systems.
   - Ⓒ Prison systems do not promote rehabilitation and reintegration despite their goal.
   - Ⓓ Rehabilitation cannot be achieved by prisons without reintegration into society.

8. Why should prisons be built near towns or cities?
   - Ⓐ Prisoners benefit from family visitations.
   - Ⓑ Workers need to be close to their homes.
   - Ⓒ Reintegration programs require resources.
   - Ⓓ Prisons contribute to the economies.

9. The author mentions all the following as necessary to prison reform EXCEPT
   - Ⓐ newer buildings
   - Ⓑ smaller institutions
   - Ⓒ vocational training
   - Ⓓ collaboration with the community

10. The paragraph following this passage most probably discusses
    - Ⓐ the goals of most state and federal prisons
    - Ⓑ the cost of prison reform
    - Ⓒ examples of models for community collaboration
    - Ⓓ problems with the current criminal justice system

Refer to pages 386–387 for the Explanatory Answers.

EXERCISE 80: Persuasion/Justification—Humanities/Business

In some questions in the Reading Section on the Internet-Based TOEFL, you will be asked to recall and relate information and content from persuasion or justification passages found in college textbooks. Choose the best answer for multiple-choice questions. For computer-assisted questions, follow the directions on the screen.

Lexicostatistical Glottochronology

Paragraph 1   Although research into language change has been undertaken since the eighteenth century, it was not until the mid-twentieth century that American linguists Swadesh and Lees developed the concept that the core vocabulary of a language is replaced at a constant rate and can thus be used to determine the length of time since two related languages diverged. Referred to as lexicostatistical glottochronology, the method is supported by two assumptions. First, it is assumed that all languages include a basic vocabulary that is more stable than other words in a language. While the concept of such a list had been informally experimented with prior to his investigations, Swadesh created a list of 100 words that every linguist could use to identify the basic vocabulary of any language. Commonly called a Swadesh list, it is still a widely used tool in the field of linguistics. To control for culturally specific concepts, words like local foods, plants, and animals are not included in the list.

2   Using the basic word list, a sample of vocabulary is taken from the languages that are being studied, the number of similar words is counted, with allowances for the processes that affect phonetic changes. Thus, the Sanskrit words for family members like *matar*, *pitar*, *bhratar*, and *svasar* are considered similar to the English words for the same relationships—mother, father, brother, and sister. Conversely, in Navajo, no relationship to English is evident in the words for family members; *shima* is the name for mother, and *shizhee* for father; *shinaai* is the name for an older brother and *shitsili* for a younger brother, while *shiadi* is for an older sister and *shideezhi* for a younger sister.

3   Second, it is assumed that every word in this core vocabulary is replaced in a process like that of radioactive decay in Carbon 14 dating, in constant percentages. Linguists hypothesize that the fewer words that are related between two languages, the longer the separation of those languages. For example, languages with 50 percent of their core vocabulary in common would have diverged earlier than languages with 75 percent in common. Swadesh and Lees took that hypothesis a step further. [A] Using several Romance languages for which the period of time since divergence from Latin was known, they calculated the correlation between the percentage of common vocabulary and the time that had intervened since their divergence. [B] On average, the languages that they studied had about 85 percent in common after one thousand years of divergence. [C] Using the percentages from a number of language comparisons, they created a table of historical divergence. [D] With the table, they were able to estimate the possible date of divergence for many of the languages in the major language families.

4   The method, though widely used, is problematic for three reasons. First, linguists have argued that it is not possible to select words that are universal to all cultures. Second, at least some of the words on the list may have cultural significance that is not accounted for. For instance, those words that refer to nature may actually have religious meaning in some but not all of the sample languages. And finally, the rate of change may not be the same for all languages. Since societies develop at different rates over different periods in their histories, it is logical that languages may develop at different rates over different periods in their histories as well. Furthermore, the hypothesis does not account for language contact and borrowing of vocabulary across languages. This is particularly significant because even a slight inaccuracy would be compounded as the analysis was taken back in time since fewer cognates would be left after a long divergence. Even if only one cognate were inaccurate, the result could affect multiple centuries of data.

5   Swadesh was aware of the limitations and relied on supportive evidence from the field of archaeology when he presented his findings. Because a viable alternative to his method has not been put forward, scholars still rely on it for their research on the relative chronology of modern languages. It should also be pointed out that Swadesh did not hypothesize that all languages developed from a universal ancestor, although others have cited his research to support such a theory.

Glossary
phonetic: the sounds of speech

1. According to paragraph 1, what is NOT true of the Swadesh list?
   Ⓐ It is a list of 100 basic vocabulary words.
   Ⓑ It includes culturally significant words.
   Ⓒ It is used for current research studies.
   Ⓓ It stays about the same over time.

2. The word that in the passage refers to
   Ⓐ vocabulary
   Ⓑ process
   Ⓒ decay
   Ⓓ word

3. Which of the sentences below best expresses the information in the highlighted statement in the passage? The other choices change the meaning or leave out important information.
   Ⓐ Languages separated for a long time will have two samples of vocabulary that agree.
   Ⓑ Vocabulary in two samples will have fewer agreements because the languages are separated.
   Ⓒ Fewer vocabulary items will agree when languages have separated a long time ago.
   Ⓓ Longer words will tend to agree even when languages have been separated.

4. How much common vocabulary could be expected after languages had been separated for 1000 years?
   - Ⓐ 14 percent
   - Ⓑ 50 percent
   - Ⓒ 75 percent
   - Ⓓ 85 percent

5. Four squares (□) indicate where the following sentence can be added to the passage.

   The table in years begins at 25,000 years ago and stops at 0 years ago, that is, the present.

   Where would the sentence best fit into the passage?
   - Ⓐ
   - Ⓑ
   - Ⓒ
   - Ⓓ

6. The word limitations in the passage is closest in meaning to
   - Ⓐ weak points
   - Ⓑ difficult instructions
   - Ⓒ dangerous results
   - Ⓓ brief conclusions

7. The word viable in the passage is closest in meaning to
   - Ⓐ recent
   - Ⓑ practical
   - Ⓒ additional
   - Ⓓ organized

8. The author mentions all of the following as criticisms of the approach, EXCEPT
   - Ⓐ some languages may change more rapidly than others
   - Ⓑ small errors compound over time
   - Ⓒ no alternative method is available
   - Ⓓ word lists may be culturally biased

9. It can be inferred from the passage that the author
   - Ⓐ is not interested in glottochronology
   - Ⓑ worked with linguists Swadesh and Lees
   - Ⓒ uses glottochronology in his own research
   - Ⓓ has a balanced view of the work by Swadesh and Lees

10. Complete a summary of the passage by selecting THREE answer choices that express the most important ideas. The other three sentences do not belong in the summary because they express ideas that are not in the passage or they do not refer to the major ideas. *This question is worth 2 points.*

Lexicostatistical glottochronology is a linguistic approach devised by Swadesh and Lees.

Ⓐ A table provides estimates for the number of years of linguistic divergence.

Ⓑ Evidence from archaeology can be used to date the language separation.

Ⓒ The Italian word *padre* and Portuguese *pai* are accepted cognates.

Ⓓ Samples of languages are compared using a carefully constructed word list.

Ⓔ Cognate words are counted, and a percentage of word agreements is calculated.

Ⓕ The word list includes names of family members.

Refer to page 387 for the Explanatory Answers.

EXERCISE 81: Persuasion/Justification—Arts/Architecture

In some questions in the Reading Section on the Internet-Based TOEFL, you will be asked to recall and relate information and content from persuasion or justification passages found in college textbooks. Choose the best answer for multiple-choice questions. For computer-assisted questions, follow the directions on the screen.

Art Appreciation

Paragraph 1   Art appreciation courses are part of most liberal arts curricula in colleges and universities, but what does it mean to "appreciate" art? [A] Although the physical process of perception is the same for everyone, when individuals look at a work of art, they don't all see the same image. [B] Nevertheless, a work of art can convey emotion, and by merely looking at it, a viewer can interpret meaning. One way to appreciate art, then, is to feel whatever emotion the work evokes in you when you view it. But to appreciate the work on a deeper level, it is important to understand *how* the artist elicited that response. [C] In other words, you must go beyond your initial perception. [D] Perhaps it is the color, the shapes, the texture, or even the topic itself. Reflecting on the reason that you are intrigued by the work is a step beyond reacting on an emotional level, and it is the beginning of a more mature appreciation.

2   When looking at a work of art, it may also be useful to see it from different vantage points or in different lighting. Sometimes the artist has a surprise hidden in the piece. Modern artist Michael Murphy creates incredible three-dimensional sculptures that require the observer to stand at a specific vantage point to see the image. For instance, when viewed from the front, one of his sculptures appears to be an image of two giraffes, but viewed from the side, it is clearly an elephant. Even when such a startling difference is not part of the structure, a work of art will look different when it is viewed in different venues or from different perspectives.

3   Moreover, our perception of a work of art can provide appreciation in the same way that looking at nature might elicit an emotional response. On that level, there is really no correct way to interpret it. The perception of a work is quite personal. However, most courses require that students look beyond their own perceptions by learning something of the background for the creation of the work, either the historical context of the art or the artist's life and experiences.

4   Knowing the date of creation allows us to understand the events that were taking place when the work was conceived and made. For example, the painting *Guernica* was completed by Picasso in 1937. By merely looking at it, most observers would feel disturbed or even horrified, but knowing that Picasso created the painting during the Spanish Civil War, when the town of Guernica was bombed, we gain a deeper understanding of the painting and the purpose that the artist had, not only in the overall composition, but also in the anti war symbolism throughout.

5   Having some background information about the artist is another way we can appreciate a work. Knowing at what point the artist was in his or her career when the piece was created is interesting, as is making a comparison of the style with the same artist's works before and after the piece. Comparing the work with that of other contemporary artists also tells us whether the work is part of a movement or a departure from it. In combination, this information gives us an insight into the mind of the artist at the time that the creation was completed.

6   Identifying the school or movement that influenced the work can also be helpful to an appreciation of the art. For instance, Egyptian painters were careful to draw persons in sizes relative to their social status and were limited to six colors. Looking at a work from the Egyptian school with that information in mind allows us to understand and appreciate a perspective that would be very different from the expected proportions of people in other artistic movements.

7   Even with a great deal of study, however, it must be acknowledged that great works of art are capable of conveying many meanings. Those that survive the test of time may, in fact, hold new meanings for a new generation of observers. What is perhaps most important in the appreciation of art is the willingness to bring contextual knowledge to the process, along with an open mind and a desire to respond to the experiences and emotions that the artist has attempted to express in the creation.

1. Which of the sentences below best expresses the information in the highlighted statement in the passage? The other choices change the meaning or leave out important information.
    Ⓐ We see images differently because of the mode of perception.
    Ⓑ Although we see images differently, the mode of perception is similar.
    Ⓒ Since the mode of perception is similar, we see images in the same way.
    Ⓓ When the mode of perception is the same, we see the same images.

2. Four squares (□) indicate where the following sentence can be added to the passage.

    For example, one person may focus on the image while another person may experience the color.

    Where would the sentence best fit into the passage?
    Ⓐ
    Ⓑ
    Ⓒ
    Ⓓ

3. The phrase intrigued by in the passage is closest in meaning to
   - Ⓐ very pleased
   - Ⓑ very confused
   - Ⓒ very interested
   - Ⓓ very surprised

4. According to paragraph 2, what is unique about Michael Murphy's work?
   - Ⓐ He limits his work to only six bright colors.
   - Ⓑ He uses lighting to hide the smaller sculptures.
   - Ⓒ Different images are seen from different vantage points.
   - Ⓓ He makes realistic models of wild animals.

5. What can be inferred about Picasso from his painting *Guernica*?
   - Ⓐ He was living in the town of Guernica when he painted it.
   - Ⓑ He was probably opposed to the Spanish Civil War.
   - Ⓒ He must not have been in Spain in the year 1937.
   - Ⓓ He was painting scenes from his imagination.

6. The word overall in the passage is closest in meaning to
   - Ⓐ general
   - Ⓑ complex
   - Ⓒ original
   - Ⓓ unique

7. Why does the author mention *Egyptian art* in paragraph 6?
   - Ⓐ To include an example of non-Western art in the discussion
   - Ⓑ To demonstrate how an artistic movement influences artists
   - Ⓒ To show the progression of an artist's work over a long period of time
   - Ⓓ To make a point about the way different generations view art

8. The word those in the passage refers to
   - Ⓐ each attentive observer
   - Ⓑ thoughts and emotions
   - Ⓒ a lifetime of experiences
   - Ⓓ great works of art

9. The author mentions all of the following ways to enhance the appreciation of art EXCEPT
   - Ⓐ understanding the artistic movement
   - Ⓑ becoming familiar with the history
   - Ⓒ experiencing the art by copying
   - Ⓓ knowing about the life of the artist

10. Complete a summary of the passage by selecting THREE answer choices that express the most important ideas. The other three sentences do not belong in the summary because they express ideas that are not in the passage or they do not refer to the major ideas. *This question is worth 2 points*.

   Art can be appreciated in various ways.
   - Ⓐ Picasso painted *Guernica* during the Spanish Civil War when the town was bombed.
   - Ⓑ Studying the historical context and the artist's life may contribute to art appreciation.
   - Ⓒ Works of art have many meanings that every individual interprets on a personal level.
   - Ⓓ Science defines perception as the recognition and interpretation of sensory data.
   - Ⓔ The school or artistic movement may also contribute to a deeper appreciation.
   - Ⓕ The title of a work of art can be the first clue to the artist's purpose.

Refer to pages 387–388 for the Explanatory Answers.

EXERCISE 82: Problem/Solution—Arts/Architecture

In some questions in the Reading Comprehension Section on the Institutional TOEFL, you will be asked to recall and relate information and content from problem-solution passages about various fields of study. Choose the best answer.

The Art World

One of the major problems in the art world is how to distinguish and promote an artist. In effect, a market must be created for an artist to be successful. The practice of signing and numbering
Line individual prints was introduced by James Abbott McNeill Whistler,
5 the nineteenth-century artist best known for the painting of his mother, called *Arrangement in Grey and Black No. 1*, but known to most of us as *Whistler's Mother*. Whistler's brother-in-law, Sir Francis Seymour Haden, a less well-known artist, had speculated that collectors might find prints more attractive if they knew that there
10 were only a limited number of copies produced. By signing the work in pencil, an artist could guarantee and personalize each print.

As soon as Whistler and Haden began the practice of signing and numbering their prints, their work began to increase in value. When other artists noticed that the signed prints commanded higher prices,
15 they began copying the procedure.

Although most prints are signed on the right-hand side in the margin below the image, the placement of the signature is a matter of personal choice. Indeed, prints have been signed within the image, in any of the margins, or even on the reverse side of the print.
20 Wherever the artist elects to sign it, a signed print is still valued above an unsigned one, even in the same edition.

1. Which of the following would be a better title for the passage?
   - Ⓐ *Whistler's Mother*
   - Ⓑ Whistler's Greatest Works
   - Ⓒ The Practice of Signing Prints
   - Ⓓ Copying Limited Edition Prints

2. What made Whistler's work more valuable?
   - Ⓐ His fame as an artist
   - Ⓑ His painting of his mother
   - Ⓒ His signature on the prints
   - Ⓓ His brother-in-law's prints

3. The word "speculated" in line 8 could best the replaced by
   - Ⓐ guessed
   - Ⓑ noticed
   - Ⓒ denied
   - Ⓓ announced

4. The word "distinguish" in line 1 is closest in meaning to
   - Ⓐ recognize differences
   - Ⓑ make improvements
   - Ⓒ allow exceptions
   - Ⓓ accept changes

5. The word "it" in line 20 refers to
   - Ⓐ the same edition
   - Ⓑ the image
   - Ⓒ the reverse side
   - Ⓓ a print

6. Where in the passage does the author indicate where an artist's signature might be found on a work?
   - Ⓐ Lines 10–11
   - Ⓑ Lines 12–15
   - Ⓒ Lines 16–19
   - Ⓓ Lines 20–21

7. What does the author mean by the statement in lines 12–13: "As soon as Whistler and Haden began the practice of signing and numbering their prints, their work began to increase in value"?
   - Ⓐ The prints that were signed and numbered were worth more.
   - Ⓑ The signing and numbering of prints was not very popular.
   - Ⓒ The signatures became more valuable than the prints.
   - Ⓓ Many copies of the prints were made.

8. What was true about the painting of Whistler's mother?
   - Ⓐ It was painted by Sir Francis Seymour Haden.
   - Ⓑ Its title was *Arrangement in Grey and Black No. 1*.
   - Ⓒ It was not one of Whistler's best paintings.
   - Ⓓ It was a completely new method of painting.

9. The author mentions all of the following as reasons why a collector prefers a signed print EXCEPT
   - Ⓐ it guarantees the print's authenticity
   - Ⓑ it makes the print more personal
   - Ⓒ it encourages higher prices for the print
   - Ⓓ it limits the number of copies of the print

10. It can be inferred from the passage that artists number their prints
    - Ⓐ as an accounting procedure
    - Ⓑ to guarantee a limited edition
    - Ⓒ when the buyer requests it
    - Ⓓ at the same place on each of the prints

Refer to page 388 for the Explanatory Answers.

EXERCISE 83: Problem/Solution—Humanities/Business

In some questions in the Reading Comprehension Section on the Institutional TOEFL, you will be asked to recall and relate information and content from problem-solution passages about various fields of study. Choose the best answer.

Negotiation

The increase in international business and in foreign investment has created a need for executives with knowledge of foreign languages and skills in cross-cultural communication. Americans,
Line   however, have not been well trained in either area and, consequently,
5   have not enjoyed the same level of success in negotiation in an international arena as have their foreign counterparts.

Negotiating is the process of communicating back and forth for the purpose of reaching an agreement. It involves persuasion and compromise, but in order to participate in either one, the negotiators
10   must understand the ways in which people are persuaded and how compromise is reached within the culture of the negotiation.

In many international business negotiations abroad, Americans are perceived as wealthy and impersonal. It often appears to the foreign negotiator that the American represents a large multimillion-
15   dollar corporation that can afford to pay the price without bargaining further. The American negotiator's role becomes that of an impersonal purveyor of information and cash, an image that succeeds only in undermining the negotiation.

In studies of American negotiators abroad, several traits
20   have been identified that may serve to confirm this stereotypical perception, while subverting the negotiator's position. Two traits in particular that cause cross-cultural misunderstanding are directness and impatience on the part of the American negotiator. Furthermore, American negotiators often insist on realizing short-term goals.
25   Foreign negotiators, on the other hand, may value the relationship established between negotiators and may be willing to invest time in it for long-term benefits. In order to solidify the relationship, they may opt for indirect interactions without regard for the time involved in getting to know the other negotiator.
30   Clearly, perceptions and differences in values affect the outcomes of negotiations and the success of negotiators. For Americans to play a more effective role in international business negotiations, they must put forth more effort to improve cross-cultural understanding.

1. What is the author's main point?
   - Ⓐ Negotiation is the process of reaching an agreement.
   - Ⓑ Foreign languages are important for international business.
   - Ⓒ Foreign perceptions of American negotiators are based on stereotypes.
   - Ⓓ American negotiators need to learn more about other cultures.

2. According to the author, what is the purpose of negotiation?
   - Ⓐ To undermine the other negotiator's position
   - Ⓑ To communicate back and forth
   - Ⓒ To reach an agreement
   - Ⓓ To understand the culture of the negotiators

3. The word "persuaded" in line 10 is closest in meaning to
   - Ⓐ respected
   - Ⓑ accused
   - Ⓒ informed
   - Ⓓ convinced

4. The word "undermining" in line 18 is closest in meaning to
   - Ⓐ making known
   - Ⓑ making clear
   - Ⓒ making brief
   - Ⓓ making weak

5. The word "that" in line 16 refers to
   - Ⓐ bargaining
   - Ⓑ role
   - Ⓒ corporation
   - Ⓓ price

6. Where in the passage does the author indicate the two criteria necessary for negotiation?
   - Ⓐ Lines 8–11
   - Ⓑ Lines 12–13
   - Ⓒ Lines 21–23
   - Ⓓ Lines 25–27

7. What does the author mean by the statement in lines 3–6: "Americans, however, have not been well trained in either area and, consequently, have not enjoyed the same level of success in negotiation in an international arena as have their foreign counterparts"?
   - Ⓐ Training is not available for Americans who must interact in international negotiations.
   - Ⓑ Foreign businesspersons negotiate less effectively than Americans because of their training.
   - Ⓒ Because their training is not as good, Americans are less successful as negotiators than their international counterparts.
   - Ⓓ Foreign businesspersons do not like to negotiate with Americans, who are not well trained.

8. According to the passage, how can American businesspersons improve their negotiation skills?
   - Ⓐ By living in a foreign culture
   - Ⓑ By getting to know the negotiators
   - Ⓒ By compromising more often
   - Ⓓ By explaining the goals more clearly

9. The American negotiator is described as all of the following EXCEPT
   - Ⓐ perceived by foreign negotiators as wealthy
   - Ⓑ willing to invest time in relationships
   - Ⓒ known for direct interactions
   - Ⓓ interested in short-term goals

10. The paragraph following the passage most probably discusses
    - Ⓐ ways to increase cross-cultural understanding
    - Ⓑ traits that cause cross-cultural misunderstanding
    - Ⓒ knowledge of foreign languages
    - Ⓓ relationships between negotiators

Refer to page 389 for the Explanatory Answers.

EXERCISE 84: Problem/Solution—Social Sciences

In some questions in the Reading Section on the Internet-Based TOEFL, you will be asked to recall and relate information and content from problem-solution passages found in college textbooks. Choose the best answer for multiple-choice questions. For computer-assisted questions, follow the directions on the screen.

Students with Special Needs

Paragraph 1   According to a recent report by the Department of Education, the number of students in the United States aged three to twenty-one who receive special education services is seven million, or 14 percent of all public school students. More than half of them have learning disabilities, and the others have a variety of mental and physical health needs, including autism, intellectual disabilities, developmental delays, and emotional disturbances.

2   The terms that educators use to refer to students with disabilities are constantly under revision. A broad identification is "students with special needs." For instance, students in wheelchairs have special needs when it comes to accessing various areas of the school or the transportation to and from school. Students with emotional issues have special needs as well. They may need strategies and support to calm down and stop their disturbing behavior before it becomes violent.

3   Most students with special needs, however, have a learning disability. These are students with normal intelligence or above who have a learning difficulty in at least one academic area that is not attributed to any other diagnosed disorder and usually includes problems with at least one of the following skills—listening, concentrating, reading, and speaking or doing mathematical calculations. Almost two million students, or about 3.5 percent of all students in the United States, receive special services for some type of reading disorder. Many have *dyslexia*, a learning disability that causes difficulties with reading and spelling. Students with dyslexia may have problems connecting letters to the sounds they produce and may reverse letters or words when they see them in print. They may also develop vocabulary more slowly. Another group of students are identified with *dysgraphia*, which is characterized by problems with the cognitive skills for memory, vocabulary retrieval, and grammar as they organize their writing as well as issues with the motor skills necessary to physically write their compositions. Students who struggle with basic mathematics and reasoning are identified with *dyscalculia*.

4   Before 1975, when Public Law 94-142 was enacted, children with special needs were often refused enrollment or were not adequately educated within the public school system. With the passage of that legislation, all students with special needs must now be given a free, appropriate public education and must be provided with the funding to support their evaluation and educational plan. In 1990, that legislation was renamed the Individuals with Disabilities Education Act (IDEA) and was expanded to include evaluation and an individualized education plan (IEP) that provides for the specific individual needs of each student. These plans require that the student be educated in the *least restrictive environment*, that is, an educational setting that is as much as possible like that in which students without special needs are receiving their education. Whenever possible, the student should be in an *inclusion* program, which allows for a full-time educational program in the school. With mainstreaming, a student with special needs is educated partially in a regular classroom with modified or supplementary services and partially in a special education classroom; a plan that is often, but not always, the best structure for an IEP.

5   The legislation has had a very positive effect on the services that students with special needs are receiving. Compared with several decades ago, many more students with special needs are receiving educational services. Although there is no consensus on whether inclusion and mainstreaming is better than separate programs for these students, recent research has encouraged services not only for students but also for their families, allowing parents and professional educators to share the evaluation, planning, and structuring of educational services. With this type of approach, special needs professionals partner with the entire family instead of developing a relationship with the student as their only client.

6   Providing education for students with special needs within the public school environment can be difficult or even disruptive for the students without special needs; however, it has been shown that students without special needs can benefit by interacting with students who are different from themselves and struggling with their disabilities.

7   At this writing, 162 countries worldwide have signed the United Nations Convention on the Rights of Persons with Disabilities. [A] The Convention includes Article 24, which stipulates that students with special needs have a right to education without discrimination. [B] The convention follows decades of work by the United Nations to change attitudes about persons with disabilities. [C] Students with special needs are not viewed as charity cases but, rather, as persons with rights. [D]

1. The word broad in the passage is closest in meaning to
   Ⓐ expensive
   Ⓑ general
   Ⓒ adequate
   Ⓓ practical

2. According to paragraph 3, what is the main problem that students face when they have dyslexia?
   Ⓐ They need more support for mathematical reasoning skills to do calculations.
   Ⓑ They require additional help to organize their writing and use grammatical structures.
   Ⓒ They need special reading instruction because of the way that they see print on the page.
   Ⓓ They benefit from instruction to improve their concentration and listening skills.

3. What was the situation for students with special needs before 1975?
   - Ⓐ They were often denied admission to public school programs.
   - Ⓑ They were referred to special schools funded by the government.
   - Ⓒ They were educated at home by a designated family member.
   - Ⓓ They had tutors to supplement their individualized school plan.

4. The IDEA legislation includes all the following EXCEPT
   - Ⓐ a legal basis for inclusion in the public schools
   - Ⓑ an individualized program requirement
   - Ⓒ special equipment for home schooling
   - Ⓓ specifications for evaluation

5. Which of the sentences below best expresses the information in the highlighted statement in the passage? The other choices change the meaning or leave out important information.
   - Ⓐ Fewer students were receiving adequate services twenty years ago.
   - Ⓑ Students had to travel long distances to receive services twenty years ago.
   - Ⓒ Services for students have not improved much in twenty years time.
   - Ⓓ Students have been receiving special services for twenty years.

6. What is the most current view of support programs for students with disabilities?
   - Ⓐ All students should be included in the regular classroom.
   - Ⓑ Parents and professionals should confer and make decisions.
   - Ⓒ Separate individualized instruction is best.
   - Ⓓ Teachers should be trained to help students with disabilities.

7. The word disruptive in the passage refers to
   - Ⓐ finding fault
   - Ⓑ causing confusion
   - Ⓒ taking charge
   - Ⓓ getting lost

8. Four squares (□) indicate where the following sentence can be added to the passage.

   The article further states that they should not be excluded from free and compulsory primary or secondary education in the school systems in their countries.

   Where would the sentence best fit into the passage?
   Ⓐ
   Ⓑ
   Ⓒ
   Ⓓ

9. It can be inferred from the passage that
   - Ⓐ most children with learning disabilities do not have normal intelligence
   - Ⓑ 7 percent of all children in the U.S. have some type of learning disability
   - Ⓒ handicapping conditions are more common than learning disabilities
   - Ⓓ disruptive or hyperactive behavior always accompanies a learning disability

10. Complete a summary of the passage by selecting THREE answer choices that express the most important ideas. The other three sentences do not belong in the summary because they express ideas that are not in the passage or they are minor points that are not as important as the three major ideas. *This question is worth 2 points.*

10 percent of the children in the U.S. receive special education services.

Ⓐ The fact that boys are more active than girls may account for the fact that their teachers refer them more often.

Ⓑ Most students with learning disabilities can graduate from high school when they have an IEP.

Ⓒ By law, students with disabilities must be served in public school settings.

Ⓓ The most recent approach to serving students with disabilities is to involve their families in the services.

Ⓔ Students with learning disabilities score average or above average on intelligence tests.

Ⓕ Most of the students with disabilities in the United States have learning disabilities.

Refer to pages 389–390 for the Explanatory Answers.

EXERCISE 85: Problem/Solution—Natural Sciences

In some questions in the Reading Section on the Internet-Based TOEFL, you will be asked to recall and relate information and content from problem-solution passages found in college textbooks. Choose the best answer for multiple-choice questions.

Resistance to Antibiotics

Paragraph 1   According to an old superstition, a bullet can be charmed to hit only a specific target. Penicillin, discovered in 1928 by Alexander Fleming, and other antibiotics that followed, were viewed by the general public as "magic bullets" because they cured diseases and infections that certainly would have proven fatal, including meningitis and pneumonia. Penicillin was also used to treat bacterial infections and greatly reduced the number of deaths and amputations in the wounded troops during World War II. According to records, only 400 million units of penicillin were available during the first six months in 1943, but, by the end of the war, U.S. pharmaceutical companies had anticipated the demand and were producing 650 billion units a month.

2   Today, more than 100 different antibiotics are available worldwide. They work by blocking the molecules in the cell walls of bacteria, preventing reproduction and growth. The reason that so many varieties of antibiotics were developed is that in any population of bacteria, there are some that are resistant to a specific antibiotic. And for those bacteria, the antibiotic actually allows them to multiply, while the nonresistant bacteria competing with them are eliminated. Thus, when one antibiotic doesn't take care of an infection, a different antibiotic has to be prescribed to eliminate the bacteria that was resistant to the first treatment.

3   The issue is that more and more bacteria have become resistant to antibiotics. By the 1990s, it was clear that resistance was a serious challenge, but developing new antibiotics was expensive, and almost every major drug company was reluctant to make an investment in yet another one with so many already on the market. By then, gene therapy was already on the horizon as the next "magic bullet," and most research and funding were being directed to a process that would replace an unhealthy gene with a healthy one. Also, as compared with drugs used to treat chronic conditions that require medication for decades, antibiotics, which treat short-term infections, do not provide a good return on investment. Of the eighteen largest pharmaceutical companies, fifteen have abandoned antibiotic research and development.

4   In the twenty-first century, serious bacterial infections that are resistant to antibiotics have become a major global health care problem. According to the World Health Organization, by 2050, resistance to antibiotics will be a contributing factor in more than ten million deaths every year, a number that would make it a leading cause of death worldwide, surpassing even cancer.

5   Among the causes for the growth of so-called "superbugs" that resist antibiotics, the over-prescription of antibiotics is at the top of the list. Although antibiotics are still the go-to solution for bacterial infections, too often they are prescribed for viral infections. Overuse encourages resistance. In addition, antibiotics have been used in live-stock and fish farming, thereby increasing their presence in humans who consume these animal products. Moreover, some people don't finish their treatment. If a patient stops taking an antibiotic too soon, all the bacteria may not be destroyed and the remaining bacteria may become resistant.

6   Many strategies have been suggested to stem this global problem. Physicians are already beginning to write fewer prescriptions for antibiotics, monitoring their use for clear cases of bacterial infection. Patients with colds and flu should not take them. This is especially concerning in countries where antibiotics are freely available without a prescription. But more steps need to be taken. First, alternatives to antibiotics must be explored. Researchers are having some success using viruses to kill bacteria, but this therapy is in its infancy. Second, governments must provide incentives for pharmaceutical companies to develop new antibiotics, since market forces do not encourage them to invest. Third, the use of antibiotics in agriculture should be curtailed, using compensation instead of penalties.

7   Finally, global travel can carry infectious diseases around the world. Nearly every case of polio and measles in the United States involves air travel, with an infected person spreading the disease among non-vaccinated travelers. But it is not always human contact that carries the threat of disease—rats or infected mosquitoes are also on board planes and ships. Therefore, for travelers to combat serious health hazards, the best means of personal defense is to make sure that preventive vaccinations are up to date.

1. The word anticipated in the passage is closest in meaning to
   Ⓐ predicted
   Ⓑ concealed
   Ⓒ investigated
   Ⓓ disregarded

2. According to paragraph 2, how do antibiotics treat infections?
   Ⓐ They interfere with the reproductive cycle of bacteria.
   Ⓑ They construct cell walls to resist bacteria.
   Ⓒ They replace the affected cells.
   Ⓓ They increase the number of healthy cells.

3. Which of the sentences below best expresses the information in the highlighted statement in the passage? The other choices change the meaning or leave out important informaiton.
   Ⓐ Some antibiotics will affect a population of bacteria much more efficiently than other varieties.
   Ⓑ There are several reasons why some bacteria do not respond to most antibiotics in the population.
   Ⓒ The effect of antibiotics on bacteria is to bind them together into one population that may not be resistant.
   Ⓓ Different antibiotics are needed because a number of bacteria in any sample will probably be resistant to a specific antibiotic.

4. According to paragraph 4, why do some bacteria benefit from antibiotics?
   - Ⓐ The antibiotic eliminates competing bacteria, allowing resistant bacteria to reproduce.
   - Ⓑ The resistant bacteria compete with the antibiotic, and the bacteria becomes stronger.
   - Ⓒ The competition helps the resistant bacteria to multiply by reproducing with the resistant type.
   - Ⓓ The properties of the antibiotic are acquired by the bacteria, making it resistant to the competition.

5. The word issue in the passage is closest in meaning to
   - Ⓐ problem
   - Ⓑ fact
   - Ⓒ news
   - Ⓓ future

6. The phrase another one in the passage refers to
   - Ⓐ a serious challenge
   - Ⓑ a new antibiotic
   - Ⓒ a major drug company
   - Ⓓ an investment

7. In paragraph 5, the author mentions all of the following reasons for drug-resistant bacteria to appear EXCEPT
   - Ⓐ Antibiotics have been overused for too many people for viral diseases.
   - Ⓑ Some patients fail to complete the full dosage of their antibiotics.
   - Ⓒ Newer antibiotics are not as strong and effective as the original antibiotics.
   - Ⓓ Animals treated with antibiotics increase the amount of antibiotics in humans.

8. According to paragraph 7, why are travelers at risk for infectious diseases?
   - Ⓐ Air travel crowds many people in a small space for extended periods of time.
   - Ⓑ Some travelers have not received the vaccinations they need to protect them.
   - Ⓒ Recently more travelers have been identified with polio and measles.
   - Ⓓ Travelers cannot be treated until they reach their destinations.

9. It can be inferred from the passage that
   - Ⓐ research to develop new antibiotics will not be necessary in the future
   - Ⓑ the scientific community was not surprised by the resistant strains of bacteria
   - Ⓒ antibiotics are not very expensive when they are made available commercially
   - Ⓓ it could take years for a new drug to be made available commercially for consumers

10. Complete a summary of the passage by selecting THREE answer choices that express the most important ideas. The other three sentences do not belong in the summary because they express ideas that are not in the passage or they are minor points that are not as important as the three major ideas. *This question is worth 2 points.*

Many strains of bacteria have become resistant to the antibiotics currently available.

Ⓐ Antibiotics have been ineffective because they were prescribed too often, consumed in animal products, and not taken as prescribed.

Ⓑ Resistance to antibiotics has contributed to the death of more than ten million people per year worldwide.

Ⓒ Alternatives to antibiotics, incentives to develop new antibiotics, and compensation to discontinue antibiotics in agriculture should be explored.

Ⓓ Some bacteria can be treated with only one type of antibiotic because it is resistant to all other varieties.

Ⓔ The best way to protect yourself from serious diseases that might require antibiotics is to keep your vaccinations current.

Ⓕ Penicillin, which was the first antibiotic, was very effective in curing bacterial infections from diseases and wounds.

Refer to page 390 for the Explanatory Answers.

PRACTICE EXERCISES
FOR WRITING

———————————————————————

Writing Section

The Writing Section of the TOEFL tests your ability to write in English on a variety of general and academic topics. This section is included in the Institutional TOEFL as an optional test.

Overview of the TOEFL® ITP Writing Section

The Writing Section on the Institutional TOEFL is optional. When it is offered, it tests your ability to write an essay in English on a general topic. You can use your personal experience and general knowledge to write your essay. Usually, you must plan, write, and edit the essay in 30 minutes. Typically, a good essay for the Writing Section will require that you write 300–350 words. The score is calculated separately from the total score on the TOEFL® ITP.

Overview of the TOEFL iBT® Writing Section

The Writing Section tests your ability to write essays in English similar to those that you would write in college courses. During the test, you will write two essays.

The Integrated Essay. First you will read an academic passage, and then you will listen to a lecture on the same topic. You may take notes as you read and listen, but notes are not graded. You may use your notes to write the essay. The reading passage will disappear while you are listening to the lecture, but the passage will return to the screen for reference when you begin to write your essay. You will have 20 minutes to plan, write, and revise your response. Typically, a good essay for the integrated topic will require that you write 150–225 words.

The Independent Essay. You will read a question on the screen. It usually asks for your opinion about a familiar topic. You will have 30 minutes to plan, write, and revise your response. Typically, a good essay for the independent topic will require that you write 300–350 words.

A clock on the screen will show you how much time you have left to complete each essay.

EXERCISE 86: Independent Essay—Agree or Disagree

In some essays in the Writing Section on the Institutional TOEFL or the Internet-Based TOEFL, you will be asked to agree or disagree with a statement. First, spend 5 minutes thinking about the topic and making notes. Based on your notes, write an essay of 300–350 words. Complete it in 20 minutes. Then, use the last 5 minutes to read your essay and make corrections.

Topic One

Do you agree or disagree with the following statement? Smoking should not be permitted in restaurants, and laws that prohibit it should be upheld. Use specific reasons and examples to support your opinion. Type your essay on a computer.

Notes

Use this space for essay notes only. Work done on this work sheet will *not* be scored.

Refer to page 392 for the Example Answer.

Topic Two

Do you agree or disagree with the following statement? All college students should be required to take classes outside of their major fields of study. Use specific reasons and examples to support your opinion. Type your essay on a computer.

Notes

Use this space for essay notes only. Work done on this work sheet will *not* be scored.

_____

_____

_____

_____

_____

_____

_____

_____

_____

_____

_____

_____

_____

_____

_____

_____

_____

_____

_____

_____

_____

_____

_____

_____

_____

Refer to pages 392–393 for the Example Answer.

EXERCISE 87: Independent Essay—Agree or Disagree

In some essays in the Writing Section on the Institutional TOEFL or the Internet-Based TOEFL, you will be asked to agree or disagree with a statement. First, spend 5 minutes thinking about the topic and making notes. Based on your notes, write an essay of 300–350 words. Complete it in 20 minutes. Then, use the last 5 minutes to read your essay and make corrections.

Topic One

Do you agree or disagree with the following statement? Retirement at age 65 should be mandatory. Use specific reasons and examples to support your opinion. Type your essay on a computer.

_____

Notes

Use this space for essay notes only. Work done on this work sheet will *not* be scored.

_____
_____
_____
_____
_____
_____
_____
_____
_____
_____
_____
_____
_____
_____
_____
_____
_____
_____
_____
_____
_____
_____

Refer to pages 393–394 for the Example Answer.

Topic Two

Do you agree or disagree with the following statement? Most celebrities are not good role models for young people. Use specific reasons and examples to support your opinion. Type your essay on a computer.

Notes

Use this space for essay notes only. Work done on this work sheet will *not* be scored.

_____

_____

_____

_____

_____

_____

_____

_____

_____

_____

_____

_____

_____

_____

_____

_____

_____

_____

_____

_____

_____

_____

_____

_____

_____

_____

Refer to pages 394–395 for the Example Answer.

EXERCISE 88: Independent Essay—Agree or Disagree

In some essays in the Writing Section on the Institutional TOEFL or the Internet-Based TOEFL, you will be asked to agree or disagree with a statement. First, spend 5 minutes thinking about the topic and making notes. Based on your notes, write an essay of 300–350 words. Complete it in 20 minutes. Then, use the last 5 minutes to read your essay and make corrections.

Topic One

Do you agree or disagree with the following statement? Social media sites offer a good way to meet people and make friends. Type your essay on a computer.

Notes

Use this space for essay notes only. Work done on this work sheet will *not* be scored.

Refer to page 395 for the Example Answer.

Topic Two

Do you agree or disagree with the following saying? "If at first you don't succeed, try, try again" means to continue working toward a goal in spite of difficulties. Use specific reasons and examples to support your opinion. Type your essay on a computer.

Notes

Use this space for essay notes only. Work done on this work sheet will *not* be scored.

_____

_____

_____

_____

_____

_____

_____

_____

_____

_____

_____

_____

_____

_____

_____

_____

_____

_____

_____

_____

_____

_____

_____

_____

_____

_____

_____

Refer to page 396 for the Example Answer.

EXERCISE 89: Independent Essay—Point of View

In some essays in the Writing Section on the Institutional TOEFL or the Internet-Based TOEFL, you will be asked to choose between two viewpoints and argue your point of view. First, spend 5 minutes thinking about the topic and making notes. Based on your notes, write an essay of 300–350 words. Complete it in 20 minutes. Then, use the last 5 minutes to read your essay and make corrections.

Topic One

Some international students choose American roommates. Others choose roommates from their own countries. Compare the advantages of having an American roommate with the advantages of having a roommate from your country. Which kind of roommate would you prefer? Why? Use specific reasons and examples to support your opinion. Type your essay on a computer.

Notes

Use this space for essay notes only. Work done on this work sheet will *not* be scored.

_____
_____
_____
_____
_____
_____
_____
_____
_____
_____
_____
_____
_____
_____
_____
_____
_____
_____
_____
_____
_____
_____
_____

Refer to pages 396–397 for the Example Answer.

Topic Two

Some people want to attend a small college. Other people think that it is better to attend a large university. Which type of school do you prefer? Why? Use specific reasons and examples to support your opinion. Type your essay on a computer.

Notes

Use this space for essay notes only. Work done on this work sheet will *not* be scored.

_____

_____

_____

_____

_____

_____

_____

_____

_____

_____

_____

_____

_____

_____

_____

_____

_____

_____

_____

_____

_____

_____

_____

_____

Refer to pages 397–398 for the Example Answer.

EXERCISE 90: Independent Essay—Point of View

In some essays in the Writing Section on the Institutional TOEFL or the Internet-Based TOEFL, you will be asked to choose between two viewpoints and argue your point of view. First, spend 5 minutes thinking about the topic and making notes. Based on your notes, write an essay of 300–350 words. Complete it in 20 minutes. Then, use the last 5 minutes to read your essay and make corrections.

Topic One

Some parents reward their children for good grades by giving them money or gifts. Other parents expect their children to earn good grades without additional incentives. What is your opinion, and why? Use specific reasons and examples to support your opinion. Type your essay on a computer.

Notes

Use this space for essay notes only. Work done on this work sheet will **not** be scored.

Refer to pages 398–399 for the Example Answer.

Topic Two

Some students in the United States work while they are earning their degrees. Others receive support from their families. Which arrangement do you agree with? Why? Use specific reasons and examples to support your opinion. Type your essay on a computer.

Notes

Use this space for essay notes only. Work done on this work sheet will *not* be scored.

Refer to pages 399–400 for the Example Answer.

Exercise 91: Integrated Essay—Academic Debate

In some essays in the Writing Section on the Internet-Based TOEFL, you will be asked to respond to a question from both a reading passage and a lecture. Most of the time, the lecture presents an opposing view. First, spend 3 minutes reading the passage. Next, listen to the lecture and take notes. Finally, write an essay of 150–225 words, based on your lecture notes and the passage. Try to complete it in 15 minutes. Use the last 5 minutes to read your essay and make corrections.

Textbook Passage

The Inca civilization and other pre-Columbian people were well-known for their exquisite decorative objects made of gold. Most of them are easily recognizable as gods or forms inspired by nature, but some sculptures are more puzzling. Among the most fascinating are a number of gold figures that look very much like jet airplanes, complete with the kind of swept wings usually reserved for supersonic flight, stabilizing tails, and landing gear. They have been found in various locations, including many coastal regions of South America. Although gold is more difficult to date than many other materials, at the Gold Museum in Bogota, Colombia, where they currently reside, anthropologists believe that these artifacts date from around 800 to 500 B.C.E.

So are they airplanes or just decorative sculptures? Three convincing arguments have been made to support the ancient airplane hypothesis. First, artists from the pre-Columbian cultures who made other objects found in similar locations and dated from about the same time were careful to render them with great accuracy and in realistic detail. Clearly, they created art from the visible world around them.

Perhaps even more persuasive is the experiment carried out in 1997 by two German researchers. They put the design to the ultimate test in a live demonstration in Florida. They created an exact model fitted with a jet engine and proved that the designs were so aerodynamic that the models could take off, fly, and land perfectly.

Finally, almost every ancient culture includes flying objects in its mythology, including the pre-Columbians of South America. A logical conclusion is that the gold objects are artists' representations of airplanes from a very advanced civilization that made contact with them in ancient times.

Lecture

🎧 **(Track 41)**

Now listen to a professor's response to the textbook passage.

Notes

Use this space for lecture notes only. Work done on this work sheet will *not* be scored.

_____

_____

_____

_____

_____

_____

_____

_____

_____

_____

_____

_____

_____

_____

_____

_____

_____

_____

_____

_____

_____

_____

_____

Writing Question:

Summarize the main points presented in the lecture, and explain how they cast doubt on specific information in the reading passage. You have 20 minutes to write 150–225 words. Type your essay on a computer.

Refer to page 402 for the Example Answer.

EXERCISE 92: Integrated Essay—Academic Debate

In some essays in the Writing Section on the Internet-Based TOEFL, you will be asked to respond to a question from both a reading passage and a lecture. Most of the time, the lecture presents an opposing view. First, spend 3 minutes reading the passage. Next, listen to the lecture and take notes. Finally, write an essay of 150–225 words, based on your lecture notes and the passage. Try to complete it in 15 minutes. Use the last 5 minutes to read your essay and make corrections.

Textbook Passage

Solar energy has many advantages. First, and perhaps the most obvious, is that it is renewable and sustainable. Unlike oil reserves, which will probably be consumed in about another forty years, the potential for solar energy is so abundant that we can almost never run out. Solar energy will be available as long as the Sun shines, which, according to NASA, should be about another six-and-a-half billion years. In addition, it is sustainable, which means that we can use it to meet our needs for energy in the present without compromising the resources of future generations. In other words, we can use solar energy without causing long-term damage to the energy source.

Second, solar energy is environmentally friendly. It is relatively free of pollution and does not emit any greenhouse gases. No smoke, gas, or chemical by-products occur during solar power production or use. Furthermore, most applications are quiet compared with other types of energy that rely on moving parts, which means that even noise pollution is avoided.

Third, solar energy is readily available and relatively cheap. The fact that everyone has equal access to the Sun means that power can be made available in remote areas where the population has not been able to purchase dependable electrical power. It also means that all nations have the potential for solar energy resources, without relying on other nations to provide natural resources that may not be available within their borders. Solar panels are simple to manufacture, and once solar power is made available, it requires a significantly lower operational cost.

Lecture

🎧 **(Track 42)**

Now listen to a professor's response to the textbook passage.

Notes

Use this space for lecture notes only. Work done on this work sheet will *not* be scored.

Writing Question:

Summarize the main points presented in the lecture, and explain how they cast doubt on specific information in the reading passage. You have 20 minutes to write 150–225 words. Type your essay on a computer.

Refer to page 403 for the Example Answer.

EXERCISE 93: Integrated Essay—Academic Debate

In some essays in the Writing Section on the Internet-Based TOEFL, you will be asked to respond to a question from both a reading passage and a lecture. Most of the time, the lecture presents an opposing view. First, spend 3 minutes reading the passage. Next, listen to the lecture and take notes. Finally, write an essay of 150–225 words, based on your lecture notes and the passage. Try to complete it in 15 minutes. Use the last 5 minutes to read your essay and make corrections.

Textbook Passage

Everyone agrees that Pacific salmon are not only an ecological resource but also an economic resource. These extraordinary fish transverse the coastal waters from California to Alaska during the migration period critical to their breeding season. The problem is that natural habitats for wild salmon have disappeared or degraded, and, consequently, wild salmon populations have been considerably reduced, and many of those that survive are being injured as they pass through the dams along the Columbia and Snake rivers; therefore, a plan that will protect them is essential.

The plan that is being proposed includes three key points. First, federal guidelines will prevent harvesting wild salmon during critical times until the endangered populations have recovered significantly. Every spring, surveys will be made of designated areas to determine a catch quota to prevent overfishing.

Second, international salmon protected areas (SPAs) will be identified along the Pacific basin, including the river sub-basins in Washington and Oregon. With a view to conserving salmon and encouraging reproduction, scientists from Russia, Canada, Japan, and the United States will manage these important SPAs. Since the land and the sub-basins belong to local, state, and federal government agencies, as well as to private individuals, the effort is complex and, consequently, protracted. It is further complicated because a number of the essential habitats cross international borders. Nevertheless, managed sanctuaries remain a key part of the plan.

Third, where populations are found to be dangerously low, natural stocks will be supplemented with hatchlings grown in fish hatcheries. In some countries, wild salmon populations are transferred to and raised in hatcheries, but for now, the plan is to release the hatchlings from the hatcheries back into the natural habitat. Of course, each area is slightly different because of the related issues of local energy sources, residential development, agriculture, and transportation, but these three interventions should allow reasonable levels of fishing to continue while stocks are being reconstituted.

Lecture

🎧 **(Track 43)**

Now listen to a professor's response to the textbook passage.

Notes

Use this space for lecture notes only. Work done on this work sheet will *not* be scored.

_____
_____
_____
_____
_____
_____
_____
_____
_____
_____
_____
_____
_____
_____
_____
_____
_____
_____
_____
_____
_____
_____

Writing Question:

Summarize the main points presented in the lecture, and explain how they cast doubt on specific information in the reading passage. You have 20 minutes to write 150–225 words. Type your essay on a computer.

Refer to pages 404–405 for the Example Answer.

EXERCISE 94: Integrated Essay—Academic Debate

In some essays in the Writing Section on the Internet-Based TOEFL, you will be asked to respond to a question from both a reading passage and a lecture. Most of the time, the lecture presents an opposing view. First, spend 3 minutes reading the passage. Next, listen to the lecture and take notes. Finally, write an essay of 150–225 words, based on your lecture notes and the passage. Try to complete it in 15 minutes. Use the last 5 minutes to read your essay and make corrections.

Textbook Passage

The Industrial Revolution produced more than machine-made products. It also created social problems, including unhealthy living standards, harsh working conditions, and increased environmental pollution. As unskilled rural workers migrated to cities, they crowded into ghettos, often living in cramped rooms without running water and sanitation. Disease accounted for many deaths in industrial urban areas. Cholera, smallpox, typhoid, and tuberculosis spread quickly in the overcrowded tenements among people whose water supplies were contaminated by sewage.

Child labor, long hours, and unsafe labor practices all contributed to the harsh working conditions. For the first time, women were recruited in the workplace, although they were paid wages considerably lower than their male counterparts. Children were given dangerous jobs. Because of their small size, younger workers were often assigned to crawl into machines to clean or repair them. Accidents commonly occurred in the workplace. A twelve-hour workday was the norm, and wages were so low that subsistence was barely achievable for factory workers, even when many family members contributed to their mutual survival.

Mass production led to the depletion of natural resources, which caused permanent environmental damage. The most obvious was deforestation, which led to the additional destruction of the habitats for wildlife in the surrounding area. The environmental contamination that resulted from factories included air, land, and water pollution, some of which is still being dealt with today.

Lecture

🎧 **(Track 44)**

Now listen to a professor's response to the textbook passage.

Notes

Use this space for lecture notes only. Work done on this work sheet will *not* be scored.

_____

_____

_____

_____

_____

_____

_____

_____

_____

_____

_____

_____

_____

_____

_____

_____

_____

_____

_____

_____

_____

_____

Writing Question:

Summarize the main points presented in the lecture, and explain how they cast doubt on specific information in the reading passage. You have 20 minutes to write 150–225 words. Type your essay on a computer.

Refer to pages 405–406 for the Example Answer.

EXERCISE 95: Integrated Essay—Academic Debate

In some essays in the Writing Section on the Internet-Based TOEFL, you will be asked to respond to a question from both a reading passage and a lecture. Most of the time, the lecture presents an opposing view. First, spend 3 minutes reading the passage. Next, listen to the lecture and take notes. Finally, write an essay of 150–225 words, based on your lecture notes and the passage. Try to complete it in 15 minutes. Use the last 5 minutes to read your essay and make corrections.

Textbook Passage

Unlike traditional school years, year-round school calendars eliminate the summer break, inserting several shorter breaks throughout the year. Several reasons to consider year-round schooling have been cited, including continuity, efficiency, and social issues. Proponents of year-round school calendars claim that, during the long summer break, many students forget what they have learned the prior year. In order to review the material, teachers spend the first month of school reinforcing previously learned concepts instead of introducing new concepts. According to the National Education Association, shorter breaks also improve retention rates.

More efficient use of school facilities has been a strong reason for year-round schools. When students are on long summer and holiday breaks, school facilities are not in use. Year-round calendars keep schools open at all times by instituting a multitrack calendar, staggering student breaks so that some classes are always in session throughout the year. Buildings are never empty, and other physical facilities like buses are in constant use.

Several social issues also support a year-round calendar. Perhaps the most pressing is that of child care. Most school-age children are from homes in which both parents work. Child care during the summer can present a number of problems for families. In addition to the concern about finding safe, dependable caregiving, for most families, the cost can be a significant burden. Especially for single-parent households, year-round school would be a good solution.

Lecture

🎧 **(Track 45)**

Now listen to a professor's response to the textbook passage.

Notes

Use this space for lecture notes only. Work done on this work sheet will *not* be scored.

_____
_____
_____
_____
_____
_____
_____
_____
_____
_____
_____
_____
_____
_____
_____
_____
_____
_____
_____
_____
_____
_____
_____

Writing Question:

Summarize the main points presented in the lecture, and explain how they cast doubt on specific information in the reading passage. You have 20 minutes to write 150–225 words. Type your essay on a computer.

Refer to pages 406–407 for the Example Answer.

EXERCISE 96: Integrated Essay—Academic Debate

In some essays in the Writing Section on the Internet-Based TOEFL, you will be asked to respond to a question from both a reading passage and a lecture. Most of the time, the lecture presents an opposing view. First, spend 3 minutes reading the passage. Next, listen to the lecture and take notes. Finally, write an essay of 150–225 words, based on your lecture notes and the passage. Try to complete it in 15 minutes. Use the last 5 minutes to read your essay and make corrections.

Textbook Passage

More than four hundred years after his death, the controversy continues surrounding the authorship of works attributed to William Shakespeare from Stratford-upon-Avon. At the heart of the issue are his background and the circumstances surrounding his death.

First, we know that William Shakespeare was very poorly educated and of common birth. His father was unable to write his own name, his wife and daughters were illiterate, and there is no evidence that Shakespeare ever attended a university, although it has been assumed that he was probably a grammar student in the King's New School for at least a short time. In addition, the man from Stratford spelled his name in a variety of ways, which may also point to a lower level of literacy than would be expected for a writer who demonstrated such a wide knowledge of the classics. In contrast, the works attributed to Shakespeare are clearly written by a man of impeccable education and probably noble background. In addition to the scholarly allusions in the works and references to exotic places that would suggest an author who had traveled widely, intimate familiarity with the Elizabethan and Jacobean courts is also evident, demonstrating knowledge that would be known only by an insider of high rank. However, there is no evidence that Shakespeare from Stratford-upon-Avon was well read or traveled, and he had certainly not been accepted into the royal court.

Second, Shakespeare's death in 1616 casts doubt on his authorship. It is well documented that Shakespeare amassed a substantial estate as a tradesman. Consequently, his will is very long and detailed, listing the possessions that one might expect of a successful trader and large landowner; however, no mention is made of books. If he were self-educated, then a large, private library should have been listed. In addition, no personal papers were included in the inventory, and the manuscripts of eighteen plays that remained unpublished at the time of his death were not mentioned either. Furthermore, when Shakespeare died, none of his contemporary authors paid tribute to him, as was the custom. If he had been such a successful author, surely his peers would have recognized his passing.

Lecture

(Track 46)

Now listen to a professor's response to the textbook passage.

Notes

Use this space for lecture notes only. Work done on this work sheet will *not* be scored.

Writing Question:

    Summarize the main points presented in the lecture, and explain how they cast doubt on specific information in the reading passage. You have 20 minutes to write 150–225 words. Type your essay on a computer.

Refer to pages 407–408 for the Example Answer.

EXERCISE 97: Integrated Essay—Academic Debate

In some essays in the Writing Section on the Internet-Based TOEFL, you will be asked to respond to a question from both a reading passage and a lecture. Most of the time, the lecture presents an opposing view. First, spend 3 minutes reading the passage. Next, listen to the lecture and take notes. Finally, write an essay of 150–225 words, based on your lecture notes and the passage. Try to complete it in 15 minutes. Use the last 5 minutes to read your essay and make corrections.

Textbook Passage

Animal studies are an unfortunate practice in which thousands of helpless creatures are injured and abused without any direct benefit to medical science. For years, mice have been the foundation of basic scientific research into human diseases, but forty years after the first cancer studies were designed and carried out in animal laboratory settings, scientists are still not even close to providing a human remedy. Much of the animal research in other areas such as Alzheimer's, diabetes, and spinal cord injury has not translated into either a prevention or a cure for human patients.

Besides the fact that the studies do not actually result in major advances in medicine, another reason to cease this useless practice is that the studies are simply unreliable. Animals are not the best research subjects because their genetic compositions, anatomies, and metabolisms are quite different from those of human beings. Therefore, we must assume that the reaction of drugs in their bodies will also be different. In fact, many drugs that pass animal tests fail in human tests.

Finally, animal testing is archaic. Many new scientific methods—including sophisticated computer modeling and cell cultures—are cheaper, faster, and more accurate. The computer models can now reconstruct human molecular structures and perform tests that predict the effects of substances without invasive experiments. Studying cell cultures in petri dishes can produce better results than animal testing because human cells can be used.

Lecture

(Track 47)

Now listen to a professor's response to the textbook passage.

Notes

Use this space for lecture notes only. Work done on this work sheet will *not* be scored.

_____
_____
_____
_____
_____
_____
_____
_____
_____
_____
_____
_____
_____
_____
_____
_____
_____
_____
_____
_____
_____
_____
_____
_____

Writing Question:

Summarize the main points presented in the lecture, and explain how they cast doubt on specific information in the reading passage. You have 20 minutes to write 150–225 words. Type your essay on a computer.

Refer to pages 408–409 for the Example Answer.

EXERCISE 98: Integrated Essay—Academic Debate

In some essays in the Writing Section on the Internet-Based TOEFL, you will be asked to respond to a question from both a reading passage and a lecture. Most of the time, the lecture presents an opposing view. First, spend 3 minutes reading the passage. Next, listen to the lecture and take notes. Finally, write an essay of 150–225 words, based on your lecture notes and the passage. Try to complete it in 15 minutes. Use the last 5 minutes to read your essay and make corrections.

Textbook Passage

Genetically modified organisms (GMOs) allow engineers to design and grow plants that exhibit improved characteristics; however, disinformation about the safety of GMO crops has caused an ongoing debate about whether they should be made available. Several dozen countries have banned the production and sale of GM plants—mostly fruit and vegetables—in spite of the overwhelming evidence that they are not only safe but even beneficial to those who eat them.

In more than thirty years since GMOs have been available in food for human consumption, thousands of studies globally have confirmed the safety of GM ingredients. In fact, some crops have been engineered to provide healthy alternatives for people with allergies. For example, there is now a peanut variety that has been engineered to prevent the allergic and often fatal reaction by people with peanut allergies.

Since genetic engineering can increase the output of various vital food crops around the world by as much as 30 percent, GMO crops can contribute to the health of people in areas where famine is a serious cause of malnutrition and even starvation. Some crops engineered for better absorption and retention of water can withstand serious droughts. Increased yields in these areas would provide more food at lower prices for hundreds of millions of critically malnourished people.

Besides the increased availability of crops, some varieties have been specifically engineered to combat disabling or deadly diseases. For example, in Australia and New Zealand, a GMO variety of rice with high levels of beta-carotene is being engineered with a view to improving chronic vitamin A deficiencies among children in areas of extreme poverty. Known as "golden rice," this GMO crop could save them from suffering blindness by boosting their vitamin A intake.

Lecture

(Track 48)

Now listen to a professor's response to the textbook passage.

Notes

Use this space for essay notes only. Work done on this work sheet will *not* be scored.

Writing Question:

Summarize the main points in the lecture, and explain how they cast doubt on specific information in the reading passage. You have 20 minutes to write 150–225 words. Type your essay on a computer.

Refer to pages 409–410 for the Example Answer.

EXERCISE 99: Integrated Essay—Academic Debate

In some essays in the Writing Section on the Internet-Based TOEFL, you will be asked to respond to a question from both a reading passage and a lecture. Most of the time, the lecture presents an opposing view. First, spend 3 minutes reading the passage. Next, listen to the lecture and take notes. Finally, write an essay of 150–225 words, based on your lecture notes and the passage. Try to complete it in 15 minutes. Use the last 5 minutes to read your essay and make corrections.

Textbook Passage

A large number of studies have been completed over the past decade to determine whether cell phones pose a potential health risk, but to date, there is no credible evidence of adverse health effects directly caused by cell phone use. Many studies have failed to find biological effects, and others claiming them have not confirmed their findings with additional research. Of 17 studies on cell phone use and brain cancer, only two have suggested an association, and those studies had relatively weak methodologies.

One study with rats has been often cited and has caused disproportionate concern; however, animal studies should not be used to draw conclusions about human cell phone usage. In the first place, an animal's exposure to radiofrequency would be different from a human subject holding a cell phone. Moreover, the anatomy of a rat, for example, is so different from that of humans that the results are simply not relevant. Ultimately, an animal's predisposition to certain cancers compared with the statistical probability for the same type of cancer occurring in human beings is difficult to control for in these types of research studies.

The assertion that cell phones cause brain tumors is not supported by statistical data. If there were a higher risk of brain tumors among cell phone users, then an increase in general cell phone usage over a certain time period should correlate with a similar increase in the number of brain tumors. Although brain tumors have increased over the past few decades, a direct correlation has not been shown. In fact, researchers have suggested that any increase in brain tumors is probably a result of an improvement in the technology used to screen and diagnose them rather than a consequence of cell phone use.

Lecture

🎧 **(Track 49)**

Now listen to a professor's response to the textbook passage.

Notes

Use this space for essay notes only. Work done on this work sheet will *not* be scored.

Writing Question:

    Summarize the main points in the lecture, and explain how they cast doubt on specific information in the reading passage. You have 20 minutes to write 150–225 words. Type your essay on a computer.

Refer to pages 411–412 for the Example Answer.

Exercise 100: Integrated Essay—Academic Debate

In some essays in the Writing Section on the Internet-Based TOEFL, you will be asked to respond to a question from both a reading passage and a lecture. Most of the time, the lecture presents an opposing view. First, spend 3 minutes reading the passage. Next, listen to the lecture and take notes. Finally, write an essay of 150–225 words, based on your lecture notes and the passage. Try to complete it in 15 minutes. Use the last 5 minutes to read your essay and make corrections.

Textbook Passage

While it is true that too much homework can actually have a negative effect on students, research is overwhelmingly in favor of continuing the practice of assigning homework to students. The studies indicate that homework improves student achievement as measured by classroom grades and test scores. A comprehensive investigation by Duke University professor Harris Cooper, in which he reviewed more than 60 research studies, concluded that the average student who did homework had a higher unit test score than the students who were not assigned homework. In addition, homework has a positive correlation with standardized test results. Research published in the *High School Journal* reported that students who spent between 30 and 90 minutes every day completing homework assignments were likely to score 40 points higher on the SAT Math test than students who did not complete homework assignments.

Homework also supports the development of life skills and study skills that will be helpful not only in the context of school but also on jobs and in leading successful lives after graduation. Some of these skills include goal setting and time management as well as self-discipline and accountability. Being responsible for a homework assignment or out-of-school project requires planning and commitment in order to meet deadlines, all of which supports success in life as an adult. Furthermore, formal studies and informal tabulations by school districts demonstrate that students who complete homework assignments are more likely to attend college and do better once they are admitted.

There is an abundance of evidence that parent involvement improves school achievement, and homework is a positive link between the school and the home. The research overwhelmingly supports it, citing help with homework assignments, reading together, or tutoring by a parent or other home caregiver as resulting in impressive results. Furthermore, the earlier that parent involvement begins, the greater the probability of higher achievement in school and after school.

In conclusion, the benefits of homework are well documented, along with the "ten-minute rule"— that is ten minutes of homework per day for each grade level. A first-grader might be expected to spend ten minutes on homework every day, whereas a sixth grader might have an hour of homework to do. This is actually much less homework than is required in many nations throughout the world but is the current standard in the United States.

Lecture

(Track 50)

Now listen to a professor's response to the textbook passage.

Notes

Use this space for essay notes only. Work done on this work sheet will *not* be scored.

_____

_____

_____

_____

_____

_____

_____

_____

_____

_____

_____

_____

_____

_____

_____

_____

_____

_____

_____

_____

_____

_____

_____

Writing Question:

Summarize the main points in the lecture, and explain how they cast doubt on specific information in the reading passage. You have 20 minutes to write 150–225 words. Type your essay on a computer.

Refer to pages 412–413 for the Example Answer.

7

EXPLANATORY ANSWERS AND AUDIO SCRIPTS FOR TOEFL PRACTICE EXERCISES

Listening

EXERCISE 1: Short Conversations—Topics

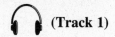 (Track 1)

Audio

1. Woman: The professor drilled and drilled until I couldn't stand it.
   Man: I heard he assigned a whole lot of exercises without explaining any of the grammar rules, too. I'm glad I went to the gym.
   Third Voice: What are the man and woman talking about?

Answer

(B) From the references to the *professor*, *assignments*, and *grammar rules*, it must be concluded that they are talking about a class. Choice (A) refers to the place the man went instead of to class. Choices (C) and (D) are not mentioned and may not be concluded from information in the conversation.

Audio

2. Man: They sell gas by the gallon here.
   Woman: Yes, and I see that the bulk food in the grocery store is sold in pounds and ounces.
   Third Voice: What are these two people most probably discussing?

Answer

(C) From the reference to *gallons*, *pounds*, and *ounces*, it must be concluded that the two people are talking about weights and measures. Choices (A), (B), and (D) are mentioned in reference to the main topic of discussion, "the English system of measurement."

Audio

3. Woman: You should have your mail held at the post office until you get back.
   Man: Good idea. I remembered to get the newspaper stopped, but I'd forgotten about that.
   Third Voice: What are these two people talking about?

Answer

(A) Since the man will be *gone*, it must be concluded that he is going on a trip. Choices (B), (C), and (D) are mentioned in reference to the main topic of discussion, "the man's vacation."

Audio

4. Man: Do you know how many students were accepted in the new doctoral program?
   Woman: Well, I saw Mary at the party last night, and she said that only six got in.
   Third Voice: What are the two people discussing?

Answer

(D) Since they are talking about the *new doctoral program*, it must be concluded that they are discussing a graduate program. Choices (B) and (C) are mentioned in reference to the main topic of discussion, "acceptance in the new doctoral program." Choice (A) is not mentioned and may not be concluded from information in the conversation.

Audio

5. Man: I applied for the exchange program to Europe this year, but I couldn't go because I got sick.
   Woman: That's too bad. Nancy went to England last year, and she said it was really a great experience.
   Third Voice: What are the man and woman discussing?

Answer

(A) Since they are talking about the man's *application* for an *exchange program* to Europe, it must be concluded that they are discussing the exchange program. The place in choice (B) refers to Nancy's trip, not to the man's trip. Choice (C) is the reason that the man could not go on the exchange program, not the topic of conversation. Choice (D) refers to the friend who went on the exchange program last year.

Audio

  6. Man: The chairs in that lecture room are really uncomfortable.

     Woman: You said it. They're so small that my children wouldn't even fit in them.

     Third Voice: What are the man and woman talking about?

Answer

(C) "The chairs in that lecture room are really uncomfortable." Choice (B) is mentioned in reference to the main topic of discussion, "the chairs." Choices (A) and (D) are not mentioned and may not be concluded from information in the conversation.

Audio

  7. Woman: I've had it with my computer. I lost another paper when I tried to save it on a disk.

     Man: You have to do something about that. Why don't you try over at Computer World?

     Third Voice: What are the two people discussing?

Answer

(A) Since the woman mentions a *problem* with her *computer*, and the man offers a suggestion, it must be concluded that they are discussing the woman's computer. Choice (B) is mentioned in reference to the main topic of discussion, "the computer." Choices (C) and (D) are not mentioned and may not be concluded from information in the conversation.

Audio

  8. Woman: I was late for class because I couldn't find a parking space.

     Man: It's because of registration week. I drove around for almost half an hour before I found one this morning.

     Third Voice: What are the two people talking about?

Answer

(C) From the references to *parking space* and *driving around to find one* [a parking space], it must be concluded that they are talking about the parking situation. Choices (A), (B), and (D) are mentioned in reference to the main topic of discussion, the "parking situation."

Audio

  9. Man: I really like Dr. Smith, but I can't say as much for her T.A.

     Woman: Sally? Oh, she's okay as long as you go to class and get the lab reports in on time.

     Third Voice: What are the man and woman discussing?

Answer

(D) A *T.A.* is a teaching assistant. Choices (A), (B), and (C) are mentioned in reference to the main topic of discussion, "the T.A., Sally."

Audio

10. Man: I used to bring my lunch to school when I was working in the Chemistry Department, but now that I'm a full-time student, I just eat at the Snack Bar.

     Woman: Me, too. It's too hard trying to get everyone ready in the morning at my house.

     Third Voice: What are the man and woman talking about?

Answer

(D) From the references to *bringing lunch to school* and eating *at the Snack Bar*, it must be concluded that they are talking about having lunch on campus. Choices (A), (B), and (C) are mentioned in reference to the main topic of discussion, "lunch on campus."

EXERCISE 2: Short Conversations—Details

 (Track 2)

Audio

1. Woman: You look awful. Do you have a hangover?

   Man: No. I've been up all night finishing a paper. All I've had to drink is coffee.

   Third Voice: What is the man's problem?

Answer

(A) "I've been up all night finishing a paper." Choice (B) is not correct because all the man has had to drink is coffee. Choice (D) is not correct because the man has finished the paper. Choice (C) is not mentioned and may not be concluded from information in the conversation.

Audio

2. Woman: Can I use my credit card to pay my fees, or do I have to give you a check?

   Man: Your card is fine as long as your credit approval goes through.

   Third Voice: How does the woman want to pay?

Answer

(B) "Can I use my credit card . . . ?" Choice (A) refers to the alternative that the woman suggests, not to her preference. Choices (C) and (D) are not mentioned and may not be concluded from information in the conversation.

Audio

3. Woman: No wonder Sharon won't see you. She probably thought that such an expensive gift was inappropriate on such short acquaintance.

   Man: It certainly is different here. In my country, men are supposed to show women that they care for them by giving them jewelry.

   Third Voice: Why did Sharon stop seeing the man?

Answer

(C) "She probably thought that such an expensive gift was inappropriate on such short acquaintance." The word *short* in Choice (A) refers to the acquaintance, not to the man. Choice (B) is true, but it is not the reason Sharon stopped seeing the man. Choice (D) is not correct because the man gave Sharon an expensive gift.

Audio

4. Woman: Why do you need to check my purse? Do you think I stole something?

   Man: Not at all. This is a standard security procedure.

   Third Voice: Why did the man look through the woman's purse?

Answer

(C) "This is a standard security procedure." Choice (A) is not correct because the man denied that he suspected the woman of theft. The word *secure* in Choice (B) and the word *standard* in Choice (D) refer to a standard security procedure, not to securing a purse or to a standard size.

Audio

5. Woman: I lost my notebook. Could I borrow yours before the test?

   Man: I'm sorry. I'd like to help you, but I just can't. I have to take it with me to work so I can study on my breaks.

   Third Voice: What does the woman want the man to do?

Answer

(D) "Could I borrow yours [your notebook] before the test?" The word *study* in Choice (A) refers to the man's plan to study, not to the woman's request. The word *break* in Choice (C) refers to the man's breaks at work, not to the woman's request. Choice (B) is not mentioned and may not be concluded from information in the conversation.

Audio

6. Woman: That looks like Steve's car, but who is that girl driving it?

    Man: Oh, that's Steve's sister. I met her last night at Mary Anne's party.

    Third Voice: Who is driving Steve's car?

Answer

(B) "Oh, that's Steve's sister." Choice (C) refers to the owner of the car, not to the driver. Choice (D) refers to the person who had a party, not to the person driving. Choice (A) is not mentioned and may not be concluded from information in the conversation.

Audio

7. Woman: The door seems to be locked. Do I need a key for the bathroom?

    Man: No. Just push hard. It sticks a little.

    Third Voice: Why won't the door open?

Answer

(C) "It [the door] sticks a little." Choice (A) refers to the woman's original conclusion, not to the real reason that the door would not open. The word *key* in Choice (B) refers to the woman's question about a key, not to the reason that the door would not open. Choice (D) is not mentioned and may not be concluded from information in the conversation.

Audio

8. Man: Can we use our calculators on the test?

    Woman: Yes, if you bring them to me at the beginning of the test, I'll check them out and return them right away so you can use them.

    Third Voice: What does the man want to do?

Answer

(B) "Can we use our calculators on the test?" The word *check* in Choice (A) refers to the woman's offer to check the calculators, not to what the man wants to do. Choices (C) and (D) are not mentioned and may not be concluded from information in the conversation.

Audio

9. Man: My roommate left, and he didn't pay his share, so I'm stuck with all the rent and utilities for last month.

    Woman: That's not fair. You should call his family.

    Third Voice: What is the woman's advice?

Answer

(C) "You should call his [your roommate's] family." Choice (A) is not correct because the woman does not think it is fair for the man to be stuck with the bills. The word *family* in Choice (B) refers to the family of the roommate, not of the man. The word *leave* in Choice (D) refers to the roommate's leaving, not the man's leaving.

Audio

10. Man: I want to apply for a student loan, please.

    Woman: All right. Fill out these forms and bring in your income tax records from last year. Then I'll review your options with you.

    Third Voice: How will the woman help the man?

Answer

(C) "Then I'll review your options with you." Choices (A), (B), and (D) refer to instructions that the woman gives the man about what he is to do before their interview, not to the way that the woman will help the man at the interview.

Exercise 3: Short Conversations—Selections   (Track 3)

Audio

1. Woman: Is Jack your cousin?
   Man: No. He seems more like a brother, really, but we are just good friends.
   Third Voice: What is the relationship between Jack and the man?

Answer

(B) "... we are just good friends." Choice (A) refers to the way that the man feels about Jack, not to their actual relationship. Choice (C) refers to the woman's assumption, not to the relationship. Choice (D) is not mentioned and may not be concluded from information in the conversation.

Audio

2. Man: So I asked Frank if we could room together next semester, and he said that he was going to room with Geoff.
   Woman: Oh, that's too bad. Well, I know that Steve is looking for a roommate.
   Third Voice: What does the woman suggest?

Answer

(C) "Well, I know that Steve is looking for a roommate." Because the woman mentions that Steve is looking for a roommate, it may be concluded that she is suggesting that the man and Steve be roommates. Choice (A) is not correct because Frank responded to the man's offer by saying that he was going to room with Geoff. Choices (B) and (D) are not correct because Frank and Geoff plan to be roommates.

Audio

3. Man: What did you get on the calculus exam?
   Woman: A *C*. And I feel lucky to have it. Mike got a *B*, but almost everyone else got *D*s and *F*s.
   Third Voice: What grade did the woman receive?

Answer

(C) "A *C*." Choice (B) refers to Mike's grade, not to the woman's grade. Choice (D) refers to the grades received by almost everyone else. Choice (A) is not mentioned and may not be concluded from information in the conversation.

Audio

4. Man: Where can I buy a computer? It doesn't have to be the best on the market.
   Woman: Um-hum. You could go to a computer store, or a discount store, but if I were you, I'd look into some of the special offers through the university. I saw something in the paper just last night.
   Third Voice: What advice does the woman give the man?

Answer

(D) "... if I were you, I'd look into some of the special offers through the university." Choices (A) and (C) refer to alternatives that the woman mentions, not to the advice she gives the man. The word *newspaper* in Choice (B) refers to an article about special offers, not to an ad for a computer.

Audio

5. Man: You didn't get your grades because your name isn't on the roster. Did you attend the class and take the exams?
   Woman: I certainly did. And I paid my fees, too.
   Third Voice: Why didn't the woman receive a grade for the course?

Answer

(D) "You didn't get your grades because your name isn't on the roster." Choice (A) is not correct because the woman paid her fees. Choice (C) is not correct because she attended class. Choice (B) is not mentioned and may not be concluded from information in the conversation.

Audio

6. Man: What size do you need?

   Woman: I'm not too sure. I wear a $5\frac{1}{2}$ or a 6 in Europe, and a 7 in Canada, but I think I need a $7\frac{1}{2}$ here.

   Third Voice: What size will the man probably bring?

Answer

(D) ". . . I think I need a $7\frac{1}{2}$ here." Choices (A) and (B) refer to the size that the woman takes in Europe, not to the size she needs here. Choice (C) refers to the size that the woman takes in Canada.

Audio

7. Woman: I have been having the worst headaches. I know some of it is stress, but I'm worried that I might have something more serious, like high blood pressure.

   Man: Well, we'll check that out, of course, but first, tell me the last time you had your glasses changed. It really sounds more like eye strain.

   Third Voice: What does the man suspect?

Answer

(A) ". . . tell me the last time you had your glasses changed. It really sounds more like eye strain." Choices (B), (C), and (D) refer to the concerns that the woman has about her health, not to the problem that the man suspects.

Audio

8. Man: Have you started writing your paper for history?

   Woman: Not yet. I'm still writing up my laboratory assignments for chemistry and studying for my midterms in English and French.

   Third Voice: For which class must the woman begin to prepare?

Answer

(A) "Have you started writing your paper for history?" "Not yet." Choices (B), (C), and (D) refer to assignments that she is doing now, not to an assignment she must begin.

Audio

9. Woman: Are you glad that you came to Washington?

   Man: Yes, indeed. I'd considered going to New York or Boston, but I've never regretted my decision.

   Third Voice: Where does the man live?

Answer

(D) "Are you glad that you came to Washington?" "Yes, indeed." Choices (A) and (B) refer to places the man considered before coming to Washington. Choice (C) is not mentioned and may not be concluded from information in the conversation.

Audio

10. Man: Something is wrong with second gear. It seems to run fine in reverse and drive, but when I shift into second, the motor stalls out.

    Woman: I hope that it won't be too difficult to fix.

    Third Voice: Which gear needs to be fixed?

Answer

(B) "Something is wrong with second gear." Choices (C) and (D) refer to gears that run fine. Choice (A) is not mentioned and may not be concluded from information in the conversation.

EXERCISE 4: Short Conversations—Reversals

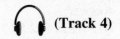 (Track 4)

Audio

1. Man: Do you need a ride to the airport?
   Woman: Thanks, anyway. I thought I would, but I have my car back now.
   Third Voice: How will the woman get to the airport?

Answer

(C) "... I have my car back now." Choice (A) refers to the man's offer and to the woman's first plan, not to the way that the woman will get to the airport. Choices (B) and (D) are not mentioned and may not be concluded from information in the conversation.

Audio

2. Man: Okay. What'll you have?
   Woman: Give me the eggs and potatoes. Oh, wait a minute. How about the eggs and pancakes?
   Third Voice: What does the woman want to eat?

Answer

(B) "How about the eggs and pancakes?" Choice (A) refers to the woman's choice before she changes her mind. Choice (D) refers to part of the woman's order but leaves out the fact that she wants eggs, also. Choice (C) is not mentioned and may not be concluded from information in the passage.

Audio

3. Woman: How many boxes of Girl Scout cookies did you order?
   Man: Four, no, five.
   Third Voice: How many boxes of cookies did the man order?

Answer

(C) "Four, no five." Choice (B) refers to the man's first thought, not to his final statement about the number of boxes he ordered. Choices (A) and (D) are not correct because the man ordered five boxes of cookies.

Audio

4. Man: What is the area code from which you are calling?
   Woman: 6-9-1. Oops, that's not right. It's 6-1-9.
   Third Voice: What is the correct area code for the woman?

Answer

(D) "It's 6-1-9." Choice (A) refers to the woman's first response, before she corrects herself. Choices (B) and (C) are not mentioned and may not be concluded from information in the conversation.

Audio

5. Woman: I thought you said it was eight cents a copy.
   Man: I did, but it's ten cents a copy when you make fewer than twenty copies, and you have only fifteen.
   Third Voice: How much per copy will the woman pay?

Answer

(B) "... it's ten cents a copy when you make fewer than twenty copies, and you have only fifteen." Choice (A) refers to the price per page for twenty copies or more. The number in Choice (C) refers to the number of copies the woman has, not to the price per copy. The number in Choice (D) refers to the number of copies required for the lower price, not to the price per copy.

Audio

6. Woman: How much to send a one-page fax?
   Man: One dollar. Oh, wait a minute. This is an overseas transmission. That's two-fifty.
   Third Voice: How much will the woman pay?

Answer

(D) "That's $2.50." Choice (B) refers to the price of a one-page domestic fax, not to the overseas transmission that the woman wants to send. The per-minute prices in Choices (A) and (C) are not mentioned and may not be concluded from information in the conversation.

Audio

7. Man: Let me see. There's a documentary about wolves on Channel Three.
    Woman: That sounds pretty interesting, but I'd rather go to the movies.
    Third Voice: What does the woman want to do?

Answer

(D) ". . . I'd rather go to the movies." Choices (A) and (C) refer to the man's preference, not to the woman's preference. Choice (B) is not mentioned and may not be concluded from information in the passage.

Audio

8. Woman: Do you want large bills or twenties?
    Man: Give me twenties, please. Oh, wait, maybe I should take two fifties and the rest in twenties.
    Third Voice: What does the man want the woman to do?

Answer

(D) ". . . I should take two fifties and the rest in twenties." Choice (A) refers to the man's request before he changed his mind. Choices (B) and (C) are not correct because he asks for some twenties.

Audio

9. Man: Where shall we go for lunch? It's your turn to choose.
    Woman: How about The Country Kitchen or, better yet, The Old House. They have great salads.
    Third Voice: Where will the man and woman eat lunch?

Answer

(C) ". . . better yet, The Old House." Choice (A) refers to the woman's first suggestion before she changed her mind. Choices (B) and (D) are not mentioned and may not be concluded from information in the conversation.

Audio

10. Woman: Will you be home late again tonight?
    Man: I'm afraid so. But I should be able to get away by six, or let's say seven, just to be on the safe side.
    Third Voice: When will the man be home?

Answer

(C) ". . . let's say seven, just to be on the safe side." The time in Choice (A) refers to the man's first estimate, not to the man's final estimate. Choices (B) and (D) are not correct because the man acknowledged that he would be home late.

EXERCISE 5: Short Conversations—Idioms 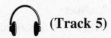 (Track 5)

Audio

1. Man: Let's go to Florida on spring break.
    Woman: You're putting me on!
    Third Voice: What does the woman mean?

Answer

(A) "You're putting me on" is an idiomatic expression that means the speaker does not think the other person is serious. Choices (B), (C), and (D) are not paraphrases of the expression.

Audio
2. Man: Can you believe it? It says in the paper that tuition is going up another hundred dollars a semester.
   Woman: That's just what I need.
   Third Voice: What does the woman mean?

Answer
(C) "That's just what I need" is an idiomatic expression that means the speaker will be inconvenienced. Choices (A), (B), and (D) are not paraphrases of the expression.

Audio
3. Man: Can you let me borrow some paper? This lecture is so long that I've run out.
   Woman: Sure. Here you go.
   Third Voice: What did the man do?

Answer
(B) "... I've run out" is an idiomatic expression that means the speaker has used all of the supply. Choices (A), (C), and (D) are not paraphrases of the expression.

Audio
4. Woman: That test was not what I studied for.
   Man: No joke. I hope I passed it.
   Third Voice: How does the man feel about the test?

Answer
(B) "No joke" is an idiomatic expression that means the speaker agrees with another person. Choices (A), (C), and (D) are not paraphrases of the expression.

Audio
5. Man: What did you say?
   Woman: Honestly, Will. You're just not all there sometimes.
   Third Voice: What does the woman mean?

Answer
(A) "You're just not all there ..." is an idiomatic expression that means the speaker does not believe the other person is very attentive. Choices (B), (C), and (D) are not paraphrases of the expression.

Audio
6. Woman: Do you remember the name of the book the professor recommended?
   Man: Off the top of my head, I'd say it was *Talk Like Ted*, but I'll check my notes when I get back to my room.
   Third Voice: What does the man mean?

Answer
(C) "Off the top of my head" is an idiomatic expression that means that the speaker is making a best guess in order to answer immediately. Choices (A), (B), and (D) are not paraphrases of the expression.

Audio
7. Man: I'll pick you up after class.
   Woman: Don't bother.
   Third Voice: What does the woman mean?

Answer
(A) "Don't bother" is an idiomatic expression that means the speaker does not want the other person to take action. Choices (B), (C), and (D) are not paraphrases of the expression.

Audio
8. Woman: Do you like ice cream?
   Man: I'll say!
   Third Voice: What does the man mean?

Answer

(A) "I'll say" is an idiomatic expression that means the speaker agrees with the other person. Choices (B), (C), and (D) are not paraphrases of the expression.

Audio

9. Man: Did you know that Joan is going to move back to Maine?
   Woman: I'll believe it when I see it.
   Third Voice: What does the woman mean?

Answer

(B) "I'll believe it when I see it" is an idiomatic expression that means the speaker is doubtful. Choices (A), (C), and (D) are not paraphrases of the expression.

Audio

10. Woman: How was your day?
    Man: Don't ask.
    Third Voice: What does the man mean?

Answer

(C) "Don't ask" is an idiomatic expression that means an emphatic no. Choices (A), (B), and (D) are not paraphrases of the expression.

EXERCISE 6: Short Conversations—Emotions 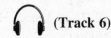 (Track 6)

Audio

1. Woman: Are you worried about getting a job after graduation?
   Man: No. I've had several good interviews, and I can always work for my dad for a while.
   Third Voice: How does the man feel?

Answer

(C) Since the man says that he has had several interviews, and that he can work for his father, and since his tone is confident, it may be concluded that he feels confident. Choice (A) is not correct because the man says he is not worried. Choices (B) and (D) are not mentioned and may not be concluded from information in the conversation.

Audio

2. Woman: That was a great movie!
   Man: Sure, if you like fairy tales.
   Third Voice: How did the man feel about the movie?

Answer

(A) Since the man compares the movie to fairy tales, and since his tone is sarcastic, it may be concluded that he thought it was a very unrealistic movie. Choices (B), (C), and (D) are not mentioned and may not be concluded from information in the conversation.

Audio

3. Man: Did you get your TOEFL scores yet?
   Woman: Not yet, but I think I got more than 100. I had 90 the first time I took it, and I know I did much better this time because I knew a lot about several of the reading comprehension passages.
   Third Voice: How does the woman feel about the TOEFL?

Answer

(B) Since the woman says she knows she did much better, it may be concluded that she thought she improved her score. Choice (A) is not correct because she knows she did much better. The number in Choice (C) refers to the score she received the first time, not this time. Choice (D) is not correct because she knew a lot about several of the reading comprehension passages.

Audio

4. Man: What page are we on? I'm just not with it today.

    Woman: Or any other day.

    Third Voice: How does the woman feel about the man?

Answer

(C) Since the woman says that the man is not *with it* any day, and since her tone is impatient, it may be concluded that she thinks he never pays attention. Choices (A), (B), and (D) are not mentioned and may not be concluded from information in the conversation.

Audio

5. Woman: If you invite Lucy, you'll have to ask Rick, too.

    Man: Forget it!

    Third Voice: How does the man feel about Rick?

Answer

(D) Since the man says to forget asking Rick, and since his tone is negative, it may be concluded that he does not want to invite them. Choice (C) is not correct because he does not want to invite Rick. Choices (A) and (B) are not mentioned and may not be concluded from information in the conversation.

Audio

6. Woman: I heard that Professor Saunders has retired.

    Man: What?

    Third Voice: What is the man's reaction to the news?

Answer

(A) Since the man says *what*, and since his tone is surprised, it may be concluded that the man is surprised by the news. Choices (B), (C), and (D) are not mentioned and may not be concluded from information in the conversation.

Audio

7. Woman: I don't care much for the way that our lab assistant grades our assignments.

    Man: Neither do I.

    Third Voice: How does the man feel about the assignments?

Answer

(C) Since the man agrees with the woman, it may be concluded that he does not like the grading system. Choice (A) misinterprets the idiom *to not care for*, which means "to not like." Choice (D) is not correct because he agrees with the woman. Choice (B) is not mentioned and may not be concluded from information in the conversation.

Audio

8. Woman: You are wrong about Terry.

    Man: If you say so.

    Third Voice: What best describes the man's opinion of Terry?

Answer

(C) Since the man agrees reluctantly, and since his tone is dubious, it may be concluded that he has his doubts about Terry. Choices (A), (B), and (D) are not mentioned and may not be concluded from information in the conversation.

Audio

9. Woman: I don't want to go to that review session.

    Man: Neither do I, but I think we should.

    Third Voice: How does the man feel about the review session?

Answer

(B) Since the man agrees with the woman when she says that she does not want to go to the review session, it may be concluded that he does not want to go. Since he says they should go, it may be concluded that he will go. Choices (A) and (C) are not correct because the man does not want to go. Choice (D) is not correct because he will go.

Audio

10. Woman: I was going to room with Carol, but when I got here, I had been assigned to live with Janine.
    Man: Bummer.
    Third Voice: How does the man feel about Janine?

Answer

(A) Since the man says *bummer*, and since his tone is sympathetic, it may be concluded that he thinks Janine would be difficult to live with. Choices (B) and (C) are not correct because the man thinks it is a bummer for the woman to have been assigned to live with Janine instead of with Carol. Choice (D) is not mentioned and may not be concluded from information in the conversation.

EXERCISE 7: Short Conversations—Suggestions    (Track 7)

Audio

1. Woman: I'll leave the tip since you got dinner.
   Man: Okay. Five dollars is about 20 percent.
   Third Voice: What does the man suggest that the woman do?

Answer

(C) Since the man says "okay" when the woman offers to leave the tip, and he calculates the amount, it must be concluded that the woman will tip the waiter after dinner. Choice (A) refers to what the man, not the woman, will do. Choice (B) is not correct because the man will pay for dinner. Choice (D) is not correct because they are leaving a tip for a waiter in a restaurant.

Audio

2. Woman: Oh, no. We're locked out of the dorm. I didn't think it was that late.
   Man: Do you have a phone number for the security guard?
   Third Voice: What does the man suggest the woman do?

Answer

(B) Since the man asks whether the woman has a phone number for the security guard, it must be concluded that he suggests phoning the guard. Choices (A), (C), and (D) are not mentioned and may not be concluded from information in the conversation.

Audio

3. Man: All the bathrooms are locked.
   Woman: That's odd. Why don't you go down to the main lobby? I think I saw a custodian there when we came in.
   Third Voice: What does the woman suggest that the man do?

Answer

(C) Since the woman mentions that she saw a custodian in the main lobby, and suggests that the man "go down to the main lobby," it must be concluded that the custodian could unlock the bathroom for the man. Choice (B) is not correct because a custodian, not a bathroom, is in the main lobby. Choice (D) is not correct because the woman mentions the main lobby in the building they are in, not in another building. Choice (A) is not mentioned and may not be concluded from information in the conversation.

Audio

4. Woman: Are you in line here?
   Man: We all are. You need to take a number.
   Third Voice: What does the man suggest that the woman do?

Answer

(B) "You need to take a number." Choices (A), (C), and (D) are not mentioned and may not be concluded from information in the conversation.

Audio

5. Man: It's only twenty dollars.
   Woman: I know, but unless you have an account with us, we can't cash your check. There's a branch of your bank across the street.
   Third Voice: What does the woman suggest that the man do?

Answer

(A) Since the woman points out that there is a branch of the man's bank nearby, it must be concluded that she suggests he go to the other bank. Choice (C) is not correct because she cannot cash his check since he does not have an account at the bank. Choice (D) is not correct because the check is already made out for twenty dollars. Choice (B) is a possible solution to the problem, but it is not mentioned and may not be concluded from information in the conversation.

Audio

6. Man: I'll be glad to pick you up at the airport. What time does your plane arrive?
   Woman: Well, it's scheduled to be here at eleven thirty-five, but it might be late if the weather is bad out of Chicago. Why don't I call you when I get in?
   Third Voice: What does the woman suggest that the man do?

Answer

(C) "Why don't I call you when I get in?" Choice (A) refers to what the man offers to do, not to what the woman suggests. Choices (B) and (D) are not mentioned and may not be concluded from information in the conversation.

Audio

7. Woman: When does Dr. Watson have her office hours this semester?
   Man: I think her hours are from two to three o'clock every day. I'm not sure, but I know it's on the syllabus.
   Third Voice: What does the man suggest that the woman do?

Answer

(A) Since the man mentions that the hours are on the syllabus, it must be concluded that he wants the woman to refer to the syllabus. The time in Choice (C) refers to the man's recollection of the office hours, not to his suggestion. Choices (B) and (D) are not mentioned and may not be concluded from information in the conversation.

Audio

8. Woman: There won't be any kids at the dinner. Maybe we should stay at home.
   Man: Why don't we get a babysitter? We could use an evening out.
   Third Voice: What does the man suggest that they do?

Answer

(C) "Why don't we get a babysitter?" Choice (A) refers to what the woman, not the man suggests. Choices (B) and (D) are not mentioned and may not be concluded from information in the conversation.

Audio

9. Man: I've tried the interlibrary loan before, and it took too long for the material to get here.
   Woman: I'd just use the internet then. You can probably find some similar references.
   Third Voice: What does the woman suggest that the man do?

Answer

(D) "I'd just use the internet then." Choice (B) refers to the way that the man has done his research in the past, not to the woman's suggestion. Choices (A) and (C) are not mentioned and may not be concluded from information in the conversation.

Audio

10. Man: I don't like carrying a lot of cards in my wallet, but then I never have the one I need.
    Woman: You could put them in a card case and leave them in your book bag.
    Third Voice: What does the woman suggest that the man do?

Answer

(B) "You could put them in a card case and leave them in your book bag." Choices (A), (C), and (D) are not mentioned and may not be concluded from information in the conversation.

EXERCISE 8: Short Conversations—Assumptions   (Track 8)

Audio

1. Man: You mean this test isn't open book?
   Woman: Not this time.
   Third Voice: What had the man assumed about the test?

Answer

(C) Since the man is surprised that the test is not open book, it must be concluded that he assumed he could use his book during the test. Choice (B) refers to a take-home test, not an open-book test. Choices (A) and (D) are not mentioned and may not be concluded from information in the conversation.

Audio

2. Woman: I just used the security deposit from my old apartment for a deposit on the new one.
   Man: So you did get your deposit back after all.
   Third Voice: What had the man assumed?

Answer

(A) Since the man is surprised that she got her deposit back, it must be concluded that he assumed she would not receive it. Choices (B), (C), and (D) are not mentioned and may not be concluded from information in the conversation.

Audio

3. Man: You mean you are going out with Phil again?
   Woman: Just for lunch.
   Third Voice: What had the man assumed about the woman?

Answer

(B) Since the man is surprised that the woman is going out with Phil again, it must be concluded that he assumed she would not start dating Phil again. Choice (C) refers to the woman's date with Phil, not with the man. Choices (A) and (D) are not mentioned and may not be concluded from information in the conversation.

Audio

4. Woman: My daughter's first birthday is Saturday. Why don't you come?
   Man: You don't mean it. She can't be a year old already.
   Third Voice: What had the man assumed about the woman's daughter?

Answer

(A) Since the man is surprised that the woman's daughter is one year old already, it must be concluded that he thought she was younger. Choice (B) refers to what the woman, not the man, says. Choices (C) and (D) are not mentioned and may not be concluded from information in the conversation.

Audio

5. Man: We're almost finished with the handouts for Anne.

   Woman: Anne is going to give the presentation for the group?

   Third Voice: What had the woman assumed about the presentation?

Answer

(C) Since the woman is surprised that Anne is going to make the presentation for the group, it must be concluded that she assumed Anne would not make the presentation. Choice (A) is not correct because they are almost finished with the handouts. Choices (B) and (D) are not mentioned and may not be concluded from information in the conversation.

Audio

6. Man: The health center is in the student services building, not in the union.

   Woman: No wonder I couldn't find it. Now I have to go all the way over to North Campus.

   Third Voice: What had the woman assumed about the health center?

Answer

(B) Since the man tells the woman that the health center is not in the union, it must be concluded that she thought it was there. Choice (A) is not correct because the woman went to the union, not to the student services building. Choice (C) refers to the place where the woman must go, not to where she had assumed the health center to be. Choice (D) is not mentioned and may not be concluded from information in the conversation.

Audio

7. Woman: I wanted to read *Saratoga Trunk* for my report in English class, but Bill had already asked for it.

   Man: Bill is reading a novel?

   Third Voice: What had the man assumed about Bill?

Answer

(C) Since the man is surprised that Bill is reading a novel, it must be concluded that the man assumed Bill did not read novels. Choices (A), (B), and (D) are not mentioned and may not be concluded from information in the conversation.

Audio

8. Woman: John must have been joking when he said he was going to drop out of the business program to apply for medical school.

   Man: I don't think so. He seemed very serious to me.

   Third Voice: What had the woman assumed about John?

Answer

(B) "John must have been joking." Choice (A) is not correct because the woman did not think the man would apply for medical school. Choice (D) is not correct because the man was already in the business program. Choice (C) is not mentioned and may not be concluded from information in the conversation.

Audio

9. Man: When we got there Mr. Brown was already in the lab getting the equipment set up.

   Woman: You mean he was on time?

   Third Voice: What had the woman assumed about Mr. Brown?

Answer

(A) Since the woman was surprised that Mr. Brown was on time, it must be concluded that she assumed he would be late. Choice (B) is not correct because she thought he would not be in the lab yet. Choices (C) and (D) are not mentioned and may not be concluded from information in the conversation.

Audio

10. Man: So we met with our study group during the break, and we each took one part of the book to outline.
    Woman: Wait a minute. Dr. Peterson actually gave you a break?
    Third Voice: What had the woman assumed about Dr. Peterson?

Answer

(C) Since the woman was surprised that Dr. Peterson gave them a break, it must be concluded that she assumed Dr. Peterson would not give them a break. The *meeting*, the *outline*, and the *book* in Choices (A), (B), and (D) are activities of the study group, not Dr. Peterson.

EXERCISE 9: Short Conversations—Predictions

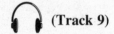 (Track 9)

Audio

1. Man: I'll have hot tea and a large glass of orange juice.
   Woman: We only have one size orange juice. It's pretty big, though. About like that.
   Third Voice: What will the man probably do?

Answer

(B) Since the man has ordered a large orange juice, he will most probably accept the size orange juice they have. Choice (A) is less probable because they have the drink that he wants. Choice (C) is less probable because there is no reason for him to change his order because of the size glass available. Choice (D) is less probable because the hot tea was ordered in addition to the orange juice, not instead of it.

Audio

2. Woman: Have you seen my chemistry book?
   Man: It was on the kitchen table yesterday. Did you have it with you when you went to the library last night? Maybe you left it there.
   Third Voice: What will the woman probably do?

Answer

(C) Since the woman went to the library last night, and the man suggests that she might have left her book there, the woman will most probably go to the library to look for her book. Choices (A) and (D) are less probable because the kitchen and the table refer to the place where the book was yesterday, not to places where the woman will go to study or eat instead of looking for the lost book. Choice (B) is less probable because in the conversation *chemistry* refers to the book, not a class.

Audio

3. Man: You have a long distance call from London. Will you accept the charges?
   Woman: I don't know anyone in London.
   Third Voice: What will the woman probably do?

Answer

(C) Since the woman does not know anyone in London, she will most probably refuse the collect call. Choice (B) is less probable because she will probably not accept the charges. Choices (A) and (D) are less probable because she does not know anyone in London.

Audio

4. Man: Is there a copy machine in this building?
   Woman: No. But there is one in the building across the street.
   Third Voice: What will the man probably do?

Answer

(B) Since the man is looking for a copy machine, and the woman directs him to a building across the street, he will most probably go across the street to make a copy. Choice (A) is less probable because she does not have access to a copy machine. Choice (C) is less probable because the building is right across the street. Choice (D) is less probable because the man wants to make copies, but he does not have them now.

Audio

5. Man: Tuesdays you can rent two DVDs for the price of one. Wednesdays you can rent any DVD you want for two dollars. And every time you have rented a total of ten, you get one free. But you have to join the club, and that costs ten dollars.

   Woman: Okay. That sounds good to me.

   Third Voice: What will the woman probably do?

Answer

(A) Since the woman says that the offer sounds good to her, she will most probably join the club. Choice (B) is less probable because the $5.00 refers to the cost of joining the club, not the price of a video. Choice (C) is less probable because the offer of one free video after renting ten is available after joining the club. Choice (D) is less probable because she is already in the video store.

Audio

6. Woman: How may I direct your call?

   Man: Reservations, please.

   Third Voice: What does the man probably want to do?

Answer

(C) Since the man asks for his call to be directed to reservations, he will most probably make a reservation. Choice (A) is less probable because his call, not he, is being directed. Choice (B) is less probable because he is already on the phone, making a call. Choice (D) is less probable because the woman is directing his call to someone else.

Audio

7. Woman: Is this where the bus to the mall stops?

   Man: No. It's on the other side of the street.

   Third Voice: What will the woman probably do?

Answer

(C) Since the woman asks where the bus will stop, she will most probably cross the street to wait for the bus. Choices (A) and (D) are less probable because she wants to take a bus. Choice (B) is less probable because the bus stop is on the other side of the street.

Audio

8. Woman: Did you drive in on I-17?

   Man: Yes, and it was already starting to get slick. By now it should be really bad. You'd better call the highway patrol before you leave to make sure it's still open.

   Third Voice: What will the woman probably do?

Answer

(B) Since the man suggests that the woman call the highway patrol, she will most probably call them. Choice (A) is less probable because the man suggests that she check with the highway patrol before leaving. Choices (C) and (D) are not mentioned and may not be concluded from the information.

Audio

9. Woman: Do you deliver?

   Man: That depends. We do if you are within three miles of the university.

   Third Voice: What will the man do?

Answer

(C) Since the man delivers within three miles of the university, he will most probably make the delivery to the woman if she is close to the university. Choice (A) is less probable because the woman has not indicated that she is at the university. Choice (B) is less probable because the woman may be within the delivery area. Choice (D) is not mentioned and may not be concluded from information in the conversation.

Audio

10. Woman: It will be about a twenty-minute wait if you want to sit indoors. We can seat you outdoors on the patio in five minutes.

    Man: Okay. I don't have twenty minutes to wait.

    Third Voice: What will the man probably do?

Answer

(B) Since the man does not have twenty minutes to wait, he will most probably wait five minutes to be seated outdoors on the patio. Choice (A) is less probable because the man says he does not have twenty minutes to wait. Choice (C) is less probable because both sections have a waiting list. Choice (D) is not mentioned and may not be concluded from the information in the conversation.

EXERCISE 10: Short Conversations—Implications   (Track 10)

Audio

1. Woman: That book is on reserve, so you can't take it out of the library. You can use it here for two hours, though. Or, you can wait until an hour before closing and check it out until the library opens at eight in the morning.

    Man: Okay. I'll come back tonight.

    Third Voice: What does the man imply?

Answer

(C) Since the man says that he will come back tonight, he implies that he will check the book out before closing. Choice (A) is less likely because he plans to return to the library. Choice (B) is less likely because he leaves the library. Choice (D) is less likely because the book is already on reserve.

Audio

2. Woman: Do you know where I can get a soda?

    Man: Isn't there a machine downstairs?

    Third Voice: What does the man imply?

Answer

(C) Since the man says that there is a machine downstairs, he implies that the woman should go downstairs to get a soda. Choice (A) is less likely because there is a soda machine downstairs. Choice (B) is less likely because he gives directions to the woman. Choice (D) is not correct because he gives directions to a soda machine.

Audio

3. Man: Why do *you* have to take the TOEFL? I thought if you graduated from an American high school, you didn't have to take it.

    Woman: I thought so, too. But the universities where I applied required a score even with an American diploma.

    Third Voice: What do we know about the woman?

Answer

(D) Since the man expresses surprise that the woman will have to take the TOEFL, and mentions that he thought those who graduated from an American high school were exempted from taking it, we know that the woman graduated from an American high school. Choice (B) is less likely because she is making application to American universities now. Choice (C) is not correct because she thought she would NOT be required to take the TOEFL, but has been required to do so by the universities to which she applied. Choice (A) is not mentioned and may not be concluded from information in the conversation.

Audio

4. Woman: How long did it take you to register? I was in line for two hours.

   Man: You were lucky.

   Third Voice: What did the man mean?

Answer

(B) Since the man says the woman was lucky to be in line for two hours, the man most probably means that he was in line longer than the woman. Choice (A) is true, but it is not what the man means by his comment. Choice (C) is not correct because the man thought the woman's two-hour wait was lucky compared to his. Choice (D) is not correct because it took the woman two hours to register.

Audio

5. Woman: If I were you, I would take a plane instead of a bus. It will take you forever to get there.

   Man: But flying makes me so nervous.

   Third Voice: What does the man prefer to do?

Answer

(C) Because the man offers an argument against taking a plane, it must be concluded that he prefers to take a bus. Choice (B) refers to the way that the woman, not the man, prefers to travel. Choices (A) and (D) are not mentioned and may not be concluded from information in the conversation.

Audio

6. Man: The name is Baker. We don't have a reservation, but we have time to wait.

   Woman: Party of four? It shouldn't be more than ten minutes, Mr. Baker. We'll call you when we have a table.

   Third Voice: Where does this conversation most likely take place?

Answer

(C) From the references to *reservation, party of four*, and *table*, it must be concluded that this conversation takes place in a restaurant. The word *reservation* in Choice (A) refers to a place saved, not to land owned by Native Americans. The word *party* in Choice (B) refers to a group, not an occasion. The word *Baker* in Choice (D) refers to a name, not to a place where bread and pastries are made.

Audio

7. Woman: Do you think that Bob is serious about Sally?

   Man: Well, I know this. I've never seen him go out so often with the same person.

   Third Voice: What conclusion does the man want us to draw from his statement?

Answer

(B) Because the man has never seen Bob go out so often with the same person, it must be concluded that Bob is serious about Sally. Choice (D) is not correct because Bob has never gone out so often with the same person. Choices (A) and (C) are not mentioned and may not be concluded from information in the conversation.

Audio

8. Woman: Whereas European nations have traditionally employed metric units, such as meters and grams, the United States has employed English units, such as feet and pounds.

   Man: Both systems are now in use in the U.S., though.

   Third Voice: What are these people most probably discussing?

Answer

(A) From the references to *metric units, meters, grams, feet,* and *pounds*, it must be concluded that the people are discussing weights and measurements. The phrase *European nations* in Choice (B) refers to the countries using the metric system, not to politics. The word *employ* in Choice (C) refers to use, not employment. The word *pounds* in Choice (D) refers to weight, not money.

Audio

9. Woman: Jane told me that she was going to quit her job. I'll certainly be sorry to see her go.
    Man: Oh, she always says that! I wouldn't buy her a going-away present if I were you.
    Third Voice: What does the man think about Jane?

Answer

(C) Because the man says that Jane always says she is going to quit her job, it must be concluded that he does not take her seriously. Choice (A) is not correct because the man does not believe Jane will quit. Choice (B) refers to the way that the woman, not Jane, feels. The word *present* in Choice (D) refers to a going-away present for Jane, not for the man.

Audio

10. Man: I wonder what happened to Betty Thompson? I don't see her anywhere.
    Woman: I don't know. She told me that she would be here at the play tonight.
    Third Voice: What do we learn about Betty from this conversation?

Answer

(D) Because they do not see her there, it must be concluded that Betty was not at the play. Choices (A) and (C) are not correct because she told the man she would be at the play. Choice (B) is not correct because the man and woman don't see her at the play.

EXERCISE 11: Short Conversations—Problems 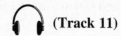 (Track 11)

Audio

1. Man: Oh, no. I've run out of checks, and the rent is due.
    Woman: Maybe you could get a cashier's check at the bank.
    Third Voice: What is the man's problem?

Answer

(B) "I've run out of checks. . . ." Choice (A) is not correct because the man has run out of checks. Choices (C) and (D) are not mentioned and may not be concluded from information in the conversation.

Audio

2. Woman: My roommate is getting married next month. I'd like to live by myself, but I really can't afford to.
    Man: Why don't you sign up on the message board in the housing office?
    Third Voice: What is the woman's problem?

Answer

(B) Since her roommate will be getting married, it must be concluded that she will be moving out. Choice (A) is not correct because she would like to live by herself, but can't afford to. Choices (C) and (D) are not mentioned and may not be concluded from information in the conversation.

Audio

3. Woman: What's the matter?
    Man: I can't register until I get my advisor's signature on my registration form, and, as usual, I can't find him.
    Third Voice: What is the man's problem?

Answer

(A) Since the man can't get registered without his advisor's signature on the registration form, it must be concluded that he needs his advisor to sign the form. Choice (B) is not correct because he is looking for his advisor. Choice (C) is not correct because he has the registration form. In Choice (D), it is his advisor, not his registration, that he can't find.

Audio

4. Woman: Can you give me a lift? My car's in the shop, and I'm already late to work.
   Man: Sure. I'll drop you off on my way to class.
   Third Voice: What is the woman's problem?

Answer

(B) Since the woman asks for a lift, it must be concluded that she needs a ride. To give someone a "lift" is an idiomatic expression that means to give them a ride. Choice (A) is not correct because her car is in the shop. Choice (C) is not correct because she is late for work, not class. Choice (D) is not correct because she is going to work, not shopping. It is her car that is in the shop.

Audio

5. Woman: Great! Professor Jones is using a different book this semester. Now I'll have to buy a new one.
   Man: Me, too. My friend let me have a copy of the book he used last semester, but that won't do me any good now.
   Third Voice: What is the problem that the man and woman are talking about?

Answer

(C) "Professor Jones is using a different book this semester." Choices (A), (B), and (D) are not mentioned and may not be concluded from information in the conversation.

Audio

6. Woman: Sorry. I have to stay here until someone comes from the phone company to install my phone.
   Man: That's too bad. I wish you could go with us to the movie.
   Third Voice: What is the woman's problem?

Answer

(A) "I have to stay here until someone comes from the phone company to install my phone." Choice (B) is not correct because she is waiting for her phone to be installed. Choice (C) refers to the movie that the man and his friends are going to see, but it is not mentioned whether the woman has seen it already. The *company* in the conversation is the phone company, not visitors, as in Choice (D).

Audio

7. Man: Excuse me. I need to exchange this sweatshirt for a larger size, but I can't find the receipt.
   Woman: That's okay, since it's an even exchange. Just take the size you want and give me that one.
   Third Voice: What is the man's problem?

Answer

(C) ". . . I can't find the receipt." Choice (B) is not correct because he needs a larger size because the sweatshirt is too small. Choice (D) is not correct because the clerk exchanges the sweatshirt. Choice (A) is not mentioned and may not be concluded from information in the conversation.

Audio

8. Woman: If the university had child care on campus, it would make my life a lot easier.
   Man: It really would. It must take a lot of time going back and forth to day care all the way across town.
   Third Voice: What is the woman's problem?

Answer

(A) Since child care on campus would make the woman's life easier, and we know that she is traveling across town, it must be concluded that she needs child care that is closer to the university. Choices (B), (C), and (D) are not mentioned and may not be concluded from information in the conversation.

Audio

9. Man: I need to get a different job. The one I have just doesn't give me enough hours anymore.

   Woman: Have you tried the library? They're always looking for help.

   Third Voice: What is the man's problem?

Answer

(B) "The one [job] I have just doesn't give me enough hours anymore." Choices (A), (C), and (D) are not mentioned and may not be concluded from information in the conversation.

Audio

10. Woman: I've been staying up until three and four in the morning trying to get all my papers and projects done. I'm exhausted.

    Man: Well, you can't do that for very long without getting sick.

    Third Voice: What is the woman's problem?

Answer

(A) Since the woman has been staying up late, and she says she is exhausted, it must be concluded that she needs to get more sleep. Choice (B) refers to the man's concern about her getting sick, not to how she feels now. Choice (C) is not correct because she is getting her papers and projects done. She says she feels tired, but being tired of school work is not mentioned and may not be concluded from information in the conversation.

EXERCISE 12: Conversations—Friends on Campus 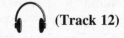 (Track 12)

Conversation One

Audio

Narrator: Listen to part of a conversation between two friends on campus.

Man: Did you see the special on Norman Rockwell last night—the one that Dr. Mitchell mentioned in class?

Woman: Yes, I did. I don't have a TV, but I went over to a friend's house. It was really good, wasn't it?

Man: It sure was. I thought it was interesting how he developed the paintings in stages starting with photographs.

Woman: I thought that was interesting, too. It never occurred to me that he would have actually employed models. I just assumed that he dreamed up all those wonderful characters. When you look at one of those magazine covers . . . which magazine was it?

Man: *The Saturday Evening Post.*

Woman: Right. Well, you can just tell what the people are thinking and feeling. The picture really tells a story.

Man: And to think that he created several hundred of those.

Woman: Amazing. Of course that was over almost sixty years. But still . . .

Man: I'd like to see the exhibit when it comes to Miami.

Woman: What exhibit?

Man: The one they mentioned after the special.

Woman: Oh. I must have turned it off before the announcement. I'd like to see it, too.

Man: Maybe we could go, take some photographs, and turn them in as an extra-credit project.

Woman: Great idea. Maybe we could package it for the reserve desk at the library.

Audio

1. What do the speakers mainly discuss?

Answer

(B) "Did you see that TV special on Norman Rockwell last night?" Choices (A), (C), and (D) are mentioned in reference to the main topic of the conversation, "the TV program about Norman Rockwell."

Audio

2. How did Rockwell paint such interesting faces?

Answer

(C) "It never occurred to me that he would have actually employed models. Choice (A) refers to the woman's assumption, not to Rockwell's method. Choice (B) refers to Rockwell's finished work, not to the source of the interesting faces. Choice (D) is not correct because the picture tells a story.

Audio

3. What do we know about Rockwell?

Answer

(A) "And to think that he [Rockwell] created several hundred of those [paintings]." Choices (B), (C), and (D) are not mentioned and may not be concluded from information in the conversation.

Audio

4. What do the students plan to do for extra credit?

Answer

(D) ". . . we could go [to the exhibit], take some photographs, and turn them in as an extra-credit project." Choice (A) is not correct because the video will not be at the reserve desk until the students package it. The exhibit in Choice (B) refers to the Rockwell exhibit that the students will see, not to an exhibit that they will bring to the library. The photographs in Choice (C) refer to the photographs that the man will take of the Rockwell exhibit, not to photographs of models.

Audio

5. What will the couple probably do?

Answer

(A) "I'd like to see the exhibit when it comes to Miami." "I'd like to see it, too." Choice (B) is not correct because they already saw the special. Choice (C) is not correct because the television special aired last night, not now. Choice (D) is not correct because they are in Miami now.

Conversation Two

Audio

Narrator: Listen to part of a conversation between two students on campus.

Bill: So Linda, how are you going to study for the final?

Linda: Me? I'm going to use my notes mostly, I guess.

Bill: You mean you aren't going to read the book?

Linda: Oh, well, yeah, I read the book, but I'm not going to spend much time reviewing it. I did that for the first couple of quizzes, but there were hardly any questions from the book on them at all. So I figured that the midterm wouldn't have that much from the book either.

Bill: Well, you were right about that. Most of the questions *did* come from the notes. And there were some from the handouts, too. Remember that question about colonial art?

Linda: Oh, yeah. That was directly from the handout, but I had some notes on that, too.

Bill: Did you? I'm not sure I did. But maybe your notes are more detailed than mine.

Linda: I don't know about that, but I try to write down everything I can in class, then I organize it afterward.

Bill: You mean you rewrite your notes? That must take a lot of time.

Linda: Well, I guess so, but still I remember better when I write something down. And now that I'm getting ready for the final, I have everything in one place. I think it actually saves me time in the long run. I think you probably spend more time reading the book. I'm just getting general background information, so I can be a better listener in class.

Bill: I do spend a lot of time reading and highlighting the book, and come to think of it, I have a lot of repetition in my notes. Uh, Linda, if you don't mind telling me, how did you do on the midterm using that system?

Linda: I got an A.

Bill: Wow. I got a B, and I studied hard for it.

Linda: Oh, and another thing, I never miss a class since the notes are so important.

Bill: Well, I think it's too late to rewrite all my notes for the final, but I sure plan to spend more time organizing and studying my notes than reviewing the book this time.

Audio

1. What are the students mainly discussing?

Answer

(B) ". . . how are you going to study for the final?" Choices (A), (C), and (D) are mentioned in reference to the main topic of the conversation, "studying for a test."

Audio

2. Why does Bill mention colonial art?

Answer

(A) "That [the question about colonial art] was . . . directly from the handout." Choice (C) is not correct because he is not sure that he had notes on colonial art. Choice (D) is not correct because the topic was on a handout, not in the book. Choice (B) is not mentioned and may not be concluded from information in this conversation.

Audio

3. How does Linda usually study for a test?

Answer

(B) "You mean you rewrite your notes?" Choice (A) is not correct because Linda does not spend much time reviewing the book. The *handouts* in Choice (C) refer to material from the professor, not Linda. Choice (D) refers to the way that the man, not the woman, usually studies for a test.

Audio

4. What kind of student is Linda?

Answer

(D) "I got an A. . . ." The grade of B in Choice (A) refers to the grade that the man received on his midterm, not to the grade that the woman tries to get. Choice (B) is not correct because she is a student who got an A. Choice (C) is not correct because she never misses a class.

Audio

5. What will Bill probably do?

Answer

(D) "I sure plan to spend more time organizing and studying my notes. . . ." Choice (B) is not correct because it is too late to rewrite the notes for the final. Choice (C) is not correct because he is not going to spend as much time reviewing the book. Choice (A) is not mentioned and may not be concluded from information in this conversation.

EXERCISE 13: Conversations—Campus Personnel/Students   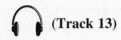 (Track 13)

Conversation One

Audio

Narrator: Listen to part of a conversation between a student and a secretary on campus.

Man: Hello, Mrs. Kelly. I'd like to pick up my test, please.

Woman: Sure. Whose class are you in?

Man: Dr. Purcell's math class.

Woman: And your name?

Man: My last name is Raleigh. R-A-L-E-I-G-H.

Woman: That's right. Jim Raleigh. Here it is.

Man: Thank you. And Terry Young's test, too, please.

Woman: Oh, I'm sorry. I can't let you take someone else's test.

Man: He's sick, and he can't come in to get it. He's my roommate.

Woman: I understand. But the privacy act won't permit it.

Man: Really? Maybe you could call him.

Woman: Not even then. I can only give a test to the student whose name appears on it. I can't even give it to a family member.

Man: That's weird.

Woman: I think so, too, frankly, but that's the law.

Man: Okay. I'll tell Terry. Thanks anyway.

Woman: You're welcome. Tell him I'll just keep his test here until he feels better and can come in for it himself.

Man: Okay. I'll do that.

Woman: Have a nice day, Jim.

Man: You, too, Mrs. Kelly.

Audio

1. What do the speakers mainly discuss?

Answer

(C) "I can't let you take someone else's test . . . the privacy act won't permit it." Choices (A), (B), and (D) are mentioned in reference to the main topic of the conversation, "school policy."

Audio

2. Why can't the woman give Terry Young's test to the man?

Answer

(A) "I can only give a test to the student whose name appears on it . . . that's the law." Choice (B) is not correct because she can't even give it [the test] to a family member. Choice (D) is not correct because Jim wants to pick up the test that Terry took. Choice (C) is not mentioned and may not be concluded from information in the conversation.

Audio

3. What is the man's last name?

Answer

(C) "My last name is Raleigh." Choice (A) is the name of the man's friend. Choice (B) is the name of the professor. Choice (D) is the name of the secretary.

Audio

4. How does the woman feel about the policy?

Answer

(B) Because the man says that the policy is *weird* and the woman agrees with him, it must be concluded that the woman thinks that the policy is "odd." Choice (A) is not correct because she agrees with the man. Choice (C) is not correct because she will not give the man his roommate's test, thereby enforcing the policy. Choice (D) is not mentioned and may not be concluded from information in this conversation.

Audio

5. What will the man most probably do?

Answer

(A) "Okay. I'll tell Terry." Choice (B) is not correct because the man is in the office and has picked up his test. Choice (D) is not correct because the man has already taken the test. Choice (C) is not mentioned and may not be concluded from information in the conversation.

Conversation Two

Audio

Narrator: Listen to part of a conversation between a student and an advisor on campus.

Woman: I usually advise first-year engineering students to take mathematics, chemistry, and an introductory engineering course the first quarter.

Man: Oh. That's only three classes.

Woman: Yes. But I'm sure that you'll be busy. They're all five-hour courses, and you'll have to meet each class every day. The chemistry course has an additional two-hour laboratory.

Man: So that would be seventeen hours of class a week.

Woman: That's right.

Man: Okay. Which mathematics course do you think I should take?

Woman: Have you taken very much math in high school?

Man: Four years. I had algebra, geometry, trigonometry. . . .

Woman: Good. Then I suggest that you take the math placement test. It's offered this Friday at nine o'clock in the morning in Tower Auditorium.

Man: Do I need anything to be admitted? I mean a permission slip?

Woman: No. Just identification. A driver's license will be fine.

Man: Do I take a chemistry test, too?

Woman: No. Chemistry 100 is designed for students who have never taken a chemistry course, and Chemistry 200 is for students who have had chemistry in high school.

Man: I've had two courses.

Woman: Then you should take Chemistry 200, Orientation to Engineering, and either Mathematics 130 or 135, depending on the results of your placement test. Come back Friday afternoon. I should have your score on the test by then, and we can finish getting you registered.

Audio

1. What is the purpose of this conversation?

Answer

(A) ". . . I should have your score on the test by then, and we can finish getting you registered." Choices (B) and (D) are mentioned as secondary themes that are used to develop the main purpose of the conversation, "to register the student for classes." Choice (C) is not mentioned and may not be concluded from information in the conversation.

Audio

2. How many classes does the woman advise the man to take?

Answer

(C) "That's only three classes." Choice (A) refers to the number of hours that the two-hour laboratory meets per week. Choice (B) refers to the number of hours that each five-hour class meets per week. Choice (D) refers to the total number of hours that the classes meet per week.

Audio

3. What does the man need to be admitted to the examination?

Answer

(A) "A driver's license will be fine." Choice (B) refers to the man's suggestion, not to what he needs. Choice (D) is not correct because the man needs identification to be admitted to the examination. Choice (C) is not mentioned and may not be concluded from information in the conversation.

Audio

4. What does the woman suggest?

Answer

(A) "Come back Friday afternoon." Choice (B) is not correct because the results of the placement test are needed before the advisor can finish the registration process. Choice (C) is not correct because the advisor says three classes will keep the man busy. Choice (D) is not correct because the advisor needs the results of a placement test before choosing between Mathematics 130 or 135.

Audio

5. What do we know about the student?

Answer

(C) Because the woman says that she advises first-year students, it must be concluded that the student is a first-year student, or a freshman. Choice (A) is not correct because he is an engineering student. Choice (B) is not correct because he has had two courses in chemistry. Choice (D) is not mentioned and may not be concluded from information in the conversation.

EXERCISE 14: Conversations—Campus Personnel/Students 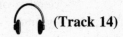 (Track 14)

Conversation One

Audio

Narrator: Listen to part of a conversation between a student and a clerk at the campus bookstore.

Kathy: Excuse me. Do you work here?

Jim: Yes, I do. How can I help you?

Kathy: Oh, well, um, I'm looking for a book for . . . for English 100.

Jim: Okay. Textbooks are in the back of the store. Did you want a new book or a used book?

Kathy: . . . I, . . . uh . . . I don't know. Is there much difference . . . in the price, I mean?

Jim: Well, that depends. We price the used books based on the, uh, depending on their condition. But in general, you can probably save, I'd say, at least 40 percent.

Kathy: Oh, great. I'll do that then.

Jim: Okay. These are the used books . . . uh . . . over here. Now, uh . . . which section did . . . are you signed up for? See, every instructor selects a book, so there are several different textbooks for each course. And English 100 is a core course, so there are, uh, a lot of sections.

Kathy: I don't remember the number, but it meets at eight o'clock.

Jim: In the morning? That sounds awful.

Kathy: Really. I registered late.

Jim: Do you know the instructor's name?

Kathy: Yes, it's Henry . . . Henley . . . uh . . . .

Jim: Hendrix?

Kathy: That's it. Hendrix.

Jim: Oh, well, that's not so bad, then. She's a good teacher. I wish I'd taken that class with her.

Kathy: That's what I was . . . what I heard. My roommate had her last semester.

Jim: Oh, then why don't you use your roommate's book? I don't think, uh, Hendrix changed the order this semester.

Kathy: Wouldn't you know? My roommate sold all her books at the end of the term.

Jim: Oh . . . so she sold the one for this course? Too bad. Well, this is the shelf . . . and you're looking for a book called, uh, *College Writing*. I think it's green, or maybe green and blue. There should be a fairly clean one here.

Kathy: Thanks . . . Look, here's one . . . oh . . . but it's pretty marked up.

Jim: Let's see it. Sometimes it actually helps to use someone else's highlighting, I mean, if you happen to get a . . . get an A student's book.

Kathy:	True, I see your point, but really, I'd really rather highlight it myself.
Jim:	Okay. That one didn't look like it belonged to an A student anyway. Hey, look at this. I don't think there's a mark in it . . . except for the name.
Kathy:	Wow! That's great.
Jim:	Wait . . . let's check on the edition.
Kathy:	The edition? Does that matter?
Jim:	Un-huh. It really does. Sometimes there's, uh, new information in a later edition, so that's why the professor . . . orders it. But the worst part is if the instructor is always referring to, say, page 50, and the information is on a different page in your edition, well, uh, it gets confusing.
Kathy:	Oh . . . anyway . . . this is the tenth edition.
Jim:	And you need, uh, the tenth edition. You really lucked out. The new one would have cost you at least thirty dollars, but this one's only fifteen.
Kathy:	Thanks.
Jim:	Wait a minute. See this? Right over here, over the shelf? It's a list of the books that Professor Hendrix ordered. And it looks like . . . yep . . . you have another book for that class. It's not required . . . but, uh, it's recommended.
Kathy:	So I don't have to buy it.
Jim:	No, it's up to you, but you . . . you'd better look . . . take a look at it . . . before you decide.
Kathy:	It looks like a handbook . . . or really, you know, a . . .
Jim:	. . . style manual.
Kathy:	Exactly.
Jim:	Well then, the instructor will probably want you to, you know, use the format and, uh, style in this book . . . for your essays.
Kathy:	I'd better get it then. Don't you think?
Jim:	I would.
Kathy:	How much is it?
Jim:	All of these are ten dollars, but they're fairly clean . . . uh, because, uh, because people don't usually write in a handbook. I mean, it's more of a reference.
Kathy:	Well, I'll take one then. . . . This one looks good.
Jim:	Okay . . . are you looking for anything else?
Kathy:	No. Just this. But I really appreciate your help. You saved me some money.
Jim:	Glad it, uh, worked out for you. I'm a student, too. I just work here part time, and, believe me, I understand the problem. Most of the textbooks are, uh, fifty or a hundred dollars. When you're taking, say, four classes, that really adds up.
Kathy:	It sure does. Anyway, thanks again.
Jim:	Sure.

Audio

1. What is the purpose of this conversation?

Answer

(B) ". . . I'm looking for a book for . . . English 100." Choice (A) is not correct because the man offers his opinion without being asked. Choices (C) and (D) are not mentioned and may not be concluded from information in this conversation.

Audio

2. Why didn't the woman use her roommate's book?

Answer

(D) "My roommate sold all her books at the end of the term." Choice (A) is not correct because her roommate had her [Dr. Hendrix] last semester. Choice (B) is not correct because Hendrix did not change the book order this semester. Choice (C) refers to a used book on the shelf, not to her roommate's book.

Audio

3. According to the man, what is the problem with using an older edition?

Answer

(A) ". . . the instructor is always referring to, say, page 50, and the information is on a different page in your edition. . . ." Choice (B) is not correct because many of the used books they are looking at do not have marks. Choice (C) is true, but it is not the problem that students have using an older edition. Choice (D) is not mentioned and may not be concluded from information in this conversation.

Audio

4. Why does the woman buy the style manual?

Answer

(C) ". . . the instructor will probably . . . want you to . . . use the format and, uh, style in this book. . . ." Choice (A) is not correct because the manual is recommended but not required. Choice (B) is not correct because the woman asks the price after she decides to buy it. Choice (D) is true, but it is not the reason why she decides to buy the manual.

Audio

5. Listen again to part of the conversation.
   Then answer the question.
   "I don't think, uh, Hendrix changed the order this semester."
   "Wouldn't you know? My roommate sold all her books at the end of the term."
   Why does the woman say this:
   "Wouldn't you know?"

Answer

(C) The question is asked with an ironic tone, in a way that invites commiseration. Choice (A) is not correct because the woman tells the man what her roommate did. She doesn't ask him. Choice (B) is not correct because the roommate's name is not mentioned. Choice (D) is not correct because the woman is using an ironic tone, not a humorous tone.

Audio

6. What can we infer about the woman?

Answer

(A) "I really appreciate your help. . . . You saved me some money." Choice (B) is not correct because the woman greets the man formally, asking whether he works in the bookstore, and because they do not call each other by name. The *A student* in Choice (C) refers to a previous owner of a used book, not to the woman. Choice (D) is not correct because the woman does not complain about her roommate when she mentions that she sold her book.

Conversation Two

Audio

Narrator: Listen to part of a conversation between a student and a librarian.

Joe: Hi. Is it true that I can search the library catalog from home? I mean, from my home computer? One of my friends at the dorm told me I could, uh, do that, but I live off campus, so I wasn't sure whether it would work for me.

Librarian: You're talking about the Oasis catalog, which is the online library catalog system. Here. It's easier if I just show you at this computer terminal.

Joe: Okay. Thanks.

Librarian: See. First, you get online.

Joe: Oh, I get it. It's all through the internet.

Librarian: Right. You click on a browser, then, uh, go to the library . . . the home page.

Joe: Wait, wait. The home page is, uh, *www.awu.org*.

Librarian: Right. See all those options? Oasis is what you want . . . for the catalog. So you click on that.

Joe: Okay . . . okay. Did you use a password or, uh, anything to get into it?

Librarian: No. All you need is an internet connection. But if you actually want to look at the books.
            . . .

Joe: I can do that?

Librarian: Sure. You want to go to a different . . . a different web site though. Here. . . . First, enter
            www.netlibrary.org. . . . There. See? This site lets you access all the e-books in our system.

Joe: Oh, well, do you have many of those?

Librarian: Thousands. They're all part of our collection, but we . . . we store them electronically, which
            means we don't have to have all that shelf space anymore.

Joe: Sounds good.

Librarian: But if you want to access Netlibrary, then you'll need to . . . you'll need a user name and a
            password.

Joe: So, how do I . . . do I just set that up online from home?

Librarian: No. You have to set up the account here in the library. You can do that on this terminal, if
            you like.

Joe: Great. Then I can . . . I can see the books on screen from my apartment.

Librarian: You can view the books from any place you have access to the internet. If you're out of
            town or you go somewhere on break, you can still use Netlibrary. Of course, we don't have
            all of our books online yet, but we're working on building the collection.

Joe: So can I go directly to Netlibrary to do a search, or um . . . do I have to go to . . . what do
            you call it . . . the Oasis catalog first?

Librarian: You can go right to the Netlibrary if you want. But that'll just show you the books and, uh,
            databases that are online. If you search Oasis, you'll have access to all of the books in print,
            I mean, the ones in the library, as well. Of course, you'll have to . . . to come into the library
            to check them out.

Joe: Let me see if I've got this. Oasis is exactly like the catalog for the library here at school,
            and so, uh, I can find all the books and materials that are on the shelves, but they . . . I can't
            see them.

Librarian: Right. But, if you want to go to Netlibrary after you use Oasis, then you can look for a
            particular resource . . . to see whether it's part of our online holdings. If it is, then you
            can just read it on your computer screen. . . . Look, you can enter a title or an author, or even
            a subject, and then you get a list of books. When you click on a title, you see the table of
            contents. You can read one chapter or the . . . the whole book if you want.

Joe: That is so great. Oh, one more thing. If I don't have time to read it all, do I just start over
            again next time, or, I mean, is there like an easy way to . . . to get back to my book?

Librarian: It's very easy. You just bookmark your place and click on your e-book when you go into
            the site next time. It'll open to the page you marked.

Joe: Well, I think the best thing for me to do is, uh, open an account, and then go back to my
            apartment and start working with it.

Librarian: There's a help screen on the site, but if you get stuck, just call the library, and someone will
            walk you through it.

Joe: And, uh, how do I pay for this? Do I have a one-time fee or a monthly charge or what?

Librarian: No charge. It's part of the library system. You're a student here, so when you log in, you'll
            be asked to enter your student ID number after your user name, and then your password,
            and, uh, that's it. Here's the screen you need to open the account . . . I'm sure you'll like
            using Netlibrary. Everyone does.

Audio

1. What is the main topic of this conversation?

Answer

(B) Because they discuss the "online library catalog" and the "Netlibrary service", it may be concluded
that the main topic is research methods on the internet. Choices (A), (C), and (D) are mentioned in
reference to the main topic, "research methods online."

Audio

2. What is *Oasis*?

Answer

(A) "... the Oasis catalog, which is the online library catalog system." Choice (C) refers to Netlibrary, not to Oasis. The name of the school in Choice (B) and the password in Choice (D) are not mentioned and may not be concluded from information in the conversation.

Audio

3. How does the man set up an account for Netlibrary?

Answer

(C) "But if you want to access Netlibrary. . . . You have to set up the account here in the library." Choice (A) is not correct because the man will not have a password until he sets up the account. Choice (B) refers to Oasis, not to Netlibrary. Choice (D) refers to how he should get help, not how he should set up the account.

Audio

4. How does the man pay for Netlibrary?

Answer

(C) "No charge. It's part of the library system." Choices (A) and (B) refer to the man's question about payment, not to the librarian's response. Choice (D) is not mentioned and may not be concluded from information in this conversation.

Audio

5. Listen again to part of the conversation.
   Then answer the question.
   "Let me see if I've got this. Oasis is exactly like the catalog for the library here at school, and so, uh, I can find all the books and materials that are on the shelves, but they . . . I can't see them."
   Why does the man say this:
   "Let me see if I've got this."

Answer

(A) The phrase *to get* something means "to understand" it. The man paraphrases the information as a comprehension check. Choices (B), (C), and (D) are not mentioned and may not be concluded from information in the conversation.

Audio

6. What will the man probably do now?

Answer

(B) Because the librarian directs him to the screen he needs to open the account, it may be concluded that he will open the account now. Choice (C) is not correct because he needs to open the account before using Netlibrary. Choice (A) is not correct because the man says the best thing to do is open an account, and then [after opening the account] go back to the apartment and start working with it. Choice (D) refers to the librarian's offer to help after he starts using Netlibrary, not now.

EXERCISE 15: Conversations—Professors/Students 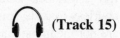 (Track 15)

Conversation One

Audio

Narrator: Listen to part of a conversation between a student and a professor on campus.

Man: I'm really sorry, Professor Irwin. I was sick yesterday.

Woman: Look, I'm not upset that you couldn't keep the appointment, but it is common courtesy to call. You know that.

Man: Yes, I do.

Woman: During registration, I have to see all my students, and sometimes they have to wait several days to get in. When someone doesn't show and doesn't call, that deprives someone else of an appointment time.

Man: You're right. I apologize. I didn't feel well, and I guess I just wasn't thinking straight at the time.

Woman: Okay, apology accepted. Now, I suppose you need to set up another appointment.

Man: Yes, I do. Can you see me now if I wait?

Woman: No. I can see you at three o'clock this afternoon or during my office hour on Tuesday or Thursday.

Man: Great. Your office hour is best. That's two o'clock, right?

Woman: That's right. Which day do you prefer?

Man: Tuesday.

Woman: Okay. Be there this time.

Man: I will be. Thanks a lot.

Audio

1. What is the main subject of the conversation?

Answer

(A) "... I'm not upset that you couldn't keep the appointment, but it is common courtesy to call." Choices (B), (C), and (D) are mentioned in reference to the main topic of the conversation, "the man's last appointment."

Audio

2. When is the man's new appointment scheduled?

Answer

(A) "That's two o'clock . . . Tuesday." Choices (B) and (C) refer to alternative times that the professor suggests, not to the time that the student chooses for the appointment. Choice (D) refers to the time that the student suggests.

Audio

3. What should the man have done about his first appointment?

Answer

(B) "... it is common courtesy to call." Choice (A) is not correct because he had an appointment that he did not keep. Choice (C) is not correct because the professor is not upset because he couldn't keep the appointment. Choice (D) is not mentioned and may not be concluded from information in the conversation.

Audio

4. What is the man's excuse?

Answer

(A) "I was sick yesterday." Choice (C) is not correct because the professor confirms, "... it is common courtesy to call. You know that," and the man responds, "Yes, I do [know that]." Choices (B) and (D) are not mentioned and may not be concluded from information in this conversation.

Audio

5. What word best describes Professor Irwin's attitude toward the student?

Answer

(D) From the tone of the conversation, it may be concluded that the professor is annoyed because the student did not call to cancel his appointment. Choice (B) refers to the student's attitude, not to that of the professor. Choices (A) and (C) are not mentioned and may not be concluded from information in the conversation.

Conversation Two

Audio

Narrator: Listen to part of a conversation between a student and a professor on campus.

Woman: Dr. Newbury, could I speak with you?
Man: Sure. Come on in.
Woman: I need to ask you to let me take the final early.
Man: May I ask why?
Woman: Yes. It's because I bought a ticket to go home for Christmas, and my flight leaves on Tuesday. That's the day before the exam.
Man: Yes, well, Penny, the exam schedule is printed in the registration materials. You had to know the dates. Why didn't you buy your ticket for the day after the exam?
Woman: Truthfully, I just made a mistake. And now, I've got a real problem because the ticket is nonrefundable, and I can't afford to buy another one.
Man: Hmmm.
Woman: Dr. Newbury, I live too far away to get home for Thanksgiving and spring break like the other students do. This is my only chance to see my family during the school year. I'm sorry that it happened, but couldn't you make an exception this time? Or could you give me an incomplete and let me make it up next semester?
Man: Okay. Anyone can make a mistake. You can take the exam on Monday.
Woman: Thank you. I really appreciate this.

Audio

1. What is the woman's main purpose in this conversation?

Answer

(C) "I need to ask you to let me take the final early." Choices (A) and (B) are mentioned in reference to the main topic of the conversation, "a change in the date of the woman's exam." Choice (D) is not correct because the woman has already scheduled her flight.

Audio

2. Why does the woman have a problem?

Answer

(C) "Truthfully, I just made a mistake [scheduling the trip]." Choice (B) is true, but it is not the problem that is the concern of the conversation. Choice (D) is not correct because the woman has not yet taken the final exam. Choice (A) is not mentioned and may not be concluded from information in the conversation.

Audio

3. On what day is the exam scheduled?

Answer

(C) "... my flight leaves on Tuesday. That's the day before the exam." Choice (A) would be the day before the flight, not the day of the exam. Choice (B) refers to the day of the flight, not to the day of the exam. Choice (D) is not mentioned and may not be concluded from information in this conversation.

Audio

4. What does the professor decide to do?

Answer

(B) "You can take the exam on Monday." Choice (A) is not correct because the woman has not taken the exam yet. Choice (D) refers to the woman's suggestion, not to the professor's decision. Choice (C) is not mentioned and may not be concluded from information in the conversation.

Audio

5. When does this conversation most probably take place?

Answer

(D) Since the woman bought a ticket to go home for Christmas, and her flight leaves on Tuesday, it may be concluded that the conversation took place in December. Choices (A), (B), and (C) are not close enough to Christmas.

EXERCISE 16: Conversations—Professors/Students

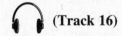 (Track 16)

Conversation One

Audio

Narrator: Listen to part of a conversation between a student and a professor.

Jim: Dr. Stephens?

Stephens: Oh, hi Jim.

Jim: I'm a little early. About . . . ten minutes. Do you want me to come back later?

Stephens: No, no, not at all. Come on in.

Jim: Thanks.

Stephens: Have a seat. I want to talk with you a little bit . . . before you take the test. You realize that this won't be . . . it isn't the same test that everyone else took in class last Friday.

Jim: Yes, I know. I, uh, I noticed that policy on the syllabus.

Stephens: Good. I try to include everything on the syllabus, but . . . well . . . students don't always read a syllabus that carefully, so. . . . The test that I gave in class was mostly multiple choice and true-false and, uh, with a few matching. In other words, it was an objective test.

Jim: Okay.

Stephens: The makeup is an essay test, with . . . uh . . . let's see, it has three questions on it. I occasionally give oral recitations instead of essays, but. . . .

Jim: Oh, I'm glad it isn't an oral exam.

Stephens: Good. In general, my makeup tests are . . . uh . . . let's say they're more difficult than the tests in class because . . . frankly, I want to discourage my students from using the makeup option.

Jim: Okay . . . I understand, Dr. Stephens. I'm just glad to . . . to have an opportunity . . . to make it up. I was so sick last Friday, believe me, I couldn't have gotten a good grade on a test.

Stephens: And . . . how are you now?

Jim: A lot better, thanks. I went over to the health center instead of going to classes last Friday, and I got some medicine, uh, some antibiotics and some kind of decongestant. By Sunday, I was starting to . . . I was feeling better. You should have seen the waiting room over there. Anyway, I was lucky. My other classes meet on Tuesdays and Thursdays, and I have, uh, one independent study. . . . I didn't miss any other classes, I mean, just yours on Friday. . . . Too bad it was a test day, though.

Stephens: Yes, well, when you finish this, you'll be all caught up.

Jim: Mostly I still have a lot of reading to do in my other classes. That medicine just knocked me out, you know, so I slept a lot. Um, am I the only one taking a makeup?

Stephens: You are. So, if you want to get started, you can just leave your books here. All you need to take with you is your pencil, and . . . just a second . . . I'll get your test. . . . Here you go.

Jim: Thanks.

Stephens: Why don't you take a look at it and, uh, I can answer any questions you have before you get started.

Jim: Okay . . . okay . . . okay. Hmmm. It's pretty straightforward, Dr. Stephens. The only thing I can think of to ask is . . . how long you want . . . uh . . . how long the essays should be . . . for each question, I mean.

Stephens: Well, the answer should be as long as it takes to respond to the question . . . but that doesn't help you much, does it? . . . I'd say you'd need, uh, two, or maybe three paragraphs, to develop each of the questions fully.

Jim: Okay.
Stephens: Anything else?
Jim: Not that I can think of.
Stephens: Okay, then. I'm going to . . . you can just leave your jacket and your backpack here. There's a conference room two doors down. And, uh, it should be quiet there. I'll show you where it is, and then when you finish, you can just bring your test back to me.
Jim: You'll be . . . ?
Stephens: I'll be in my office.
Jim: Oh, Dr. Stephens. Sorry . . . I just thought of another question. How long do I have to finish?
Stephens: Of course. I'm glad you asked. Fifty minutes, which is just about the same amount of time you would have had in class. But, knowing you, I think you'll probably finish long before that. Do you have a watch on?
Jim: Yes.
Stephens: Good. I don't think there's a clock in the conference room. In any case, if you haven't turned in the test by 1:45, I'll . . . I'll come to the room to collect it, okay?
Jim: Okay. Well, thanks again . . . I appreciate this.
Stephens: You're welcome, Jim. Good luck.

Audio
1. What is the main topic of this conversation?
Answer
(B) Because the purpose of the man's appointment is to take a makeup test, it is the main topic of conversation. Choices (A), (C), and (D) are mentioned in reference to the main topic, "the makeup test."

Audio
2. Why did the man need to take the test?
Answer
(A) ". . . I didn't miss any other classes, I mean, just yours on Friday . . . a test day . . . ." Choice (B) is not correct because he missed class in the past, not that he will miss class. Choice (C) is true, but he is not taking the test for the independent-study course. Choice (D) is not mentioned and may not be concluded from information in this conversation.

Audio
3. What kind of test will the man take?
Answer
(C) "The makeup is an essay test." Choices (A) and (B) refer to the test that the professor gave in class, not to the makeup test. Choice (D) refers to an option that the professor occasionally uses but not to this makeup test.

Audio
4. How long does he have to complete the test?
Answer
(C) "Fifty minutes, which is just about the same amount of time you would have had in class." Choice (A) refers to the amount of time early that Jim arrived. Choices (B) and (D) refer to the clock time, 1:45, when the test must be turned in.

Audio
5. Listen again to part of the conversation.
   Then answer the question.
   "Fifty minutes, which is just about the same amount of time you would have had in class. But, knowing you, I think you'll probably finish long before that."
   Why does the professor say this:
   "But, knowing you, I think you'll probably finish long before that."

Answer

(B) The professor expresses a positive opinion based on her knowledge of the student's abilities. The tone is encouraging, and should increase the student's self-confidence. Choices (A), (B), and (D) are not correct because the professor has already told him that he has fifty minutes to finish the test.

Audio

6. What can we assume about the man?

Answer

(C) "I noticed that policy on the syllabus." Choice (A) is not correct because Jim has read the syllabus and has arranged for a makeup test. Choice (B) is not correct because Jim is a lot better. Choice (D) is not mentioned and may not be concluded from information in this conversation.

Conversation Two

Audio

Narrator: Listen to part of a conversation between a student and a professor.

Marge: Dr. Jones?

Jones: Hi, Marge.

Marge: Hi . . . I was wondering whether I should . . . whether to make an appointment with you or, uh, whether I should come back while the secretary's here.

Jones: Do you have time to talk now? My two o'clock canceled, so . . . I'm free.

Marge: That'd be great.

Jones: What do you have on your mind?

Marge: Well . . . I need your advice. Um . . . I like your class. I mean, it's my favorite one.

Jones: I'm glad. Are you a biology major?

Marge: Uh . . . premed, but biology is my emphasis.

Jones: Good. And, I'm looking at my grade book, and, uh, you have a B+ in the class. . . . You could probably pull that up to an A before the end of the semester.

Marge: I know I could [deep breath] if I had the time to study. But the problem is . . . well you see . . . I took six classes this semester . . . and that's okay. I can handle that. I've taken six classes before, and I've done all right, but . . . but two of my classes are lab classes . . . so I have the labs and the lab assignments on top of the classes, and I'm . . . I'm really in over my head.

Jones: I see. Labs do take a lot of time.

Marge: They do, if you do them right. So . . . so, I thought, uh, if you'd sign, I mean, if you'd give me permission to drop your biology class, then I'd take it over again next semester.

Jones: Well, it's very late in the semester to drop a course. You have only two weeks left before the final.

Marge: I know. I can't do it without the professor's, I . . . I mean, without your signature. But I . . . I just don't see any other way.

Jones: Marge, I'm sure you've thought this through, so . . . can you tell me why you decided to drop the biology class? You said it was your favorite class, and you're doing well in it . . . so, uh, I'm a little surprised that you didn't decide to, perhaps, drop another class instead.

Marge: Oh, no. You see, I'll have to take the course that I drop over again . . . from the beginning I mean, next semester . . . and I really like biology . . . and I really like the way you teach it, so I thought . . . I wouldn't mind repeating it as much as, well, some of my other classes.

Jones: I see . . . Well, have you considered taking an incomplete?

Marge: Not really. I've never done that. I'm not even, uh, not sure what it means.

Jones: Marge, what you would do is continue attending class, but . . . you wouldn't have to turn in your lab reports and take your final until next semester.

Marge: Is . . . is that possible?

Jones: Not always . . . but in this case, I'm willing to do it . . . with one condition.

Marge: What's that?

Jones: I want you to write a memo to your advisor explaining that the eighteen-hour schedule was too much . . . and, uh, that you have indicated to me that . . . that . . . you don't plan to take so many hours again. And, I'd like to have a copy of the memo for my file.

Marge: Oh, Dr. Jones, I'd be glad to do that. I've really learned my limits this semester . . . I mean, I know . . . and, and . . . I don't ever plan to get myself in this mess again.

Jones: Good. Then, I'll fill out the paperwork when I turn in my grades, and you'll see an *I* on your grade report. . . . And Marge, I should tell you that if you don't complete the requirements for the course by the end of next semester, then . . . you'll receive an F for the class.

Marge: That won't happen. I'll finish my lab reports and study for the final over the break, and . . . if it's okay with you, I'll, uh, I'll just take the exam as soon as we get back . . . in January, I mean.

Jones: That's a good plan.

Audio

1. What is the purpose of this conversation?

Answer

(C) Because the woman asks permission to drop a course in order to decrease her course load, it may be concluded that the purpose of the conversation is to talk about her workload. Choices (A), (B), and (D) are mentioned in reference to the main topic, "the workload."

Audio

2. What does Marge mean when she says she is "over her head"?

Answer

(B) "Labs do take a lot of time." The idiom *in over one's head* means to be "overwhelmed." Choice (A) is not correct because the woman has a B+ and could have an A before the end of the semester. Choice (C) is not correct because it is her favorite class. Choice (D) is true because she has a premed major with a biology emphasis, but it is not the meaning of the phrase *in over one's head*.

Audio

3. Why does Marge want to drop the biology class?

Answer

(C) "I thought I wouldn't mind repeating it [the biology class] . . . ." Choice (A) is not correct because she says biology is her favorite class. Choice (B) is not correct because she has a B+ in the grade book. Choice (D) is not correct because she likes the way the professor teaches the course.

Audio

4. Why does Marge need the professor's signature?

Answer

(B) "I can't do it [drop the class] without the professor's, I mean without your signature." Choice (A) is not correct because she has the professor's permission to take the exam at the beginning of next term, but she does not need the professor's signature. Choice (C) is not correct because she has not asked for excused absences. Choice (D) is not correct because she has a grade of B in the class.

Audio

5. Listen again to part of the conversation.
   Then answer the question.
   "I see. . . . Well, have you considered taking an incomplete?"
   Why does the professor say this:
   "Well, have you considered taking an incomplete?"

Answer

(C) Speakers often ask whether the listener has considered something as a way to make a suggestion without being too direct. Choice (A) is not correct because the consideration of an option would not provide information about the student's academic record. Choice (B) is not correct because the student has already told him that she cannot complete the work for the class. Choice (D) is not correct because the student has already explained the problem.

Audio

6. Why does Dr. Jones want Marge to write a memo to her advisor?

Answer

(A) Because the memo states that she will not "plan to take so many hours again," it may be concluded that the purpose of the memo is to prevent her advisor from allowing her to register for so many hours. Choice (B) refers to the grade that she will receive if she does not complete the course, not to the grade that she already has. Choice (D) is not mentioned and may not be concluded from information in this conversation.

EXERCISE 17: Conversations—Professors/Students 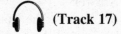 (Track 17)

Conversation One

Audio

Narrator: Listen to a conversation between a student and his academic advisor.

Student: Hi Professor Watson.

Professor: Hi. What brings you in today, Paul?

Student: I was hoping you could help me think through a decision I need to make about my major.

Professor: I'll try. What seems to be the problem?

Student: Well, I declared my major in history my freshman year because I enjoy reading history books and I always get good grades in history. But . . .

Professor: But . . .

Student: Now that I'm starting my senior year, I'm wondering what kind of job I can get with a major in history. But please don't tell me to teach. I know I wouldn't be good at that.

Professor: Okay. Scratch the teaching jobs. Do you like doing research?

Student: You mean research in history?

Professor: Well yes, but other things, too. I was thinking about a job as either a researcher for a government agency, perhaps, or maybe a librarian.

Student: Truthfully, neither one of those options sounds appealing. I guess I have really dug myself into a hole.

Professor: Not necessarily. Would you consider postgraduate studies? Here's where I'm going with this. A large number of lawyers have undergraduate degrees in history.

Student: Well, the truth is I would love to go to law school . . . I've always wanted to be a lawyer, but I really need to work after I graduate to make some money and pay off some of my student loans. More student loans for law school? I don't know.

Professor: Okay then. Would you consider changing majors? Maybe something related to history?

Student: But wouldn't that mean that I would have to go an extra semester or even a whole year longer to graduate?

Professor: Not necessarily. We might be able to fit those history courses into your program as electives. I notice that you have taken quite a few economics courses.

Student: Yes. I really like that aspect of history.

Professor: Well, there are certainly more job opportunities with a major in economics. Why don't you give me a day or so to try to put together a new program for you with an economics major and maybe a minor in history? You know, if you ever decide to go to law school at some time in the future, the economics major would be just as good as a history major.

Audio

1. What is the purpose of this conversation?

Answer

(D) When the professor asks what brings the student in, he answers directly, "I was hoping you could help me think through a decision I need to make about my major." Choice (A) refers to the job opportunities that the student would have after graduation, not to a job that he is looking for now. Choice (B) is not correct because, although it is true that the student would like to go to law school, that is not the reason for the conversation. Choice (C) is not correct because the student says he needs to work to pay off the loans he has, and he does not want more loans.

Audio

2. Why did the man decide to major in history?

Answer

(B) "I declared my major in history my freshman year because I enjoy reading history books." Choice (A) is not correct because he tells the professor not to tell him to teach. Choice (C) is a suggestion that the professor makes, not the man's plan. Choice (D) is true, but he took the courses after he declared his major.

Audio

3. Listen again to part of the conversation.
   Then answer the question.
   "But please don't tell me to teach. I know I wouldn't be good at that."
   "Okay. Scratch the teaching jobs."
   Why does the professor say this:
   "Okay. Scratch the teaching jobs."

Answer

(A) "Scratch" means to "mark it out" or "eliminate" it. Choice (B) is not correct because the professor does not agree that Paul wouldn't be a good teacher, she just agrees to eliminate the option because he is not interested. Choices (C) and (D) are not correct because the professor does not express any emotion in her tone.

Audio

4. According to the student, what is the problem with law school?

Answer

(A) "I've always wanted to be a lawyer, but I really need to work after I graduate to make some money and pay off some of my student loans." Choice (B) is not correct because he has always wanted to be a lawyer. Choice (C) is not correct because his major is history. He is considering changing from history to another major. Choice (D) is not correct because he doesn't think he would be a good teacher, but he would like to be a lawyer.

Audio

5. What is Professor Watson's final recommendation to the student?

Answer

(B) "Why don't you give me a day or so to try to put together a new program for you with an economics major and maybe a minor in history?" Choices (A) and (D) are suggestions that the professor made and the student turned down, not the final recommendation. Choice (C) is not correct because the student wants to work to pay for his student loans, not his tuition.

Audio

6. What will Paul probably do?

Answer

(A) Since Professor Watson asks him to "give her a day or so to put together a new program," Paul will probably return in a few days to see it. Choice (B) is not correct because he is not satisfied with the program he is in. Choice (D) is not correct because he is already majoring in history. Choice (C) is not correct because withdrawing from school is not mentioned and may not be concluded from information in this conversation.

Conversation Two

Audio

Narrator: Listen to a conversation between a financial aid officer and a student.

Officer: Anna?

Student: Yes. Thanks for seeing me.

Officer: Of course. How can I help you?

Student: Well, I'm hoping that you can give me some advice about financial aid.

Officer: That's what I do here. Tell me a little about yourself. That will help me narrow down your options.

Student: Okay. I'm a junior, and I'm majoring in engineering.

Officer: You're an international student, right?

Student: Yes.

Officer: So how have you been funding your education so far?

Student: My parents have been helping me, but now it's hard for them because my brother is starting his college program this year, so there are two of us now.

Officer: Well, there are a few scholarships for international students, but I'll be honest with you, they are very competitive. Did you bring your transcripts?

Student: Yes. I have them here.

Officer: Well, your grades are certainly outstanding. I can think of two scholarships that you might qualify for—a general university scholarship for international students. But I have to tell you, we only award two of them every year, and more than fifty students apply. Most general university scholarships go to instate students, that is, students who have graduated from high schools in Wisconsin. Still, you should submit an application online. Go to the university site and click on financial aid, then general scholarships. You'll find it there. And I should tell you that the essay is an important factor in the selection process.

Student: Good to know. Thank you.

Officer: The other possibility is the Danburry scholarship—an engineering scholarship for women sponsored by the Danburry family. It isn't a full tuition scholarship like the general university scholarship, but it *is* $2,000 per semester, and once you are awarded the scholarship, you can apply to continue the award until you graduate. As long as your grades are good—and yours are—so that should be no problem.

Student: And how do I apply for that one?

Officer: Well, first you fill out an application online, and for this one, you need three letters of reference from faculty or other university personnel. After you complete the application online, then I can schedule you for an interview with the scholarship committee. I'll give you all the information before you leave.

Audio

1. What is the main purpose of this conversation?

Answer

(A) When the man asks how he can help her, the student replies, "Well, I'm hoping that you can give me some advice about financial aid." Choice (B) is not correct because the woman is already a successful engineering student. Choice (C) is not correct because the woman needs letters of reference from faculty or other university personnel to apply for the Danburry scholarship, but she does not ask the man to write one for her. The woman shows her transcripts to the financial aid officer, but Choice (D) is not the purpose of the conversation.

Audio

2. How has the woman been paying for her tuition?

Answer

(A) The woman tells the financial aid officer that "her parents have been helping" her. Choices (B), (C), and (D) are not mentioned and may not be concluded from information in this conversation. Since her brother is starting college this year, it is not probable that he has been sending money.

Audio

3. Listen again to part of the conversation.
   Then answer the question.
   "Well, there are a few scholarships for international students, but I'll be honest with you, they are very competitive."
   Why does the man say this:
   ". . . but I'll be honest with you, they are very competitive."

Answer

(B) By telling her honestly that the scholarships are competitive, he is preparing her to be realistic about her chances. Choices (A), (C), and (D) cannot be concluded from his comment.

Audio

4. What can we assume about the university?

(C) Since "instate students" have graduated from high schools in the state of Wisconsin, it can be assumed that the university is in the state of Wisconsin. The conversation does not include evidence about the size of the school in Choice (A) or the number of international students in Choice (B). The difficulty in Choice (D) refers to the competition for a scholarship, not for admission.

Audio

5. What does the man tell the woman about the Danburry scholarship?

Answer

(B) "The other possibility is the Danburry scholarship—an engineering scholarship for women."
Choice (A) is not correct because scholars can continue to receive the award if their grades are good, not if they have financial need. Choice (C) is not correct because the Danburry scholarship "isn't a full tuition scholarship like the general university scholarship. . . ." Choice (D) refers to the meeting with the scholarship committee, but it is not mentioned whether the Danburry family is on the committee.

Audio

6. What will the woman probably do to apply for the Danburry scholarship?

Answer

(B) ". . . first you fill out an application online. . . ." Choice (A) is not correct because the man has already seen her transcripts. The essay in Choice (C) refers to the general scholarship, not to the Danburry scholarship. Choice (D) is not mentioned and may not be concluded from information in this conversation.

EXERCISE 18: Conversations—Professors/Students   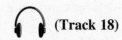 (Track 18)

Conversation One

Audio

Narrator: Listen to part of a conversation in a professor's office.

Smith: You wanted to talk about the results of your laboratory experiment. Did you have any problems with it?

Bob: Yes, Professor Smith. We did.

Smith:	And you two are lab partners?
Bob:	Yes, we are.
Smith:	Well, then, can you go over the procedure for me?
Anne:	Sure. First we put ten grams of crushed limestone in a bottle.
Smith:	Anything special about the bottle?
Bob:	It was a gas-collecting bottle with a one-hole stopper and bent glass tubing.
Smith:	Very good. So you put the limestone in a gas-collecting bottle. Then what?
Anne:	Then we poured in ten milligrams of hydrochloric acid, put on the stopper, and collected a bottle of carbon dioxide.
Smith:	Right. What was the method of collection?
Anne:	Water displacement.
Smith:	Good.
Anne:	Then, we lit a magnesium ribbon and put it in the bottle of carbon dioxide.
Bob:	And carbon deposits began to form on the bottom of the bottle. You see, we didn't have any problem with procedure . . .
Anne:	Well, we had a little problem getting the magnesium ribbon to stay lit until we could get it into the bottle.
Bob:	Okay. But we did it. The big problem was that we really didn't understand what happened. Did the magnesium combine with the oxygen in the carbon dioxide?
Smith:	You have just answered your own question, Bob. The burning magnesium broke the carbon-oxygen bonds in the carbon dioxide, and then the oxygen combined with the magnesium to produce magnesium oxide.
Anne:	And the carbon was freed to deposit itself on the bottle.
Smith:	Exactly.

Audio

1. What is the purpose of this conversation?

Answer

(A) "You wanted to talk about the results of your laboratory experiment." Choices (B) and (C) are mentioned as secondary themes that are used to develop the main theme of the discussion, "the results of the lab experiment." Choice (D) is not correct because the students had already done the lab experiment.

Audio

2. What was deposited on the bottom of the gas bottle?

Answer

(C) "And carbon deposits began to form on the bottom of the bottle." Choice (A) refers to the ribbon that was lit, not to the deposits. Choice (B) refers to the material that was put in the bottle at the beginning of the experiment, not to what was deposited at the end. Choice (D) refers to the method of collection, water displacement.

Audio

3. What caused the deposits?

Answer

(C) "The burning magnesium broke the carbon-oxygen bonds in the carbon dioxide, and then the oxygen combined with the magnesium to produce magnesium oxide." Choices (A), (B), and (D) are not correct because burning magnesium broke the carbon-oxygen bonds.

Audio

4. Where does this conversation take place?

Answer

(D) "Listen to part of a conversation in a professor's office." The *lab* in Choice (A) refers to the place where the experiment took place, not to where the conversation is taking place. Choices (B) and (C) are not mentioned and may not be concluded from information in this conversation.

Audio
5. What can we infer from this conversation?
Answer
(B) Since the students are able to explain the procedures for the experiment, it may be concluded that they performed the experiment correctly. Choice (C) is not correct because in spite of a little problem, the students completed the experiment. Choice (D) refers to the fact that there is burning magnesium, not a fire in the lab. Choice (A) is not mentioned and may not be concluded from information in the discussion.

Conversation Two

Audio

Narrator: Listen to part of a conversation with a professor.

Tom: Dr. Anderson, could you please clarify the requirements for this course? Some of us are a little bit confused about the final examination.

Anderson: Oh? Well, you have two options in this course. You can either take a final examination or you can write a research paper instead.

Tom: Excuse me, Dr. Anderson. That's the point I need you to clarify. What kind of research paper did you have in mind? An original study? A report? A book review, perhaps?

Anderson: A report. A summary really, based upon a reading list of current research in the field.

Jane: How long should the reports be?

Anderson: Length is really not important. I should think that it would take at least ten pages in order to develop the topic, however.

Jane: And should we check the topic with you before we begin writing?

Anderson: You may, if you wish. But the only requirement is that it relate to current trends in United States foreign policy. Are you considering writing a paper, Jane?

Jane: I'm not sure. I think that I'd like to know a little bit more about the examination.

Anderson: All right. One hundred multiple-choice questions covering both the lectures and the outside readings.

Tom: Didn't you say that you would give us one hour for the examination?

Anderson: Yes, I did.

Tom: I'm going to do the paper, then.

Jane: Me, too.

Audio
1. What prompted the conversation?
Answer
(A) "Dr. Anderson, could you please clarify the requirements for this course?" Choice (B) refers to Jane and Tom, not to all the students. Choice (C) is not correct because the professor is clarifying the requirements he has previously explained. Choice (D) is not mentioned and may not be concluded from information in the conversation.

Audio
2. What kind of research paper has Dr. Anderson assigned?
Answer
(A) "What kind of research paper did you have in mind? An original study? A report? A book review, perhaps?" "A report." Choices (B) and (C) refer to options that the student, not the professor, mentions. Choice (D) is not mentioned and may not be concluded from information in the discussion.

Audio

3. What kind of examination has Dr. Anderson prepared?

Answer

(B) "One hundred multiple-choice questions covering both the lectures and the outside readings." From the reference to *multiple-choice* questions, it must be concluded that it is an objective test. Choices (A), (C), and (D) are not mentioned and may not be concluded from information in the conversation.

Audio

4. Which option do the students choose?

Answer

(B) When the man says, "I'm going to do the paper, then," the woman agrees. The *lectures* in Choice (A) refer to one source of the questions on the examination, not to the option that the students choose. Choice (C) refers to the *reading list* that will be required for the paper, not to a separate option. Choice (D) refers to the option that the students decide not to choose.

Audio

5. Based on the conversation, which course does Dr. Anderson most probably teach?

Answer

(C) From the reference to current trends in *U.S. foreign policy*, it must be concluded that Dr. Anderson teaches political science. Choices (A), (B), and (D) are not mentioned and may not be concluded from information in the conversation.

EXERCISE 19: Conversations—Professors/Students 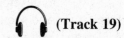 (Track 19)

Conversation One

Audio

Narrator: Listen to part of a conversation between a student and a professor.

Larry: Hi, Professor Davidson.

Professor: Oh, hello, Larry.

Larry: Um . . . I know it's not your office hour right now, but I saw you, and I . . . I wondered if . . .

Professor: Sure, come in. What can I do for you?

Larry: I just want to check something out with you, uh, from the lecture on Wednesday. I want to get it straightened out before . . . before class tomorrow, because . . . uh, because . . .

Professor: . . . because it might be on the quiz.

Larry: Well, yes.

Professor: Okay. Fire away.

Larry: It's about hot spots. Under the ocean. I've got two questions. First, you said that hot spots appear to be fixed in place for . . . let's see . . . tens or even hundreds of millions of years . . . and, uh, they're stable even when the litho . . . litho . . . spheric plates move over them. And then you said that volcanic activity is stronger at hot spots.

Professor: Right so far.

Larry: Then, I have in my notes here . . . that in Hawaii . . . I think it was Hawaii because I have Iceland scratched out and Hawaii written in . . . so I think it was in Hawaii . . . where the hot spots have, uh, have active volcanoes under the ocean . . . and, uh, the volcanoes continue to erupt and . . . and . . . that builds the island.

Professor: Right again.

Larry: Now here's the part that gets confusing. I wrote this down, "The quantity of lava produced by hot-spot volcanoes is so large that such volcanoes are the tallest topographic features on Earth's surface."

Professor: Larry, that's exactly what I said in my lecture.

Larry: But then . . . this is what I can't figure out . . . I wrote that the, uh, mountains in Hawaii are only about 4,500 meters above sea level.

Professor: Oh, now I see your problem. The island actually rises 5,500 meters . . . that is . . . 5,500 meters from the sea floor to the surface of the ocean.

Larry: From the surface of the ocean. So, then . . . okay . . . I need to add 5,500 meters to the 4,500 to calculate the actual elevation from the surface of the planet . . . which is actually the ocean floor.

Professor: Exactly.

Larry: Well, that takes care of one of my questions.

Professor: Okay. What else do you have?

Larry: It's about hot spots again . . . the ones remaining in place as the uh . . . the uh . . . plate moves over them. What did you say about chains of islands? Like, well, like Hawaii, to use that example again.

Professor: Okay. Visualize a hot spot on the ocean floor. It doesn't move. But the plate moves over it, and the plate carries one of the Hawaiian Islands that the hot spot has created . . . away from the hot spot that formed it.

Larry: But uh . . . the hot spot is still active, so . . . so it's still building an undersea formation . . . that, I mean, the undersea formation . . . will, uh, become another island close to the first island. Okay. And then . . . the plate moves the second island away from the hot spot, so . . . so a chain of islands . . . that's how a chain is formed . . . from the same hot spot.

Professor: From the hot spot and the movement of the lithospheric plates.

Larry: The litho . . . litho . . .

Professor: The lithospheric plates . . . *Lithospheric* just means Earth's crust and the upper part of the mantle.

Larry: So this process is going on all the time.

Professor: It is. In fact, if volcanic activity continues at its present rate, another island may be appearing at the end of the Hawaiian chain.

Larry: Really?

Professor: We've given it a name already—Loihi. Of course, we won't actually see it above the surface of the ocean for another ten to forty thousand years, and you and I won't see it at all . . . but uh . . . we are observing it closely as it continues to build under water.

Larry: That is so cool.

Professor: It is, isn't it? And to get back to your original question, when Loihi is only a few feet above the water, it will already be a very significant topographical feature.

Larry: Because . . . because of the height it has reached . . . before breaking the surface.

Professor: Well said. You should do just fine on that quiz.

Audio

1. What is the purpose of the conversation?

Answer

(A) "I want to get it straightened out . . . because it might be on the quiz." Choice (B) is true, but the reason he wants to know is because it will probably be a quiz question. The *quiz* in Choice (C) refers to the next quiz, not to the last quiz. Choice (D) is not correct because Larry refers to the lecture on Wednesday.

Audio

2. What is the main topic of this conversation?

Answer

(D) "It's about hot spots." Choices (A), (B), and (C) are all mentioned in reference to the main topic, "hot spots."

Audio

3. What is the altitude of Hawaii?

(D) "So . . . I need to add 5,500 meters to the 4,500 to calculate the actual elevation from the surface of the planet . . . which is actually the ocean floor." Choice (A) sounds like 4,500 meters [forty-five hundred], which is the elevation above sea level, not the total altitude. Choice (B) is the elevation above sea level but does not include the elevation below the surface of the ocean. Choice (C) is the elevation below the surface of the ocean but does not include the elevation above sea level.

Audio

4. What does the professor say about the newest Hawaiian island?

Answer

(D) ". . . when Loihi is only a few feet above water, it will already be a very significant topographical feature." Choice (A) is not correct because the island is named Loihi. Choice (B) is not correct because it will appear in ten to forty thousand years. Choice (C) is not correct because it will not appear for ten to forty thousand years.

Audio

5. Listen again to part of the conversation.
   Then answer the question.
   "Of course, we won't actually see it above the surface of the ocean for another ten to forty thousand years . . . and you and I won't see it at all . . . but uh . . . we are observing it closely as it continues to build under water."
   Why does the professor say this:
   ". . . and you and I won't see it at all. . . ."

Answer

(C) Because the island will not appear for thousands of years, the professor makes a joke of the fact that they cannot expect to live long enough to see it. Choice (B) is not correct because the island is not visible yet and not well-known, and therefore, it is not a concrete example. Choice (D) is not correct because the student is asking questions, not presenting an argument. Choice (A) is not correct because it is not mentioned and may not be concluded from information in the consultation.

Audio

6. Put the following events in order to explain how island chains are formed.

Answer

(B) (A) (C) (D) ". . . the plate moves over it [the first island], and the plate carries one of the Hawaiian islands . . . away from the hot spot that formed it. . . . But . . . the hot spot is still active, . . . so it is still building . . . another island close to the first island."

Conversation Two

Audio

Narrator: Listen to part of a conversation between a student and a professor.

Ronda: Hi, Dr. Gilbert. Are you busy?

Gilbert: Just getting organized for my class.

Ronda: Oh. . . . Do you want me to come back later?

Gilbert: No, no. Come in. This is an open office hour. I was just working on some notes until someone showed up, so . . .

Ronda: Thanks. I wanted to talk about . . . about my term paper. I have a topic . . . but I'm not sure where to begin. I'm finding so many references, I, well, I couldn't possibly read them all.

Gilbert: Okay. What's the topic?

Ronda: The baroque style.

Gilbert: The baroque style?

Ronda: Yes, I really like the . . . the . . .

Gilbert: Opulence is the word usually associated with baroque.

Ronda: I was thinking of "over the top," but opulence is even better. I'm attracted to it.

Gilbert: Well, that's good. You want to choose a topic you're interested in, or, uh, attracted to. But let's talk about the problem you're having. Ronda, it's no wonder that you are finding so much material. That topic is extremely broad. To really do it justice, you'd have to write a dissertation. Remember, your paper is supposed to be only ten to twelve pages long.

Ronda: Well, I haven't started writing yet. Do you think maybe I should choose another topic?

Gilbert: Another topic? No, I didn't say that. I said the topic was too broad. What you need to do is, uh, narrow it down. Look at, uh, one aspect of the baroque style, perhaps architecture or painting or sculpture, or you could do some research on one artist and, uh, demonstrate . . . discuss how the baroque style is . . . is reflected in the work. You could probably even narrow it down to one work by one artist and still have more than enough material for such a short paper.

Ronda: Oh, okay. Actually, that sounds really good. A lot more manageable. Thanks, Dr. Gilbert.

Gilbert: Wait a minute, Ronda. Let's talk a little more about the research you've been doing, and, uh, maybe we can find a topic.

Ronda: Really? That would be perfect. I have my research on my laptop, but . . .

Gilbert: Just talk to me about it.

Ronda: Okay. I started out with some general sources, and I . . . I found a lot on, uh, Bernini.

Gilbert: Umhum. That makes sense. Bernini was certainly at the center of the baroque movement. But even that topic would be very broad since he was such a Renaissance man—hard to imagine someone who could be a sculptor, a painter, and an architect. I think he even wrote plays and composed music. So what else did you find?

Ronda: Well, I had a lot on Versailles. And, you know, the Hall of Mirrors. And the Spanish painters of the period.

Gilbert: Diego Velazquez.

Ronda: Uh-huh . . . and, oh, did I mention Saint Peter's Cathedral in Rome?

Gilbert: So you have Italy, France, and Spain in your research.

Ronda: More than that. I've got some information on the Dutch baroque, too . . . although I think it seems different from the rest somehow. Wasn't Rembrandt Dutch?

Gilbert: Right you are.

Ronda: So . . .

Gilbert: Hold on a minute, Ronda. Of everything you've read, what's the one person or building, or work of art, or fact that you found the most interesting?

Ronda: Let me see, well, probably . . . the architecture.

Gilbert: And which structure stands out in your mind?

Ronda: Oh, that's easy. Versailles. The inside though, not the outside, which to me has at least some classical influence. Don't you think so? It isn't as typical of baroque as the magnificent rooms inside the palace.

Gilbert: I would agree with that.

Ronda: I . . . I actually saw Versailles when my family was living in Europe five years ago. My dad was transferred to London, and . . . it was so great . . . we traveled a lot while we were there. The trains go everywhere, but you probably know that. I didn't get to Italy and Spain, though. I'd like to some day.

Gilbert: Well, let's see what we've accomplished. You started out with baroque, which was very broad, then you said that you were interested in architecture . . . which limited the topic somewhat . . . and, uh, let's see . . . then you found one building.

Ronda: Versailles.

Gilbert: And, as I understood you, you eliminated the outside . . . the outside of Versailles . . . so your topic is much more narrow now . . . if you choose to write about the interior of Versailles. Frankly, that's still a major topic.

Ronda: Is it? So, do you think I should narrow it even more?

Gilbert:	I do. Remember a ten-page paper is only a few thousand words. And, uh, I should think, uh, fifteen to twenty sources should be more than enough.
Ronda:	Well then . . . how do I put this? Do you think I could . . . I could find enough to write about, I mean, if I just focused on the Hall of Mirrors? I think I have more than twenty sources about that in my list already.
Gilbert:	I'm sure you could. In fact, you should probably think about an even more specific aspect of the hall . . . something that would interest you. There has been a tremendous amount of research on it. Look, why don't you go back to your research files, and, uh, try to come up with a title? We can talk about it more after you do . . . after you have a title . . . and then, uh, I'll try to direct you to some specific resources if you don't have enough material already. How's that?
Ronda:	That would be perfect. Maybe I can have it figured out . . . I mean, I'll try to have it by class tomorrow.

Audio

1. What is Ronda's problem?

Answer

(B) "That topic is extremely broad." Choice (A) is not correct because Ronda's topic is *the baroque style*. Choice (D) is not correct because she is finding so many references that she can't read them all. Choice (C) is not mentioned and may not be concluded from information in this conversation.

Audio

2. How long should the paper be?

Answer

(B) "Remember, your paper is supposed to be only ten to twelve pages." The number in Choice (A) refers to how many years ago Ronda and her family lived in Europe. Choices (C) and (D) are not mentioned and may not be concluded from information in this conversation.

Audio

3. What does Dr. Gilbert suggest?

Answer

(C) ". . . try to come up with a title. We can talk about it more after you do. . . ." Choice (A) is not correct because the professor tells Ronda that he didn't say she should find another topic. Choice (B) refers to the offer to direct Ronda to specific *resources*, but he has not given her resources in the past. Choice (D) is not mentioned and may not be concluded from information in this conversation.

Audio

4. Where did Ronda's family live five years ago?

Answer

(D) "My dad was transferred to London. . . ." Choices (A) and (B) refer to places she would like to visit some day, not to where she has lived. Choice (C) refers to a place she visited, not to where she has lived.

Audio

5. Listen again to part of the conversation.
   Then answer the question.
   "Hi, Dr. Gilbert. Are you busy?" "Just getting organized for my class."
   Why does the student ask this:
   "Are you busy?"

Answer

(C) Speakers who are interrupting someone in an office setting often ask the question, *Are you busy?* to give the other person the opportunity to postpone the conversation. Choice (A) is not correct because she asks a general question, but she does not ask for specific details. Choice (B) is not correct because she asks the question before she begins to chat. Choice (D) is not mentioned and may not be concluded from information in the conversation.

Audio

6. What will Ronda most probably do?

Answer

(A) "... do you think I could ... find enough to write about I mean, if I just focused on the Hall of Mirrors?" "I'm sure you could." Choice (B) is not correct because she already has more than twenty sources. Choice (C) is not correct because the Hall of Mirrors is a topic in the baroque period. Choice (D) is not correct because she has not started writing a draft yet.

EXERCISE 20: Conversations—Professors/Students 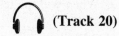 (Track 20)

Conversation One

Audio

Narrator: Listen to part of a conversation between a student and a professor.

Jim: Hi Professor Wilson.

Professor: Hi Jim. What can I do for you today?

Jim: Well, we have a test coming up.

Professor: Yep. On Monday.

Jim: Right. So this is the first test I've taken in one of your classes. Uh, most of the other students have had other classes with you. But, uh, but I'm a transfer student.

Professor: Oh, that's right. You took the prerequisites for this class at Community College, didn't you?

Jim: Yeah. It was a lot different there.

Professor: Okay. Well, I think I mentioned in class that it would be ten short-answer questions.

Jim: Yeah. I have that in my notes from class on Wednesday. But I'm not sure what that is. I'm used to multiple-choice tests. So do you want an essay for, uh, for each question?

Professor: Not exactly. That would take a lot longer than an hour.

Jim: That's what I was thinking.

Professor: Look, you'll have a question. Then you should just respond to it with a few sentences. No more than a short paragraph. In fact, if you can provide a complete answer in one sentence, that's fine.

Jim: Okay ...

Professor: So if I ask you for a definition of a term, for example, you could probably answer that in one sentence, but if I asked you to explain a process, you would need more detail and that would maybe mean you'd need to write a paragraph.

Jim: Oh. I think I get it now.

Professor: And Jim, I suggested that you pay close attention to the summaries at the end of each of the chapters in the e-book.

Jim: Right. I have that in my notes, and I plan to answer all the summary questions to get ready for the test.

Professor: Well then, I think you'll do just fine. By the way, how are you getting along with everything else? A transfer to a large university from a small community college can be a little ... overwhelming at first.

Jim: Oh, it's going fine. It *is* a big change, but I have a terrific roommate, and he's been great. And the professors have been willing to help me figure things out, like you have today. So it's all good.

Professor: Glad to hear it. Come back anytime if you have questions about the course requirements or anything else that I could help you with.

Jim: Thanks. I really appreciate that.

Audio

1. What is the student mainly discussing with his professor?

Answer

(D) "Well, we have a test coming up. . . . I'm used to multiple-choice tests. So do you want an essay for, uh, for each question?" Choice (A) is mentioned because the man is a transfer student, but it is not the main topic of discussion. Choice (B) is mentioned briefly when they are discussing the student's previous school, but it is not the main topic. The professor mentions the summaries in Choice (C) when she is helping the student prepare for the tests, but it is not the main topic.

Audio

2. When will the test be given?

Answer

(A) "Well, we have a test coming up." "Yep. On Monday." Choices (B), (C), and (D) are not mentioned as test days.

Audio

3. Why is the man worried about the test?

Answer

(A) (B) "So this is the first test I've taken in one of your classes. Uh, most of the other students have had other classes with you. . . . I'm used to multiple-choice tests." Choices (C) and (D) are not mentioned and may not be concluded from information in the conversation.

Audio

4. What does the professor suggest?

Answer

(A) "And Jim, I suggested that you pay close attention to the summaries at the end of each of the chapters in the e-book." The notes in Choice (B) are mentioned because the student has information about the summaries in his notes, but the professor does not suggest going over the notes. Choices (C) and (D) are not mentioned and may not be concluded from information in the conversation.

Audio

5. Listen again to part of the conversation. Then answer the question.

"So if I ask you for a definition of a term, for example, you could probably answer that in one sentence, but if I asked you to explain a process, you would need more detail and that would maybe mean you'd need to write a paragraph."

"Oh. I think I get it now."

What does Jim mean when he says this:

"Oh. I think I get it now."

Answer

(B) To "get it" means to *understand*. Choices (A), (C), and (D) are not implied when the student indicates that he understands.

Audio

6. What can we assume about the man?

Answer

(B) Since the man is a transfer student from a smaller school, and he says that it is "a big change," we learn that he has an adjustment to make. When he says that his roommate and the professors are helpful, and that it is "all good," we know that he is adjusting to the larger school. Choice (A) is not correct because he says he has a "terrific roommate." Choice (C) is not correct because he took the prerequisite at his former school. Choice (D) is not correct because he refers to his notes when he is talking with the professor.

Conversation Two

Audio

Narrator: Listen to part of a conversation between a student and a professor.

Student: Hi Professor Lee.

Professor: Hi Martha. Come on in.

Student: You wanted to see me?

Professor: Yes. I just wanted to see whether you needed any help locating resources for your paper. Your previous paper was very well written, but you lost points because you didn't have enough citations. The list was too short.

Student: I know.

Professor: I think you told me that you aren't using the library.

Student: No, I don't. Well, I do, but just to study because it's quiet, and the campus coffee shop is there. I don't use it to do my research. But Professor Lee, nobody I know uses the library to check out books anymore.

Professor: Yes, well I've heard that before. So, Martha, how are you locating your sources?

Student: Oh, to tell the truth, at the beginning of the term, when I did that first paper, I was just doing a general Google search, for the topic, and I really didn't know which ones to use. They all looked about the same to me. Except the really good articles that you had to pay for. So I just used what I could find for free.

Professor: And now?

Student: I'm using Google Scholar now, and that's working much better for me. There are a lot of free articles, but they're a lot better than the ones I was finding in the general Google search.

Professor: So you don't need any help then?

Student: I don't think so. But . . .

Professor: But?

Student: But, uh, if you wouldn't mind, I could bring in a list of my citations when I get the first draft done, if you . . .

Professor: Sure. I think that's a good plan. Let me take a look, and if you need any additional sources, then I can give you some suggestions.

Student: That would be awesome. I'm almost done with the draft now.

Professor: Well, I have office hours on Tuesday morning.

Student: Um, I'm not sure I'll have it ready by then.

Professor: Okay, how about coming in after class on Friday? That way you'd have the weekend to check out any new sources that you might want to use before the paper is due next Monday.

Student: That's perfect. Well, I'll see you in class on Friday then. Thank you so much for everything.

Audio

1. Why did the professor want to see the student?

Answer

(D) "I just wanted to see whether you needed any help locating resources for your paper." Choice (B) refers to a short conversation about the use of the library, but not to the reason that the professor wanted to see the student. Choices (A) and (C) are not mentioned and may not be concluded from information in the conversation.

Audio

2. Why did the student lose points on her last paper?

Answer

(B) "Your previous paper was very well written, but you lost points because you didn't have enough citations." Choice (A) is not correct because the professor says that the paper was "well written." Choice (C) is not correct because it was the number, not the quality of the citations, that caused her to lose points. The length in Choice (D) refers to the list of citations, not to the length of the paper itself.

Audio

3. How does the student do her research now?

Answer

(C) "I'm using Google Scholar now. . . ." Choice (A) refers to how she did her research in the past, not now. Choice (B) is not correct because she tries to find "free articles." Choice (D) is not correct because she uses the library to study but not to do her research.

Audio

4. Listen again to part of the conversation.
    Then answer the question.
    "So you don't need any help then?"
    "I don't think so. But . . ."
    "But?"
    Why does the professor say this:
    "But?"

Answer

(A) Repeating a word or phrase that leaves a sentence unfinished is a way to encourage the other person to continue. Choices (B), (C), and (D) are not expressed by repetition.

Audio

5. How will the professor help the student?

Answer

(C) ". . . if you need any additional sources, then I can give you some suggestions." Choice (A) is not correct because he does not offer to read the paper. Choice (B) is not correct because he will give her suggestions after he sees the list of sources that she has. Choice (D) is not correct because she needs help with the citations.

Audio

6. When will they meet again?

Answer

(B) ". . . how about coming in after class on Friday?" Choice (A) refers to the day that the paper is due, not to the day of the meeting. Choices (C) and (D) refer to office hours, but since the student will not have the paper finished by then, it is too early to meet.

EXERCISE 21: Talks—Professor 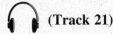 (Track 21)

Lecture One

Audio

Narrator: Listen to part of a talk by a college professor.

Professor:

Your test on Friday will cover material from both of your textbooks, my lecture notes, and your lab assignments. There will be fifty multiple-choice questions and five short-answer essay questions. The multiple-choice will count half of your grade, and the essay questions will count half of your grade.

I will tell you right now that there won't be any math problems, but that doesn't mean that you shouldn't review the formulas and know what they are used for.

I wouldn't bother much with the notes from my first lecture since that was an overview of the course, but you'll probably want to look at them when you study for the final.

Oh yes, this test represents twenty-five percent of your total grade for the semester. The lab reports are twenty-five percent, attendance ten, and your final forty.

Any questions?

Audio

1. What is the purpose of the announcement?

Answer

(B) "Your test on Friday will cover material from both of your textbooks, my lecture notes, and your lab assignments." Choice (A) refers to the first lecture, not to this lecture. Choice (C) refers to the test on Friday. Choice (D) refers to the material to be tested, not to the purpose of the lecture.

Audio

2. On the test, how much will the multiple-choice questions count?

Answer

(D) "The multiple-choice will count half of your grade [on the test]." Choice (A) refers to the credit toward the final grade for attendance, not to the credit on the test for multiple-choice questions. Choice (B) refers to the credit toward the final grade for the test and for the lab report, not to the credit for the multiple-choice questions. Choice (C) refers to the credit toward the final grade for the final exam.

Audio

3. For what percentage of the total grade will the test count?

Answer

(B) "Oh yes, this test represents twenty-five percent of your total grade for the semester." Choice (A) refers to the credit toward the final grade for attendance, not for the test. Choice (C) refers to the credit toward the final grade for the final exam. Choice (D) refers to the credit on the test for the multiple-choice questions and for the essay questions.

Audio

4. What does the speaker say about math problems?

Answer

(B) "I will tell you right now that there won't be any math problems . . ." Choice (A) refers to the notes from the first lecture, not to all of the notes. Choice (C) is not correct because the speaker reveals that there will be no math problems on the test. Choice (D) is not correct because the speaker encourages students to review the formulas.

Audio

5. In which class would this announcement occur?

Answer

(C) "Your test on Friday will cover material from both of your textbooks, my lecture notes, and your lab assignments . . . there won't be any math problems, but that doesn't mean that you shouldn't review formulas . . ." Choices (A), (B), and (D) would be less likely to have *lab assignments* and *formulas*.

Lecture Two

Audio

Narrator: Listen to part of a talk by a college professor.

Professor:

Before you start writing your term papers, I would like to clarify the differences among paraphrasing, quoting, and plagiarizing. All of these activities involve the use of someone else's ideas, but whereas paraphrasing and quoting are legitimate writing strategies, plagiarizing is a serious offense.

In your term papers, I expect you to paraphrase, that is, to summarize someone else's ideas in your own words. I also expect you to quote, that is to copy information from another source and enclose it in quotation marks in your paper.

When you paraphrase and quote, be sure to cite the source of your information. If you do not cite the source, then you are plagiarizing. You are stealing the ideas and using them as your own. If I discover that you have plagiarized on your term paper, you will receive a zero for the paper and an F for the course.

Audio

1. What is the main topic of this talk?

Answer

(A) "I would like to clarify the differences among paraphrasing, quoting [which are legitimate strategies], and plagiarizing." Choices (B) and (C) are mentioned as secondary themes that are used to develop the main theme of the talk, "the difference between plagiarism and legitimate writing strategies." Choice (D) is not mentioned and may not be concluded from information in the talk.

Audio

2. What is *plagiarizing*?

Answer

(D) "If you do not cite the source, then you are plagiarizing." Choices (B) and (C) refer to quoting, not to plagiarizing. Choice (A) is not mentioned and may not be concluded from information in the lecture.

Audio

3. What are two legitimate writing strategies?

Answer

(C) ". . . whereas paraphrasing and quoting are legitimate writing strategies . . ." Choices (A) and (B) are not correct because plagiarizing is not a legitimate writing strategy. Choice (D) is not correct because copying [without citing the source] is not a legitimate writing strategy.

Audio

4. What will happen to a student who plagiarizes on the term paper?

Answer

(D) "If I discover that you have plagiarized on your term paper, you will receive a zero for the paper and an F for the course." Choices (A), (B), and (C) are not mentioned as alternatives and may not be concluded from information in the lecture.

Audio

5. Who is the speaker?

Answer

(D) Since the speaker is teaching the audience how to write a term paper, it may be concluded that the speaker is a teacher. Choices (A) and (B) refer to the audience, not to the speaker. Choice (C) is less probable because a librarian does not usually assign term papers.

EXERCISE 22: Lectures—Professor

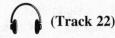 (Track 22)

Lecture One

Audio

Narrator: Listen to part of a lecture by a college professor.

Professor:

The first few pages of the syllabus are an outline of, uh, the topics for each session. As you can see, you'll be responsible for reading the material before you come to class so, uh, you'll have enough background to be able to . . . follow the lecture. For example, on September 3, when you come to class, you should already have read the first two chapters in the text, so, uh, we can discuss the history of psychology in that session. The following week, you should have a grasp of chapters three and four, so . . . so we can cover biology and the psychology of the brain. And so on.

Now, let's take a few minutes to look at the policies and procedures listed on page three of the course syllabus. Uh . . . refer to the section under assignments first, please. You'll notice that all assignments must be typewritten and submitted on the due date . . . in order for you to receive full credit and, uh, the grade for a late assignment will be lowered by one letter for each day past the due date.

Now, look at the section under examinations. As you see, all exams must be completed on the dates and times, uh, scheduled in the syllabus. If you must be absent . . . I mean for an exam, then try to call me to let me know what your problem is. My office phone is on the syllabus, and . . . and my home phone is listed in the telephone directory. Of course, e-mail is best, and you have my e-mail address on page one, uh, it's right under my name on the syllabus. A makeup exam must be arranged within one week of the scheduled date of the exam. And, I must warn you, the questions on the makeup will not be the same as the questions on the regular exam. In fact, I, uh, usually give multiple-choice tests, but I always give short-answer tests for makeups. And, my students tell me . . . they say the makeups are quite a bit more difficult than the regularly scheduled exams.

Oh, yes, let's take a minute to clarify my attendance policy. I suggest that you come to class. I'll be assigning you a seat. . . . Yes, yes, I know you'd rather choose your own seat, but, uh, this is a large class, and it would take up too much time to call the roll every session, so I'll just mark those people absent who aren't present in their seats by the time the class begins. Better late than never, but, uh, if you're late, you'd better check in with me after class so I can change my attendance records. Remember that attendance is 10 percent . . . sorry . . . 15 percent of the grade, which usually makes the difference between an A and a B, or a B and a C. Let's not even talk about Ds and Fs.

One more thing . . . if you need to request an incomplete, please remember that I only approve them for illness or for a serious personal problem, not just for a . . . because you ran out of time. And you must submit a request form with a signed statement of explanation to my office in order for your incomplete to be considered. Otherwise, you'll have to register and take the entire course over again to get credit.

Audio
1. What is the main purpose of this lecture?
Answer
(C) "Let's take a few minutes to look at the policies and procedures listed on page three . . ." Choices (A) and (B) are mentioned as secondary themes that are used to develop the main purpose of the talk, "to explain course policies and procedures." Choice (D) is not mentioned and may not be concluded from information in the lecture.

Audio
2. What is the speaker's policy for late assignments?
Answer
(C) "The grade for a late assignment will be lowered by one letter for each day past the due date." Choice (A) is not correct because assignments must be submitted on the due date for students to receive full credit. Choice (B) is not correct because grades for late assignments will be lowered. Choice (D) is not mentioned and may not be concluded from information in the lecture.

Audio
3. What is the professor's attendance policy?
Answer
(D) "It would take up too much time to call the roll . . . so I will just mark those people absent who are not present in their seats . . ." Choice (A) is not correct because the professor says it would take too much time to call the roll. Choice (B) is not correct because he mentions his attendance records. Choice (C) is not correct because only students who are late should check in with the professor.

Audio
4. What is the procedure for a student to receive a grade of incomplete?
Answer
(A) ". . . you must submit a request form with a signed statement of explanation . . ." Choice (B) refers to the procedure for being absent from an exam, not to the procedure for an incomplete. Choice (C) refers to the procedure for a makeup exam. Choice (D) refers to the consequences of failing to comply with the procedure, not to the procedure itself.

Audio

5. Listen again to part of the lecture.
   Then answer the question.
   "Better late than never, but, uh, if you're late, you'd better check in with me after class so I can change my attendance records. Remember that attendance is 10 percent . . . sorry . . . 15 percent of the grade, which usually makes the difference between an A and a B, or a B and a C."
   Why does the professor say this:
   "Remember that attendance is 10 percent . . . sorry . . . 15 percent of the grade . . ."

Answer

(C) Professors occasionally need to correct a previous statement. In this case, the professor apologizes for the error by saying "sorry" and provides the correct number. Choice (A) is not correct because he makes the statement without comment. Choice (B) is not correct because the correction is for a misstatement, but the policy is not changed. Choice (D) is not correct because he has already reminded students to attend.

Audio

6. What can we infer about the speaker?

Answer

(C) Because the professor announces that his ". . . home phone is listed in the telephone directory," it may be concluded that he does not mind receiving calls at home. Choice (A) is not correct because the syllabus is very detailed and organized. Choice (D) is not correct because he refers to a section under *examinations* on the syllabus. Although the professor appears to be strict, Choice (B) cannot be concluded from information in this lecture.

Lecture Two

Audio

Narrator: Listen to part of a class clarification by a professor.

Professor:

I've been getting quite a few e-mails with, uh, with questions about grading for the group projects, so let me clarify that before we start class today. Each group has five members in it, except one group that . . . that has six. The group project includes a presentation and a written report. But I'll be giving you three grades and, uh, averaging them for a final grade on the project. First, I'll be grading the written report as a whole, and every member of the group will receive the same grade on the written report, so, uh, so it'll be to your benefit to divide the work and produce the best report you can. How do you divide the work? Well, uh, in the past, some of my students have actually divided the report into sections, and each group member does . . . has written one of the sections. That's certainly a possibility, especially for groups who may have a problem finding mutual meeting times. But, uh, some of the other groups have assigned tasks to the group members. For example, two members might do the research, two members might write the report, and another member might, uh, provide editing and . . . and formatting . . . of the final draft. In my experience, it's been difficult for a group of five or six people to write . . . to do the actual writing, line by line, but I have had a few groups do it that way. So, you can see that you have a lot of flexibility in . . . how to prepare the report. However, remember that everyone will receive the same grade for it.

   That brings us to the second grade, which is a group grade for the presentation. Again, I suggest that you share the labor here. If you have a group member who's . . . artistic, you could . . . you could capitalize on that talent . . . maybe by having posters, overheads, or, uh, visuals as part of the presentation. If you have an excellent speaker . . . someone who likes presenting . . . that person might be responsible for . . . for the majority of the oral presentation. Another person who writes well but prefers not to speak could, uh, prepare the handout, if you choose to provide one. I think you see what I mean.

   The best way to get a high grade is to play to the strength of every group member. I mean that you shouldn't ask someone to perform a task that is outside his or her unique ability. And remember, everyone has the potential to contribute something to the group. But, uh, about the grade . . . again . . . there will be one grade for the group presentation, and everyone will receive the same grade. The major problem for previous groups, and, uh, I'll alert you to it right now . . . is preparing too much material for the time frame. Remember, you have thirty minutes, and that might seem like a lot of time, but, uh, many groups haven't been able to complete their presentations, and of course, they have had points deducted because of it.

So what about the third grade? This is an individual grade based on your contribution to the group. I'll be asking you to prepare a list of your activities as a group member, and I . . . I'll be giving you a grade based on participation. Let me explain that a little more. Let's say that one group member has an impressive list. How will I know that it's, uh, accurate? Not that anyone in this class would exaggerate, but to be as fair as possible, your list will not be complete without . . . I'll be asking for the signatures of every group member, uh, verifying that your list is appropriate for the work you've done. Then, you see, I can evaluate your performance on an individual basis.

So, I'll have the three grades, and, uh, and I'll add them together and average them to give you a total grade. I've found that this system discourages hitchhikers. By that I mean, someone who belongs to the group but doesn't contribute to the group. Let's say I have a group member with a grade of A for the group report, a grade of . . . A for the group presentation, but a grade of D for the participation . . . then that student will have a B or, uh, even a C . . . for the final grade, whereas someone in the same group who has an A for participation will have an A for the final grade. I think that uh . . . makes the grading a little more fair.

Audio

1. What is the purpose of this lecture?

Answer

(C) "I've been getting . . . questions about grading for the group projects . . . so let me clarify that. . . ." Choices (A) and (B) are not correct because the projects have not been graded yet. Choice (B) is not correct because the students are not participating in the clarification while the professor speaks.

Audio

2. How will the written report be graded?

Answer

(B) ". . . every member of the group will receive the same grade on the written report." Choice (A) refers to the grade for participation, not to the grade for the written report. Choices (C) and (D) refer to the way that the group project will be graded, not to the way that the written report will be graded.

Audio

3. How will the final grade be calculated for each student?

Answer

(B) "So, I'll have the three grades [two group grades and one individual grade], and, uh, I'll add them together and average them to give you a total grade." Choices (A), (C), and (D) are not mentioned as options for grading and may not be concluded from information in the clarification.

Audio

4. How will the professor know what each individual has contributed?

Answer

(C) "I'll be asking you to prepare a list of your activities as a group member . . . [but] your list will not be complete without . . . the signatures of every group member, uh, verifying that your list is appropriate." Choice (B) is part of the procedure, but the verification is the way that the professor will know that the list is accurate. Choices (A) and (D) are not mentioned and may not be concluded from information in the clarification.

Audio

5. Listen again to part of the lecture.

Then answer the question

"How do you divide the work? Well, uh, in the past, some of my students have actually divided the report into sections, and each group member does . . . has written one of the sections."

Why does the professor ask this:

"How do you divide the work?"

Answer

(C) Professors often ask and answer rhetorical questions. In this case, he is preparing to offer advice about dividing the work. Choices (A) and (B) are not correct because he does not pause long enough to invite student responses. Choice (D) is not correct because the students have not organized the work yet.

Audio

6. Why does the professor most probably use such a complicated grading system?

Answer

(A) "I think that uh . . . makes the grading a little more fair." Choice (B) is true, but it is not the reason that he is using the system. Choice (D) is not correct because the professor has been getting a lot of questions, and he is taking the time to answer them in class. Choice (C) is not mentioned and may not be concluded from information in this clarification.

EXERCISE 23: Talks—Professor

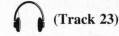 (Track 23)

Lecture One

Audio

Narrator: Listen to part of a lecture in a history class. The professor will discuss gold coins.

Professor:

In 1792, Congress passed an act authorizing the coinage of gold eagles valued at ten dollars, half eagles valued at five dollars, and quarter eagles valued at two dollars and fifty cents. These gold coins were standardized to silver on a fifteen-to-one ratio, that is, fifteen ounces of silver to one ounce of gold. Although the ratio was reasonable at the time that the bill was passed, by the turn of the century, the ratio in Europe had reached fifteen and three quarters to one, and the overvalued gold coins in the United States were either smuggled out of the country or melted down. Gold therefore disappeared from circulation until 1834, when a new law reduced the weight of gold pieces. Soon afterward, gold coins appeared in a smaller size and returned to circulation. The new interest and demand for gold encouraged the mint to strike twenty-dollar double eagles and a smaller number of fifty-dollar gold coins.

The financial uncertainty during the Great Depression of 1929 encouraged hoarding of gold coins by individuals, a situation that became so serious that the government finally ordered all gold coins to be turned in. During the next several years, a number of amendments exempted certain kinds of gold coins and allowed limited collecting. Since then, the interest in collecting gold coins has increased, and the restrictions have decreased. Now, there are no restrictions regarding the export, import, purchase, sale, or collecting of gold coins in the United States.

Audio

1. What is the main topic of this lecture?

Answer

(B) "In 1792, Congress passed an act authorizing the coinage of gold eagles . . . by the turn of the century . . . gold disappeared from circulation until 1834. . . . The financial uncertainty during the Great Depression . . . encouraged hoarding of gold. . . . Now, there are no restrictions. . . ." Choices (A), (C), and (D) are mentioned as secondary themes that are used to develop the main theme of the lecture, "the history of gold coins in the United States."

Audio

2. What was the value of the original gold eagle?

Answer

(B) "In 1792, Congress passed an act authorizing the coinage of gold eagles valued at ten dollars, half eagles valued at five dollars, and quarter eagles valued at two dollars and fifty cents." Choice (C) refers to the half eagle, not to the gold eagle. Choice (D) refers to a quarter eagle, not to a gold eagle. Choice (A) refers to the double eagle that was minted later.

Audio

3. What was the value of silver to gold in 1792?

Answer

(A) "In 1792 . . . gold coins were standardized to silver on a fifteen-to-one ratio." Choice (C) refers to the value by the turn of the century or 1800. Choices (B) and (D) are not mentioned and may not be concluded from information in the lecture.

Audio

4. What happened after the law of 1834?

Answer

(B) "Gold therefore disappeared from circulation until 1834, when a new law reduced the weight of gold pieces. Soon afterward, gold coins appeared in a smaller size. . . ." Choice (A) refers to 1929, not 1834. Choice (C) refers to 1929, the Great Depression. Choice (D) refers to the years following the Great Depression.

Audio

5. What are the restrictions on collecting gold coins today?

Answer

(A) "Now, there are no restrictions regarding the export, import, purchase, sale, or collecting of gold coins in the United States." Choice (B) is not correct because there are no restrictions on the export of gold coins. Choices (C) and (D) refer to the period after the Great Depression, not to today.

Lecture Two

Audio

Narrator: Listen to part of a lecture in a music appreciation class. The professor is discussing the work of Stephen Foster.

Professor:

Stephen Foster was one of the most prolific songwriters of his time, contributing more than 200 songs during his twenty-year career. His first attempt, when he was fourteen, was a forgettable composition called the "Tioga Waltz," a melody for three flutes that debuted at a school exhibition. His first published piece appeared only three years later in 1844. It was called "Open Thy Lattice, Love," and it was rather typical of the sentimental tunes of the time. Still, it was a good effort for a seventeen-year-old composer.

But, it was minstrel music for which Foster will always be remembered. The songs of Southern black slaves in the pre–Civil War days evoked nostalgic themes, like the plantation era that was already fated to pass into history. His first successful piece, "Oh, Susanna," became popular throughout the world and is still widely sung. "Camptown Races" followed with similar success. The most successful song written by an American to that date was Stephen Foster's "Old Folks at Home," which appeared in 1851. Some of you may recall it as "Way Down Upon the Swanee River," since it was also referred to by that title as well. In any case, an item in the *Musical World* of New York stressed the unprecedented sales. At a time when half of all the sheet music published was a total failure, and a sale of 5,000 copies was considered highly successful, "Old Folks at Home" sold nearly 100,000 copies. "Old Kentucky Home" which came out two years later, capitalized on the reputation that Foster was making for himself and was also a huge seller.

Now what is interesting about the success of Stephen Foster is that he himself was ambivalent about it. Sometimes he hid his identity with pseudonyms, sometimes he requested that his name be withheld from the cover to the sheet music, and other times he insisted that his name be displayed. Out of the context of the times, none of this seems to make sense, but when we contrast the musical world of high society with that of the common people, it becomes clear. Stephen Foster's success came from writing "plantation songs" for popular entertainment. The music was easy to remember, very repetitious, and available to everyone in the popular music halls. But the music that was considered serious and appropriate for society events was quite different. Foster proved that he could write such music and perhaps had some secret desire to succeed on those terms, but that type of music didn't enjoy the widespread popularity of the plantation melodies that we still recognize today. Most school children have heard "Jeannie with the Light Brown Hair" and "Beautiful Dreamer," but none would recognize the saccharine ballads and hymns that were considered by a genteel few his "better music."

Audio

1. What kind of music is associated with Stephen Foster?

Answer

(B) "Foster's success came from writing 'plantation songs' for popular entertainment." Choice (A) refers to the type of music that was popular at the time. Choices (C) and (D) refer to the kind of music that Foster occasionally wrote but that did not enjoy much success.

Audio

2. Which piece was the most successful song written by an American?

Answer

(C) "The most successful song written by an American to that date was Stephen Foster's 'Old Folks at Home'. . . ." Choice (A) refers to the first song that Foster published, not to the most successful song written. Choices (B) and (D) refer to popular songs but not to the most successful song written by an American.

Audio

3. Why did Stephen Foster withhold his name from the cover to some of his sheet music?

Answer

(C) ". . . the music that was considered serious and appropriate for society events was quite different [from that written by Foster]." Choice (A) is not correct because he wrote for more than twenty years. Choice (B) is not correct because he was famous for his plantation songs. Choice (D) is not mentioned and may not be concluded from information in the lecture.

Audio

4. What best describes Stephen Foster's most popular songs?

Answer

(A) "The music was easy to remember, very repetitious, and available to everyone in the popular music halls." Choice (C) is not correct because his music was popular in the music halls, not at society events. Choice (D) is not correct because his most popular songs were not among the serious ballads and hymns that a few considered his "better music." Choice (B) is not mentioned and may not be concluded from information in the lecture.

Audio

5. What do we know about Stephen Foster?

Answer

(A) "Stephen Foster was one of the most prolific songwriters of his time, contributing more than 200 songs during his twenty-two year career." Choice (B) is not correct because he wrote many popular songs, seven of which are mentioned in the passage. Choice (C) is not correct because "Oh, Susanna" was his first successful piece, and other songs met with similar success. Choice (D) refers to the fact that most school children have heard his music, but it was not written specifically for children.

EXERCISE 24: Talks—Professor

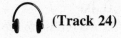 **(Track 24)**

Lecture One

Audio

Narrator: Listen to part of a lecture in a psychology class. The professor will discuss heredity and environment.

Professor:

Good morning. I trust that you have all read the assignment and that we can proceed with today's lecture. As you know from your text, both heredity and environment play a role in the development of the personality.

In addition, research at the University of Texas at Arlington has shown that the order of one's birth in relationship to brothers and sisters may be a significant factor. Those born first tend to develop personality traits that make them domineering, ambitious, and highly motivated to achieve. And the same is true for only children. In contrast, children born later in the family tend to be more socially adept, likable, talkative individuals.

Also interesting in the research is the fact that a woman with older brothers and a man with older sisters seem to be able to interact more easily with the opposite sex. Having older opposite-sex siblings seems to be important in being able to establish social relationships with members of the opposite sex.

There is also some evidence that the youngest child may develop a very charming personality in order to be included in the activities of the older group. Of course, if the other children are no longer living at home, the youngest child is more likely to develop the characteristics of an only child.

Audio

1. What is the main subject of this lecture?

Answer

(C) "... research at the University of Texas at Arlington has shown that the order of one's birth in relationship to brothers and sisters may be a significant factor." Choices (A), (B), and (D) are mentioned as secondary subjects that are used to develop the main subject of the lecture, "birth order."

Audio

2. What should the students know before they hear this lecture?

Answer

(B) "As you know from your text, both heredity and environment play a role in the development of the personality." Choice (A) refers to the topic of the lecture, not to what students should know before the lecture. Choices (C) and (D) refer to the information in the lecture.

Audio

3. Which one of the people would probably be the most comfortable interacting with a member of the opposite sex?

Answer

(B) "... a woman with older brothers and a man with older sisters seem to be able to interact more easily with the opposite sex." Choice (A) is not correct because a man with older sisters is able to interact more easily. Choices (C) and (D) are not correct because a woman with older brothers is able to interact more easily.

Audio

4. What personality trait will firstborn children probably exhibit?

Answer

(B) "Those born first tend to develop personality traits that make them domineering, ambitious, and highly motivated to achieve." Choices (A), (C), and (D) refer to personality traits of children born later in the family.

Audio

5. According to the research, what might be the dominant personality trait of the youngest child?

Answer

(A) "Those born first tend to develop personality traits that make them . . . highly motivated . . . children born later . . . tend to be . . . talkative individuals . . . There is also some evidence that the youngest child may develop a very charming personality in order to be included. . . ."

Lecture Two

Audio

Narrator: Listen to part of a lecture in an English literature class. The professor will be talking about American writers in the early nineteenth century.

Professor:

Today we will discuss the Knickerbocker School, which was a rather informal group of writers who met in New York City during the early 1800s. The name Knickerbocker—let me write that down for you—was a tribute to Diedrich Knickerbocker, a character created by one of their members, the writer Washington Irving.

At any one time, about twenty writers belonged to the group, including the three most important figures in early American literature—William Cullen Bryant, the editor of the *New York Evening Post*; Washington Irving, a well-known poet and storyteller; and novelist, James Fenimore Cooper.

Although Irving gained recognition in Europe as America's first legitimate man of letters, and his stories "Rip Van Winkle" and "The Legend of Sleepy Hollow" were widely published as serials, it was James Fenimore Cooper who achieved success with subjects and settings that were typically American. Cooper created the frontier novel, with a hero who embodied the American frontier spirit. In the *Leatherstocking Tales*, five novels about frontier life, the affable old scout Natty Bumppo evolves into a philosopher and even, some say, an epic hero. Bumppo is a frontiersman who knows how to live close to nature and possesses all the skills necessary for a rugged pioneer existence, but he is also an observer of life. He sees that the settlers are a civilizing influence. He respects the social order that they create. But he also sees the thoughtless and sometimes selfish abuse of the natural environment.

The best of all the *Leatherstocking Tales* has to be *The Last of the Mohicans*, which, I believe at least some of you have seen on video. You may recall that the story recounts the conflict between the French and the English during the early years of independence, with Indians fighting on both sides. I personally feel that this represents some of Cooper's best writing, especially in those passages that recount the death of the Mohican chief's son in a noble attempt to avenge the murder of his love.

Of course, there were others who had membership in the Knickerbocker School, but if you are familiar with the three major writers that we have discussed today, you'll have a feel for early American literature.

Audio

1. What is the main focus of this lecture?

Answer

(A) "Today we will discuss the Knickerbocker School. . . ." Choices (B), (C), and (D) are mentioned as secondary themes that are used to develop the main focus of the lecture, "the Knickerbocker School."

Audio

2. What are the *Leatherstocking Tales*?

Answer

(B) "In the *Leatherstocking Tales*, five novels about frontier life. . . ." Choice (A) refers to Natty Bumppo, the hero of the *Leatherstocking Tales*. Choices (C) and (D) refer to characters in the novels.

Audio

3. What kind of character is Natty Bumppo?

Answer

(A) "... Bumppo evolves into ... an epic hero ... a frontiersman who knows how to live close to nature. ..." Choice (B) is not correct because Bumppo possesses all the skills necessary for a rugged pioneer existence. Choices (C) and (D) refer to other characters in the *Leatherstocking Tales*, not to Natty Bumppo.

Audio

4. Who was one of the most important members of the Knickerbocker School?

Answer

(B) "... the three most important figures in early American literature—William Cullen Bryant ... Washington Irving ... and ... James Fenimore Cooper." Choice (A) refers to a character in a story by Washington Irving, not to a writer of the Knickerbocker School. Choice (C) refers to the Native American tribe in a story by James Fenimore Cooper. Choice (D) refers to the character, also created by Irving, for whom the group was named.

Audio

5. Which of the following best describes James Fenimore Cooper?

Answer

(A) "William Cullen Bryant, the editor of the *New York Evening Post* ... Irving ... [whose story] 'The Legend of Sleepy Hollow' was widely published ... and James Fenimore Cooper ... who embodied the American spirit in the *Leatherstocking Tales*. ..." Choice (B) refers to Washington Irving. Choice (C) refers to William Cullen Bryant. Choice (D) is not mentioned and may not be concluded from information in the lecture.

EXERCISE 25: Lectures—Professor 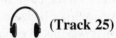 (Track 25)

Lecture One

Audio

Narrator: Listen to part of a lecture in a biology class.

Professor:

The concept of a half-life is mentioned in your textbook, but I'm going to take a few minutes to discuss it with you. The method is called *radiometric dating*. Okay.... Physicists use the term half-life to describe the average time it takes ... for half of a group of radioactive isotopes to undergo decay. Trefil and Hazen have an excellent analogy. It's in the chapter assigned for next week. Okay.... They compare the group of isotopes to a batch of microwave popcorn. If you watch one kernel in the batch, it'll pop at a specific time, but all the kernels don't pop at the same time. And although you can't predict the exact time that the ... the one kernel will pop, uh, you do know for how many minutes to set the microwave, because you can predict the amount of time necessary for the batch. Okay ... to get back to the radioactive nuclei, some nuclei will decay immediately, while ... while others will take much

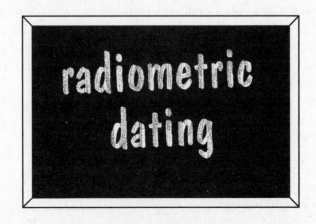

longer. The important thing is that . . . that the percentage of nuclei that decay in each second remains more or less constant. Okay . . . let's go back to that definition. Remember, a half-life is the average time that it takes for half of the group to undergo decay. So let's just use 100 nuclei as an example, and if . . . and if it takes thirty minutes for fifty of them to undergo radioactive decay, then the half-life of that nucleus is . . . thirty minutes. And if we continue observing for another thirty minutes, you'll have half of the fifty, or twenty-five . . . that have decayed, leaving you twenty-five. Okay . . . and at the end of thirty more minutes, you'll have twelve or thirteen, and so on, and so on. But this is why the popcorn example that, uh, Trefil and Hazen came up with is so useful. If a nucleus has a half-life of thirty minutes, all the nuclei won't wait half an hour before they all begin to decay . . . they don't all decay at the same moment. Each one will decay at a different moment, like the popcorn. A half-life of thirty minutes means that, on the average, an individual nucleus will take thirty minutes to decay.

Okay, this is the interesting part. Since the half-life is relatively easy to measure, it's a very useful tool in determining the age of both . . . uh natural and man-made materials. The method is called *radiometric dating*, or since the isotope carbon-14 is the most commonly used nucleus, you may hear the term *carbon-14 dating*, but that isn't really accurate since many different isotopes can be used in the process, uh, not just carbon-14. Anyway, let's turn our attention to carbon to . . . uh . . . to see why the dating system is so effective and why carbon-14 is such a good choice for dating fossils.

Every living organism uses carbon. Right now, you're using carbon from the food you ate earlier, and . . . and . . . through a series of complex processes, you're turning it into living tissue. Plants take in carbon dioxide from the air, so I think you can agree that carbon is essential to all living things. Okay, most of the carbon is carbon-12, probably close to 99 percent, and the other 1 percent is almost all carbon-13, but, uh, there's a minuscule amount of carbon-14 . . . that's the important one for the purposes of dating, because, uh, carbon-14 has a half-life of approximately . . . 5,700 years.

Now, remember that all living things are taking in carbon, all the time, including carbon-14, but at . . . at the point of death, the carbon begins to decay. In radiometric dating, we can determine the age of wood or bone or . . . or other materials that have once been alive by, uh, by measuring the carbon-14 that remains in comparison with the amount that we know must have been present when it was a living plant or animal. And . . . and . . . that's pretty exciting.

But, of course, carbon-14 can go back in time only about 50,000 years until the amount of carbon is so small that it's no longer a useful measure, uh, to date geological formations, like rocks and minerals. So . . . what about rocks that are millions or even billions of years old? Well, the same process can be applied, but we have to use isotopes that have longer half-lives. For example, uh, uh, for example, uranium-238 with a half-life of about 4.5 billion years . . . or . . . or even rubidium-87 with a half-life of almost 50 billion years. So, most of the dates that we'll refer to in this class will have been determined by the use of radiometric dating using carbon-14, since we'll be dealing with living organisms but, uh, but it's important for you to understand that the method has application in other sciences that don't treat carbon-based life forms. Okay. Any questions so far?

Audio
1. What is the main topic of this lecture?
Answer
(B) "The concept of a half-life is mentioned in your textbook, but I'm going to take a few minutes to discuss it with you. . . . The method is called *radiometric dating*. . . ." Choice (A) refers to an analogy that the professor uses to explain radiometric dating. Choice (C) is the most commonly used nucleus for radiometric dating, but it is not the correct term for the topic. Choice (D) is mentioned in reference to the main topic, "radiometric dating."

Audio
2. What is the definition of a *half-life*?
Answer
(A) "Physicists use the term half-life to describe the average time it takes . . . for half of a group of radioactive isotopes to undergo decay." Choices (B), (C), and (D) are not mentioned and may not be concluded from information in this lecture.

Audio

3. Why does the professor mention popcorn?

Answer

(C) "Trefil and Hazen have an excellent analogy. . . . They compare the group of isotopes to a batch of microwave popcorn." Choice (A) is true, but it is not the reason that the professor mentions it. Choices (B) and (D) are not mentioned and may not be concluded from information in this lecture.

Audio

4. What do we know about carbon-14?

Answer

(D) "Every living organism uses carbon. . . . We can determine the age of . . . materials that have once been alive by, uh, measuring the carbon-14 that remains." Choice (A) is not correct because uranium-238 and rubidium-87 are also used in radiometric dating. Choice (B) is not correct because carbon-14 represents a very small percentage of the carbon in living things, compared with carbon-12 and carbon-13. Choice (C) is not correct because carbon-14 has a half-life of 5,700 years.

Audio

5. Listen again to part of the lecture.
   Then answer the question.
   "So what about rocks that are millions or even billions of years old? Well, the same process can be applied, but we have to use isotopes that have longer half-lives."
   Why does the professor ask this question:
   "So what about rocks that are millions or even billions of years old?"

Answer

(A) Professors often ask and answer rhetorical questions. In this case, he is asking a question and providing a response to extend the concept he has been discussing. Choices (B) and (D) are not correct because he does not pause long enough to invite student responses. Choice (C) is not correct because he extends the concept that he has been discussing by demonstrating how the process can be used with non-carbon-based elements.

Audio

6. Which of the following would NOT be dated using carbon-14?

Answer

(D) Choices (A), (B), and (C) are all carbon-based life forms, but Choice (D) is a geological formation that requires an isotope with a longer half-life, as, for example, uranium-238.

Lecture Two

Audio

Narrator: Listen to a lecture in an anthropology class.

Professor:

Evidence of systematic planning, now called *city planning*, has been uncovered during archaeological excavations of ancient cities from as early as 3500 B.C. It isn't surprising is it . . . that the locations of these cities have revealed certain basic requirements for life in ancient times, including not only the necessities of water and arable land but also the requirement of a strategic fortification against invaders.

By about 3000 B.C., cities along the Indus Valley had regular patterns of streets. Houses with shared walls were built around courtyards, with differences in the height of the house and the width of the street as an . . . an . . . as outward indications of social rank among inhabitants. At about the same time, in Pompeii, a central marketplace was already in evidence, with a regular pattern of streets and sidewalks extending out from the commercial area. Less than a thousand years later, Egyptian cities were being built with, uh, parallel streets. In contrast with the Greek cities on the mainland, colonial cities incorporated a . . . gridiron pattern for streets, and by that I mean a pattern of square blocks. Rome itself was somewhat hap . . . haphazard at the time, but again, Roman colonies and military camps were being built in gridiron patterns throughout what is, uh, now Europe. In China and Japan, a central commercial area was in evidence in cities from this time period. The marketplace, in fact, was the most universal feature of cities throughout uh . . . the ancient world.

Now, I'm going to skip ahead to the Middle Ages, which was the second interesting historic period in city planning. About uh . . . the tenth century, heavily fortified garrisons were replaced by towns of a few thousand inhabitants. The towns were only about one square mile in size, and, uh, many were located in strategic areas near rivers or . . . or along the seacoast . . . where larger cities would later flourish. But, uh, in spite of the earlier examples of organized grid patterns from the Roman Empire, the streets in these small towns were narrow and winding, often projecting out in an arbitrary way . . . from a public square that was often built around a church or a mosque. Gated walls usually surrounded the city, and a custom house for the collection of tolls was . . . it was almost always constructed on a conspicuous site.

Let me see. . . . Uh, that brings us to the Renaissance. The Renaissance began near the end of the Middle Ages and continued into the 1600s. It was a period in city planning in which huge plazas were erected to overcome the overcrowding of the earlier towns. In order to accommodate burgeoning populations . . . and, uh, new modes of transportation, cities were planned with wide boulevards, spacious parks, and . . . symmetrical, ordered streets. It is in this period that we start to see . . . intricate patterns of circles with diagonals radiating out like the spokes in a wheel. And this was popular, especially in Europe.

Moving into the 1700s and 1800s, which roughly correspond to, uh, the Industrial Revolution, the . . . the towns that had been planned for 2,000 inhabitants became very overcrowded, as people moved into the urban areas to work in factories. In North America and Europe, the streets that had been designed for pedestrians and horses were much too narrow, and sanitation, uh, became a major concern near the factories where workers were crowding into dirty, noisy neighborhoods. Although governments tried to regulate housing, in many cases proposing the separation of housing from industrial zones, uh, city planning could simply not keep pace with the migration of workers from rural areas to urban centers.

City planning in the nineteenth and twentieth centuries has been chiefly a response to the need to improve living conditions in, uh, overcrowded urban areas, and by that I mean not only a city but also, more recently, sprawling suburbs. The mass production of automobiles in . . . after World War I . . . made, uh, cars a viable means of transportation for a larger segment of the population and opened up areas beyond the immediate downtown for residential use. The need for streets to accommodate more and more vehicles has been one of the modern-day challenges. And a movement called the "garden city plan," which was exported from Britain to the former colonies, . . . the plan called for public land and buildings to serve as a green belt, and this was an attempt to, uh, limit the urban sprawl that was . . . characteristic of this period. In Europe, after World War II, the reconstruction of cities devastated by bombing necessitated even more attention to the concept of city planning.

Do we still have a few minutes? Let's go to the modern period of, uh . . . of, uh . . . city planning. Today, there are three types of cities. The decentralized metropolitan city in . . . in developed nations with high automobile ownership, like metropolitan areas in the United States. And the centralized and heavily planned metro areas in European nations, Singapore, and Japan, where land is limited and the high cost of . . . of fuel discourages suburban living. And densely populated cities in nations where automobile ownership is still out of reach for most people, like some areas in Latin America, where we see new towns springing up on the fringes of cities almost overnight. I know I went over that rather quickly, but, uh, I advise you to refer to the three types of cities in your book. It's an important concept.

Audio

1. What is this lecture mainly about?

Answer

(C) "Evidence of systematic planning, now called *city planning*, has been uncovered during archaeological excavations of ancient cities from as early as 3500 B.C." Choices (A), (B), and (D) are mentioned as secondary themes that are used to develop the main theme of the lecture, "city planning."

Audio

2. What feature of ancient cities appears throughout most of the world?

Answer

(B) "The marketplace, in fact, was . . . the most universal feature of cities throughout . . . the ancient world." Choice (A) includes features of cities in the Middle Ages, not those in the ancient world. Choice (C) includes features of cities in the Renaissance. Choice (D) is a feature of colonial cities of the Roman and Greek Empires but not a feature throughout the world.

Audio

3. When were symmetrical streets with circular patterns introduced?

Answer

(B) "[During] the Renaissance . . . symmetrical, ordered streets [in] . . . intricate patterns of circles with diagonals radiation out." Choice (A) was noted for a gridiron pattern. Choice (C) was noted for narrow streets. Choice (D) was noted for urban sprawl.

Audio

4. What was the problem for city planners during the Industrial Revolution?

Answer

(A) (B) "the towns . . . became very overcrowded, as people moved into the urban areas to work in factories . . . and sanitation . . . became a major concern." Choices (C) and (D) refer to the nineteenth and twentieth centuries, not to the Industrial Revolution.

Audio

5. Listen again to part of the lecture.
   Then answer the question.
   "I know I went over that rather quickly, but uh . . . I advise you to refer to the three types of cities in your book. It's an important concept."
   Why does the professor say this:
   "I advise you to refer to the three types of cities in your book."

Answer

(B) Because the professor says that she has gone over the material quickly, it may be concluded that she did not have time to talk about the concept in depth. Choice (C) is not correct because the students, not the teacher, will refer to their books. Choices (A) and (D) are not mentioned and may not be concluded from information in the passage.

Audio

6. Classify each of these cities, matching them with their type.

Answer

(A) Singapore is *Centralized*.

(B) Mexico City is *Densely populated*.

(C) Los Angeles is *Decentralized*.

EXERCISE 26: Lectures—Professor 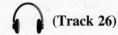 (Track 26)

Lecture One

Audio

Narrator: Listen to part of a lecture in an environmental science class.

Professor:
Hydrogen is the most recent and, I'd say, one of the most promising in a long list of alternatives to petroleum. Some of the possibilities include batteries, methanol, natural gas, and, well, you name it. But hydrogen fuel cells have a couple of advantages over some of the other options. First of all, they're really quiet, and they don't pollute the atmosphere. Besides that, hydrogen is the most abundant element

in the universe, and it can be produced from a number of sources, including ammonia, or . . . or even water. So, it's renewable, and there's an almost unlimited supply.

Okay. Now fuel cells represent a radical departure from the conventional internal combustion engine and even a fairly fundamental change from electric battery power. Like batteries, fuel cells run on electric motors; however, batteries use electricity from an external source and store it for use in the battery while the fuel cells create their own electricity through a chemical process that uses hydrogen and oxygen from the air. Are you with me? Look, by producing energy in a chemical reaction rather than through combustion, a fuel cell can convert, say, 40–60 percent of the energy from the hydrogen into electricity. And when this ratio is compared with that of a combustion engine that runs at about half the efficiency of a fuel cell, well, it's obvious that fuel-cell technology has the potential to revolutionize the energy industry.

So, fuel cells have the potential to generate power for almost any kind of machinery or equipment that fossil fuels run, but, the most important, let's say goal, the goal of fuel-cell technology is the introduction of fuel-cell-powered vehicles. Internationally, the competition is fierce to commercialize fuel-cell cars. I guess all of the leading automobile manufacturers worldwide have concept cars that use fuel cells, and some of them can reach speeds of as high as 90 miles per hour. Even more impressive is the per-tank storage capacity. Can you believe this? Some of those cars can run for 220 miles between refills. But many of those cars were designed decades ago, so . . . what's the holdup?

Well, the problem in introducing fuel-cell technology is really twofold. In the first place, industries will have to invest millions, maybe even billions of dollars to refine the technology—and here's the real cost—the infrastructure to support the fueling of the cars. And by infrastructure, I mean basic facilities and services like hydrogen stations to refuel cars and mechanics who know how to repair them. I think you get the picture. And then, consumers will have to accept and use the new products powered by fuel cells. So, we're going to need educational programs to inform the public about the safety and convenience of fuel cells, if we're going to achieve a successful transition to fuel-cell products. But, unfortunately, major funding efforts get interrupted. Here's what I mean. When oil prices are high, then there seems to be more funding and greater interest in basic research and development, and more public awareness of fuel cells, and then the price of oil goes down a little, and the funding dries up, and people just go back to using their fossil-fueled products. And this has been going on for more than thirty years.

Some government-sponsored initiatives have created incentives for fuel-cell powered vehicles, but probably one of the most successful programs, at least in my opinion, is the STEP program, which is an acronym for the Sustainable Transportation Energy Program. STEP is a demonstration project sponsored by the government of Western Australia. Now, in this project, gasoline-driven buses have been replaced with fuel-cell buses on regular transportation routes. I think that British Petroleum is the supplier of the hydrogen fuel, which is produced at an oil refinery in Kwinana, south of Perth. So, we need to watch this carefully. Another collaborative research effort is being undertaken by the European Union and the United States. Scientists and engineers are trying to develop a fuel cell that's effectively engineered and attractive to the commercial market. Now, under an agreement signed in about 2000, if memory serves, it was 2003, but anyway, the joint projects include the writing of codes and standards, the design of fueling infrastructures, the refinement of fuel-cell models, and the demonstration of fuel-cell vehicles. In Europe, the private sector will combine efforts with government agencies in the public sector to create a long-term plan for the introduction of fuel cells throughout the EU. And the World Bank is providing funding to promote the development and manufacture of fuel-cell buses for public transportation in China, Egypt, Mexico, and India, and we're starting to see some really interesting projects in these areas. So, uh, clearly, fuel-cell technology is an international effort.

Okay, at the present time, Japan leads the way in addressing the issues of modifying the infrastructure. Several fueling stations that dispense hydrogen by the cubic meter are already in place, with plans for more. But even when a nationwide system is completed, decisions about how and where to produce the hydrogen and how to transport it will still have to be figured out. Most countries share the view that fleets of vehicles have significant advantages for the introduction of fuel-cell-powered transportation because, well, obviously, they can be fueled at a limited number of central locations. And, uh, and other benefits of a fleet are the opportunity to provide training for a maintenance crew and for the drivers. As for consumer education, no one country seems to have made the advances there that . . . that would serve as a model for the rest of us. But perhaps, when the demonstration projects have concluded and a few model cars are available to the public, well, more attention will be directed to public information programs.

Audio

1. What is this lecture mainly about?

Answer

(A) An overview of fuel-cell technology. The professor discusses the process for producing energy, the efficiency of the cells, the problems, and some model programs mentioned in Choices (B), (C), and (D).

Audio

2. What do we know about hydrogen?

Answer

(D) "Besides that, hydrogen is the most abundant element in the universe, and it can be produced from a number of sources, including ammonia, or . . . or even water." Choice (A) is not correct because the professor says that energy is produced "in a chemical reaction rather than through combustion." Choice (C) is not correct because "a combustion engine . . . runs at about half the efficiency of a fuel cell." Choice (B) is not mentioned and may not be concluded from information in the lecture.

Audio

3. Why does the professor mention the STEP program in Australia?

Answer

(D) ". . . probably one of the most successful programs, at least in my opinion, is the STEP program. . . ." He thinks it is a very good example of a project. Choice (C) is not correct because, although the professor mentions a program in Japan, he does not directly compare it with the STEP program. Choices (A) and (B) are not mentioned and may not be concluded from information in the lecture.

Audio

4. Listen again to part of the lecture.
   Then answer the following question.
   "Now, under an agreement signed in about 2000, if memory serves, it was 2003, but anyway, the joint projects include the writing of codes and standards, the design of fueling infrastructures, the refinement of fuel-cell models, and the demonstration of fuel-cell vehicles."
   Why does the professor say this:
   ". . . if memory serves, it was 2003 . . ."

Answer

(D) To show that he is uncertain about the date. The phrase "if memory serves" indicates that the information is probably correct, but the memory could possibly be inaccurate. The phrase would not be used for Choices (A), (B), and (C).

Audio

5. What are some of the problems associated with fuel-cell technology?

Answer

(B) (D) " . . . here's the real cost—the infrastructure to support the fueling of the cars . . . and . . . we're going to need educational programs. . . ." Choice (A) is not correct because the professor mentions that fuel cells are "really quiet." Choice (C) is not correct because hydrogen is "the most abundant element in the universe."

Audio

6. What is the professor's attitude toward fuel cells?

Answer

(B) He is hopeful about their development in the future. He would like more attention to be directed to public information programs, which would solve one of the major problems for fuel-cell technology.

Choice (A) is not correct because he says that combustion engines are only half as efficient as fuel cells. Choices (C) and (D) are not correct because the professor's tone is positive.

Lecture Two

Audio

Narrator: Listen to part of a lecture in a literature class.

Professor:

Today we'll discuss transcendentalism . . . transcendentalism . . . which is a philosophical and literary movement that developed in New England in the early nineteenth century. transcendentalism began with the formation in 1836 of the Transcendental Club in Boston, Massachusetts, by a group of artists and writers. There's evidence that the group was involved in somewhat of a protest against the intellectual climate of Harvard. Interestingly enough, many of the transcendentalists were actually Harvard educated, but they never met in Cambridge. Remember, at this time, Harvard had only eleven professors, and at least eleven members could be expected to attend a meeting of the Transcendental Club. So, their intellectual community was large enough to rival the Harvard faculty.

All right then. Their criticism of Harvard was that the professors were too conservative and old-fashioned. Which, come to think of it, isn't an unusual attitude for students when they talk about their professors. But, in fairness, the classroom method of recitation that was popular at Harvard required the repetition of a lesson without any operational understanding of it. In contrast, the transcendentalists considered themselves modern and liberal because they preferred a more operational approach to education. Bronson Alcott translated transcendentalism into pedagogy by encouraging the students to think, using dialogues and journals to develop and record their ideas. Language was viewed as the connection between the individual and society. In 1834, Alcott established the Temple School near Boston Commons and later founded a form of adult education, which he referred to as *Conversation*. This was really a process whereby the give and take in a conversation became more important than the doctrine that a teacher might have been inclined to pass on to students, an approach that stood in diametric opposition to the tradition at Harvard that encouraged students to memorize their lessons.

The transcendental group also advanced a reaction against the rigid Puritanism of the period, especially insofar as it emphasized society at the expense of the individual—the Puritans, I mean. According to the transcendentalists, the justification of all social organizations is the improvement of the individual. So, in the literature of the time, the transcendentalists insisted that it was basic human nature to engage in self-expression, and many interpreted this as encouragement for them to write essays and other opinion pieces. One of the most distinguished members of the club was Ralph Waldo Emerson, who served as editor of the transcendentalist's literary magazine, the *Dial*. His writing stressed the importance of the individual. In one of his best-known essays, "Self-Reliance," he appealed to intuition as a source of ethics, asserting that people should be the judge of their own actions, without the rigid restrictions of society. You can imagine the reaction of the church, in particular, the Unitarian Church, in which many of the intellectuals held membership. If individuals were responsible for their own code of ethics, then the clergy and the entire church organization was threatened.

Perhaps because they were encouraged to think for themselves, the transcendentalists came up with several options for living out their philosophies. Many were devoted to the idea of a Utopian society or at least to a pastoral retreat without class distinctions, where everyone would be responsible for tending the gardens and maintaining the buildings, preparing the food, and so forth. And quite a few were involved in some sort of communal living. Brook Farm was probably the most successful of these cooperatives, although it lasted only six years. Brook Farm and some of the other experimental communities brought to the surface the problem that the transcendentalists faced when they tried to reconcile a cooperative society and individual freedom. Both Emerson and Thoreau declined to participate in Brook Farm because they maintained that improvement had to begin with an individual, not a group.

From 1841 to 1843, Emerson and Thoreau lived and worked together in Emerson's home, exchanging ideas, developing their philosophies, and writing. Upon leaving Emerson's home, Thoreau built a small cabin along the shores of Walden Pond near Concord, Massachusetts, where he lived alone for two years. Devoting himself to the study of nature and to writing, he published an account of his experiences in *Walden*, a book that's generally acknowledged as the most original and sincere contribution to literature by the transcendentalists.

But I'm getting ahead of myself. transcendentalism didn't change the educational system, and it certainly didn't reform the church in any significant way, but it did, in a sense, change the direction of American social and political culture, because transcendentalism evolved from its initial literary roots into a force that shaped the way a democratic society was interpreted on the North American continent.

Audio

1. What does this lecturer mainly discuss?

Answer

(A) The professor states the topic directly. "Today we'll discuss transcendentalism."
Choices (B), (C), and (D) are all mentioned as part of the discussion, but they are not the main topic.

Audio

2. Listen again to part of the lecture.
   Then answer the following question.
   "All right then. Their criticism of Harvard was that the professors were too conservative and old-fashioned. Which, come to think of it, isn't an unusual attitude for students when they talk about their professors."
   Why does the professor say this:
   "Which, come to think of it, isn't an unusual attitude for students when they talk about their professors."

Answer

(A) Her tone implies that she is joking with the students. Choices (B), (C), and (D) are not implied by the tone.

Audio

3. According to the professor, what was true about the Puritans?

Answer

(C) They believed that society should be respected above persons. " . . . the rigid Puritanism of the period . . . emphasized society at the expense of the individual." Choice (A) refers to the transcendentalists, not the Puritans. Choice (B) is not correct because many leaders were educated at Harvard. Choice (D) is not correct because neither Emerson nor Thoreau supported communal living.

Audio

4. Why did the church oppose the transcendental movement?

Answer

(A) "If individuals were responsible for their own code of ethics, then the clergy and the entire church organization was threatened." Choice (B) is not correct because the leaders were as well educated as the clergy, many at Harvard. Choices (C) and (D) are not mentioned and may not be concluded from information in the lecture.

Audio

5. Why did the professor mention *Walden*?

Answer

(B) " . . . *Walden*, a book that's generally acknowledged as the most original and sincere contribution to literature by the transcendentalists." Choice (A) is probably true, but it is not the reason that the book is mentioned. Choices (C) and (D) are not mentioned and may not be concluded from information in the lecture.

Audio

6. According to the professor, what was the most lasting contribution of transcendentalism?

Answer

(D) "Transcendentalism didn't change the educational system, and it certainly didn't reform the church in any significant way, but it did, in a sense, change the direction of American social and political culture. . . ." Choices (A) and (B) are not correct because the professor says that "Transcendentalism didn't change the educational system, and it certainly didn't reform the church in any significant way. . . ." Choice (C) is not correct because it is mentioned briefly, not as a major contribution.

EXERCISE 27: Talks—Professor/Students 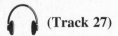 (Track 27)

Lecture One

Audio

Narrator: Listen to part of a discussion in an education class.

Sally: I'm sorry. I just don't agree with you at all.

Paul: Look. Take the example of an international student applying for university admission. If the student has a 550 on the TOEFL or an 80 on the Michigan Test, most admissions officers will accept the applicant. The student with a 547 or 79 won't be considered. The officer won't even look at transcripts.

Sally: Right. But I think that proves my point, not yours.

Paul: How?

Sally: Well, it's the admissions officer who decides *how* to use the test. The TOEFL and the Michigan are good English proficiency tests, but that's all they are. And English proficiency is necessary for success in an American university, but so are several other factors, including good academic preparation.

Paul: Good academic preparation is more important.

Sally: Maybe. I don't really know. But what I'm trying to explain to you is that admissions officers should use the proficiency test as one of many considerations, and as such, they really shouldn't insist on a rigid cutoff score like 550 or 80.

Ayers: Isn't this the basic disagreement: that Paul thinks the tests are bad in themselves, and Sally believes that the tests are good, but that many people don't use them for their intended purpose?

Paul: I don't agree with having the tests, Professor Ayers, and that's my position.

Sally: But Paul, what would you do to evaluate the English proficiency of a student ten thousand miles away without a standardized test?

Paul: I admit that's a big problem.

Sally: It sure is.

Ayers: Okay, class. For Wednesday, let's consider the problem of evaluation without standardized tests like the TOEFL, the SAT, GMAT, and GRE. Paul says that there ought to be an alternative. Sally doesn't seem to believe that there is an appropriate alternative. Please bring in your ideas and suggestions, and we'll discuss them.

Audio

1. What do the speakers mainly discuss?

Answer

(B) "The TOEFL and Michigan are good English proficiency tests [for college admissions]." Choice (A) refers to the name of a test, the Michigan Test, not to admissions standards at the University of Michigan. Choice (C) is mentioned as a secondary theme that is used to develop the main theme of the talk, "the use of standardized tests for college admissions." Choice (D) refers to the topic assigned for Wednesday, not to the main theme of the lecture.

Audio

2. What is Paul's opinion about the TOEFL and the Michigan Test?

Answer

(D) "I don't agree with having the tests, Professor Ayers, and that's my position." Choice (A) refers to Sally's, not Paul's, opinion. Choices (B) and (C) are not mentioned and may not be concluded from information in the discussion.

Audio

3. What does Sally say about the admissions officers?

Answer

(A) ". . . Sally believes that the tests are good, but that many people don't use them for their intended purpose." Choice (C) refers to what the admissions officers do, not to what Sally believes they should do. Choices (B) and (D) refer to what Paul believes admissions officers should do, not to what they actually do.

Audio

4. How does the professor handle the disagreement?

Answer

(B) "Isn't this the basic disagreement: that Paul thinks the tests are bad in themselves, and Sally believes that the tests are good, but that many people don't use them for their intended purpose?" Choices (A) and (D) are not correct because Professor Ayers does not comment after he restates each student's position. Choice (C) is not mentioned and may not be concluded from information in this discussion.

Audio

5. Where did this discussion most probably take place?

Answer

(A) "Okay, class." From the reference to *class*, it must be concluded that this conversation took place in a classroom. Choices (B), (C), and (D) are not mentioned and may not be concluded from information in the discussion.

Lecture Two

Audio

Narrator: Listen to part of a discussion in a linguistics class.

Baker: Since so many of you have asked me about how to learn a language, I thought it might be useful to take some class time today to discuss it. Betty, you speak several languages, don't you?

Betty: Yes, I speak Spanish and French.

Baker: And what helped you most in learning those languages?

Betty: What helped me most. . . . Well, I studied both languages in high school, and I'm still studying Spanish here at the university, but I think that travel has probably been the most help to me. You see, I've been lucky in that I've lived in Europe. Believe me, I didn't speak very well before I moved there.

Bill: You're right, Betty. After studying a language, practice is very useful. When you live in a country where the language is spoken, it's ideal. But, you know, sometimes it's difficult to make friends in a new place, even when the people are very friendly.

Betty: Yes, I know what you mean. Especially if you don't speak the language too well. I had some problems when I first moved to Europe.

Baker: And, of course, some people are shy.

Betty: That's true.

Bill: Professor Baker, whether or not I'm living in a country where the language is spoken, I always go to movies, and whenever I can, I watch TV or listen to the radio in the language I'm trying to learn.

Betty: Me, too. And reading is another good way to learn. Books are good, but I think that newspapers and magazines are even better.

Baker: Probably the best way to learn is to combine all of these ideas: traveling, talking with people, going to movies, watching TV, listening to the radio, and reading books, newspapers and magazines. What do you think?

Betty: I agree with that, Professor Baker.

Bill: So do I. But I don't believe that it's possible to take advantage of practice opportunities without some knowledge of the language first.

Betty: Sure. First it's a good idea to study grammar, vocabulary . . .

Bill: . . . and listening, perhaps even reading.

Betty: Then practice is very, very helpful.

Audio

1. What do the speakers mainly discuss?

Answer

(D) "Since so many of you have asked me how to learn a language, I thought that it might be useful to take some class time to discuss it." Choices (A), (B), and (C) are mentioned as secondary themes that are used to develop the main theme of the talk, "learning a foreign language."

Audio

2. Why does Professor Baker begin the discussion by calling on Betty?

Answer

(C) "Betty, you speak several languages, don't you?" The shy person in Choice (A) is a reference to language learners, not to Betty. Choice (B) is true, but Betty mentions it after she is called on. Choice (D) is not mentioned and may not be concluded from information in this discussion.

Audio

3. What helped Betty most in learning Spanish?

Answer

(B) ". . . I think that travel has probably been the most helpful to me." Choice (C) refers to what Betty did before traveling. Choice (D) refers to what helped Bill, not Betty. Choice (A) is not mentioned and may not be concluded from information in the discussion.

Audio

4. What is Professor Baker's opinion?

Answer

(A) "Probably the best way to learn is to combine all of these ideas: traveling, talking with people, going to movies, watching TV, listening to the radio, and reading books, newspapers and magazines." Choice (B) is true, but incomplete. Choice (D) refers to Betty's opinion, not to Professor Baker's opinion. Choice (C) is not mentioned and may not be concluded from information in the discussion.

Audio

5. How can we best describe Professor Baker?

Answer

(B) Since Professor Baker encourages the students to express their opinions, it may be concluded that he is respectful of them. Choice (A) is not correct because Professor Baker rephrases the students' comments and combines them into a better answer. Choice (C) is not correct because the students interact informally without waiting to be called on. Choice (D) refers to Betty, not to Professor Baker.

EXERCISE 28: Lectures—Professor/Students

Lecture One

Audio

Narrator: Listen to part of a lecture in an art class.

Stephens: Let me remind you that this is a seminar, so, uh . . . I won't uh . . . I won't be lecturing. This is a discussion format, and that means that I expect you to respond to the reading assignments. No need to raise your hand. Just be moderately courteous about taking turns. Remember that uh . . . 30 percent of your grade is based on class participation. Okay? . . . Now, with that in mind, let's begin our discussion of Chapter 22 in the main textbook. What is *pop art*?

Julia: I'll start. Pop art, as I understand it, was . . . a movement that began in, um, the early 60s when painters . . . I think it was mostly painters . . . began to use popular . . . I mean commercial objects . . . like bottles, comic strips, um . . . cigarette packages, and like that as subjects for their art.

Stephens: Okay. So I'll ask the obvious question: Why paint these objects . . . when they're everywhere?

Tom: Well, first, let me mention that, although there were several artists who were . . . part . . . who were associated with the pop movement, it's uh . . . it's probably Andy Warhol whose paintings best represent it, and I uh . . . I believe Warhol had a response for that question. I think he said, "Everything is art. Everything is beautiful."

Stephens: Yes, he did say that. I'm glad you mentioned it. So let's focus on Warhol for a few minutes. There are some examples of his work on . . . let's see . . . on page 524 of your textbook . . . As you see, he painted enormous Campbell's soup cans, lines of Coca-Cola bottles, and rows of Martinson coffee cans. Any ideas about these particular subjects?

Tom: Well, of course the story is that uh . . . that uh Warhol actually ate soup for lunch every day for twenty years, so when he decided to paint objects in the environment, then . . . then the soup can naturally came to mind. Do you think that's true, Dr. Stephens?

Stephens: Tom, it certainly is a widespread myth, but uh . . . probably closer to reality is the fact that Warhol was once a commercial artist and that it was a logical transition for him, personally, to paint products. He went from commercial ads to art, well, that gave expression to the same kinds of objects. But he painted people, too. Any thoughts on that?

Julia: Well, he painted faces, actually—huge images of the popular . . . the celebrities of the sixties. There were several of Marilyn Monroe and Elvis Presley.

Karen: And at least one of Jacqueline Kennedy. But . . . but I was thinking that they really weren't portraits in the strictest sense.

Stephens: That's interesting. What do you mean?

Karen: I'm not sure, but . . . besides the giant canvases . . . well . . . well the way that they were presented . . . it also had a commercial feel. I don't know . . . I'm not saying that too well.

Stephens: No, I think you're on to something. Do you mean perhaps that the people are commercialized in a sense, like a brand name?

Karen: Exactly. I think the book identified the subjects in the face series as um . . . as popular icons . . . that was it . . . of the 60s . . . so maybe their faces do have commercial appeal.

Julia: Yes, and he wasn't always very . . . wasn't very flattering, was he?

Stephens: No, he wasn't. What did you think about the colors?

Julia: That's what I mean! Sometimes the colors are almost . . . psychedelic. Again, that's very . . . I mean . . . you know . . . very 60s.

Stephens: Let's go back to one of the Marilyn Monroe paintings in your book. Let me see . . . here it is. Turn to page 526. You can't see it very well here, but uh . . . on the original, the paint actually gives the impression of colored ink, and . . . and there's usually . . . often a black stencil over it, which produces a unique effect. See how the orange background contrasts with the yellow hair, and there's a pink and a . . . a purple tone on the face? Then there's this green eye shadow. And, to me, it looks like he stenciled the black over the . . . the flat surfaces of the face. It's not a lovely portrait. And the critics agreed with you, Julia. Some critics even called it grotesque. But uh . . . it is . . . absolutely original.

Tom: Original, but dated, don't you think? I mean, years from now, will . . . will anyone be eating Campbell's soup, or drinking Coca-Cola, or really, for that matter, uh . . . will anyone remember Marilyn Monroe?

Stephens: Interesting observation. So, Tom, you're saying that since pop art . . . since it depends on the popular culture, which by its very nature is uh, transient, you're asking . . . will the subject matter of the pop art movement doom its artists to temporary recognition?

Tom: Exactly. Which, I'm thinking, is really different from . . . well, unlike a painter who chooses to create landscapes, which don't change.

Audio

1. What is this lecture mainly about?

Answer

(B) "Although there were several artists who are associated with the pop movement . . . it's . . . probably Andy Warhol whose paintings best represent it." Choices (A), (C), and (D) are mentioned as secondary themes that are used to develop the main theme of the lecture, "Andy Warhol's art."

Audio

2. According to the lecturer, why did Warhol paint objects in the environment?

Answer

(A) "Probably closer to reality is the fact that Warhol was once a commercial artist, and that it was a logical transition for him personally to go from commercial ads to art that gave expression to the same kinds of objects." Choice (C) refers to the story, rather than the fact. Choices (B) and (D) are not mentioned and may not be concluded from information in the lecture.

Audio

3. Whose faces did Warhol paint?

Answer

(A) (B) "There were several [faces] of Marilyn Monroe and Elvis Presley. . . ." Warhol also painted Jacqueline Kennedy, but John Kennedy in Choice (C) is not mentioned and may not be concluded from information in the lecture. There is also no mention of a self-portrait, as in Choice (D).

Audio

4. What problem does Tom mention?

Answer

(D) "The problem with Warhol is that unlike a painter who chooses to create landscapes, his subject matter is very dated. . . . Will the subject matter of the pop art movement doom its artists to temporary recognition?" Choices (A), (B), and (C) are not mentioned as problems.

Audio

5. Listen again to part of the lecture.

Then answer the question.

"I mean, years from now, will . . . will anyone be eating Campbell's soup, or drinking Coca-Cola, or really, for that matter, uh . . . will anyone remember Marilyn Monroe?" "Interesting observation. So, Tom, you're saying that since pop art . . . since it depends on the popular culture, which by its very nature is uh, transient, you're asking . . . will the subject matter of the pop art movement doom its artists to temporary recognition?"

Why does the professor say this:

"So, Tom, you're saying that since pop art . . . since it depends on the popular culture, which by its very nature is uh, transient, you're asking . . . will the subject matter of the pop art movement doom its artists to temporary recognition?"

Answer

(D) Professors often restate a student's comment to improve or clarify it. In this case, Tom provides several examples, and Professor Stephens restates them by making a generalization. Choice (A) is not correct because it is the professor, not the student, who restates the comment. Choice (B) is not correct because the professor restates the student's idea without agreement or disagreement. Choice (C) is not correct because the professor restates the previous question. He does not answer the question.

Audio

6. Select a drawing that is done in the Andy Warhol style.

Answer

(C) The objects from the environment are typical of the subject matter in the Andy Warhol style. Choice (A) is a traditional portrait, unlike the huge faces that Warhol created. Choice (B) is a landscape, which does not represent popular culture.

Lecture Two

Audio

Narrator: Listen to part of a lecture in an environmental science class. The professor is discussing the *web of life*.

Green: To review from yesterday's lecture, *ecology* is the study of organisms in relation to their environment. The total complex of relationships . . . is referred to as the *web of life*. Now, you'll remember that when the relationships don't change much from year to year . . . when they don't change, we observe a balance of nature. Today, we'll discuss what occurs when the balance of nature's disturbed, either . . . either by a geological change such as a change of climate . . . or . . . or a local agitation such as a fire, like the recent forest fire north of here. Now, after the balance of nature has been disturbed . . . when it's disturbed, a period of rehabilitation must occur. And the first life to appear has traditionally been called . . . pioneer flora and fauna. But, the pioneer life is temporary and soon replaced by other forms of life. In turn, these forms are . . . these forms are replaced by others. That is, a series of transitional life forms successively appears, preparing the environment for the forms that will replace them.

Mike: Excuse me, Dr. Green, would that be what the book refers to as *ecological succession*?

Green: It is. For example, after a forest fire, pioneer plants will appear, and . . . and they are usually herbs or ground cover. Now, soon they'll be replaced by shrubs. Shrubs will be replaced by trees. And so it goes in succession, which is where we get the term *ecological succession*. Now, until very recently, it was assumed that plants and animals would . . . form a climax community, and . . . and that's a final stage in the ecological succession, and that tended to be stable for a long time. So, in the case of the forest fire, when the appearance . . . when a permanent climax flora appeared, we would have assumed that the environment had finally stabilized in balance with the fauna, minerals, and water supply. And the theory was interesting, because a climax community . . . because it usually didn't have the same kinds of plants and animals as . . . as the community that had been prevalent before the balance of nature was disturbed. Now, what was essential to the concept of a climax was that . . . that the balance of nature permitted the community . . . to continue in spite of other organic competition for the area. But the notion of a stable, symbiotically functioning community has been mostly abandoned by scientists. Currently, we believe that . . . that natural ecosystems are much too complex to be neatly organized into predictable stages with a final stable community. So what we can expect in the case of the fire is the . . . the emergence of patches of former landscapes, and probably these patches will be at different stages in the same local environment. Question?

Mike: So the patches are in different stages, and that would be . . . a *polyclimax* condition?

Green: That's exactly right, Mike. *Poly* means *many*, so *polyclimax* refers to adjoining ecosystems at different but mature stages. I believe it's explained as *dynamic equilibrium* in your text.

Mike: Thank you. That's very helpful.

Green: Janet?

Janet: Yes. I was wondering what your opinion was of that wildfire. You know, the one near here. In . . . in the book, it was mentioned that sometimes . . . that fire is now recognized . . . how did they say it? Fire is a natural part of uh . . . fire is a natural part of an ecosystem, and . . . and at least some experts have been quoted in news reports . . . that they feel fire-prevention strategies may have contributed to that disaster. So, um . . . do you agree with that?

Green: I do. That particular ecosystem had an enormous amount of undergrowth, and I think that it may have fueled the fire. Now, in my opinion, if we had purposely burned some of the undergrowth in what we call a *cool fire*, we would have removed the accumulation of brush that contributed to . . . to the destructive *hot fire* that destroyed more than . . . I think I read that it was 50,000 acres of wilderness . . . Yes?

Janet: Is a cool fire a controlled burn?

Green: Yes, it's referred to as a *controlled burn*. But back to your original question, I have to tell you that everyone wouldn't agree with my opinion. Critics call that policy the "let it burn" policy. Now, of course, many people have a . . . a . . . let's say a vested interest in fire suppression, because so many people have built their homes close to the natural environments, they don't want any fires started in their immediate vicinity. So, like your textbook indicates, it's a very controversial topic.

Audio

1. What is the main topic of today's lecture?

Answer

(D) "Today we will discuss what occurs when the balance of nature is disturbed, either by a geological change such as a change of climate, or a local agitation such as a fire." Choices (A), (B), and (C) are mentioned as secondary ideas that are used to develop the main idea, "a disturbance in the balance of nature."

Audio

2. How does the scientific community view the theory of a stable climax community?

Answer

(A) "But the notion of a stable, symbiotically functioning [climax] community has been mostly abandoned by scientists." Choice (B) is not correct because the professor says it was an interesting theory. Choice (C) refers to the terminology used in the textbook to describe the new theory, not the older stable climax theory. Choice (D) is not correct because it was *polyclimax* that replaced the stable climax theory.

Audio

3. According to the lecturer, why is pioneer life important?

Answer

(A) "The pioneer life is temporary and soon replaced by other forms of life . . . preparing the environment for the forms that will replace them." Choice (B) is not correct because it is temporary and soon replaced by other forms of life. Choices (C) and (D) are not correct because pioneer plants are replaced by shrubs and shrubs are replaced by trees.

Audio

4. What is Dr. Green's opinion of a *controlled burn*?

Answer

(A) "In my opinion, if we had purposely burned some of the undergrowth in what we call a *cool fire*, we would have removed the accumulation of brush that contributed to . . . to the destructive *hot fire* . . . It's [a cool fire] referred to as a *controlled burn*."

Choice (B) is not correct because the professor says he agrees with the book about fire-prevention strategies. Choice (C) is not correct because the professor admits that it is a very controversial topic and that everyone would not agree with his opinion. Choice (D) contradicts the fact the professor agrees with the news reports in which fire-prevention strategies were blamed for the disaster.

Audio

5. Listen again to part of the lecture.
   Then answer the question.
   "That is, a series of transitional life forms successively appears, preparing the environment for the forms that will replace them."
   "Excuse me, Dr. Green, would that be what the book refers to as *ecological succession?*"
   Why did the student ask this question:
   "Excuse me, Dr. Green, would that be what the book refers to as *ecological succession?*"

Answer

(B) Professors encourage students to relate information from their textbooks to information in the lectures. In this case, the student is trying to understand the meaning of technical terms. Choice (D) is not correct because the student is polite and he asks a sincere question. Choices (A) and (C) are not mentioned and may not be concluded from information in the lecture.

Audio

6. The professor describes the process of *ecological succession* that occurs after the balance of nature has been disturbed. Summarize the process by putting the events in order.

Answer

(A) (D) (C) (B) "The first life to appear is called pioneer flora and fauna. The pioneer life is temporary and soon replaced by other forms of life . . . a series of transitional life forms successively appears. . . . The final stage . . . in transition tends to be stable. . . . It is called a *climax association.*"

EXERCISE 29: Talks—Professor/Visuals

 (Track 29)

Lecture One

Audio

Narrator: Listen to part of a lecture in an art class. The professor has been discussing the art nouveau school.

Professor:

By the last quarter of the nineteenth century, Louis Tiffany had begun experimenting with different methods of adding color to blown glass. Finally, he produced a unique, iridescent glass which he called Tiffany *favrile*. It was this glass that he shaped and pieced together with metals to form lamps, windows, and other objects of art. This is a typical example of a Tiffany lamp. Look at the way that the pieces are fitted together. You've probably seen one or a reproduction of one at one time or another.

From 1890 to about 1920, Tiffany's favrile glass became very popular throughout the world. It regained popularity in the 1960s and is still prized by many glass collectors today.

In addition, Tiffany created floral jewelry that was considered very stylish at the turn of the century. Rebelling against current fashion that dictated the use of precious stones, Tiffany began working with new materials, creating symbolic, dramatic forms. As a member of the art nouveau movement, he tried to create new and unusual pieces, with delicate designs and curved lines.

Although his name is associated with glass and jewelry today, Tiffany was probably best known during his lifetime for the interior designs that he created. It was Tiffany who was commissioned to design the altar in the Cathedral of Saint John the Divine in New York City and to redecorate the reception rooms in the White House during the administration of President Chester Arthur. The spectacular glass curtain at the National Theater in Mexico City was perhaps his crowning achievement.

His estate on Long Island was filled with beautiful furnishings and decorations, many of them designed by Tiffany himself. When it was sold, the proceeds were transferred to the Louis Tiffany Foundation for Art Students to provide scholarships for aspiring artists. The jewelry store on Fifth Avenue in Manhattan that his father had founded still bears the name Tiffany & Co., and it is still considered a highly fashionable shop for wealthy clientele.

Audio

1. What is the main purpose of this lecture?

Answer

(B) Since most of the information is about Louis Tiffany's work, it must be concluded that his work is the main purpose of the lecture. Choices (A), (C), and (D) are mentioned as secondary themes that are used to develop the main theme of the lecture, "the work of Louis Tiffany."

Audio

2. What characterized Tiffany's jewelry?

Answer

(D) ". . . Tiffany created floral jewelry . . . with delicate designs and curved lines." Choice (A) refers to the material Tiffany used in his lamps and windows. Choice (B) is not correct because Tiffany rebelled against the use of precious stones. Choice (C) is not correct because Tiffany created new and unusual pieces, not traditional designs.

Audio

3. How did Tiffany help aspiring artists?

Answer

(C) ". . . the proceeds [from his estate] were transferred to the Louis Tiffany Foundation for Art Students to provide scholarships for aspiring artists." Choices (A), (B), and (D) are not mentioned and may not be concluded from information in the lecture.

Audio

4. For which interior design was Tiffany NOT commissioned?

Answer

(D) "It was Tiffany who was commissioned to design the altar in the Cathedral of Saint John the Divine . . . and to redecorate the reception rooms in the White House. . . . The spectacular glass curtain at the National Theater in Mexico City was perhaps his crowning achievement." Choice (D) refers to the area where Tiffany's father founded a jewelry store.

Audio

5. Select the example of a Tiffany *favrile* design.

Answer

(B) ". . . he produced a unique, iridescent glass which he called Tiffany *favrile*." Choice (B) is an example of Tiffany favrile glass. Choice (A) is an example of carved furniture, not favrile glass. Choice (C) is a piece of pottery, not favrile glass.

Lecture Two

Audio

Narrator: Listen to part of a lecture in a botany class. The professor will discuss cacti.

Professor:

The cactus is one example of the way that plants adapt to extreme conditions of climate. A cactus like this one has the same basic structure as all other plants, but the function of leaves is carried out by the stems and branches of the plant.

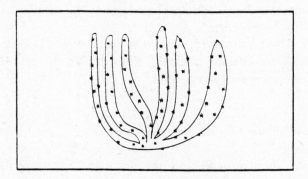

Here are some more examples of the most familiar cacti—the barrel, the Saguaro, and the prickly pear. As you see, they all have stems, branches, or spines, but no leaves. In spring, they may have beautiful blossoms.

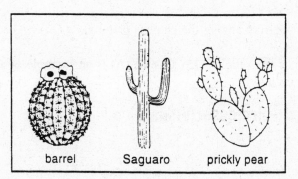

barrel   Saguaro   prickly pear

It is assumed that the predecessors of the modern cactus had leaves, but that during millions of years of changes in the climate, resulting in desert conditions, the cactus gradually adapted to the hotter, drier environment. The roots spread out and began to grow closer to the surface, so that water could be absorbed more quickly. The roots and spongy or hollow stem of the cactus began to serve as a storage container for water, and the outer layer of the plant developed thick, waxy walls to prevent the water from draining out. Some varieties of cactus actually have ribbed folds that expand and contract depending on the volume of water stored inside the stem.

Although there are a few members of the cactus family that retain their leaves, in most cacti, they have evolved into spines, needles, or hairs to protect the plant in areas where little green vegetation is available for foraging animals. In cacti without leaves, the stems and branches carry out the nutritive functions that usually take place in the thin-leafed surfaces of other plants.

Audio

1. What is the lecture mainly about?

Answer

(A) "A cactus . . . has the same basic structure as all other plants . . ." Choices (B), (C), and (D) are mentioned as secondary ideas that are used to support the main idea of the lecture, "The structure of the cactus."

Audio

2. What is assumed about cactus plants millions of years ago?

Answer

(B) "It is assumed that the predecessors of the modern cactus had leaves, but . . . the cactus gradually adapted to the hotter, drier environment." Choices (A), (C), and (D) are not mentioned and may not be concluded from information in the lecture.

Audio

3. According to the lecturer, why have cacti developed spines and needles?

Answer

(C) ". . . leaves . . . have evolved into spines, needles, or hairs to protect the plant in areas where little green vegetation is available for foraging animals." Choices (A), (B), and (D) are not mentioned as reasons why the cacti developed spines and needles.

Audio

4. Where is the nutritive function of the cactus carried out?

Answer

(C) "In cacti without leaves, the stems and branches carry out the nutritive functions that usually take place in the thin-leafed surfaces of other plants." Choice (A) refers to the place where the nutritive function of thin-leafed plants, not cacti, takes place. Choice (B) is not mentioned and may not be concluded from information in the lecture. Choice (D) refers to the place where water is stored.

Audio

5. Select the Saguaro cactus from among the choices pictured.

Answer

(C) As shown in the visuals from the lecture, Choice (A) is an example of a prickly pear. Choice (B) is an example of a barrel cactus.

EXERCISE 30: Lectures—Professor/Visuals   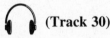 (Track 30)

Lecture One

Audio

Narrator: Listen to part of a lecture in an anthropology class. The professor is preparing the students for a field trip.

Professor:

Today the lecture's about petroglyphs, but before we begin, we . . . let's go over our plans for the field trip. As you'll remember, next week we'll be meeting in the parking lot of . . . the lot outside this building . . . at eight o'clock in the morning. The bus will be leaving by eight-fifteen so, um, we can be at the petroglyph site by ten o'clock. A heads up. Please wear comfortable shoes because we'll be doing quite a lot of walking. And the area at the site . . . it's laid out with paths . . . so we won't actually be doing any climbing. In fact, climbing on the rocks is against the law since, um, since the area's a protected site. But it's a rather long walk from the bus parking area over there to the site, and . . . and then we'll be walking the paths to view the petroglyphs, so you'll be glad you've got comfortable shoes on.

That said, let's begin our discussion of . . . petroglyphs. What are they? Well, the general definition's very broad, including any symbols that have been carved or . . . or hammered into rocks. The term "petroglyph" comes from two Greek words: *petro*, which means "rock," and *glyph*, which means "carving." But, um . . . why were they carved in the first place? For a variety of reasons really. Some petroglyphs simply appear to mark a trail or identify the presence of water or good hunting grounds, but many petroglyphs record important events in the history of the people, or they invoke some uh . . . magical presence in religious ceremonies.

The major culture in the area that we'll be exploring on our field trip is the Hohokam . . . who, uh, probably lived at the site from about A.D. 300 to A.D. 1450. Since there are no current inhabitants, it's difficult to interpret the symbols on the rock art, but their modern descendants . . . the descendants of the Hohokam have provided some insights. In addition, uh, some of the symbolism is shared by many cultures and, therefore, we're able to . . . we can interpret a few of the symbols that we see there, um, either by researching other similar symbols or by relying on interpretations by current cultural groups with similar inscriptions.

Okay. There are four basic types of symbols common to the area we're going to explore . . . which I've drawn on the handout . . . the one I passed out at the beginning of class. So let's refer to the first drawing, which looks like this. As you can see, it's a figure of a person.

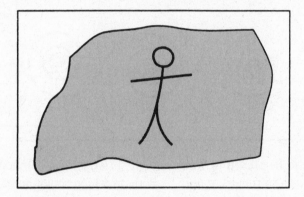

You'll see these on . . . on many of the rocks. Some of them illustrate activities that may have been . . . significant to the Hohokam. Drawings of this kind are called *anthropomorphs*.

The second set of symbols . . . and these are called *zoomorphs* . . . are animal figures. S . . . Some of the more common zoomorphs are deer, sheep, snakes, lizards, coyotes, and birds . . . all of which are still found in the area. But besides the obvious allusion to a successful hunt or um . . . when they are drawn close to . . . close to other drawings, like a reference to a historic event, then these zoomorphs might also represent clans or family groups that are named for animals. Look at this deer.

Here's what I mean. It could be a reference to a family that . . . a family that had taken the deer as the symbol for their clan.

So . . . a third set of symbols—and again I am referring to the handout—these are various representations of circles, especially concentric circles. In most cultures, symbols like this . . . represent the sun, which usually figures prominently in religious ceremonies. Here are several examples.

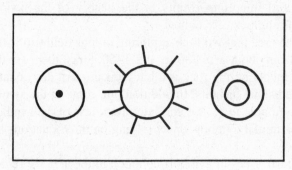

Finally, I want you to watch for spirals like these.

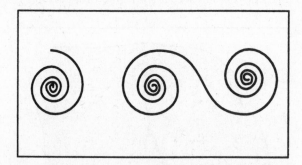

The spiral is thought to be related to water, which . . . which can symbolize life or migration, but more often is interpreted as a spiritual symbol. . . . Perhaps a representation of the emergence . . . of the first people from, uh, the spiritual world to this place.

Let me also mention that—when we go—you may see some crosses carved into some of the rocks, um, which are frankly very difficult to interpret. Some scholars believe that the cross could . . . may represent the important stars such as Venus or the Morning Star, but . . . but other scholars remind us that many missionaries passed through the desert and may have carved the symbol of the cross on the rocks a thousand years or more after the original carvings were made. Which reminds me, just a word about the site that we're going to visit. . . . This entire area has a . . . highly significant spiritual meaning to the Native Americans, so . . . so I expect our group to treat it as a sacred place. You can bring a camera if you wish since there's no objection to our taking photographs, but we should be respectful. Any questions?

Audio
1. What is the main purpose of this lecture?
Answer
(B) "Today the lecture is about petroglyphs." Choices (A), (C), and (D) are mentioned as secondary themes that are used to develop the main purpose of the lecture, to introduce "common petroglyphs."

Audio
2. What are *petroglyphs*?
Answer
(B) ". . . the general definition [of petroglyphs] is very broad, including any symbols that have been carved or hammered into rocks." Choices (A), (C), and (D) are not mentioned in the definition of petroglyphs.

Audio

3. How are anthropologists able to interpret the symbols?

Answer

(B) (C) "Since there are no current inhabitants, it is difficult to interpret the symbols on the rock art, but their descendants have provided some insights. In addition, some of the symbolism is shared by many cultures . . ." Choice (A) is not probable because the lecturer does not mention it. Choice (D) is not correct because the petroglyphs sometimes represent ideas such as life or migration as well as clan names and spiritual symbols.

Audio

4. What might be represented by a *zoomorph*?

Answer

(B) (C) ". . . besides the obvious allusion to a successful hunt or, when shown with other drawings, the reference to an historic event, these zoomorphs might also represent clans or family groups of the same name." Choices (A) and (D) are not mentioned in reference to zoomorphs.

Audio

5. Listen again to part of the lecture.
   Then answer the question.
   "But, um . . . why were they carved in the first place? For a variety of reasons really. Some petroglyphs simply appear to mark a trail or identify the presence of water or . . . or good hunting grounds, but many petroglyphs record important events in the history of the people, or they invoke some, uh, magical presence in religious ceremonies."
   Why did the professor say this:
   "But, um . . . why were they carved in the first place?"

Answer

(B) Professors often ask and answer rhetorical questions. In this case, she is asking a question that she answers in the following statement. Choices (C) and (D) are not correct because she continues her lecture without pausing long enough to invite student responses. Choice (A) is not mentioned and may not be concluded from information in the lecture.

Audio

6. Select the petroglyph that is a spiritual symbol of life.

Answer

(A) "The spiral is thought to be related to water, which can symbolize life . . ." Choice (B) is the symbol for the sun, which figures prominently in religious ceremonies. Choice (C) is an anthropomorph, which is a figure of a person.

Lecture Two

Audio

Narrator: Listen to part of a lecture in an astronomy class. The professor will discuss comets.

Professor:
Comets are small bodies from the outer solar system that are characterized by gaseous emissions and consist of a solid nucleus, a cloudy atmosphere, which is called the *coma*, and a tail. Let me say that again. Comets are small bodies from the outer solar system that are characterized by gaseous emissions and consist of a solid nucleus, a cloudy atmosphere, which is called the *coma*, and a tail. This is an example of a typical comet.

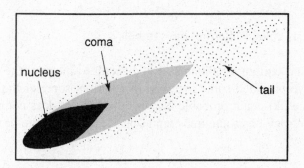

You can't really see it in this diagram, but, uh, the nucleus is made of ice with rocks and dust particles encrusted in it. When it's far from the Sun, the nucleus of a comet may be completely frozen, and most are quite small. But, as . . . as a comet approaches the sun, some of the ice on the surface vaporizes, and, uh, the gas and dust particles that were embedded in the ice of the nucleus . . . are released and blown back by the solar wind . . . and that's what forms a hydrogen atmosphere, and, uh, the tail of the comet. It's important to note that the tails of comets always point away from the Sun because, uh, the solar wind pushes them back.

Most comets have a nucleus . . . that is less than, say, a body ten miles in diameter, but the comas can extend out nearly one million miles. And some exceptional tails have been known to trail 100 million miles behind their comets.

We classify comets as, uh, either short-period comets or long-period comets, depending on how long they take to orbit the Sun. And you may want to write this down. Short-period comets require fewer than 200 years, whereas long-period comets need more than 200 years. . . . The key number there is 200 years. So, when you do the math, you see that, uh, short-period comets tend to recur often enough to be . . . well, anticipated by the scientific community. For example, Edmund Halley used Newton's law of gravitation to . . . to calculate a comet's seventy-six year orbit and predicted that it would return in 1758. When it appeared on schedule, the comet was named Halley's comet, and as many of you know, it passed near Earth on schedule in 1986, and, uh, when we add 76 years, we should see it again in 2061. Well, maybe *you* will, even if I don't.

A little more on, uh, on short-period comets. They're nearer the Sun, so consequently, they're heated and . . . and lose their ice by a process called sublimation. So, their supply of gas may be depleted after only a few hundred revolutions . . . leaving them devoid of the coma and tail . . . and all but invisible. But, let me back up a minute. What I'm really saying is that, uh, the gaseous envelope burns up, leaving only a nucleus, which is virtually impossible to see.

As far as we can tell, the short-period comets have their origin in a belt of comets that . . . that lies just beyond the orbit of Pluto. And, uh, since they are constantly burning up, in maybe less than a million years, all of the short-period comets . . . that's the short-period comets we're talking about now . . . they would have disappeared if it hadn't been for something called *capture*, a process whereby the planets, especially Jupiter, attract comets that have originated farther away, replacing those that are, uh, that are decaying, and maintaining the population of the short-period group at a more or less stable level. By the way, capture doesn't usually occur on the first pass but may happen after many passes. And . . . and eventually, the comets that have been captured . . . they detach themselves and start moving toward the Sun, like other short-period comets.

Okay, let's just touch on the long-period comets now. We think that the long-period comets come from a cloud of comets one thousand times farther away than Pluto. One thousand times. Consequently, they may be seen only once in . . . in recorded history. It's also worth thinking about that . . . that most of these comets travel in, uh, elongated orbits that . . . that cross the circular orbits of the planets. Thus, the possibility of collision does exist at the points where the orbits intersect. Here. . . . Look at this drawing, which . . . which shows the orbits of four planets with several comets intersecting them. See what I mean? Where they cross?

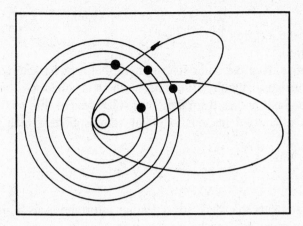

Oh, yes, another interesting point. Some of the craters on the satellites of the outer planets . . . are probably evidence of past cometary collisions. In fact, the *Galileo* spacecraft on its way to Jupiter got some fantastic photographs of impacts on Jupiter's right side. And . . . and . . . even the craters on Earth's moon could have been caused by comets.

Audio
1. What is the main purpose of this lecture?
Answer
(B) Most of the information in the lecture is about the structure and nature of comets. Choices (A), (C), and (D) are mentioned as secondary themes that are used to develop the two main themes of the lecture, "the structure and the nature of comets."

Audio
2. What causes the tail of a comet to point away from the Sun?
Answer
(B) "The tails of comets always point away from the Sun because the solar wind pushes them back." Choice (A) refers to the way that we classify comets, not to the reason that the tail points away from the Sun. Choice (C) refers to the cloudy atmosphere that projects out from the nucleus. Choice (D) refers to the origin of comets, not to the reason the tails of comets point away from the Sun.

Audio
3. What is the difference between a short-period comet and a long-period comet?
Answer
(D) "We classify comets as either short-period comets or long-period comets, depending on how long they take to orbit the Sun." Choice (A) refers to the difference between comets and planets, not to the difference between types of comets. Choices (B) and (C) are not mentioned as factors that differentiate between comets.

Audio
4. What is *capture*?
Answer
(B) ". . . *capture*, a process whereby the planets . . . attract comets that have originated farther away [long-period], replacing those [short-period] that are decaying." Choice (A) is not correct because the comets eventually detach themselves. Choices (C) and (D) are occasionally true, but neither is a definition of *capture*.

Audio

5. Listen again to part of the lecture.

    Then answer the question.

    "Comets are small bodies from the outer solar system that are characterized by gaseous emissions and consist of a solid nucleus, a cloudy atmosphere, which is called the *coma*, and a tail. Let me say that again. Comets are small bodies from the outer solar system that are characterized by gaseous emissions and consist of a solid nucleus, a cloudy atmosphere, which is called the *coma*, and a tail."

    Why does the man say this:

    "Let me say that again."

Answer

(A) Professors often tell students that they are repeating information as a signal for them to write it down. Choice (B) is not correct because he repeats it in exactly the same words. Choice (C) is not correct because he does not suggest that students pay attention. He simply repeats a definition. Choice (D) is not correct because students are not interacting with the professor in class.

Audio

6. Identify the orbit of a comet.

Answer

(B) "Most comets travel in elongated orbits that cross the circular orbits of the planets." Choice (A) refers to the orbit of a planet, not a comet. Choice (C) is not mentioned and may not be concluded from information in the lecture.

Evaluation of Speaking—Independent Tasks

Responses on general topics can be evaluated by referring to the checklist printed below and the rubric on page 499. Examples of level 4 talks for Exercises 31–33 follow.

NO ⇨ ⇨ ⇨ YES
0 1 2 3 4

✓ The response answers the topic question.

✓ The point of view or position is clear.

✓ The talk is direct and well-organized.

✓ The sentences are logically connected to each other.

✓ Details and examples support the main idea.

✓ The speaker expresses complete thoughts.

✓ The meaning is easy for the listener to comprehend.

✓ A wide range of vocabulary is used.

✓ There are only minor errors in grammar and idioms.

✓ The response is within a range of 100–150 words.

Speaking

Narrator 2: This is the script for the speaking exercises. During each exercise, you will respond to a speaking question. You may take notes as you listen. The reading passages and the questions are printed in the book, but most of the directions will be spoken. Ready? Let's begin.

EXERCISE 31: Independent Task 1—Agree or Disagree

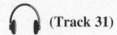 (Track 31)

Topic One

Audio
Narrator 2:
Exercise 31, Topic One. Listen for a question that asks your opinion about a familiar topic. After you hear the question, you have 15 seconds to prepare and 45 seconds to record your answer.

Narrator 1:
State whether you agree or disagree with the following position.

A college education should be free for all qualified students.

Be sure to use specific reasons and examples to support your opinion.

Narrator 2:
Please prepare your answer after the beep.

Beep

[Preparation Time: 15 seconds]

Narrator 2:
Please begin speaking after the beep.

Beep

[Recording Time: 45 seconds]

Example Notes
not free
   someone pays
   taxpayers
motivation
   less pressure
   pay—more motivated
responsibility
   college less—quality
   funding—not from student

Example Speaking Answer
I disagree that a college education should be free to all qualified students because ultimately someone will have to pay for it. Calling it free doesn't make it free. So in most cases, it would be another burden for taxpayers, and many of them wouldn't be able to go to college themselves. They would have to work harder to support someone else's opportunity. Also, if college were free, some of the pressure on students to succeed might be removed. I mean that when students are paying for their educations, they might feel more motivated to get something for their investment, and they'd study harder. And some of

the responsibility that colleges have to provide a quality education to their students might be diminished because their source of funding would no longer be directly from those students and their families.

Beep

Topic Two

Audio
Narrator 2:
Exercise 31, Topic Two. Listen for a question that asks your opinion about a familiar topic. After you hear the question, you have 15 seconds to prepare and 45 seconds to record your answer.

Narrator 1:
State whether you agree or disagree with the following position.

Young people spend too much time on their phones.

Be sure to use specific reasons and examples to support your opinion.

Narrator 2:
Please prepare your answer after the beep.

Beep

[Preparation Time: 15 seconds]

Narrator 2:
Please begin speaking after the beep.

Beep

[Recording Time: 45 seconds]

Example Notes
replaced devices
   alarm clock
   calculator
   map—directions
print
   dictionary
   newspaper
   schoolwork
   catalog
   game
communicate
   friend
   family

Example Speaking Answer
I disagree that we young people spend too much time on our phones. The fact is that phones have replaced many other devices, so when we're using our phones, we may be setting an alarm clock, using a calculator, or reading a map for directions. Print has also been replaced, so we could be checking a word in a dictionary, reading a newspaper, doing schoolwork, shopping from a catalog, or playing a game. The way we communicate has changed as well, so we might be talking with a friend or with family. Older people are performing the same tasks and enjoying games and friends, but they are using older technology, and probably spending more time doing it.

Beep

EXERCISE 32: Independent Task 1—Two Options

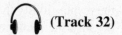 (Track 32)

Topic One

Audio

Narrator 2:

Exercise 32, Topic One. Listen for a question that asks your opinion about a familiar topic. After you hear the question, you have 15 seconds to prepare and 45 seconds to record your answer.

Narrator 1:

Some teachers encourage competition among their students. Others help students learn how to collaborate and study in groups. Which approach do you think is better for learning, and why do you think so? Be sure to use specific reasons and examples to support your opinion.

Narrator 2:

Please prepare your answer after the beep.

Beep

[Preparation Time: 15 seconds]

Narrator 2:

Please begin speaking after the beep.

Beep

[Recording Time: 45 seconds]

Example Notes

Teachers should help students collaborate because

    employment—teams and committees

    biographies—successful people collaborate

    business and industry—win-win situation

Example Speaking Answer

I think teachers should help students learn how to study in groups because after students leave school, they'll have to rely on collaboration in order to succeed. Um . . . teams and committees get the job done in most employment settings. There are very few positions in which the responsibility and the credit for a project belong to one individual. In the biographies of successful people, they . . . it's clear that they owe their success to others, and . . . and that they've had to collaborate in order to achieve it. And, competition implies that, uh, someone must lose in order for another to win, and the current thinking in business and industry is to try to work out a win-win situation, and that means that all parties have to collaborate.

Beep

Topic Two

Audio
Narrator 2:
Exercise 32, Topic Two. Listen for a question that asks your opinion about a familiar topic. After you hear the question, you have 15 seconds to prepare and 45 seconds to record your answer.

Narrator 1:
Some people cope with stress by exercising. Others talk with family or friends. How do you handle stressful situations? Be sure to use specific reasons and examples to support your opinion.

Narrator 2:
Please prepare your answer after the beep.

Beep

[Preparation Time: 15 seconds]

Narrator 2:
Please begin speaking after the beep.

Beep

[Recording Time: 45 seconds]

Example Notes
cope—depending on why I'm upset
    situation I can do something about—talk + express feelings
    part of life—long walks
        rhythm + fresh air
        clear mind + calm down

Example Speaking Answer
I use several methods to cope with stress depending on why I'm feeling upset. If it's a situation I can do something about, I try to talk with the people involved. For example, when I'm angry with my friend, I'll tell him so, um . . . and I'll try to resolve the problem with him directly. I feel better—less stressed—when I express my feelings. But sometimes stressful things happen that you can't really do much about. For example, when I have a lot to do at school, it's just part of life. So, when that happens, then I take long walks. I'm not sure whether it's the rhythm of the walking or maybe the fresh air, but I do know that it always helps me clear my mind and calm down, so, uh, I can go back to the stressful situation again, without feeling so out of control.

Beep

EXERCISE 33: Independent Task 1—Three Options

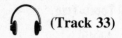 **(Track 33)**

Topic One

Audio

Narrator 2:

Exercise 33, Topic One. Listen for a question that asks your opinion about a familiar topic. After you hear the question, you have 15 seconds to prepare and 45 seconds to record your answer.

Narrator 1:

You are applying for a work-study job on campus, and you have three opportunities: a job in the library, in the cafeteria, or in a professor's office. For which job would you apply? Be sure to give specific reasons and examples for your choice.

Narrator 2:

Please prepare your answer after the beep.

Beep

[Preparation Time: 15 seconds]

Narrator 2:

Please begin speaking after the beep.

Beep

[Recording Time: 45 seconds]

Example Notes

library—better study area
   quiet
   resources—copy machine, reserve
learn
   resources
   research
meet—informal
   researchers
   professors

Example Speaking Answer

A work-study position allows students to study when the work's completed for their scheduled time, so my choice for a work-study position would be a job in the library because it would offer a better place to study. The cafeteria and even an office area wouldn't be as quiet, and there wouldn't be any resources available for personal use, such as a copy machine, reserve, or other materials. Another good reason to prefer the library position is so I could learn on the job about the resources in the library that I might want to use for my own research. By helping other students locate what they need, I'd know more about what was available. And the library position would allow me to meet researchers and professors who use the library. Getting to know them in the library environment is a little less formal than the classroom and could prove useful.

Topic Two

Audio

Narrator 2:

Exercise 33, Topic Two. Listen for a question that asks your opinion about a familiar topic. After you hear the question, you have 15 seconds to prepare and 45 seconds to record your answer.

Narrator 1:

The International Student Association is planning a fund-raiser. Three possibilities are being considered: a talent show with music and dancing from around the world, a dinner with food from various countries, and a fair with booths featuring international items for sale. Which option would you support and why? Be sure to give specific reasons and examples for your choice.

Narrator 2:

Please prepare your answer after the beep.

Beep

[Preparation Time: 15 seconds]

Narrator 2:

Please begin speaking after the beep.

Beep

[Recording Time: 45 seconds]

Example Notes

dinner

    more people—restaurants packed

    students prepare

    dining hall

fair—items don't sell

show—equipment + venue

Example Speaking Answer

I support a dinner as the fund-raiser for the International Club because more people would probably buy a ticket. The number of restaurants around any campus proves that student and other people on campus enjoy eating out. The restaurants are always packed, and you usually have to wait to get a seat. All the students in the club would know how to prepare something typical of their countries, so they could do the work themselves, and they wouldn't have to buy anything that might not sell in a fair. A talent show would require a lot of equipment and a good venue that might have to be rented for the night, but the club members could probably decorate one of the dining halls on a weekend and serve the dinner there, since many campus dining halls close at least one night a week.

Evaluation of Speaking—Integrated Tasks

Responses on campus and academic topics can be evaluated by referring to the checklist printed below and the rubric on page 499. Examples of Level 4 talks for Exercises 34–40 follow.

NO ⇨ ⇨ ⇨ YES
0   1   2   3   4

✓ The response answers the topic question.

✓ There are only minor inaccuracies in the content.

✓ The response is direct and well-organized.

✓ The sentences are logically connected to each other.

✓ Details and examples support the main idea.

✓ The speaker expresses complete thoughts.

✓ The meaning is easy for the listener to comprehend.

✓ A wide range of vocabulary is used.

✓ The speaker paraphrases, using his or her own words.

✓ The speaker credits the lecturer with wording when necessary.

✓ There are only minor errors in grammar and idioms.

✓ The response is within a range of 100–150 words.

EXERCISE 34: Integrated Task 2—Campus Reports

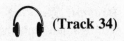 **(Track 34)**

Topic One

Audio

Narrator 2:

Exercise 34, Topic One. Read a short passage and listen to a talk on the same topic. Then listen for a question about them. After you hear the question, you have 30 seconds to prepare and 60 seconds to record your answer.

Narrator 1:

The administration at City College is considering a proposal for an accelerated bachelor's degree program. Read the notice from a poster on campus. You have 50 seconds to complete it (refer to page 62). Please begin reading now.

[Reading Time: 50 seconds]

Narrator 1:

Now listen to a student who is speaking to an advisor. She is expressing her opinion about the new program.

Woman student:

First, I'd like you to know that I probably qualify for the accelerated program because I'm an honors student, but I'm not going to apply because I don't agree with the plan. You see, the idea is to select some students for special treatment, and I don't think that's fair. If you limit the classes to twenty students each, then the big lecture classes for the rest of the students will just have to get bigger and more impersonal than they already are. Look, I'm already accelerating my program by taking extra classes every term. Students don't need a new program to do that. Besides, it will cost money, and that always means higher tuition and fees.

Narrator 1:

The student expresses her opinion about the college's plans for an accelerated three-year degree program. Summarize her opinion and the reasons she gives for having that opinion.

Narrator 2:

Please prepare your answer after the beep.

Beep

[Preparation Time: 30 seconds]

Narrator 2:

Please begin speaking after the beep.

Beep

[Recording Time: 60 seconds]

Example Notes

special treatment unfair
    regular classes bigger to limit accelerated
not necessary
    take more courses every term
cost → higher tuition + fees

Example Speaking Answer

The woman feels that the accelerated program is unfair because the large lecture classes—the ones for the students who aren't admitted to the program, I mean the new program—those classes will probably be even larger in order to limit the number of students in the accelerated classes to twenty. She's also concerned that the accelerated program will be expensive to administer, and the additional cost could result in, uh, in an increase in tuition for all the students. Um . . . she also points out that it isn't necessary to create an accelerated program for students to complete their degrees in three years because . . . because she's already doing that by taking more than the usual number of classes every term.

Beep

Topic Two

Audio

Narrator 2:

Exercise 34, Topic Two. Read a short passage and listen to a talk on the same topic. Then listen for a question about them. After you hear the question, you have 30 seconds to prepare and 60 seconds to record your answer.

Narrator 1:

The administration at State University is considering a proposal to close the dorms during spring break. Read the notice from the campus newspaper. You have 50 seconds to complete it (refer to page 63). Please begin reading now.

[Reading Time: 50 seconds]

Narrator 1:

Now listen to a student who is speaking at the meeting. He is expressing his opinion about the new program.

Man student:

Well, I'm all for a plan that will help the university save money, but not like this. When we sign our dorm contracts, the university agrees to provide us with a home, and it isn't right to tell us that we can't stay in our home over the break if we choose to. Besides, we keep some valuable possessions in our rooms, like computers and audio equipment. I live in Norman Hall, and I don't want someone else living in my room. Do I have to move all my stuff out, or do I just hope that the person who is staying there won't bother it? I don't think that the university has thought this through.

Narrator 1:

The student expresses his opinion about the proposal for closing the dorms over spring break. Summarize his opinion and the reasons he gives for having that opinion.

Narrator 2:

Please prepare your answer after the beep.

Beep

[Preparation Time: 30 seconds]

Narrator 2:

Please begin speaking after the beep.

Beep

[Recording Time: 60 seconds]

Example Notes
should be able to stay
    dorm contracts→home
    Norman Hall—valuable possessions = computers + audio

Example Speaking Answer
The man thinks that students should be able to stay in their dorm rooms over spring break if they choose to. He argues that the dorm students have a contract with the university. He also says that, um, the students consider the dorm their home, and . . . and they should be able to stay home during a break if they want to. Um, his strongest argument is probably that the students in Norman Hall would have to let strangers stay in their dorm rooms over the break, so um, they would either have to move their valuables out, or . . . or they would have to trust the person staying in their rooms not to damage their computers and audio equipment. So . . . he doesn't think that the university has considered all the potential problems.

Beep

EXERCISE 35: Integrated Task 2—Campus Reports

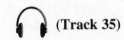 (Track 35)

Topic One

Audio
Narrator 2:
Exercise 35, Topic One. Read a short passage and listen to a conversation on the same topic. Then listen for a question about them. After you hear the question, you have 30 seconds to prepare and 60 seconds to record your answer.

Narrator 1:
The administration at City College has decided to shorten the hours for on-site registration. Read the notice that students received. You have 50 seconds to complete it (refer to page 64). Please begin reading now.

[Reading Time: 50 seconds]

Narrator 1:
Now listen to a conversation between two students. The man is expressing his opinion about the change.

Man: I think registration is going to be worse than ever.
Woman: Oh, maybe not. A lot of people will just use the internet to register online.
Man: I won't. And a lot of other people won't either. For one thing, the website keeps going down whenever there's heavy use, and there will be during registration week.
Woman: That's true, but it's still better than standing around waiting your turn at all those tables in the gym.
Man: Okay, but what about the problems that you can't work out online? Like the professor's signature for an override when there are too many students in the class? If you register on-site, the professor's right there to do it.
Woman: That's true. And sometimes the advisors can help.
Man: Right, they can keep you from taking the wrong course. But the real problem is going to be the long lines. If people have to register in three days instead of five, it's going to be more crowded than ever. It was just getting manageable because of the internet option.

Narrrator 1:
The man expresses his opinion about the changes in the registration procedure. Report his opinion and explain the reasons he gives for having that opinion.

Narrator 2:
Please prepare your answer after the beep.

Beep

[Preparation Time: 30 seconds]

Narrator 2:
Please begin speaking after the beep.

Beep

[Recording Time: 60 seconds]

Example Notes
registration worse
    heavy use → web site goes down
    problems can't work out online
        professor's signature for override
        advisor for wrong course
    crowded
        long lines
        three days instead of five

Example Speaking Answer
The man thinks that the changes in registration will cause problems for the students. The university claims that students will be able to register online, but the man won't use that option because the web site is unreliable during peak use, um, like a registration period. He also maintains that there are problems that require a professor's signature, for example, when a student wants permission to register for a class that's already full. That can't be done on the computer. And he says that it's helpful for students to see their advisors to be sure they're signing up for the right courses. Um . . . but his biggest concern is that the three-day registration schedule on-site is going to be even more crowded than in the past because the same number of people will be trying to register in a . . . a shorter time frame.

Beep

Topic Two

Audio
Narrator 2:
Exercise 35, Topic Two. Read a short passage and listen to a conversation on the same topic. Then listen for a question about them. After you hear the question, you have 30 seconds to prepare and 60 seconds to record your answer.

Narrator 1:
The fall career fair is being planned. Read the notice that appeared in the campus newspaper. You have 50 seconds to complete it (refer to page 65). Please begin reading now.

[Reading Time: 50 seconds]

Narrator 1:
Now listen to a conversation between two students. The woman is expressing her opinion about the career fair.

Man: I can't decide whether to go to the career fair.
Woman: Well, I'm going to go. I missed it last year, but I was just a junior. Now that I'm a senior, I'm serious about finding a job.
Man: Yeah, but there will be so many other people trying to talk to the representatives, all at the same time. Maybe it's not worth it.
Woman: Look, you have to, you know, make an impression. I'm working really hard on my resume, and I'm going to wear a suit, even if it is Saturday. I think this is an opportunity to stand out from the crowd. And besides that, where else can you find people from 100 companies in the same room? I'm saving a lot of work later by deciding which companies *I* really want to work for.
Man: You mean, you won't send applications to companies that don't impress *you*.
Woman: Right. But probably the best reason to go is because my friend Carla got her job at a company that interviewed her at the career fair last year. It works.

Narrator 1:
The woman expresses her opinion about the career fair. Report her opinion and explain the reasons that she gives for having that opinion.

Narrator 2:
Please prepare your answer after the beep.

Beep

[Preparation Time: 30 seconds]

Narrator 2:
Please begin speaking after the beep.

Beep

[Recording Time: 60 seconds]

Example Notes
woman going to fair
   senior
   serious about job
make impression
   resume
   suit
100 companies
   deciding which companies
friend got job at fair last year

Example Speaking Answer
The woman has a very positive opinion about the career fair because she's a senior and she's a serious candidate for a position, and she thinks that by presenting a good resume and dressing well, she'll make a good impression on the recruiters, which will give her an edge on the competition. She also points out that it's a good opportunity to form opinions about the companies—the companies that participate in the fair. She mentions that there are 100 companies participating, and this will give her a chance to

talk to a lot of representatives. Um . . . after the fair, she'll only pursue positions with the companies that she chooses, based on her conversations. She says that her friend interviewed at the career fair last year and was hired by one of the companies, so she knows that it's possible to get a job by attending the fair, and that's probably the best reason for her favorable opinion.

Beep

Exercise 36: Integrated Task 3—Academic Concepts 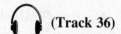 (Track 36)

Topic One

Audio
Narrator 2:
Exercise 36, Topic One. Read a short passage and listen to a lecture on the same topic. Then listen for a question about them. After you hear the question, you have 30 seconds to prepare and 60 seconds to record your answer.

Narrator 1:
Now read the passage about a village. You have 50 seconds to complete it (refer to page 66).
Please begin reading now.

[Reading Time: 50 seconds]

Narrator 1:
Now listen to part of a lecture on the same topic.

Professor:
Thomas Jefferson was probably the first to refer to a college campus as an "academic village." This term seems appropriate because the campus that Jefferson created when he designed the University of Virginia included all of the qualities that are found in the definition of a traditional village. His plan was realized in the shape of a large rectangle. It featured a grassy lawn with the rotunda library at the center and ten pavilions along two sides of the lawn, each to house the classrooms for one branch of learning. Behind the pavilions, he created formal gardens with another set of buildings on each side to serve as residences and dining halls. Quite soon, businesses grew up around the periphery of the rectangle to support all manner of basic services as well as to provide areas for social and educational exchange.

It is interesting to reflect on the impression that the classical architecture and the balanced pattern of the campus may have had on the self-concept of the students and faculty. Clearly, Jefferson had provided them with the outward structure of an organized, rational academic community.

Narrator 1:
Refer to Thomas Jefferson's definition of a college campus presented in the lecture, and explain how the information in the anthropology text supported Jefferson's view.

Narrator 2:
Please prepare your answer after the beep.

Beep

[Preparation Time: 30 seconds]

Narrator 2:
Please begin speaking after the beep.

Beep

[Recording Time: 60 seconds]

Example Notes
"academic village"
University of Virginia
   large rectangle—library center
   pavilions—classrooms
   gardens—residences + dining halls
   periphery—businesses for basic services + social
classical architecture
   balanced pattern
   organized + rational

Example Speaking Answer
Jefferson called a college campus an "academic village," and the definition of a traditional village in the anthropology text supports his view. First, a village is self-contained, and so is a campus because . . . because there are facilities for daily life—residences, dining halls, and classrooms. Second, a village can store most of the goods and services inside its limits, and so does a campus because businesses for basic services and social life . . . they spring up around the main area. Um . . . third, residents in a traditional village have common objectives, and so do the students and faculty of a college campus who are united by, um, educational goals. And um . . . last, a traditional village reflects the spirit of the community. By using classical architecture, Jefferson designed the University of Virginia to . . . to give the impression of a rational academic village.

Beep

Topic Two

Audio
Narrator 2:
Exercise 36, Topic Two. Read a short passage and listen to a lecture on the same topic. Then listen for a question about them. After you hear the question, you have 30 seconds to prepare and 60 seconds to record your answer.

Narrator 1:
Now read the passage about entrepreneurs. You have 50 seconds to complete it (refer to page 67). Please begin reading now.

[Reading Time: 50 seconds]

Narrator 1:
Now listen to part of a lecture on the same topic. The professor is talking about Levi Strauss.

Professor:
Levi Strauss is a good example of the kind of entrepreneur that is described in your textbook. He came to the United States from Bavaria as a teenager. After selling clothing and dry goods from door to door for several years in New York, he made the journey to California with a supply of canvas. The gold rush was at its peak, and Strauss got the idea to sell tents to the gold miners.

    When he discovered that the miners were not very interested in purchasing tents, he wasted no time in recycling the brown canvas cloth into sturdy pants, a product in great demand in the mining camps. Later he began making work pants in a blue cotton fabric imported from France, called "serge de Nimes" but known in America as "denim." Along with Jacob Davis, a tailor from Nevada, Strauss patented a pattern of copper rivets to strengthen the stress points on pants, especially the pockets. They first became known as "waist overalls," then "levis." They became so popular that Strauss concentrated most of his effort on the manufacture and sales of durable work pants.

Narrator 1:
Referring to both the lecture and the reading passage, explain why the experience of Levi Strauss is typical of small-business owners.

Narrator 2:
Please prepare your answer after the beep.

Beep

[Preparation Time: 30 seconds]

Narrator 2:
Please begin speaking after the beep.

Beep

[Recording Time: 60 seconds]

Example Notes
Strauss = entrepreneur
   teenager—sold clothing + dry goods
   California—canvas tents to miners
   miners not interested—wanted work pants
   recycled canvas into pants—later blue denim
   patent for copper rivets—strengthen stress points

Example Speaking Answer
Levi Strauss is representative of the small-business owners described in the reading passage. He was already employed full time as a teenager selling clothing and dry goods. He showed a strong desire for independence, uh, when he journeyed to California and . . . and a high level of initiative when he followed through on his idea to sell tents to miners. Then, when he realized that the miners needed work pants more than they needed tents, he was quick to take advantage of the opportunity. First, he recycled the canvas fabric from his tents into sturdy pants, and later, uh, he made work pants in denim. The patent for the copper rivets to protect the stress points on pockets was very . . . uh . . . very innovative. Finally, like so many successful entrepreneurs, Strauss didn't follow a fixed business plan. He reacted to coincidence and, uh, he responded to opportunity.

Beep

EXERCISE 37: Integrated Task 3—Academic Concepts 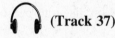 (Track 37)

Topic One

Audio
Narrator 2:
Exercise 37, Topic One. Read a short passage and listen to a lecture on the same topic. Then listen for a question about them. After you hear the question, you have 30 seconds to prepare and 60 seconds to record your answer.

Narrator 1:
Now read the passage about architecture. You have 50 seconds to complete it (refer to page 68). Please begin reading now.

[Reading Time: 50 seconds]

Narrator 1:
Now listen to part of a lecture on the same topic.

Professor:
Let me make a few remarks about the Sydney Opera House. There has been a great deal of discussion among architects as to which architectural movement it represents, but I submit to you that, although it does have aspects of several modern schools of architecture, it's a magnificent example of expressionism in architecture, and I've arrived at that conclusion for a number of reasons.

First, the design was totally innovative. I think you'll agree that there's nothing like it in the world. Second, architect Jorn Utzon was inspired by the forms, functions, and colors in nature. In interviews, he stated that he was influenced in the design by bird wings, the shape and form of clouds, shells, and other natural elements in the harbor where the building would be placed, which is why it seems so right for the site in which it was built. The unique series of shells on the roof structure appear to many who view it for the first time very like white sails on a fleet of ships in the harbor. Third, new structural engineering practices, technologies, and materials allowed him to collaborate with engineers to build a structure that wouldn't have been possible prior to the construction of the opera house. If I'm not mistaken, it was one of the first structures to be supported by computer design techniques. And finally, for anyone who sees it, it produces an emotional response. Of course, the location itself is spectacular, but the opera house fits into the harbor beautifully, and unlike so many buildings that are constructed along waterfronts, it enhances the view.

Personally, I think it's a masterwork of architecture for a number of reasons, but primarily because it's totally unique—a blend of art and architecture, engineering and technology. And it fits into expressionism better than it does into any of the other modern movements in architecture.

Narrator 1:
Referring to both the lecture and the reading passage, explain why the Sydney Opera House is an example of expressionism.

Narrator 2:
Please prepare your answer after the beep.

Beep

[Preparation Time: 30 seconds]

Narrator 2:
Please begin speaking after the beep.

Beep

[Recording Time: 60 seconds]

Example Notes
SOH = Expressionism
  innovative
  Jorn Utzon natural forms—wings, clouds, shells
    roof white sails
  new engineering—technologies, materials
    computer design
  emotional response

Example Speaking Answer

The beautiful site in Sydney harbor provides a backdrop for an iconic building that combines all of the aspects of expressionistic architecture identified in the reading passage. First, the Sydney Opera House was innovative for its time, in fact it was and continues to be absolutely unique. Second, architect Jorn Utzon was inspired by the forms and colors of nature, including bird wings, clouds, and shells, all of which fit into the harbor site. Third, the engineers used novel materials and new technologies to erect a building that wouldn't have been possible earlier, including the very new techniques made possible by computer design. Fourth, anyone who's seen the Sydney Opera House will agree that it elicits an emotional response. To many, it looks like an idyllic fleet of ships in full sail.

Beep

Topic Two

Audio

Narrator 2:

Exercise 37, Topic Two. Read a short passage and listen to a lecture on the same topic. Then listen for a question about them. After you hear the question, you have 30 seconds to prepare and 60 seconds to record your answer.

Narrator 1:

Now read the passage about the Pygmalion effect. You have 50 seconds to complete it (refer to page 69). Please begin reading now.

[Reading Time: 50 seconds]

Narrator 1:

Now listen to part of a lecture on the same topic.

Professor:

Let me tell you about an experiment by Rosenthal and Jacobson that's often cited as proof of the Pygmalion effect. In the study, all the students at an elementary school were given intelligence tests. Then the teachers at the school were told that about 20 percent of the children had been identified in the test at a stage in which they would experience a rapid period of intellectual growth in that school year, achieving at a much higher level than that of their classmates. The names of the children who were identified as higher achievers were given to their teachers. But, of course, these were children chosen at random from all of those tested.

Now Rosenthal and Jacobson predicted that the random group of students would, in fact, achieve at a higher level during the school year, in spite of the fact that there was nothing in the test that actually identified them as higher achievers. Why? Because the teachers expected them to do better than the others and began to treat them in subtly different ways. They paid more attention to them and gave them more encouragement. And that's exactly what happened in each of the 18 classrooms.

So what does this mean? Well, according to Rosenthal and Jacobson, biased expectations could affect performance. So labeling in school is an important issue to consider. When teachers expect certain behavior and intellectual gains from their students, their interactions with them may create an environment of self-fulfilling prophesy. And if high expectations result in high achievement, then, conversely, low expectations could result in low achievement as well.

Narrator 1:

Referring to both the lecture and the reading passage, explain how the Pygmalion effect was demonstrated in the Rosenthal and Jacobson experiment.

Narrator 2:
Please prepare your answer after the beep.

Beep

[Preparation Time: 30 seconds]

Narrator 2:

Please begin speaking after the beep.

Beep

[Recording Time: 60 seconds]

Example Notes
Rosenthal + Jacobson—Pygmalion effect
    all students IQ tests
    names random 20% = high achievers
    teachers expected—more attention, encouragement
    labeling affects
    low expectations = low

Example Speaking Answer
The Pygmalion effect occurs when expectations influence improved performance. In an experiment by Rosenthal and Jacobson, elementary school students were given IQ tests, and then their teachers received a list of those students who would be expected to achieve at a higher level than their classmates. Since the children were chosen at random, the only reason for their higher achievement would be the expectation of the teachers and the additional attention and encouragement they received. So at the end of the school year, the 20 percent of the children selected at random showed significantly higher gains, proving that expectations count and probably influence the quality of interactions between teachers and students. Conversely, labeling students as low achievers could have detrimental effects on their success in school.

Beep

EXERCISE 38: Integrated Task 4— Academic Summaries   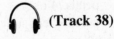 (Track 38)

Topic One

Audio
Narrator 2:
Exercise 38, Topic One. Listen to part of a lecture. Then listen for a question about it. After you hear the question, you have 20 seconds to prepare and 60 seconds to record your answer.

Narrator 1:
Now listen to part of a lecture in a botany class. The professor is discussing flowering plants.

Professor:
Flowering plants have traditionally been divided into two major classes—dicots and monocots. The actual basis for the distinction is the number of cotyledons. Remember, cotyledons are the seed leaves that the embryo produces. In monocots, there is a single seed leaf, and in dicots, there are two seed leaves. Although there are a number of other characteristics that distinguish them, two are particularly useful—the number of flower parts and the leaf vein patterns are different in the two classes. The

petals of the flowers or other flower parts are divisible by three in monocots, whereas they are divisible by four or five in dicots. And a parallel leaf structure is usual in monocots, but dicots tend to have numerous auxiliary veins that connect the major veining.

That seems relatively straightforward then, right? Wrong. Botanists are not always in agreement regarding several families of flowering plants because they have a combination of characteristics that don't fit neatly into the classifications. For example, water lilies have leaf veining like dicots, but it appears that there is only a single seed leaf as would be expected in a monocot. So how can this happen? Well, we believe that the two groups may actually have a shared ancestor, a basic group probably more similar to the dicots, from which the monocots have evolved. This means that no one characteristic of a flowering plant—the number of flower parts, leaf veining, or even the number of seed leaves— is going to be sufficient to identify it as either a monocot or a dicot.

Narrator 1:
Referring to the main points and examples from the lecture, describe the two general groups of flowering plants. Then explain the problem for classification that the professor presents.

Narrator 2:
Please prepare your answer after the beep.

Beep

[Preparation Time: 20 seconds]

Narrator 2:
Please begin speaking after the beep.

Beep

[Recording Time: 60 seconds]

Example Notes
flowering plants

Dicots	Monocots
two seed leaves (cotyledons)	single seed leaf
petals /4 or 5	/3
parallel leaf structure	auxiliary veins

problem
    combination characteristics
    water lilies veining like dicot + single seed leaf like monocot
shared ancestor
    dicots → monocots
no one characteristic to identify

Example Speaking Answer
Dicots and monocots are the two major classes of flowering plants. Basically, a monocot has one seed leaf, and a dicot has two. In monocots, the number of petals can be divided evenly by three, but in dicots, the number can be divided evenly by four or five. Also, monocots have parallel veins in their leaves, but dicots have, um, numerous veins with connecting patterns. Now, the problem in classification is that sometimes the characteristics overlap. The professor's example is the . . . the water lily, which has characteristics from both the monocot and the dicot. The professor explains that the two classifications may have descended from a common ancestor, and that makes classification of a plant

on the basis of any one characteristic . . . that one characteristic is insufficient to identify it as either a monocot or a dicot.

Beep

Topic Two

Audio
Narrator 2:
Exercise 38, Topic Two. Listen to part of a lecture. Then listen for a question about it. After you hear the question, you have 20 seconds to prepare and 60 seconds to record your answer.

Narrator 1:
Now listen to part of a lecture in an engineering class. The professor is discussing bridge construction.

Professor:
Okay, let's talk about bridge construction, specifically, arch bridges and suspension bridges. Arch bridges have been a standard for bridge construction since ancient times because they are very stable structures. In an arch, the force of the load is carried outward from the top to the ends of the arch where abutments prevent the ends from pulling apart. So, you see, an arch bridge can be designed so that no part of it has to withstand tension. Another advantage of arch bridges is the fact that they can be constructed from such a wide variety of materials, including stone, brick, timber, cast iron, steel, or reinforced concrete. It's also adaptable. The deck can be propped above the arch or hung below the arch. One major disadvantage of the arch bridge though—the bridge is completely unstable until the two spans meet in the middle, so that can make an arch bridge a little tricky to build.

Now, a suspension bridge consists of a deck suspended from cables. The two largest cables or main cables are hung from towers with the cable ends buried in huge concrete blocks or rock called anchorages. The cables support the weight of the bridge and transfer the load to the anchorages and the towers. Suspension bridges are considered aesthetically beautiful, and because they are relatively light and strong, they can be used for the longest spans. The cables, usually of high tensile wire, can support an immense weight. But the design does have the disadvantage of potential bending in the roadway. And because suspension bridges are light and flexible, wind is always a serious concern.

Narrator 1:
Referring to the main points and examples from the lecture, describe the two types of bridge construction presented by the professor. Then explain the specific advantages and disadvantages of each type.

Narrator 2:
Please prepare your answer after the beep.

Beep

[Preparation Time: 20 seconds]

Narrator 2:
Please begin speaking after the beep.

Beep

[Recording Time: 60 seconds]

Example Notes

<u>Arch bridge</u>

advantages

   stable—force load top to ends

      abutments prevent ends apart

   materials—stone, brick, timber, iron, steel, concrete

   adaptable—deck above or below

disadvantage

   unstable until two spans meet middle

<u>Suspension bridge</u>

   deck suspended from cables

   cables hung from towers

   cables buried in anchorages

advantages

   beautiful

   light

   strong—support weight

disadvantage

   bending

   wind

Example Speaking Answer

The professor describes two types of bridges—the arch bridge and the suspension bridge. Arch bridges are very stable because the weight is distributed from the top to the ends of the arch, where abutments keep the ends from separating. In addition to stability, an advantage of arch bridges is that they can be constructed from many different materials, like wood, steel, stone, brick, or concrete. The problem is that an arch is difficult to build because it's unstable until the middle span is complete. Now suspension bridges. They have a deck suspended from cables that are hung from towers. So the cables support the weight and distribute the load to anchorages of concrete or rock and to the towers as well. Suspension bridges are beautiful, and they're light and strong, which makes them appropriate choices for the longest spans. The problem is that the deck of a suspension bridge may bend, and they're not appropriate for very windy areas.

Beep

EXERCISE 39: Integrated Task 4— Academic Summaries

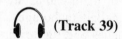 (Track 39)

Topic One

Audio

Narrator 2:

Exercise 39, Topic One. Listen to part of a lecture. Then listen for a question about it. After you hear the question, you have 20 seconds to prepare and 60 seconds to record your answer.

Narrator 1:

Now listen to part of a lecture in an anatomy class. The professor is discussing the functions of the liver.

Professor:

So that brings us to our discussion of the liver, the largest internal organ in the human body. As you already know, it's part of the digestive system, and it performs more than 500 functions. Today, we'll talk about the three primary functions of the liver. First, the liver functions as a storage system. The liver stores energy in the form of *glycogen*, which is made from a type of sugar called *glucose*. When the glucose levels in the blood are high, the liver uses the glucose to create glycogen and stores it as energy that can be used later. When the glucose level in the blood falls below the minimum level, the liver changes glycogen into glucose for energy. The liver also stores essential vitamins, such as A, D, K, and the B vitamins, all of which are critical to maintain good health.

    In addition to storing energy and vitamins, the liver produces essential chemicals, including important proteins like albumin, which retains calcium and regulates the movement of water from the bloodstream to the tissues. And globin, which is key to maintaining the immune system. And, uh, cholesterol, an important part of the cell membrane, which is used to transport fats in the blood to tissues in the body.

All right, the last crucial function of the liver is to help eliminate toxic substances such as alcohol and drugs from the bloodstream. To clear these harmful substances, the liver absorbs them, then chemically alters them, and finally, excretes them into bile. And the bile works its way out of the system through the small intestine of the digestive tract.

Narrator 1:
Referring to the main points and examples from the lecture, describe the three basic functions of the liver presented by the professor.

Narrator 2:
Please prepare your answer after the beep.

Beep

[Preparation Time: 20 seconds]

Narrator 2:

Please begin speaking after the beep.

Beep

[Recording Time: 60 seconds]

Example Notes
liver = largest internal organ
500 functions
primary functions
   stores energy
      glucose levels in blood high glucose→glycogen
      levels low glycogen→glucose energy
      stores vitamin A, D, K, B
   produces chemicals = proteins
      albumin—regulates water from blood to tissues
      globin—immune system
      cholesterol—transports fat from blood to tissues
   eliminates toxic from bloodstream—alcohol + drugs
      liver absorbs, alters, excretes into bile
      bile through small intestine

Example Speaking Answer
The liver has more than 500 functions, but the professor concentrates on three. First, the liver is used as a storage system. The liver regulates the glucose levels in the blood, and when it's too high, the liver converts glucose into glycogen and stores it as energy for later use. When the glucose level's too low, it changes the glycogen back into glucose for energy. The liver also stores vitamins A, B, D, and K. Second, the liver is a chemical system . . . it produces essential proteins, um, proteins that transport water and fats from the blood to, uh, tissues in the body, and they also support the immune system. Third, the liver eliminates toxic material from the blood, for example, drugs and alcohol. Um . . . the

liver absorbs them and changes their chemical composition and excretes them into bile that gets eliminated through the small intestine.

Beep

Topic Two

Audio
Narrator 2:
Exercise 39, Topic Two. Listen to part of a lecture. Then listen for a question about it. After you hear the question, you have 20 seconds to prepare and 60 seconds to record your answer.

Narrator 1:
Now listen to part of a lecture in a psychology class. The professor is discussing how behavior can be predicted.

Professor:
In addition to describing behavior, psychologists try to predict future performance. We do this by designing studies that determine relationships between the behavior that we expect with the behavior that we can actually record. We use a statistical measurement called a *correlation* to tell us whether two variables, like perhaps two test scores, whether they vary together in the same way. For example, studies have shown a positive correlation between a student's performance on the SAT, that's the Scholastic Aptitude Test, and the same student's performance in college courses. It's a *positive* correlation because the higher the score on the SAT, the better we can expect the college grades to be.

But what about a *negative* correlation? Well, other studies suggest that getting a lot of sleep the night before taking the SAT will result in fewer errors on the verbal section. So in a negative correlation like that, the variables move in the opposite direction. The more hours sleep, the fewer verbal errors.

Now, that's all well and good, but the problem occurs when we try to understand *why* correlations exist. That gets us into *causality*. You see, there are so many potentially uncontrolled or unknown factors that the two variables we are studying may appear to be connected, but they may both be responding to a common third variable. Let's go back to the SAT verbal example. What if the students who slept well the night before the SAT were all very intelligent, or were more prepared for the verbal section, or by chance, many words that they already knew showed up on the exam? Then the real cause wouldn't be the sleep at all.

Narrator 1:
Referring to the main points and examples from the lecture, describe two types of research correlations that the professor presents. Then explain causality.

Narrator 2:
Please prepare your answer after the beep.

Beep

[Preparation Time: 20 seconds]

Narrator 2:
Please begin speaking after the beep.

Beep

[Recording Time: 60 seconds]

Example Notes

correlation = whether two variables vary together same way

positive correlation—SAT + college courses

    higher SAT → better grades

negative correlation—sleep + errors verbal section

    more sleep → fewer verbal errors

problem = why correlations exist = causality

    uncontrolled or unknown factors

    two variables appear connected but responding to common third variable

    students slept well ← all intelligent, more prepared, knew words

    (real cause wasn't sleep)

Example Speaking Answer

A correlation indicates whether two variables correspond—I mean whether they vary in the same way. The professor uses the example of students' scores on the SAT and their performances in college to demonstrate a positive correlation. If a student has a high SAT score, we can expect good grades in college. The variables move in the same direction. Um . . . the professor uses the example of getting a good night's sleep before taking the SAT and, uh, the number of incorrect answers on the verbal section . . . that's an example of a negative correlation. If a student gets a good night's sleep, we can expect fewer errors. The variables move in opposite directions. But . . . but even when a correlation can be shown, we don't know the cause. The two variables could be affected by a third factor they have in common. As an example, the students in the study might be more prepared for the verbal section and would have performed well whether they were rested or not.

Beep

EXERCISE 40: Integrated Task 4—Academic Summaries (Track 40)

Topic One

Audio

Narrator 2:

Exercise 40, Topic One. Listen to part of a lecture. Then listen for a question about it. After you hear the question, you have 20 seconds to prepare and 60 seconds to record your answer.

Narrator 1:

Now listen to a lecture in a sociology class. The professor is discussing crime.

Professor:

In the United States, there are two primary classifications of criminal offenses, including felonies and misdemeanors, and each of these is distinguished by how serious the crime is and the amount of punishment that can be inflicted for the crime. So let's look at each of these, starting with the most serious, that is, felonies. These are usually crimes that are punishable by more than a year in prison, including murder, rape, assault with a weapon, armed robbery, and the theft of something with a high value.

In contrast, a misdemeanor is not considered as serious as a felony. Some minor assault charges, drunken behavior, trespassing, and petty theft—which is stealing something of a small value—these are common examples of a misdemeanor.

But here's the tricky part. Each state has the authority to issue its own classifications and punishments for crimes, so in one state what would be considered only a misdemeanor elsewhere is a felony in that state. And to make things even more complicated, the punishment is based on guidelines that are often determined by the degree of the crime. So that means that assault with a deadly weapon is a felony, but assault when a person is unarmed is a misdemeanor. In the first case, if convicted, the person can go to prison, but in the second case, a fine might be all of the punishment the court would demand.

Let's look at theft. Shoplifting could be either a felony or a misdemeanor, depending on the value of an item. If valued higher than $1,500, it might be considered a felony in some states, with a prison sentence attached to the crime, but under $100 could be a misdemeanor with a fine and no jail time. Possession of less than one ounce of marijuana might be a misdemeanor, but possession of more than an ounce might be viewed as intent to sell to others and could be treated as a felony. Okay, let's go back to the problem of state authority. In some states, possession of even a small amount of a restricted substance like marijuana is a serious crime, whereas in other states, it isn't even a misdemeanor.

Narrator 1:
Referring to the main points and examples from the lecture, describe the two classifications of crimes presented by the lecturer, and the reasons why it is difficult to distinguish between them.

Narrator 2:
Please prepare your answer after the beep.

Beep.

[Preparation Time: 20 seconds]

Narrator 2:
Please begin speaking after the beep.

Beep.

[Recording Time: 60 seconds]

Example Notes
felony—murder, rape, assault w/weapon, theft++
    prison
misdemeanor—drunk, trespass, theft - -
    fine
states or degree crime
    shoplifting $1,500 f /$100 m some states
    −1 oz marijuana = m   +1 oz = f
    some states serious/others not m

Example Speaking Answer
Felonies and misdemeanors are the two major kinds of crimes in the U.S. Felonies are the most serious, like murder, rape, armed robbery, or stealing something valuable, or assault with a weapon, and the punishment is usually a year or more in prison. A misdemeanor is less serious than a felony, and some examples are stealing something of little value, assault without a weapon, drunkenness, or trespassing. The punishment is often a fine. But each state can determine the classifications and punishments for crimes, and the punishment is often decided by how serious the crime is. Shoplifting items worth $1,500 could be a felony, but under $100 a misdemeanor. Assault with a weapon is a felony, but without a weapon is a misdemeanor. Possession of an ounce of marijuana is a serious crime in some states but not even a misdemeanor in others.

Beep

Topic Two

Audio

Narrator 2:
Exercise 40, Topic Two. Listen to part of a lecture. Then listen for a question about it. After you hear the question, you have 20 seconds to prepare, and 60 seconds to record your answer.

Narrator 1:
Now listen to a lecture in an environmental science class. The professor is discussing fossil fuels.

Professor:
There are three major types of fossil fuels, including coal, oil, and natural gas. Together they account for a little more than 80 percent of the global energy supply, but their use has serious consequences, many of which are already apparent.

The main disadvantage of fossil fuels, of course, is the pollution that results when they're burned. Fossil fuels are the largest source of carbon dioxide, a greenhouse gas that causes consequences for both the environment and for human health. And even though it's called "clean coal," coal causes the emission of sulfur dioxide, one of the major contributors to acid rain. Also concerning is that drilling and mining operations produce a huge amount of wastewater containing heavy metals and radioactive material. This wastewater has the potential to leak into aquifers and other water supplies, contaminating them with pollutants that are known to cause cancer.

Less well known is the relationship between fossil fuels and earthquakes, but there's growing evidence that water from oil and natural gas production may strengthen the magnitude of earthquakes by placing stress on fault lines in oil-producing areas. Although this problem isn't new, recent studies show that the water may be penetrating deeper into the cracks, creating force on the underlying faults, making them less stable, and leading to an increase in the number of higher magnitude earthquakes. And I should mention the salty water that's a by-product of drilling is often injected back into the ground, further increasing the stress on the fault lines.

Obviously, fossil fuels are nonrenewable resources, which means that eventually, once they're used, they can't be replaced. Our depleting reserves of oil, coal, and natural gas could become a pressing issue by the end of this century, which should be enough motivation to seek alternative, renewable sources for the world's energy needs.

Narrator 1:
Referring to the main points and examples from the lecture, explain the issues surrounding the continuing use of fossil fuels.

Narrator 2:
Please prepare your answer after the beep.

Beep.

[Preparation Time: 20 seconds]

Narrator 2:
Please begin speaking after the beep.

Beep.

[Recording Time: 60 seconds]

Example Notes
coal, oil, natural gas—80%
disadvantages
    pollution—co2 greenhouse, sulfur dioxide acid rain, wastewater metals, radioactive/cancer
    earthquakes—saltwater faults stability
    nonrenewable—end of century

Example Speaking Answer
The lecture identifies coal, oil, and natural gas as the three kinds of fossil fuels that supply more than 80 percent of the world's energy. Then the disadvantages are discussed. First, fossil fuels cause pollution in the form of carbon dioxide that contributes to greenhouse gases, sulfur dioxide that falls as acid rain, and wastewater that leaks heavy metals and radioactive waste into the water supplies. The second problem is that the water from the production of oil and natural gas leaks into the deep cracks in the fault lines, destabilizing them and contributing to higher magnitude earthquakes. And the saltwater from the drilling process goes back into the ground, and that stresses the faults, too. The third issue is that fossil fuels are not renewable resources, and they'll be seriously depleted by the end of this century. So alternatives to fossil fuels need to be found.

Beep.

Structure

EXERCISE 41: Sentences—Verbs

1. **(C)** The verb *fail* requires an infinitive in the complement. Choices (A) and (D) are *-ing* forms, not infinitives. Choice (B) is an infinitive, but it expresses a past time and does not maintain the point of view established by the verb *fails*.

2. **(B)** Because the verb phrase *to get through* requires an *-ing* form in the complement, *to lay* should be *laying*.

3. **(A)** *If* is used before the noun *endangered species* and the present verb *are* followed by the infinitive *to be* to express the result of a condition with *must*. Choice (B) is a verb word, not a present verb. Choices (C) and (D) are modals.

4. **(C)** The infinitive *to complete* is used to express purpose. Choice (A) includes the unnecessary word *for*. Choice (B) is an *-ing* form, not an infinitive. Choice (D) expresses manner, not purpose.

5. **(B)** *Not* is used before the infinitive *to be* in the clause after the verb *agreed*. "Doctors agreed that they shouldn't be truthful" would also be correct. The verb *agree* requires an infinitive in the complement. Choice (A) is an infinitive, but the negative *don't* is used instead of *not*. The modal in Choice (C) requires a verb word, not the participle *been*. Choice (D) uses *not* as the negative, but *been* is a participle, not an infinitive.

6. **(A)** *In* is used after *interested*. The *-ing* form *establishing* is used after the preposition *in*. The preposition in Choice (B) is *for*, not *in*. Choice (C) does not have the correct preposition, *in*. Choice (D) is an infinitive, not a preposition with an *-ing* form.

7. **(C)** The infinitive *to communicate* is used to express purpose. Choice (A) is an *-ing* form after the preposition *to*, not an infinitive. In Choice (B), *for*, not *to*, is used. In Choice (D), *for* is used with a past verb.

8. **(C)** The subject *art* is used before the verb phrase *tends to be* followed by *worth* and the indefinite amount *more* to express value. The words in Choices (A), (B), and (D) are related in meaning to *worth*, but they are not idiomatic expressions with *to be*.

9. **(A)** *Let* is used as a causative to express permission before the complement *their offspring* followed by the verb word *build*. Choice (B) is a present verb, not a verb word. Choice (C) is an *-ing* form. Choice (D) is an infinitive.

10. **(C)** An infinitive is used to express purpose. *To reading* should be *to read*.

11. **(A)** A present verb in the condition requires a present modal such as *will* in the result. *Will* expresses future time. Choice (B) is a past form, not a present modal. Choice (C) is a past modal. Choice (D) is an *-ing* form.

12. **(C)** An infinitive is used to express purpose. *To understanding* should be *to understand*.

13. **(B)** Every English sentence must have a subject and a main verb. Choices (A), (C), and (D) do not include a main verb.

14. **(B)** In contrary-to-fact clauses, *were* is the only accepted form of the verb BE. *Was* should be *were*.

15. **(A)** The anticipatory clause *it is generally accepted that* introduces a subject and a verb, *schools are*. Choice (B) is a subject clause that requires a verb, not a subject and verb. The clauses in Choices (C) and (D) do not introduce a subject and verb.

16. **(A)** The word order for a passive sentence is a form of BE followed by a participle. *Found* should be *was founded*. *Found* means "discovered." *Founded* means "established."

17. **(D)** An infinitive that expresses purpose such as *to relieve pain* introduces a verb word that expresses a manner to accomplish that purpose. Choice (A) is an *-ing* form, not a verb word. Choice (B) is an infinitive. Choice (C) is a participle.

18. **(C)** For scientific results, a present form in the condition such as *mixes* requires a present or future form in the result, *will occur*. Choice (A) is a past, not a present, form. Choice (B) is *had* followed by a participle. Choice (D) is a noun.

19. **(A)** The verb *refuse* requires an infinitive in the complement. Choice (B) is an *-ing* form, not an infinitive. Choice (C) is a noun. Choice (D) is a verb word.

20. **(C)** A form of *make* with something such as *the vocal chords* [*them*] and a verb word expresses a causative. Choice (A) is an infinitive, not a verb word. Choice (B) is an *-ing* form. Choice (D) is a noun.

EXERCISE 42: Sentences— Auxiliary Verbs

1. **(B)** *Ought* is used before *to* to express obligation. *A healthy heart should pump* would also be correct. Choices (A), (C), and (D) are modals that are used before verb words, not before *to*.

2. **(B)** *Wrote* should be *written* because the auxiliary *had* requires a participle. *Wrote* is a past form. *Written* is a participle.

3. **(C)** *Will have* is used before the participle *decreased* to predict the future, *by the second year of production*. The modals in Choices (A) and (D) require a verb word, not past and present forms of the verb. Choice (B) expresses a past, not a future, point of view.

4. **(B)** A passive sentence is used to focus on the *structures* rather than on the *builders*. In a passive sentence, a form of *be* is followed by a participle. *Build* should be *built*.

5. **(A)** Every sentence must have a main verb. *Having* should be *has*.

6. **(B)** Every sentence must have a main verb. *Composed* should be *are composed*.

7. **(D)** *Won't* means will not. *Won't* is used before *be* followed by the participle *developed* in a passive to express the importance of the *cure*. "Scientists won't develop a cure until more funds are allocated" would also be correct to express the importance of the *scientists*. Choices (B) and (C) do not express future. Choice (A) is not a passive.

8. **(B)** The past form of the verb *to spend* is *spent*. *Spended* should be *spent*.

9. **(A)** *Had better* requires a verb word. Choice (B) is an *-ing* form, not a verb word. Choice (C) is a noun. Choice (D) is a past verb.

10. **(B)** The participle is used after a form of BE in a passive sentence. *Finding* should be *found* after *to be*.

11. **(C)** Every English sentence must have a subject and a main verb. Choice (A) is an infinitive, not a main verb. Choice (B) is an *-ing* form. Choice (D) is a main verb, but it does not agree with the plural subject *cones*.

12. **(A)** A verb word must be used in a clause after the verb *to require*. *Taken* should be *be taken*.

13. **(A)** A verb word must be used in a clause after an impersonal expression such as *it is important that*. *Is* should be *be*.

14. **(C)** *Had hoped that* introduces a clause with a subject and *would* followed by a verb word. Choice (A) is a verb word without *would*. Choice (B) is *had* followed by a participle. Choice (D) is an *-ing* form.

15. **(C)** *Used to* requires a verb word to express a custom in the past. *Was used to be carried* should be *used to be carried*.

16. **(C)** *Must* followed by *be* and an *-ing* form expresses a logical conclusion about an event that is happening now. *Save* should be *saving*.

17. **(D)** *Unless* introduces a clause with a subject and a main verb. *Be* should be *is* to maintain the point of view established by *is* in the previous clause, *jewelry is*.

18. **(B)** The modal *can* followed by a verb word expresses ability. The infinitive in Choice (A), the *-ing* form in Choice (C), and the verb word in Choice (D) do not express ability.

19. **(A)** A form of HAVE followed by a participle expresses a duration of time. The participle *been* is a form of BE used with the participle *caused* in a passive before the agent *by the aphids or pollution*. *Been caused* should be *has been caused*.

20. **(B)** A form of HAVE followed by a participle expresses a duration of time. The infinitive is *to have*. *Had been* should be *have been* after *to*.

EXERCISE 43: Sentences—Nouns

1. **(A)** Either an *-ing* form or an infinitive may be used as the subject of a sentence. *The understanding* should be *Understanding* or *To understand*. "The understanding of electricity" would also be correct.

2. **(B)** Singular and plural expressions of noncount nouns such as *mail* occur in idiomatic phrases, often *piece* or *pieces of*. *Mails* should be *pieces of mail*.

3. **(A)** *Kinds of* is used before the plural count noun *magnets* to express classification. *Kind* in Choices (B) and (C) is used before a singular count noun or a noncount noun, not a

plural count noun. In Choice (D), the preposition *of* does not follow *kinds*.

4. **(A)** *Ice* is a noncount noun because it is a natural substance that can change shape according to natural laws. Choices (B) and (D) are not noncount nouns. Choice (C) implies specific *ice*, but is incomplete without a qualifying phrase.

5. **(D)** No article before a plural count noun such as *dogs* has the same meaning as *all dogs*. Choice (A) is redundant and incorrect. *That* in Choice (B) introduces a subject clause before a main verb, but only the subject follows, *that dogs can live to be more than fifteen years old*. Choice (C) also provides a subject clause with no main verb.

6. **(B)** *Plant* should be *plants* to imply *one* of many.

7. **(B)** The plural of leaf is *leaves*. Choices (A), (C), and (D) do not provide the correct plural noun.

8. **(D)** *Fruit* is usually a noncount noun, and *vegetables* is a count noun. In Choices (A) and (B), *vegetable* is used as a noncount, not a count, noun. *The* in Choice (C) implies specific *fruit* and *vegetables*, but there is no qualifying phrase.

9. **(A)** Singular and plural expressions of noncount nouns such as *thunder* occur in idiomatic phrases. *Thunder* should be *a clap of thunder* to mean one, or *thunder* to mean *all thunder*.

10. **(B)** The determiner *an* is used before singular count nouns that begin with a vowel sound such as *a* in *area*. The determiner *a* in Choice (A) is used before singular count nouns that begin with consonant sounds, not vowel sounds. *The* in Choice (C) is incomplete without a specific qualifying phrase. Choice (D) requires a determiner because it is a count noun.

11. **(B)** No article before a plural count noun such as *beavers* has the same meaning as *all beavers*. Choices (A) and (C) do not agree with the plural verb *were* in the sentence. *That* in Choice (D) introduces a subject clause for a main verb, but only the subject follows, *that beavers were hunted for their pelts*.

12. **(D)** The noun *children* is the irregular plural form of *child*. *Childrens* should be *children*.

13. **(D)** It is logical to assume that there is more than one museum throughout the United States. *Museum* should be *museums*.

14. **(D)** *Types of* is used before plural count nouns to express classification. *Ten types* should be *ten types of*.

15. **(B)** An *-ing* form such as *spraying* may be used as a noun. *The* precedes the noun when a prepositional phrase such as *of designs on a wall* qualify the noun. Choice (A) is incomplete without *the*. Choices (C) and (D) are not *-ing* forms.

16. **(B)** No article before a plural count noun such as *novels* has the same meaning as *all novels*. The singular noun *novel* in Choices (A), (C), and (D) does not agree with the verb *are* in the sentence.

17. **(D)** The noun clause *that computers have made communications faster and easier through the use of e-mail and the internet* is a very long subject of the main verb *is*. Choices (A), (B), and (C) cannot function as the subject of the main verb.

18. **(A)** Either an infinitive or an *-ing* form can be used as the subject of a sentence. *Provide* should be *to provide* or *providing*.

19. **(A)** Singular and plural expressions of noncount nouns such as *equipment* occur in idiomatic phrases, often *piece* or *pieces of*. *Equipments* should be *pieces of equipment*.

20. **(D)** Although *damage* is a count noun in many other languages, *damage* is a noncount noun in English. The article *a* in Choice (A) and the plural *-s* ending in Choice (B) are forms that are correct for singular and plural, but not for noncount nouns. Choice (C) implies specific *damage* but is incomplete without a qualifying phrase.

EXERCISE 44: Sentences—Pronouns

1. **(D)** There must be agreement between pronoun and antecedent. Choices (A), (B), and (C) do not agree in number, gender, and case with the singular, neuter, objective antecedent *crime rate*. Choice (A) is plural. Choice (B) is masculine. Choice (C) is possessive.

2. **(B)** There must be agreement between pronoun and antecedent. *Its* should be *their* to agree with the plural antecedent *sloths*.

3. **(D)** Object pronouns are used after prepositions such as *from. Their* should be *them.*

4. **(B)** A reflexive pronoun is used when the subject and complement refer to the same person. Only *themselves* in Choice (B) is a reflexive pronoun. *Them* in Choice (A) is an object pronoun. *They* in Choice (C) is a subject pronoun. *Their* in Choice (D) is a possessive pronoun.

5. **(B)** *Him* should be *he* because it is part of the subject, with *Drs. Daniel Nathan* and *Hamilton Smith*, of the verb *were awarded. He* functions as a subject. *Him* functions as a complement.

6. **(C)** *Which* should be *who* because it refers to people, not things.

7. **(D)** *Each other* is used to express mutual acts such as *trade.* Choices (A), (B), and (C) are not idiomatic. "One another" would also be correct.

8. **(D)** There must be agreement between pronoun and antecedent. *Their* should be *our* to agree with the second-person antecedent *those of us.*

9. **(C)** Object pronouns are used after prepositions such as *for.* Choices (A) and (B) are subject, not object, pronouns. Choice (D) is a possessive pronoun.

10. **(D)** *Each other* is used to express mutual acts. Choices (A), (B), and (C) are not idiomatic. "One another" would also be correct.

11. **(A)** There must be agreement between pronoun and antecedent. *Which* should be *who* to refer to the antecedent *George Herman Ruth. Which* refers to things. *Who* refers to persons.

12. **(B)** There must be agreement between pronoun and antecedent. Only *its* in Choice (B) agrees with the singular noun *the constellation.* Choice (A) would agree with *you,* not *the constellation.* Choice (C) would agree with a plural, not a singular, noun. Choice (D) would agree with *she.*

13. **(C)** *Whom* should be *whose,* a pronoun used as an adjective to modify *creative genius.*

14. **(B)** There must be agreement between pronoun and antecedent. *Themselves* refers to the plural antecedent *wolves.* Choices (A) and (C) would agree with a singular, not a plural, noun. Choice (D) is not a word in

standard English, although it does occur in some nonstandard dialects.

15. **(A)** There must be agreement between pronoun and antecedent. *Which* refers to the antecedent *very hardy plants. Which* refers to things. *What* and *where* in Choices (B) and (D) do not logically refer to *plants. Who* in Choice (C) refers to persons, not things, such as *plants.*

16. **(A)** Possessive pronouns are used before *-ing* nouns. *Result from* should be followed by a noun, not a clause with a subject and verb as in Choice (B). The infinitive in Choice (C) is not idiomatic after the preposition *from.* Choice (D) is an object pronoun, not a possessive pronoun.

17. **(D)** *Themself* should be *himself* to agree with the singular noun, *the patient.*

18. **(D)** Object pronouns are used after prepositions such as *for. They* should be *them.*

19. **(C)** There must be agreement between pronoun and antecedent. *Their eggs* should be *her eggs* to refer to the antecedent, a *female* sea horse.

20. **(B)** *Whom* is the complement of the subject *Cooper* and the verb *created.* Choice (A) is used as a subject, not a complement. Choice (C) refers to things, not to a person, like *Hawkeye.* Choice (D) is used as a possessive, not a complement.

EXERCISE 45: Sentences—Modifiers

1. **(C)** The *-ing* form adjective *interesting* is used to describe the noun *data.* Choice (A) is not logical since the *scientist,* not the *data,* would be *interested.* Choice (B) is a noun, not an adjective. Choice (D) would also be correct without the adverb *very.*

2. **(C)** *Any other* excludes all others. *The other* should be *other.*

3. **(B)** *Real* is an adjective used in colloquial speech as an adverb. *Real great* should be *very great* in standard, written English.

4. **(D)** *No* is used before the noun *earthquakes.* Choice (A) is a pronoun that would take the place of the noun, *serious earthquakes.* Choices (C) and (D) must be used with a verb such as *have not* before the participle *had.* "The New England states have not had any serious earthquakes" would also be correct.

5. **(B)** *Almost* is used before *all* to express approximation. Choices (A), (C), and (D) are not idiomatic. "Nearly all" would also be correct.

6. **(D)** *Others* is used consecutively with *some*. Choice (A) is not a word in English unless it has an apostrophe in it. Choice (B) is used consecutively with *one*, not *some*. Choice (C) is used before a noun.

7. **(B)** *So* is used before the adjective *great* to express cause. *As* should be *that* to introduce the clause of result.

8. **(B)** When two nouns occur together, the first noun functions as an adjective. Adjectives do not change form when the noun that follows is plural. *Light year* should be *light years* to agree with the plural number *500 million*.

9. **(C)** *A large number of* is used before the plural count noun *doctors*. Choice (A) is used before a noncount noun, not a plural count noun. In Choices (B) and (D), the article *a* is missing.

10. **(A)** *None of* should be *no*. *No* before a noun means *not any*.

11. **(A)** A cardinal number is used after a noun. *The* is used with an ordinal number before a noun. Choice (B) is incomplete because it does not include *the* before the ordinal number. Choice (C) is not used after a noun. Choice (D) is incomplete because it does not have a *-th* ending. "President four" would also be correct, but not as idiomatic.

12. **(B)** *As* should be *that* to introduce a clause of result after *so* and an adjective.

13. **(D)** Both *a few* and *a little* are used after *only*, but *a few* must be used with the count noun *nations*. "Few nations in the world" would also be correct.

14. **(A)** An adjective is used before *enough* to express sufficiency. In Choice (B), there is an adverb used after *enough*. In Choice (C), the adjective is used after, not before, *enough*, and the word *as* is unnecessary and incorrect. In Choice (D), the word *as* is unnecessary and incorrect.

15. **(B)** Most adverbs of manner are formed by adding *-ly* to adjectives. *Careful* should be *carefully* to qualify the manner in which *you must listen*.

16. **(D)** An adjective is used before *enough* to express sufficiency. *As* should be deleted.

17. **(D)** When two nouns occur together, the first noun functions as an adjective. Choice (A) is not logical because it implies ownership of the *restaurants* by a *chain*. In Choice (B), the adjective is plural, but adjectives in English do not change form to agree in number with the nouns they modify. In Choice (C), the singular noun *restaurant* does not agree with the two nouns, *McDonald's* and *Kentucky Fried Chicken*, to which it refers.

18. **(B)** *Too* means excessively. When an infinitive follows, *too* expresses cause, as in *too old*, and the infinitive expresses result, as in *to return*. Choice (A) would be followed by a clause with *that*, not an infinitive. Choices (C) and (D) would be used to compare *Glen* to others, but a comparison is not implied in the sentence.

19. **(A)** *The* can be used before a noncount noun that is followed by a qualifying phrase. *The art* is qualified by the phrase *that is known as art deco*. Choices (B) and (C) use plural and singular forms for the noncount noun *art*. The count noun *artist* in Choice (D) requires either *the* or *an* for singular or *-s* for plural.

20. **(A)** The number *second* appears as the first in a series of hyphenated adjectives. Choice (B) reverses the order of the number with the other adjective. Choice (C) is redundant and indirect. In Choice (D), the adjective *magnitude* had a plural form, but adjectives in English do not change form to agree in number with the nouns they modify.

EXERCISE 46: Sentences—Comparatives

1. **(C)** *As high as* is used before the amount of money *fifty thousand dollars* to establish a limit. None of the words after *high* in Choices (A), (B), and (D) is idiomatic.

2. **(B)** *The same* is used with a quality noun such as *color* followed by *as* in comparisons. *Than* should be *as*.

3. **(B)** The comparative adjective *better* is used for separate comparisons of two, including *PNG* and *JPEG*.

4. **(D)** *Much too much* is a phrase that is used to express excess. Choice (A) introduces a clause with *that*, not a phrase with *for*. Choice (B) is incomplete. In Choice (C), *very* does not express excess. "The cost is too

much for most businesses" would also be correct.

5. **(B)** *The most longest* should be *the longest.* Because *long* is a one-syllable adjective, the superlative is formed by adding *-est. Most* is used with two-syllable adjectives that do not end in *-y.*

6. **(D)** *The same* is used with a quality noun such as *age* followed by *as* in comparisons. *Old* is an adjective. *Old* should be *age.*

7. **(A)** The comparative of a three-syllable adverb is formed by using *more* before the adverb and *than* after the adverb. Choice (B) is an adverb, but it is not a comparative with *more.* Choices (C) and (D) are an adjective comparative and superlative, not adverbs.

8. **(B)** *The larger* should be *the largest.* Because it is logical that there were more than two newspapers in the colonies, a superlative form with *-est* should be used to compare three or more.

9. **(D)** *Same* should be *the same as* between two comparable nouns, *the area where a microchip is manufactured* and *that* [the area] *of an operating room.*

10. **(C)** Multiple comparatives like *half* are expressed by the multiple number followed by the phrases *as . . . as.* Choice (A) is a multiple with an incomplete phrase. In Choices (B) and (D), the multiples are not first, and the phrases that follow are incomplete.

11. **(A)** The verb *differ* is used with *from* to express general difference. *Differ* should be *differ from.*

12. **(D)** When the degree of one quality, *the pulse,* is dependent upon the degree of another quality, *the heart rate,* two comparatives are required, each of which must be preceded by *the. Quicker* should be *the quicker.*

13. **(B)** A two-syllable adjective like *severe* forms the comparative by using *more* or *less* before the adjective form followed by *than.* In Choice (C), the adjective is after, not before, *than.* Choices (A) and (D) use the incorrect form *lesser.*

14. **(C)** Comparisons must be made with logically comparable nouns. *That of* is used instead of repeating a singular noun, and *those of* is used instead of repeating a plural noun. Choice (A) illogically compares *two stages of development* with *marsupials.* Choice (B) would be correct for a singular, not a plural,

noun like *stages.* In Choice (D), *of* is not used after *those.*

15. **(C)** *More than* is used before a specific number like *fifty* to express an estimate that exceeds the number. Choice (A) is incomplete without *than.* Choice (B) uses *as,* not *than,* with *more.* Choice (D) uses *most,* not *more,* with *than.*

16. **(B)** *As many as* is used before a count noun to express an estimate that does not exceed the number. *Much* in Choice (A) would be correct with a noncount noun, not a count noun with a number. Choices (C) and (D) are incomplete because *as* is used only once, before or after *many.*

17. **(A)** Comparatives require *than.* Choices (B) and (C) use *that* and *as* instead of *than.* Choice (D) is incomplete without *than.*

18. **(D)** *Faster* is the comparative form of the adjective *fast,* used to compare two activities, *the Coachella Music Festival* and *any other musical event.* Choice (A) is a superlative that would be used to compare more than two activities. Choice (C) needs a comparative adjective before *than.* Choice (B) is not complete without *as* before *fast.* "As fast as any other musical event" would also be correct.

19. **(A)** *Like* is a preposition. *Alike* should be *like.*

20. **(C)** Comparatives with adverbs such as *strenuously* require *as* before and *as* after the adverb. In Choice (A), *as* appears before, but not after, the adverb. Choice (B) uses *more,* not *as,* before the adverb. Choice (D) uses *that,* not *as,* after the adverb.

EXERCISE 47: Sentences—Connectors

1. **(B)** The preposition *from* is used before the *-ing* form *watching* to express cause. Choices (A) and (D) express purpose, not cause. In Choice (C), there is a verb word, not an *-ing* form, after the preposition.

2. **(B)** The preposition *to* is used after the verb *prefer.* None of the words in Choices (A), (C), and (D) is idiomatic with *prefer.*

3. **(B)** *Such as* introduces an example. *Such* should be *such as* before the examples of metals.

4. **(B)** *When* is used before the subject *it* and the present verb *ages* to express a general truth. Choice (A) is a modal, not a present verb. Choice (C) expresses present time, but it is

not the simple present verb that is required in clauses after *when*. Choice (D) is a past, not a present, verb.

5. **(B)** *But* is used before the noun *smell* to express exception. The words in Choices (A), (C), and (D) do not mean *except*.

6. **(A)** *Because* introduces a clause with a subject and verb. *Because of* introduces a phrase. *Because* should be *because of* before the nouns *expense . . . and concern*. "Because traditional fuels were expensive, there was concern . . ." would also be correct.

7. **(B)** *Instead of* is used before a noun to indicate replacement. Choice (A) does not have the preposition *of*. The word *that* in Choice (C) introduces a clause with a subject and verb, but no verb follows. The word *instead* at the end of a sentence or clause as in Choice (D) would not include two options, in this case, both kinds of *current*. "The lights and appliances in most homes use alternating current instead" would also be correct.

8. **(A)** *In* is used between numbers to express a fraction. *On* should be *in*.

9. **(B)** *In* is used before the month *December*. Choice (A) is used before dates. Choice (C) is used before clock time. Choice (D) is used before duration of time.

10. **(D)** *By* is used before the *-ing* form *increasing* to express method. Choices (A) and (C), which express purpose, not method, are not logical in this sentence. Choice (B) has a verb word, not an *-ing* form, after the preposition *for*.

11. **(B)** *Among* refers to three or more nouns. *Between* refers to two nouns. *Among* should be *between* to refer to the two nouns *speed* and *pressure*.

12. **(B)** Subject-verb order is used in the clause after a question word connector such as *what*. In Choices (A) and (D), subject-verb order is reversed. In Choice (C), the auxiliary *did* is unnecessary and incorrect.

13. **(B)** *So* is commonly used as a purpose connector in spoken English, but *so that* should be used in written English.

14. **(C)** *In spite* should be *in spite of* because *in spite of* introduces a condition with an unexpected result. "Despite" would also be correct.

15. **(C)** Affirmative agreement with *so* requires verb-subject order and an affirmative

verb that refers to the verb in the main clause. Choices (A) and (B) have verb-subject order, but the verbs DO and HAVE do not refer to the verb BE in the main clause. In Choice (D), *so* is used at the end, not at the beginning, of the clause, and there is no verb.

16. **(A)** *Because* is used before a subject and verb to introduce cause. Choices (B) and (C) are not accepted for statements of cause. Choice (D) is used before a noun, not before a subject and verb.

17. **(C)** *On* is used before the street name *Beacon*. *In* is used before the city *Boston*. Choices (A), (B), and (D) all use inappropriate prepositions before the street name *Beacon*. Choices (B) and (D) use inappropriate prepositions before the city *Boston*.

18. **(B)** *Besides* means "in addition to." Choice (A) means "near," not "in addition." In Choice (C), *in addition* is used without *to*. *Also* in Choice (D) is used with verbs, not a noun like *the original document*.

19. **(C)** *But* should be *but also*, which is used in correlation with the inclusive *not only*.

20. **(C)** Negative agreement requires verb-subject order and an affirmative verb after *neither*, or subject-verb order and a negative verb before *either*. In Choices (A) and (D), there are no verbs. In Choice (B), the verb is affirmative, not negative, with *either*.

EXERCISE 48: Sentences—Sentences and Clauses

1. **(A)** *Are* is the main verb of the subject *some ancient units*. Choices (B), (C), and (D) are all part of subject classes that would require a main verb after *today*.

2. **(D)** *Was issued* is the main verb of the subject *paper money*. Choices (A) and (C) are part of subject clauses that would require a main verb after *American Revolution*. Choice (B) is an active verb before a passive agent.

3. **(C)** *That are* should be *are* to provide a main verb for the subject *the plastic arts*.

4. **(B)** *Is taken* is the main verb of the subject *The Scholastic Aptitude Text*. Choices (A) and (C) are part of subject clauses that would require a main verb after *many colleges*. Choice (D) is an active verb before a passive agent.

5. **(A)** *That* should be deleted to provide a main verb [*help*] for the subject *ocean currents*.

6. **(D)** *Is* is the main verb of the subject *Camp David*. Choice (A) is part of a subject clause that would require a main verb after *U.S. presidents*. Choices (B) and (C) are redundant because the subject pronoun *it* is used consecutively with the subject noun *Camp David*.

7. **(C)** *Forming* should be *form* to provide a main verb for the subject *gas and dust*.

8. **(A)** *Which* should be deleted to provide a main verb [*regulated*] for the subject *ordinances*.

9. **(B)** The subject *blue chip stock* and the verb *is* are simple and direct. In addition, *is considered* provides for parallelism with *is favored*. Choices (A), (C), and (D) are redundant.

10. **(B)** *That* introduces a subject and verb in the clause. *Exhibiting* in Choices (A) and (C) cannot be used as a verb without a form of BE. Choice (D) is redundant because the pronoun *they* is used consecutively with the noun *seed*.

11. **(D)** *Is named* is the main verb of the subject *La Guardia Airport*. Choices (A) and (B) are part of subject clauses that would require a main verb after *most popular mayors*. The active verb in Choice (C) is not logical because it implies that the *airport* did the *naming*.

12. **(D)** *Are valued* is the main verb of the subject *intelligence and ability*. Choices (A) and (C) are not logical because they imply that the *intelligence and ability* can *value* something or someone. Choice (B) is part of a subject clause that would require a main verb after *social position or wealth*.

13. **(B)** *Which it feed* should be *feeds* to provide a main verb for the subject *the larva*.

14. **(B)** *95 percent of them* is the subject, and *are filed* is the verb. The usual word order of subject and verb is not followed in Choice (A). Choices (C) and (D) are redundant, and the usual word order is not followed.

15. **(B)** Choice (B) is an example of a dependent clause. Choice (A) is incomplete without the verb *was written* in the clause. Choice (C) is incomplete without *which*, the subject of the clause. Choice (D) is a clause that is not connected to the main clause by a clause marker.

16. **(C)** *Cats and dogs* is the subject of the verb *are kept*. Choices (A) and (D) are part of a subject clause that would require a main verb after *in the world*. The word order in Choice (B) would be correct for a question, but not for a sentence with a period.

17. **(B)** *Which* should be *which are* to provide a verb for the clause.

18. **(D)** *Is* is the main verb of the subject *PTA*, and *a group* is the complement. Choice (A) is redundant because the subject pronoun *it* is used consecutively with the subject noun *PTA*. Choice (B) is part of a subject clause that would require a main verb after *other activities*. *Which* in Choice (C) requires a verb in the clause.

19. **(B)** *Appears* should be *which appears* to provide a subject for the clause. The sentence is also correct without the verb *appears*.

20. **(B)** Choice (B) is the main clause that introduces a dependent clause. Choice (A) is part of a subject clause that would require a main verb after *latitude*. The appositive in Choice (C) would be correct with a comma before it and a comma after it. Choice (D) is redundant because the subject pronoun *it* is used consecutively with the subject noun *the jet stream*.

EXERCISE 49: Sentences— Point of View

1. **(A)** The adverbial phrase *in 1970* establishes a point of view in the past. *Are* should be *were* to maintain the point of view.

2. **(B)** The verb *cannot make* establishes a point of view in the present. *Were* should be *are* to maintain the point of view.

3. **(A)** The reference to an activity before the subject's death establishes a point of view in the past. *Publishes* should be *published* to maintain the point of view.

4. **(B)** The adverbial phrase *seven o'clock in the morning when the sun comes up* establishes a point of view in the present. *Disappeared* should be *disappears* to maintain the point of view.

5. **(C)** The adverbial phrase *Before the 1800s* establishes a point of view in the past. The modal *could* in Choice (C) maintains the point of view. Choices (A) and (B) are present, not past. Choice (D) is a participle without a verb.

6. **(C)** The adverbial phrase *seven months before the stock market crashed in 1929* and the verb *said* establish a point of view in the past. *Is* should be *was* to maintain the point of view.

7. **(C)** The adverbial phrase *In the Middle Ages* establishes a point of view in the past. The verb *was* in Choice (C) maintains the point of view. Choice (A) is also a past verb, but it is an active, not a passive, verb. A passive verb is required by the agent *by a journeyman*. Choice (B) is a present, not a past, verb. Choice (D) is an active verb.

8. **(B)** The adverbial phrase *for about twelve thousand years* establishes a point of view that begins in the past. *Are living* should be *have been living* to maintain the point of view.

9. **(A)** The adverbial clause *although we once thought* establishes a point of view in the past. *Has* should be *had* to maintain the point of view.

10. **(D)** Activities of the dead logically establish a point of view in the past. Choice (D) maintains the point of view. Choices (A) and (C) are present, not past, verbs. Choice (B) is a past verb with a noun, not an adjective, to describe *Carver*.

11. **(D)** Activities of historical figures known to be dead logically establish a point of view in the past. The verb *reported* further establishes that point of view. Choices (A) and (C) are present, not past, verbs. Choice (B) is a past verb, but it is an active verb.

12. **(D)** The adverbial phrase *In 1900* establishes a point of view in the past. *Is* should be *was* to maintain the point of view.

13. **(C)** The adverbial phrase *in 1605* and the verb *founded* establish a point of view in the past. *Builds* should be *built* to maintain the point of view.

14. **(C)** The adverbial phrase *in 2000* establishes a point of view in the past. *Are passed* should be *were passed* to maintain the point of view.

15. **(B)** The adverbial phrase *on June 17, 1775* establishes a point of view in the past. *Occurs* should be *occurred* to maintain the point of view.

16. **(D)** The *development of language* is a historical event that logically establishes a point of view in the past. Choice (D) is a past verb that maintains the point of view. Choice (A) is an infinitive, not a past verb. Choice (B) is a present verb. Choice (C) is a noun.

17. **(B)** The adverb *originally* establishes a point of view in the past. *Is* should be *was* to maintain the point of view.

18. **(A)** Activities of the dead logically establish a point of view in the past. Choice (A) is a past verb. Choice (B) is an *-ing* form, not a past verb. Choice (C) is a present verb. Choice (D) is a verb word.

19. **(B)** The phrase *ancient cultures* establishes a point of view in the past. *Begin* should be *began* to maintain the point of view.

20. **(B)** The phrase *remember when* establishes a point of view in the past. Choice (B) is a past verb. Choice (A) is a present, not a past, verb. Choices (C) and (D) are *-ing* forms.

Exercise 50: Sentences—Agreement

1. **(B)** There must be agreement between subject and verb. *Is* should be *are* to agree with the plural subject *both a term paper and a final exam*.

2. **(A)** There must be agreement between subject and verb. *Were* should be *was* to agree with the singular subject *the popularity*.

3. **(D)** *Are* is used before *there* to refer to the noun *notes* at the specific place in the musical scale and to maintain word order for questions. The singular verb *is* in Choices (A) and (B) does not agree with the plural phrase *many musical notes*. Choice (C) reverses the word order for questions.

4. **(B)** There must be agreement between subject and verb. *Develop* should be *develops* to agree with the singular subject *not one*.

5. **(D)** There must be agreement between subject and verb. *Live* in Choice (D) agrees with the plural subject *nine of every ten people*. Choice (A) is an *-ing* form, not a verb. Choice (B) is redundant because the noun subject is followed by the pronoun subject *they*. Choice (C) would agree with a singular, not a plural, subject.

6. **(D)** There must be agreement between pronoun and antecedent. *Their* should be *its* to agree with the third-person-singular neuter noun *the eagle*.

7. **(D)** There must be agreement between subject and verb. *Require* should be *requires* to agree with the singular subject *the Blue Spruce*.

8. **(A)** There must be agreement between subject and verb. *Is* should be *are* to agree with the plural subject *few airports*.

9. **(C)** *There* is used before *is* to refer to the noun *salt* at the specific place *in the ocean*.

10. **(B)** There must be agreement between subject and verb. *Were* should be *was* to agree with the singular subject *work*.

11. **(C)** There must be agreement between subject and verb. The verb *is* in Choice (C) agrees with the singular subject *the average temperature of rocks*. Choice (A) is a verb word, not a verb that can agree with a subject. Choice (B) is a verb that would agree with a plural, not a singular, subject. Choice (D) is a participle without an auxiliary verb that would agree with a subject.

12. **(B)** There must be agreement between pronoun and antecedent. *Their* should be *his* or *her* to agree with the singular subject *each voter*.

13. **(B)** There must be agreement between pronoun and antecedent. *They* should be *one* or *he* to agree with the impersonal antecedent *one*.

14. **(A)** There must be agreement between subject and verb. *Are* should be *is* to agree with the singular subject *a large percentage*.

15. **(B)** There must be agreement between subject and verb. The verb *has* in Choice (B) agrees with the singular subject *a mature grove*. The verbs in Choices (A) and (C) would agree with a plural, not a singular, subject. Choice (D) is an *-ing* form, not a verb that can agree with a subject.

16. **(D)** There must be agreement between subject and verb. *Is* should be *are* to agree with the plural subject *coins*.

17. **(C)** There must be agreement between subject and verb. *Are* should be *is* to agree with the inverted singular subject *evidence*.

18. **(D)** There must be agreement between subject and verb. *Are contained* should be *is contained* to agree with the plural subject *the urinary system*.

19. **(C)** There must be agreement between subject and verb. The verb *were* in Choice (C) agrees with the plural subject *flying dinosaurs*. Choice (A) does not contain a verb. The verb

in Choice (B) would agree with a singular, not a plural, subject. Choice (D) agrees with the subject, but *have* with a participle does not express a completed past action or state. Since dinosaurs are extinct, the simple past verb correctly expresses completion.

20. **(D)** There must be agreement between subject and verb. *Were* should be *was* to agree with the singular subject *art deco*.

EXERCISE 51: Sentences—Introductory Verbal Modifiers

1. **(A)** An introductory verbal phrase followed by a comma should immediately precede the noun that it modifies. *After finishing Roots* is misplaced because it does not modify the noun it precedes, *author Alex Haley*.

2. **(A)** An introductory verbal phrase followed by a comma should immediately precede the noun that it modifies. *A competitive sport* is misplaced because it does not modify the noun it precedes, *gymnasts*.

3. **(B)** An introductory verbal phrase followed by a comma should immediately precede the noun that it modifies. *Carefully soaking* should be [*you*] *carefully soak them* to provide a noun and a verb for the introductory verbal phrase *to remove stains from permanent press clothing*.

4. **(C)** An introductory phrase should immediately precede the noun that it modifies. Only Choice (C) provides a noun that could be logically modified by the introductory phrase *An abstract painter and pioneer of Surrealism*. Neither *Miro's works* nor *the works of Miro* nor *bright colors* could logically be *painters* as would be implied by Choices (A), (B), and (D).

5. **(A)** An introductory verbal phrase followed by a comma should immediately precede the noun that it modifies. *Found in Tanzania by Mary Leakey* is misplaced because it does not precede the noun it modifies, *the three-million-year-old fossils*.

6. **(D)** An introductory verbal phrase followed by a comma should immediately precede the noun that it modifies. *Columbus's final resting place* should be *Columbus is now buried* because the man, not the place, is modified by the verbal phrase *Originally having been buried in Spain*.

7. **(A)** An introductory phrase should immediately precede the noun that it modifies. Only Choice (A) provides a noun that could be logically modified by the introductory phrase *the largest hotel on Earth*. In Choice (C), *7350 rooms* could not logically be a *hotel*. Choices (B) and (D) are sentences, not nouns.

8. **(B)** An introductory verbal phrase followed by a comma should immediately precede the noun that it modifies. *Audiences are still thrilled* should be *Phantom of the Opera still thrills audiences*, because the play, not the audiences, is modified by the introductory verbal phrase, *With music written by Andrew Lloyd Webber*.

9. **(A)** An introductory verbal phrase followed by a comma should immediately precede the noun that it modifies. *Dental floss should be used* should be *[you] use dental floss* to provide a noun for the introductory verbal phrase *to prevent cavities*.

10. **(A)** An introductory verbal phrase followed by a comma should immediately precede the noun that it modifies. *The Senate committee's discovery* should be *The Senate committee discovered* because the *committee*, not the *discovery*, is modified by the verbal phrase *while researching the problem of violent crime*.

11. **(B)** An introductory phrase should immediately precede the noun that it modifies. Neither *one-third of North America* nor *North America* nor *the water* could logically be a *river* as would be implied by Choices (A), (C), and (D).

12. **(A)** An introductory verbal phrase followed by a comma should immediately precede the noun that it modifies. *After reviewing the curriculum* is misplaced because it does not precede the noun it modifies, *faculty*.

13. **(D)** An introductory verbal phrase followed by a comma should immediately precede the noun that it modifies. *Barry Bond's record* should be *Barry Bond* because the *man*, not the *record*, is modified by the verbal phrase *having hit more home runs in one year than any other player in the history of baseball*.

14. **(A)** An introductory verbal phrase followed by a comma should immediately precede the noun that it modifies. *Banned in the U.S.* is misplaced because it does not precede the noun it modifies, *fluorocarbons*.

15. **(B)** An introductory verbal phrase should immediately precede the noun that it modifies. Only Choice (B) provides a noun that could logically be modified by the introductory phrase *while trying to build a tunnel*. Neither *coal* nor *the construction site* could logically *build a tunnel* as would be implied by Choices (A) and (C). Choice (D) is wordy and indirect.

16. **(A)** An introductory verbal phrase followed by a comma should immediately precede the noun that it modifies. *To avoid jet lag* is misplaced because it does not precede the noun it modifies, *patients*.

17. **(B)** An introductory verbal phrase followed by a comma should immediately precede the noun that it modifies. *Named for women* is misplaced because it does not precede the noun it modifies, *a hurricane*.

18. **(C)** An introductory verbal phrase should immediately precede the noun that it modifies. Only Choice (C) provides a noun that could logically be modified by the introductory verbal phrase, *published by Pocket Books*. *Pearl Buck* would not logically be *published* as would be implied by Choice (A). Choices (B) and (D) are wordy and indirect.

19. **(B)** An introductory verbal phrase should immediately precede the noun that it modifies. Only Choice (A) provides a noun that could logically be modified by the introductory phrase *born in 1892*. Neither *the library* nor *at the library* could logically *be born* as would be implied by Choices (A) and (D). Choice (C) is awkward because it has two introductory phrases used consecutively.

20. **(A)** An introductory verbal phrase followed by a comma should immediately precede the noun that it modifies. *Founded in 1919* is misplaced because it does not precede the noun it modifies, *the Institute for International Education*.

EXERCISE 52: Sentences— Parallel Structure

1. **(B)** Ideas after inclusives should be expressed by parallel structures. *Not only popular* should be *popular not only* to provide parallelism between the adverbial phrases *in the United States* and *abroad*.

2. **(A)** Ideas in a series should be expressed by parallel structures. *Making* should be *to make* to provide parallelism with the infinitive *to control*.

3. **(B)** Ideas after exclusives should be expressed by parallel structure. The correlative conjunction *neither* requires *nor*. Choice (B) has a verb word after *nor* to provide parallelism with the verb word *read* after *neither*. Choice (A) has a pronoun, not a verb word, after *nor*. The word *or* in Choice (C) and *neither* in Choice (D) are not the correct correlative conjunction for *neither*.

4. **(D)** Ideas in a series should be expressed by parallel structures. *Signing your name* should be *the signature* to provide parallelism with the nouns *the address*, *the inside address*, *the salutation*, *the body*, and *the closing*.

5. **(D)** Ideas in a series should be expressed by parallel structures. The noun *diagnosis* in Choice (D) provides parallelism with the nouns *cooking* and *telecommunications*. Choice (A) is an infinitive, not a noun. Choice (B) is an *-ing* form. Choice (C) is a past verb.

6. **(A)** Ideas in a series should be expressed by parallel structures. *Being introduced* should be *to be introduced* to provide parallelism with the infinitive *to read*.

7. **(A)** Ideas in a series should be expressed by parallel structures. *Ice skating* should be *to go ice skating* to provide parallelism with the infinitive *to go skiing*.

8. **(C)** Ideas in a series should be expressed by parallel structures. *Avoiding* should be *avoid* to provide parallelism with the verb words *drink* and *eat*.

9. **(A)** Ideas after exclusives should be expressed by parallel structures. The verb word *transmit* in Choice (A) provides parallelism with the verb word *conduct*. Choice (B) is an *-ing* form, not a verb word. Choices (C) and (D) are nouns.

10. **(D)** Ideas in a series should be expressed by parallel structures. *There are* should be deleted to provide parallelism among the nouns *the flag*, *the airplane*, and *the gowns*.

11. **(D)** Ideas after inclusives should be expressed by parallel structures. *The House of Representatives* should be *by the House of Representatives* to provide parallelism with the phrase *by the Senate*.

12. **(B)** Ideas in a series should be expressed by parallel structures. The noun phrase *the energy* in Choice (B) provides parallelism with the noun phrase *the heat*. Choice (A) is a question word conjunction, not a noun phrase. Choices (C) and (D) are nouns, but they are not noun phrases with the determiner *the*.

13. **(D)** Ideas in a series should be expressed by parallel structures. *With ease* should be *easily* to provide parallelism with the adverbs *safely* and *efficiently*.

14. **(C)** Ideas after exclusives should be expressed by parallel structures, and exclusives should be used in coordinating pairs. *But also* should be *but* to coordinate with *not*.

15. **(C)** Ideas in a series should be expressed by parallel structures. The adjective *decorated* in Choice (C) provides parallelism with the adjectives *cast* and *carved*. Choice (A) is a noun, not an adjective. Choice (B) is an *-ing* form. Choice (D) is a verb word.

16. **(C)** Ideas in a series should be expressed by parallel structures. *Also they* should be deleted to provide parallelism among the verb words *stick out, move*, and *retract*.

17. **(C)** Ideas after inclusives should be expressed by parallel structures, and inclusives should be used in coordinating pairs. *Also* should be *but also* to coordinate with *not only*.

18. **(D)** Ideas in a series should be expressed by parallel structures. *Move* should be *the movement of* to provide parallelism with the noun phrase *the maintenance of*.

19. **(D)** Ideas in a series should be expressed by parallel structures. The verb *help* in Choice (D) provides parallelism with the verbs *report* and *give*. Choices (A) and (B) are *-ing* forms, not verbs. Choice (C) is a parallel verb, but when the verb *help* is used as a causative, it requires a verb word after it, not an *-ing* form.

20. **(D)** Ideas in a series should be expressed by parallel structures. *To control* should be *the control of* to provide parallelism with the nouns *techniques, capitalization*, and *specialization*.

EXERCISE 53: Sentences—Redundancy

1. **(D)** Repetition of a word by another word with the same meaning is redundant. *Again* should be deleted because it means *repeat*.

2. **(A)** Repetition of the subject by a subject pronoun is redundant. *It* should be deleted.

3. **(B)** Redundant, indirect phrases should be avoided. The adverb *uniformly* in Choice (B) is simple and more direct than the phrases in Choices (A) and (C). Choice (D) is not an adverb and cannot describe the manner in which the *gas expands*.

4. **(D)** Indirect phrases instead of adverbs are redundant. *In an impartial manner* should be *impartially*.

5. **(C)** Repetition of the subject by the subject pronoun is redundant. *They* should be deleted.

6. **(D)** Repetition of a word by another word with the same meaning is redundant. *Back* should be deleted because it means *return*.

7. **(B)** Redundant, indirect phrases should be avoided. Choice (B) is the simplest, most direct choice. Choice (A) is redundant because the pronoun *it* is used consecutively after the noun clause subject *that witches cause disasters and misfortunes*. Choice (C) is redundant because the phrase *in a wide way* is used instead of the simpler, more direct adverb *widely*. Choice (D) is an additional clause that does not provide a main verb for the noun clause subject that precedes it, *that witches cause disasters and misfortunes*.

8. **(B)** Repetition of a word by another word with the same meaning is redundant. *Enough* should be deleted because it means *sufficiently*.

9. **(B)** Words or phrases that do not add information are redundant. *In nature* should be deleted.

10. **(C)** Repetition of a subject by a subject pronoun is redundant. *They* should be deleted.

11. **(C)** Redundant, indirect phrases should be avoided. Choice (C) is the simplest, most direct choice. Choices (A), (B), and (D) are redundant because they all use the subject pronoun *it* along with the subject noun *Joshua tree*.

12. **(B)** Redundant, indirect phrases should be avoided. The adverb in Choice (B) is the simplest, most direct choice. Choices (A), (C), and (D) are all redundant phrases.

13. **(C)** Repetition of a word by another word with the same meaning is redundant. *New* should be deleted because it means *innovations*.

14. **(D)** Repetition of a word by another word with the same meaning is redundant. *By name* should be deleted.

15. **(B)** Repetition of a word by another word with the same meaning is redundant. *Forward* should be deleted because it means *advances*.

16. **(B)** Repetition of the subject by a subject pronoun is redundant. *It* should be deleted.

17. **(C)** Indirect phrases instead of adverbs are redundant. *With rapidity* should be *rapidly*.

18. **(B)** Redundant, indirect phrases should be avoided. Choice (B) provides a verb and a modified adjective in the complement. Choice (A) is redundant because the subject pronoun *they* is used consecutively with the noun phrase subject *digital clocks*. Choice (C) requires a verb before *not*. Choice (D) requires a modal before *not*.

19. **(C)** Using words with the same meaning consecutively is repetitive. *Both, together*, and *with* in Choices (A), (B), and (D) all have the same meaning.

20. **(A)** Repetition of the subject by a subject pronoun is redundant. *It* should be deleted.

EXERCISE 54: Sentences— Word Choice

1. **(D)** *Equal to* is a prepositional idiom. *As* should be *to*.

2. **(B)** *Raise* means "to move to a higher place." *Is risen* should be *is raised*.

3. **(C)** *Compare with* is a prepositional idiom. *Comparing* should be *compared with*.

4. **(D)** The past verb *borrowed* is used to maintain the past point of view established by the past adverbial phrase *in 1620*. Choices (B) and (C) are not past verbs. Choice (A) is not logical since the Pilgrims received the money. To *borrow* means to "receive." To *lend* means "to give." "An English company lent the Pilgrims seven thousand dollars" would also be correct.

5. **(C)** *Effects on* is a prepositional idiom. *In* should be *on*.

6. **(C)** *Let* means "allow." *Leave* should be *let*.

7. **(A)** *Effective* is not the correct part of speech. *Effective* should be *effect* to provide a noun as the subject of *is*.

8. **(A)** *The cops* is a colloquial expression. *The cops* should be *the police*.

9. **(B)** In order to refer to *residue*, *leave* should be used. *To leave* means "to let something [*residue*] remain." *To let* in Choice (A) means "to allow." *Residue* in Choice (C) cannot be used as a verb. Choice (D) is not idiomatic.

10. **(A)** In order to refer to a range of *frequencies*, *lie* should be used. *To lie* means "to occupy a place" [within the range]. *To lay* in Choice (B) means "to put in a place." Choices (C) and (D) are -*ing* forms, not verbs to agree with the subject *the audible range*.

11. **(A)** *To suspicion* is not idiomatic. *Suspicions* should be *suspects*.

12. **(A)** *Menkind* is not idiomatic. *Menkind* should be *mankind* or *humankind*.

13. **(A)** *As a whole* means "generally." Choices (B) and (D) are not idiomatic. Choice (C) means "completely."

14. **(A)** *The classify* is not the correct part of speech. *Classify* should be *Classification* to provide a noun as the subject of *begins*.

15. **(A)** *The develop* is not the correct part of speech. *Develop* should be *development* to provide a noun as the object of the preposition *with*.

16. **(C)** Become *bored with* is a prepositional idiom. Choices (A), (B), and (D) are not idiomatic expressions with *bored*.

17. **(A)** *An understand* is not the correct part of speech. *Understand* should be *understanding* to provide a noun as the subject of the verb *is*.

18. **(B)** *Presided over* is a prepositional idiom. *Presided* should be *presided over*.

19. **(C)** *Next to* is a prepositional idiom. Choices (A) and (B) are not idiomatic. Choice (D) means "almost," not "beside." "Near" would also be correct.

20. **(B)** *Depends on* is a prepositional idiom. *Depends to* should be *depends on*.

EXERCISE 55: Sentences— Comprehensive Structures

1. **(C)** *Most* is used before a noncount noun to express a quantity that is larger than half the amount. A singular verb follows the noncount noun. Choice (A) does not have a verb. In Choice (B), the verb is before, not after the noun. In Choice (D), *the* is used before *most*.

2. **(B)** An adjective is used before *enough* to express sufficiency. In Choice (A), *goodly* is ungrammatical. The adverbial form of the adjective *good* is *well*. In Choice (C), *as* is unnecessary and incorrect. In Choice (D), the adjective is used after, not before *enough*.

3. **(A)** *The* can be used before a noncount noun that is followed by a qualifying phrase. *Population* should be *the population* before the qualifying phrase *of the Americas*.

4. **(C)** An adjective clause modifies a noun in the main clause. *That the earliest cultures evolved* modifies *the way*. Choice (A) is a clause marker *that* and a noun. Choice (B) is a verb and a noun. Choice (D) is a clause marker *which* and a noun.

5. **(C)** A sentence has a subject and a verb. Choice (A) is redundant because the subject pronoun *it* is used consecutively with the subject *calculus*. Choice (B) has the marker *that* to introduce a main clause. Choice (D) is redundant because it has a verb that replaces the main verb *can reduce*.

6. **(B)** Subject-verb order and a negative verb with *either* expresses negative agreement. Negative agreement with *neither* requires verb-subject order and an affirmative verb. In Choice (A), verb-subject order is reversed. In Choice (C), verb-subject order is reversed, and *neither* is used at the beginning, not at the end of the clause. In Choice (D) *either*, not *neither*, is used with verb-subject order and an affirmative verb. "Neither did Mexico" would also be correct.

7. **(D)** A sentence has a subject and a verb. Choice (A) does not have a verb. Choices (B) and (C) introduce a main clause subject and verb.

8. **(C)** The anticipatory clause *it is accepted that* introduces a subject and verb, *the*

formation . . . began. Choices (A), (B), and (D) are incomplete and ungrammatical.

9. **(A)** The word order for a passive sentence is a form of BE followed by a participle. Only Choice (A) has the correct word order. Choice (B) does not have a BE form. Choice (C) has a HAVE, not a BE form. Choice (D) is a present tense verb, not BE followed by a participle.

10. **(C)** Subject-verb order is used in the clause after a question word connector such as *how much*. In Choice (A), subject-verb order is reversed. In Choice (B), the auxiliary *does* is unnecessary and incorrect. In Choice (D), the verb *are* is repetitive. "The Consumer Price Index lists how much every car *is*" would also be correct.

11. **(C)** A logical conclusion about the past is expressed by *must have* and a participle. Choices (A), (B), and (D) are not logical because they imply that the *theater* will act to restore *itself*.

12. **(A)** The verb *to want* requires an infinitive complement. Choice (B) is an *-ing* form, not an infinitive. Choice (C) is a verb word. Choice (D) is ungrammatical.

13. **(C)** An introductory verbal phrase should immediately precede the noun that it modifies. Only Choice (C) provides a noun that could be logically modified by the introductory verbal phrase, *after seeing the movie.* Neither *the books* nor *the reading* could logically *see a movie* as would be implied by Choices (A), (B), and (D).

14. **(A)** An introductory phrase should immediately precede the subject noun that it modifies. It does not have a main verb. Choices (B) and (C) contain both subjects and verbs. Choice (D) does not modify the subject noun, *Carl Sandburg.*

15. **(B)** A form of *make* with someone such as *you* and a verb word expresses a causative. Choice (A) is an *-ing* form, not a verb word. Choice (C) is a past form. Choice (D) is an infinitive.

16. **(A)** *Responsible for* is a prepositional idiom. *Responsible the* should be *responsible for the.*

17. **(B)** A form of BE is used with the participle in passive sentences. *Practice* should be *practiced.*

18. **(C)** There must be agreement between pronoun and antecedent. *Their* should be *our* to agree with the second-person antecedent *those of us.*

19. **(B)** *Wrote* should be *written* because the auxiliary *had* requires a participle. *Wrote* is a past form. *Written* is a participle.

20. **(A)** *Would have* and a participle in the result require *had* and a participle in the condition. Because *would have won* is used in the result, *would have* should be *had* in the condition.

21. **(B)** There must be agreement between pronoun and antecedent. *Which* should be *who* to refer to the antecedent *Shirley Temple Black. Which* refers to things. *Who* refers to persons.

22. **(D)** Comparative forms are usually followed by *than.* After the comparative *more reasonable, as* should be *than.*

23. **(D)** *To know* should be *to know how* before the infinitive *to use. To know* is used before nouns and noun clauses. *To know how* is used before infinitives.

24. **(C)** *There* introduces inverted order, but there must still be agreement between subject and verb. *Has been* should be *have been* to agree with the plural subject *two major factions.*

25. **(A)** In order to refer to occupying a place on the battlefields, *lain* should be used. *To lay* means "to put in a place," and the participle is *laid. To lie* means "to occupy a place," and the participle is *lain.*

26. **(B)** *Purposeful* should be *purposes. Purposeful* is an adjective. *Purposes* is a noun.

27. **(B)** *Large* should be *largest.* Because there were more than two ethnic groups, a superlative form must be used.

28. **(B)** The determiner *a* is used before a singular count noun. *Results* should be *result.*

29. **(B)** Most adverbs of manner are formed by adding *-ly* to adjectives. *Calm* should be *calmly* to qualify the manner in which the talking should be done.

30. **(B)** When the degree of one quality, *the heat,* is dependent upon the degree of another quality, *the humidity,* two comparatives are used, each preceded by *the. The worst* should be *the worse* because it is a comparative.

31. **(B)** A dependent clause modifies an independent clause. *Which are* should be *are* to provide a verb for the subject *statistical data*, of the independent clause.

32. **(D)** Ideas in a series should be expressed by parallel structures. *The Assassinate* should be *The Assassination of* to provide for parallelism with the nouns *Causes*, *Economy*, and *Strategies*.

33. **(A)** *Despite of* is a combination of *despite* and *in spite of*. Either *despite* or *in spite of* should be used.

34. **(A)** Because it is a prepositional phrase, in a comparison *as every nation* should be *like every nation*. *As* functions as a conjunction. *Like* functions as a preposition.

35. **(A)** A verb word must be used in a clause after the phrase *It is necessary*. *Met* should be *meet*. *Met* is a past form. *Meet* is a verb word.

36. **(A)** *Are* should be *were* to maintain the point of view in the past established by the phrase *Until recently*.

37. **(C)** *More cheaper* should be *cheaper*. Because *cheap* is a one-syllable adjective, the comparative is formed by adding *-er*. *More* is used with two-syllable adjectives that do not end in *-y*.

38. **(A)** The verb *thought* establishes a point of view in the past. *Will* should be *would* in order to maintain the point of view.

39. **(D)** Because the verb *enjoy* requires an *-ing* form in the complement, *to play* should be *playing*.

40. **(D)** Ideas in a series should be expressed by parallel structures. *To plant* should be *planting* to provide parallelism with the *-ing* forms *plowing* and *rotating*.

Reading

EXERCISE 56: Narration/Sequence— Popular Culture

1. **(B)** The main idea is found in the concluding sentence, "Although he created the game of basketball . . ." Choices (A), (C), and (D) are major points that support the main idea, "the development of basketball."
2. **(D)** ". . . basketball was introduced as a demonstration sport in the 1904 Olympic Games . . ." Choice (A) refers to the date that Naismith organized the first basketball game, not to its introduction in the Olympics. Choice (C) refers to the date that five players became standard. Choice (B) is not mentioned and may not be concluded from information in the passage.
3. **(A)** In the context of this passage, *balk* means to "resist." Choices (B), (C), and (D) are not accepted meanings of the word *balk*.
4. **(C)** In the context of this passage, *fierce* means "extreme." Choices (A), (B), and (D) are not accepted meanings of the word *fierce*.
5. **(C)** "First he attempted to adapt outdoor games such as soccer and rugby to indoor play, but he soon found *them* [outdoor games] unsuitable for confined areas." The pronoun *them* does not refer to Choices (A), (B), or (D).
6. **(C)** "Five years later, a championship tournament was staged in New York City, which was won by the Brooklyn Central YMCA." The other lines do not discuss the winner of the first basketball championship tournament.
7. **(B)** Choice (B) is a paraphrase of the statement. The phrase to "quickly spread throughout the world" means to "become popular worldwide." Choices (A), (C), and (D) do not paraphrase what the author means.
8. **(C)** "Dr. Naismith noticed a lack of interest in exercise among students during the wintertime." Choice (A) is not correct because Dr. Naismith tried to adapt soccer and rugby. Choice (D) is not correct because basketball is played indoors. Choice (B) is not mentioned and may not be concluded from information in the passage.
9. **(B)** Choice (A) is mentioned in line 16. Choice (C) is mentioned in line 15. Choice (D) is mentioned in lines 17–18. Choice (B) is not correct because running with the ball was a violation.
10. **(C)** Because someone had to climb a ladder to retrieve the ball every time a goal was made, it may be concluded that the original baskets did not have a hole in the bottom. Choice (A) is not correct because someone had to climb a ladder to retrieve the ball. Choice (B) is not correct because a metal hoop was introduced in 1906. Choice (D) is not correct because the baskets were hung at either side of the gymnasium.

EXERCISE 57: Definition/Illustration— Popular Culture

1. **(A)** The main idea is found in the concluding sentence, "Mickey Mouse was not Walt Disney's first successful cartoon creation, but he is certainly his most famous one." Choices (B), (C), and (D) are major points that support the main idea, "the image of Mickey Mouse."
2. **(B)** "In the third short cartoon, *Steamboat Willie*, Mickey was whistling and singing through the miracle of the modern sound track" Choice (C) is not correct because Minnie was a costar in the first cartoon, *Plane Crazy*. Choices (A) and (D) are not mentioned and may not be concluded from information in the passage.
3. **(B)** In the context of this passage, *pervasive* means "widespread." Choices (A), (C), and (D) are not accepted meanings of the word *pervasive*.
4. **(A)** In the context of this passage, *appealing* means "attractive." Choices (B), (C), and (D) are not accepted meanings of the word *appealing*.
5. **(A)** "Although he has received a few minor changes throughout his lifetime, most notably the addition of white gloves and the rounder forms of a more childish body, he has remained true to his nature since *those* [cartoons] first cartoons." The pronoun *those* does not refer to Choices (B), (C), or (D).
6. **(A)** "But we do know that Disney had intended to call him Mortimer until his wife Lillian intervened and christened him

Mickey Mouse." The other lines do not indicate Disney's first choice of a name for Mickey Mouse.

7. **(D)** Choice (D) is a paraphrase of the statement. "Nature" means "personality." Choices (A), (B), and (C) do not paraphrase what the author means.

8. **(C)** "Perhaps that was Disney's own image of himself." Choices (A) and (D) are true, but they are not what Disney means when he says that "There is a lot of the mouse in me." Choice (B) is not mentioned and may not be concluded from information in the passage.

9. **(D)** Choices (A) and (C) are mentioned in lines 7–8. Choice (B) is mentioned in line 4. Choice (D) is the exception because the gloves were added later.

10. **(B)** Because the last sentence of this passage mentions one image in popular culture, it may be concluded that the paragraph following the passage most probably discusses other images in popular culture. Choices (A) and (D) are referred to only as they relate to the Mickey Mouse image. Choice (C) is not mentioned and may not be concluded from information in the passage.

EXERCISE 58: Narration/Sequence— Social Sciences

1. **(C)** The main idea is found in the topic sentence, "Federal policy toward the Native Americans has a long history of inconsistency, reversal, and failure." Choice (A) contradicts the fact that the policies have been inconsistent. Choice (B) contradicts the fact that today government policies are unclear. Choice (D) is a major point that supports the main idea, "inconsistent and unclear policies."

2. **(B)** ". . . expulsion of the major Southeastern tribes to . . . what is now Oklahoma . . . which the Cherokee Nation refers to as the 'Trail of Tears' . . ." Choice (A) refers to the Dawes Severalty Act, not to the "Trail of Tears." Choice (C) refers to policies before the "Trail of Tears." Choice (D) refers to policies in the 1950s.

3. **(B)** In the context of this passage, *ambivalent* means "experiencing contradictory feelings." Choices (A), (C), and (D) are not accepted meanings of the word *ambivalent*.

4. **(A)** In the context of this passage, *culminated* means "ended." Choices (B), (C), and (D) are not accepted meanings of the word *culminated*.

5. **(A)** "At the same time, the government supported missionary groups in their efforts to build churches, schools, and model farms for those tribes that permitted *them* [missionary groups] to live in their midst."

6. **(C)** "Congress passed the Dawes Severalty Act, and for the next forty years Indian agents and missionaries attempted to destroy the tribal system by separating the members. It was during this time that the government boarding schools were established to educate Native-American youth outside of the home environment." The other lines do not refer to the congressional act that allowed Native-American students to be sent to boarding schools.

7. **(D)** Choice (D) is a paraphrase of the statement. In both sentences, the president gives the order, but Congress and the Supreme Court oppose it. None of the other choices paraphrases what the author means.

8. **(A)** ". . . the government had discovered that some of the land allocated as permanent reservations for the Native Americans contained valuable resources. Congress passed the Dawes Severalty Act. . . ." Choice (B) refers to the plan that was put in place after the act was passed in order to break up the tribes. Choice (C) refers to a policy from the 1950s, not from the 1800s. Choice (D) refers to the attitude of some government officials today, not during the era of the Dawes Severalty Act.

9. **(C)** Choices (A) and (D) are mentioned in paragraph 1, sentence 1. Choice (B) is mentioned in paragraph 2, sentence 3.

10. **(A)** Because the last sentence of this passage mentions the ambivalence of the Native Americans about the role of the federal government in their affairs, it may be concluded that the paragraph following the passage most probably discusses the Native Americans' point of view regarding government policies today. Choices (B), (C), and (D) are not mentioned and may not be concluded from information in the passage.

EXERCISE 59: Narration/Sequence—Arts/Architecture

1. **(C)** The main idea is found in the concluding sentence, ". . . his work chronicled his life." Choice (A) contradicts the fact that the first six lines of the passage describe his life before he began writing. Choice (B) contradicts the fact that the last twelve lines of the passage describe his work. Choice (D) refers to the fact that his characters were portraits of himself and his family, not to the theme of the passage.

2. **(C)** "The play [*Beyond the Horizon*] won the Pulitzer Prize for the best play of the year. O'Neill was to be awarded the prize again in 1922, 1928, and 1957." Choice (A) refers to the number of times that O'Neill won the Nobel, not the Pulitzer, Prize. Choice (B) refers to the number of times that O'Neill won the Pulitzer Prize in addition to the first time. Choice (D) refers to the total number of times that O'Neill was awarded the Pulitzer and Nobel prizes.

3. **(B)** In the context of this passage, *briefly* means "for a short time." Choices (A), (C), and (D) are not accepted meanings of the word *briefly*.

4. **(B)** In the context of this passage, *struggle* means "conflict." Choices (A), (C), and (D) are not accepted meanings of the word *struggle*.

5. **(B)** "It [the one-act *Bound East for Cardiff*] was produced on Cape Cod by the Provincetown Players, an experimental theater group that was later to settle in the famous Greenwich Village theater district in New York."

6. **(B)** "Upon returning from voyages to South Africa and South America, he was hospitalized for six months to recuperate from tuberculosis." The other lines do not indicate the reason for O'Neill's hospitalization.

7. **(A)** Choice (A) is a paraphrase of the statement. In both sentences, family members were characters in his plays. None of the other choices paraphrases what the author means.

8. **(D)** "Although he did not receive the Pulitzer Prize for it, *Mourning Becomes Electra*, produced in 1931, is arguably his most lasting contribution to the American theater." Choices (A), (B), and (C) refer to plays that were awarded the Pulizer Prize, not to the play that the author identified as the most important to the American theater.

9. **(A)** Choice (B) is mentioned in paragraph 1, sentence 5. Choices (C) and (D) are mentioned in paragraph 3, sentence 1.

10. **(C)** ". . . several themes emerge, including the ambivalence of family relationships, the struggle between the sexes, the conflict between spiritual and material desires, and the vision of modern man as a victim." Choice (A) contradicts the fact that the themes mentioned were controversial. Choice (B) contradicts the fact that most of the characters were portraits of himself and his family. Choice (D) contradicts the fact that O'Neill's plays won so many awards.

EXERCISE 60: Narration/Sequence—Humanities/Business

1. **(D)** Choice (A) is mentioned in paragraph 2, sentence 1. Choice (B) is mentioned in paragraph 2, sentence 5. Choice (C) is mentioned in paragraph 1, sentence 2.

2. **(D)** "Several forms of moveable type were invented in China in the eleventh century, using clay and glue to create individual characters, which, when fired, became durable porcelain squares. Later, iron plates were used to hold *them* [porcelain squares], making it possible to print an entire page." The pronoun *them* does not refer to Choices (A), (B), or (C).

3. **(C)** ". . . European inventors independently experimented with block printing as a way to replace manuscript copying." Choices (A) and (D) are not correct because there is no direct evidence that typesetting in any form was transferred from either China or Egypt to Europe. Choice (B) refers to the printing press, not to block printing.

4. **(B)** In the context of this passage, crucial means "very significant." Choices (A), (C), and (D) are not accepted meanings of the word *crucial*.

5. **(D)** Because Gutenberg engaged in years of lengthy experiments, it may be concluded that he worked for a long time to perfect his printing process. Choice (B) is not correct because he was alive after the Bibles were printed. Choice (C) is not correct because he was a goldsmith, not a painter. Choice (A)

is not mentioned and may not be concluded from information in the passage.

6. **(C)** Paraphrase is a transitional device that connects the inserted sentence with the previous sentence. The previous sentence indicates that Gutenberg "had to give the equipment and . . . Bibles" to his business partner, which implies that he did not benefit financially. In the inserted sentence, the paraphrase is ". . . he did not receive the financial remuneration that he deserved." Choices (A), (B), and (D) do not include transitional devices that connect with the sentences marked in the passage.

7. **(B)** Choice (B) is a paraphrase of the statement If "owning books was no longer the exclusive privilege of scholars," then "scholars were not the only people who could own books." Choices (A), (C), and (D) change the meaning of the statement.

8. **(D)** Choice (A) is mentioned in paragraph 7, sentence 3. Choice (B) is mentioned in paragraph 7, sentence 4. Choice (C) is mentioned in paragraph 8, sentence 2.

9. **(B)** Because stories and songs were "standardized," it must be concluded that they changed less often. Choice (A) is not correct because, although print standardized popular culture, the effect of the oral tradition on print is not mentioned. Choices (C) and (D) are not mentioned and may not be concluded from information in the passage.

10. **(A) (B) (E)** summarize the passage. Choice (F) is true, but it is a minor point that is mentioned in the context of Gutenberg's invention. Choices (C) and (D) are not mentioned in the passage.

Exercise 61: Narration/Sequence— Natural Sciences

1. **(B)** "The base usually moves slower than the internal, more plastic flow of the glacier, which results in something called *basal slip*. . . . It [*basal slip*] is often caused when the bottom of the glacier becomes heated by friction with the bedrock, which, in turn, causes a small amount of melting, lubricating the area where the rock and ice meet, and causing the glacier to move faster." Choice (D) is not correct because it refers to a surge, not a basal slip. Choices (A) and (C) are not

correct because they are not mentioned and may not be concluded from information in the passage.

2. **(B)** ". . . a process called *ice regelation*, which is one way that the glacier secures rock and debris in the basal layer, thus facilitating its movement downhill." Choice (A) is not correct because it does not prevent dangerous crevasses from forming. Choice (C) is not correct because it is stated that "the glacier secures rock and debris in the basal layer." Choice (D) is not mentioned and may not be concluded from information in the passage.

3. **(B)** "Surges are thought to be caused by meltwater at the base of a glacier, which would result in water pressure sufficient to temporarily detach the top of the glacier from the rock in a soft bed of saturated sediment under the glacier. The top then floats forward." Choice (A) is not correct because the snow is on top of the glacier, but it is the pressure on the bottom that causes the surge. Choice (C) is not correct because the sediment is saturated with water, not dry, and the top, not the bottom, moves. Choice (D) is not mentioned and may not be concluded from information in the passage.

4. **(A)** In the context of this passage, abrupt means "unexpected." Choices (B), (C), and (D) are not accepted meanings of the word *abrupt*.

5. **(A)** In the context of this passage, *precise* means "exact." Choices (B), (C), and (D) are not accepted meanings of the word *precise*.

6. **(B)** "the ice absorbs red light, leaving the blue reflection that is visible to the eye." Choice (A) is not correct because air bubbles do not absorb red light. Choice (C) is not correct because it is not mentioned and may not be concluded from information in the passage. Choice (D) is not correct because the air pockets in the ice crystals are not blue.

7. **(A)** Noun reference is a transitional device that connects the inserted sentence with the previous sentence. The two sentences are related by the reference to "ice fields" in the previous sentence and "these fields" in the inserted sentence. Choices (B), (C), and (D) do not include transitional devices that connect the sentences marked in the passage.

8. **(C)** "... extending 5.4 million square miles or approximately the combined area of the United States and Mexico." Choice (A) is not correct because it does not identify the locations of ice fields. Choice (B) is not correct because it does not explain the formation of large icebergs. Choice (D) is not correct because it references glacial movement, not the size of a glacier.

9. **(A)** Choice (B) is mentioned in paragraph 1, sentence 1. Choice (C) is mentioned in paragraph 1, sentence 4. Choice (D) is mentioned in paragraph 6, sentence 1.

10. **(A) (C) (E)** summarize the passage. Choice (B) is true, but it is a minor point that is mentioned in reference to the movement of a glacier. Choices (D) and (F) are not mentioned in the passage.

Exercise 62: Definition/Illustration—Humanities/Business

1. **(C)** The main idea is found in the topic sentence, "Canada is a constitutional monarchy with a parliamentary system of government modeled after that of Great Britain." Choices (A), (B), and (D) are major points that support the main idea, "the Canadian system of government."

2. **(B)** "When a government loses its majority support in a general election, a change of government occurs." Choices (A), (C), and (D) are not correct because the government is elected by the voters. In Choice (A), the governor-general represents the queen, but he does not appoint the government. Choice (C) is not correct because the prime minister chooses a cabinet, not a government. Choice (D) is not correct because the House of Commons holds a great deal of power in the government, but does not choose the government.

3. **(D)** In the context of this passage, *dissolved* means "dismissed." Choices (A), (B), and (C) are not accepted meanings of the word *dissolved*.

4. **(B)** In the context of this passage, *varied* means "different." Choices (A), (C), and (D) are not accepted meanings of the word *varied*.

5. **(B)** "The system is referred to as responsible government, which means that the cabinet members sit in parliament and are directly responsible to *it* [parliament], holding power only as long as a majority of the House of Commons shows confidence by voting with them."

6. **(B)** "The actual head of government is the prime minister, who is responsible for choosing a cabinet." The other lines do not indicate whose responsibility it is to choose the cabinet.

7. **(C)** Choice (C) is a paraphrase of the statement. If the system of government is "modeled after that of Great Britain" then the two countries must have "very similar systems of government." None of the other choices paraphrases what the author means.

8. **(C)** "Although major and minor political parties were not created by law, they are recognized by law in Canada. The party that wins the largest number of seats in a general election forms the government, and its leader becomes the prime minister." Choice (A) is not correct because political parties are recognized by law. Choice (B) is not correct because the party that wins the general election forms the [official] government. Choice (D) may be true, but it is not mentioned and may not be concluded from information in the passage.

9. **(B)** Choices (A) and (C) are mentioned in paragraph 1, sentence 3. Choice (D) is mentioned in paragraph 3, sentence 1. Choice (B) contradicts the fact that the actual head of government is the prime minister.

10. **(D)** Because a change of government occurs when a government loses its majority support in a general election, it may be concluded that the voters in Canada determine when a change of government should occur. Choice (A) contradicts the fact that the prime minister chooses the cabinet. Choice (C) contradicts the fact that the members of the House of Commons are elected directly by voters in general elections. Choice (B) is not mentioned and may not be concluded from information in the passage.

Exercise 63: Definition/Illustration—Natural Sciences

1. **(A)** The main idea is found in the topic sentence, "It [hydrogen] is among the ten most

common elements on Earth as well and one of the most useful for industrial purposes." It is repeated in the first sentence in the second paragraph "hydrogen . . . has several properties that make it valuable for many industries." Choices (B), (C), and (D) are major ". . . points that support the main idea, "the industrial uses of hydrogen."

2. **(D)** ". . . hydrogen is used with oxygen for welding torches that produce temperatures as high as 4,000 degrees F and can be used in cutting steel." Choice (A) is not correct because the hydrogen is heated, and the steel is not cooled. Choice (B) is not correct because the hydrogen is heated, not cooled. Choice (C) is not correct because the hydrogen, not the temperature of the steel, is heated.

3. **(D)** In the context of this passage, *readily* means "easily." Choices (A), (B), and (C) are not accepted meanings of the word *readily*.

4. **(D)** In the context of this passage, *combining* means "adding." Choices (A), (B), and (C) are not accepted meanings of the word *combining*.

5. **(B)** "Hydrogen also serves to prevent metals from tarnishing during heat treatments by removing the oxygen from *them* [metals]."

6. **(D)** "Hydrogen is also one of the coolest refrigerants. [because] It does not become a liquid until it reaches temperatures of –425 degrees F." None of the other lines explains why hydrogen is used as a refrigerant.

7. **(D)** Choice (D) is a paraphrase of the statement. In both sentences, the oxygen and hydrogen are combined, and then heated. None of the other choices paraphrases what the author means.

8. **(B)** "Pure hydrogen seldom occurs naturally, but it exists in most organic compounds. . . . Moreover, hydrgoen is found in inorganic compounds." Choices (A) and (C) are not correct because pure hydrogen seldom occurs naturally. Choice (D) is not correct because hydrogen is added, not released, during hydrogenation.

9. **(D)** Choice (A) is mentioned in paragraph 2, sentence 1. Choice (B) is mentioned in paragraph 4, sentence 4. Choice (C) is mentioned in paragraph 3, sentence 2. Choice (D) contradicts the fact that liquids are changed to semi solids, not the reverse.

10. **(B)** Because several uses for hydrogen in a number of industries are mentioned in the passage, it may be concluded that hydrogen has many purposes in a variety of industries. Choices (A) and (D) contradict the fact that several industrial purposes are mentioned in the passage. Choice (C) contradicts the fact that hydrogen has several properties that make it valuable for many industries.

EXERCISE 64: Definition/Illustration— Social Sciences

1. **(C)** "For some large retail chain stores that has been true [they would disappear] . . . because online options would not have the overhead of a physical location and would be able to offer lower prices. . . ." Choice (B) is not correct because the retail stores had to charge higher prices than the online stores. Choice (D) is not correct because when stores closed, there were many empty buildings available. Choice (A) is not mentioned and may not be concluded from information in the passage.

2. **(A)** In the context of this passage, *merging* means "combining." Choices (B), (C), and (D) are not accepted meanings of the word *merging*.

3. **(B)** "One disadvantage for retail stores is that customers often use them to preview products and then shop online . . . ." Choice (C) is not correct because many online stores have virtual shopping assistants to offer advice. Choice (D) is not correct because customers use online sites to compare prices instead of going to several stores. Choice (A) is not mentioned and may not be concluded from information in the passage.

4. **(C)** In the context of this passage, *obsolete* means "discontinued." Choices (A), (B), and (D) are not accepted meanings of the word *obsolete*.

5. **(B)** ". . . small retailers . . . are able to develop products and brands online without the large startup costs of a physical store." Choice (A) is not correct because they use social media to market their products, not to locate investors. Choice (D) is not correct because they don't have to rely on local customers since the "internet offers a global market for their merchandise . . . ." Choice (A) is not

mentioned and may not be concluded from information in the passage.

6. **(C)** "Customers rely on reviews to choose" paraphrases "Online reviews are also influencing the choices that customers are making." ". . . similar products" paraphrases "products that are almost alike," and a "retail or online store" paraphrases "online or in a retail setting." Choices (A), (B), and (D) change the meaning of the statement.

7. **(B)** The fact that local stores are offering free delivery "like online stores" implies that they are competing for business. Although it is true that online stores have large warehouses as mentioned in Choice (A), that is not the reason that they offer free home delivery. Choice (C) is not correct because the limited shelf space is the reason for shipping to online warehouses, not the reason for free home delivery. Choice (D) is not mentioned and may not be concluded from information in the passage.

8. **(D)** Choices (A) and (B) are mentioned in paragraph 7, sentence 4. Choice (C) is mentioned in paragraph 7, sentence 2.

9. **(A)** Example is a transitional device that connects the insert sentence with the previous sentence. The "putting greens" refer to "fun" and provide another example such as "play areas" and "sports and fitness centers" in the previous sentence. Choices (B), (C), and (D) do not include transitional devices that connect the insert sentence with the sentences marked in the passage.

10. **(A)**, **(B)**, and **(D)** refer to online stores. **(C)** and **(E)** refer to local retail stores.

EXERCISE 65: Definition/Illustration— Arts/Architecture

1. **(B)** In the context of this passage, *particular* means "specific." Choices (A), (C), and (D) are not accepted meanings of the word *particular*.

2. **(B)** Reference is a transitional device that connects the insert sentence with the previous sentence. "The C an octave above" refers to "middle C." Choices (A), (C), and (D) do not include transitional devices that connect the insert sentence with the sentences marked in the passage.

3. **(B)** "In Western music, the octave is divided into eight tones represented by seven letters; however, on the piano you will find thirteen keys in an octave." Choice (A) is not correct because seven refers to the number of letters to label the pitches, not to the number of pitches themselves. Choice (C) is not correct because twelve refers to the number of half steps, not to the number of pitches. Choice (D) is not correct because thirteen refers to the number of keys.

4. **(A)** In the context of this passage, *adjacent* means "beside each other." Choices (B), (C), and (D) are not accepted meanings of the word *adjacent*.

5. **(A)** Choice (A) is a paraphrase of the statement. "Some Classical Persian musicians reject the notion . . ." means ". . . the idea is not accepted by some Persian musicians." Choices (B), (C), and (D) change the meaning of the statement.

6. **(A)** "Ancient musical instruments such as the bone flute . . . . One of the oldest examples . . . is more than 40,000 years old." Choice (B) is not correct because it does not introduce the topic. Choice (C) is not correct because the flute is not mentioned to compare traditions. Choice (D) is not mentioned and may not be concluded from information in the passage.

7. **(D)** Choice (A) is mentioned in paragraph 5, sentence 2. Choice (B) is mentioned in paragraph 7, sentence 2. Choice (C) is mentioned in paragraph 6, sentence 4.

8. **(B)** ". . . the span from the lowest to the highest note, with a frequency ratio of 2:1 is still referred to as an octave." Choice (A) is not correct because octaves do not always have an even number of tones. Choice (C) is not correct because the scales in the octave are not always the same. Choice (D) is not correct because Western music is an eight-note octave, but other cultures have different octaves.

9. **(D)** Choices (A) and (C) are mentioned in paragraph 3, sentence 1. Choice (B) is mentioned in paragraph 3, sentence 4. Choice (D) refers to Persian and Arabic music, not European music.

10. **(B) (D) (E)** summarize the passage. Choice (A) is true, but it is a minor point that is mentioned as an example of a common scale.

Choice (C) is true, but it is a minor point that is mentioned as an example of how one culture labels pitches. Choice (F) is not mentioned in the passage.

EXERCISE 66: Classification—Humanities/Business

1. **(C)** The main idea is found in the topic sentence, after the introduction, "There are four basic types of competition in business that form a continuum . . ." Choices (A) and (B) are major points that support the main idea, "the competition continuum." Choice (D) is not mentioned and may not be concluded from information in the passage.
2. **(D)** "The classic example of monopolistic competition is coffee and tea." Choice (A) is an example of pure competition, not monopolistic competition. Choice (B) is an example of a monopoly, not monopolistic competition. Choice (C) is an example of an oligopoly.
3. **(A)** In the context of this passage, *tolerate* means "permit." Choices (B), (C), and (D) are not accepted meanings of the word *tolerate*.
4. **(B)** In the context of this passage, *dominate* means "control." Choices (A), (C), and (D) are not accepted meanings of the word *dominate*.
5. **(A)** "In oligopoly, serious competition is not considered desirable because *it* [competition] would result in reduced revenue for every company in the group."
6. **(A)** "At one end of the continuum, pure competition results when every company has a similar product." The other lines do not explain pure competition.
7. **(A)** Choice (A) is a paraphrase of the statement. "Not unusual" means "usual." None of the other choices paraphrases what the author means.
8. **(A)** "In these cases [of monopolies], it is government control, rather than competition, that protects and influences sales." The chart that represents the competition continuum shows "monopoly" as the business with the least competition, and therefore, the most control. Choices (B), (C), and (D) are positioned on the continuum with increasingly more competition, and therefore less control.

9. **(A)** Choice (B) is mentioned in paragraph 4, sentence 3. Choice (C) is mentioned in paragraph 4, sentence 2. Choice (D) is mentioned in paragraph 4, sentence 1. Choice (A) refers to monopolistic competition, not to monopoly.
10. **(A)** Because the purpose of the passage is to teach the differences among the basic types of competition in business, it may be concluded that the passage was first printed in a business textbook. It is not as probable that an expository passage of this kind would be printed in any of the other choices—(B), (C), or (D).

EXERCISE 67: Classification—Social Sciences

1. **(C)** The main idea is developed in the first paragraph, "Whether one is awake or asleep, the brain emits electrical waves. During wakefulness . . . small waves. With . . . sleep, the waves become larger. . . ." Choices (A), (B), and (D) are major points that support the main idea, "two types of sleep."
2. **(B)** "In a period of eight hours, most sleepers experience from three to five instances of REM sleep." Choice (A) refers to the number of hours, not the times per night. Choice (C) refers to the number of minutes that each instance of REM sleep lasts. Choice (D) refers to the number of minutes interval between instances of REM sleep.
3. **(B)** In the context of this passage, *vague* means indefinite. Choices (A), (C), and (D) are not accepted meanings of the word *vague*.
4. **(D)** In the context of this passage, *essential* means "necessary." Choices (A), (B), and (C) are not accepted meanings of the word *essential*.
5. **(C)** ". . . sleep is essential because in some way *it* [sleep] regenerates the brain and the nervous system."
6. **(D)** "Sleep is essential because it regenerates the brain and the nervous system." The other lines do not explain why sleep is essential.
7. **(D)** Choice (D) is a paraphrase of the statement. "Physical activity" is "muscle control." None of the other choices paraphrases what the author means.
8. **(C)** "REM sleep is emotionally charged. The heart beats irregularly, and blood pressure

may be elevated. In contrast, the body is so still that the dreamer may appear to be paralyzed." Choices (A), (B), and (D) are all mentioned as typical of REM sleep. Choice (C) is not typical because the body is still.

9. **(A)** Choice (B) is mentioned in paragraph 2, sentence 1. Choice (C) is mentioned in paragraph 2, sentence 3. Choice (D) is mentioned in paragraph 2, sentence 4. Choice (A) refers to slow-wave sleep, not to REM sleep.

10. **(C)** Because REM sleep is important for mental activity, it may be concluded that students who are writing term papers need REM sleep to restore mental functioning. Choice (A) contradicts the fact that slow-wave sleep is helpful in restoring muscle control, not mental activity. Choice (B) contradicts the fact that one kind of sleep will not compensate for the lack of another kind of sleep. Choice (D) is not mentioned and may not be concluded from information in the passage.

EXERCISE 68: Classification—Arts/Architecture

1. **(B)** "In fact" is a transitional device that connects the insert sentence with the previous sentence. The reference to the "Ionic column" as a "female form" further supports the previous idea of the "... graceful Ionic style." Choices (A), (C), and (D) do not include transitional devices that connect the insert sentence with the sentences marked in the passage.

2. **(B)** Choice (A) is mentioned in paragraph 5, sentence 6. Choice (C) is mentioned in paragraph 4, sentence 3. Choice (D) is mentioned in paragraph 5, sentence 8.

3. **(B) (C)** "In addition, the Romans developed two styles of their own—the Tuscan and the Composite." Choices (A) and (D) refer to styles that were developed by the Greeks, not the Romans.

4. **(B)** "The Romans also created rules for a superimposed order in which successive stories included multiple orders, one on top of *the other* [orders]." The phrase does not refer to Choices (A), (C), or (D).

5. **(C)** "The Colosseum is a well-known example of the superimposed order." Choice (A), the Acropolis, is a building with Ionic columns. Choice (B), the Parthenon, is a building with Doric columns. Choice (D), the Temple of Apollo, is a building with classical Corinthian columns.

6. **(C)** "The height of a Corinthian column [is] ten times the diameter" [of its base]. Choice (A) is not correct because the formula refers to a Doric column, not to a Corinthian column. Choice (B) is not correct because the formula refers to an Iconic column. Choice (D) is not correct because it is not mentioned in reference to any of the columns in the passage.

7. **(B)** Because the height of the Corinthian column is ten times the diameter of its base, as compared with smaller ratios for the other columns, it may be concluded that the Corinthian column is the slimmest. Choice (D) is not correct because the Tuscan column is even simpler than the Doric. Choices (A) and (C) are not mentioned and may not be concluded from information in the passage.

8. **(B)** In the context of this passage, the phrase *far-reaching* means "very large." Choices (A), (C), and (D) are not accepted meanings of the phrase *far-reaching*.

9. **(D)** "... the Roman invention of concrete allowed them to build without relying solely on stone or wood." Choice (A) is not correct because they borrowed the architecture from the Greeks, not the engineering. Choice (B) is not correct because concrete allowed them to build, using materials in addition to stone and wood. Choice (C) is not correct because the Romans took their styles to the colonies.

10. **(C)** and **(D)** refer to the *Doric order*. **(E)** and **(F)** refer to the *Ionic order*. **(A)** and **(G)** refer to the *Corinthian order*. Choice (B) is not mentioned in the passage.

EXERCISE 69: Classification—Natural Sciences

1. **(B)** "... astronomers generally include stars within 10,000 light years from the center in the bulge and those farther away to be party of the halo." Choices (A), (C), and (D) are not mentioned and may not be concluded from information in the passage.

2. **(A)** If "spiral galaxies with large bulges tend to have less interstellar gas," then logically, "spiral galaxies with small bulges have more gas." Choices (B), (C), and (D) change the meaning of the sentence and leave out important information.

3. **(A)** "... in the barred spiral galaxies, like the Milky Way ... the arms emerge from there." [the nucleus]. Choice (B) is not correct because all spiral galaxies have a halo. Choice (C) is not correct because all spiral galaxies contain interstellar gas and dust. Choice (D) is not correct because the Milky Way is a barred galaxy in which the arms emerge from the nucleus, not the bulge.

4. **(C)** Choice (A) is mentioned in paragraph 5, sentence 1. Choice (B) is mentioned in paragraph 5, sentence 3. Choice (D) is mentioned in paragraph 5, sentence 3.

5. **(A)** In the context of this passage, *remnants* means "remains." Choices (B), (C), and (D) are not accepted meanings of the word *remnants*.

6. **(B)** In the context of this passage, *devoid* means "empty." Choices (A), (C), and (D) are not accepted meanings of the word *devoid*.

7. **(D)** "Elliptical galaxies ... differ from spiral galaxies in large measure because they do not have a substantial disk." Choice (B) is not correct because elliptical galaxies have little gas and dust. Choice (C) is not correct because irregularly shaped galaxies are included in the irregular category, not in the elliptical category. Choice (A) is not correct because the size of the halo of an elliptical galaxy is not mentioned and may not be determined from information in the passage.

8. **(D)** Example is a transitional device that connects the insert sentence with the previous sentence. The two sentences are related by the reference to "dwarf elliptical galaxies" in the "local group" in the previous sentence and the specific example of a "dwarf elliptical galaxy" in the inserted sentence. Choices (A), (B), and (C) do not include transitional devices that connect the sentences marked in the passage.

9. **(D)** Choice (A) is mentioned in paragraph 9, sentence 5. Choice (B) is mentioned in paragraph 9, sentence 4. Choice (C) is mentioned in paragraph 9, sentence 1.

10. **(B)** and **(F)** are typical of *spiral galaxies*. **(A)** and **(G)** are typical of *elliptical galaxies*. **(D)** and **(H)** are typical of *irregular galaxies*. Choices (C) and (E) are not mentioned in the passage.

EXERCISE 70: Comparison/Contrast— Humanities/Business

1. **(C)** The main idea is found in the topic sentence, "Most languages have several levels of vocabulary that may be used by the same speakers." Choices (A), (B), and (D) are major points that support the main idea, "different types of usage."

2. **(D)** "Slang ... refers to words and expressions understood by a large number of speakers but not accepted as good formal usage by the majority." Choice (A) refers to standard usage. Choice (B) is not correct because colloquial expressions and even slang may be found in standard dictionaries. Choice (C) is not correct because slang is understood by a large number of speakers.

3. **(A)** In the context of this passage, *obscurity* means "disappearance." Choices (B), (C), and (D) are not accepted meanings of the word *obscurity*.

4. **(C)** In the context of this passage, *appropriate* means "correct." Choices (A), (B), and (D) are not accepted meanings of the word *appropriate*.

5. **(B)** "In some cases, the majority never accepts certain slang phrases but nevertheless retains *them* [slang phrases] in their collective memories."

6. **(B)** "Both colloquial usage and slang are more common in speech than in writing." The other lines do not explain where one is more likely to find colloquial language and slang used.

7. **(C)** Choice (C) is a paraphrase of the statement. If colloquialisms are "not considered acceptable," then they are probably "not found" in more formal language. None of the other choices paraphrases what the author means.

8. **(A)** "Standard usage includes those words and expressions understood, used, and accepted by a majority of the speakers of a language in any situation regardless of the level of formality." Choice (B) is not correct because colloquial expressions and slang are more common in speech than in writing, but standard language is used in speech, especially in formal settings. Choice (C) is not correct because standard usage is understood, used, and accepted by a majority of speakers, not

esclusively by the upper classes. Choice (D) is true, but it is not mentioned and may not be concluded from information in the passage.

9. **(D)** Choices (A) and (C) are mentioned in paragraph 3, sentence 2. Choice (B) is mentioned in paragraph 2, sentence 4.

10. **(C)** Because the author states without judgment that most speakers of English will select and use standard, colloquial, and slang expressions in appropriate situations, it may be concluded that the author approves of slang and colloquial speech in appropriate situations. Choices (A), (B), and (D) contradict the fact that the author points out there are appropriate situations for slang and colloquial speech.

EXERCISE 71: Comparison/Contrast— Arts/Architecture

1. **(A)** The main idea is found in the concluding sentences, "Chiefly through the efforts of Steiglitz, modern photography [the Photo-Secession movement] had seceded from painting and had emerged as a legitimate art form. In summary, the Aesthetic movement rejected reality for beauty, but the Photo-Secessionists embraced realism as even more beautiful." Choices (B), (C), and (D) are major points that support the main idea, "The Photo-Secession movement."

2. **(B)** ". . . they [earlier photographs] were cloudy. . . . In contrast, the straightforward photographers produced images that were sharp and clear." Choices (C) and (D) refer to modern, not earlier, photographs. Choice (A) is not mentioned and may not be concluded from information in the passage.

3. **(D)** In the context of this passage, a *defect* means an "imperfection." Choices (A), (B), and (C) are not accepted meanings of the word *defect*.

4. **(B)** In the context of this passage, *chiefly* means "mostly." Choices (A), (C), and (D) are not accepted meanings of the word *chiefly*.

5. **(B)** "Since *they* [aesthetic prints] were cloudy because of the gum bichromate plate that allowed for manual intervention, the aesthetic prints were easily distinguished from the more modern prints, which came to be called straightforward photographs."

6. **(C)** "The subjects included nature in its undisturbed state and people in everyday situations." The other lines do not identify the subjects that modern photographers used.

7. **(B)** Choice (B) is a paraphrase of the statement. If "mechanical precision" was considered a defect by members of the Aesthetic movement, then they must have engaged in "criticism" of it. None of the other choices paraphrases what the author means.

8. **(B)** "Founded by Alfred Steiglitz in New York City in 1902, Photo-Secession had as its proposition the promotion of straightforward photography through exhibits and publications. One of its publications, *Camera Work*, has been recognized among the most beautiful journals ever produced. . . . Photo-Secessionists embraced realism as even more beautiful." Choice (B) is not true because the magazine encouraged Photo-Secessionists, not members of the older Aesthetic movement.

9. **(D)** Choice (A) is mentioned in paragraph 2, sentence 2. Choice (B) is mentioned in paragraph 1, sentence 4. Choice (C) is mentioned in paragraph 1, sentence 4. Choice (D) refers to the Aesthetic movement, not to the Photo-Secession movement.

10. **(D)** Because the author credits Steiglitz with the establishment of modern photography and the publication of one of the most beautiful journals ever produced, it may be concluded that the author admired Alfred Steiglitz. Choices (B) and (C) contradict the fact that the author praises Steiglitz for his work. Choice (A) is not mentioned and may not be concluded from information in the passage.

EXERCISE 72: Comparison/Contrast— Social Sciences

1. **(B)** Example is a transitional device that connects the insert sentence with the previous sentence. The fact that the "process was very controlled, or structured" introduces the example of the "responses that were limited to 'yes' or 'no.'" Choices (A), (C), and (D) do not include transitional devices that connect the insert sentence with the sentences marked in the passage.

2. **(C)** In the context of this passage, *consistently* means "uniformly." Choices (A), (B),

and (D) are not accepted meanings of the word *consistently*.

3. **(B)** Because "... even experienced observers did not work consistently and complex experiences were difficult to analyze," it must be concluded that self-observation may not provide accurate data. Choice (A) is not correct because the method is being criticized, not advanced. Choices (C) and (D) are not mentioned and may not be concluded from information in the passage.

4. **(D)** In the context of this passage, *fundamental* means "necessary." Choices (A), (B), and (C) are not accepted meanings of the word *fundamental*.

5. **(A)** "... behavior could be changed using reinforcement such as a reward. ..." Choice (C) is not correct because it refers to functionalism. Choices (B) and (D) are not mentioned and may not be concluded from information in the passage.

6. **(D)** "William James was pioneering a different school of psychology called *functionalism*. ... Influenced by Darwin, he [James] argued that it was necessary to understand the purpose of mental operations. ..." Choice (A) is not correct because, although evolutionists were influential, they were biologists, not psychologists. Choice (B) is not correct because behaviorists were interested in observable behavior, not the purpose of that behavior. Choice (C) is not correct because structuralists were interested in the content, not the purpose of experience.

7. **(D)** Choice (A) is mentioned in paragraph 6, sentence 1. Choice (B) is mentioned in paragraph 6, sentence 4. Choice (C) is mentioned in paragraph 6, sentence 2.

8. **(B)** "Although one school of thought may have dominated the discipline at a particular time in the history of psychology, psychologists today do not generally identify themselves according to any one school of psychology, and most would agree that each [school] has made a significant contribution to the field." The adjective *each* does not refer to Choices (A), (C), and (D).

9. **(C)** Choice (A) is mentioned in paragraph 3, sentence 4. Choice (B) is mentioned in paragraph 4, sentence, 4. Choice (D) is mentioned in paragraph 1, sentence 3 and paragraph 3, sentence 1.

10. **(A) (B) (F)** summarize the passage. Choice (C) is true, but it is a minor point that is mentioned in reference to psychoanalysis. Choice (D) is true, but it is a minor point that is mentioned as an example of functional psychology. Choice (E) is not mentioned in the passage.

EXERCISE 73: Comparison/Contrast— Natural Sciences

1. **(D)** In the context of this passage, *roles* means "positions." Choices (A), (B), and (C) are not accepted meanings of the word *roles*.

2. **(C)** In the context of this passage, *phenomenon* means "occurrence." Choices (A), (B), and (D) are not accepted meanings of the word *phenomenon*.

3. **(C)** Restatement is a transitional device that connects the insert sentence with the previous sentence. "To say that another way" introduces a restatement. Choices (A), (B), and (D) do not include transitional devices that connect the insert sentence with the sentences marked in the passage.

4. **(A)** "... engineering technologists discover problems in the designs. ..." Choice (B) is not correct because engineers develop new products. Choice (C) is not correct because scientists perform basic research. Choice (D) is probably true, but it is not mentioned and may not be concluded from information in the passage.

5. **(D)** Choice (D) is a paraphrase of the statement. "Engineering technologists are responsible for making the tools" paraphrases "tools ... are made by engineering technologists." The "tools that engineers need ... and scientists use" paraphrases "tools for engineering projects and scientific research." Choice (A) is not correct because it does not include scientists and their research. Choices (B) and (C) change the meaning of the statement.

6. **(A)** "As an example of how scientists, engineers, and engineering technologists might collaborate on a project, consider the problem of building a structure that will withstand a specific type of earthquake. ..." Choice (C) is not correct because it is a reference to engineers. Choice (D) is not correct because it is about education, not earthquakes. Choice (B) is not

mentioned and may not be concluded from information in the passage.

7. **(C)** "... those interested in engineering would need math and science, but would also require specialized courses...." Choice (D) is not correct because it is in reference to scientists. Choices (A) and (B) are not mentioned and may not be concluded from information in the passage.

8. **(C)** Choice (A) is mentioned in paragraph 7, sentence 1. Choices (B) and (D) are mentioned in paragraph 7, sentence 3.

9. **(B)** Because the author offers information about career choices, it may be concluded that this passage would be published in an orientation book for engineering students. Choice (A) is not correct because the focus is not on mathematics. Choice (C) is not correct because the information is too basic for an advanced textbook. Choice (D) is not correct because engineering technology is only one of three career fields explained.

10. **(A) (C) (E)** summarize the passage. Choice (B) is true, but it is a minor point that is mentioned to compare engineers and technologists. Choice (D) is true, but it is a minor point that is mentioned to introduce the main topic—the differences among career fields for engineers, scientists, and engineering technologists. Choice (F) is not mentioned in the passage.

EXERCISE 74: Cause/Effect— Natural Sciences

1. **(A)** The main idea is found in the topic sentence, "Light from a living plant or animal is called bioluminescence or cold light...." Choices (B), (C), and (D) are major points that support the main idea, "cold light."

2. **(B)** "... some primitive plants and animals continue to use the light for new functions such as mating or attracting prey." Choices (A) and (D) refer to the original purposes of bioluminescence, not to the reason it has continued in modern plants and animals. Choice (C) refers to incandescence, not to bioluminescence.

3. **(A)** In the context of this passage, *primitive* means "very old; at an early stage of development." Choices (B), (C), and (D) are not accepted meanings of the word *primitive*.

4. **(A)** In the context of this passage, *relatively* means "comparatively." Choices (B), (C),

and (D) are not accepted meanings of the word *relatively*.

5. **(C)** "Light from a living plant or animal is called bioluminescence, or cold light, to distinguish *it* [bioluminescence, or cold light] from incandescence, or heat-generating light."

6. **(B)** "Living light occurs when luciferin and oxygen combine in the presence of luciferase." The other lines do not explain how living light occurs.

7. **(A)** Choice (A) is a paraphrase of the statement. The phrase "little or no measurable heat" means "without heat." None of the other choices paraphrases what the author means.

8. **(D)** "The earliest recorded experiments with bioluminescence in the late 1800s are attributed to Raphael Dubois, who extracted a luminous fluid from a clam, observing that it continued to glow in the test tube for several minutes. He named the substance *luciferin*...." Choice (A) is not correct because *luciferin* was discovered in the late 1800s, not recently. Choice (C) is not correct because *luciferase* was always present with *luciferin*. Choice (B) refers to oxygen, which may have been poisonous to life forms on early Earth.

9. **(D)** Choice (A) is mentioned in paragraph 1, sentence 4. Choice (B) is mentioned in paragraph 2, sentences 4 and 5. Choice (C) is mentioned in line 1. Choice (D) refers to oxygen in the earth's early atmosphere, not to bioluminescence.

10. **(D)** Because the last sentence of this passage mentions that some primitive plants and animals continue to use bioluminescence for new functions, it may be concluded that the paragraph following the passage most probably discusses bioluminescence in modern plants and animals. Choices (A), (B), and (C) have already been discussed earlier in the passage.

EXERCISE 75: Cause/Effect— Social Sciences

1. **(A)** The main idea is found in the concluding sentence of the paragraph, "This population trend has been referred to as the graying of America." Choices (B), (C), and (D) are major points that support the main idea, "the graying of America."

2. **(C)** "Among females, the life span increased from 78.3 years in 2000 ..." Choice (A) refers to the average male life span in 2000. Choice

(B) refers to the average male life span in 2005. Choice (D) refers to the average female life span in 2005, not 2000.

3. **(A)** In the context of this passage, a *pool* means a "group of people." Choices (B), (C), and (D) are not accepted meanings of the word *pool*.

4. **(D)** In the context of this passage, *trends* means "general directions." Choices (A), (B), and (C) are not accepted meanings of the word *trends*.

5. **(C)** "Because the birth rates among this specialized population were very high, *their* [this specialized population's] children, now among the elderly, are a significant segment of the older population."

6. **(B)** "Although the increase in the birth rate is the most dramatic factor, the decline in the death rate is also significant." The other lines do not explain what has influenced life expectancy.

7. **(A)** Choice (A) is a paraphrase of the statement. If the second factor is "also significant," then they are "both . . . significant." None of the other choices paraphrases what the author means.

8. **(C)** ". . . and by 2025, there will be 59 million elderly Americans, representing 21 percent of the population in the United States." Choices (A) and (D) refer to the years when the "baby boom" will become the "senior boom." Choice (B) is not mentioned and may not be concluded from information in the passage.

9. **(D)** Choice (A) is mentioned in paragraph 2, sentence 3. Choice (B) is mentioned in paragraph 4, sentence 2. Choice (C) is mentioned in paragraph 3, sentence 2.

10. **(A)** Because older people tend to get gray hair, it may be concluded that the word *gray* is a reference to the hair color of older people. Choices (B), (C), and (D) are not mentioned and may not be concluded from information in the passage.

EXERCISE 76: Cause/Effect—Arts/Architecture

1. **(C)** In the context of this passage, *major* means "important." Choices (A), (B), and (D) are not accepted meanings of the word *major*.

2. **(A)** Choice A is a paraphrase of the statement. "People engaged in business and trade" paraphrases "merchants and manufacturers" and

no "monarch was in power" paraphrases "in the absence of a monarch." Choices (B), (C), and (D) change the meaning of the statement.

3. **(A)** In the context of this passage, *acquire* means "achieve." Choices (B), (C), and (D) are not accepted meanings of the word *acquire*.

4. **(C)** "Probably in keeping with their ethical and religious standards, art collectors tended to choose smaller works. . . ." Choice (A) is not correct because they chose smaller works instead of the lavish decorations typical of the Italian baroque period. Choice (B) is not correct because the system of commissions was being replaced. Choice (D) is not mentioned and may not be concluded from information in the passage.

5. **(A)** ". . . art collectors tended to choose . . . landscapes, still lives, and portraits. . . ." Choices (B) and (C) are not correct because they were typical of the Italian baroque period, not the Dutch Republic. Choice (D) is not mentioned and may not be concluded from information in the passage.

6. **(A)** Choice (B) is mentioned in paragraph 7, sentence 1. Choice (C) is mentioned in paragraph 7, sentence 3. Choice (D) is mentioned in paragraph 7, sentence 3.

7. **(D)** "Many artists settled their debts by decorating businesses with their art. This practice was especially popular among innkeepers and tavern owners, who often became art dealers. . . ." Choice (C) is true, but both innkeepers and tavern owners became art dealers for the same reason at the same time. One did not influence the other. Choices (A) and (B) are not mentioned and may not be concluded from information in the passage.

8. **(B)** Implication is a transitional device that connects the insert sentence with the previous sentence. The previous sentence states that "precise prices" would be difficult to determine. The insert sentence mentions a range of prices "from very cheap to extravagantly expensive" as implied possibilities. Choices (A), (C), and (D) do not include transitional devices that connect the sentence with the sentences marked in the passage.

9. **(C)** Choice (A) is mentioned in paragraph 5, sentence 1. Choice (B) is mentioned in paragraph 2, sentence 5. Choice (D) is mentioned in paragraph 6, sentence 2.

10. **(B) (C) (F)** summarize the passage. Choice (A) is true, but it is a minor point that is mentioned in reference to the rise of the merchant class. Choice (D) is true, but it is a minor point that is mentioned in contrast to the preferences of the Dutch collectors. Choice (E) is not mentioned and may not be concluded from information in the passage.

EXERCISE 77: Cause/Effect— Social Sciences

1. **(D)** Choice (A) is mentioned in paragraph 2, sentence 2. Choice (B) is mentioned in paragraph 2, sentence 6. Choice (C) is mentioned in paragraph 3, sentence 1.

2. **(B)** "In many cases, the dust drifted like snow." Choice (A) is not correct because the dust was not white. Choices (C) and (D) are not mentioned and may not be concluded from information in the passage.

3. **(B)** "To discourage cattle grazing . . . the Department of Agriculture purchased more than eight million head of cattle. . . ." Choice (A) is not correct because, although it is true that the government became the largest cattle owner in the world, it was not the reason that they purchased the cattle. Choices (C) and (D) are not mentioned and may not be concluded from information in the passage.

4. **(B)** Choice (B) is a paraphrase of the statement. A government *subsidy* is a payment to farmers for "not growing crops." Choices (A), (C), and (D) change the meaning of the statement.

5. **(D)** In the context of this passage, *alter* means "modify." Choices (A), (B), and (C) are not accepted meanings of the word *alter*.

6. **(B)** "However, with several consecutive years of good rainfall and the increased demand and higher prices for grain during World War II, many homesteaders abandoned the practices that the SCS had encouraged *them* [homesteaders] to institute on their farms." The pronoun *them* does not refer to Choices (A), (C), and (D).

7. **(A)** "At the height of the disaster, 100 million acres had been eroded. . . ." Choice (C) refers to the number of cattle purchased by the government. Choice (D) refers to the number of acres still vulnerable to erosion by 1940. Choice (B) is not mentioned and may not be concluded from information in the passage.

8. **(A)** In the context of this passage, *potential* means "probable." Choices (B), (C), and (D) are not accepted meanings of the word *potential*.

9. **(C)** Because the farmers replaced grasslands with crops when the price of wheat rose, it may be concluded that the Great Plains is a wheat-producing region in the United States. Choice (A) is not correct because ranchers were grazing cattle, not buffalo. Choice (B) is not correct because the high prices for grain during World War II had a negative effect on the policies that previously had ended the Dust Bowl. Choice (D) is not correct because, although 2.5 million people migrated, all of the homesteaders did not abandon their farms.

10. **(B) (E) (F)** summarize the passage. Choice (A) is true, but it is a minor point that is mentioned as an example of how federal agencies intervened. Choice (C) is true, but it is a minor point that is mentioned to demonstrate the extent of the devastation. Choice (D) is not mentioned and may not be concluded from information in the passage.

EXERCISE 78: Persuasion/ Justification—Natural Sciences

1. **(C)** The main topic is found in the title, "Endangered Species," and in the topic sentence: "There are three valid arguments to support the preservation of endangered species." Choices (A) and (B) are mentioned in reference to the major point, "aesthetic justification," one of the three arguments. Choice (D) is mentioned in reference to the major point, "ecological self-interest," one of the three arguments.

2. **(D)** ". . . proponents of a *moral justification* contend that all species have the right to exist." Choice (A) is not correct because it supports the experience of humankind, not that of animals. Choice (B) is not correct because it is an argument that supports protection of animals for their benefit to humans. Choice (C) is not correct because it is the same argument as the ecological argument, supporting the benefits to the human species, not animal rights.

3. **(D)** In the context of this passage, *perspective* means "view." Choices (A), (B), and (C) are not accepted meanings of the word *perspective*.

4. **(C)** In the context of this passage, *unique* means "special." Choices (A), (B), and (D) are not accepted meanings of the word *unique*.

5. **(C)** "Furthermore, if humankind views itself as the stewards of all the creatures on Earth, then it is incumbent upon human beings to protect *them* [the creatures] and to ensure the continued existence of all species."

6. **(C)** "Some advocates of the ecological argument contend that important chemical compounds derived from rare plants may contain the key to a cure for one of the diseases currently threatening human beings." The other lines do not explain how rare species contribute to the health of human beings.

7. **(D)** Choice (D) is a paraphrase of the statement. Choices (A), (B), and (C) change the meaning of the statement.

8. **(B)** "By preserving all species, we retain a balance of nature that is ultimately beneficial to humankind. Recent research on global ecosystems has been cited as evidence that every species contributes important or even essential functions that may be necessary to the survival of our own species." Choices (A), (C), and (D) are true, but they are not what is cited in the passage from research on global ecosystems.

9. **(C)** Choice (A) is mentioned in paragraph 2, sentence 4. Choice (B) is mentioned in paragraph 1, sentences 2 and 4. Choice (D) is mentioned in paragraph 3, sentence 1.

10. **(C)** Because the author states that there are three valid arguments to support the preservation of endangered species, it may be concluded that the author supports all of the arguments. Choice (A) is not correct because the author refers to the members of deep ecology as "they," not "we." Choice (B) is not correct because the author included ecological self-interest as one of the three valid arguments. Choice (D) is not mentioned and may not be concluded from information in the passage.

EXERCISE 79: Persuasion/ Justification—Social Sciences

1. **(A)** The main idea is found in the topic sentence in the second paragraph, after the introduction, "Although the stated objective of most prison systems . . . is to rehabilitate the inmates . . . the systems themselves do not support such a goal. . . . If prisons are . . . to achieve the goal . . . then the prisons themselves will have to change." Choice (D) contradicts the fact that the goal is rehabilitation and reintegration. Choices (B) and (C) are major points that support the main idea, "that prisons must be restructured."

2. **(B)** ". . . only one-third of the inmates have vocational training opportunities or work release options." Choice (D) refers to the percentage rate for rearrest. Choices (A) and (C) are not mentioned and may not be concluded from information in the passage.

3. **(B)** In the context of this passage, *recidivism* refers to people who "return to a former activity," in this case to criminal activity that leads to prison after release. Choices (A), (C), and (D) are not accepted meanings of the word *recidivism*.

4. **(C)** In the context of this passage, *options* means "alternatives." Choices (A), (B), and (D) are not accepted meanings of the word *options*.

5. **(B)** "Although the stated goal of most prison systems, on both federal and state levels, is to rehabilitate the inmates and reintegrate *them* [the inmates] into society, the systems themselves do not support such a goal."

6. **(B)** "Even more shocking is the fact that the number and rate of imprisonment has more than doubled over the past twenty years, and the recidivism—that is, the rate for rearrest— is more than 60 percent." The other lines do not explain the rate of imprisonment over the past twenty years.

7. **(C)** Choice (C) is a paraphrase of the statement. The phrase "not support" means "not promote." None of the other choices paraphrases what the author means.

8. **(C)** "Second, *they* [prisons] will have to be built in or near population centers with community resources available for gradual reintegration into society." Choices (A), (B), and (D) are not mentioned and may not be concluded from information in the passage.

9. **(A)** Choice (B) is mentioned in paragraph 3, sentence 2. Choice (C) is mentioned in paragraph 3, sentence 4. Choice (D) is mentioned in paragraph 3, sentence 3.

10. **(C)** Because the last sentence of this passage mentions models for collaborative efforts between the criminal justice system and the community, it may be concluded that the paragraph following the passage most probably discusses examples of models for community collaboration. Choices (A) and (D) have already been discussed earlier in the passage. Choice (B) is not mentioned and may not be concluded from information in the passage.

EXERCISE 80: Persuasion/Justification—Humanities/Business

1. **(B)** Choice (A) is mentioned in paragraph 1, sentence 4. Choice (C) is mentioned in paragraph 1, sentence 5. Choice (D) is mentioned in paragraph 1, sentence 3.

2. **(B)** "Second, it is assumed that every word in this core vocabulary is replaced in a process like *that* [process] of radioactive decay in Carbon 14 dating, in constant percentages." The pronoun *that* does not refer to Choices (A), (C), and (D).

3. **(C)** Choice (C) is a paraphrase of the statement. "Fewer words" means "fewer vocabulary items" and the "longer the separation" means "separated a long time ago." Choices (A), (B), and (D) change the meaning of the statement.

4. **(D)** "On average, the languages that they studied had about 85 percent in common after one thousand years of divergence." The number in Choice (A) refers to the Carbon 14 dating system. The numbers in Choices (B) and (C) refer to the example that compares earlier and later divergence, not one thousand years of divergence.

5. **(D)** Reference is a transitional device that connects the insert sentence with the previous sentence. The two sentences are related by the reference to "a table of historical divergence" in the previous sentence by "the table in years" in the insert sentence. Choices (A), (B), and (C) do not include transitional devices that connect the sentences marked in the passage.

6. **(A)** In the context of this passage, *limitations* means "weak points." Choices (B), (C), and (D) are not accepted meanings of the word *limitations*.

7. **(C)** In the context of this passage, *viable* means "practical." Choices (A), (B), and (D) are not accepted meanings of the word *viable*.

8. **(C)** Choice (A) is mentioned in paragraph 4, sentence 5. Choice (B) is mentioned in paragraph 4, sentence 8. Choice (D) is mentioned in paragraph 4, sentence 3. Choice (C) is true, but it is a justification for using the method, not a criticism of it.

9. **(D)** Because the passage includes criticism as well as an unbiased presentation of the approach, it may be concluded that the author has a balanced view of the work. Choice (A) is not correct because there are no comments that would indicate a lack of interest. Choices (B) and (C) are not mentioned and may not be concluded from information in the passage.

10. **(A) (D) (E)** summarize the passage. Choice (B) is true, but it is a minor point that is mentioned in reference to the criticisms of the method. Choice (F) may be concluded from the examples, but it is not a major idea. Choice (C) is logical, but it is not mentioned in the passage.

EXERCISE 81: Persuasion/Justification—Arts/Architecture

1. **(B)** Choice (B) is a paraphrase of the statement. The phrase "perception is the same" paraphrases "perception is similar" and "don't all see the same image" paraphrases "we see images differently." Choices (A), (C), and (D) change the meaning of the statement.

2. **(B)** Example is a transitional device that connects the insert sentence with the previous sentence. The two sentences are related by the reference to the fact that "they don't all see the same image" in the previous sentence and the specific example of "one person . . . another person" in the insert sentence. Choices (A), (C), and (D) do not include transitional devices that connect the sentences marked in the passage.

3. **(C)** In the context of this passage, the phrase *intrigued by* means "very interested." Choices (A), (B), and (D) are not accepted meanings of the phrase *intrigued by*.

4. **(C)** ". . . Michael Murphy creates incredible three-dimensional sculptures that require the

observer to stand at a specific vantage point to see the image." Choice (A) refers to Egyptian painters, not to Michael Murphy. Choice (B) is not correct because it was not directly stated that a "smaller sculpture" is hidden. Choice (D) is not mentioned and may not be concluded from information in the passage.

5. **(B)** ". . . the purpose that the artist had . . . in the anti war symbolism throughout." Choices (A), (C), and (D) are not mentioned and may not be concluded from information in the passage.

6. **(A)** In the context of this passage, *overall* means "general." Choices (B), (C), and (D) are not accepted meanings of the word *overall*.

7. **(B)** "Looking at a work from the Egyptian school . . . allows us to understand and appreciate a perspective that would be very different from the expected proportions of people in other artistic movements." Choices (A), (C), and (D) are not mentioned and may not be concluded from information in the passage.

8. **(D)** ". . . great works of art are capable of conveying many meanings. *Those* [great works of art] that survive the test of time . . ." The pronoun *Those* does not refer to Choices (A), (B), and (C).

9. **(C)** Choice (A) is mentioned in paragraph 6, sentence 1. Choices (B) and (D) are mentioned in paragraph 3, sentence 4.

10. **(B) (C) (E)** summarize the passage. Choice (A) is true, but it is an example of the major point that history contributes to appreciation of art. Choices (D) and (F) are not mentioned in the passage.

EXERCISE 82: Problem/Solution— Arts/Architecture

1. **(C)** The main idea is found in the topic sentence, "The practice of signing and numbering individual prints was introduced by James Abbott McNeill Whistler . . ." Choices (A) and (B) are major points that support the main idea, "the practice of signing prints." Choice (D) is not mentioned and may not be concluded from information in the passage.

2. **(C)** "As soon as Whistler and Haden began signing and numbering their prints, their work began to increase in value." Choice (A) is not correct because it is not mentioned as a reason why Whistler's work was

more valuable. Choice (B) refers to Whistler's best-known work, but not to the reason that his work increased in value. Choice (D) refers to the prints that were signed along with those of Whistler.

3. **(A)** In the context of this passage, *speculate* means "guess." Choices (B), (C), and (D) are not accepted meanings of the word *speculate*.

4. **(A)** In the context of this passage, *distinguish* means "recognize differences." Choices (B), (C), and (D) are not accepted meanings of the word *distinguish*.

5. **(D)** "Wherever the artist elects to sign *it* [the print], a signed print is still valued above an unsigned one, even in the same edition."

6. **(C)** "Although most prints are signed on the right-hand side in the margin below the image, the placement of the signature is a matter of personal choice." The other lines do not indicate where one might find an artist's signature on his work.

7. **(A)** Choice (A) is a paraphrase of the statement. To "increase in value" means to be "worth more." None of the other choices paraphrases what the author means.

8. **(B)** ". . . James Abbott McNeill Whistler . . . [was] best known for the painting of his mother, called *Arrangement in Grey and Black No. 1* but known to most of us as *Whistler's Mother*." Choice (A) refers to Whistler's brother-in-law, who, along with Whistler, began the practice of signing and numbering prints. Choices (C) and (D) are not mentioned and may not be concluded from information in the passage.

9. **(C)** Choices (A) and (B) are mentioned in paragraph 1, sentence 3. Choice (D) is mentioned in paragraph 1, sentence 2. Choice (C) is true, but it is not a reason why a collector prefers a signed print.

10. **(B)** Because Whistler's brother-in-law speculated that collectors would find prints more attractive if there were only a limited number of copies produced and an artist could guarantee and personalize each print, it may be concluded that artists number their prints to guarantee a limited edition. Choice (C) contradicts the fact that there are a limited number. Choice (D) contradicts the fact that the placement of the signature and the number is a matter of personal choice. Choice (A) is not mentioned and may not be concluded from information in the passage.

EXERCISE 83: Problem/Solution—Humanities/Business

1. **(D)** The main idea is found in the topic sentence, "For Americans to play a more effective role in international business negotiations, they must put forth more effort to improve cross-cultural understanding." Choices (A), (B), and (C) are major points that support the main idea, "that American negotiators need to learn more about other cultures."

2. **(C)** "Negotiating is the process of communicating back and forth for the purpose of reaching an agreement." Choice (B) refers to the process, not to the purpose of negotiation. Choice (D) refers to an important aspect of international negotiations. Choice (A) is not mentioned and may not be concluded from information in the passage.

3. **(D)** In the context of this passage, *persuade* means "convince." Choices (A), (B), and (C) are not accepted meanings of the word *persuade*.

4. **(D)** In the context of this passage, *undermining* means "making weak." Choices (A), (B), and (C) are not accepted meanings of the word *undermining*.

5. **(B)** "The American negotiator's role becomes *that* [the role] of an impersonal purveyor of information and cash."

6. **(A)** "*It* [Negotiating] involves persuasion and compromise, but in order to participate in either one, the negotiators must understand the ways in which people are persuaded and how compromise is reached within the culture of the negotiation." The other lines do not indicate the two criteria necessary for negotiation.

7. **(C)** Choice (C) is a paraphrase of the statement. The phrase to "not enjoy the same level of success" means to be "less successful." None of the other choices paraphrases what the author means.

8. **(B)** "... American negotiators often insist on realizing short-term goals. Foreign negotiators, on the other hand, may value the relationship established between negotiators and may be willing to invest time in it for long-term benefits." Choices (A), (C), and (D) are true, but they are not mentioned and may not be concluded from information in the passage.

9. **(B)** Choice (A) is mentioned in paragraph 3, sentence 1. Choice (C) is mentioned in paragraph 4, sentence 2. Choice (D) is mentioned in paragraph 4, sentence 3. Choice (B) refers to foreign negotiators, not to the American negotiator.

10. **(A)** Because the last sentence of this passage mentions efforts to improve cross-cultural understanding, it may be concluded that the paragraph following the passage most probably discusses ways to increase cross-cultural understanding. Choices (B), (C), and (D) have already been discussed earlier in the passage.

EXERCISE 84: Problem/Solution—Social Sciences

1. **(B)** In the context of this passage, *broad* means "general." Choices (A), (C), and (D) are not accepted meanings of the word *broad*.

2. **(C)** "... *dyslexia*, a learning disability that causes difficulties with reading and spelling ... The students may have problems connecting letters to the sounds they produce and may reverse letters or words when they see them in print." Choice (A) refers to *dyscalculia*, not to *dyslexia*. Choice (B) refers to *dysgraphia*. Choice (D) is mentioned in reference to general learning disabilities, not specifically to *dyslexia*.

3. **(A)** "Before 1975 ... children with special needs were often refused enrollment or were not adequately educated within the public school system." Choices (B), (C), and (D) are not mentioned and may not be concluded from information in the passage.

4. **(C)** Choices (A) and (D) are mentioned in paragraph 4, sentence 2. Choice (B) is mentioned in paragraph 4, sentence 3.

5. **(A)** Choice (A) is a paraphrase of the statement. If "many more students" are receiving services today, then "fewer children were receiving services" in the past. Choices (B), (C), and (D) change the meaning of the statement.

6. **(B)** "... recent research has encouraged services not only for students but also for their families, allowing parents and professional educators to share the evaluation, planning, and structuring of educational services." Choice (A) is not correct because mainstreaming in the regular classroom is not always the best structure. Choice (C) is not correct because inclusion is recommended whenever possible. Choice (D) is true, but it is not mentioned and may not be concluded from information in the passage.

7. **(B)** In the context of this passage, *disruptive* means "causing confusion." Choices (A), (C), and (D) are not accepted meanings of the word *disruptive*.

8. **(B)** Addition is a transitional device that connects the insert sentence with the previous sentence. "The article further states" adds information to the previous sentence about *Article 24*. Choices (A), (C), and (D) do not include transitional devices that connect the insert sentence with the sentences marked in the passage.

9. **(B)** Because "14 percent of all public school students" are receiving special education services, and "half of them have learning disabilities," it may be concluded that 7 percent of the students in the U.S. have some type of learning disability. Choice (A) is not correct because students with a learning disability have normal intelligence. Choices (C) and (D) are not mentioned and may not be concluded from information in the passage.

10. **(C) (D) (F)** summarize the passage. Choice (B) is logical since students with learning disabilities are of normal intelligence, but it is not one of the major points. Choice (E) is true, but it is a detail in the major point that refers to learning disabilities. Choice (A) is not mentioned and may not be concluded from information in the passage.

EXERCISE 85: Problem/Solution— Natural Sciences

1. **(A)** In the context of this passage, *anticipated* means "predicted." Choices (B), (C), and (D) are not accepted meanings of the word *anticipated*.

2. **(A)** "They work by blocking the molecules in the cell walls of bacteria, preventing reproduction and growth." Choice (B) is not correct because antibiotics block the construction of cell walls, but they do not construct walls. Choices (C) and (D) are not mentioned and may not be concluded from information in the passage.

3. **(D)** Choice (D) is a paraphrase of the statement. "Different antibiotics" paraphrases "many varieties," and "sample" paraphrases "population." Choices (A), (B), and (C) change the meaning of the statement.

4. **(A)** "... the antibiotic actually allows it [the resistant bacteria] to multiply, while the non resistant bacteria competing with it is eliminated." Choice (B) is not correct because the resistant bacteria compete with other bacteria, not with the antibiotic. Choice (C) is not correct because the competition is wiped out. Choice (D) is not mentioned and may not be concluded from information in the passage.

5. **(A)** In the context of this passage, *issue* means "problem." Choices (B), (C), and (D) are not accepted meanings of the word *issue*.

6. **(B)** "By the 1990s, it was clear that there was a serious challenge, but developing a new antibiotic was expensive and almost every major drug company was reluctant to make an investment in yet *another one* [new antibiotic] with so many already on the market." The phrase *another one* does not refer to Choices (A), (C), and (D).

7. **(C)** Choice (A) is mentioned in paragraph 5, sentence 2. Choice (B) is mentioned in paragraph 5, sentence 5. Choice (D) is mentioned in paragraph 5, sentence 4.

8. **(B)** "... Nearly every case ... involves ... an infected person spreading the disease among non-vaccinated travelers." Choices (A), (C), and (D) are not mentioned and may not be concluded from information in the passage.

9. **(D)** Because antibiotics "do not provide a good return on investment," and fifteen of the largest eighteen pharmaceutical companies have "abandoned antibiotic research and development," it must be concluded that it could take a long time for a new antibiotic to be made available. Choice (A) is not correct because new antibiotics are necessary to solving the resistance problem. Although it is logical that the expense of development would be passed along to the consumer, the price of antibiotics in Choice (C) is not mentioned. Choice (B) is not mentioned and may not be concluded from information in the passage.

10. **(A) (C) (E)** summarize the passage, providing the reasons why the resistance has occurred, the solutions for the problem, and the alternative to using antibiotics. Choice (B) is a detail, not a major point. Choice (F) is part of an introduction to the main idea that bacteria have become resistant to the new antibiotics. Choice (D) is not mentioned in the passage.

Evaluation of Writing—Independent Essays

Essays on general topics can be evaluated by referring to the checklist printed below. Examples of Level 5 essays for Exercises 86–90 follow.

NO   ⇨   ⇨   ⇨   ⇨   YES
0   1   2   3   4   5

✓ The essay answers the topic question.

✓ The point of view or position is clear.

✓ The essay is direct and well-organized.

✓ The sentences are logically connected to each other.

✓ Details and examples support the main idea.

✓ The writer expresses complete thoughts.

✓ The meaning is easy for the reader to understand.

✓ A wide range of vocabulary is used.

✓ Various types of sentences are included.

✓ There are only minor errors in grammar and idioms.

✓ The general essay is within a range of 300–350 words.

Writing

EXERCISE 86: Independent Essay— Agree or Disagree

Topic One
Example Notes

Outline

Smoking should not be permitted in restaurants.
• Health problems are caused by secondary smoke.
• Smoke affects the taste of food.
• Nonsmoking areas are ineffective.

The state law in California makes it easy for restaurant proprietors to do the right thing.

Map

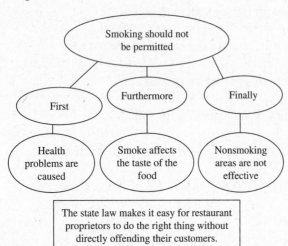

Example Essay One

In my view, smoking should not be permitted in restaurants for a number of reasons. First, many health problems are caused by secondary smoke. Although smokers make a choice to endanger their health, the other people in their immediate area are not involved in that choice. For a long time, we have been informed about the dangers of smoke inhaled by nonsmokers. It is only responsible for restaurant owners to protect their nonsmoking customers.

Furthermore, smoke affects the taste of the food. Part of the pleasure of a meal is the aroma of the food with its unique blend of spices and flavorings. If it isn't possible to smell the dishes, the experience is diminished. Moreover, the

senses of smell and taste are related. I would argue that with smoke permeating the restaurant, the food absorbs the taste of smoke, and the customers have a different meal than they would enjoy without the smoke-filled environment.

Finally, it is important to mention that non-smoking areas are not effective in most restaurants. Although the hostess may seat diners in an area designated for nonsmoking customers, it is very difficult, if not impossible, to confine smoke. The smokers may be segregated in a different area, but the smoke itself drifts into the nonsmoking side of the restaurant. Besides the unpleasant experience of eating in a smoke-filled environment, the diners go home with the smell of smoke on their clothing and hair.

In short, the state law in California makes it easy for restaurant proprietors to do the right thing without directly offending their customers. I think it is a very good law.

Topic Two
Example Notes

Outline

College curriculum
• Increase knowledge
• Career possibilities
• More leisure time

Map

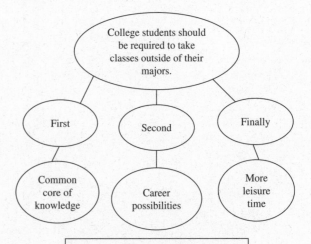

Example Essay Two

I agree that college students should be required to take classes outside of their major fields of study in order to graduate. Although it could be argued that these classes do not contribute to the career goals of students and, furthermore, require investments of additional time and tuition, I contend that there are three important reasons for the requirement.

First, exposure to a variety of subjects provides a common core of knowledge for all educated people. If students limited their courses to their major fields of study, they would not have a broad view of the world. Their perspective would be very narrow, and they would not be able to exchange views with others whose education had been limited to the study of a different field. Taking courses in many subjects allows the free flow of information and ideas among members of an educated society.

Second, many students entering college are unsure of their career goals. By selecting courses in a variety of fields during the first two years, students have an opportunity to experiment and learn about several career possibilities. Many students find their life's work in a class that they never would have taken if they had not been required to do so. Furthermore, many people change careers several times during their lives. Early exposure to many subjects in college can be valuable when a career ends, either by choice or by circumstance. Alternatives explored during college could be pursued long after graduation.

Finally, the amount of leisure time available is expanding. Past generations worked longer hours. Moreover, the life expectancy did not afford as many people with the possibility of a long retirement. Today, however, a large number of college graduates can expect to enjoy several decades of recreational activities after they have stopped working full-time. The interests that they may have developed during their college years as a result of taking a wide range of courses could be helpful in making choices for a happy retirement.

To summarize, there is more to education than merely training for a career. By taking courses outside of their major fields, students prepare not only for successful professions but also for lives that include intellectual exchange with other educated people and the pursuit of interests outside of the workplace.

Exercise 87: Independent Essay—Agree or Disagree

Topic One
Example Notes

Outline

I strongly disagree that people should be forced to retire at age 65.
- Some people are mentally and physically healthier.
- Average life expectancy has been extended.
- Some older people do not have enough money to retire.

Mandatory retirement is a discriminatory practice that really doesn't benefit society.

Map

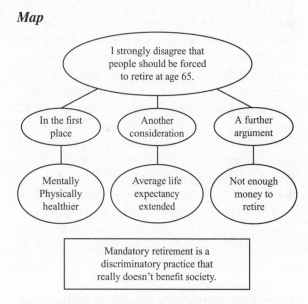

Example Essay One

I strongly disagree that people should be forced to retire at age 65 because it is an arbitrary number that does not consider individual health and circumstances.

In the first place, at age 65, some people are mentally and physically healthier than people who are much younger. Their chronological age might force them to abandon their work before their biological age would demand that they retire. For example, one of my grandmothers is in her late seventies, but she continues to teach and make a contribution to her field and mentor the younger generation of teachers in her school. Mandatory retirement would have denied her many productive years and would have deprived many young teachers of her experience and guidance. In contrast, my other grandmother has been ill since she was in her fifties. She retired before the arbitrary age of 65. Clearly, individual evaluation makes more sense.

Another consideration is that the average life expectancy has been extended by several decades. A person 65 years old might reasonably expect to live twenty years after a mandatory retirement. Without the purpose and the structure of employment, many people would find themselves living an aimless life. With no reason to get up in the morning, they could develop both physical and mental health issues. Besides, because many friendships are formed in the workplace, social isolation would also be a negative consequence of mandatory retirement.

A further argument against mandatory retirement is the fact that some older people do not have enough money to retire comfortably at age 65. Although they receive a government check, it isn't enough to afford the lifestyle that they were accustomed to when they had a regular salary. For some, it would even push them into living at the poverty level. Women especially would be faced with economic discrimination because they often take time away from their careers to care for young children and elderly parents, resulting in fewer total years in a retirement system. Unless they are able to continue working past the mandatory age of 65, their contribution to a retirement system will be much less than that of most of their male colleagues.

If an older person wants to or needs to work, it seems to me that they should be able to make that choice. Mandatory retirement is a discriminatory practice that really doesn't benefit society.

Topic Two
Example Notes

Outline
I agree that most celebrities are not good role models for young people.
• False image
• Failed relationships
• Extreme lifestyle

Ordinary people such as family or neighbors would be better role models because they are real, develop healthy relationships, and have realistic lifestyles.

Map

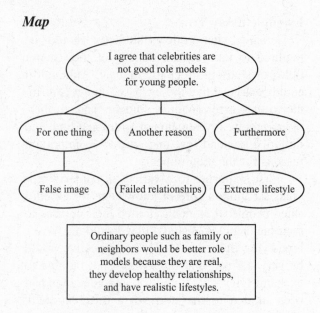

Example Essay Two
Although some celebrities use their fame to promote positive causes, I agree that most celebrities are not good role models for young people because their publicity promotes a false image. For one thing, you can't really believe what you read in the magazines and online. As an example, a model might say that she never has to worry about what she eats because she has always been thin, when in reality, she has to control her diet very carefully and may be eating a very unhealthy diet to retain the required look for her career. A basketball player may claim to wear only a certain brand of shirts when he is promoting it in a commercial, but you might never see an unplanned photo of him wearing one. In short, celebrities have an image, and it would be the image, not a real person, that would be the unrealistic role model.

Another reason that celebrities fail to measure up to the standard for a role model is that so many of them fail to achieve long-term, loving relationships. The statistics for divorce among celebrities speaks for itself. The gossip columns expose affairs, abusive relationships, and neglected children. Part of their failure in this important area may be due to their use of drugs and alcohol, which also plays out in the press, or to the fact that their continued popularity rests on their being able to retain their looks or their athleticism, and that contributes to self-involvement.

Furthermore, Hollywood stars and sports idols have a lifestyle based on extreme wealth. They live in homes that most people can never aspire to own, they travel on private jets, and wear clothing and jewelry that are far above the means of the average person. If young people see this lifestyle as a goal, they will probably be very disappointed with a good but moderate income and the lifestyle that it affords. When they compare their looks or their lives with celebrities, young people may feel unhappy with what they have, even when they are attractive and blessed with so much more than most.

Ordinary people such as family or neighbors would be better role models because they are real, they develop healthy relationships, and have realistic lifestyles.

Exercise 88: Independent Essay— Agree or Disagree

Topic One
Example Notes

Outline
I agree that social media sites offer a good way to meet people and make friends.
- Online sites are safer than alternative places.
- Sites provide a way to connect with people at a distance.
- Less stressful than traditional dating.

The best thing is to be careful no matter how you meet new people and to go slowly while you are developing a friendship.

Map

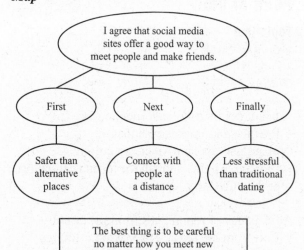

Example Essay One

I strongly agree that social media sites offer a good way to meet new people and make friends. Although there are many benefits to using them, the most compelling are that online sites are safer than most alternative places, they allow you to meet people who may not be in your area, and they help young people avoid awkward moments on a first date.

First, meeting someone new at a party or a bar can be dangerous, and the encounter can get out of control, but on social media sites, it is much safer. You aren't really in the same room with the people you see online, and you never have to meet them in person if you choose not to. You can provide as much or as little information about yourself as you want. You can be totally safe in your room and start a conversation or just look at the profiles for people who like the same things that you do.

Next, social media sites provide a wonderful way to connect with people who live at a distance. I have personally interacted with people from many countries online and have learned a lot about different cultures. One of my online friends tutors me in Spanish, and I tutor her in English. It is a friendship that I wouldn't have had the opportunity to enjoy if I hadn't gone on the site that offered international language partners. I will probably never meet her in person, but I consider her a friend.

Finally, traditional dating can be stressful for young people, but meeting online allows you to get acquainted first, before deciding whether to meet. If the person seems compatible, you can choose to have a face-to-face meeting for coffee or a meal. When you do, you feel much more comfortable because you have already talked online and it is like meeting someone you already know. For a shy person like me, that is a definite advantage.

To sum up, although the argument is often made that the pictures and profiles online could be completely false, people you meet in person can also lie to you if they aren't honest. The best thing is to be careful no matter how you meet new people and to go slowly while you are developing a friendship.

Topic Two
Example Notes

Outline

The motto "if at first you don't succeed, try, try again" is one that I agree with.

Examples of struggle to maintain a healthy weight
• Low-calorie plan
• Rigorous exercise plan
• The Zone

What is important is not to give up and to learn from each failure.

Map

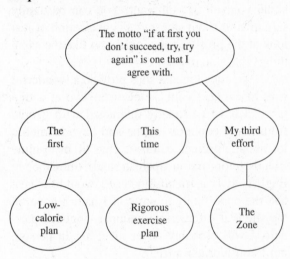

Example Essay Two

The motto "if at first you don't succeed, try, try again" is one that I agree with. In my life, I have made an effort to persevere, using several different approaches to a problem or goal in order to be successful. One example that comes to mind is a long-term struggle to maintain a healthy weight. Even as a child, I preferred sedentary activities such as reading to sports. Truthfully, I would still rather have ice cream than an apple. Nevertheless, I have launched several campaigns to lose weight.

My first weight-loss program was a low-calorie plan. For six weeks, I ate fewer than fifteen hundred calories a day, counting every calorie carefully. I learned to choose foods, such as lettuce, because it did not add many calories to my total. At the end of six weeks, I had lost twelve pounds! The problem was I felt hungry and tired all the time, and I missed the foods that I had eliminated

from my life. I gained the weight back almost as quickly as I had lost it.

Although I had failed in my first effort, I decided to try again. This time, I followed a rigorous exercise plan. I walked two miles every morning instead of sleeping in. I parked my car at the farthest end of the parking lot so that I would have to walk. I joined a gym and used machines to lift weights. Although I didn't lose as much weight as I had on the low-calorie plan, I began to receive compliments from friends on my appearance. Nevertheless, I found myself sleeping later, missing walks and workouts because I was "too busy." Parking the car so far from the door wasn't possible because I was arriving late. I gained weight again.

But I tried again. My third effort was a program called The Zone, a diet that balances food intake. Forty percent of each meal is from the carbohydrate group, including fruits, vegetables, and bread. Thirty percent is from the protein group, including meat, cheese, and eggs, and thirty percent is from good fats such as olive oil, fish oil, and almonds. By limiting the portions, by walking three times a week, and by following this meal plan, I have slowly reached my goal. It has been two years since I started The Zone, and I feel confident that I can maintain this plan.

So, as you see, I tried and tried again, but at last I succeeded in finding a program that worked for me. What is important is not to give up and to learn from each failure.

EXERCISE 89: Independent Essay— Point of View

Topic One
Example Notes

Outline

Advantages of American roommates
• Practice and improve English
• Share and explain American culture
• Provide insights and advice for new situations at the university

Advantages of roommates from my country
• Rest from the stress of speaking a foreign language
• Have a more familiar lifestyle—food
• Offer better suggestions for situations— experience

I view my home as a place to relax, not as an extension of my learning environment.

Map

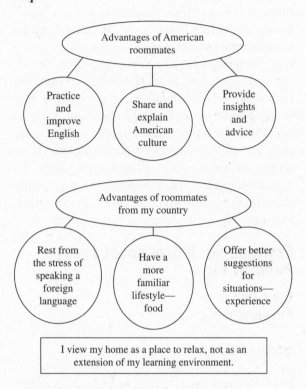

I view my home as a place to relax, not as an extension of my learning environment.

Example Essay One

There are many advantages to living with American roommates. Perhaps the most obvious is the opportunity to practice and improve your English. By interacting all the time with your roommates and their friends in English, your language skills would naturally improve. In addition, American roommates would share and explain many aspects of American culture. I know of many international students who receive their degrees in the United States without ever being invited to an American home. American roommates would probably invite you to celebrate holidays with their families. Moreover, the culture of the campus itself can be confusing. It would be very helpful to have American roommates to provide their insights and advice when new situations occurred at the university.

On the other hand, the advantages of living with roommates from your own culture should be considered. Although speaking English all the time is beneficial, it is also very tiring. The opportunity to communicate in your own lan-

guage at home would give you a much needed rest from the stress of speaking a foreign language. Even though sharing another culture is interesting and would contribute to your education, it is also more comfortable to have a more familiar lifestyle. For example, cooking and eating the food you are used to would be appealing, especially over a period of several years while you are in school. Finally, when situations arise on campus, American insights would certainly be helpful, but international students have many experiences that are unique, and most Americans don't have the knowledge to provide good advice in many cross-cultural situations. Other international students from your country may have gone through and solved the same problems and would therefore be able to offer better suggestions.

As for me, roommates from my own country would be a better choice because I view my home as a place to relax, not as an extension of my learning environment. However, I also think that it would be very important to make American friends in order to practice English, appreciate the culture more fully, and have some resources for friendly advice. By inviting American friends to my home, my roommates and I could have the best of both worlds.

Topic Two
Example Notes

Outline

Advantages of small colleges
- Professors have more interaction with their students
- The expense of a car can be saved
- Students make lifelong friendships

Advantages of a large university
- Professors have national, international reputations
- The library will offer greater resources
- Frequency and quality of cultural events would be greater

I consider cross-cultural exchange a major part of my education, and it would be more likely to occur in a small college atmosphere.

Map

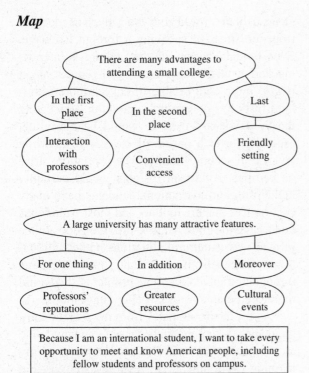

Because I am an international student, I want to take every opportunity to meet and know American people, including fellow students and professors on campus.

Example Essay Two

There are many advantages to attending a small college. In the first place, the professors at small colleges have more interaction with their students. Because the campus is small, you see each other more often in informal settings such as the student union or the library. In such an environment, it is more likely that the professor will know your name and view you as a person, not just a number on a roster. In the second place, you can usually walk to all of the buildings on campus in a short time, and often, it is possible to walk downtown. The expense of a car can be saved, and the money can be used toward academic tuition, fees, and books. Last, a small college tends to be a more friendly setting. Students know each other by name and make lifelong friendships. Although these kinds of close relationships are possible on a larger campus, a smaller college encourages them through frequent contact and shared activities.

On the other hand, a large university has many attractive features. For one thing, on a large campus, you are more likely to find professors who have national or even international reputations for research. In addition, the library will probably offer greater resources for students. Moreover, the frequency and quality of cultural events on campus would be greater on a large campus because the facilities would accom-

modate a larger audience and would there fore provide more revenue to sponsor major events.

With so many advantages for both a small college and a large university, it is difficult to make a choice. However, in my view, a small college would be best for me. Because I am an international student, I want to take every opportunity to meet and know American people, including fellow students and professors on campus. I consider cross-cultural exchange a major part of my education, and it would be more likely to occur in a small college atmosphere. After I complete my undergraduate degree, perhaps the large university environment will have more appeal. As a graduate student, professors who are engaged in important research would be useful to my career. For now, the small college is better for me.

Exercise 90: Independent Essay— Point of View

Topic One
Example Notes

Outline

I believe that parents should provide an incentive for good grades and reward their children when they are successful.
- Transition from external to internal motivation
- Setting and accomplishing goals
- Positive association from work to reward

It is all part of learning how to succeed as adults, which is, after all, what parents should be teaching their children.

Map

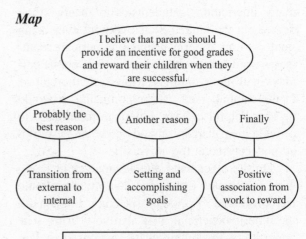

It is all part of learning how to succeed as adults, which is, after all, what parents should be teaching their children.

Example Essay One

I believe that parents should provide an incentive for good grades and reward their children when they are successful. As part of parenting, some system of consequences and rewards is usually in place to help children monitor their behavior in a number of ways, and grades easily fit into that learning process.

Probably the best reason to create an incentive for children in school is to support their developmental transition from external to internal motivation. Some children are intrinsically motivated to achieve from a young age, whereas others require an external incentive to motivate them. A gift or money provides that incentive until the time when children who aren't intrinsically motivated reach a point in their development when success is its own reward.

Another reason to implement a system of rewards in childhood is to teach children how to set and accomplish goals, one of the primary lessons for succeeding not only in school but in every aspect of life. The gift or money is only the end of the lesson. Parents should begin by setting the goal of good grades and supporting their children in steps toward accomplishing that goal.

Finally, an incentive for good grades is a good idea because it establishes a positive association between work and reward. In adulthood, people who work to achieve a goal are often rewarded, as, for example, when an employer provides high producers with a trip or a team receives a day off for successfully completing a project ahead of schedule. When children experience the satisfaction of a reward after a term of hard work at school, they begin to understand the connection.

By instituting a reward system for children, parents provide a bridge between extrinsic and intrinsic motivation, help children learn how to set and achieve goals, and create an association between work and rewards. It is all part of learning how to succeed as adults, which is, after all, what parents should be teaching their children.

For my part, I must argue in favor of family support. While I study at an American university, my older brother will send me money every month. Because I don't have to work, I can spend more time studying, and I can get better grades. My family is proud because I am on the dean's list of honor students. When I finish my degree and find a good job, I will send my younger sister

to a school or university. I will repay my family by helping her. It may not be a better way, but it is the way that my society rewards.

Topic Two
Example Notes

Outline

Advantages of working
• Friends would praise them for their initiative and perseverance
• Future employers might be impressed by their work records
• They might derive satisfaction from their personal investments

Advantages of family support
• Friends would praise them for efforts on behalf of their families
• Future employers would not expect a work record
• They might feel greater responsibility toward others in their families

For my part, I must argue in favor of family support. It is the way that my society rewards.

Map

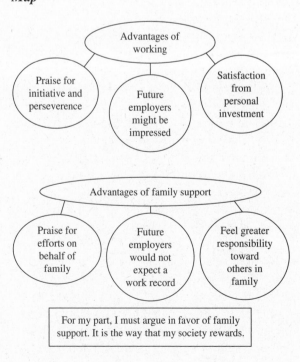

For my part, I must argue in favor of family support. It is the way that my society rewards.

Example Essay Two

Some students in the United States work while they are earning their degrees; others receive support from their families. Both approaches have advantages and disadvantages. In this essay, I will name some of the advantages of each approach, and I will argue in favor of family support.

In a society where independence and individual accomplishment are valued, students who have earned their degrees by working would be greatly admired. Friends would praise them for their initiative and perseverance. Future employers might be impressed by their work records. They might derive greater satisfaction from their personal investment.

On the other hand, in a society where cooperation and family dependence are valued, students who have received support would be better understood. Friends would praise them for their efforts on behalf of their families. Future employers would not expect a work record from students. They might feel greater responsibility toward others in their families because the accomplishment was shared. Thus, not one but every family member would be assured some opportunity or benefit.

Evaluation of Writing—Integrated Essays

Essays on academic topics can be evaluated by referring to the checklist printed below. Examples of Level 5 essays for Exercises 91–100 follow.

NO	⇨	⇨	⇨	⇨	YES
0	1	2	3	4	5

✓ The essay answers the topic question.

✓ There are only minor inaccuracies in the content.

✓ The essay is direct and well-organized for the topic.

✓ All arguments from the lecture are included.

✓ The sentences are logically connected to each other.

✓ Details and examples support the main idea.

✓ The writer expresses complete thoughts.

✓ The meaning is easy for the reader to comprehend.

✓ A wide range of vocabulary is used.

✓ The writer paraphrases, using his or her own words.

✓ The writer credits the author with wording when necessary.

✓ There are only minor errors in grammar and idioms.

✓ The academic essay is within a range of 150–225 words.

EXERCISE 91: Integrated Essay—Academic Debate

 (Track 41)

Audio
Narrator: Now listen to a professor's response to the textbook passage.

Professor:
Okay, let's talk about the pre-Columbian sculptures referred to in the reading. First, what can we make of the gold figures that have been described as jet airplanes? Well, if we ask some of the more traditional researchers, we hear a very different story. As you already know, the Inca and other pre-Columbian artisans produced a large number of small gold artifacts that represented plants and animals from their natural environment. In fact, the book alluded to this and mentioned that these objects were created to realistically represent subjects from nature. So, as we look at the sculptures, it is possible that we are seeing insects, birds, bats, or even flying fish, all of which would have been part of the known world at the time that the artifacts were fashioned.

Now the experiment is a little more difficult, but not impossible, to explain. If an object were able to fly, then a model of the object would be able to fly. So far, so good. But this doesn't necessarily mean that the object is an airplane. Bees, condors, and flying fish achieve flight. They are engineered to fly just like airplanes are. Are the protrusions on the artifacts really landing lights or just large eyes? I think you see what I mean. A lot of this is subject to interpretation.

As for the mythology that supports contact with flying objects, there are an abundance of myths or histories with descriptions of flying machines, but it isn't a very big leap of the imagination from visible flying objects in nature to flying objects that would facilitate manned flight. Even ancient imaginations could have seen birds and imagined winged flight. So even if you think that the gold objects are ancient versions of airplanes, it doesn't necessarily follow that the shapes are jet engines, and it doesn't mean that pre-Columbian peoples had actual contact with aliens who landed supersonic planes in ancient cities.

Example Notes
Passage Reference
Sculptures jet planes
1 pre-C culture artists realistic
2 experiment 1997 model flew
3 myths flying objects

Lecture Notes
Prof refutes
1 shape realistic—insects, bats, birds, fish
2 experiment—model flying bee = aerodynamic
3 myth—see animals fly + imagine humans fly

Example Essay
The professor refutes all three arguments supporting the claim that the pre-Columbian sculptures referred to in the reading passage are depictions of supersonic jet airplanes. She concludes that the shape of the sculptures are not planes but rather realistic representations of insects, bats, birds, and flying fish, all of which would have been found in the natural surroundings in the Inca empire. Furthermore, she proposes a very different interpretation of the experiment in which engineers constructed a model of the sculptures. Although she concedes that the model flew, she argues that flying animals are also engineered to fly. In other words, if the sculpture is a representation of a bee, a model of the bee would also be aerodynamic. Finally, she refers to the ancient mythology that mentions flying machines; however, she accounts for these stories as constructs of the imagination. She suggests that the pre-Columbian peoples could have witnessed flight by animals in their natural environment and imagined the possibility of human flight without ever having seen alien jet planes.

Exercise 92: Integrated Essay—Academic Debate

 (Track 42)

Audio
Narrator: Now listen to a professor's response to the textbook passage.

Professor:
On the surface, it seems that solar power should be the answer to the world's energy needs; however, as we look more closely at the advantages, we find that there are some problems associated with solar energy. Let's take this one step at a time. First, it is true that solar power is renewable and sustainable, but that does not necessarily mean that it is efficient and reliable. In the first place, because not all the light from the sun is absorbed by the solar panels, we can anticipate about a 40 percent efficiency rate. On the flip side, that means that 60 percent of the power is wasted. And unlike other renewable sources, which can be operated at night, well, solar panels are useless in the dark.

That brings us to the second advantage—that solar power is environmentally friendly. Yes and no. True, there are no by-products, but most of the photo panels are made of silicon and other toxic metals such as mercury, lead, and cadmium, so that makes solar less friendly to the environment long term.

Finally, let's look at the issue of equal access to the Sun. The fact is that the location of solar panels in areas that have cloud cover and fog will produce power at a reduced rate and will require more panels to generate power. In addition, areas with trees or high buildings may also block the Sun and substantially diminish the efficiency of solar power. And, while solar power does have a low operating cost, the initial cost of purchasing and installing solar panels is substantial—so much so that without subsidies and tax incentives from government sources, the cost is often prohibitive.

Example Notes
Passage Reference
Solar advantages
1 renewable/sustainable
2 environmentally friendly
3 available/cheap

Lecture Notes
Prof diff view solar
1 not efficient/reliable—60% not absorbed/night 0
2 not friendly environment—panels toxic ex lead, mercury, cadmium
3 not available—cloudy, foggy, trees, buildings
   unaffordable—cost panels, installation

Example Essay
The professor offers a different view of solar power than the very positive assessment in the passage. He maintains that solar energy is not very efficient or reliable in spite of the fact that it is renewable and sustainable. In fact, he claims that 60 percent of the power is unavailable for use because it is not absorbed by the solar panels, and at night, solar panels cannot be used at all.

The passage asserts that solar power is friendly to the environment because it does not emit greenhouse gases, it is not noisy, and it does not cause pollution, but the professor points out that the solar panels themselves are made of toxic metals, including lead, mercury, and cadmium, which could cause long-term damage to the environment.

He also addresses the claim that the Sun is available to everyone and can be used in rural areas that have traditionally not had a reliable source for electricity. According to the professor, cloudy skies, fog, and even trees and tall buildings can interfere with the efficiency required for solar power to be useful. Perhaps even more concerning is the cost of the panels, as well as the expensive installation charges, which can make solar power unaffordable for the remote areas that could most benefit from solar power.

EXERCISE 93: Integrated Essay—Academic Debate

 (Track 43)

Audio
Narrator: Now listen to a professor's response to the textbook passage.

Professor:
The plan for protecting threatened and endangered wild salmon in the Columbia and Snake rivers is disappointing and, I am afraid, doomed to failure. But let's look at each of the key points that are being proposed. First, let me address the federal guidelines that are supposed to regulate the harvesting of wild salmon during peak migratory periods until the populations begin to recover. Well, in response to that, harvesting the salmon really has a very small impact on the problem. In fact, all sport, tribal, and commercial fishing combined accounts for only about 5 percent of human-induced mortality among salmon populations. In addition, the punitive measures are so minor that they probably won't serve as a deterrent.

Second, the SPAs, those international salmon protected areas, well, here's the problem with that proposal: Salmon use a variety of habitats and cross multiple international borders, which make conservation areas difficult to organize and even more difficult to manage. But, for purposes of argument, let's just say that the SPAs can be identified, organized, and managed with international cooperation. Okay, that would take care of about 15 percent of the problem for salmon survival.

Which brings us to number three, that is, the hatchery reform. So increasing hatchery stocks is a good thing, but the plan really doesn't provide any new practices. Increasing hatchery stocks has been around for a long time, and it has not made up for the losses of the wild salmon populations, partly because even hatchery fish die in the river when the river is stressed. My position is that the plan fails to deal with the real issue—the reason that salmon are impacted—and that is the federal hydroelectric power dams all along the river, which account for as high as 80 percent of all salmon mortality. While all of the points in the plan are good, until a proposal includes how to prevent massive dam-related mortalities, we can't expect to solve the problem.

Example Notes
Passage Reference
Key points plan
1 harvesting guidelines
2 international protected areas
3 hatcheries supplement

Lecture Notes
Lect convinced efforts fail
1 harvesting—fishing/5% problem
2 conservation areas—problem build/manage across borders/15% problem
3 hatcheries—not achieved in past/salmon don't survive when released
Successful plan—changes legislation/regulation hydroelectric power dams/80% mortality

Example Essay
The passage lists three points that are proposed in the plan to protect wild salmon, including restrictions on harvesting salmon, identification of protected habitats, and supplementation of wild salmon by fish grown in hatcheries and released into the wild. However, the lecturer is convinced that these efforts will fail. He states that the proposal to regulate harvesting, even if successful, would only address fishing, which accounts for only 5 percent of the problem. The legislation that would establish conservation areas, besides being problematic to build and manage across international borders, would

only solve the issue of mortality in habitats, which is 15 percent of the problem. The lecturer points out that the plan to increase hatcheries is not new and has not achieved the desired result in the past because salmon from hatcheries often do not survive and thrive when they are released into the river. According to the lecturer, a successful plan for protecting wild salmon must include changes in the legislation and regulation of federal hydroelectric power dams, which cause 80 percent of the mortality in the wild salmon population.

EXERCISE 94: Integrated Essay—Academic Debate

 (Track 44)

Audio
Narrator: Now listen to a professor's response to the textbook passage.

Professor:
Everything that you have read about the Industrial Revolution is true, but there is another side to the story. Yes, the living conditions were primitive in the newly settled neighborhoods, but most lower-income families were living without running water and sanitation systems whether they were working in factories or on farms. Diseases like cholera, smallpox, typhoid, and tuberculosis were prevalent in subsistence farm communities as well as in the newly settled urban areas. I concede that disease spread more rapidly in the crowded ghettos of the cities, but it was a lack of hygiene and ignorance about the relationship between sanitation and disease that caused so many deaths among the poor, whether they were farmers or factory workers.

Now let's look at working conditions. Mass production set the stage for a factory system that provided many jobs at higher wages than unskilled workers had ever achieved. Instead of spending years to learn a trade by apprenticing with a craftsman, these workers could learn to use a machine in a few days. Although women at a factory were paid only one-third the salary of their male coworkers, it should be pointed out that before they were offered jobs with salaries, most women had toiled without pay on farms and in cottage industries owned by male family members. As for child labor, poor children in the 18th century did not attend schools and were expected to work and contribute to the family as soon as they were able. The hours at factories were not any longer than the hours that children worked on farms and at lower paying unskilled jobs in the cities.

Before the Industrial Revolution, subsistence farming was, for the most part, environmentally friendly. With mechanization, water and air pollution increased, and I won't argue that. What I will say is that it took a while for steam-engine technologies to be fully understood, and when the pollution problem was identified, steps were taken to develop cleaner industries.

Example Notes
Passage Reference
I Rev created social problems
1 unhealthy living standards—disease
2 harsh working conditions—women low wages/long hrs/children dangerous jobs
3 environmental damage—deforestation/air, land, water pollution

Lecture Notes
Lect different perspective
1 Living conditions unhealthy for low-income families factory city or rural farm—diseases ex. Cholera, small pox, typhoid, tb
2 Working conditions women not paid for farm labor/poor children no school rural areas, long hrs farm
3 Pollution after problem understood—cleaner methods air, water

Example Essay

Although the lecturer agrees with the passage, she adds information that provides a different perspective. She concedes that living conditions were crowded and unhealthy in ghetto neighborhoods where factory workers lived, but she points out that low-income families in rural areas also faced problems caused by lack of sanitation. The poor, whether they were factory workers in cities or farm workers in rural America, were susceptible to diseases like cholera, small pox, typhoid, and tuberculosis.

Again, the lecturer acknowledges the working conditions in factories where women were not paid equal salaries, children did not attend schools, and hours were long; however, she explains that women were not paid at all for farm labor, poor children did not attend schools in rural areas, and hours for farm labor were not any longer than those for factory workers.

She admits that farming during the period corresponding to the Industrial Revolution was more environmentally friendly, but she argues that after the problem of pollution was understood, factory owners made an effort to use cleaner methods that did not contaminate the air and water as much.

In short, the lecturer claims that the living conditions and working conditions for the poor, whether they were farmers or factory workers, were about the same, and the problem of pollution caused by mechanization was being addressed.

EXERCISE 95: Integrated Essay—Academic Debate

 (Track 45)

Audio

Narrator: Now listen to a professor's response to the textbook passage.

Professor:

The discussion about year-round schooling wasn't very even-handed in your textbook, so let me present the other side of the debate. First, let's talk about continuity. While there is some evidence that retention rates are better when students have shorter breaks from school, for certain students who are disabled or developmentally younger, attending school for longer periods of time without traditional breaks may cause inattention and behavioral problems instead of providing continuity and retention.

Now think about the efficiency argument. Although schools are never closed in a year-round system, and that makes it seem like the facilities are being used at maximum efficiency, the cost of keeping the schools open year-round has to be factored into the equation. Utilities during the summer months can be very costly because of air conditioning, and other school maintenance costs can increase up to 10 percent per year on the multitrack calendar.

As for the social issues, here is where the real argument has intensified. On the surface, it may seem that working parents would benefit from year-round schools because they would not need to arrange for child care during the long summer months. But actually, in communities where year-round schools have been instituted, working parents have been very vocal about the problems caused by multitrack schedules. When families have children at different schools on different tracks, then their child care planning is more complicated and more costly because they are not contracting for care at the same times for all of their children. In addition, when school days are longer, after-school activities like sports and the arts may be cut from the budget. And let's not forget that summer offers non traditional opportunities for children to learn in informal, experiential ways. Camps and recreational programs offered in the summer by camps and city parks as well as family trips are important to learning and the experiences that contribute to childhood development.

Example Notes

Passage Reference

Proponents yr-round school

1 continuity—improve retention

2 efficiency—facilities constant use

3 social issues—child care summer/working parents

Lecture Notes

Prof refutes yr-round school superior
1 shorter breaks—attention/behavior problems for disabled/immature
2 not efficient—utilities/maintenance + 10 percent yr
3 working parents w/2+ child—problem different tracks
Summer non-trad learning—camps, recreational prog, trips

Example Essay

The professor refutes the claim that year-round schooling is superior to the traditional school calendar. First, she argues that shorter breaks do not encourage continuity and retention for all students. In fact, she claims that the year-round calendar can cause attention and behavior problems for disabled or immature students who tend to do better after longer, traditional breaks.

Second, the professor disagrees that keeping schools open all year is efficient, citing the cost of utilities and maintenance, which can increase the budget as much as 10 percent annually. She uses the high cost of utilities during the summer months to support her claim.

Finally, she provides evidence that working parents do not actually benefit from the multitrack calendar because families with more than one child often have to plan for different child care options when children do not attend the same school or are on different tracks. She also reminds us that a longer summer break allows children to take advantage of nontraditional learning opportunities, for example, camps, recreational programs, and family trips.

EXERCISE 96: Integrated Essay—Academic Debate

 (Track 46)

Audio

Narrator: Now listen to a professor's response to the textbook passage.

Professor:

Although many scholars still question William Shakespeare's authorship of the works attributed to him, the evidence that they provide can be reexamined and, in my view, refuted, merely by studying it within the context of the historical period. At the heart of the controversy is the fact that Shakespeare from Stratford-on-Avon was not a nobleman with a university education. True enough, but there is evidence that he had access to a large book collection owned by Richard Field, a childhood friend who lived on the same street as Shakespeare and later became a bookseller and publisher in London. It seems possible, even probable, that he used this and other sources to create the exotic settings that he had never seen in his own travels. As to whether he could have written about the aristocracy and court life without being part of it—well, his critics correctly point out many errors in his works that would support the claim that he was not, in fact, intimately familiar with court life. It is also interesting to note that Ben Jonson, the most popular playwright of the Elizabethan reign, was the son of a bricklayer with very little formal education; however, his command of classical literature was legend, and he enjoyed the patronage of the aristocracy. Clearly noble birth and a university education were not requisite for success as a playwright in Shakespeare's time.

Now let's look at the arguments surrounding Shakespeare's death. I think we have already touched on the fact that he had access to at least one large library and, therefore, probably did not have to purchase expensive books for his own collection. In his will, he registered bequests to fellow actors and theatrical entrepreneurs. It is curious that the passage does not document the recognition by fellow actors, playwrights, and writers that appeared after his death, perhaps because several of the most important eulogies were published years later in dedications and folios of Shakespeare's published works. For example, Ben Jonson's eulogy to "the Memory of My Beloved, the Author" appears in the preface of the First Folio of Shakespeare's plays, printed in 1623.

Example Notes

Passage Reference

Controversy Shakespeare's works
1 Background—poorly educated/common birth
2 Circumstances death—will/euologies

Lecture Notes

Lect challenged theory WS not author
1 Commoner/poor education—not familiar court life + foreign settings
Friend's research library/critics found inaccuracies/Ben J not aristocrat/university ed
2 WS death—will no personal papers, books, manuscripts/no eulogies
Friend's private library, bequests friends theater/eulogies posthumously 1st Folio 7 yrs after death

Example Essay

The lecturer challenged the theory put forward in the passage that William Shakespeare was not, in fact, the author of the works attributed to him. According to the passage, Shakespeare, born a commoner, was too poorly educated to write about the court life and foreign places that were used as settings for Shakespearean plays; however, the lecturer contended that Shakespeare was able to use a friend's extensive library for research. Moreover, he reported that contemporary critics found many inaccuracies in the way that Shakespeare portrayed court life. Finally, he observed that Ben Jonson had neither an aristocratic background nor a university education; nevertheless, Jonson was the most popular playwright of the Elizabethan era.

The lecturer also contradicted the argument that Shakespeare's will did not include a listing of the assets that a writer might be expected to possess, specifically books, personal papers, and manuscripts. He explained that Shakespeare most probably did not purchase books because he was using his friend's private library, and noted that several bequests were made to his friends in the theater. The lecturer also mentioned eulogies to Shakespeare that were published posthumously in dedications and folios of his work, including a tribute to his memory in the First Folio of Shakespeare's plays, which appeared seven years after his death.

Exercise 97: Integrated Essay—Academic Debate

 (Track 47)

Audio

Narrator: Now listen to a professor's response to the textbook passage.

Professor:

Let's take these arguments one at a time. First, although the reading passage cites a handful of advances that were not attributed to animal studies, nearly every medical breakthrough in the past 100 years is the direct result of animal research. Let me mention only a few. The discovery of insulin, which has saved the lives of millions of diabetics, was tested in animal laboratories. The polio vaccine, which has reduced the global outbreak of polio from 350,000 cases in 1988 to 233 cases in 2012, was tried in research studies with monkeys. Pacemakers have saved more than 200 million lives since they were developed in the 1950s, but they were first shown to be effective in animal experiments. The American Cancer Society emphasizes that animal research is our best hope for finding a cure for many types of cancer, even if it is taking longer than anyone would like.

Second, according to the passage, animals are not the best research subjects because their bio-logical makeup is not similar to human beings, but when we compare DNA across species, we get a different picture. For example, mice are 98 percent genetically similar to humans, and chimpanzees are 99 percent similar. In addition, all mammals have the same organs, which function in essentially the same ways. Moreover, it is simply not true that animals do not contract the same diseases that plague humans. Animal rights organizations simply fail to mention that the lives of animals are also saved by the medical advances developed as a result of animal experimentation precisely because they do suffer from the same diseases that humans do, and consequently, benefit from the research. Veterinarians have a whole new arsenal of treatments for their animal patients as a result of animal research studies.

Of course it is imperative that new methods such as computer modeling and cell cultures be vigorously pursued as an addition to animal testing, not as a substitute.

Example Notes
Passage Reference
Animal studies no direct benefit medical science
1 studies do not result in advancements—cancer, Alzheimer's, diabetes, spinal injury
2 research unreliable—genes, anatomy, metabolism different—drug reaction different
3 testing archaic—computer modeling/cell cultures better

Lecture Notes
Lect disagrees w/arguments in passage
1 animal research breakthroughs past 100 yrs—insulin, polio vaccine, pacemakers/saved millions
2 mice–humans 98% genetic code/chimps 99%—mammals same organs, functions, diseases
3 computer model + cell cultures—support, not replace

Example Essay
The lecturer disagrees with the arguments in the reading passage. He asserts that animal research has advanced medical science, citing important advances in treatments and cures during the past one hundred years, including the discovery of insulin, the polio vaccine, and pacemakers. He asserts that animal research has saved millions of lives and is the best way to research and find a cure for cancer.

He also disputes the assumption in the passage that animals are not similar enough to humans to be good research subjects. According to the lecturer, mice and humans share 98 percent of their genetic code, and chimpanzees share 99 percent. He also claims that all mammals have the same organs, which, for the most part, function in the same ways. Moreover, animals suffer from the same diseases as humans.

Although he agrees with the text that computer modeling and the study of human cell cultures is important to the future of medical science, he believes that these new methods should support, not replace, animal studies.

EXERCISE 98: Integrated Essay—Academic Debate

 (Track 48)

Audio
Narrator: Now listen to a professor's response to the textbook passage.

Professor:
Now let's take a look at the arguments that are put forward in support of GMOs. First, that GM crops can provide alternatives for people with allergies. While it is true that food allergies are a growing concern, some researchers point to the fact that during the same time period that GMOs have been introduced in the food we eat, food allergies, especially in children, have almost doubled, and studies are underway to determine whether there's a link between GMOs and this spike in allergies. In an article in the *New England Journal of Medicine*, researchers reported that a GM soybean caused allergic reactions in people with nut allergies because one of the proteins introduced to improve the crop contained Brazil nuts.

As for the claim that drought-resistant crops could solve the problem of hunger in areas of the world where famines still occur, here's the problem with that. A half dozen major companies control most of the GM crop production, and they're not engineering the plants to increase yield by producing drought tolerance but rather by working with pesticides to combat weeds. So any increase in yield comes with a huge health risk from the pesticides that are more effective with GM plants. And there are better ways to combat famine, such as improving the soil, preventing crops being exported from areas of food shortage, and expanding the chain of distribution from areas where food is plentiful.

Probably the most compelling reason to support GMOs is the possibility that engineered food could be used medicinally. That's certainly the hope in the Golden Rice Project. But so far, it's been difficult to engineer a variety that contains enough of a specific vitamin to solve some of the diseases that are caused by malnutrition. At least for now, providing vitamin capsules would be cheaper and more effective.

At this time, 26 nations ban the cultivation of GM crops, mainly because of genetic contamination that occurs when a natural variety of a crop is unintentionally cross-pollinated, thereby changing its structure and even impacting other natural plant and animal life in the habitat. In addition, although current research is interesting, it provides data from only a couple of decades. The long-term use of GMOs for animal feed and human consumption is virtually unknown.

Example Notes
Passage Reference
GMO safe
1 healthy alternatives
2 increased yields—withstand drought
3 combats diseases—Golden Rice Vitamin A

Lecture Notes
prof casts doubt
1 food allergies × 2—soybean w/Brazil nut
2 yields not drought—work w/pesticides
3 g rice not enough vitamin—better capsules
26 nations banned

Example Essay
Although the reading states that some countries have banned the cultivation and sale of GMOs, the passage supports their use, stating that GMOs provide healthy alternatives, increase production in areas of cyclical famine, and combat diseases. However, the professor provides a rebuttal for all three arguments.

First, she points out that food allergies have doubled during the time period in which GMOs have been introduced in our food. Furthermore, a protein in a GM soybean actually produced an unanticipated allergic reaction in people with nut allergies because it had been engineered with Brazil nuts.

Second, the professor points out that only a few major companies control GM crop production and claims that they are more committed to experimentation to increase yields by weed control, using GMOs that improve the results of pesticides. If the claim is true, then the GM crops are a health risk, not an improvement. Besides that, the argument that drought areas will benefit from the engineering is false if the companies have another purpose for their research.

Finally, the potential for medically beneficial plants is addressed. The golden rice that was engineered to boost vitamin A has not yet been engineered with enough vitamin content to be effective in the battle against diseases caused by malnutrition. In fact, the professor suggests that vitamin capsules would be less expensive and more beneficial.

She feels that we should be concerned that 26 nations have banned GM crops because of cross-contamination, and the lack of long-term studies on the effect of GMOs on both animals and humans should cause us to slow down the consumption of these products until we know more about them.

Exercise 99: Integrated Essay—Academic Debate

 (Track 49)

Audio

Narrator: Now listen to a professor's response to the textbook passage.

Professor:

The problem is that most environmental agents or toxins don't cause cancer after only a few years of exposure, for example, smoking cigarettes. If you start smoking at age 16, you won't have lung cancer at age 20. It'll probably take a few decades of smoking until the symptoms start to occur. So we just haven't had enough time to study people who use cell phones, and saying that there's no evidence now doesn't mean very much in the long run, since most of the research was done using ten years or less as the base line for the cell phone usage. In Nordic nations where cell phones have been used for the longest period of time, researchers report 30 to over 200 percent more brain tumors for cell phone users than for nonusers. Another concern is that the technology continues to change, and most of the studies were done when the cell phone networks were using only 2G or 3G technologies. So additional research using 5G should be considered.

Okay then, let's consider the animal studies. While I agree that human studies are more relevant, the evidence of tumors in the hearts, brains, and adrenal glands of rats exposed to cell phone radio frequency radiation in the National Toxicology Program by the U.S. Department of Health sounds another warning bell. Animal studies aren't meant to provide definitive conclusions anyway. They're meant to help us design human studies, which we should do.

Finally, while it's true that brain tumors haven't increased in direct proportion to the increase in cell phone use, the most serious type of brain cancer *has* increased in areas of the brain closest to where people hold their cell phones, I mean, on the side of the head where the phone's being held. The greatest increase has been observed among adolescents and young adults. So while that isn't conclusive, it's suspicious, isn't it?

My argument is that we really shouldn't wait until we have irrefutable evidence. With almost half of the world using cell phones, we probably ought to find some ways to make them safer or, like a few countries are beginning to do, at least issue a warning.

Example Notes

Passage Reference

cell phones not risk

1 No credible evidence last decade

2 rat study—animal anatomy + predisposition

3 no correlation—increase cell use + brain tumor

Lecture Notes

lecturer contradicts claims

1 no long-term studies + no 5G

2 rat study—caution

3 young people more brain cancer—phone side

½ world users—make safe or warning

Example Essay

According to the reading passage, there is "no credible evidence" of a health risk when cell phones are used. Neither research studies with animals and humans nor statistical data on brain tumors supports the allegation that cell phone use causes cancer or other health issues.

However, the lecturer contradicts each of those claims.

First, he offers a very strong argument against the studies cited because the data that was collected did not include long-term studies and cell phone use is so recent. Using cigarette smoking as an example, he reminds us that most carcinogens require more than ten years to manifest their effects. He also expresses concern about the fact that most of the studies were completed before the more powerful 5G networks were introduced.

While he recognizes that the results of animal studies are not meant to provide final recommendations for human health, he thinks that we should pay attention to the study by the U.S. Department of Health in which rats developed cancer after exposure to cell phone radiation. It is suggestive and should be a reason for caution for cell phone users.

In conclusion, the lecturer addresses the problem of statistical correlations. Although the number of brain cancers has not increased in direct proportion to the increase in cell phone use, it is concerning that adolescents and young people have experienced more instances of brain cancer, and that they have occurred on the side of their heads where they held their phones.

The lecturer makes a chilling observation to bring his argument to a close. Half of the world is using cell phones. Waiting for conclusive evidence before issuing a warning may not be wise.

Exercise 100: Integrated Essay—Academic Debate

 (Track 50)

Audio

Narrator: Now listen to a professor's response to the textbook passage.

Professor:

Here's the problem with the case for homework. For every study that's cited in favor of it, another study can be found that argues against it. For example, an article recently reported in the *Review of Educational Research* concluded that among elementary school students, there was no correlation between homework and achievement, using their grades in school or on standardized tests as indicators. In fact, students who were assigned more than 45 minutes of homework actually scored at lower levels. A study by researchers at the University of Michigan found that reading for pleasure had much greater benefits on achievement tests than doing homework.

As for the value of life skills, although homework may be one way to learn life skills like accountability and time management, it isn't the *only* way or even the *best* way. Being responsible for chores at home, interacting and playing with other children, helping others in the family or in the neighborhood, and taking care of a sibling or pet are all ways to learn and grow without extending the lessons of the school day into the home. And it's easier and more natural for parents to teach their children in these contexts. For older students, a part-time job or an internship may be more valuable than more of the same kind of activities that they've been engaging in all day at school but see repackaged in a homework assignment.

So now, let's explore the benefits of parent involvement. I'm not going to argue the fact that parents have a positive influence on their children's education, but the *kind* of involvement shouldn't necessarily be limited to participation in their child's homework assignments. For one thing, many parents simply don't understand the homework assignments and find it very difficult to help their children with them. Besides that, low-income families may not have the resources to help. A computer and internet access may not be available at home. And a consideration that's seldom discussed is the fact that some children have to work on weekends or after school or they have to babysit younger brothers and sisters while their parents work. That's not to say that parents can't be involved in their child's education, but homework may actually be a very disadvantageous requirement for some families.

Finally, let's talk about the "ten-minute rule." Teachers and school districts that have abandoned that rule in favor of less or no homework have had some interesting results. Students exhibit less anxiety, depression, and anger. Families report fewer conflicts and less tension in the home when there's more time for sports, music, or just relaxing as a family.

Example Notes
Passage Reference
homework improves classroom grades + test scores
1 Harris Cooper 60 studies tests/SAT scores
2 life skills + study skills—goals, time, accountability
3 parent involvement = achievement in/after school
10-min rule

Lecture Notes
prof casts doubt
1 studies against—Rev Ed Research no correlation/U Michigan reading
2 life skills—chores, care sibs + pets
3 parent involve—don't understand how, no resources, working

Example Essay

The reading makes a case for assigning homework to students, citing the Harris Cooper study and arguing that homework produces better grades and better test scores, teaches life skills as well as academic content, and encourages parent involvement.

In response, the professor casts doubt on all of these assumptions. She asserts that there is also a body of research that does not support the Cooper study; for example, the report in the *Review of Educational Research* that showed no relationship between homework and either school grades or scores on standardized tests.

She also suggests that there are alternative ways for students to learn life skills, including taking responsibility for chores at home or for the care of younger siblings or pets. Older students might benefit more from a part-time job than from homework as they begin to learn life skills.

While she agrees that parent involvement in the school is important, she points out that many parents find homework assignments difficult to understand and that some families may not have the means to provide computers or other resources for their children so that the assignments can be completed at home.

Finally, she makes the observation that some children need to work from a very young age or watch their siblings while their parents work. For these families, homework may be burdensome and divisive. They may be struggling and exhausted, and homework may not be a priority, or if it is, it may come at the end of a very long day for both the parents and the children, robbing them of relaxation and sleep.

The professor strengthens her case against homework by citing school districts that have reduced or eliminated homework assignments. They report that students are less anxious and depressed, and families experience reduced tensions and conflict when they have time for relaxing or playing together.

MODEL TESTS

ITP Model Test Answer Sheet

Section 1	Section 2	Section 3
1 Ⓐ Ⓑ Ⓒ Ⓓ	1 Ⓐ Ⓑ Ⓒ Ⓓ	1 Ⓐ Ⓑ Ⓒ Ⓓ
2 Ⓐ Ⓑ Ⓒ Ⓓ	2 Ⓐ Ⓑ Ⓒ Ⓓ	2 Ⓐ Ⓑ Ⓒ Ⓓ
3 Ⓐ Ⓑ Ⓒ Ⓓ	3 Ⓐ Ⓑ Ⓒ Ⓓ	3 Ⓐ Ⓑ Ⓒ Ⓓ
4 Ⓐ Ⓑ Ⓒ Ⓓ	4 Ⓐ Ⓑ Ⓒ Ⓓ	4 Ⓐ Ⓑ Ⓒ Ⓓ
5 Ⓐ Ⓑ Ⓒ Ⓓ	5 Ⓐ Ⓑ Ⓒ Ⓓ	5 Ⓐ Ⓑ Ⓒ Ⓓ
6 Ⓐ Ⓑ Ⓒ Ⓓ	6 Ⓐ Ⓑ Ⓒ Ⓓ	6 Ⓐ Ⓑ Ⓒ Ⓓ
7 Ⓐ Ⓑ Ⓒ Ⓓ	7 Ⓐ Ⓑ Ⓒ Ⓓ	7 Ⓐ Ⓑ Ⓒ Ⓓ
8 Ⓐ Ⓑ Ⓒ Ⓓ	8 Ⓐ Ⓑ Ⓒ Ⓓ	8 Ⓐ Ⓑ Ⓒ Ⓓ
9 Ⓐ Ⓑ Ⓒ Ⓓ	9 Ⓐ Ⓑ Ⓒ Ⓓ	9 Ⓐ Ⓑ Ⓒ Ⓓ
10 Ⓐ Ⓑ Ⓒ Ⓓ	10 Ⓐ Ⓑ Ⓒ Ⓓ	10 Ⓐ Ⓑ Ⓒ Ⓓ
11 Ⓐ Ⓑ Ⓒ Ⓓ	11 Ⓐ Ⓑ Ⓒ Ⓓ	11 Ⓐ Ⓑ Ⓒ Ⓓ
12 Ⓐ Ⓑ Ⓒ Ⓓ	12 Ⓐ Ⓑ Ⓒ Ⓓ	12 Ⓐ Ⓑ Ⓒ Ⓓ
13 Ⓐ Ⓑ Ⓒ Ⓓ	13 Ⓐ Ⓑ Ⓒ Ⓓ	13 Ⓐ Ⓑ Ⓒ Ⓓ
14 Ⓐ Ⓑ Ⓒ Ⓓ	14 Ⓐ Ⓑ Ⓒ Ⓓ	14 Ⓐ Ⓑ Ⓒ Ⓓ
15 Ⓐ Ⓑ Ⓒ Ⓓ	15 Ⓐ Ⓑ Ⓒ Ⓓ	15 Ⓐ Ⓑ Ⓒ Ⓓ
16 Ⓐ Ⓑ Ⓒ Ⓓ	16 Ⓐ Ⓑ Ⓒ Ⓓ	16 Ⓐ Ⓑ Ⓒ Ⓓ
17 Ⓐ Ⓑ Ⓒ Ⓓ	17 Ⓐ Ⓑ Ⓒ Ⓓ	17 Ⓐ Ⓑ Ⓒ Ⓓ
18 Ⓐ Ⓑ Ⓒ Ⓓ	18 Ⓐ Ⓑ Ⓒ Ⓓ	18 Ⓐ Ⓑ Ⓒ Ⓓ
19 Ⓐ Ⓑ Ⓒ Ⓓ	19 Ⓐ Ⓑ Ⓒ Ⓓ	19 Ⓐ Ⓑ Ⓒ Ⓓ
20 Ⓐ Ⓑ Ⓒ Ⓓ	20 Ⓐ Ⓑ Ⓒ Ⓓ	20 Ⓐ Ⓑ Ⓒ Ⓓ
21 Ⓐ Ⓑ Ⓒ Ⓓ	21 Ⓐ Ⓑ Ⓒ Ⓓ	21 Ⓐ Ⓑ Ⓒ Ⓓ
22 Ⓐ Ⓑ Ⓒ Ⓓ	22 Ⓐ Ⓑ Ⓒ Ⓓ	22 Ⓐ Ⓑ Ⓒ Ⓓ
23 Ⓐ Ⓑ Ⓒ Ⓓ	23 Ⓐ Ⓑ Ⓒ Ⓓ	23 Ⓐ Ⓑ Ⓒ Ⓓ
24 Ⓐ Ⓑ Ⓒ Ⓓ	24 Ⓐ Ⓑ Ⓒ Ⓓ	24 Ⓐ Ⓑ Ⓒ Ⓓ
25 Ⓐ Ⓑ Ⓒ Ⓓ	25 Ⓐ Ⓑ Ⓒ Ⓓ	25 Ⓐ Ⓑ Ⓒ Ⓓ
26 Ⓐ Ⓑ Ⓒ Ⓓ	26 Ⓐ Ⓑ Ⓒ Ⓓ	26 Ⓐ Ⓑ Ⓒ Ⓓ
27 Ⓐ Ⓑ Ⓒ Ⓓ	27 Ⓐ Ⓑ Ⓒ Ⓓ	27 Ⓐ Ⓑ Ⓒ Ⓓ
28 Ⓐ Ⓑ Ⓒ Ⓓ	28 Ⓐ Ⓑ Ⓒ Ⓓ	28 Ⓐ Ⓑ Ⓒ Ⓓ
29 Ⓐ Ⓑ Ⓒ Ⓓ	29 Ⓐ Ⓑ Ⓒ Ⓓ	29 Ⓐ Ⓑ Ⓒ Ⓓ
30 Ⓐ Ⓑ Ⓒ Ⓓ	30 Ⓐ Ⓑ Ⓒ Ⓓ	30 Ⓐ Ⓑ Ⓒ Ⓓ
31 Ⓐ Ⓑ Ⓒ Ⓓ	31 Ⓐ Ⓑ Ⓒ Ⓓ	31 Ⓐ Ⓑ Ⓒ Ⓓ
32 Ⓐ Ⓑ Ⓒ Ⓓ	32 Ⓐ Ⓑ Ⓒ Ⓓ	32 Ⓐ Ⓑ Ⓒ Ⓓ
33 Ⓐ Ⓑ Ⓒ Ⓓ	33 Ⓐ Ⓑ Ⓒ Ⓓ	33 Ⓐ Ⓑ Ⓒ Ⓓ
34 Ⓐ Ⓑ Ⓒ Ⓓ	34 Ⓐ Ⓑ Ⓒ Ⓓ	34 Ⓐ Ⓑ Ⓒ Ⓓ
35 Ⓐ Ⓑ Ⓒ Ⓓ	35 Ⓐ Ⓑ Ⓒ Ⓓ	35 Ⓐ Ⓑ Ⓒ Ⓓ
36 Ⓐ Ⓑ Ⓒ Ⓓ	36 Ⓐ Ⓑ Ⓒ Ⓓ	36 Ⓐ Ⓑ Ⓒ Ⓓ
37 Ⓐ Ⓑ Ⓒ Ⓓ	37 Ⓐ Ⓑ Ⓒ Ⓓ	37 Ⓐ Ⓑ Ⓒ Ⓓ
38 Ⓐ Ⓑ Ⓒ Ⓓ	38 Ⓐ Ⓑ Ⓒ Ⓓ	38 Ⓐ Ⓑ Ⓒ Ⓓ
39 Ⓐ Ⓑ Ⓒ Ⓓ	39 Ⓐ Ⓑ Ⓒ Ⓓ	39 Ⓐ Ⓑ Ⓒ Ⓓ
40 Ⓐ Ⓑ Ⓒ Ⓓ	40 Ⓐ Ⓑ Ⓒ Ⓓ	40 Ⓐ Ⓑ Ⓒ Ⓓ
41 Ⓐ Ⓑ Ⓒ Ⓓ		41 Ⓐ Ⓑ Ⓒ Ⓓ
42 Ⓐ Ⓑ Ⓒ Ⓓ		42 Ⓐ Ⓑ Ⓒ Ⓓ
43 Ⓐ Ⓑ Ⓒ Ⓓ		43 Ⓐ Ⓑ Ⓒ Ⓓ
44 Ⓐ Ⓑ Ⓒ Ⓓ		44 Ⓐ Ⓑ Ⓒ Ⓓ
45 Ⓐ Ⓑ Ⓒ Ⓓ		45 Ⓐ Ⓑ Ⓒ Ⓓ
46 Ⓐ Ⓑ Ⓒ Ⓓ		46 Ⓐ Ⓑ Ⓒ Ⓓ
47 Ⓐ Ⓑ Ⓒ Ⓓ		47 Ⓐ Ⓑ Ⓒ Ⓓ
48 Ⓐ Ⓑ Ⓒ Ⓓ		48 Ⓐ Ⓑ Ⓒ Ⓓ
49 Ⓐ Ⓑ Ⓒ Ⓓ		49 Ⓐ Ⓑ Ⓒ Ⓓ
50 Ⓐ Ⓑ Ⓒ Ⓓ		50 Ⓐ Ⓑ Ⓒ Ⓓ

1 1 1 1 1 1 1 1 1 1 1 1

ITP Model Test

Section 1: Listening Comprehension

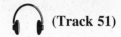 (Track 51)

50 QUESTIONS 35 MINUTES

In this section of the test, you will demonstrate your ability to understand spoken English in conversations and talks. There are three parts in the section with special directions for each part. You may take notes, but you may not write in your test book when you take the ITP.

Part A

Directions: In Part A, you will hear short conversations between a man and a woman. The conversations will not be repeated. After each conversation, a narrator will ask a question. In your test book, you will see four possible answer choices. Choose the best answer among the choices for the question that you have heard. Then, on your answer sheet, mark the letter of the answer you have chosen. Fill in the oval completely.

1. (A) Car repairs should be done at a garage.
   (B) The price was not too high.
   (C) The garage took advantage of the woman.
   (D) The car had serious problems.

2. (A) Have a party
   (B) Attend the International Students' Association
   (C) Go to work
   (D) Get some rest

3. (A) Leave immediately
   (B) Watch the game on TV
   (C) Start to play
   (D) Eat a sandwich

4. (A) He went to see the foreign student advisor.
   (B) He went to Washington.
   (C) He wrote to the passport office.
   (D) He reported it to the passport office.

5. (A) It is the policy of the bank.
   (B) The man was not helpful at all.
   (C) Her account at the bank is in order.
   (D) The check should be cashed.

6. (A) Ask Dr. Tyler to clarify the assignment
   (B) Show a preliminary version to Dr. Tyler
   (C) Let her see the first draft before Dr. Tyler sees it
   (D) Talk to some of the other students in Dr. Tyler's class

7. (A) Dr. Clark is a good teacher.
   (B) Statistics is a boring class.
   (C) Two semesters of statistics are required.
   (D) The students do not like Dr. Clark.

8. (A) He cannot do them.
   (B) They are finished.
   (C) It will be a difficult job.
   (D) They will be ready Saturday afternoon.

GO ON TO THE NEXT PAGE ▶

1 1 1 1 1 1 1 1 1 1 1 1

9. (A) A concert
   (B) An art museum
   (C) A flower shop
   (D) A restaurant

10. (A) He is at lunch.
    (B) He is at the office.
    (C) He is in class.
    (D) He is at home.

11. (A) Take the ten o'clock bus
    (B) Come back in five minutes
    (C) Go to New York another day
    (D) Call the airport

12. (A) A teacher
    (B) A textbook
    (C) An assignment
    (D) A movie

13. (A) Make corrections on the original
    (B) Make copies
    (C) Deliver the copies to Mr. Brown
    (D) Find the original

14. (A) She was Sally Harrison's cousin.
    (B) She was Sally Harrison's sister.
    (C) She was Sally Harrison's friend.
    (D) She was Sally Harrison.

15. (A) The desk drawer won't open.
    (B) The pen is out of ink.
    (C) She cannot find her pen.
    (D) She is angry with the man.

16. (A) John is usually late.
    (B) John will be there at eight-thirty.
    (C) John will not show up.
    (D) John is usually on time.

17. (A) She does not agree with the man.
    (B) She needs a larger home.
    (C) She regrets the cost of their vacation.
    (D) She thinks that houses are very
        expensive.

18. (A) He did not make a presentation.
    (B) He got confused during the
        presentation.
    (C) He should have spoken more loudly.
    (D) He did a very complete job.

19. (A) He has decided not to mail the
        invitations.
    (B) He wants to get Janet's opinion.
    (C) He is waiting for Janet to answer the
        phone.
    (D) He does not want to invite Janet.

20. (A) The baby is asleep.
    (B) The baby is very active.
    (C) The baby is not staying with the
        woman.
    (D) The baby is just about to start walking.

21. (A) The results of the tests are not
        available.
    (B) The experiment had unexpected results.
    (C) He has not completed the experiment
        yet.
    (D) It is taking a lot of time to do the
        experiment.

22. (A) She does not put much effort in her
        studies.
    (B) She is very likable.
    (C) She prefers talking to the woman.
    (D) She has a telephone.

23. (A) See the doctor
    (B) Get another job
    (C) Go to the counter
    (D) Buy some medicine

24. (A) She will try her best.
    (B) She has to save her money.
    (C) She is still undecided.
    (D) She needs an application.

GO ON TO THE NEXT PAGE ➡

1 1 1 1 1 1 1 1 1 1 1

25. (A) She is glad to meet Robert.
    (B) She is surprised to hear from Robert.
    (C) She does not enjoy talking with Robert.
    (D) She was ready to call Robert.

26. (A) The man must stop working.
    (B) There is a little more time.
    (C) The test is important.
    (D) It is time for the test.

27. (A) The woman's roommate took a different class.
    (B) The book is very expensive.
    (C) The textbook may have been changed.
    (D) The course is not offered this semester.

28. (A) Sally may get a bike for Christmas.
    (B) Sally already has a bike like that one.
    (C) Sally likes riding a bike.
    (D) Sally may prefer a different gift.

29. (A) He does not want to give Carol a ride.
    (B) He does not have a car.
    (C) He cannot hear well.
    (D) He does not know Carol.

30. (A) Take a break
    (B) Go to work
    (C) Do the other problems
    (D) Keep trying

Part B

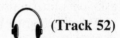 (Track 52)

Directions: In Part B, you will hear longer conversations. After each conversation, a narrator will ask several questions. The conversations and questions will not be repeated. In your test book, you will see four possible answer choices for each question. Choose the best answer among the choices for the question that you have heard. Then, on your answer sheet, mark the letter of the answer you have chosen. Fill in the oval completely.

31. (A) A lecture in a science class
    (B) Dr. Morgan's teaching style
    (C) Science fiction movies
    (D) A quiz in their class

32. (A) She is preparing for a test.
    (B) She was late to class.
    (C) She missed class last week.
    (D) She did not understand the lecture.

33. (A) The gas in outer space is very dense.
    (B) Space has very few atoms.
    (C) No sound waves are in space.
    (D) No one is there to hear the sounds.

34. (A) Most of the movies are very realistic.
    (B) The shows should have more explosions.
    (C) The woman missed a good science fiction movie.
    (D) The scenes in space should be without sound.

GO ON TO THE NEXT PAGE ➤

1 1 1 1 1 1 1 1 1 1 1

35. (A) Travel in New England
    (B) Hudson River paintings
    (C) A field trip to an art gallery
    (D) A report that the man wrote

36. (A) He thought it was a modern art exhibit.
    (B) He did not think the woman would go.
    (C) He does not like landscapes.
    (D) He does not like Dr. Brown's class.

37. (A) Western landscapes
    (B) The modern art room
    (C) Thomas Cole paintings
    (D) New England portraits

38. (A) Write her report
    (B) Travel to the American West
    (C) Take an art class
    (D) Go back to the gallery

Part C

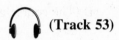 (Track 53)

Directions: In Part C, you will hear several short talks and lectures. After each talk, a narrator will ask some questions. The talks or lectures and questions will not be repeated. In your test book, you will see four possible answer choices for each question. Choose the best answer among the choices for the question that you have heard. Then, on your answer sheet, mark the letter of the answer you have chosen. Fill in the oval completely.

39. (A) Private industry
    (B) Advances in medicine
    (C) Space missions
    (D) Technological developments

40. (A) Contact lenses
    (B) Cordless tools
    (C) Food packaging
    (D) Ultrasound

41. (A) To monitor the condition of astronauts in spacecraft
    (B) To evaluate candidates who wanted to join the space program
    (C) To check the health of astronauts when they returned from space
    (D) To test spacecraft and equipment for imperfections

42. (A) Archaeologists and astronauts were compared.
    (B) Astronauts made photographs of the Earth later used by archaeologists.
    (C) Archaeologists have used advances in medical technology developed for astronauts.
    (D) Space missions and underwater missions are very similar.

43. (A) Transportation on the Pacific Coast
    (B) History of California
    (C) Orientation to San Francisco
    (D) Specifications of the Golden Gate Bridge

44. (A) Golden Gate
    (B) San Francisco de Asis Mission
    (C) Military Post Seventy-six
    (D) Yerba Buena

GO ON TO THE NEXT PAGE ➡

1   1   1   1   1   1   1   1   1   1   1

45. (A) Gold was discovered.
    (B) The Transcontinental Railroad was completed.
    (C) The Golden Gate Bridge was constructed.
    (D) Telegraph communications were established with the East.

46. (A) Eighteen miles
    (B) 938 feet
    (C) One mile
    (D) Between five and six miles

47. (A) The term "essay"
    (B) Prose writing
    (C) Personal viewpoint
    (D) Brainstorming

48. (A) The work of Alexander Pope
    (B) The difference between prose and poetry
    (C) The general characteristics of essays
    (D) The reason that the phrase "personal essay" is redundant

49. (A) It is usually short.
    (B) It can be either prose or poetry.
    (C) It expresses a personal point of view.
    (D) It discusses one topic.

50. (A) They will prepare for a quiz.
    (B) They will write their first essay.
    (C) They will read works by Pope.
    (D) They will review their notes.

THIS IS THE END OF THE LISTENING COMPREHENSION SECTION.

DO NOT READ OR WORK ON ANY OTHER SECTION OF THE TEST.

2 2 2 2 2 2 2 2 2 2 2

Section 2: Structure and Written Expression

40 QUESTIONS 25 MINUTES

This section of the test measures your ability to identify language that is correct in standard, written English. There are two types of questions with special directions for each type.

Structure

Directions: Questions 1–15 are incomplete sentences with four answer choices below each one. Choose the letter of the choice that completes the sentence best. Then, on your answer sheet, mark the letter of the answer you have chosen. Fill in the oval completely.

1. Based on the premise that light was composed of color, the Impressionists came to the conclusion ---------- not really black.

    (A) which was that shadows
    (B) was shadows which
    (C) were shadows
    (D) that shadows were

2. ---------- a parliamentary system, the prime minister must be appointed on the basis of the distribution of power in the parliament.

    (A) The considered
    (B) To be considered
    (C) Considering
    (D) Considers

3. ---------- of the play *Mourning Becomes Electra* introduces the cast of characters and hints at the plot.

    (A) The act first
    (B) Act one
    (C) Act first
    (D) First act

4. As soon as -------- with an acid, salt, and sometimes water, is formed.

    (A) a base will react
    (B) a base reacts
    (C) a base is reacting
    (D) the reaction of a base

5. The Internal Revenue Service ------- their tax forms by April 15 every year.

    (A) makes all Americans file
    (B) makes all Americans to file
    (C) makes the filing of all Americans
    (D) makes all Americans filing

6. Although one of his ships succeeded in sailing all the way back to Spain past the Cape of Good Hope, Magellan never completed the first circumnavigation of the world, and ---------- .

    (A) most of his crew didn't too
    (B) neither most of his crew did
    (C) neither did most of his crew
    (D) most of his crew didn't also

7. To answer accurately is more important than ---------- .

    (A) a quick finish
    (B) to finish quickly
    (C) finishing quickly
    (D) you finish quickly

GO ON TO THE NEXT PAGE →

2   2   2   2   2   2   2   2   2   2   2

8. Weathering ---------- the action whereby surface rock is disintegrated or decomposed.

(A) it is
(B) is that
(C) is
(D) being

9. A telephone recording tells callers ---------.

(A) what time the movie starts
(B) what time starts the movie
(C) what time does the movie start
(D) the movie starts what time

10. The people of Western Canada have been considering ---------- themselves from the rest of the provinces.

(A) to separate
(B) separated
(C) separate
(D) separating

11. It costs about two hundred fifty dollars to have a tooth ----------.

(A) filling
(B) to fill
(C) filled
(D) fill

12. Not until a student has mastered algebra ---------- the principles of geometry, trigonometry, and physics.

(A) he can begin to understand
(B) can he begin to understand
(C) he begins to understand
(D) begins to understand

13. Although Margaret Mead had several assistants during her long investigations of Samoa, the bulk of the research was done by ---------- alone.

(A) herself
(B) she
(C) her
(D) hers

14. ---------- war correspondent, Hemingway used his experiences for some of his most powerful novels.

(A) But a
(B) It is a
(C) While
(D) A

15. Sixty-two national sites are known as parks, another eighty-four as monuments, and ----------.

(A) the another eighty-nine as historical sites
(B) the other eighty-nine as historical sites
(C) more eighty-nine others as historical sites
(D) as historical sites eighty-nine other

GO ON TO THE NEXT PAGE

2 2 2 2 2 2 2 2 2 2 2

Written Expression

Directions: In questions 16–40, each sentence has four underlined words or phrases. The four underlined parts of the sentence are marked (A), (B), (C), and (D). Identify the **one** underlined word or phrase that must be changed in order for the sentence to be correct. Then, on your answer sheet, find the number of the question and fill in the space that corresponds to the letter of the answer you have chosen.

16. Interest in data processing has grown rapid since the first large calculators were
          (A)   (B) (C) (D)
    introduced in 1950.

17. Vaslav Nijinsky achieved world recognition as both a dancer as well as a choreographer.
                   (A)   (B)   (C)   (D)

18. Airports must be located near to major population centers for the advantage of air transportation
                   (A)   (B)   (C)
    to be retained.
        (D)

19. It is said that Einstein felt very badly about the application of his theories to the creation of
      (A)   (B) (C)   (D)
    weapons of war.

20. The plants that they belong to the family of ferns are quite varied in their size and structure.
           (A)   (B)   (C)   (D)

21. Despite of the increase in air fares, most people still prefer to travel by plane.
      (A)   (B) (C)   (D)

22. All of we students must have an identification card in order to check books out of the library.
          (A)   (B)   (C)(D)

23. Columbus Day is celebrated on the twelve of October because on that day in 1492, Christopher
                  (A)   (B)   (C)   (D)
    Columbus first landed in the Americas.

24. One of the most influence newspapers in the U.S. is *The New York Times,* which is widely distributed
            (A)   (B)   (C)   (D)
    throughout the world.

25. During the Great Depression, an unexpected raise in the cost of living as well as a decline in
                                        (A)   (B)
    employment opportunities resulted in the rapid creation by Congress of new government programs
                          (C)   (D)
    for the unemployed.

GO ON TO THE NEXT PAGE ➤

2 2 2 2 2 2 2 2 2 2 **2**

26. <u>It is</u> imperative that a graduate student <u>maintains</u> a grade point average <u>of</u> "B" in <u>his</u> major field.
    (A)   (B)   (C)   (D)

27. Coastal and inland waters <u>are inhabited</u> <u>not only</u> by fish but also by <u>such</u> <u>sea creature</u> as shrimps
                              (A)   (B)   (C)   (D)
    and clams.

28. Economists have tried <u>to discourage</u> <u>the use</u> of the phrase "underdeveloped nation" and
                          (A)   (B)
    <u>encouraging</u> <u>the more</u> accurate phrase "developing nation" in order to suggest an ongoing process.
        (C)   (D)

29. A gas <u>like</u> propane will <u>combination</u> with water molecules in a saline solution <u>to form</u> a solid
            (A)   (B)   (C)
    <u>called</u> a hydrate.
        (D)

30. Although <u>it</u> cannot <u>be proven,</u> <u>presumable</u> the expansion of the universe will slow down as
                (A)   (B)   (C)
    <u>it approaches</u> a critical radius.
        (D)

31. <u>Regardless of</u> your teaching method, the objective of any conversation class <u>should be</u> for the
        (A)   (B)
    students <u>to practice</u> <u>speaking words</u>.
             (C)   (D)

32. A City University professor reported that he <u>discovers</u> a vaccine <u>that</u> has been 80 percent effective
                                                (A)   (B)
    <u>in reducing</u> the instances of tooth decay <u>among</u> small children, but it is not yet approved.
        (C)   (D)

33. North American baseball teams, <u>once</u> the only contenders for the world championship, could now
                                   (A)
    <u>be</u> challenged <u>by</u> <u>either</u> Asian teams and Latin American teams.
    (B)   (C) (D)

34. When they <u>have been</u> <u>frightened,</u> as, for example, <u>by</u> an electrical storm, dairy cows may refuse
                  (A)   (B)   (C)
    <u>giving</u> milk.
        (D)

35. Miami, Florida, is <u>among</u> the few cities in the United States <u>that</u> <u>has been founded</u>
                       (A)   (B)   (C)
    <u>by</u> a woman.
    (D)

GO ON TO THE NEXT PAGE ➤

2 2 2 2 2 2 2 2 2 2 **2**

36. <u>No other</u> quality is more important <u>for</u> a scientist to acquire <u>as</u> to observe <u>carefully</u>.
    (A)   (B)   (C)   (D)

37. After <u>the police</u> try <u>unsuccessfully</u> to determine to <u>who</u> the stolen property belongs, they
            (A)   (B)   (C)

    auction <u>it</u> locally or online.
         (D)

38. Fertilizers <u>are used</u> <u>primarily</u> to enrich <u>soil</u> and <u>increasing</u> yield.
           (A)   (B)   (C)   (D)

39. If the ozone gases of the atmosphere <u>did not filter out</u> the ultraviolet rays of the sun, life <u>as we</u>
                                      (A)   (B)

    know <u>it</u> would not have evolved <u>on Earth</u>.
       (C)   (D)

40. The regulation requires that everyone <u>who</u> <u>holds</u> a nonimmigrant student visa <u>reports</u> <u>an</u> address
                                   (A) (B)   (C) (D)

    change to the university within ten days.

THIS IS THE END OF THE STRUCTURE AND WRITTEN EXPRESSION SECTION.

IF YOU FINISH BEFORE 25 MINUTES HAS ENDED, CHECK YOUR WORK ON SECTION 2 ONLY.

DO NOT READ OR WORK ON ANY OTHER SECTION OF THE TEST.

3 3 3 3 3 3 3 3 3 3   3

Section 3: Reading Comprehension

50 QUESTIONS 55 MINUTES

In this section of the test, you will demonstrate your ability to understand written English in general interest and academic reading passages.

Directions: In this section, you will read five short passages. After each passage, you will see ten questions followed by four answer choices. Choose the best answer among the choices for each question. Then, on your answer sheet, mark the letter of the answer you have chosen. Fill in the oval completely.

Answer all questions about the information in a passage on the basis of what is **stated** or **implied** in that passage.

Questions 1–10

Precipitation, commonly referred to as rainfall, is a measure of the quantity of water in the form of either rain, hail, or snow that reaches the ground. The average annual precipitation over the whole of the United States is thirty-six inches. It should be understood,
Line however, that a foot of snow is not equal to a foot of precipitation. A general formula for
(5) computing the precipitation of snowfall is that ten inches of snow is equal to one inch of precipitation. In New York State, for example, twenty inches of snow in one year would be recorded as only two inches of precipitation. Forty inches of rain would be recorded as forty inches of precipitation. The total annual precipitation would be recorded as forty-two inches.

The amount of precipitation is a combined result of several factors, including location,
(10) altitude, proximity to the sea, and the direction of prevailing winds. Most of the precipitation in the United States is brought originally by prevailing winds from the Pacific Ocean, the Gulf of Mexico, the Atlantic Ocean, and the Great Lakes. Because these prevailing winds generally come from the West, the Pacific Coast receives more annual precipitation than the Atlantic Coast. Along the Pacific Coast itself, however, altitude causes some diversity
(15) in rainfall. The mountain ranges of the United States, especially the Rocky Mountain Range and the Appalachian Mountain Range, influence the amount of precipitation in their areas. East of the Rocky Mountains, the annual precipitation decreases substantially from that west of the Rocky Mountains. The precipitation north of the Appalachian Mountains is about 40 percent less than that south of the Appalachian Mountains.

1. What does this passage mainly discuss?

   (A) Precipitation
   (B) Snowfall
   (C) New York State
   (D) A general formula

2. Which of the following is another word that is often used in place of *precipitation*?

   (A) Humidity
   (B) Wetness
   (C) Rainfall
   (D) Rain-snow

3. The term *precipitation* includes

   (A) only rainfall
   (B) rain, hail, and snow
   (C) rain, snow, and humidity
   (D) rain, hail, and humidity

GO ON TO THE NEXT PAGE

3 3 3 3 3 3 3 3 3 3 3

4. What is the average annual rainfall in inches in the United States?

(A) Thirty-six inches
(B) Thirty-eight inches
(C) Forty inches
(D) Forty-two inches

5. If a state has 40 inches of snow in a year, by how much does this increase the annual precipitation?

(A) By two feet
(B) By four inches
(C) By four feet
(D) By 40 inches

6. The phrase "proximity to" in line 10 is closest in meaning to

(A) communication with
(B) dependence on
(C) nearness to
(D) similarity to

7. Where is the annual precipitation highest?

(A) The Atlantic Coast
(B) The Great Lakes
(C) The Gulf of Mexico
(D) The Pacific Coast

8. Which of the following was NOT mentioned as a factor in determining the amount of precipitation that an area will receive?

(A) Mountains
(B) Latitude
(C) The sea
(D) Wind

9. The word "substantially" in line 17 could best be replaced by

(A) fundamentally
(B) slightly
(C) completely
(D) apparently

10. The word "that" in line 19 refers to

(A) decreases
(B) precipitation
(C) areas
(D) mountain ranges

Questions 11–20

  Course numbers are an indication of which courses are open to various categories of students at the university. Undergraduate courses with the numbers 100 or 200 are generally introductory courses appropriate for freshmen or sophomores, whereas courses with the numbers 300 or 400
Line often have prerequisites and are open to juniors and seniors only. Courses with the numbers
(5) 800 or above are open only to graduate students. Certain graduate courses, generally those devoted to introductory material, are numbered 400 for undergraduate students who qualify to take them and 600 for graduate students. Courses designed for students seeking a professional degree carry a 500 number for undergraduate students and a 700 number for graduate students. Courses numbered 99 or below are special interest courses that do not carry academic
(10) demic credit. If students elect to take a special interest course, it will not count toward the number of hours needed to complete graduation requirements.
  A full-time undergraduate student is expected to take courses that total twelve to eighteen credit hours. A full-time graduate student is expected to take courses that total ten to sixteen credit hours. Students holding assistantships are expected to enroll for proportionately fewer
(15) hours. A part-time graduate student may register for a minimum of three credit hours.

GO ON TO THE NEXT PAGE

3   3   3   3   3   3   3   3   3   3   3

An overload, that is, more than the maximum number of hours, may be taken with the approval of an academic advisor. To register for an overload, students must submit the appropriate approval form when registering. Overloads above twenty-four hours will not be approved under any circumstances.

11. Where would this passage most likely be found?

(A) In a syllabus
(B) In a college catalog
(C) In an undergraduate course
(D) In a graduate course

12. What is the purpose of the passage?

(A) To inform
(B) To persuade
(C) To criticize
(D) To apologize

13. The word "prerequisites" in line 4 is closest in meaning to

(A) courses required before enrolling
(B) courses needed for graduation
(C) courses that include additional charges
(D) courses that do not carry academic credit

14. The word "those" in line 6 refers to

(A) graduate students
(B) graduate courses
(C) introductory courses
(D) course numbers

15. Which classification of students would be eligible to enroll in Mechanical Engineering 850?

(A) A graduate student
(B) A part-time student
(C) A full-time student
(D) An undergraduate student

16. If an undergraduate student uses the number 520 to register for an accounting course, what number would a graduate student probably use to register for the same course?

(A) Accounting 520
(B) Accounting 620
(C) Accounting 720
(D) Accounting 820

17. How is a student who registers for eight credit hours classified?

(A) Full-time student
(B) Graduate student
(C) Part-time student
(D) Non-degree student

18. Which of the following courses would not be included in the list of courses for graduation?

(A) English 90
(B) English 100
(C) English 300
(D) English 400

19. A graduate student may NOT

(A) enroll in a course numbered 610
(B) register for only one one-hour course
(C) register for courses if he has an assistantship
(D) enroll in an introductory course

20. The phrase "under any circumstances" in line 18 is closest in meaning to

(A) without cause
(B) without permission
(C) without exception
(D) without a good reason

GO ON TO THE NEXT PAGE

3 3 3 3 3 3 3 3 3 3 3

Questions 21–30

During the nineteenth century, women in the United States organized and participated in
a large number of reform movements, including movements to reorganize the prison system,
improve education, ban the sale of alcohol, and, most importantly, to free the slaves. Some
Line women saw similarities in the social status of women and slaves. Women such as Elizabeth
(5) Cady Stanton and Lucy Stone were feminists and abolitionists who supported the rights of
both women and blacks. A number of male abolitionists, including William Lloyd Garrison
and Wendell Philips, also supported the rights of women to speak and participate equally with
men in antislavery activities. Probably more than any other movement, abolitionism offered
women a previously denied entry into politics. They became involved primarily in order to
(10) better their living conditions and the conditions of others.

When the Civil War ended in 1865, the Fourteenth and Fifteenth Amendments to the
Constitution adopted in 1868 and 1870 granted citizenship and suffrage to blacks but not to
women. Discouraged but resolved, feminists influenced more and more women to demand the
right to vote. In 1869, the Wyoming Territory had yielded to demands by feminists, but eastern
(15) states resisted more stubbornly than before. A women's suffrage bill had been presented to
every Congress since 1878, but it continually failed to pass until 1920, when the Nineteenth
Amendment granted women the right to vote.

21. With what topic is the passage primarily
concerned?

(A) The Wyoming Territory
(B) The Fourteenth and Fifteenth Amendments
(C) Abolitionists
(D) Women's suffrage

22. The word "ban" in line 3 most nearly
means to

(A) encourage
(B) publish
(C) prohibit
(D) limit

23. The word "supported" in line 5 could best
be replaced by

(A) disregarded
(B) acknowledged
(C) contested
(D) promoted

24. According to the passage, why did women
become active in politics?

(A) To improve the conditions of life that
existed at the time
(B) To support Elizabeth Cady Stanton for
president
(C) To be elected to public office
(D) To amend the Declaration of
Independence

25. The word "primarily" in line 9 is closest in
meaning to

(A) above all
(B) somewhat
(C) finally
(D) always

GO ON TO THE NEXT PAGE ➡

3 3 3 3 3 3 3 3 3 3 | 3

26. What had occurred shortly after the Civil War?

  (A) The Wyoming Territory was admitted to the Union.
  (B) A women's suffrage bill was introduced in Congress.
  (C) The eastern states resisted the end of the war.
  (D) Black people were granted the right to vote.

27. The word "suffrage" in line 12 could best be replaced by which of the following?

  (A) pain
  (B) citizenship
  (C) freedom from bondage
  (D) the right to vote

28. What does the Nineteenth Amendment guarantee?

  (A) Voting rights for blacks
  (B) Citizenship for blacks
  (C) Voting rights for women
  (D) Citizenship for women

29. The word "it" in line 16 refers to

  (A) bill
  (B) Congress
  (C) Nineteenth Amendment
  (D) vote

30. When were women allowed to vote throughout the United States?

  (A) After 1866
  (B) After 1870
  (C) After 1878
  (D) After 1920

Questions 31–40

Fertilizer is any substance that can be added to the soil to provide chemical elements essential for plant nutrition. Natural substances such as animal droppings and straw have been used as fertilizers for thousands of years, and lime has been used since the Romans introduced
Line it during the empire. It was not until the nineteenth century, in fact, that chemical fertilizers
(5) became popular. Today, both natural and synthetic fertilizers are available in a variety of forms.

A complete fertilizer is usually marked with a formula consisting of three numbers, such as 4-8-2 or 3-6-4, which designate the percentage content of nitrogen, phosphoric acid, and potash in the order stated.
(10) Synthetic fertilizers are available in either solid or liquid form. Solids, in the shape of chemical granules, are popular because they are easy to store and apply. Recently, liquids have shown an increase in popularity, accounting for about 50 percent of the nitrogen fertilizer used throughout the world. Formerly, powders were also used, but these were found to be less convenient than either solids or liquids.
(15) Fertilizers have no harmful effects on the soil, the crop, or the consumer as long as they are used according to recommendations based on the results of local research. Occasionally, however, farmers may use more fertilizer than necessary, damaging not only the crop but also the animals or humans that eat it. Accumulations of fertilizer in the water supply accelerate the growth of algae and, consequently, may disturb the natural cycle of life, contributing to the
(20) death of fish. Too much fertilizer on grass can cause digestive disorders in cattle and in infants who drink cow's milk.

GO ON TO THE NEXT PAGE

31. With which of the following topics is the passage primarily concerned?

    (A) Local research and harmful effects of fertilizer
    (B) Advantages and disadvantages of liquid fertilizer
    (C) A formula for the production of fertilizer
    (D) Content, form, and effects of fertilizer

32. The word "essential" in line 2 could best be replaced by which of the following?

    (A) limited
    (B) preferred
    (C) anticipated
    (D) required

33. In the formula 3-6-4

    (A) the content of nitrogen is greater than that of potash
    (B) the content of potash is greater than that of phosphoric acid
    (C) the content of phosphoric acid is less than that of nitrogen
    (D) the content of nitrogen is less than that of phosphoric acid

34. Which of the following has the smallest percentage content in the formula 4-8-2?

    (A) Nitrogen
    (B) Phosphorus
    (C) Acid
    (D) Potash

35. What is the percentage of nitrogen in a 5-8-7 formula fertilizer?

    (A) 3 percent
    (B) 5 percent
    (C) 7 percent
    (D) 8 percent

36. The word "designate" in line 8 could be replaced by

    (A) modify
    (B) specify
    (C) limit
    (D) increase

37. Which of the following statements about fertilizer is true?

    (A) Powders are more popular than ever.
    (B) Solids are difficult to store.
    (C) Liquids are increasing in popularity.
    (D) Chemical granules are difficult to apply.

38. The word "these" in line 13 refers to

    (A) powders
    (B) solids
    (C) liquids
    (D) fertilizer

39. The word "convenient" in line 14 is closest in meaning to

    (A) effective
    (B) plentiful
    (C) easy to use
    (D) cheap to produce

40. What happens when too much fertilizer is used?

    (A) Local research teams provide recommendations.
    (B) Algae in the water supplies begin to die.
    (C) Animals and humans may become ill.
    (D) Crops have no harmful effects.

GO ON TO THE NEXT PAGE ➤

3 3 3 3 3 3 3 3 3 3 3

Questions 41–50

In 1626, Peter Minuit, governor of the Dutch settlements in North America known as New Amsterdam, negotiated with Canarsee Indian chiefs for the purchase of Manhattan Island for merchandise valued at sixty guilders or about $24.12. He purchased the island for the
Line Dutch West India Company.
(5)   The next year, Fort Amsterdam was built by the company at the extreme southern tip of the island. Because attempts to encourage Dutch immigration were not immediately successful, offers, generous by the standards of the era, were extended throughout Europe. Consequently, the settlement became the most heterogeneous of the North American colonies. By 1637, the fort had expanded into the village of New Amsterdam, and other small communities had
(10) grown up around it, including New Haarlem and Stuyvesant's Bouwery, and New Amsterdam began to prosper, developing characteristics of religious and linguistic tolerance unusual for the times. By 1643, it was reported that eighteen different languages were heard in New Amsterdam alone.

Among the multilingual settlers was a large group of English colonists from Connecticut
(15) and Massachusetts who supported the English king's claim to all of New Netherlands set out in a charter that gave the territory to his brother James, the Duke of York. In 1664, when the English sent a formidable fleet of warships into the New Amsterdam harbor, Dutch governor Peter Stuyvesant surrendered without resistance.

When the English acquired the island, the village of New Amsterdam was renamed New
(20) York in honor of the duke. By the onset of the revolution, New York City was already a bustling commercial center. After the war, it was selected as the first capital of the United States. Although the government was eventually moved, first to Philadelphia and then to Washington, D.C., New York City has remained the unofficial commercial capital.

During the 1690s, New York became a haven for pirates who conspired with leading mer-
(25) chants to exchange supplies for their ships in return for a share in the plunder. As a colony, New York exchanged many agricultural products for English manufactured goods. In addition, trade with the West Indies prospered. Three centuries after his initial trade with the Indians, Minuit's tiny investment was worth more than seven billion dollars.

41. Which of the following would be the best title for this passage?

(A) A History of New York City
(B) An Account of the Dutch Colonies
(C) A Biography of Peter Minuit
(D) The First Capital of the United States

42. What did the Indians receive in exchange for their island?

(A) Sixty Dutch guilders
(B) $24.12 U.S.
(C) Goods and supplies
(D) Land in New Amsterdam

43. Where was New Amsterdam located?

(A) In Holland
(B) In North America
(C) On the island of Manhattan
(D) In India

44. The word "heterogeneous" in line 8 could best be replaced by

(A) liberal
(B) renowned
(C) diverse
(D) prosperous

GO ON TO THE NEXT PAGE →

45. Why were so many languages spoken in New Amsterdam?

    (A) The Dutch West India Company was owned by England.
    (B) The Dutch West India Company allowed freedom of speech.
    (C) The Dutch West India Company recruited settlers from many different countries in Europe.
    (D) The Indians who lived there before the Dutch West India Company purchase spoke many languages.

46. The word "formidable" in line 17 is closest in meaning to

    (A) powerful
    (B) modern
    (C) expensive
    (D) unexpected

47. The name of New Amsterdam was changed

    (A) to avoid a war with England
    (B) to honor the Duke of York
    (C) to attract more English colonists
    (D) to encourage trade during the 1690s

48. The word "it" in line 21 refers to

    (A) revolution
    (B) New York City
    (C) the island
    (D) the first capital

49. Which city was the first capital of the new United States?

    (A) New Amsterdam
    (B) New York
    (C) Philadelphia
    (D) Washington

50. On what date was Manhattan valued at $7 billion?

    (A) 1626
    (B) 1726
    (C) 1656
    (D) 1926

THIS IS THE END OF THE READING COMPREHENSION SECTION .

IF YOU FINISH BEFORE 55 MINUTES HAS ENDED, CHECK YOUR WORK ON SECTION 3 ONLY.

DO NOT READ OR WORK ON ANY OTHER SECTION OF THE TEST.

To check your answers for the ITP Model Test, refer to the answer key on page 445.

Optional Essay

Directions: Although the Institutional TOEFL® Program (ITP) does not include a Writing Section, many institutions administer an essay test along with the ITP.

When you take this Model Test essay, you should use one sheet of paper, both sides. Time the Model Test carefully. After you have read the topic, you should spend 30 minutes writing. For results that would be closest to the actual testing situation, it is recommended that an English teacher score your test, using the guidelines on page 391 of this book.

In your opinion, what is the best way to choose a marriage partner? Use specific reasons and examples why you think this approach is best.

Notes

ITP Model Test Scripts for the Listening Comprehension Section

Section 1

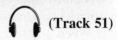 (Track 51)

50 QUESTIONS 35 MINUTES

In this section of the test, you will demonstrate your ability to understand spoken English in conversations and talks. There are three parts in the section with special directions for each part. You may take notes, but you may not write in your test book when you take the ITP.

Part A

Directions: In Part A, you will hear short conversations between a man and a woman. The conversations will not be repeated. After each conversation, a narrator will ask a question. In your test book, you will see four possible answer choices. Choose the best answer among the choices for the question that you have heard. Then, on your answer sheet, mark the letter of the answer you have chosen. Fill in the oval completely.

1. Woman: You'd better take the car to the garage from now on. They charged me seventy-five dollars for a few minor repairs.
    Man: That's not too bad.
    Narrator: What does the man mean?

(Note: There should be a 12-second pause after each test question in this section.)

2. Man: The International Students' Association is having a party Saturday night. Can you come, or do you have to work at the hospital?
    Woman: I wish I could.
    Narrator: What will the woman probably do?

3. Woman: I think that the game starts at eight.
    Man: Good. We have just enough time to get there.
    Narrator: What will the speakers probably do?

4. Woman: What did you do after you lost your passport?
    Man: I went to see the foreign student advisor, and he reported it to the passport office in Washington.
    Narrator: What did the man do after he lost his passport?

5. Man: If you don't have an account here, I can't cash your check. I'm sorry, but that's the way it is.
    Woman: Well, thanks a lot! You're a big help!
    Narrator: What does the woman mean?

6. Man: I'm not sure what Dr. Tyler wants us to do.
    Woman: If I were you, I'd write a rough draft and ask Dr. Tyler to look at it.
    Narrator: What does the woman suggest the man do?

7.   Man: Dr. Clark is the only one teaching statistics this term.

       Woman: You mean we have to put up with her for another semester?

       Narrator: What does the woman mean?

8.   Man: Do you think that you can have these shirts finished by Friday morning?

       Woman: I'm sorry. I couldn't possibly get them done by then. Saturday afternoon would be the earliest that you could have them.

       Narrator: What does the woman say about the shirts?

9.   Woman: The music and the flowers are lovely.

       Man: Yes. I hope that the food is good.

       Narrator: What kind of place are the speakers probably talking about?

10.   Man: Hello, Anne. This is Larry at the office. Is Fred at home?

       Woman: No, Larry, He's in class now. He'll be home for lunch though.

       Narrator: What do we know about Fred?

11.   Man: When does the next bus leave for New York?

       Woman: Buses leave for New York every half hour. You just missed the nine-thirty bus by five minutes.

       Narrator: What will the man probably do?

12.   Woman: Did we have an assignment for Monday? I don't have anything written down.

       Man: Nothing to read in the textbook, but we have to see a movie and write a paragraph about it.

       Narrator: What are the speakers discussing?

13.   Man: Make thirty copies for me and twenty copies for Mr. Brown.

       Woman: As soon as I make the final corrections on the original.

       Narrator: What is the woman probably going to do?

14.   Man: Excuse me. Are you Sally Harrison's sister?

       Woman: No, I'm not. I'm her cousin.

       Narrator: What had the man assumed about the woman?

15.   Woman: I can't find my pen. It was right here on the desk yesterday, and now it's gone. Have you seen it?

       Man: Yes. I put it in the desk drawer.

       Narrator: What is the woman's problem?

16.   Woman: When is John coming?

       Man: Well, he said he'd be here at eight-thirty, but if I know him, it will be at least nine o'clock.

       Narrator: What does the man imply about John?

17.   Man: I suppose we should look for a bigger house, but I don't see how we can afford one right now.

       Woman: If only we hadn't spent so much money on our vacation this year.

       Narrator: What does the woman mean?

18.   Man: Did you see Jack's presentation?
        Woman: Yes. What happened? He didn't seem to know up from down.
        Narrator: What does the woman imply about Jack?

19.   Woman: Shall I send out the invitations?
        Man: Let's hold off on that until I can talk to Janet.
        Narrator: What does the man mean?

20.   Man: How's the baby? Is she walking yet?
        Woman: Oh, yes. I can't keep up with her!
        Narrator: What does the woman mean?

21.   Woman: How is your experiment coming along?
        Man: It's finished, but it didn't turn out quite like I thought it would.
        Narrator: What does the man mean?

22.   Woman: Barbara sure likes to talk on the phone.
        Man: If only she liked her classes as well!
        Narrator: What does the man imply about Barbara?

23.   Woman: My allergies are really bothering me. I guess I'll have to go to the doctor.
        Man: If I were you, I'd try some over-the-counter medications first. They usually do the job.
        Narrator: What does the man suggest the woman do?

24.   Man: What did you decide about the scholarship? Did you fill out the application?
        Woman: I'm going to give it all I've got.
        Narrator: What does the woman mean?

25.   Man: Hello, Anne. This is Robert.
        Woman: Oh, hi, Robert. I was just about to call you.
        Narrator: What does the woman mean?

26.   Man: Could I have a few more minutes to finish?
        Woman: I'm afraid not. It's a timed test.
        Narrator: What does the woman mean?

27.   Woman: The best part is I can use my roommate's book.
        Man: I'm not so sure about that. I think they're using a different book this semester.
        Narrator: What does the man imply?

28.   Man: I'm going to get Sally a bike for Christmas.
        Woman: Are you sure she'd like one?
        Narrator: What does the woman imply?

29.   Woman: Carol needs a ride downtown, and I said you'd take her.
        Man: Oh, no. Please say you didn't!
        Narrator: What can be inferred about the man?

30.	Man:	I just can't get the answer to this problem. I've been working on it for three hours.
	Women:	Maybe you should get some rest and try it again later.
	Narrator:	What does the woman suggest that the man do?

Part B

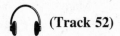 **(Track 52)**

Directions: In Part B, you will hear longer conversations. After each conversation, a narrator will ask several questions. The conversations and questions will not be repeated. In your test book, you will see four possible answer choices for each question. Choose the best answer among the choices for the question that you have heard. Then, on your answer sheet, mark the letter of the answer you have chosen. Fill in the oval completely.

[Remember, you are allowed to take notes, but you cannot write on your test pages.]

Questions 31–34. Listen to a conversation between two students.

Woman:	Thanks for meeting me.
Man:	No problem. You didn't miss much.
Woman:	That's what I was hoping. Professor Morgan usually reviews a lot of information from the previous class before she starts her lecture.
Man:	And she did that today, too. So where did you come in? I mean, when did you start taking notes?
Woman:	The first thing I heard her say was "And that's why there is no sound in space." So I wrote down "No sound in space."
Man:	But you don't know why.
Woman:	Not a clue.
Man:	Okay. On Earth, we have sound waves that rise and fall with the pressure around them. She said we have trillions of gas atoms that push into our eardrums.
Woman:	But there are sound waves in space, too, right?
Man:	Oh, yeah, but the interstellar gas has a really low density, so only a few atoms per second would hit a human eardrum, because . . .
Woman:	. . . because of the size of the eardrum and the density of the gas.
Man:	Right. So, in spite of the sound waves and shock waves, space is silent.
Woman:	And all those science fiction movies that have explosions and sound tracks are just for show.
Man:	Uh-huh. If they wanted to make the scenes in space more realistic, or more scientific at least, then they should just turn the sound off.
Woman:	Was that all I missed?
Man:	That was it.

Narrator:	31.	What topic are the man and woman discussing?

(Note: There should be a 12-second pause after each test question in this section.)

32. Why does the woman need the man's help?

33. According to the man, why is space so quiet?

34. What does the man say about science fiction movies?

<u>Questions 35–38</u>. Listen to a conversation between two college students.

Woman:	How did you like the field trip to the art galley?
Man:	I did.
Woman:	Really? I'm surprised to hear you say that. You weren't very excited about it when Dr. Brown announced the field trip a few weeks ago.
Man:	Yeah. I surprised myself. I hadn't expected to enjoy it, but after I got there, I really got into it. I thought it would be a lot of modern art, and that turns me off, but it wasn't like that at all.
Woman:	Good. So what did you like best?
Man:	The landscapes. Especially the White Mountain painters.
Woman:	Oh, well that makes sense. You're from New Hampshire, aren't you?
Man:	Yeah, I am. But I hadn't seen the White Mountain paintings before. Before the field trip, I mean.
Woman:	Right. Did you notice those Thomas Cole paintings in that little room off the main gallery?
Man:	That was where I spent a lot of my time there.
Woman:	So I guess you are going to write your report on Thomas Cole then?
Man:	Probably. How about you?
Woman:	Well, I actually liked the Hudson River School better. You know, they were a little more romantic in their approach, and they had expanded the subject matter from the White Mountains to other locations in New England and even the American West.
Man:	I liked some of the Western landscapes, but it was harder to relate to them because I've never traveled outside of New England.
Woman:	Me either, but I want to. I'd love to see some of those Western sunsets someday.
Narrator:	35. What is the topic of this conversation?
	36. Why was the man upset about the field trip when it was announced?
	37. Which exhibit did the man prefer?
	38. What does the woman want to do?

Part C

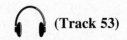 **(Track 53)**

Directions: In Part C, you will hear several short talks and lectures. After each talk, a narrator will ask some questions. The talks or lectures and questions will not be repeated. In your test book, you will see four possible answer choices for each question. Choose the best answer among the choices for the question that you have heard. Then, on your answer sheet, mark the letter of the answer you have chosen. Fill in the oval completely.

[Remember, you are allowed to take notes, but you cannot write on your test pages.]

<u>Questions 39–42</u>. Listen to "Breakthroughs in Science," a weekly radio program.

Since the National Aeronautical and Space Administration was established in 1961, NASA has been engaged in an extensive research effort, which, in cooperation with private industry, has transferred technology to the international marketplace. Hundreds of everyday products can be traced back to the space mission, including cordless electrical tools, airtight food packaging, water purification systems, and even scratch coating for eyeglasses.

In addition, many advances in medical technology can be traced back to NASA laboratories. First used to detect flaws in spacecraft, ultrasound is now standard equipment in almost every hospital for diagnosis and assessment of injuries and disease; equipment first used by NASA to transmit images from space to Earth is used to assist in cardiac imaging; and lasers first used to test satellites are now used in surgical procedures. Under-the-skin implants for the continuous infusion of drugs and small pacemakers to regulate the heart were originally designed to monitor the physical condition of astronauts in space.

Finally, with the help of images that were obtained during space missions, and NASA technology, archaeologists have been able to explore the Earth. Cities lost under desert sands have been located and rediscovered, and the sea floor has been mapped using photographs from outer space.

Narrator: 39.   What is the talk mainly about?

(Note: There should be a 12-second pause after each test question in this section.)

                     40.   Which of the products listed is NOT mentioned as part of the technology development for space missions?

                     41.   According to the speaker, why did NASA develop medical equipment?

                     42.   Why does the speaker mention archaeology?

<u>Questions 43–46</u>. Listen to a talk by a tour guide on a bus.

The first permanent settlement was made at this site in 1776, when a Spanish military post was established on the end of that peninsula. During the same year, some Franciscan fathers founded the Mission San Francisco de Asis on a hill above the post. A trail was cleared from the military post to the mission, and about halfway between the two, a station was established for travelers called *Yerba Buena*, which means "good herbs."

For thirteen years, the village had fewer than one hundred inhabitants. But in 1848, with the discovery of gold, the population grew to ten thousand. That same year, the name was changed from Yerba Buena to San Francisco.

By 1862, telegraph communications linked San Francisco with eastern cities, and by 1869, the first transcontinental railroad connected the Pacific coast with the Atlantic seaboard. Today, San Francisco has a population of almost seven million. It is the financial center of the West and serves as the terminus for trans-Pacific steamship lines and air traffic. The port of San Francisco, which is almost eighteen miles long, handles between five and six million tons of cargo annually.

And now, if you will look to your right, you should just be able to see the Golden Gate Bridge. The bridge, which is more than one mile long, spans the harbor from San Francisco to Marin County and the Redwood Highway. It was completed in 1937 at a cost of thirty-two million dollars and is still one of the largest suspension bridges in the world.

Narrator: 43.   What is the main purpose of this talk?

              44.   According to the tour guide, what was the settlement called before it was renamed San Francisco?

              45.   According to the tour guide, what happened in 1848?

              46.   How long is the Golden Gate Bridge?

<u>Questions 47–50</u>. Listen to a short lecture by a college instructor in an English class.

So many different kinds of writing have been called essays, it is difficult to define exactly what an essay is. Perhaps the best way is to point out four characteristics that are true of most essays. First, an essay is about one topic. It does not start with one subject and digress to another and another. Second, although a few essays are long enough to be considered a small book, most essays are short. Five hundred words is the most common length for an essay. Third, an essay is written in prose, not poetry. True, Alexander Pope did call two of his poems essays, but that word is part of a title, and after all, the "Essay on Man" and the "Essay on Criticism" really are not essays at all. They are long poems. Fourth, and probably most important, an essay is personal. It is the work of one person whose purpose is to share a thought, idea, or point of view. Let me also state here that since an essay is always personal, the term "personal essay" is redundant. Now, taking into consideration all of these characteristics, perhaps we can now define an essay as a short prose composition with a personal viewpoint that discusses one topic. With that in mind, let's brainstorm some topics for your first essay assignment.

Narrator: 47.   What is the instructor defining?

              48.   What is the main point of the talk?

              49.   According to the lecture, which of the characteristics are NOT true of an essay?

              50.   What will the students probably do as an assignment?

Answer Key—ITP

Section 1: Listening Comprehension

1. **B**	11. **A**	21. **B**	31. **A**	41. **D**
2. **C**	12. **C**	22. **A**	32. **C**	42. **B**
3. **A**	13. **A**	23. **D**	33. **B**	43. **C**
4. **A**	14. **B**	24. **A**	34. **D**	44. **D**
5. **B**	15. **C**	25. **D**	35. **C**	45. **A**
6. **B**	16. **A**	26. **A**	36. **A**	46. **C**
7. **D**	17. **C**	27. **C**	37. **C**	47. **A**
8. **D**	18. **B**	28. **D**	38. **B**	48. **C**
9. **D**	19. **B**	29. **A**	39. **D**	49. **B**
10. **C**	20. **B**	30. **A**	40. **A**	50. **B**

Section 2: Structure and Written Expression

1. **D**	11. **C**	21. **A**	31. **D**
2. **B**	12. **B**	22. **A**	32. **A**
3. **B**	13. **C**	23. **C**	33. **D**
4. **B**	14. **D**	24. **B**	34. **D**
5. **A**	15. **B**	25. **A**	35. **C**
6. **C**	16. **C**	26. **B**	36. **C**
7. **B**	17. **D**	27. **D**	37. **C**
8. **C**	18. **B**	28. **C**	38. **D**
9. **A**	19. **C**	29. **B**	39. **A**
10. **D**	20. **A**	30. **C**	40. **C**

Section 3: Reading Comprehension

1. **A**	11. **B**	21. **D**	31. **D**	41. **A**
2. **C**	12. **A**	22. **C**	32. **D**	42. **C**
3. **B**	13. **A**	23. **D**	33. **D**	43. **B**
4. **A**	14. **B**	24. **A**	34. **D**	44. **C**
5. **B**	15. **A**	25. **A**	35. **B**	45. **C**
6. **C**	16. **C**	26. **D**	36. **B**	46. **A**
7. **D**	17. **C**	27. **D**	37. **C**	47. **B**
8. **B**	18. **A**	28. **C**	38. **A**	48. **B**
9. **A**	19. **B**	29. **A**	39. **C**	49. **B**
10. **B**	20. **C**	30. **D**	40. **C**	50. **D**

iBT® Model Test

Reading Section

30 QUESTIONS 54 MINUTES

Directions: This section tests your ability to understand reading passages like those in college textbooks. After each passage, you will answer 10 questions about it. You will have 18 minutes to read each passage and answer the comprehension questions. You may use notes to answer. There are two types of reading comprehension questions. The multiple-choice questions require that you choose the best of four possible answers. The computer-assisted questions require that you follow directions on the page or on the screen. You may return to previous questions to change answers or answer questions that you may have left blank.

Reading 1

Social Norms

Paragraph 1   Norms are the expectations and rules that govern social behavior. Although norms vary greatly across cultural groups, and they are basically subjective, they provide guidance so that members of social groups can make decisions about how to behave in situations and how to judge the behaviors of others. For example, in the United States, appropriate behavior in an elevator would include facing toward the front where the door will open, looking at the number pad, or asking which floor another rider would like. People who insist on personal conversation or turn their backs to the elevator door may be considered odd or even dangerous.

2   Sociologists consider at least four types of norms, including mores, folkways, laws, and taboos. *Mores* are violations of moral codes that are dictated by the values or ethics of a culture and are considered essential to the survival of the society. Mores are clear indicators of the difference between right and wrong and are often associated with religious practices. For example, violent crimes such as murder and theft are not only strongly disapproved of but also subject to serious punishments. Those who violate mores can be imprisoned or exiled. They are viewed as sinful or malicious, and in some societies, may even be executed.

3   In contrast, *folkways* are customs that are expected but not considered morally right or wrong. Folkways organize casual interactions and are learned by repetition and routines. How we greet people, dress ourselves, or go about our daily activities are regulated by conventions in society, and others have expectations for them. Folkways distinguish between polite and rude behavior. The ways that folkways are enforced may vary among cultures, but ridicule and gossip usually keep most people from violating them. Those who insist on behaving outside the expectations for customary behavior are considered strange or eccentric.

4   [A] Next, *laws* exist to discourage behavior that could cause harm to others, especially crimes that damage property or inflict violence on innocent people. [B] Laws are norms that are formally inscribed at the state or national level and enforced by organizations such as the police or designated members of society, who have the right to exercise force, if necessary, to control those who violate the norms. [C] When they break the laws of their society, criminals may be incarcerated or, for the most serious violations, even subject to a death penalty. [D]

5   There is a close relationship between mores and laws; for instance, a society might have a high value on respect for property, and people who steal would be considered morally, as well as legally, wrong. There would be a law to punish the offender, but collectively, people in the community would probably inform others about the thief or shun the family as well. Ironically, laws can be changed more easily than mores and folkways, which means that legislation may not perfectly reflect the values or morals of the community.

6   Finally, *taboos* prohibit certain behaviors that are considered either too sacred for the public or too repulsive for society. Breaking a taboo is generally very objectionable; however, the same taboos are not practiced across cultures. In many societies, only the priests can touch religious objects. Certain dietary restrictions are also taboos, as, for example, eating pork in Muslim or Jewish communities or eating meat of any kind in Hindu societies. Taboos about appropriate marriage partners restrict unions between close family members in many cultures throughout the world.

7   In order for a society to function, its members must internalize the social norms and teach them to their children. There is considerable pressure to conform to social norms, and most of us generally do conform to the mores, folkways, laws, and taboos of our societies, in part because individual behavior can affect groups. In fact, some group members are held responsible for the behavior of the entire group; as, for example, when an organization provides incentives for employees on teams, and every team member must accomplish a goal for the entire team to be rewarded; when a family is held responsible for the actions of all of its members; or when all the troops in a military unit are punished for the infractions of one person in the unit. Even without such obvious group accountability, social norms provide communities with organization and order. We learn the norms of our cultures in order to predict the responses of other people and establish social relationships.

1. The author uses the example of people riding in an elevator in paragraph 1 in order to
   Ⓐ explain moral rules that deal with property and safety
   Ⓑ contrast social rules as they are practiced in various cultures
   Ⓒ demonstrate appropriate behaviors for a formal social situation
   Ⓓ illustrate how social control occurs when norms are broken

2. All of the following are mentioned as ways to enforce mores EXCEPT
   Ⓐ gossip
   Ⓑ death
   Ⓒ imprisonment
   Ⓓ exile

3. According to paragraph 3, people who do not observe folkways are considered
   Ⓐ dangerous
   Ⓑ odd
   Ⓒ sinful
   Ⓓ uneducated

4. The word them in paragraph 3 refers to
   Ⓐ ways
   Ⓑ folkways
   Ⓒ cultures
   Ⓓ people

5. Look at the four squares [□] that indicate where the following sentence can be added to the passage. Choose the best place to insert the sentence.

   Those who break the law are identified as criminals.
   Ⓐ
   Ⓑ
   Ⓒ
   Ⓓ

6. Which of the following statements best expresses the essential information in the highlighted sentence in the passage? *Incorrect* answer choices change the meaning or leave out information.
   Ⓐ Changes in the society require changes in the laws to uphold the morals and values that they protect.
   Ⓑ Laws may not be an exact expression of the ethical standards of the society because it is not as difficult to amend them.
   Ⓒ The morals of a society are the basis for the laws that are constantly modified as the society changes its values.
   Ⓓ Mores and folkways change along with new laws that are passed to better reflect the values of the society.

7. The word considerable in the passage is closest in meaning to
   Ⓐ huge
   Ⓑ regular
   Ⓒ new
   Ⓓ changing

8. The word predict in the passage is closest in meaning to
    Ⓐ expect
    Ⓑ control
    Ⓒ judge
    Ⓓ observe

9. According to the passage, what do folkways, mores, laws, and taboos have in common?
    Ⓐ They are experienced subjectively.
    Ⓑ They are all viewed as equally important.
    Ⓒ They are formalized and enforceable.
    Ⓓ They are all considered norms.

10. Complete the summary by choosing THREE answer choices that express the most important
    ideas in the passage. The other answer choices do not belong in the summary because they
    express ideas that are not in the passage or they do not refer to the major points.
    This question is worth two points.

    Norms are social rules that specify appropriate and inappropriate behavior in given situations.
    Ⓐ Folkways provide conventional standards for daily activities such as grooming.
    Ⓑ People who violate mores are usually subject to harsh punishment for their behavior.
    Ⓒ Beliefs are the basis for many of the norms and values of a given culture.
    Ⓓ Group members may experience either advantage or harm from the actions of associates.
    Ⓔ Laws are rules that are enforced by a political organization with legitimate authority.
    Ⓕ Strict norms that control moral and ethical behavior are referred to as mores.

Reading 2

The Death of Stars

Paragraph 1   It is not an oversimplification to view the life of stars as a constant battle between the force of gravity on the surface and the nuclear fires at the core. Using our Sun as an example, when the gas cloud began to contract, gravity compressed it inward in an effort to cause it to collapse, but the increase in temperature in the core raised the pressure in the interior and balanced the force of gravity. However, long-term gravity has the advantage. In other words, a star can only combat gravity as long as it has hydrogen to fuel the fires in the core.

2   When the hydrogen is depleted, gravity will prevail. Through a series of nuclear reactions, the residual hydrogen in the core will begin to burn around the extinguished core and the helium in the core. Eventually, they will result in *helium burning*, in which the helium core burns to form carbon. Because the temperature is never quite high enough to ignite the carbon, the helium core is surrounded by a burning hydrogen layer, a process that can continue for a very long time.

3   Every star eventually depletes its fuel, but what happens next is determined by the mass of the star, because that, in turn, determines the maximum temperature that can be reached in the core. A As a star begins fusing hydrogen into helium, a star that has a low mass will fuse it into helium only and will never get hot enough to fuse the helium into carbon. B Thus, a star with a pure helium composition, that is, all M class stars, becomes a red dwarf. C About three-quarters of all stars fall into this category. D As a result, red dwarfs usually cannot be seen with the naked eye from the Earth.

4   In stars about the size of the Sun, the core will fuse the last of its hydrogen into helium, at which point the core will start to shrink, and heat is released as a result of the sudden compression of the layers of gas. The center of the core collapses first, leaving a hydrogen shell that burns and causes the radius to expand to 250 times its original size, transforming itself into a red giant. The core will expand and cool, and upper layers will eject material around it, forming a planetary nebula, which is a very large sphere of gas and dust. During the final stages, the core will cool into a white dwarf, a small dense star about the size of a planet, and eventually into a black dwarf, which is really just a white dwarf that has cooled and no longer emits heat or light. It isn't a fast process, however. For the entire cycle to be completed, it will take several billion years.

5   Stars that are more massive than the Sun will not only fuse
hydrogen and helium into carbon, but, after that, the core will become
hot enough to fuse the carbon into heavier elements such as oxygen,
neon, magnesium, and iron. In less than one second, the iron core, no
longer able to burn, shrinks, reheats, and explodes, releasing energy
and material into space and eventually transforming itself into a
spectacular supernova. The outer layers of the star are blown off in
the explosion, suddenly increasing in brightness. The shock waves
from these massive stars and the material that bursts out from the
supernova can actually create new stars, but this process is very rare.

6   But what will happen to planet Earth when our Sun loses
its battle with gravity? When the core burns out and the burning
hydrogen surrounding it is pulled in, a temporary collapse will
increase the energy, and the surface of the Sun will expand past the
orbits of Mercury and Venus but the solar wind will probably push
the planets out, leaving only Mercury as a casualty at this point.
However, life will not be possible because the temperature will
increase, the oceans will evaporate, and nitrogen and carbon dioxide
will probably become the major components of the atmosphere.
Fortunately, we don't have to worry about this any time soon, because
the Sun has only reached middle age and shouldn't even begin the
process for another five billion years.

11. Which of the following sentences best expresses the essential information in the highlighted sentence in the passage? *Incorrect* answer choices change the meaning or leave out information.
    Ⓐ A star burns hydrogen because of gravity.
    Ⓑ The force of gravity pulls a star's hydrogen in.
    Ⓒ While a star is burning hydrogen, it can resist gravity.
    Ⓓ Hydrogen will burn for a long time before gravity affects it.

12. The word depleted in the passage is closest in meaning to
    Ⓐ scattered
    Ⓑ consumed
    Ⓒ propelled
    Ⓓ exposed

13. According to paragraph 2, what happens in *helium burning*?
    Ⓐ Carbon creates hot ashes that burst into flame.
    Ⓑ Hydrogen forms a shell around the helium.
    Ⓒ Temperatures continue to rise as the helium burns.
    Ⓓ The helium prevents nuclear reactions.

14. Look at the four squares [□] that indicate where the following sentence can be added to the passage. Choose the best place to insert the sentence.

    In about one hundred million years, the helium is completely exhausted.
    Ａ
    Ｂ
    Ｃ
    Ｄ

15. What is NOT true of the largest stars in the universe?
    Ⓐ They have the potential to create new stars.
    Ⓑ They will eventually create a huge explosion.
    Ⓒ They are not a very common class of stars.
    Ⓓ They burn their fuel more quickly than smaller stars.

16. The word massive in the passage is closest in meaning to
    Ⓐ hotter
    Ⓑ brighter
    Ⓒ larger
    Ⓓ older

17. According to paragraph 5, how are new stars created?
    - Ⓐ Their iron core shrinks and explodes.
    - Ⓑ Heavy elements combine and create a mass.
    - Ⓒ Hydrogen and helium fuse into a carbon core.
    - Ⓓ The material from a supernova produces them.

18. According to information in the passage, what can be inferred about the Sun?
    - Ⓐ Solar winds are probably beginning to increase now.
    - Ⓑ The age of the Sun is estimated at 2.25 billion years.
    - Ⓒ The Sun is about halfway through its natural cycle.
    - Ⓓ The Sun will destroy three planets when it expands.

19. According to paragraph 6, all of the following are true of the final stages of the Sun EXCEPT
    - Ⓐ the solar winds accelerate
    - Ⓑ the surface of the Sun expands
    - Ⓒ Mercury is consumed by the Sun
    - Ⓓ the carbon core turns the Sun black

20. Complete the table below by classifying each of the answer choices. Two choices will not be used.
    - Ⓐ Red giant
    - Ⓑ Red dwarf
    - Ⓒ White giant
    - Ⓓ White dwarf
    - Ⓔ Black dwarf
    - Ⓕ Black hole
    - Ⓖ Supernova

Low mass M class stars	
Stars like our Sun	
The largest stars	

Reading 3

Methods for Sculpture

Modeling

Paragraph 1   Modeled sculptures are created when a soft material is built up or shaped over a metal framework. The most common material is clay because it is very pliable and can be found in most parts of the world. Because it can be reworked as long as the clay is wet, modeling clay is often used by sculptors in the same way that painters use a sketch pad to do a trial drawing before putting the final work on canvas. Sculptors continue working the clay until they are satisfied with a final shape that may be part of a larger work or may be redone in a different technique or material.

2   When clay is heated to a very hot temperature, it becomes hard and is very durable . Often referred to by the Italian phrase *terra cotta*, many examples of firing clay have survived since ancient times. One of the most famous of these is the terra cotta army, more than 7,000 life-sized soldiers and horses buried 2,200 years ago in China and discovered in 1974.

Casting

3   Casting is quite a different process. ⒶSculptures that are cast are made from a material that is melted down, usually metal. Ⓑ Because bronze becomes molten when heated and can be poured into small crevices in a mold, it is especially popular with artists who use the casting method. Ⓒ Also, when it hardens, bronze is both beautiful and strong. Ⓓ

4   The lost wax process is the most common method for casting metal. Also referred to as the "replacement method" or *cire perdue*, the steps are very basic. First a model of the sculpture is made in wax. Then the wax object is covered with a fireproof clay mold. When the clay is hardened, it is heated so that the wax melts and runs out of the mold; that is, the wax is "lost," leaving the shape of the sculpture inside the clay mold. The metal is poured into the mold, replacing the wax. After the metal cools, the mold is broken, any flaws that have resulted in the process are repaired, and the metal is polished. Since the mold is broken in the process, only one sculpture is produced.

5   The oldest known example of this technique is a charm from the Indus Valley, estimated at about 6,000 years old, but other ancient casts have also been found in Africa. Today, however, the process has been modified to allow for multiple copies of the sculpture by using materials that can be preserved; for example, synthetic rubber can be used to form a mold around a solid sculpture. Melted wax is then applied inside the mold, and after it hardens, the hollow wax casting is encased in plaster. The plaster copy is called the

investment. The metal is poured into the investment, and when the investment is heated, the wax runs out, and the investment is broken to free the metal sculpture. Unlike the ancient lost wax method, however, the modern method preserves the rubber mold from the investment for future use.

Carving

6   In carving, the artist cuts or chips away a shape from a block of stone, wood, or some other hard material until the form emerges. In contrast to both modeling and casting, which require the addition of material to create the sculpture, this process is a subtractive method whereby material is eliminated from the outside. The variety of wood or the type of stone must be considered when selecting material for carving. Sculptors like marble because it is relatively soft and easy to work with, comes in many shades, and tends to become more beautiful with age. With both wood and stone, the artist must work with the grain of the block to avoid splintering or cracking. Throughout history, carvers have sought out local materials for carving, learned their properties, and developed tools and techniques to create their works.

Assembling

7   Like modeling, another additive process is assembling, in which sculptors gather and join different items to create, that is *assemble*, a work of art. The objects can be either natural or manufactured and are often found either in nature or in discarded recyclables. Assemblage creates art through the juxtaposition of objects, using glue, nails, or other materials to connect them.

21. Which of the following can be inferred from paragraph 1?
    ⓐ The author prefers modeling to all of the other methods of sculpture.
    ⓑ A sculptor might experiment with a clay sculpture before creating it in marble.
    ⓒ Clay is not easy to work with because it can get hard before the piece is finished.
    ⓓ Artists who are talented at drawing often create sculptures as well as paintings.

22. Why does the author mention a "sketch pad" in paragraph 1?
    ⓐ To prove that drawing is easier than sculpting
    ⓑ To name several techniques that artists use
    ⓒ To compare the sketch pad with clay
    ⓓ To suggest a trial drawing before sculpting

23. The word durable in the passage is closest in meaning to
    ⓐ strong
    ⓑ fine
    ⓒ practical
    ⓓ smooth

24. Look at the four squares [□] that indicate where the following sentence can be added to the passage. Choose the best place to insert the sentence.

    All but the simplest bronze sculptures are cast in two pieces and then welded together.
    Ⓐ
    Ⓑ
    Ⓒ
    Ⓓ

25. The word flaws in the passage is closest in meaning to
    ⓐ enhancements
    ⓑ hazards
    ⓒ defects
    ⓓ innovations

26. According to paragraph 5, from which of the following materials is the investment in the modern process made?
    ⓐ Clay
    ⓑ Plaster
    ⓒ Metal
    ⓓ Rubber

27. What is the advantage of investment casting?
    ⓐ The sculpture is stronger because it is solid.
    ⓑ Copies of the sculpture may be made.
    ⓒ The method is faster than regular casting.
    ⓓ Rubber is easier to work with than clay.

28. The phrase this process in paragraph 6 is closest in meaning to
   Ⓐ carving
   Ⓑ modeling
   Ⓒ casting
   Ⓓ sculpture

29. According to the passage, all of the following considerations are important in carving EXCEPT
   Ⓐ the type of stone
   Ⓑ the grain of the wood
   Ⓒ the nature of the tools
   Ⓓ the age of the material

30. Complete the summary by choosing THREE answer choices that express the most important ideas in the passage. The other answer choices do not belong in the summary because they express ideas that are not in the passage or they do not refer to the major points. *This question is worth two points.*

   There are four methods that are still used for sculpture.
   Ⓐ The lost wax process is the most common method for casting metal sculptures.
   Ⓑ The qualities of bronze make it a popular material for casting sculptures.
   Ⓒ Many ancient sculptures have survived because they were buried in wet clay.
   Ⓓ Modeling and assembling are additive methods for sculpture.
   Ⓔ In carving, the sculptor must work aggressively to remove the material.
   Ⓕ Rubber molds have improved the casting method because they can be reused.

Listening Section

39 QUESTIONS 57 MINUTES

Directions: This section tests your ability to understand campus conversations and academic lectures in English. You will hear each conversation and lecture one time. You may take notes while you listen. After each conversation or lecture, you will answer questions about it. You may use your notes to answer. There are two types of listening comprehension questions. The multiple-choice questions require that you choose the best of four possible answers. The computer-assisted questions require that you follow directions on the page or screen. You must answer each question in order to go to the next question. You cannot return to previous questions.

Part One: Listening 1

 (Track 54)

Directions: Choose the best answer for multiple-choice questions. Follow the directions on the page for computer-assisted questions.

1. What is the main purpose of the conversation?
   - Ⓐ The student is looking for help in his English class.
   - Ⓑ The student wants a job as a tutor in the Learning Center.
   - Ⓒ The student is there to attend a workshop in writing.
   - Ⓓ The student needs to take a math placement test.

2. What kinds of services are available at the Learning Center?
   Choose 2 answers.
   - Ⓐ Workshops
   - Ⓑ Placement tests
   - Ⓒ Tutoring sessions
   - Ⓓ English classes

3. Why is the man having problems in his psychology class?
   - Ⓐ The research is very difficult for him.
   - Ⓑ He has too many assignments to read.
   - Ⓒ Writing the paper takes him a long time.
   - Ⓓ He doesn't understand the syllabus.

4. What does the woman suggest that the man do next?
   - Ⓐ Register for Workshop 7
   - Ⓑ Request individualized tutoring
   - Ⓒ Bring his class notes to the woman
   - Ⓓ Put on a sweater or a jacket

5. Why does the man say this:
   "I don't mean to be rude, but that doesn't sound like enough time to get me squared away."
   - Ⓐ He is trying to disagree respectfully.
   - Ⓑ He wants a refund for the registration.
   - Ⓒ He thinks he has misunderstood.
   - Ⓓ He is surprised about the break.

Listening 2

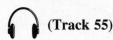 (Track 55)

6. What is the professor mainly discussing?
   Ⓐ Victorian designs and decorations
   Ⓑ The Arts and Crafts style
   Ⓒ Mass production in the industrial age
   Ⓓ The East Aurora Workshop

7. Why does the professor say this:
   "As you will recall from our study of the Victorians, theirs was an age of quantity."
   Ⓐ To introduce the class to the Victorian period
   Ⓑ To criticize the Victorian style of decoration
   Ⓒ To refer to a previous lecture about the Victorian age
   Ⓓ To give an example of the Victorian style

8. What are two design elements of Arts and Crafts chairs?
   Choose 2 answers.
   A Comfortable cushions
   B Carved legs and arms
   C Large proportions
   D Rich fabrics

9. What did the motto "hand, head, and heart" mean?
   Ⓐ Craftsmen should love their work.
   Ⓑ Artisans should live together.
   Ⓒ Tradition is important for artists.
   Ⓓ No machines should be used.

10. According to the professor, why did the Arts and Crafts bungalows become so popular?
    Ⓐ They had front porches that could be used as outdoor rooms.
    Ⓑ They were not as expensive as the homes of the Victorian era.
    Ⓒ The workmanship on the bungalows impressed the neighbors.
    Ⓓ They were like the farm homes that the middle class had moved from.

11. Why did the professor use the example of the Van Briggle Pottery Works?
    Ⓐ To prove her point about the continuing popularity of the Arts and Crafts style
    Ⓑ To demonstrate one of the advantages of the matte glazing process
    Ⓒ To give an example of highly prized antique Arts and Crafts sculptures
    Ⓓ To show how the Van Briggle Pottery designs changed over time

Listening 3

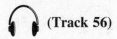 **(Track 56)**

12. What is the class mainly discussing?
    - (A) A class project in a business course
    - (B) A business in the community
    - (C) A case study from their book
    - (D) A hypothetical situation

13. Why does the professor say this:
    "Anyone?"
    - (A) She wants the students to continue speaking.
    - (B) She wants a volunteer to lead the discussion.
    - (C) She wants a student to answer the question.
    - (D) She wants the students to pay attention.

14. What does the professor mean when she says this:
    "That's it in a nutshell."
    - (A) It is not a complete answer.
    - (B) It is a good summary.
    - (C) It is an estimate of the cost.
    - (D) It is not very logical.

15. How did the mistake occur?
    - (A) The salesperson made an error in writing up the order.
    - (B) The workers forgot to assemble the furniture.
    - (C) The account supervisor did not include assembly in the bid.
    - (D) The warehouse delivered the wrong furniture.

16. Based on information in the lecture, indicate whether the statements refer to the way that the manager responded to the error.
    For each sentence, click in the YES or NO column.

	YES	NO
(A) He was angry because no one took responsibility for the error.		
(B) His position was that the procedures needed to be changed.		
(C) He reprimanded the employee who made the mistake.		
(D) He remained calm while he chaired the open meeting.		

17. What conclusion did the students make about the management style?
    - (A) They agreed that he should have acted differently when the employees concealed the error.
    - (B) They thought that he turned the problem into an opportunity to improve the company.
    - (C) They were surprised that he admitted the mistake in a meeting of all his employees.
    - (D) They felt that he was willing to accept too many excuses when the problem was discovered.

Part Two: Listening 4

 (Track 57)

18. Why does the student go to see the professor?
    Ⓐ To make an appointment for tomorrow
    Ⓑ To interview with him for a scholarship
    Ⓒ To get advice about her scholarship application
    Ⓓ To turn in her essay before the due date

19. What information is required in the essay?
    Choose 2 answers.
    Ⓐ The applicant's financial situation
    Ⓑ The personal background of the applicant
    Ⓒ The goals that the applicant has set
    Ⓓ The names of professors who support the applicant

20. When does the woman need to turn in her application to the committee?
    Ⓐ Today
    Ⓑ Tomorrow
    Ⓒ This Friday
    Ⓓ Next week

21. Why does the professor say this:
    "Your grade point average is what . . . a 4.0?"
    Ⓐ To determine whether she would qualify for the scholarship
    Ⓑ To verify the number that she has written on the application
    Ⓒ To encourage her and give her more self-confidence
    Ⓓ To ask her to think about the advice that he has given her

22. Why does Professor Walters tell the woman to pretend she is writing about her friend Kathy?
    Ⓐ Because she needs to practice writing an essay
    Ⓑ Because Kathy is a good candidate for a scholarship
    Ⓒ Because she is embarrassed to write about herself
    Ⓓ Because she is Kathy's best friend

Listening 5

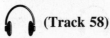 (Track 58)

23. What is this lecture mainly about?
    Ⓐ Manipulation of the reproductive cycles of pests
    Ⓑ The use of new pesticides to kill pests
    Ⓒ The genetic modification of plants to manage pests
    Ⓓ Integrated strategies to control pests

24. According to the professor, what are *pheromones*?
    Ⓐ A technical term for a female moth
    Ⓑ A sterilization process for male moths
    Ⓒ A chemical that attracts male moths
    Ⓓ A predator that controls the moth population

25. Why does the professor mention the example of ladybugs?
    Ⓐ To prove that all insects are not harmful
    Ⓑ To show how a predator can control pests
    Ⓒ To demonstrate how to control weeds
    Ⓓ To explain why pest management is necessary

26. Which changes in farming practices support pest management?
    Choose 2 answers.
    Ⓐ Planting crops that contain natural pesticides near other crops
    Ⓑ Plowing under habitats where pests usually survive the winter
    Ⓒ Planting the same crop to repeat and strengthen the same pest control
    Ⓓ Leaving weeds in the field to attract the pests away from the crop

27. Why does the professor ask the following question:
    "Did I say generic?"
    Ⓐ To emphasize the importance of the concept
    Ⓑ To determine whether students have understood
    Ⓒ To correct the misuse of a word in the lecture
    Ⓓ To include information that he forgot to mention

28. What does the professor imply about genetic modification of plants?
    Ⓐ It is a very cost effective way to manage pests.
    Ⓑ It may have serious consequences for the ecosystem.
    Ⓒ It could be a major export to other countries.
    Ⓓ It results in a lower yield when plants are modified.

Part Three: Listening 6

 **Track 59**

29. What are the speakers mainly discussing?
    - Ⓐ Sports
    - Ⓑ High school
    - Ⓒ Friends
    - Ⓓ Classes

30. How did the man make friends in high school?
    - Ⓐ He was friends with the people in his classes.
    - Ⓑ He had friends on the basketball team.
    - Ⓒ He made friends in online sites.
    - Ⓓ He went to a lot of school activities.

31. Why does the woman say this:
    "Go on."
    - Ⓐ She is asking the student to say more.
    - Ⓑ She is trying to end the conversation.
    - Ⓒ She implies that she doesn't believe it.
    - Ⓓ She shows that she is impressed.

32. What does the counselor suggest that the man do?
    - Ⓐ Find a roommate in the residence hall
    - Ⓑ Call his friends from high school
    - Ⓒ Sign up to play intermural sports
    - Ⓓ Try out for the school basketball team

33. How can a student join an intermural team?
    - Ⓐ By competing against other players
    - Ⓑ By playing in four or five games
    - Ⓒ By going online to find a team
    - Ⓓ By sending a check to the university

Listening 7

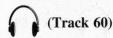 **(Track 60)**

34. What is the purpose of this lecture?
    - Ⓐ To discuss the effect of the internet on social interaction
    - Ⓑ To prove that computers have had a positive influence on life
    - Ⓒ To report that almost all college students use the internet
    - Ⓓ To design an experiment that will measure internet use by the class

35. Why does the professor say this:
    "Go on."
    - Ⓐ He wants to give someone else a turn to speak.
    - Ⓑ He is asking the student to give a more complete answer.
    - Ⓒ He disagrees with the student's answer to the question.
    - Ⓓ He is telling the student to try another answer.

36. What were the results of the research study?
    Choose 2 answers.
    - Ⓐ People who used the internet were less likely to feel lonely.
    - Ⓑ internet users had less communication with family who lived nearby.
    - Ⓒ More depression was reported by those who used the internet.
    - Ⓓ Mental health improved when people used the internet more.

37. The professor gives an example of a person who exchanges recipes with someone on the internet. What does this example demonstrate?
    - Ⓐ Who is likely to make friends on the internet
    - Ⓑ Why the internet is good for someone in a rural area
    - Ⓒ How to get good advice on the internet
    - Ⓓ What to expect from an internet friend

38. Why does the professor question the results of the research?
    - Ⓐ Because the study lasted only a few months
    - Ⓑ Because there were very few subjects in the study
    - Ⓒ Because there was only one study done
    - Ⓓ Because the findings were not conclusive

39. What is the attitude of the professor toward the students?
    - Ⓐ He wants them to wait for him to call on them.
    - Ⓑ He expects them to agree with him about the research.
    - Ⓒ He respects their opinions on the topic of discussion.
    - Ⓓ He does not like them to ask many questions.

Speaking Section

4 QUESTIONS 17 MINUTES

Directions: This section tests your ability to communicate in English in an academic context. The directions are both spoken and written. There are two types of speaking questions. The independent speaking questions require that you talk about personal preferences related to topics presented in the questions. You may take notes as you prepare. In the independent speaking questions, you should express your opinions. The integrated speaking questions require that you respond to an academic reading or a lecture. You may take notes as you read and listen. In the integrated speaking questions, you should NOT express opinions. Your response should be based on the information in the reading and lecture material.

Independent Speaking Task 1

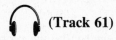 **(Track 61)**

Question:
Some people feel that it is important to be on time for every meeting, whether it is a business appointment or a party with friends. Other people feel that being on time is important only for business and professional appointments, but social occasions do not require that the participants arrive on time. Which approach do you think is better and why? Be sure to use specific reasons and examples to support your opinion.

Preparation Time: 15 seconds
Recording Time: 45 seconds

Integrated Speaking Task 2

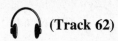 **(Track 62)**

Reading Time: 50 seconds

Question:

Notice Concerning Parking Proposal
State University administration is discussing how to improve the parking situation for students who commute to the campus. Although there are more than 5,000 students who live off campus, only 1,000 parking spaces are available in the student parking lots. The university is considering a plan that would link a campus bus system to the city bus lines in an effort to solve the problem. This plan will be discussed at a meeting in the student union on Saturday, May 2, at 9:30 a.m.

The student expresses his opinion about the university's plans for improving the parking situation at State University. Report his opinion and explain the reasons that he gives for having that opinion.

Preparation Time: 30 seconds
Recording Time: 60 seconds

Integrated Speaking Task 3

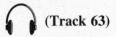 **(Track 63)**

Reading Time: 50 seconds

Question:

Land-Use Planning
Land-use planning is a system of evaluation that attempts to balance the needs and desires of the population with the characteristics and value of a particular land resource. An evaluation includes the exploration of alternatives for the use of a particular piece of land before changes are made to it. The problem inherent in any land-use decision is that competing uses may all be important, but it may not be possible to serve all interests in the final plan. A basic premise of land-use planning is to make as few changes as possible in order to accommodate the economic or recreational needs of the population.

Explain what the land-use committee believed to be the problem in their area and what they recommended to solve it. Explain how their decision reflects the fundamental principles of land-use planning.

Preparation Time: 30 seconds
Recording Time: 60 seconds

Integrated Speaking Task 4

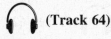 **(Track 64)**

Question:
Referring to the main points and examples from the lecture, describe the properties that make X-rays useful. Then describe the specific purposes of X-rays that the professor presents.

Preparation Time: 20 seconds
Recording Time: 60 seconds

Writing Section

2 QUESTIONS 50 MINUTES

Directions: This section tests your ability to write essays in English similar to those that you would write in college courses. There are two types of essay questions. The integrated essay requires that you respond to an academic reading passage and a lecture. You may take notes as you read and listen. In the integrated essay, you should NOT express opinions. Your response should be based on the information in the reading and lecture material. The independent essay requires that you state and support your opinion about a topic presented in the question.

Integrated Essay

Directions: You have 20 minutes to plan, write, and revise your response to a reading passage and a lecture on the same topic. First, read the passage below and take notes. Then, listen to the lecture and take notes. Finally, write your response to the writing question. Typically, a good response will require that you write 200–250 words.

Music history, also referred to as historical musicology, is the study of composition, performance, and critique over time. For example, a historical study of music would include biographical information about each composer and the way that a specific piece relates to other works, the development of styles of music, the relationship of music to social life, and the techniques associated with performance. In theory, music history could treat the study of any type of music, but in practice, it has a very narrow perspective.

In the first place, music history has heavily favored Western music, and in particular, classical music. This perspective is problematic for two reasons. First of all, it dismisses music from other cultures. Because classical music was developed in nineteenth-century Europe, it is representative of Western culture; however, Eastern music has a rich, and a very different tradition, which is virtually absent from the field of music history.

Another problem is that music history arbitrarily ignores popular music, even Western music that has been composed post nineteenth century. The fact that popular music has a very simple melody but a complex rhythmic structure makes it too different from the classical pattern. Furthermore, the fact that the rise of classical music coincided with the practice of musical notation elevated music that has a written tradition. Jazz, for example, would be considered less important because it relies on improvisation instead of sheet music. Music from cultures that are not part of a written tradition is not considered important enough to include in the historical records.

Finally, music history is a field that is dominated by male professors, relegating women to the role of music teacher in elementary schools, which allows for a very limited perspective in music research. The marginalization of women as researchers has also excluded them from the mention they deserve as composers and musicians in the historical records.

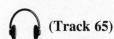 **(Track 65)**

Now listen to a lecture on the same topic as the passage that you have just read.

Writing Question:
Summarize the main points in the lecture, referring to the way that they cast doubt on the research presented in the reading.

Notes

Use this space for essay notes only. Work done on this work sheet will *not* be scored.

Essay

Independent Essay

Directions: You have 30 minutes to plan, write, and revise your essay. Typically, a good response will require that you write a minimum of 300 words.

Question:
Some students enjoy taking distance-learning courses on the computer or by television. Other students would rather take all of their courses with a teacher in a classroom. Which of these options do you think is better? Use specific reasons and examples in support of your opinion.

Notes

Use this space for essay notes only. Work done on this work sheet will *not* be scored.

Essay

iBT® Model Test Scripts for the Listening Section

This section tests your ability to understand campus conversations and academic lectures in English. You will hear each conversation and lecture one time. You may take notes while you listen. After each conversation or lecture, you will answer questions about it. You may use your notes to answer. There are two types of listening comprehension questions. The multiple-choice questions require that you choose the best of four possible answers. The computer-assisted questions require that you follow directions on the screen. You must answer each question in order to go to the next question. You cannot return to previous questions.

Part One: Listening 1

 (Track 54)

Narrator: Listen to a conversation between a student and a secretary at the Learning Center on campus.

Student:	Is this the Learning Center?
Secretary:	Yes.
Student:	I'd like to see someone about tutoring or maybe workshops.
Secretary:	Well, what kind of help do you need?
Student:	Sorry?
Secretary:	We offer workshops in reading, math, time management, public speaking, and writing. But we also provide individualized tutoring in specific subject areas.
Student:	I'm having problems in my English class. It's English 101.
Secretary:	Oh. Did you take placement tests at the Testing Center the beginning of the semester?
Student:	Yes, and I placed into English 101, but I'm not keeping up.
Secretary:	Are you having any problems in your other classes?
Student:	I'm doing okay in my algebra class and my computer science. I'm a little behind in my psychology class. The paper is sort of hard. I mean it's not researching it. Writing it takes a lot of time.
Secretary:	Well, it sounds like you could use some help with your writing. We have workshops and individualized tutoring.
Student:	Do I have to choose? Uh, could I take a workshop and then see whether I want to sign up for the tutoring?
Secretary:	Absolutely. That's what most students do. So . . . we have a workshop for freshman writing on Saturday morning at 10.
Student:	Tomorrow?
Secretary:	Yes. It's here at the Learning Center in the workshop area—that's the large room behind those glass doors.
Student:	Sounds good. How do I . . . ?
Secretary:	You can register now if you like. The registration forms are on the computer over there. Be sure to enter Workshop 7 . . . that's the one you want.
Student:	Okay. Great. Should I bring anything?
Secretary:	Oh, yes. Bring the syllabus for your English course and any essays you have already submitted. Most of the material will be on handouts that you can download to your laptop, so you'll want to bring that, but you'll probably want to take a few notes as well, so bring whatever you use to take notes in your classes. And you may want to bring a sweater or a light jacket. For some reason, that room is always cold.

Student:	Thanks. Oh, uh, how long does the workshop last?
Secretary:	Two hours, with a ten-minute break.
Student:	I don't mean to be rude, but that doesn't sound like enough time to get me squared away.
Secretary:	No, it isn't. But it will get you on the right track. At the end of the workshop, you'll know whether to sign up for the next workshop or whether you need some individualized tutoring.

Now get ready to answer the questions.

1. What is the main purpose of the conversation?
2. What kinds of services are available at the Learning Center?
3. Why is the man having problems in his psychology class?
4. What does the woman suggest that the man do next?
5. Listen again to part of the conversation. Then answer the question.

"Thanks. Oh, uh, how long does the workshop last?"
"Two hours, with a ten-minute break."
"I don't mean to be rude, but that doesn't sound like enough time to get me squared away."

Why does the man say this:
"I don't mean to be rude, but that doesn't sound like enough time to get me squared away."

Listening 2

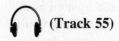 (Track 55)

Narrator: Listen to part of a lecture in an art history class.

Professor:
The Arts and Crafts movement was a reaction to the mass production of the industrial period. It began at the very end of the nineteenth century, but it's generally considered a twentieth-century movement, and, really, there's no clear end to it. In fact, arguably, there's still evidence of an Arts and Crafts school today. So, what identifies Arts and Crafts? I'm going to talk about four characteristics: quality, simplicity, comfort, and hand craftsmanship. But to really understand the philosophy, and it is a philosophy, we should compare all of those characteristics with the qualities from the Victorian age that preceded the Arts and Crafts movement. As you'll recall from our study of the Victorians, theirs was an age of quantity. That is to say, every surface was covered with pictures, ornaments, and objects. Also, the Victorians were noted for extravagance, and uh . . . even excess in decoration. And, they were impressed by the new machine reproductions that were being mass-produced at, uh, reasonable prices. Finally, don't forget that style and show were more important to them than comfort, and by that I mean the Victorians were more interested in . . . in impressing the guests that came to call than uh, than uh, than making them comfortable.

Now, with that in mind, let's go back and compare the Victorians with the Arts and Crafts artisans that came after them. 1. Quality instead of quantity. In other words, the Arts and Crafts artisans thought that it was better to have a few fine objects than . . . than a clutter of objects that were less valuable. 2. Simplicity instead of excess. A room decorated in the Arts and Crafts style would have looked . . . well, people who were accustomed to Victorian opulence would probably have thought it was quite bare. Simple lines replaced the carvings that . . . that seemed to cover every inch of furniture and architectural ornamentation in Victorian homes. 3. Comfort instead of display. And this was especially evident in the Arts and Crafts chairs that were uh . . . uh . . . softly padded with leather cushions and rounded edges. The Victorian chairs were more like, well, really like tiny thrones and were built for people to perch on, but the Arts and Crafts chairs were practical, big, and roomy. You could sink into the chairs. And the rest of the furniture was also practical, with . . . with clean lines and comfort built in. The Eastwood chair comes to mind, although Gustav Stickley was also producing chairs in a Mission style that's still popular today. And . . . and that's what I meant about not having a clear end to the movement since it's still an alternative for decorative arts today.

Okay. How did the movement begin? Well, the industrial age caused a reaction among artists in many places, but William Morris in England was certainly in the forefront, along with Elbert Hubbard who . . . Hubbard founded the East Aurora Workshop. The East Aurora motto was "hand, head, and heart" which probably sums up the movement as concisely as anything. Originally the workshop was a group of fifty artisans living in a community, and they followed the tradition of medieval craftsmen, although they used machines as tools for their crafts. I think they were probably best known for hand-bound books, but the East Aurora Workshop also produced, uh . . . pieces of hammered metalwork and . . . and furniture, primarily oak and chestnut furniture. Remember that motto, "hand, head, and heart." Well, according to Hubbard, if you love the work and work with integrity, the rest will follow. So that was his way of living the motto. In 1914 . . . sorry . . . 1915 . . . that was the date when Hubbard died, and the community dispersed, but almost one hundred years later, the pieces of Roycroft furniture that they produced there are highly prized.

So, let's see . . . what was happening in the outside world? Farmers were moving to the cities to work in factories, and there was an . . . an expansion of the middle class. The Victorian homes were too expensive, too ornate, and the Arts and Crafts bungalow home emerged as the affordable, well-constructed alternative to, uh, the castle-like mansions of the Victorian era. Bungalows were charming, homey, and affordable. They often had open living and dining areas that gave a more spacious feel to a smaller space, and built-in cabinets that reduced the need to buy furniture. The front porches became outdoor rooms with simple, comfortable tables and chairs. Instead of the Victorian facade that was built to impress the neighbors, the porch was . . . was unadorned but welcoming. In many ways, these bungalows became the standard for middle-class neighborhoods. But when we look at them today, they're impressive in their own way. The workmanship, in many cases, is just superb. The wood beams and natural wood floors, the fireplaces, and the cabinetry are . . . let's say . . . unpretentious but exquisitely crafted. And the tile work should also be mentioned. The name to remember for tile is Henry Chapman Mercer, who founded the Moravian Pottery and Tile Works in Pennsylvania. While working with apprentices, he supervised every piece, and they decorated them all by hand. The maker was part of the product and often signed the tiles.

I guess what strikes me as an art historian about the Arts and Crafts movement is the fact that the designs are so timeless. Van Briggle Pottery, for example, was founded in Colorado Springs almost one hundred years ago by Artis Van Briggle, who demanded that the function of pottery . . . uh . . . the utility . . . be combined with the art. Van Briggle created designs that were shaped to resemble sculptures, and then he developed a unique glaze that came out of the firing with a matte finish, which was really new since the pottery of the time was, uh, very highly polished. But my point is that the Van Briggle Pottery Works continues to operate today, using those original designs. That's what I mean by timeless.

Now get ready to answer the questions.

---

6. What is the professor mainly discussing?
7. Listen again to part of the lecture. Then answer the question.
   "As you'll recall from our study of the Victorians, theirs was an age of quantity. That is to say, every surface was covered with pictures, ornaments, and objects. Also, the Victorians were noted for extravagance, and uh . . . even excess in decoration."
   Why does the professor say this: "As you'll recall from our study of the Victorians, theirs was an age of quantity."
8. What are two design elements of Arts and Crafts chairs?
9. What did the motto "hand, head, and heart" mean?
10. According to the professor, why did the Arts and Crafts bungalows become so popular?
11. Why did the professor use the example of the Van Briggle Pottery Works?

Listening 3

 (Track 56)

Narrator: Listen to part of a class discussion in a business management class.

Professor: First, let me say that managing success requires a certain set of managing skills, and we're usually focusing on how to be successful managers, but it's also, uh, inevitable that all managers will have to deal with failure—their own or their staff's, or the people they have delegated responsibility to. I assume that you've all read the case study for the Anderson Company. That's on page 347 of your textbook. So, let's summarize that study and use it for the . . . uh . . . our discussion on how to manage failure. Because, believe me, as a manager, you must be able to identify and intervene when mistakes occur. Okay. Back to the Anderson Company. What happened?

Student 1: Well, first of all, the Anderson Company was a distributor for office supplies, and they lost money because they . . . they underbid a job for a client . . . an important client. So that was the mistake they made.

Professor: Right. And why did they underbid? Anyone?

Student 2: I don't have my book here, but I think I remember it. There was a large order for furniture . . . wasn't it office furniture? So there was a large order, which was good, but somehow there wasn't any charge in the estimate for assembly of the furniture, so the client expected delivery of desks and chairs, and I think filing cabinets, ready to go, completely assembled, but uh . . . there wasn't any cost figured in for the labor. It was a fairly large figure, too, maybe three thousand dollars.

Professor: Thanks, Anne. That's it in a nutshell. So what was the manager's response when the problem became known?

Student 1: Well, at first, everybody started pointing fingers at everybody else. And no one was taking responsibility. But, then, uh, the manager called a meeting, and . . . and he said he wanted explanations, not excuses. I remembered that line because I wrote it down. I thought it was really good. And he said that the problem wasn't that something had gone wrong. It was that the cause . . . um . . . the reason why the mistake happened . . . that was what was important . . . because that meant that they could make the same mistake twice.

Professor: So how did the manager handle the meeting? Do you recall?

Student 1: Oh, yeah. That was good, too. He was really calm and not angry at all. And um . . . he said that every mistake was the result of an error in the company, not the employees . . . so the company needed to be modified so the mistake wouldn't happen again, and he told everyone at the meeting that it wasn't his intention to punish anyone for the mistake unless there was an effort to cover it up.

Professor: So the manager's position was to depersonalize the failure and try to prevent it from happening again.

Student 1: Exactly.

Professor: Okay. Then what happened? Joe?

Student 3: Um, well, the salesperson who sold the furniture recognized that he forgot to mention the uh . . . the agreement to assemble the furniture before delivery . . . he forgot that when he gave the order to the account supervisor, but it was written on the order. Anyway, he ended up taking some responsibility because it was an unusual request, and he thought he should have maybe pointed it out. Then, the account supervisor admitted that she'd gone through the order very quickly, and . . . and she hadn't seen the word "assembled" on the order, so she didn't figure in the cost when she sent the bid.

Professor: So, once the guilty parties were found, what did the manager do?

Student 2:   I remember that part. He didn't focus on the error at all. He went directly to brainstorming a procedure that would prevent the same error from being made in the future, and they came up with asking the sales team to identify each furniture order as "assembly required" or "no assembly required" after each item, and the account supervisor . . . she was asked to be alert to the instruction on each order so . . . so she could factor in the cost on the bids.

Professor: Okay. What do you think about the manager's style?

Student 1:   Well, I was surprised that he called . . . that it was an open meeting, I mean to resolve the problem. I would have thought that he might have just talked with the people who made the mistake, you know, privately.

Student 2:   That occurred to me, too, when I read the case study, but then I was thinking he was probably running into so many excuses that he needed to just bring it out into the open.

Student 1:   Oh, okay. That makes sense.

Student 3:   I think he was also trying to demonstrate that the company procedures were the problem, not just the employees who had made the error.

Professor: Do you think that the employees should have been reprimanded? After all, the mistake could have been avoided, couldn't it?

Student 2:   Sure, sure, the mistake shouldn't have happened, but I think the manager . . . I think he probably gained more in terms of . . . what do you call it? . . . team building. Probably there was more of a willingness on the part of the employees to come up with positive changes in the procedure, too. I mean, I think that was more valuable than the three thousand dollars, and he wouldn't have accomplished that by calling in employees privately to give them a reprimand.

Professor: Okay. And it turned out fine because the people responsible stepped up and accepted their responsibility. But what if they hadn't done that? What do you think the manager would have done . . . in that case?

Student 2:   I think he would have been very firm about concealing the mistake, and he . . . I think he probably would have acted very differently.

Professor: You mean he would have reprimanded them in some way?

Student 2:   I think he would have.

Now get ready to answer the questions.

---

12. What is the class mainly discussing?
13. Listen again to part of the discussion. Then answer the question.
    "Right. And why did they underbid? Anyone?"
    Why does the professor say this: "Anyone?"
14. What does the professor mean when she says this: "That's it in a nutshell."
15. How did the mistake occur?
16. Based on information in the lecture, indicate whether the statements refer to the way that the manager responded to the error.
17. What conclusion did the students make about the management style?

Part Two: Listening 4

 (Track 57)

Narrator: Listen to a conversation between a student and a professor.

Student: Hi, Professor Walters.

Walters: Hi, Jan. How are you doing?

Student: Great, thanks. How are you?

Walters: Just fine. What can I do for you?

Student: Well, um . . . I'd really appreciate your help with my scholarship application.

Walters: Oh, good. I'm glad you applied. Oh, wait, that deadline is the end of next week, isn't it?

Student: It's . . . it's this Friday. But I have everything done on the computer, so, uh, any changes will be easy to fix. And, uh, it shouldn't take long to finish it up.

Walters: Okay.

Student: Actually, the main problem I'm having is with . . . I'm not sure my essay is what they're looking for. You know, I find it a little embarrassing to, well, to tell them what a great person I am, if you know what I mean.

Walters: Have you written anything yet?

Student: Just an outline. Here it is.

Walters: Okay. But before I look at this, do you have the directions for the application, or better yet, for the essay?

Student: Yeah, right here. I have the, um, instructions for the application right here.

Walters: Let me see that first, because the committee usually wants . . . has some specific points that they're looking for. This is sponsored by a private donor as I recall, and it's open only to women who are seniors in the college of business.

Student: Right. And I'll be a senior next year, so it's . . . it would be perfect.

Walters: But there have to be some more, uh, more specific requirements here . . . somewhere. . . . Oh, here we are. Look at this. They want to know about your personal background, then they want you to tell them about, uh, the first three years of your college education, and . . . and last, they want specifics about your goals.

Student: Uh-oh. Well, I didn't do this right then. Hmmm. I just wrote why I needed the scholarship.

Walters: And that may be okay for the part about your college education, or, uh, you might even be able to put it in with the part about your goals . . . uh . . . but I can assure you that you'll lose points if you don't follow these directions and write . . . it appears to me they want a three-part essay—personal background, college education, and goals. Listen, I've been involved in quite a few scholarship committees, and in order to be as . . . as fair as possible, we all read the applications and assign points to them—usually one hundred—just because it's easy to figure up, but anyway, there will be a certain number of points for the essay, and because this almost has to be a three-part essay, um . . . you'll probably get one-third of the points for each part. So . . . if you don't write about your personal background, for example, uh . . . you'll lose one-third of the points for the essay, and that, uh, that could mean the difference between being in the final group that gets called in for an interview or not moving into the final group at all.

Student: Wow. I almost blew it. I'd better go back and rewrite this. Professor Walters, uh . . . could you possibly give me another appointment . . . before Friday? I mean, so I can show you my essay? My new essay?

Walters:	Sure, Jan. But, the sooner, the better. Even if the committee doesn't meet for a month, what usually happens is the secretary will stamp a date on every application packet. And uh . . . any packets with dates after the deadline . . . those will be eliminated first. There will probably be over a hundred applications. I'm just guessing here, but there will be a lot of them, and using the date as the first screening is . . . is pretty common.
Student:	Well, it's only three paragraphs, so I could have that done by tomorrow, but . . . but I don't know if you could see me then?
Walters:	Tomorrow's fine. I'll be here between one and three.
Student:	Great. When. . . .
Walters:	You don't need an appointment. I'll see you when you get here.
Student:	Thanks so much, Dr. Walters. That's so great.
Walters:	No problem. I can see from the way that you have your application prepared that . . . I can tell you've taken a lot of time to work on this. Besides that, Jan, you're an excellent student. Your grade point average is what . . . a 4.0?
Student:	So far, I have all As.
Walters:	See what I'm saying? I think you're a good candidate for this scholarship, and I'd like to see you give it your best shot.
Student:	Thanks.
Walters:	And Jan, that part about being embarrassed to tell the committee how good you are? Pretend you're writing this essay about your best friend. You're good friends with Kathy, right?
Student:	She's my best friend for sure.
Walters:	Well then, pretend you're writing this essay about her. Just use the information about *you* when you do it. Okay?
Student:	Okay. Like you said, I'm going to give it my best shot.

Now get ready to answer the questions.

18. Why does the student go to see the professor?
19. What information is required in the essay?
20. When does the woman need to turn in her application to the committee?
21. Listen again to part of the conversation. Then answer the question.
    "Your grade point average is what . . . a 4.0?"
    "So far, I have all As."
    "See what I'm saying?"
    Why does the professor say this: "Your grade point average is what . . . a 4.0?"
22. Why does Professor Walters tell the woman to pretend she is writing about her friend Kathy?

Listening 5

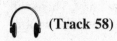 **(Track 58)**

Narrator: Listen to part of a lecture in an environmental science class.

Professor:
Today I'd like to introduce the topic of integrated pest management. Now unlike the previous methods that, uh, relied on . . . on pesticides alone, integrated pest management requires a complete analysis of the . . . ecology of the crop—which pests it might be susceptible to, how the pests interact with parasites or predators, how the climate affects the pests, and . . . and how beneficial insects can be, uh, encouraged. It's also important to . . . to understand the points of vulnerability in the life cycles of pests. Now reproduction is especially important, as you can imagine, because . . . because if you can reduce the number of new pests, then the population will be dramatically affected . . . I'm talking about during the next crop season. For example, during the mating stage of some species of moths, a chemical called a pheromone . . . pheromone spelled with a p-h . . . so a pheromone is released by females to attract males. Believe it or not, the males can detect pheromones from, well, as far away as two miles—that's nearly three kilometers. So spraying an area with a pheromone or something synthetic like a pheromone . . . that confuses the males, that makes them . . . they are unsuccessful finding females to mate with, and . . . and the moth population the following year is greatly reduced. So, there are fewer pests to deal with. Of course, another option is male sterilization, which has been very effective, especially with certain varieties of flies. The screwworm fly can actually kill large grazing animals like cattle or goats, but since the female mates only once in her life cycle, the population can be controlled by, uh, developing sterile males . . . and they do this in . . . in lab settings, and then they release them into the environment. So, as you can see, manipulating the reproductive cycles is one very good way to manage pests.

Now another management strategy is to use a predator to control the pests. Most of you are familiar with the ladybug, but you may not know that the ladybug is a natural predator of aphids, and aphids attack citrus trees and reduce crop yields. So by increasing the ladybug population, the aphid population . . . it naturally decreases. And ladybugs aren't harmful to other plants. Okay, I should mention that the definition of a pest extends to vegetation. Weeds are pests too, and they can be controlled effectively by introducing predators as well. Uh, the criteria are a little bit tricky though, since weeds are plants, and uh . . . it's important to find a predator that attacks the weeds but it doesn't like the crop, so it leaves the plant crop alone. But, it can be done, like the case of several species of beetles that feed on a wetlands weed called purple loosestrife. The problem is the loosestrife crowds out cattails and other native vegetation in the wetlands ecosystem. So, the beetles are introduced, and they reduce the loosestrife . . . don't quote me on this, but I think it is as much as 90 percent in some areas.

So, that brings us to the use of bacteria to kill pests, which I'll just mention briefly. One example of an effective intervention is the introduction of *Bacillus thuringiensis* . . . let me write that on the board for you . . . *Bacillus thuringiensis* . . . which releases a toxin that destroys large populations of mosquitoes and caterpillars and is especially efficient in ridding crop areas of the caterpillars that become adult leaf-eating moths.

Actually, the modification of farming practices can make a . . . a huge difference in pest management. For one thing, there are some naturally occurring pesticides in plants. Marigolds control soil nematodes, and, uh, garlic controls some species of beetles, so you see, planting these crops along with another crop that needs protection can, uh, really help. Another thing . . . destroying crop residues by plowing them under . . . that eliminates an environment where pests may live during the winter, and they die out so there aren't as many and that reduces the need for insecticides in the spring. Oh yes, the old practice of crop rotation has become popular again too, because it prevents a buildup of the same pests year after year.

But uh . . . the latest strategy in pest management involves the genetic modification of the plants themselves. Now in the next decade, we hope to be able to . . . to engineer high-yield plant varieties, and, uh . . . they'll be much more resistant to insects and diseases. Although this is a simplification, in general, generic engineering . . . did I say generic? . . . genetic engineering, that's genetic engineering . . . involves the insertion of genes from other species into crop plants in order to develop beneficial traits. One example that is very exciting is the insertion of bacterial genes, and these genes will . . . support the plant's production of a natural, uh, pesticide that . . . the pesticide will protect it against its primary pest. And in another successful project, genes are being inserted to . . . to protect the crop from the pesticides that are used to control weeds. So that could be a real breakthrough. Of course, there are ethical considerations and cost effectiveness issues. In fact, uh, some countries won't import genetically engineered plants because there are still so many unknowns. Can we really know the result to the total ecosystem that the introduction of a biotechnologically engineered plant will cause?

In any case, you can see that there are a number of alternatives for integrated pest management, including pesticides, but also using intervention in the reproductive cycle, the introduction of natural predators, substitution of bacteria for pesticides, modification of farming practices, and . . . and even genetic modification of the plants themselves. Most management plans will, in fact, use a number of these strategies for, uh . . . in a complete plan.

Now get ready to answer the questions.

23. What is this lecture mainly about?
24. According to the professor, what are *pheromones*?
25. Why does the professor mention the example of ladybugs?
26. Which changes in farming practices support pest management?
27. Listen again to part of the lecture. Then answer the question.
    "Although this is a simplification, in general, generic engineering . . . Did I say generic? . . . genetic engineering, that's genetic engineering . . . involves the insertion of genes from other species into crop plants in order to develop beneficial traits."
    Why does the professor ask the following question: "Did I say generic?"
28. What does the professor imply about genetic modification of plants?

Part Three: Listening 6

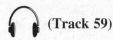 (Track 59)

Narrator: Listen to part of a conversation between a counselor and a student.

Counselor: You wanted to see me?

Student: Yes. Uh, this is kind of embarrassing.

Counselor: Don't worry. This is a confidential conversation.

Student: Well, first let me tell you that I was very popular in high school. I had a lot of friends. It was a small school, but still . . . In fact, I was captain of the basketball team.

Counselor: Go on.

Student: But here, I don't know anyone. I don't have anyone to talk to or go out with.

Counselor: That's odd. What about your roommate? I see that you are living in a residence hall.

Student: In a single. I thought that would be better because I could have a quiet study space.

Counselor: Okay. How about the other students in your classes?

Student: A lot of them seem really nice, but it's just "hi" and "bye" and everybody rushes for the door and goes in different directions after class. Everybody's busy, I guess.

Counselor: That sounds pretty typical. Well, do you go to any of the school activities?

Student: Not really.

Counselor: Okay, you said you had a lot of friends in high school. Who were friends there?

Student: Sorry?

Counselor: Who did you hang out with in high school?

Student: Oh. Mostly the other guys on the basketball team.

Counselor: And are you playing sports here on campus? Sounds like you were a good player in high school.

Student: I was, actually, but being on a team is a huge commitment. No. I thought that would take up too much time, so I didn't go out for the basketball team.

Counselor: And you aren't playing on an intermural team either?

Student: No. I thought about that.

Counselor: Well, I think that's a good first step to making some friends here on campus. Look, you join a team, and you play one game a week for four or five weeks, and then, if your team makes the playoffs, you play one more game.

Student: How do you . . . make the team?

Counselor: Just go online at www.intermuralsportsatstateuniversity.org and choose the sport you are interested in and the day of the week that you are free to play.

Student: So you don't have to compete to make the team?

Counselor: No. That's not the purpose of intermural sports. It's just for fun—until the playoff week, that is. What do you think?

Student: I'll go online and check it out.

Counselor: Let me know how you're doing, okay?

Student: Okay.

Now get ready to answer the questions.

29. What are the speakers mainly discussing?
30. How did the man make friends in high school?
31. Listen again to part of the conversation. Then answer the question.
    "I had a lot of friends. In fact, I was captain of the basketball team."
    "Go on."
    Why does the woman say this:
    "Go on."
32. What does the counselor suggest that the man do?
33. How can a student join an intermural team?

Listening 7

 (Track 60)

Narrator: Listen to part of a discussion in a sociology class. The professor is talking about the internet.

Professor: I'm sure if I asked you, everyone present would respond positively to the question, "Do you use the internet?" I know this because the use of the internet among college students is almost 100 percent. We shop on the computer, we learn on the computer, we're entertained on the computer. And more and more we use the computer as a primary means of communication not only with, uh, business associates but also with friends and family. Chat rooms are becoming more and more popular, and, uh, . . . and list-serves connect people from around the world with the information that's important to their group. We even find our prospective mates by using the internet. So the question is: What effect does the internet have on social interaction? Any ideas?

Student 1:   Well, from what you said, I think it would be a very positive influence.

Student 2:   Me, too. I mean, in my case, I write e-mails to my family 'cause it's just so easy to jump from what I'm doing at school, a paper or something, to the email program, and you know, write a few lines to my sister. I'd never take the time to write her a letter, buy a stamp, take it to the post office. You know.

Student 1:   Right.

Student 3:   Maybe, but a lot of people aren't using the net to talk to family or friends. It's a more superficial thing. Well, more of a way to communicate anonymously with, uh . . . with strangers. Half the time they aren't even using their real names.

Student 4:   That's true. Besides, what about all the time people spend playing computer games alone instead of doing something with another person?

Professor: Good observations on both sides. And basically, you've brought out the arguments that have been made for and against internet use. Some people think that the computer facilitates social interaction, and others feel that it impedes it. So, to find the answer, to investigate how internet use affects social relationships, a team of psychologists at Carnegie Mellon University . . . they conducted a longitudinal study of internet users. More than 150 people were monitored for one to two years. The subjects were recruited from among people who hadn't used the internet previously. In exchange for their participation, they received a computer, free software, and internet hookup. Before they began using their computers, they were assessed for mental health and, uh, social well-being. After an extended period of internet use, the team found that time on the computer was, uh, it was detrimental to both mental health and social well-being. In fact, increased use of the internet correlated with less communication among family members and friends in the local area. Also interesting was the incidence of . . . the highest users . . . reported increased loneliness and a higher degree of depression.

Student 1:   Hmmm. So why did that happen, did they think?

Professor: What do *you* think?

Student 1:   Disappointment maybe.

Professor: Go on.

Student 1:   Well, maybe they expected too much from their internet friends. I mean, if you think that a person you meet on the internet is going to be your special someone, that probably isn't going to happen. Someone who has internet friends probably enjoys that, and probably has a lot of . . . of relationships on the net.

Student 3:   Or they may be neglecting important friendships while they spend time online, and later, well they may find that they are damaging those . . . those relationships.

Professor: Both of those ideas sound reasonable. The researchers put it this way: The relationships on the internet were weak. Example: You might exchange recipes with someone online through a website, but that person won't probably . . . won't offer help and support when you need it, at least not like some of the friends that you might make at school, work, church, or in your community. So . . . when you say you shouldn't expect too much from an internet friend, that's uh . . . that's good advice, Nancy. And Rob, when you say that important friendships could be neglected, that's part of the picture, too. But, do you see anything about the findings that we should question?

Student 2:   Well, everybody doesn't use the internet for the same purposes. So, uh, maybe how the internet is being used . . . they should probably look at that.

Professor: Good point. Anything else?

Student 1:   Some people aren't going to make those other kinds of friendships anyway, so, you know, the internet at least allows them to have some social interaction.

Professor: That seems reasonable, too, especially in the case of isolated living situations, like, uh, rural areas where there might not be many face-to-face resources. I'd also like to point out that we need more research to draw conclusions. Because this was only one study.

Now get ready to answer the questions.

---

34. What is the purpose of this lecture?
35. Listen again to part of the lecture. Then answer the question.
    "What do *you* think?" "Disappointment maybe." "Go on." "Well, maybe they expected too much from their internet friends. I mean, if you think that a person you meet on the internet is going to be your special someone, that probably isn't going to happen."
    Why does the professor say this: "Go on."
36. What were the results of the research study?
37. The professor gives an example of a person who exchanges recipes with someone on the internet. What does this example demonstrate?
38. Why does the professor question the results of the research?
39. What is the attitude of the professor toward the students?

iBT® Model Test Scripts for the Speaking Section

Directions: This section tests your ability to communicate in English in an academic context. The directions are both spoken and written. There are two types of speaking questions. The independent speaking questions require that you talk about personal preferences related to topics presented in the questions. You may take notes as you prepare. In the independent speaking questions, you should express your opinions. The integrated speaking questions require that you respond to an academic reading or a lecture. You may take notes as you read and listen. In the integrated speaking questions, you should NOT express opinions. Your response should be based on the information in the reading and lecture material.

Narrator 2: This is the speaking section of the TOEFL Model Test. During the test, you will respond to four speaking questions. You may take notes as you listen. The reading passages and the questions are printed in the book, but most of the directions will be spoken.

Independent Speaking Task 1

 (Track 61)

Narrator 2:
Number 1. Listen for a question that asks your opinion about a familiar topic. After you hear the question, you have 15 seconds to prepare and 45 seconds to record your answer.

Narrator 1:
Some people feel that it is important to be on time for every meeting, whether it is a business appointment or a party with friends. Other people feel that being on time is important only for business and professional appointments, but social occasions do not require that the participants arrive on time. Which approach do you think is better and why? Be sure to use specific reasons and examples to support your opinion.

Narrator 2:
Please prepare your answer after the beep.

Beep

[Preparation Time: 15 seconds]

Narrator 2:
Please begin speaking after the beep.

Beep

[Recording Time: 45 seconds]

Beep

Integrated Speaking Task 2

 (Track 62)

Narrator 2:
Number 2. Read a short passage and then listen to a talk on the same topic. Then listen for a question about them. After you hear the question, you have 30 seconds to prepare and 60 seconds to record your answer.

Narrator 1:
The administration at State University recognizes that there are not enough parking spaces for commuter students. Read the notice from a poster on campus. You have 50 seconds to complete it (refer to page 467). Please begin reading now.

[Reading Time: 50 seconds]

Narrator 1:
Now listen to a student who is speaking at the open meeting. He is expressing his opinion about the parking problem.

Student:
I understand that there are good reasons to use public transportation, but for many of us, it just isn't practical. If you look at the number of married students with children, you'll see that there are quite a few who have to take children to school, go to work, and then come to campus, and it wouldn't be very convenient to try to do all that by bus. Besides, a lot of times, I stay really late at the library, but the public buses stop running at nine. And to tell the truth, I don't think students will use the buses, so the parking problem won't be solved anyway.

Narrator 1:
The student expresses his opinion about the university's plans for improving the parking situation at State University. Report his opinion and explain the reasons that he gives for having that opinion.

Narrator 2:
Please prepare your answer after the beep.

Beep

[Preparation Time: 30 seconds]

Narrator 2:
Please begin speaking after the beep.

Beep

[Recording Time: 60 seconds]

Beep

Integrated Speaking Task 3

 (Track 63)

Narrator 2:
Number 3. Read a short passage and then listen to a lecture on the same topic. Then listen for a question about them. After you hear the question, you have 30 seconds to prepare and 60 seconds to record your answer.

Narrator 1:
Now read the passage about land-use planning. You have 50 seconds to complete it (refer to page 468). Please begin reading now.

[Reading Time: 50 seconds]

Narrator 1:
Now listen to part of a lecture in an environmental science class. The professor is talking about a land-use problem.

Professor:
Recently, there was an opportunity for a recreational area to be established on public land in Arizona, with funding from a large private benefactor, but the area had traditionally been used for ranching. It seems that a special use permit had been granted to several large ranchers who had been grazing cattle on the land for years. So the problem for the land-use committee was how to resolve the dispute. On the one hand, public sentiment favored using public land for recreation that would benefit the community. On the other hand, the permits had been issued, and the ranchers were influential and politically well-connected.

One obvious solution was to designate the public land for a particular type of use and to locate a similar area nearby for the other purpose. But the committee decided to allow the recreational area to be established on the rangeland and to continue to grant range rights to the ranchers. Although the ranchers resented the intrusion of the hikers and campers, and the people who participated in recreational activities were not happy about the herds of cattle on what they considered a wilderness area, the committee was firm about the shared use.

Narrator 1:
Explain what the land-use committee believed to be the problem in their area, and what they recommended to solve it. Explain how their decision reflects the fundamental principles of land-use planning.

Narrator 2:
Please prepare your answer after the beep.

Beep

[Preparation Time: 30 seconds]

Narrator 2:
Please begin speaking after the beep.

Beep

[Recording Time: 60 seconds]

Beep

Integrated Speaking Task 4

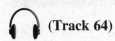 **(Track 64)**

Narrator 2:
Number 4. Listen to part of a lecture. Then listen for a question about it. After you hear the question, you have 20 seconds to prepare and 60 seconds to record your answer.

Narrator 1:
Now listen to part of a lecture in a science class. The professor is discussing X-rays.

Professor:
Okay, let's review what we talked about yesterday, about X-rays, I mean. Remember, X-rays are electromagnetic waves that range in wavelength from as large as 100 nanometers to as small as 0.1 nanometers. That's smaller than an atom. But, these waves, though small, have a very high frequency, and consequently, a very high-energy output. So X-rays can penetrate several centimeters into most objects.

But what makes X-rays really important is the fact that they are absorbed by varying degrees, right? This property is why X-rays are commonly used in medical science—to capture visual images of the skeleton and organs in the human body—because bones and teeth absorb X-rays more efficiently than soft tissues like skin or muscle, and well, a detailed picture of the internal organs can be formed in an image. Another very important function of X-rays is to make images of manufactured structures in industries where welded parts are joined. Using X-rays, it's possible to locate defects and correct them as part of the inspection process, again because materials will absorb the X-rays in varying degrees. The transportation industry relies heavily on this technology to inspect automobiles and aircraft. And X-ray scanners are standard equipment for security, as for example, in the machines at airports that check the contents of baggage. Other possibilities for X-rays are being explored in atomic research. As more powerful X-rays are developed, we believe that it'll be possible to use beams to study the exact position of atoms in something as small and delicate as a crystal. Then we'll be able to explore the properties of matter with much greater precision.

Narrator 1:
Referring to the main points and examples from the lecture, describe the properties that make X-rays useful. Then describe the specific purposes of X-rays that the professor presents.

Narrator 2:
Please prepare your answer after the beep.

Beep

[Preparation Time: 20 seconds]

Narrator 2:
Please begin speaking after the beep.

Beep

[Recording Time: 60 seconds]

Beep

iBT® Model Test Scripts for the Writing Section

Directions: This section tests your ability to write essays in English similar to those that you would write in college courses. There are two types of essay questions. The integrated essay requires that you respond to an academic reading passage and a lecture. You may take notes as you read and listen. In the integrated essay, you should NOT express opinions. Your response should be based on the information in the reading and lecture material. The independent essay requires that you state and support your opinion about a topic presented in the question.

Integrated Essay

 (Track 65)

Narrator: Now listen to a lecture on the same topic as the passage that you have just read.

Professor:
Although your textbook criticizes music history for the narrow perspective that has traditionally defined the field, I am glad to say that this view has changed considerably for the better among historical musicologists. The problems cited were legitimate even a few decades ago but not really mainstream today. Comparative musicology evolved into ethnomusicology in the early twentieth century, when anthropologists were the driving force behind the study of music in other cultures, and recently, the field of non-Western compositions in historical musicology has exploded. A current review of the literature reveals a definite shift in the paradigm from Western classical music to a more multicultural approach, which has been true of most of the humanities, and to an extent the other arts, for some time. It is now almost mandatory to include the history of Asian music, Indian classical music, African music, and Middle Eastern music in musicology books if authors want their manuscripts to be accepted for publication, and recent articles in the field of music history are expected to have at least a passing reference to music from other parts of the world. Whereas anthropologists were the primary historians in comparative and ethnomusicology, today most mainstream musical historians are on board with multicultural musicology.

In addition, we see a change in emphasis. Although classical music still enjoys pride of place in music history, greater attention is being given to modern popular music, including folk music, jazz, rock and roll, musical theater, and experimental composition. And, in spite of the preference for modern musical notation, which was ushered in by the classical music era, traditional musical notation, and by association, classical music has suffered criticism in recent years. For example, it has been observed that traditional notation, which is written from left to right, makes it very difficult to set music to scripts that are read right to left. Moreover, many modern composers are using digital recordings instead of the traditional system of notation. So technology is changing everything, including music history.

Finally, although musicology is still dominated by male professors and researchers, women are achieving top ranking positions, and their voices are making a difference. Carolyn Abbate and Susan McClary are probably the most well-known and active in an increasingly long list of women in the field. Through them, we are learning more and more about women composers and performers throughout history, filling in the blanks left by their absence in prior accounts.

Answer Key—iBT®

Reading

Reading 1	Reading 2	Reading 3
1. **B**	11. **C**	21. **B**
2. **A**	12. **B**	22. **C**
3. **B**	13. **B**	23. **A**
4. **B**	14. **B**	24. **D**
5. **C**	15. **D**	25. **C**
6. **B**	16. **C**	26. **D**
7. **A**	17. **D**	27. **B**
8. **A**	18. **C**	28. **A**
9. **D**	19. **B**	29. **D**
10. **A, E, F**	20. Low Mass: **B**	30. **A, D, E**
	Like Sun: **A, D, E**	
	Largest: **G**	

Listening

Part One	Part Two	Part Three
1. **A**	18. **C**	29. **C**
2. **A, C**	19. **B, C**	30. **B**
3. **C**	20. **C**	31. **A**
4. **A**	21. **C**	32. **C**
5. **A**	22. **C**	33. **C**
6. **B**	23. **D**	34. **A**
7. **C**	24. **C**	35. **C**
8. **A, C**	25. **B**	36. **D**
9. **A**	26. **A, B**	37. **B**
10. **B**	27. **C**	38. **C**
11. **A**	28. **B**	39. **B**
12. **C**		
13. **C**		
14. **B**		
15. **C**		
16. NO: **A, C** YES: **B, D**		
17. **B**		

Speaking

For evaluation of this section, refer to checklists and rubrics on pages 327, 334, and 499.

Writing

For evaluation of this section, refer to checklists and rubrics on pages 391, 401, and 499.

SCORE ESTIMATES

Score Scales for Institutional (ITP) Model Test

Section 1: Listening Comprehension		Section 2: Structure and Written Expression		Section 3: Reading Comprehension	
Correct Answers	*Scaled Score*	*Correct Answers*	*Scaled Score*	*Correct Answers*	*Scaled Score*
50	68	40	68	50	67
48–49	66	38–39	67	48–49	66
45–47	60	36–37	65	45–47	63
42–44	57	33–35	60	42–44	60
39–41	55	30–32	57	39–41	57
36–38	53	27–29	54	36–38	55
33–35	51	24–26	51	33–35	53
30–32	49	21–23	48	30–32	51
27–29	48	18–20	46	27–29	49
24–26	46	15–17	43	24–26	47
21–23	45	12–14	39	21–23	45
18–20	43	9–11	34	18–20	42
15–17	40	6–8	27	15–17	38
12–14	37	3–5	24	12–14	33
9–11	32	0–2	21	9–11	28
6–8	30			6–8	26
3–5	27			3–5	23
0–2	25			0–2	21

How to Calculate the Estimated Score

1. Add the number of items correct for Section 1 on the Institutional (ITP) Model Test, and locate the scaled score in the chart that corresponds to it. For example, if you have 10 items correct, your scaled score for Section 1 is 32.
2. Use the same procedure for Sections 2 and 3.
3. Now add all three numbers from Sections 1, 2, and 3.
4. Multiply the total by 10, and divide that number by 3.

Example of Estimated Score

Section 1:   40 items correct = 55
Section 2:   36 items correct = 65
Section 3:   43 items correct = 60

TOTAL = 180

$180 \times 10 = 1800 \div 3 = 600$

Score Scales for Internet-Based (iBT®) Model Test

Reading Section

Correct Answers	Scaled Score
30	30
29	29
28	28
27	27
26	26
25	25
24	24
23	23
22	22
21	21
20	20
19	19
18	18
17	17
16	16
15	15
14	14
13	13
12	12
11	11
10	10
9	9
8	8
7	7
6	6
5	5
4	4
3	3
2	2
1	1
0	0

Listening Section

Correct Answers	Scaled Score
39	30
38	29
37	28
36	27
35	26
34	26
33	25
32	24
31	23
30	23
29	22
28	21
27	20
26	20
25	19
24	18
23	17
22	16
21	16
20	15
19	14
18	13
17	13
16	12
15	11
14	10
13	10
12	9
11	8
10	7
9	6
8	6
7	5
6	4
5	3
4	3
3	2
2	1
1	0
0	0

Speaking Section

Rubric Score	Scaled Score
4.0	30
3.5	27
3.0	23
2.5	19
2.0	15
1.5	11
1.0	8

Rubrics for Speaking

Good   3.5–4.0
Very comprehensible pronunciation
Accurate content
Fluent speech
Wide range of vocabulary
Few errors in grammar
Well-organized ideas
Logical progression
Easy to understand

Fair   2.5–3.0
Mostly comprehensible pronunciation
Some hesitation in speech
Somewhat limited vocabulary
Errors in grammar
Content not fully developed
Fairly logical progression
Able to communicate

Limited   1.5–2.0
Pronunciation that interferes with
     comprehension
Frequent hesitation in speech
Very limited vocabulary
Errors in grammar that confuse meaning
Partial response

Weak   0–1.0
Incomplete response
Difficult to understand

Writing Section

Rubric Score	Scaled Score
5.0	30
4.5	28
4.0	25
3.5	22
3.0	20
2.5	17
2.0	14
1.5	11
1.0	8

Rubrics for Writing

Good   4.0–5.0
Very comprehensible essay
Accurate content (integrated essay)
Clear relationship between reading and
     lecture (integrated essay)
Wide range of vocabulary
Few errors in grammar
Well-organized ideas
Logical progression
Easy to understand

Fair   2.5–3.5
Mostly comprehensible essay
Some important ideas that are unclear
Partial relationship between reading and
     lecture (integrated essay)
Incorrect word usage
Grammatical errors that interfere with
     comprehension
Communicates general idea

Limited   1.0–2.0
Partially comprehensible essay
Comprehension of content not demonstrated
     (integrated essay)
Unclear relationship between reading and
     lecture (integrated essay)
Very limited vocabulary
Errors in grammar that confuse meaning
Requires interpretation to understand

Weak   0
Incomplete response
Different topic

How to Calculate the Estimated iBT® Score

1. Add the number of items correct for the Reading Section on the iBT® Model Test, and locate the scaled score in the chart that corresponds to it. For example, if you have 30 items correct, your scaled score for the Reading Section is 30.
2. Use the same procedure for the Listening Section.
3. Now use the rubrics to score the Speaking Section. Locate the scaled score in the chart that corresponds to your rubric score. For example, if your rubric score is 3.0, your scaled score for the Speaking Section is 23.
4. Use the same procedure for the Writing Section.
5. Now add all four numbers for a total score.

Example of Estimated Score

Reading Section	27 items correct = 27
Listening Section	28 items correct = 21
Speaking Section	3.5 rubric score = 27
Writing Section	4.0 rubric score = 25

TOTAL = 100

SCORE COMPARISONS

Common European Framework (CEFR)	Internet-Based TOEFL (iBT®)	Institutional TOEFL® (ITP)
C1	110–120	627–677
B2	87–109	543–626
B1	57–86	460–542

Note: TOEFL scores are also reported as they relate to the Common European Framework of Reference (CEFR), which is an internationally recognized measure of language proficiency. The equivalency chart above cites equivalencies determined by major research studies; however, they are only estimates of individual scores.

10

BONUS CHAPTER

TOEFL Vocabulary

Vocabulary is not tested in a separate section on either the Institutional TOEFL® (ITP) or on the Internet-Based TOEFL (iBT®). Both TOEFL formats present vocabulary questions in the context of the Reading Sections. Nevertheless, it is very important to study and increase your vocabulary in English. If you do, you will improve your score not only in the Reading Section but also in all of the other sections of the TOEFL.

The words in this bonus chapter have been carefully selected from the same Academic Word List that was used to develop the TOEFL.

Academic Vocabulary List

Note: The words in this list may have other meanings, but the definitions here are those that are referred to in the Academic Word List (AWL) developed by Averil Coxhead in 2000 and used as part of the research corpus for the TOEFL iBT®. The entries may also have additional words in the word family, but the most common words for each word family are included.

achieve v. **to accomplish a goal, acquire**
achievement n., achievable adj.
Many companies value team players because they work well with others to <u>achieve</u> objectives.

acquire v. **come into possession of an object, obtain, achieve**
acquisition n.
The largest museum in the world, the Smithsonian <u>acquires</u> thousands of objects each year through
    donations.

analysis n. **a detailed examination**
analyze v., analytical adj., analytically adv.
Linguistic fieldwork in anthropology requires an <u>analysis</u> of not only the language but also the
    culture of the society under investigation.

approach n. or v. **method, procedure**
approachable adj.
Research in learning styles suggests that teachers should use a variety of <u>approaches</u> in their
    classrooms to provide experiences for students who learn in different ways.

appropriate adj. **correct, suitable, relevant**
appropriately adv.
A gesture that is <u>appropriate</u> in one culture may be inappropriate in another culture.

area n. **a field of study, a space with boundaries, place**
Recent graduates have many opportunities for employment in the <u>area</u> of information technology.

aspects n. **characteristics, features**
The most compelling <u>aspects</u> of the setting in a literary work are the weather, surroundings, and time
    of day.

assessment n. **evaluation, judgment**
assess v., assessable adj.
Psychological <u>assessment</u> may be either informal or formal.

assistance n. **help, support**
assist v., assistant n. person who helps
Service animals provide <u>assistance</u> for students with disabilities.

assume v. **to suppose or believe, usually without proof**
assumption n.
Based on the evidence, it is reasonable to <u>assume</u> that several explorers reached the coast of North
    America before Columbus.

authority   n.   control, power to make decisions, responsibility
authorize   v.,   authoritative   adj.
For the most part, locally elected school boards have the <u>authority</u> to govern the schools within their
    districts.

available   adj.   accessible, convenient, offered
availability   n.
Very few studies are <u>available</u> to inform the development of creativity in early educational programs.

benefit   n. or v.   advantage or to provide an advantage, help
beneficial   adj.,   beneficiary   n.,   person who receives benefit
Improvements in technology have <u>benefited</u> researchers, especially those who work in remote
    locations.

chapter   n.   part, section, division
An introductory <u>chapter</u> usually defines the purpose of a book.

commission   n. or v.   authorization, appointment or to authorize, appoint
commissioner   n.,   person who authorizes
The Roman Coliseum <u>was commissioned</u> by Emperor Vespasian.

community   n.   group, social unit
The internet has introduced the idea of an online <u>community</u> with common interests that is not
    defined by a physical location.

compute   v.   calculate, figure
computation   n.,   calculation   n.,   computer machine that calculates
Although machines are better at <u>computing</u> complex numeric calculations faster than humans, the
    human brain still integrates information better.

concept   n.   idea, notion
conceptualize   v.,   to create an idea
Abraham Maslow included the <u>concept</u> of self-esteem in his hierarchy of human needs.

conclusion   n.   finish, completion, end
conclude   v.,   to close, finish, end
A scientific <u>conclusion</u> statement will summarize your experiment and report whether you proved or
    disproved your hypothesis.

consequence   n.   result, outcome
consequently   adv.
Nearly every organ in the human body is harmed as a <u>consequence</u> of smoking.

consistent   adj.   the same, ordered, regular, compatible
consist   v.,   consistently   adv.
If findings are <u>consistent</u> with a hypothesis, then the hypothesis may be considered reasonable
    because it has not yet been disproven.

constitute   v.   establish, form, compose
constitutional   adj.
Nutritionists don't always agree on what <u>constitutes</u> a healthy diet.

construct   v.   **make, build, create**
construction   n.
Although earlier Moghul buildings were primarily <u>constructed</u> of red sandstone, the Taj Mahal is a
   white marble structure inlaid with semiprecious stones.

consumer   n.   **a person who purchases goods and uses services, customer, buyer**
consume   v.,   consumption   n.,   the act of consuming
Marketing studies show that <u>consumers</u> are more receptive to small improvements rather than drastic
   changes in products.

context   n.   **setting, environment, circumstances, conditions**
contextualize   v.,   contextual   adj.
Literature should be studied in its historical <u>context</u> in order to fully understand it.

contract   v.   **get smaller**
contraction   n.,   the process of becoming smaller
Most substances <u>contract</u> when cooled.

create   v.   **make, invent, design**
creative   adj.,   creation   n.,   invention creator   n.,   person who invents
Scientists are continually trying to <u>create</u> heavier synthetic elements to add to the periodic table.

culture   n.   **customs and traditions from a specific society**
cultural   adj.,   culturally   adv.
According to E. Adamson Hoebel, <u>culture</u> can be learned, not inherited.

data   n.   **information, facts, evidence from which conclusions may be drawn**
<u>Data</u> from census records are valuable for marketing research.

definition   n.   **meaning, explanation**
define   v.
Technical terms that are specific to a field of study are usually listed with their <u>definitions</u> in the
   glossary at the back of a textbook.

derived   adj.   **developed or formed from something else, not original**
derive   v.,   derivation   n.
Petroleum is <u>derived</u> from ancient fossilized organic materials, such as zooplankton and algae.

distinction   n.   **differentiation, difference**
distinct   adj.,   distinctive   adj.,   distinction   n.,   distinctly   adv.
The crucial <u>distinction</u> between classical and operant conditioning involves the type of participation
   on the part of the subject, either passive or active.

distribution   n.   **spread, dispersion, supply**
distribute   v.,   distributor   n.,   person who distributes
Urban expansion has negatively affected the production and <u>distribution</u> of food.

economic   adj.   **financial**
economy   n.,   economical   adj.,   economically   adv.
Competition in the marketplace stimulates strong <u>economic</u> growth.

element   n.   **component, part, piece**
elemental   adj.
Included in the eight basic <u>elements</u> of music are melody and harmony.

environment   n.   **conditions, situation, surroundings**
environmental   adj.,   environmentalist   n.,   person who preserves the environment
Many traditional universities also offer a virtual learning <u>environment</u> for students who prefer to
      work at home on their computers.

equate   v.   **describe as similar or equal**
equation   n.,   formula
Research indicates that qualifications on paper do not necessarily <u>equate</u> to success on the job.

established   adj.   **recognized, official**
establish   v.,   establishment   n.
Einstein's theory that light could be bent by the gravitational force of the Sun was <u>established</u> using
      data from the eclipse of May 29, 1919.

estimate   n.   **approximation, evaluation, appraisal, judgment, calculation**
estimate   v.,   to make an approximation
The Centers for Disease Control conducts <u>estimates</u> every year to determine how well the flu vaccine
      protects against the current viruses.

evaluate   v.   **assess, judge, appraise, estimate, calculate**
evaluation   n.
A document on the internet should be <u>evaluated</u> for reliability and accuracy before citing it in your
      research.

evidence   n.   **proof, confirmation**
evident   adj.,   evidently   adv.
Some <u>evidence</u> is not admissible in a trial because the person providing it is not considered an expert
      witness.

export   v.   **to sell or send merchandise or services abroad, to send from a device**
exports   n.,   merchandise   exporter   n.,   a person who exports
Farmers in the United States <u>export</u> about 20 percent of their corn production to China, Canada,
      Mexico, Japan, and Europe.

factor   n.   **something that contributes to a result, element, component, issues, circumstances**
Sulfur dioxides are a major <u>factor</u> in the production of acid rain.

feature   n.   **attribute, aspect, characteristic, quality**
featured   adj.
Arthropods have several distinct <u>features</u> including a hard exoskeleton.

final   adj.   **concluding, closing, last, ultimate**
finalize   v.,   finally   adv.
The <u>final</u> novel of the Harry Potter series by J. K. Rowling was released globally in ninety-three
      countries.

financial   adj.   fiscal, monetary, related to money
finances   n.,   finance   v.,   financially   adv.
<u>Financial</u> institutions include not only banks but also credit unions and savings and loan associations.

formula   n.   fixed pattern, procedure, process
A proven <u>formula</u> for success includes visualizing what you want, setting a goal, and continuing to
    work toward that goal until you accomplish it.

function   n.   purpose, role, use
function   v.,   functional   adj.,   functionally   adv.
The largest organ in the body, the liver has as its primary <u>function</u> to filter potentially harmful
    substances in order to maintain healthy blood.

identify   v.   know, recognize, distinguish, name
identification   n.,   identifiable   adj.
Today many psychologists <u>identify</u> themselves with more than one school of thought.

impact   n.   effect, influence
The <u>impact</u> of social media on communication is profound.

income   n.   earnings
The price of bread in relationship to the <u>income</u> of a family is often used to calculate the cost of
    living.

indicate   v.   show, identify, point out, make reference to
indication   n.,   indicative   adj.
Four arrows <u>indicate</u> the directions of a compass on a map.

individual   n.   a human being, person
individually   adv.,   individual   adj.,   single, separate, one
Each <u>individual</u> snowflake is virtually unique in structure.

interpretation   n.   explanation, subjective report
interpret   v.
Before Freud's work on the <u>interpretation</u> of dreams, early civilizations considered a dream as a
    message of divine origin.

involve   v.   engage, participate, associate
involvement   n.,   involved   adj.
Research studies prove that students who are <u>involved</u> in clubs and activities on campus tend to make
    better grades.

issue   n.   situation, event, subject, topic
Childhood obesity is a pressing <u>issue</u> for health care not only now but also when these children
    become adults.

item   n.   article, detail, particular, point
itemize   v.
The Phoenicians traded many <u>items</u> of silver, bronze, and ivory as well as purple dye and salt for
    gold, cotton, and wheat.

labor   n.   physical or mental work
labor   v.,   work
The United Nations has passed several resolutions to protect children from <u>labor</u> that is inappropriate for them.

legal   adj.   authorized, lawful, legitimate
legally   adv.
The most widespread <u>legal</u> system in the world is civil law, derived from Roman codes under Emperor Justinian I.

legislation   n.   laws, rules
legislate   v.,   legislator   n.,   person who makes laws
Some <u>legislation</u> differs from one state to another because the states maintain certain rights.

major   adj.   greater, important, key
majority   n.
Concern for environmental protection is a <u>major</u> factor in the recovery of oil and gas reserves.

method   n.   strategy, system, procedure, process
methodology   n.,   methodical   adj.
<u>Methods</u> for data collection may vary slightly from one field of study to another, but accuracy is the goal for all types of research.

normal   adj.   regular, natural, usual
normally   adv.
Anger is a <u>normal</u> emotion with a wide range of intensity, from mild irritation to rage.

occur   v.   happen, exist, result
occurrence n.
Volcanic eruptions <u>occur</u> when the Earth's plates pull apart, causing magma to rise to the surface, either on land or under the sea.

participate   v.   take part, share
participation   n.,   act of participating   participant   n.,   person who participates
Many professors require that their students <u>participate</u> in class discussions as part of their final evaluations.

percent   n.   part, portion (of a hundred)
percentage   n.
Approximately 95 <u>percent</u> of the animals on Earth are insects.

period   n.   amount of time, division, part, section, interval
periodic   adj.,   periodically   adv.
The <u>period</u> of time between exposure and symptoms of an infectious illness can be a few days or a few years, depending on the disease.

policy   n.   course of action, plan, procedure, rule
Typically, community colleges have a <u>policy</u> of open admission for anyone who wants to take classes, but in order to be accepted into a degree program, applicants must have a high school diploma or equivalent.

positive   adj.   optimistic, affirmative, encouraging, certain, definite
positively   adv.
<u>Positive</u> attitudes have been shown to reduce stress and contribute to better health.

potential   adj.   possible, probable, likely to happen
potentially   adv.
Because computer systems are vulnerable to many <u>potential</u> threats, security must be constantly updated.

previous   adj.   preceding, prior, before
previously   adv.
Archaeologists often find the remains of <u>previous</u> cultures below the site that they are excavating.

principle   n.   basic assumption, generalization, rule
Several <u>principles</u> of relativity have been widely assumed in many scientific disciplines.

procedure   n.   course of action, method, process
proceed   v.
Standard operating <u>procedures</u> for airport security vary from one country to another.

process   n.   course of action to achieve a result, procedure
The <u>process</u> for changing the U.S. Constitution requires that two-thirds of both houses of Congress propose an amendment.

range   n.   limit, extent
Online courses cover a wide <u>range</u> of topics.

region   n.   area, district, zone, territory, location
regional   adj.,   regionally   adv.
A large <u>region</u> near the tropics has a temperate climate.

regulations   n.   rules, laws
regulate   v.
The Australian Department of Immigration and Border Protection provides <u>regulations</u> for obtaining various types of visas.

relevant   adj.   applicable, pertinent, appropriate
relevance   n.
Although libraries have changed in the digital age, they are still <u>relevant</u> to communities today.

required   adj.   compulsory, mandatory, obligatory, necessary
requirement   n.,   require   v.
After the <u>required</u> courses have been completed, students may take elective courses.

research   n.   investigation, inquiry, study that is often academic
researcher   n.,   person who researches
Climate change requires further <u>research</u> before conclusions may be made.

reside   v.   live in a certain place, be located
residential   adj.,   residence   n.,   place to live   resident   n.,   person who lives in a place
The United Nations headquarters <u>resides</u> in an international territory in New York City.

resources   n.   assets, reserves, properties
Canada has abundant natural <u>resources</u>, including oil and gas.

response   n.   reply, answer, reaction
respond   v.,   responsive   adj.
When an organism stops its <u>response</u> to a repeated stimulus—for example, a loud noise—it is
   habituated to the stimulus.

role   n.   part, function, purpose
The <u>role</u> of language teachers is changing dramatically due to the increased accessibility of
   collaborative technologies.

section   n.   portion, piece, segment, division, part
A Shakespearean sonnet is divided into four <u>sections</u>.

sector   n.   segment, area, division, part
The public <u>sector</u> refers to businesses and organizations concerned with providing government
   services.

secure   adj.   safe, stable, strong, protected
secure   v.,   security   n.,   securely   adv.
A <u>secure</u> channel allows for the transfer of confidential data.

select   v.   choose
selection   n.,   selectively   adv.
It is essential to <u>select</u> a representative sample for a research study.

significant   adj.   remarkable, meaningful, large, important
significance   n.,   signify   v.,   significantly   adv.
Images taken by satellites have made a <u>significant</u> contribution to the field of geology.

similar   adj.   almost the same, comparable, alike
similarity   n.,   similarly   adv.
Plants and green algae are <u>similar</u> in that they both rely on photosynthesis for energy.

source   n.   origin, basis, beginning, original reference
Very few foods in nature provide a <u>source</u> of vitamin D.

specific   adj.   particular, definite, explicit, exact
specify   v.,   specification   n.,   specifically   adv.
Art historians classify art as movements in which artists promote a <u>specific</u> philosophy or goal.

strategy   n.   design, approach, tactic, plan
strategic   adj.,   strategically   adv.,   strategist   n.   person who strategizes
Applicants should develop a <u>strategy</u> for gaining admission to the colleges they want to attend.

structure   n.   organization, arrangement, construction, building, system
structure   v.,   structural   adj.,   structurally   adv.
In the human eye, the <u>structure</u> of the retina includes ten distinct layers.

survey   v.   overview, analyze, examine, inspect
survey   n.,   analysis, inspection
To improve reading comprehension, <u>survey</u> the passage first.

text   n.   words in a written work, topic, theme, subject
The complete <u>text</u> of the Gettysburg Address is only 270 words, but it is considered one of the most
     outstanding speeches by an American president.

theory   n.   assumption, hypothesis, proposal
theoretical   adj.,   theoretically   adv.,   theorist   n.,   person who proposes theories
Published in 1718, *The Doctrine of Chances* was the first textbook to explain a <u>theory</u> of probability.

traditional   adj.   customary, usual, conventional
tradition   n.,   traditional   adj.,   traditionally   adv.
The <u>traditional</u> method of marketing still uses print publications such as newspapers and magazines.

transfer   v.   relocate, move
transfer   n.,   transferable   adj.
Some course credits earned at another institution cannot <u>be transferred</u> when a student changes
     schools.

variables   n.   something that changes, factors, attributes
vary   v.,   variability   n.,   the potential for variation   variation   n.,   change
<u>Variables</u> are controlled in psychology experiments to determine which factors are causing the results.

Practice Exercises for Academic Vocabulary

 Bonus Exercise 1: Academic Vocabulary

In some questions in the Reading Section on the Institutional TOEFL and on the Internet-Based TOEFL, you will be asked to identify synonyms for vocabulary words in the passage. Choose the correct synonym from the four choices below the sentence.

1. Unlike water, metals tend to <u>contract</u> when the temperature is cold.

   The word contract in the sentence is closest in meaning to
   - Ⓐ gets smaller
   - Ⓑ gets worse
   - Ⓒ gets clearer
   - Ⓓ gets simpler

2. <u>Evidence</u> for the movement of continents on tectonic plates is extensive.

   The word Evidence in the sentence is closest in meaning to
   - Ⓐ Criticism
   - Ⓑ Advantages
   - Ⓒ Prevention
   - Ⓓ Confirmation

3. An initial <u>assessment</u> is usually carried out by a social worker.

   The word assessment in the sentence is closest in meaning to
   - Ⓐ warning
   - Ⓑ visitation
   - Ⓒ evaluation
   - Ⓓ fine

4. A solar eclipse <u>occurs</u> when the Moon passes between the Sun and the Earth.

   The word occurs in the sentence is closest in meaning to
   - Ⓐ resumes
   - Ⓑ results
   - Ⓒ repeats
   - Ⓓ reverses

5. According to the critics, Myazaki's last film was a departure from works created <u>previously</u>.

   The word previously in the sentence is closest in meaning to
   - Ⓐ well
   - Ⓑ before
   - Ⓒ quickly
   - Ⓓ frequently

6. Edible products <u>derived from</u> oil crops include preserved olives, butter, nuts, and candy, as well as some soya products.

The phrase derived from in the sentence is closest in meaning to
Ⓐ developed from
Ⓑ similar to
Ⓒ in addition to
Ⓓ except for

7. A photograph is not as subject to <u>individual</u> interpretation as a painting.

The word individual in the sentence is closest in meaning to
Ⓐ predictible
Ⓑ traditional
Ⓒ single
Ⓓ arbitrary

8. An essay in English usually contains three <u>sections</u>.

The word sections in the sentence is closest in meaning to
Ⓐ problems
Ⓑ questions
Ⓒ examples
Ⓓ parts

9. Many social <u>variables</u>, including income, social status, and relationships with family and friends, will affect health.

The word variables in the sentence is closest in meaning to
Ⓐ adjustments
Ⓑ factors
Ⓒ obstacles
Ⓓ disadvantages

10. Observations by Hubble in the 1920s <u>indicated</u> that the universe was expanding.

The word indicated in the sentence is closest in meaning to
Ⓐ shed light on
Ⓑ had no regard for
Ⓒ saw in the future
Ⓓ made reference to

Bonus Exercise 2: Academic Vocabulary

In some questions in the Reading Section on the Institutional TOEFL and on the Internet-Based TOEFL, you will be asked to identify synonyms for vocabulary words in the passage. Choose the correct synonym from the four choices below the sentence.

1. Several <u>issues</u> divided the nation leading up to a civil war.

   The word issues in the sentence is closest in meaning to
   Ⓐ suggestions
   Ⓑ events
   Ⓒ disagreements
   Ⓓ purchases

2. Because companies believe that Columbus, Ohio, is a typical American city, residents are often recruited to <u>participate in</u> market research.

   The phrase participate in in the sentence is closest in meaning to
   Ⓐ put up with
   Ⓑ do without
   Ⓒ take part in
   Ⓓ set up

3. It is remarkable that the questions asked by Socrates 1,600 years ago are still <u>relevant</u> today.

   The word relevant in the sentence is closest in meaning to
   Ⓐ appropriate
   Ⓑ available
   Ⓒ doubtful
   Ⓓ pleasing

4. Bavarian artist Alois Senefelder <u>created</u> several processes that eventually led to modern lithography.

   The word created in the sentence is closest in meaning to
   Ⓐ opposed
   Ⓑ accumulated
   Ⓒ interrupted
   Ⓓ designed

5. In general, orchids prefer <u>environments</u> with high humidity and low light.

   The word environments in the sentence is closest in meaning to
   Ⓐ occasions
   Ⓑ conditions
   Ⓒ schedules
   Ⓓ alternatives

6. Most theories of the origin of life on Earth <u>assume</u> that it began in water.

   The word assume in the sentence is closest in meaning to
   - (A) contradict
   - (B) suppose
   - (C) insist
   - (D) observe

7. Five <u>major</u> schools of thought have dominated psychology since it became an independent discipline.

   The word major in the sentence is closest in meaning to
   - (A) very important
   - (B) very detailed
   - (C) very different
   - (D) very new

8. One <u>potential</u> problem with robots is that they do not have a moral compass to govern their decisions.

   The word potential in the sentence is closest in meaning to
   - (A) small
   - (B) continuing
   - (C) possible
   - (D) specific

9. In most states, auto insurance is <u>required</u>.

   The word required in the sentence is closest in meaning to
   - (A) adequate
   - (B) necessary
   - (C) expensive
   - (D) available

10. Weather forecasts are made by collecting and analyzing <u>data</u> about current atmospheric conditions.

    The word data in the sentence is closest in meaning to
    - (A) comments
    - (B) summaries
    - (C) images
    - (D) information

Bonus Exercise 3: Academic Vocabulary

In some questions in the Reading Section on the Institutional TOEFL and on the Internet-Based TOEFL, you will be asked to identify synonyms for vocabulary words in the passage. Choose the correct synonym from the four choices below the sentence.

1. Some of the most important <u>principles</u> of design refer to the color wheel as a reference.

    The word principles in the sentence is closest in meaning to
    Ⓐ generalizations
    Ⓑ problems
    Ⓒ transformations
    Ⓓ questions

2. The <u>distribution</u> of fresh water on Earth is very uneven.

    The word distribution in the sentence is closest in meaning to
    Ⓐ safety
    Ⓑ inspection
    Ⓒ supply
    Ⓓ discovery

3. The Vienna Convention provides a process for <u>establishing</u> diplomatic relations among nations.

    The word establishing in the sentence is closest in meaning to
    Ⓐ studying
    Ⓑ recognizing
    Ⓒ predicting
    Ⓓ preventing

4. Many <u>factors</u> will contribute to the response rate of surveys.

    The word factors in the sentence is closest in meaning to
    Ⓐ risks
    Ⓑ circumstances
    Ⓒ modifications
    Ⓓ incentives

5. The Australian Museum in Sydney has <u>acquired</u> a notable collection of aboriginal art and artifacts for the permanent exhibits.

    The word acquired in the sentence is closest in meaning to
    Ⓐ enlarged
    Ⓑ concealed
    Ⓒ restored
    Ⓓ obtained

6. Studies that link cell phone usage to health issues are not <u>consistent with</u> the findings of other equally important studies.

   The phrase consistent with in the sentence is closest in meaning to
   Ⓐ in opposition to
   Ⓑ as good as
   Ⓒ the same as
   Ⓓ more recent than

7. Geological <u>periods</u> document the existence of Earth from about 4,600 billion years ago to the present.

   The word periods in the sentence is closest in meaning to
   Ⓐ locations
   Ⓑ activities
   Ⓒ divisions
   Ⓓ experts

8. Cloud-based services have simplified the way that large files <u>are transferred</u>.

   The phrase are transferred in the sentence is closest in meaning to
   Ⓐ made easier to understand
   Ⓑ kept safe from theft
   Ⓒ changed from one language to another
   Ⓓ moved to another place

9. Speakers often <u>conclude</u> with a famous quotation.

   The word conclude in the sentence is closest in meaning to
   Ⓐ bring their presentations to an end
   Ⓑ make their presentations more interesting
   Ⓒ put humor in their presentations
   Ⓓ give their presentations a title

10. It is <u>normal</u> for an individual to experience emotional stress a few hours or even days or months after a traumatic event.

    The word normal in the sentence is closest in meaning to
    Ⓐ easy
    Ⓑ rare
    Ⓒ usual
    Ⓓ temporary

Bonus Exercise 4: Academic Vocabulary

In some questions in the Reading Section on the Institutional TOEFL and on the Internet-Based TOEFL, you will be asked to identify synonyms for vocabulary words in the passage. Choose the correct synonym from the four choices below the sentence.

1. The natural resources in industries such as agriculture, forestry, fishing, and mining are exploited by the primary <u>sector</u> of the economy.

    The word sector in the sentence is closest in meaning to
    (A) purpose
    (B) user
    (C) service
    (D) part

2. The charter of the United Nations gives it <u>authority</u> for international law.

    The word authority in the sentence is closest in meaning to
    (A) responsibility
    (B) assistance
    (C) protection
    (D) examples

3. The network of interactions among organisms <u>defines</u> an ecosystem.

    The word defines in the sentence is closest in meaning to
    (A) disrupts
    (B) explains
    (C) complicates
    (D) removes

4. One <u>positive</u> result of the Black Death in the Middle Ages was a higher standard of living for the smaller population worldwide that survived the epidemic.

    The word positive in the sentence is closest in meaning to
    (A) visible
    (B) ongoing
    (C) general
    (D) encouraging

5. Unlike the standard tests of intelligence, newer <u>theories</u> include multiple ways of measuring IQ.

    The word theories in the sentence is closest in meaning to
    (A) assumptions
    (B) examinations
    (C) inventions
    (D) substitutions

6. Unlike most countries, the United States issues both federal and state <u>regulations</u> for banks.

The word regulations in the sentence is closest in meaning to
Ⓐ sites
Ⓑ laws
Ⓒ currency
Ⓓ employees

7. The first Neanderthal genome sequence is <u>available</u> online for researchers at no cost.

The word available in the sentence is closest in meaning to
Ⓐ debated
Ⓑ offered
Ⓒ revised
Ⓓ simplified

8. Although many entrepreneurs are admired for their <u>impact</u>, Steve Jobs certainly improved lives and provided employment for a very large number of people.

The word impact in the sentence is closest in meaning to
Ⓐ philanthropy
Ⓑ intelligence
Ⓒ influence
Ⓓ merchandise

9. A study of the <u>response to</u> medications on the part of genetically different subjects is called pharmacogenetics.

The phrase response to in the sentence is closest in meaning to
Ⓐ compatibility with
Ⓑ exposure from
Ⓒ abuse of
Ⓓ reaction by

10. TOEFL raters give more points to talks and essays that contain <u>specific</u> details.

The word specific in the sentence is closest in meaning to
Ⓐ current
Ⓑ exact
Ⓒ interesting
Ⓓ valuable

Bonus Exercise 5: Academic Vocabulary

In some questions in the Reading Section on the Institutional TOEFL and on the Internet-Based TOEFL, you will be asked to identify synonyms for vocabulary words in the passage. Choose the correct synonym from the four choices below the sentence.

1. Great works of art and literature are subject to different <u>interpretations</u> based on the historical context for the critic.

   The word interpretations in the sentence is closest in meaning to
   Ⓐ techniques
   Ⓑ explanations
   Ⓒ acknowledgments
   Ⓓ emphases

2. There is evidence that rear-facing car seats keep infants and children under the age of two years <u>more secure</u> than front-facing seats.

   The phrase more secure in the sentence is closest in meaning to
   Ⓐ safer
   Ⓑ cheaper
   Ⓒ better
   Ⓓ newer

3. In general, the <u>function</u> of petals is to attract insects and animals to the plant for pollination.

   The word function in the sentence is closest in meaning to
   Ⓐ advantage
   Ⓑ movement
   Ⓒ shape
   Ⓓ purpose

4. As a result of media, trade, travel, and technology, a global <u>culture</u> appears to be emerging.

   The word culture in the sentence is closest in meaning to
   Ⓐ disaster
   Ⓑ tradition
   Ⓒ union
   Ⓓ plan

5. Among many species, females <u>choose</u> their mates on the basis of ornamentation and courtship displays.

   The word choose in the sentence is closest in meaning to
   Ⓐ escape
   Ⓑ select
   Ⓒ dominate
   Ⓓ approach

6. Studying patterns of words to learn how to spell in English is an alternative to the traditional <u>approach</u>, which requires memorization of unrelated words on a list.

   The word approach in the sentence is closest in meaning to
   - Ⓐ manual
   - Ⓑ academy
   - Ⓒ method
   - Ⓓ subject

7. Color is very important as a strategy to <u>identify</u> a brand, for example, a specific color of green used by Deere & Company.

   The word identify in the sentence is closest in meaning to
   - Ⓐ recognize
   - Ⓑ distribute
   - Ⓒ transform
   - Ⓓ appreciate

8. Researchers commonly use a grid to record where each <u>item</u> is found in an archaeological dig site.

   The word item in the sentence is closest in meaning to
   - Ⓐ relic
   - Ⓑ discovery
   - Ⓒ article
   - Ⓓ prize

9. It has been shown in recent studies that people who write down their goals are more likely to <u>achieve</u> them.

   The word achieve in the sentence is closest in meaning to
   - Ⓐ clarify
   - Ⓑ comprehend
   - Ⓒ articulate
   - Ⓓ accomplish

10. Both pronunciation and vocabulary distinguish <u>regional</u> dialects within a language group.

    The word regional in the sentence is closest in meaning to
    - Ⓐ commonly heard
    - Ⓑ part of a specific area
    - Ⓒ the most prestigious
    - Ⓓ difficult to understand

Bonus Exercise 6: Academic Vocabulary

In some questions in the Reading Section on the Institutional TOEFL and on the Internet-Based TOEFL, you will be asked to identify synonyms for vocabulary words in the passage. Choose the correct synonym from the four choices below the sentence.

1. Problems with joints or muscles can cause a restricted <u>range</u> of motion not only in humans but also in animals.

   The word range in the sentence is closest in meaning to
   Ⓐ limit
   Ⓑ ability
   Ⓒ view
   Ⓓ effort

2. <u>Traditionally</u>, jazz is characterized by improvisation of the horns and accompaniment by percussion instruments.

   The word Traditionally in the sentence is closest in meaning to
   Ⓐ Amazingly
   Ⓑ Exclusively
   Ⓒ Definitely
   Ⓓ Customarily

3. Most viruses, which are smaller than cells, are very simple <u>structures</u>.

   The word structures in the sentence is closest in meaning to
   Ⓐ organizations
   Ⓑ creatures
   Ⓒ examples
   Ⓓ comparisons

4. Recent models <u>estimate</u> the age of Saturn's giant moon at one billion years old.

   The word estimate in the sentence is closest in meaning to
   Ⓐ challenge
   Ⓑ calculate
   Ⓒ recognize
   Ⓓ exclude

5. A monetary <u>policy</u> that increases interest rates for borrowers will tend to decrease the amount of money circulating in the economy.

   The word policy in the sentence is closest in meaning to
   Ⓐ supervisor
   Ⓑ objection
   Ⓒ business
   Ⓓ plan

6. The degree of formality for the situation determines when slang is <u>appropriate</u>.

   The word appropriate in the sentence is closest in meaning to
   Ⓐ humorous
   Ⓑ surprising
   Ⓒ suitable
   Ⓓ appreciated

7. According to Adam Smith, it is <u>labor</u> that should determine the value of goods, not supply and demand.

   The word labor in the sentence is closest in meaning to
   Ⓐ need
   Ⓑ work
   Ⓒ time
   Ⓓ money

8. New technologies require that current <u>legislation</u> be extended or interpreted.

   The word legislation in the sentence is closest in meaning to
   Ⓐ goals
   Ⓑ equipment
   Ⓒ laws
   Ⓓ training

9. Many artists and writers who <u>resided</u> in Europe after World War I gathered at Gertrude Stein's home on Saturday evenings.

   The word resided in the sentence is closest in meaning to
   Ⓐ studied
   Ⓑ traveled
   Ⓒ lived
   Ⓓ worked

10. The proteins in the great white shark and human beings are <u>similar</u>.

    The word similar in the sentence is closest in meaning to
    Ⓐ almost the same
    Ⓑ very complex
    Ⓒ likely to change
    Ⓓ easy to see

Bonus Exercise 7: Academic Vocabulary

In some questions in the Reading Section on the Institutional TOEFL and on the Internet-Based TOEFL, you will be asked to identify synonyms for vocabulary words in the passage. Choose the correct synonym from the four choices below the sentence.

1. The <u>concept</u> of time varies significantly from one cultural group to another.

   The word concept in the sentence is closest in meaning to
   - Ⓐ experience
   - Ⓑ value
   - Ⓒ control
   - Ⓓ idea

2. A large number of companies are <u>involved in</u> research to take advantage of renewable energy reserves.

   The phrase involved in in the sentence is closest in meaning to
   - Ⓐ actively participating in
   - Ⓑ leading the way for
   - Ⓒ trying to stop
   - Ⓓ not very informed about

3. According to some of the local legends, after the immense stone figures at Easter Island were <u>constructed</u>, they were used for ancestor worship.

   The word constructed in the sentence is closest in meaning to
   - Ⓐ moved
   - Ⓑ built
   - Ⓒ returned
   - Ⓓ found

4. The <u>formula</u> for Gatorade was developed by a football coach and a team of physicians in order to replace the fluids and electrolytes that the players were losing during games.

   The word formula in the sentence is closest in meaning to
   - Ⓐ notion
   - Ⓑ demand
   - Ⓒ process
   - Ⓓ container

5. The Council for the Arts provides <u>resources</u> for aspiring artists.

   The word resources in the sentence is closest in meaning to
   - Ⓐ promotion
   - Ⓑ management
   - Ⓒ assets
   - Ⓓ instruction

6. It can be argued that the Magna Carta was the most <u>important</u> influence on constitutional law.

   The word important in the sentence is closest in meaning to
   Ⓐ significant
   Ⓑ unique
   Ⓒ trivial
   Ⓓ thorough

7. In the plant kingdom, there is a clear <u>distinction</u> in the appearance of flowering and nonflowering plants.

   The word distinction in the sentence is closest in meaning to
   Ⓐ relationship
   Ⓑ difference
   Ⓒ origin
   Ⓓ pattern

8. Language is one of the most important and recognizable <u>aspects</u> found in social identity.

   The word aspects in the sentence is closest in meaning to
   Ⓐ amusements
   Ⓑ obstacles
   Ⓒ dilemmas
   Ⓓ characteristics

9. In general, teamwork is <u>beneficial</u> for new employees.

   The word beneficial in the sentence is closest in meaning to
   Ⓐ easy
   Ⓑ helpful
   Ⓒ practical
   Ⓓ common

10. Matter <u>constitutes</u> the physical world that we are able to see around us.

    The word constitutes in the sentence is closest in meaning to
    Ⓐ forms
    Ⓑ replaces
    Ⓒ changes
    Ⓓ locates

Bonus Exercise 8: Academic Vocabulary

In some questions in the Reading Section on the Institutional TOEFL and on the Internet-Based TOEFL, you will be asked to identify synonyms for vocabulary words in the passage. Choose the correct synonym from the four choices below the sentence.

1. In modern agriculture, the soil is <u>analyzed</u> to determine the nutrient, contaminant, and acidic content.

   The word analyzed in the sentence is closest in meaning to
   Ⓐ examined
   Ⓑ combined
   Ⓒ relocated
   Ⓓ enriched

2. The pointed arch is probably the most recognizable <u>feature</u> of Gothic churches.

   The word feature in the sentence is closest in meaning to
   Ⓐ reinforcement
   Ⓑ technique
   Ⓒ mistake
   Ⓓ quality

3. Archaeological findings provide details about the <u>source</u> of Greek mythology.

   The word source in the sentence is closest in meaning to
   Ⓐ role
   Ⓑ origin
   Ⓒ accuracy
   Ⓓ period

4. The production of ethanol from corn is a relatively simple <u>process</u>.

   The word process in the sentence is closest in meaning to
   Ⓐ invention
   Ⓑ objective
   Ⓒ procedure
   Ⓓ probability

5. International relief organizations <u>assist</u> victims worldwide after earthquakes, floods, droughts, and other natural disasters.

   The word assist in the sentence is closest in meaning to
   Ⓐ save
   Ⓑ find
   Ⓒ help
   Ⓓ move

6. The <u>consequences</u> of plagiarism include a failing grade in the course in which it occurs, or even expulsion from the college or university that the student is attending.

   The word consequences in the sentence is closest in meaning to
   - Ⓐ repetition
   - Ⓑ results
   - Ⓒ risks
   - Ⓓ rewards

7. The <u>role</u> of oxygen in photosynthesis is important, but it is really a byproduct of the process in which energy is stored.

   The word role in the sentence is closest in meaning to
   - Ⓐ amount
   - Ⓑ story
   - Ⓒ importance
   - Ⓓ purpose

8. In order to <u>judge</u> the value of a work of art, it is useful to compare it with similar works sold at auction.

   The word judge in the sentence is closest in meaning to
   - Ⓐ evaluate
   - Ⓑ classify
   - Ⓒ exhibit
   - Ⓓ purchase

9. A crisis in the <u>financial</u> sector can be avoided by changes in public policies.

   The word financial in the sentence is closest in meaning to
   - Ⓐ related to health
   - Ⓑ related to employment
   - Ⓒ related to money
   - Ⓓ related to production

10. Like so many important discoveries in astronomy, the <u>method</u> for studying binary stars was found by accident.

    The word method in the sentence is closest in meaning to
    - Ⓐ solution
    - Ⓑ effort
    - Ⓒ reason
    - Ⓓ system

Bonus Exercise 9: Academic Vocabulary

In some questions in the Reading Section on the Institutional TOEFL and on the Internet-Based TOEFL, you will be asked to identify synonyms for vocabulary words in the passage. Choose the correct synonym from the four choices below the sentence.

1. Michelangelo was <u>commissioned</u> in 1501 to sculpt a likeness of David from a large piece of damaged marble.

   The word commissioned in the sentence is closest in meaning to
   Ⓐ appointed
   Ⓑ inspired
   Ⓒ discovered
   Ⓓ forced

2. Important knowledge from the ancient world has been lost because the <u>texts</u> were destroyed when the cities housing the great libraries were conquered by invaders.

   The word texts in the sentence is closest in meaning to
   Ⓐ large buildings
   Ⓑ written works
   Ⓒ important authors
   Ⓓ very old secrets

3. The separation of two nuclei into individual cells occurs during the <u>final</u> stage of mitosis.

   The word final in the sentence is closest in meaning to
   Ⓐ complex
   Ⓑ unusual
   Ⓒ amazing
   Ⓓ last

4. Large quantities of natural resources, including iron ore, coal, crude oil, natural gas, copper, and aluminum, <u>are exported</u> by Australian companies.

   The phrase are exported in the sentence is closest in meaning to
   Ⓐ used locally
   Ⓑ produced cheaply
   Ⓒ sold abroad
   Ⓓ found easily

5. One of the objectives for nineteenth-century anthropologists was to complete fieldwork with <u>communities</u> when languages were becoming extinct.

   The word communities in the sentence is closest in meaning to
   Ⓐ religious books
   Ⓑ oral histories
   Ⓒ art in caves
   Ⓓ groups of people

6. A merger often requires a <u>strategic</u> change in the mission of the two organizations that are involved.

   The word strategic in the sentence is closest in meaning to
   - Ⓐ interesting
   - Ⓑ huge
   - Ⓒ planned
   - Ⓓ frequent

7. Social psychology is about understanding individual behavior in a social <u>context</u>.

   The word context in the sentence is closest in meaning to
   - Ⓐ revolution
   - Ⓑ environment
   - Ⓒ civilization
   - Ⓓ gathering

8. The opportunity to increase your <u>income</u> is dependent in part on the region in which you live.

   The word income in the sentence is closest in meaning to
   - Ⓐ earnings
   - Ⓑ opportunities
   - Ⓒ contacts
   - Ⓓ recreation

9. All carbohydrates, including sugar, contain three basic <u>elements</u>.

   The word elements in the sentence is closest in meaning to
   - Ⓐ parts
   - Ⓑ needs
   - Ⓒ rules
   - Ⓓ types

10. An international team of geologists has <u>surveyed</u> various alternatives for using satellites and smartphones to predict earthquakes.

   The word surveyed in the sentence is closest in meaning to
   - Ⓐ abandoned
   - Ⓑ examined
   - Ⓒ restricted
   - Ⓓ approved

Bonus Exercise 10: Academic Vocabulary

In some questions in the Reading Section on the Institutional TOEFL and on the Internet-Based TOEFL, you will be asked to identify synonyms for vocabulary words in the passage. Choose the correct synonym from the four choices below the sentence.

1. For many people, retirement signals an opportunity to begin a new <u>chapter</u> in their lives, which may include a new job or moving to a new city.

    The word chapter in the sentence is closest in meaning to
    Ⓐ change
    Ⓑ division
    Ⓒ view
    Ⓓ goal

2. Whereas goods may be <u>consumed</u> immediately, services will probably be delivered over a longer period of time.

    The word consumed in the sentence is closest in meaning to
    Ⓐ purchased
    Ⓑ destroyed
    Ⓒ shipped
    Ⓓ built

3. The exact <u>percentage</u> of all species on Earth living in the oceans cannot be determined because exploration is still ongoing.

    The word percentage in the sentence is closest in meaning to
    Ⓐ report
    Ⓑ location
    Ⓒ portion
    Ⓓ behavior

4. Although it is usual for a wife to assume her husband's last name when they marry, it is not required <u>legally</u> in many societies.

    The word legally in the sentence is closest in meaning to
    Ⓐ according to customs
    Ⓑ according to the law
    Ⓒ according to religion
    Ⓓ according to schools

5. A simple <u>procedure</u> for determining whether a substance is pure is to find its melting point and compare it with that of a pure sample.

    The word procedure in the sentence is closest in meaning to
    Ⓐ idea
    Ⓑ probability
    Ⓒ answer
    Ⓓ method

6. For the most part, immigration influences the rate of population growth in urban <u>areas</u> that have already absorbed previous immigrant groups.

   The word areas in the sentence is closest in meaning to
   Ⓐ times
   Ⓑ places
   Ⓒ people
   Ⓓ things

7. Both the Egyptians and the Babylonians were able to <u>compute</u> the value of π as early as 2000 B.C.E.

   The word compute in the sentence is closest in meaning to
   Ⓐ appreciate
   Ⓑ imagine
   Ⓒ figure
   Ⓓ exchange

8. In 1820, Thomas Malthus and David Ricardo participated in one of the first debates on <u>economic</u> principles.

   The word economic in the sentence is closest in meaning to
   Ⓐ logical
   Ⓑ political
   Ⓒ cultural
   Ⓓ financial

9. Physical fitness is important, but it does not necessarily <u>equate with</u> good health, which also requires emotional stability.

   The phrase equate with in the sentence is closest in meaning to
   Ⓐ mean the same thing as
   Ⓑ cause a change in
   Ⓒ take the place of
   Ⓓ do more than

10. <u>Researching</u> the satellites that orbit Jupiter may provide insights about the properties of our early solar system.

    The word Researching in the sentence is closest in meaning to
    Ⓐ Naming
    Ⓑ Contrasting
    Ⓒ Finding
    Ⓓ Studying

Answer Key for Vocabulary Exercises

Bonus Exercise 1
1. A
2. D
3. C
4. B
5. B
6. A
7. C
8. D
9. B
10. D

Bonus Exercise 2
1. B
2. C
3. A
4. D
5. B
6. B
7. A
8. C
9. B
10. D

Bonus Exercise 3
1. A
2. C
3. B
4. B
5. D
6. C
7. C
8. D
9. A
10. C

Bonus Exercise 4
1. D
2. A
3. B
4. D
5. A
6. B
7. B
8. C
9. D
10. B

Bonus Exercise 5
1. B
2. A
3. D
4. B
5. B
6. C
7. A
8. C
9. D
10. B

Bonus Exercise 6
1. A
2. D
3. A
4. B
5. D
6. C
7. B
8. C
9. C
10. A

Bonus Exercise 7
1. D
2. A
3. B
4. C
5. C
6. A
7. B
8. D
9. B
10. A

Bonus Exercise 8
1. A
2. D
3. B
4. C
5. C
6. B
7. D
8. A
9. C
10. D

Bonus Exercise 9
1. A
2. B
3. D
4. C
5. D
6. C
7. B
8. A
9. A
10. B

Bonus Exercise 10
1. B
2. A
3. C
4. B
5. D
6. B
7. C
8. D
9. A
10. D

Track Number References

Track 1	Exercise 1: Short Conversations—Topics
Track 2	Exercise 2: Short Conversations—Details
Track 3	Exercise 3: Short Conversations—Selections
Track 4	Exercise 4: Short Conversations—Reversals
Track 5	Exercise 5: Short Conversations—Idioms
Track 6	Exercise 6: Short Conversations—Emotions
Track 7	Exercise 7: Short Conversations—Suggestions
Track 8	Exercise 8: Short Conversations—Assumptions
Track 9	Exercise 9: Short Conversations—Predictions
Track 10	Exercise 10: Short Conversations—Implications
Track 11	Exercise 11: Short Conversations—Problems
Track 12	Exercise 12: Conversations—Friends on Campus
Track 13	Exercise 13: Conversations—Campus Personnel/Students
Track 14	Exercise 14: Conversations—Campus Personnel/Students
Track 15	Exercise 15: Conversations—Professors/Students
Track 16	Exercise 16: Conversations—Professors/Students
Track 17	Exercise 17: Conversations—Professors/Students
Track 18	Exercise 18: Conversations—Professors/Students
Track 19	Exercise 19: Conversations—Professors/Students
Track 20	Exercise 20: Conversations—Professors/Students
Track 21	Exercise 21: Talks—Professor
Track 22	Exercise 22: Lectures—Professor
Track 23	Exercise 23: Talks—Professor
Track 24	Exercise 24: Talks—Professor
Track 25	Exercise 25: Lectures—Professor
Track 26	Exercise 26: Lectures—Professor
Track 27	Exercise 27: Talks—Professor/Students
Track 28	Exercise 28: Lectures—Professor/Students
Track 29	Exercise 29: Talks—Professor/Visuals
Track 30	Exercise 30: Lectures—Professor/Visuals
Track 31	Exercise 31: Independent Task 1—Agree or Disagree
Track 32	Exercise 32: Independent Task 1—Two Options
Track 33	Exercise 33: Independent Task 1—Three Options
Track 34	Exercise 34: Integrated Task 2—Campus Reports
Track 35	Exercise 35: Integrated Task 2—Campus Reports
Track 36	Exercise 36: Integrated Task 3—Academic Concepts
Track 37	Exercise 37: Integrated Task 3—Academic Concepts
Track 38	Exercise 38: Integrated Task 4—Academic Summaries
Track 39	Exercise 39: Integrated Task 4—Academic Summaries
Track 40	Exercise 40: Integrated Task 4—Academic Summaries
Track 41	Exercise 91: Integrated Essay—Academic Debate
Track 42	Exercise 92: Integrated Essay—Academic Debate
Track 43	Exercise 93: Integrated Essay—Academic Debate
Track 44	Exercise 94: Integrated Essay—Academic Debate
Track 45	Exercise 95: Integrated Essay—Academic Debate
Track 46	Exercise 96: Integrated Essay—Academic Debate
Track 47	Exercise 97: Integrated Essay—Academic Debate

Track 48   **Exercise 98: Integrated Essay—Academic Debate**
Track 49   **Exercise 99: Integrated Essay—Academic Debate**
Track 50   **Exercise 100: Integrated Essay—Academic Debate**

Track 51   **ITP Model Test: Section 1—Listening Comprehension Part A**
Track 52   **ITP Model Test: Section 1—Listening Comprehension Part B**
Track 53   **ITP Model Test: Section 1—Listening Comprehension Part C**
Track 54   **iBT Model Test: Listening Section—Listening 1**
Track 55   **iBT Model Test: Listening Section—Listening 2**
Track 56   **iBT Model Test: Listening Section—Listening 3**
Track 57   **iBT Model Test: Listening Section—Listening 4**
Track 58   **iBT Model Test: Listening Section—Listening 5**
Track 59   **iBT Model Test: Listening Section—Listening 6**
Track 60   **iBT Model Test: Listening Section—Listening 7**

Track 61   **iBT Model Test: Speaking Section—Task 1**
Track 62   **iBT Model Test: Speaking Section—Task 2**
Track 63   **iBT Model Test: Speaking Section—Task 3**
Track 64   **iBT Model Test: Speaking Section—Task 4**

Track 65   **iBT Model Test: Writing Section—Integrated Writing Lecture**

There are long pauses in the Speaking Section exercises and test questions to provide you with preparation and recording times that simulate the iBT TOEFL.